The Silver Market Phenomenon

Florian Kohlbacher · Cornelius Herstatt

Editors

The Silver Market Phenomenon

Marketing and Innovation
in the Aging Society

Second Edition

 Springer

Editors
Dr. Florian Kohlbacher
German Institute for
Japanese Studies (DIJ)
Jochi Kioizaka Bldg. 2F
7-1 Kioicho
Chiyoda-ku, Tokyo 102-0094
Japan
kohlbacher@dijtokyo.org

Professor Dr. Cornelius Herstatt
TU Hamburg-Harburg
AB Technologie- und
Innovationsmanagement
Schwarzenbergstr. 95
21073 Hamburg
Germany
c.herstatt@tu-harburg.de

ISBN 978-3-642-14337-3   e-ISBN 978-3-642-14338-0
DOI 10.1007/978-3-642-14338-0
Springer Heidelberg Dordrecht London New York

Library of Congress Control Number: 2010938945

Cover design: WMXDesign GmbH, Heidelberg, Germany

Printed on acid-free paper

Springer is part of Springer Science+Business Media (www.springer.com)

Preface and Introduction

In the developed countries, the dominant factor in the next society will be something to which most people are only beginning to pay attention: the rapid growth in the older population and the rapid shrinking of the younger generation.

Peter F. Drucker

In 2008 we presented the first edition of this book. Since then, the issue of demographic change and the aging phenomenon have raised the attention of more and more scholars, business leaders, and politicians in many parts of the world. We strongly believe that aging is one of the decisive mega-trends, and societies all over the world will have to tackle aging and shrinking populations along with the related challenges.

Globally, the number of persons aged 60 or over is expected almost to triple, increasing from 737 million in 2009 to 2 billion by 2050. In the more developed regions, 21% of the population is already aged 60 years or over and that proportion is projected to reach 33% in 2050. As a matter of fact, in developed countries as a whole, the number of older persons has already surpassed the number of children (persons under age 15), and by 2050 the number of older persons in developed countries will be more than twice the number of children. But this trend is not restricted to the developed world. In developing countries as a whole, even though just 8% of the population is today aged 60 years or over, that proportion will more than double by 2050, reaching 20% that year. Visualizing the demographic change in terms of population aging and shrinking helps in grasping these massive figures. Figure 1 shows the percentage of people 65 years and older in relation to the total population for a number of selected countries. This percentage can be seen as a good proxy for the aging of these populations. Figure 2 shows the growth or shrinkage respectively of the populations in selected countries between 2005 and 2050.

We assume these unprecedented trends to heavily affect societies, companies, and politics. We further expect this development to be relevant for industrialized nations as well as for certain emerging economies. Against this backdrop, it is all the more surprising to see that research on the implications of the demographic change on societies, industries, and companies is still in its infancy. Most accounts of the so-called demographic "problem" deal, as the term already suggests, with the challenges and threats of the demographic development. These discussions feature, for example, the shrinking workforce, welfare effects, social

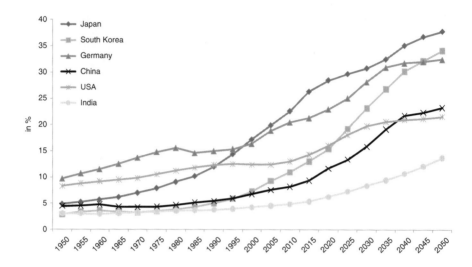

Fig. 1 Percentage of population age 65 or over (middle variant)
Source: UN Population Division DESA, World Population Prospects – the 2008 Revision Population Database 2009

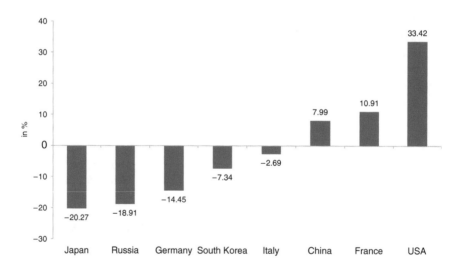

Fig. 2 Population change 2005–2050 in % (middle variant)
Source: UN Population Division DESA, World Population Prospects – the 2008 Revision Population Database 2009

conflicts, etc. At the same time, chances and opportunities are often neglected. The emergence of new markets, the potential for innovations, the integration of older people into jobs and work places, the joy of active aging, and their varied roles within society are just a few examples of how what at first sight appears to be a crisis could be turned into an opportunity. All in all, countries and industries are reacting very differently – from still neglecting to proactively looking for and developing solutions.

One particularly essential implication of the demographic shift is the emergence and constant growth of the "graying market" or "silver market," the market segment more or less broadly defined as those people aged 50 or 55 and older. Increasing in number and share of the total population while at the same time being relatively well-off, this market segment can be seen as very attractive and promising, although still very underdeveloped in terms of product and service offerings. Note that this is true for the B2C as well as the B2B sector, as the workforce of organizations is also aging. This means that machines and tools, etc. also need to be adapted to fit the needs of an aging workforce.

Given the importance and the vast implications of demographic change for the business world, it is surprising to see how little academic research in the field of business and management studies has been conducted so far. Academia is only slowly taking up this challenge. In particular, empirically grounded work is missing. We need to know how companies and whole industries are coping with demographic change. We need to know what the needs of aging/aged people are compared to other age groups, and we need to look for practical solutions to their needs. There is also a lack of concepts, processes, and practical solutions in various fields and functions of management: How to segment and approach the silver market? How to adapt product development, design, and delivery of value to the silver market? How to grasp the latent needs and wants of the potential silver customers?

This new edition offers a thorough and up-to-date analysis of the challenges and opportunities in leveraging innovation, product development, and marketing for older consumers and employees. But it is much more focused than the first edition, and we put more emphasis on product development and design as well as marketing activities. This second edition features a total of nine brand-new chapters, and all remaining chapters have been carefully checked and updated where necessary. The authors are leading experts with backgrounds in various fields and disciplines, and are engaged in leading-edge academic scholarship or business practice or even both.

We still want to reach a rather broad target audience and offer helpful guidance for decision-makers, managers responsible for innovation, technology and R&D, marketing managers, strategic management (including CEOs, governmental and political decision-makers), but also interested scholars, teachers, and students.

We strongly believe in the relevance of the topic, and hope that this work helps to stimulate the development of innovation on different levels (product, services, and social). We further want to bridge between disciplines, such as the social sciences, engineering, health care/medical etc., and to foster networking among these, favoring the creation of valuable silver market solutions.

This is an edited volume, and without the positive response and active (writing) support of all the contributing authors it would never have been thinkable, nor possible. We therefore want to express our gratitude and thanks here to all authors.

Further, we would like to thank our publisher Springer, and specifically Dr. Martina Bihn and her colleagues, for accepting and realizing this ambitious project.

Structure of the Book: Overview

This book is structured into three parts. In the first section, Part I (Innovation, Design and Product Development for the Silver Market) authors present their concepts and processes for successfully approaching the silver market, leading to innovative solutions in the form of new products and services that better fulfill the specific needs and desires of this target market. The authors clearly demonstrate that an important element of these approaches is to carefully assess the needs of older consumers and empathize with them, to ensure adequate and early integration of representatives of this market (customers and users) into product and service development, and to design solutions that truly correspond to their needs and desires.

Part II (Marketing for the Silver Market) of this book addresses marketing-related issues in connection with serving the silver market. Authors in this section look at pricing, distribution, and promoting and positioning issues, as well as segmentation approaches corresponding to silver markets. They discuss the applicability of classical marketing-mix-related activities in combination with silver markets, and present innovative approaches in employing these within this specific context.

The final section of the book, Part III (Industry Challenges and Solutions) presents a series of concrete examples or solutions (innovative products and services for the silver market) from various industries and countries.

Structure of the Book: Detailed Overview

Part I: Innovation, Design and Product Development for the Silver Market

The first part of our book includes ten chapters. The first chapter in this section by *Florian Kohlbacher, Cornelius Herstatt and Tim Schweisfurth* (Product Development for the Silver Market) can be seen as an introduction to this section. The accelerated aging of many populations and the demographic shift are expected to have major implications for innovation management and new product development across all industries. One major challenge lies in the assessment and understanding of the needs of the silver market, since chronological age by itself is not a sufficient segmentation criterion. A promising dimension is the need for autonomy, which increases with age and which is correlated to social isolation and other individual drawbacks. Thus, focusing on autonomy as a guideline to develop products and services that support people in maintaining or regaining their independence is a viable approach to developing innovation for the silver market, hence "silver products." In this chapter, the authors present four cases from different industry settings where silver products were developed that help users to sustain or regain autonomy in combination with different functions (e.g., hearing, continence, vision). They present different approaches to technological and functional complexity and newness in these innovation projects, and depict related approaches to marketing and market research.

The second chapter in this section (Silver Age Innovators: A New Approach to Old Users) by *Britt Östlund* is about user-driven innovation. When designing innovations for the silver age, it is not sufficient only to discover old people's needs. In addition, one also has to discover the new roles of old people as consumers, citizens and innovators. Since this is a group that until recently has been given few opportunities to make its voice heard, there is a requirement for methods that identify their needs and demands. More importantly, we need to study and use methods that reveal the sources of innovation behind their expressed problems and lifelong habits as users of technology. Three attempts to identify old people's needs and demands by involving them in the design process are presented, drawn from design projects implemented in Sweden from 2005 to 2009. One project explores how the furniture market can be opened to new segments of older consumers. Another project concerns the development of services. The third project links older people's lifelong habit of looking at the TV to the development of communication via the television medium. The results were analyzed from two points of view: How do we recognize a need that can be explored in design? When discovered, how do we know that this is a worthwhile need to explore? The first attempt shows that older people can present needs as active users with expressed and specific demands; the second attempt shows that older users can have a need to support the solution to problems which are not yet expressed and activated; and the third attempt shows them as users with latent needs that originate from their lifelong experiences and needs to keep up with daily routines.

Pia Helminen (Disabled Persons as Lead Users for Silver Market Customers), looks at the key aspect of integrating customers/users into the process of developing innovative products and services. She argues how important it is to deeply understand needs of (silver-)customers when developing new products. User-centered design provides tools for learning about the user needs in question, but studying only the target market customers may result in constricted need data because of the functional fixedness of these customers. The lead user approach, in contrast, aims to learn from the lead users of a certain target group in order to find better solutions for the needs in the target market. In this chapter, Helminen shows through a study on mobile phones how disabled persons can be seen as lead users when developing products for silver market customers. She also presents methods to explore the needs and solutions that disabled users possess.

The fourth chapter in this section (Integration of the Elderly into the Design Process), by *Karin Schmidt-Ruhland* and *Mathias Knigge*, is somewhat related to the work of Helminen. They argue that with demographic change looming in the background there is an ever-greater need for products and aids for the growing target group of elderly people. Both authors state that classical methods in product development and design have often failed to develop attractive and helpful solutions that meet the wishes and needs of this age group. They then introduce new approaches and concepts, which have been developed in the "sentha Research Project." "sentha" stands for "seniorengerechte Technik im häuslichen Alltag" (Everyday Technology for Senior Households). In this interdisciplinary research, project designers from the Berlin University of the Arts work closely in cooperation with the Technical Universities of Berlin and Cottbus as well as the Berlin Institute for Social Research. The goal was to develop products and services for an increasingly aging society so that seniors can maintain their independence in daily life as long as possible. This includes the development and positioning of senior-friendly products and services. In their projects, the focus was on specific wishes and needs of elderly people, without limiting themselves in form and function solely to this one target group. The article elucidates specific design approaches, methods for integrating elderly people, and shows a selection of real-world designs.

Florian Kohlbacher and *Chang Chieh Hang* (Leveraging Disruptive Innovations for the Silver Market) propose that the silver market might be an ideal field of application for disruptive technologies and innovation, and that there are important business opportunities in this market segment that could be leveraged through them. This chapter builds and extends on their previous research by (a) analyzing how changes in the external reality of the firm can create new opportunities for the development of disruptive innovations and how R&D has to grasp and react to these changes, and (b) analyzing the important role of disruptive innovations in aging societies. This chapter aims to contribute to the stream of research on the front-end question of technology creation and to the area of purposeful R&D to create disruptive technologies. R&D should consciously match these with potential markets in order to accelerate the pace of business growth through disruptive innovations, by investigating R&D efforts for disruptive innovations catering to the needs of the emerging market segment of the so-called silver market. The chapter also contributes to the knowledge of analyzing disruptive potential in R&D activities, and adds to efforts to clarify the concept of disruptive innovations in general. Finally, the authors also aim to give recommendations to practitioners such as R&D and product managers.

Ryoko Fukuda (Gerontechnology for a Super-aged Society) argues that various rapidly developed technologies are supporting the daily lives of younger users, but have left older adults behind. However, in a super-aged society, technologies could (and should) contribute to helping older adults maintain independent lives. The chapter introduces "gerontechnology," which means the study of technology and aging, for the improvement of the daily functioning of the elderly. Through such means as behavior observation, eye tracking, and the subjective evaluation of participants in a daily situation, the difficulties older adults encounter in using technologies are clarified, and products aimed at the elderly are designed and produced based on the obtained data. More empirical studies are still required to verify the effectivity of products aimed at the elderly. At the same time, efforts should be made to help more people become familiar with gerontechnology.

Deana McDonagh and *Dan Formosa* (Designing for Everyone, One Person at a Time) contend that products that surround us have a profound impact upon our lives. When they empower us to complete daily tasks with ease, speed and dignity, they contribute to our well-being and independence. When they generate negative experiences, they can strip us of dignity and erode our independence. Many companies confuse age with ability which can diminish the value of the final product. This chapter discusses two techniques that address ability by adding empathy to the design process. Real People targets specific individuals. Empathic Modeling simulates physical challenges that designers can experience for themselves.

Oliver Gassmann and *Gerrit Reepmeyer* (Universal Design – Innovations for All Ages), strongly argue for a product design that bridges between the needs of different age groups. In their view, demographics require companies to abandon the concept of solely targeting young customers. They need to create new products that are attractive to *both* younger *and* older customers. For both authors the key to success is Universal Design. Products that follow the principles of Universal Design do not separate but integrate customer groups, and they substantially increase a company's target markets. This chapter not only highlights the economic potential of Universal Design, it also shows how Universal Design can be implemented within any corporation. A successful implementation makes it necessary to (1) define a suitable Universal Design strategy, (2) establish adequate processes within the firm, (3) design the products correctly, and (4) market the products appropriately to customers. The chapter concludes by illustrating attractive areas for universally designed innovations.

James J. Pirkl writes his chapter on the design of living, or what he calls transgenerational housing (Transgenerational Design: A Heart Transplant for Housing). Responding to his past research and the realities of the aging process, the author describes why and how he designed and built the first fully accessible house aiming directly at baby-boomers and beyond. His project offers a vehicle for broadening consumer awareness of, and increasing the demand for, "transgenerational" housing and household products. This uniquely innovative design neutralizes many restrictive effects of aging, accidents, illness or chronic conditions. It also demonstrates that attractive transgenerational houses can be designed to promote, provide and extend independent living, remove barriers, offer wider options, supply greater choices, and enhance the quality of life for all – the young, the old, the able, the disabled – without penalty to any group.

The last chapter in this section of the book takes the perspective of services and innovations in service (Service Innovation: Towards Designing New Business Models for Aging Societies, by *Patrick Reinmoeller*). This author claims that the aging of industrialized countries requires firms to fundamentally rethink their business models. Firms active in Japan have to reconsider how to deal with unprecedented demographic change that alters the resources available to satisfy the shifting demand. Throughout the supply chain, aging of human talent and retirement requires firms to anticipate and prevent the negative effects of losing knowledge and skills. Adjusting the supply chain, developing new products, and/or augmenting products with services to target the silver market may offer short-term benefits, but is not enough to sustain success. Firms need to develop and implement new business models, leveraging service innovation to meet the needs in aging societies. Examples of service innovations and the case study of the shared business model innovation of Seven Eleven Japan and Yamato Transport illustrate how companies can seize the opportunities to create and capture more value in aging societies.

Part II: Marketing for the Silver Market

This section includes ten chapters. *Gunnar Arnold* and *Stephanie Krancioch* (Current Strategies in the Retail Industry for Best-Agers) take a closer look at retailing in combination with the silver market. In their view of the demographic transformation, the retail trade faces a clear challenge to reconsider existing retailing concepts, and to better include older target groups in marketing planning. In this chapter, the authors look first at the factor of location, one of the central success factors in the retail trade. Next, they examine the preferences of German best-agers for certain types of businesses, such as shops close to home in comparison with out-of-town malls. They then proceed to discuss the effects of changed customer needs with regard to the design of the assortments and of packaging resulting from their decreasing physical capabilities. Finally, the authors present examples from the daily practice of the trade, and conclude with a brief overview of foreseeable trends in the retail trade.

Stefan Lippert (Silver Pricing: Satisfying Needs Is Not Enough – Balancing Value Delivery and Value Extraction Is Key) presents the next piece of work. In his view also, the silver market provides a highly lucrative opportunity for businesses willing and able to meet the needs of Japan's senior generation. International and domestic players have been pursuing these new opportunities in the last few years. Thoroughly understanding the needs of the silver generation is a key to capitalizing on it. However, this is just one side of the value coin. A need is not the same as demand, and demand is not the same as profitable business. To turn a profit, you have to balance value delivery and value extraction. Value delivery is relatively easy: it requires market research, appropriate products and services, and an effective distribution system. Value extraction is difficult: you need to set and implement the right prices across products, regions, and channels. A marketing strategy based solely on demographic and socioeconomic data, customer needs, and buying power is simplistic, misleading, and in some cases dangerous. Capitalizing on the silver market requires a systematic approach to developing and profitably selling products and services tailored to the older generation. It takes a solid understanding of customer requirements, value-to-customer, ability and willingness to pay, price elasticities, and revenue and profit functions. The best way to achieve this is by means of a professional pricing process covering and connecting pricing strategy, price setting, and price implementation.

The chapter "Changing Consumer Values and Behavior in Japan: Adaptation of Keio Department Store, Shinjuku" by *Nozomi Enomoto* looks (again) closer at issues concerning retailing for the silver market. Retailers in Japan now face various changes in the business environment – including demographic change, economic globalization, development of information technology, and changes in consumer values and behavior. Consumer values and behavior in Japan reflect a characteristic transition in the retail sector, in which department stores have been a major force. The Keio Department Store Co. Ltd. in Shinjuku has been gearing its business toward seniors since the mid-1990s. The purpose of this study is to examine how an organization adapts to a changing business environment by exploring Keio Department Store, Shinjuku as a case of a senior-focused retailer, extracting factors that are important in tailoring business practices.

Lynn Sudbury and *Peter Simock* (Bargain Hunting Belongers and Positive Pioneers: Key Silver Market Segments in the UK) argue that although the importance of older consumers to marketers is well-documented, there exists a relative paucity of UK-based empirical studies into the attitudes, values, and behaviors of these consumers. Moreover, silver consumers are often treated as a homogenous mass. Based on an extensive survey into a range of socio-demographic, health and physical, socio-psychological, psychographic, and behavioral variables amongst adults aged between 50 and 79 years ($n = 650$), their study confirms that the older consumer market is not homogeneous. Rather, analysis of the data leads to the first comprehensive segmentation model of the older consumer market in the UK. This chapter profiles two of the major segments to emerge from this analysis, which differ considerably from each other on a range of variables, including consumer behaviors. The marketing implications for targeting these different segments are discussed.

The next chapter in this section, "Grey Power: Developing Older Customer Strategies" by *Sue Tempest*, *Christopher Barnatt* and *Christine Coupland*, explores the increasing importance of "grey power" in the labor market and the marketplace. To fully understand grey market potential, companies need to develop an understanding of individual older customers and their broader social contexts, in terms of both their varying immediate household compositions and their intergenerational relationships. In this chapter, the authors first challenge stereotypes and then introduce a model of older-person segmentation. The frame of analysis is then extended beyond the individual older customer in order to assess the range of "future households" in which the old will increasingly play a key role when purchasing decisions are being made. The authors provide a wealth/health segmentation for firms seeking to develop older customer strategies, and supplement this with a categorization of future households and the issues raised by intergenerational dynamics. This is then used to challenge false assumptions about older household compositions in the twenty-first century. In turn, this provides a segmentation of the old as workers and as customers in a variety of social contexts, which offers some useful tools for companies seeking to capitalize on grey power now and into the future.

Simone Pettigrew, with her work on "Catering to Older Consumers' Customer Service Needs," discusses her observation that older consumers have distinct customer service needs that can constitute a source of competitive advantage for forward-thinking marketers who seek to attract this large and relatively affluent segment. Her chapter focuses on the supermarket, financial planning, and health-care industries to demonstrate the importance of providing personalized attention to allow for the older person's deteriorating physical and cognitive abilities and shrinking social networks. In particular, emphasis is placed on the need to allow older customers to form meaningful relationships with service staff. This strategy has implications for the recruitment, training, and retention of staff members who are able to demonstrate genuine concern for the welfare of the older consumer.

George Moschis and *Simone Pettigrew* (Business Strategies for Enhancing Quality of Life in the Later Years) emphasize the importance of understanding the factors that enhance well-being in later life, and suggest strategies that can be adopted by marketers to assist consumers to achieve this objective. This emphasis on developing strategies that enhance well-being entails a change in philosophy, involving a more holistic approach to marketing that focuses on both profits and enhancing consumer well-being.

Michael Prieler, Florian Kohlbacher, Shigeru Hagiwara, and *Akie Arima* (Silver Advertising: Older People in Japanese TV Ads) contend that choosing the right models and portraying them appropriately are crucial tasks in marketing management and advertising creation. The way older television viewers feel represented by a company has an influence on the overall company image and purchase intentions. This chapter reports that despite a strong increase in older people in Japanese television advertisements between 1997 and 2007, there is still an under-representation of older people. This is especially the case for older women. These findings are in accordance with extant research from different parts of the world. However, our study also finds that when represented, older models are overwhelmingly depicted in major roles. Overall, this study adds not only a Japanese perspective, but is also the first one that compares two periods in time. In terms of product categories the authors found finance/insurance and real estate/housing to feature the largest number of older people. Finally, results from a survey of Japanese consumers give further insight into the phenomenon of older people in Japanese TV ads and how Japanese think about them. Even though the content analysis had revealed a strong under-representation of older people, the consumer survey shows that TV ads are not seen as showing too few older models, and the vast majority of respondents refuted the idea that they did not want to see older people in television advertising. Implications for advertising research and practice are discussed.

Chuck Nyren (Advertising Agencies: The Most Calcified Part of the Process) also looks into the issues of advertising in connection with the silver market. From his perspective, today's advertising industry needs a minor revolution. Talented men and women in their 40s, 50s, and 60s must be brought into the fold if you want to target the silver market. This includes copywriters, graphic artists, producers, video directors, and creative directors. If companies plan on implementing a marketing strategy that includes baby-boomers as a primary, secondary, or tertiary market, and turn it over to only people in their 20s and 30s, they will forfeit the natural sensibilities required to generate vital campaigns. Companies can analyze marketing fodder all day and night, read countless books about marketing to baby-boomers, attend advertising and marketing conventions around the world, and soak up everything all the experts have to say. However, the bottom line is this: if the right people are not in the right jobs, what happens is what happens in all arenas of business – failure and mediocrity. And the reverse is true. If a company had a product or service for the late-teens and twenty-somethings, and had walked into an advertising agency with a creative team made up of only people in their 50s and 60s, the company would and should be very, very worried.

The last chapter in this section (The Importance of Web 2.0 to the 50-Plus) by *Dick Stroud* looks into the importance of Web 2.0 for older people. This chapter addresses this issue, and provides suggestions on how organizations can use Web 2.0 to improve their online interactions with the older market. The chapter analyses the differences between the historical way that web sites have been created and used and the opportunities and dangers of using Web 2.0 technologies. Social networking and web video are the two best-known applications of Web 2.0, and are discussed in detail. The author shows that whilst both these applications are associated with young people, they are intrinsically "age-neutral" and are equally appropriate to older Web users. The chapter describes how social networking and web video are likely to develop, and the resulting implications upon the channel strategy of organizations targeting the older web user.

Part III: Industry Challenges and Solutions

Altogether we present 13 chapters here. The first, "The Business of Aging: Ten Successful Strategies for a Diverse Market" by *Hiroyuki Murata*, starts with the observation that in Japan, an increasing number of enterprises have been focusing on developing new products and services for older adults or for the baby-boomer generation, but actually most of them failed to do so. One reason for this is that often their visions or approaches were too narrowly defined. Many enterprises consider the older adult market or the boomer market as single homogeneous icebergs. However, it seems not to be enough to say that the boomers represent a large part of the market just by sheer numbers. Another reason is that the nature of today's markets is very different from those of the past. This chapter gives readers a perspective of how to view the baby-boomer market or senior market, and gives insights in how to successfully serve markets in this realm.

Kim Walker (The Age-Neutral Customer Journey) claims that nobody wants to feel old as a result of choosing or using a particular product or service. For this reason, age-based products and positionings will have limited appeal for mature consumers, particularly the aging baby-boomer generation. These marketing-wise, life-experienced consumers will expect any purchase experience to be age-neutral. This will require just about every consumer business to make subtle or even radical changes to their product-development, marketing and after-sales approach: changes that accommodate the relentless effects of physiological aging. This chapter demonstrates why and how businesses and brands should become age-neutral. Using three distinct case studies, the author introduces SilverAudit, a unique process that measures and monitors age neutrality by applying 150 "experiences" of the customer journey against 15 identified "effects" of aging. By making products, services and the entire customer experience "age-neutral," businesses can understand, measure, and ultimately remove the barriers between their products and services and mature customers, thereby unlocking the vast spending power of the "senior" markets.

The next chapter looks closer at the case of Germany (The Discovery and Development of the Silver Market in Germany). The authors *Carolin Eitner*, *Peter Enste*, *Gerhard Naegele* and *Verena Leve* report a paradigm shift which is emerging in Germany with regard to the silver economy, and which is resulting in an increasing focus on the economic potential and the economic power of the elderly. Given the much increased buying power of the elderly, and the increased heterogeneity of consumption wishes and needs corresponding to the differentiation of old age, as well as the empirical evidence for an age-specific change in consumption requirements, it stands to reason to look for inherent impulses for economic growth and employment by dint of new "age-sensitive" product ranges and services, and to promote their development and expansion. Today, in fact, the silver economy comprises products and services in very diverse and by no means only "social" market segments and, in addition to the health economy, affects such diverse sectors as mobility and IT. This contribution provides an insight into the development of the silver economy in Germany and its future prospects.

Chikako Usui (Japan's Population Aging and Silver Industries) shows that the "aging problem" should not be viewed as an economic encumbrance. It is better viewed in the context of the robustness of the economy. Expansion of the carrying capacity of the active labor force, as well as active aging among older adults, will decrease the burden on society. This chapter draws out social and cultural implications of demographic changes in the context of Japan's transformation from a Fordist to post-Fordist economy. The distinction shifts attention to the social organization of technology-based service industries. The growing number of older persons and senior households means immense business opportunities for developing new solutions, products, and services. Older adults are potent consumers, willing and economically able to maintain independent living and a high quality of life. This chapter discusses a number of emerging silver industries, including housing and real estate, food, pets, robotics, senior care appliances, and the funeral market.

The perspective of India is presented by *Suresh Paul Antony*, *P.C. Purwar*, *Neelam Kinra*, and *Janakiraman Moorthy* (India: Opportunities and Challenges of

Demographic Transition). India is in the middle of its demographic transition. The 60-plus age group (elderly population) is projected to quadruple by 2050, while the 0–14 age group (child population) remains stagnant. India's population structure and distribution would then closely resemble that of nations currently with a high aging index. The high index, as seen now in nations like Russia and the UK, indicates that the elderly population is larger than the child population. Such changes in the size, structure, and distribution of the population will have implications for public policy as well as business. The Government of India has launched a slew of initiatives to meet this challenge. On the business front, many products and services have been launched that specifically target the elderly. However, there are many other products and services used by all age groups. These may have to be repositioned, if the motivations of the different age groups are not similar. Both from the angle of public policy and business, decision makers in India should closely examine the experience of nations with a high aging index, and respond to the challenges of demographic transition.

The chapter "Silver Markets and Business Customers: Opportunities for Industrial Markets?" by *Peter Mertens*, *Steve Russell* and *Ines Steinke* looks at the impact of demographic change on industrial markets and B2B. Companies can react on many different levels. On the one hand, they can make it a business opportunity by developing and selling products and services that support older people. On the other hand, companies will have to cope with fewer younger workers. The authors discuss several ways to do this (1) to prevent loss of skills from retirement, (2) to accommodate older workers, and (3) to survive with fewer workers. These could lead to Business-to-Business (B2B) products and services that can help companies to solve the issues involved. The authors look at these possibilities in turn, and find that they each lead to ideas that have one or more of the following properties (1) they are actually Business-to-Consumer (B2C) products, (2) they are management or organizational solutions or services, and/or (3) their benefits are not specific to older workers but benefit all employees. Thus, the authors are led to the conclusion that the technical products best suited for the B2Industry silver market will not be "silver-specific" products, but products "designed for all" with an emphasis on usability and problem solving.

Part III includes further a number of chapters discussing different industries, and solutions within these, for the silver market automotive industry. The first of these (Business Opportunities in Personal Transportation: Traffic Safety for Older Adults) by *Kazutaka Mitobe* starts with a view on business opportunities in the safety of personal transportation for older adults. In order to achieve traffic safety for older adults, it is important to support the declining sense and cognitive functions. The author discusses the process of how to reduce traffic accidents involving pedestrians in an aged society. A first business opportunity lies in the establishment of inspection technology. A second business opportunity would be the establishment of training technology. A third business opportunity would lie in the establishment of the market of assistive devices that can compensate for the older adult's declining sense and cognitive functions. From the human factor study using a VR technology, the detailed situations of pedestrian traffic accidents will become clear. Effective assistive technology might be developed based on the risk factor of traffic accidents.

A related piece of work is next presented by *Joachim Meyer* (In-Vehicle Telematic Systems and the Older Driver). He starts his argument with the fact that cars in general are rapidly changing. In addition to its traditional driving-related functions, the car has become a platform for various services and devices. Some of these are involved in the driving task and can improve its ease, comfort, and safety. Others are unrelated to driving, and allow the driver to engage in various activities while driving. The aging of the driving population, and the tendency of older people in many parts of the world to continue driving for as long as possible, pose major challenges regarding the design of such devices and their deployment in cars. Some advantages, as well as some limitations, which these devices may have for older drivers are pointed out. Design of future in-vehicle telematic systems will have to consider these issues in order to provide maximum benefits for the older driver.

"The Golden Opportunity of Silver Marketing: The Case of Housing and Financial Services," by *Kenneth Alan Grossberg*, examines two areas that promise major commercial opportunities because of such a vast socio-demographic change linked to a huge pool of liquid assets. Those areas are, firstly, catering to the financial needs of the country's senior citizens and, secondly, responding to their particular preferences and requirements for housing. In Japan's generally sluggish market for housing and financial services, the silver market provides one of the richest segments available, but successfully offering such services to this population requires skill, sensitivity, and an understanding of the evolving consumer mindset in Japan. In addition, the added impact of the recession of 2008 will make it even more difficult to persuade this target market to part with their diminished personal assets, but it also opens opportunities for financial service providers whose offerings best suit the anxieties and fears of these aging investors.

In the next chapter, the author *Mark Miller* takes the perspective of the media industry (The End of Mass Media: Aging and the US Newspaper Industry). Miller observes that the baby-boom generation, the largest in US history, grew up with mass media and is by far the largest constituency for newspapers, television, and magazines. However, as audiences age and fragment, the economic foundations of these traditional media are challenged. The pain is especially sharp in the newspaper industry, giving rise to worries about the future of American journalism.

Junichi Tomita (Material Innovation in the Japanese Silver Market) takes yet another industry perspective. His work argues what the material innovation process in the Japanese silver market should be like. Material suppliers are continually attempting to contribute to an aging society through material innovation. Although they are not always successful in their intentions to meet the needs of users, they at times discover the actual needs of the users, which are slightly different from the perceived needs. Subsequently, these suppliers work on improving the new materials so as to meet the actual needs of users by developing a close contact with them. The case of superabsorbent polymer (SAP), studied in this chapter, is a typical example of this. The author terms this material innovation process an emergent process. The SAP "Aqualic CA" launched on the market by Nippon Shokubai Co., Ltd., in 1983 is a raw material that facilitated the popularity of disposable diapers in the Japanese market. It also currently holds a large share in the American and European markets. However, it was not originally designed for use in disposable diapers, and the process it underwent from development to marketing was not linear. His case study describes how, after failure in its technological development and supply agreements, success was finally achieved. Further, it indicates the effectiveness of developing evaluation technologies in the process through an end-user oriented approach. As a result, his study should prove to be a valuable aid in helping material suppliers understand effective innovation management.

Another industry perspective is presented by *Helinä Melkas* (Effective Gerontechnology Use in Elderly Care Work: From Potholes to Innovation Opportunities). The use of information and communication technologies (ICT), including safety alarm technologies, is increasing. Its influence on service personnel in elderly care has implications on the possibilities for rooting technological innovations into care work. Human impact assessment methodologies have been employed to assess competence related to technology use, needs for orientation to technology use, and well-being of care personnel. Safety alarms are considered useful both for actual care work and for the administrative part of the care organization. Care personnel appeared not to be fully informed on the technical characteristics and resulting organizational changes. At individual and work community levels, regular human impact assessment of new technologies may stimulate their adoption by the professional carers. The chapter is based on empirical research in a large research and development project in Finland. The research focused on safety telephones and high-tech well-being wristbands. "Potholes" lying in safety alarm systems were identified – taking into account the technology as well as services and organizational networks. The potholes may also be looked into as sources and opportunities for potential future innovation. Social, organizational, process, and marketing innovations – combined with technology – are significant parts of the innovation activity related to the aging of the population.

Finally, in their chapter "Senior Educational Programs to Compensate for Future Student Decline in German Universities," the German authors *Doreen Schwarz*, *Janine Steidelmüller* and *Christiane Hipp* discuss the opportunities of the silver market for (German) universities. Germany's population is expected to fall from about 82 million people in 2008 to, at worst, 65 million people in 2060. Simultaneously, the average age of the population is increasing. In particular, the coming years in East Germany will be characterized by an expected strong decline in the number of young people and a significant increase in the number of elderly. However, demographic change does not automatically imply negative consequences but also creates room for opportunities. In this chapter, the authors explore opportunities to enlarge the purpose of the educational silver market by an economic component because of two developments (1) current and upcoming generations of seniors increasingly spend their spare time studying intellectual and cultural subjects, and (2) traditional universities will experience a shortage of students. The authors propose incentives to include more people aged 65 and over in educational issues, and thus to create a win–win situation for third agers and institutions of higher education.

Lessons Learned and the Challenges and Opportunities Ahead

> Concerning aging, we are talking too much about technology and not about innovation. But what counts is not what is technically possible. What counts is what people want.
>   Professor Joseph F. Coughlin, Director, AgeLab, MIT

Despite the vast amount of valuable information, insights and analyses in this book, there still remain many questions unanswered and a great deal of work to be done. But, we did not – and could not – aim for completeness but rather for variety, and wished to highlight the differences between distinct industries and countries. Thus, we could only present a first fraction of the global silver market phenomenon and some of the industries working on ways of catering for the needs of older people. The need for further research, as well as practice, is obvious.

Lessons Learned

The lessons learned are of course legion. We won't repeat all the lessons learned from each individual chapter here, and it would be somewhat unfair to stress only the lessons learned from some chapters. But one of the most crucial insights is without doubt the fact that the silver market is by no means a homogenous market segment, in that the so-called 50-plus market covers a wide range of different customers and consumers with an equally wide range of values, attitudes, needs and wants. Thus, the silver market actually consists of various different silver markets. In a similar vein, we should not forget that marketing has, for a long time, already gone beyond the simplistic segmentation by age and that, despite the tremendous business potential of the 50-plus, we should resist the temptation of merely looking at a person's age.

The second crucial insight is that the silver market is not necessarily restricted to the silver generation only. Or, put differently, who is silver is not determined by age (alone), and younger consumers can also have silver hair, so to speak. This of course refers to the powerful concepts of universal and transgenerational design as well as ageless or age-neutral marketing. Managers and scholars alike should bear in mind that the best products, services and solutions are often those that can be attractive to a variety of customers regardless of their age, and that they can also be used or consumed regardless of age and physical or mental condition. Beware of ageism, think transgenerationally!

Challenges Ahead

Of course, the challenges ahead are numerous. Ever more countries are affected by demographic change. Think about China, for example. The population structure continuously shifts from young to old due to the effects of the one-child policy, for example. Even currently very young countries such as Vietnam and Thailand are also aging, though the population is not going to shrink over the next decades. However, despite the importance and the vast implications of population aging and shrinking in many nations, we should not forget that population growth still remains a major challenge in many developing countries. Lord Adair Turner of Ecchinswell, Former Chairman of the UK Pensions Commission, for example argues that:

> ... across the world the biggest demographic challenge is rapid population growth in parts of the developing world, not the manageable problems of aging in rich developed countries. [1]

Even though this issue goes beyond the scope of this book, this fact should not be forgotten when discussing demographic change.

Another crucial challenge derives from a combination of the financial situation and the health condition of senior people. Especially with the (mostly affluent) baby-boomer generation that is approaching age 60 and beyond in many countries, the focus of most silver market strategies are the "rich and young-at-heart" elderly, while the "poor and weak-of-limb" elderly are often neglected. True, there are ever-more helpful gerontechnologies and assistive and supportive devices, etc. available, but these are often costly. What happens to those who cannot afford to pay by themselves and are at the same time not sufficiently covered by social and welfare systems? We believe that there might be a new silver market phenomenon on the horizon, which will even be more challenging to governments, policy makers and corporations. The number of those older people whose financial and health situation is not favorable might strongly increase over the next decades. Prahalad [2] has written a book "The Fortune at the Bottom of the Pyramid," where he refers to those consumers at the bottom of the income and wealth pyramid, especially those in developing countries. Kohlbacher and Hang [3] were the first to apply this idea to the silver market, where those in need will be those at the top of the population pyramid (while being at the bottom of the income and wealth pyramid). They warn:

> Firms should be careful not to exclude those customers at the bottom of the innovation pyramid, not only because – as is the case with many baby boomers – the fortune at the bottom of this pyramid is enormous, but also because of corporate social responsibility, as they can benefit both individuals and societies with "gerontechnologies" and related products and services [3].

Bringing the issue of (corporate) social responsibility and social innovation to the discussion of the silver market, or bringing the silver market phenomenon onto the agenda of the CSR and social business debate, will be an important development for both areas.

Opportunities Ahead

Finally, the opportunities ahead will not be less than the challenges. The baby-boomers will continue to age and retire, and so will their children in the future. The silver market phenomenon will not only be an opportunity for business but also an opportunity for innovation and invention, creativity, learning, and social response and responsibility. The lead market Japan could certainly serve as an interesting role model, as can other countries such as the USA, Germany and the Scandinavian nations, but also India and China.

We strongly hope that this book has contributed to this opportunity for business, innovation and invention, creativity, learning, and social response and responsibility. We also hope that it will be a helpful tool in making sense of the silver market phenomenon and that it will encourage an active and creative debate as well as real action in tackling the challenges and opportunities of demographic change.

Tokyo, Japan   Florian Kohlbacher
Hamburg, Germany   Cornelius Herstatt
May 2010

References

1. A. Turner, Population aging: What should we worry about? Philos. Trans. R. Soc. B **364**, 3009–3021 (2009)
2. C.K. Prahalad, *The Fortune at the Bottom of the Pyramid: Eradicating Poverty Through Profits* (Wharton School Publishing, Upper Saddle River, 2006)
3. F. Kohlbacher, C.C. Hang, in *Proceedings of the 2007 IEEE International Conference on Industrial Engineering and Engineering Management (IEEM)* (2007), pp. 1915–1919

From the World Demographic and Ageing (WDA) Forum

Long life expectancy is both a privilege and an achievement that is due largely to successful economic development and improvement in public health. However, it is also a challenge that will impact on all aspects of twenty-first century society. For example, the consequences of improved life expectancy on demographics is illustrated by the fact that the number of people aged 60 and over is expected to rise from the approximately 600 million people reported in 2000 to 1.2 billion in 2025 and 2 billion in 2050. Likewise, whereas today about two-thirds of all older people live in the developing world, by 2025 it will be three-quarters. At the same time, the fastest-growing population group in the developed world is the over-80s, and because women outlive men in virtually all societies, women constitute the majority at a ratio of 2:1.

Thus, population growth and population ageing pose great challenges to industrialised and developing countries alike. As with every challenge, it is not just about facing the problem but about seizing the chance to identify and shape the opportunities that lie within. We have the right and the responsibility to define today what effect and impact population ageing will have on our society, on our social and political framework, on our economy and on our position within the global framework. It is our task and opportunity to shape our future and to think for generations ahead. The WDA Forum strives to identify these unique opportunities by looking at the broad spectrum of issues so that sustainable solutions can be developed. For that purpose, the WDA Forum has created an international, interdisciplinary, intergenerational and permanent platform for demographic and generational issues – a forum designed to facilitate the analysis, discussion and exchange of ideas.

We believe that addressing this challenge requires serious effort and cooperation, not only from the public sector but from all stakeholders. Yet, the action plans and programmes initiated to date, the most prominent being the 1982 First World Assembly on Ageing (Vienna, Austria), and the 2002 Second World Assembly on Ageing (Madrid, Spain), point to few correlations between facing this challenge and global political agendas. Rather, we are still far from an actual global coordination of the multiple initiatives and projects suggested locally, let alone adequate institutionalisation to deal with the challenge.

Moreover, whereas the international debate is important in raising awareness, it is also vital to realise that all people are highly affected by this change on both an individual and a collective level. As the challenges are multiple, so must the responses be manifold, because every human being will deal with the situation in his or her own individual way. Thus, it is important to acknowledge that ageing is not disconnected from social integration, gender progression, and financial and economic stability or poverty.

As a result, modern societies, with their complex social security systems and social infrastructure, will be confronted with effects that are not easily estimated, let alone absorbed. However, individuals too will have to face the consequences of an unexpectedly extended lifespan, and will have to adapt their life course in terms of career, family and financial planning. These challenges will be of particular concern to the so-called Baby Boomers, those individuals born between 1946 and 1964, who will make up a large portion of those over 60 by 2030.

These boomers do and always have innovated and redefined trends and values, challenging the standards and practises of pre-modern society through their political, social or economic views. Indeed, they founded social modernism through their legendary "anti-war" and "free love" movements in the 1960s, reinvented professional careers by aiming for the professional integration of women, and redefined social concepts like family life and active ageing.

Today, the boomers continue to "do it their way" and forge new ground as they go. Thus, because of the high population percentage their group represents, they are challenging today's notion of retirement and, even more, today's perception of "being old". Never before have retirees been so well-educated, so healthy, and so active. Most importantly, this generation grew up comfortable with a consumption-based lifestyle of which they still, because of their high purchasing power, are a main pillar. Thus, whereas earlier generations would refrain in old age from spending their hard-earned money, today's retirees are active: travelling, serving in Senior Expert Service (SES), renovating their houses or even buying high-end cars. Consequently, it comes as no surprise that the average age of a Porsche buyer is said to be 58.

As a result, being above 60 no longer means looking, behaving and acting like a grandfather or grandmother. Rather, instead of simply adapting their services and products to this newly discovered consumer group, multiple commercial services and industries are creating and redefining "age" as sexy, inventing euphemisms for "old" and making it easy for the older consumer to identify with the "young old". Much of this change in mindset manifests among the "Woopies" (well-off old people) or "Best Agers". Above all, this phenomenon reflects a change in the perception of what it means to be old today.

Nevertheless, today's and tomorrow's retirees are more than just the 1968 generation. They are selective consumers with several decades of consumer experience: not only do they know what they want, what quality they strive for and what price they are willing to pay, but most importantly, they can afford to be selective. These trends are particularly reflected in housing and banking for the elderly, but are apparent in many areas.

Despite these changes, and no matter how great the opportunities for new markets, it is imperative that the international community responds to the extraordinary variability in opportunities and challenges. Specifically, we must recognise the limits as well as the benefits of ageing societies by offering our older citizens the opportunity to contribute in a meaningful way.

Thus, we must start thinking of what can be, and learn to cooperate to achieve what should be: a meaningful and peaceful community of all generations. Or, as Nitin Desai, Special Advisor to the Secretary-General, United Nations, stated in the foreword to the World Ageing Situation 2000: *"We are all constituents of an ageing society, rural and city dwellers, public and private sector identities, families and individuals, old and young alike. It is crucial that societies adjust to this human paradigm as record numbers of people live into very old age, if we are to move towards a society for all ages. [Let us]...continue the dialogue and build on partnerships that can bring us closer to a society that weaves all ages into the larger human community in which we thrive"*.

Alfonso Sousa-Poza, Secretary of the Foundation, WDA Forum & Professor of Economics, University of Hohenheim, Germany

Contents

Contributors

Suresh Paul Antony Marketing Area, XLRI School of Business and Human Resources, Jamshedpur, India

Akie Arima Department of Communication, Tokyo Woman's Christian University, Tokyo, Japan

Gunnar Arnold Freelance Market Researcher, London, UK

Christopher Barnatt Department of Computing & Organizations, Nottingham University Business School, Nottingham, UK

Christine Coupland Department of Organizational Behaviour, Nottingham University Business School, Nottingham, UK

Carolin Eitner Department Work, Economy and Technology, Institute of Gerontology, Technische Universität Dortmund, Dortmund, Germany

Nozomi Enomoto School of Management, Tokyo University of Science, Saitama, Japan

Peter Enste Department of Health Industries and Quality of Life, Institute for Work and Technology, Germany

Dan Formosa Smart Design, New York City, USA

Ryoko Fukuda Department of Environment and Information Studies, Keio University, Japan

Oliver Gassmann Institute of Technology Management, University of St. Gallen, St. Gallen, Switzerland

Kenneth Alan Grossberg Waseda Business School, Waseda Marketing Forum, Waseda University, Tokyo, Japan

Shigeru Hagiwara Institute for Media and Communications Research, Keio University, Tokyo, Japan

Chang Chieh Hang Division of Engineering & Technology Management, National University of Singapore, Singapore

Pia Helminen BIT Research Centre, Aalto University School of Science and Technology, Aalto, Finland

Cornelius Herstatt Institute for Technology and Innovation Management, Hamburg University of Technology, Hamburg, Germany

Christiane Hipp Institute of Economics, Brandenburg University of Technology, Cottbus, Germany

Neelam Kinra Marketing Area, Indian Institute of Management, Lucknow, India

Mathias Knigge Grauwert – Office for Demographically Proven Products and Services, Hamburg, Germany

Florian Kohlbacher German Institute for Japanese Studies, Tokyo, Japan

Stephanie Krancioch Independent Financial Adviser, London, UK

Verena Leve Department Work, Economy and Technology, Institute of Gerontology, Technische Universität Dortmund, Dortmund, Germany

Stefan Lippert MBA Program, Kenichi Ohmae Graduate School of Business, Tokyo, Japan

Deana McDonagh Department of Industrial Design, University of Illinois at Urbana, Champaign, USA

Helinä Melkas Lahti School of Innovation, Lappeenranta University of Technology, Lappeenranta, Finland

Peter Mertens Innovation Strategy, Siemens AG, Corporate Technology, Chief Technology Office, Germany

Joachim Meyer Department of Industrial Engineering and Management, Ben Gurion University of the Negev, Beer Sheva, Israel

Mark Miller President, 50+Digital LLC, Author, Retire Smart syndicated newspaper column, Publisher/Editor, RetirementRevised.com, US

Kazutaka Mitobe Department of Engineering and Resource Science, Akita University, Akita, Japan

Janakiraman Moorthy Marketing Area, Indian Institute of Management, Calcutta, India

George Moschis Alfred Bernhardt Research Professor & Director of the Center for Mature Consumer Studies, Georgia State University, Atlanta, USA

Hiroyuki Murata Murata Associates, Inc., Smart Ageing International, Research Center, Tohoku University, Sendai, Japan

Gerhard Naegele Institute of Gerontology, Technische Universität Dortmund, Dortmund, Germany

Chuck Nyren Author, Advertising to Baby Boomers (copyright 2005, 2007), Paramount Market Publishing A Classroom Resource for The Advertising Educational Foundation, US

Britt Östlund Department of Design Sciences, Lund University, Lund, Sweden

Simone Pettigrew Department of Marketing, UWA Business School, University of Western Australia, Perth, Australia

James J. Pirkl All-University Gerontology Center, Syracuse University, Syracuse, NY, USA

Michael Prieler School of Communications, Hallym University, Gangwon-do, South Korea

P.C. Purwar Marketing Area, Indian Institute of Management, Lucknow, India

Gerrit Reepmeyer Institute of Technology Management, St. Gallen, Switzerland

Patrick Reinmoeller Strategic Management and Business Environment, Rotterdam School of Management, Erasmus University, Erasmus, The Netherlands

Steve Russell Knowledge Management, Siemens Corporate Research, Princeton, NJ, USA

Karin Schmidt-Ruhland Design of Playing and Learning, Burg Giebichenstein, University of Art and Design, Halle, Germany

Doreen Schwarz Institute of Economics, Brandenburg University of Technology, Cottbus, Germany

Tim Schweisfurth Institute for Technology and Innovation Management, Hamburg University of Technology, Hamburg, Germany

Peter Simcock Liverpool Business School, Liverpool John Moores University, Liverpool, UK

Alfonso Sousa-Poza World Demographic & Ageing (WDA) Forum, St. Gallen, Switzerland; Department of Economics, University of Hohenheim, Hohenheim, Germany

Janine Steidelmüller Institute of Economics, Brandenburg University of Technology, Cottbus, Germany

Ines Steinke Corporate Technology, User Interface Design CT IC 7, Siemens AG, Munich, Germany

Dick Stroud 20plus30 Consulting, Salisbury, UK

Lynn Sudbury Liverpool Business School, Liverpool John Moores University, Liverpool, UK

Sue Tempest Department of Strategic Management, Nottingham University Business School, Nottingham, UK

Junichi Tomita Department of Business Administration, Toyo University, Tokyo, Japan

Chikako Usui Department of Sociology, University of Missouri–St. Louis, St. Louis, USA

Kim Walker Silver Group Asia Pacific, Singapore

Part I
Innovation, Design and Product Development for the Silver Market

Chapter 1
Product Development for the Silver Market

Florian Kohlbacher, Cornelius Herstatt, and Tim Schweisfurth

Abstract The accelerated aging of many populations and the demographic shift are expected to have major implications for innovation management and new product development across all industries. One major challenge lies in the assessment and understanding of the needs of the silver market, since chronological age by itself is not a sufficient segmentation criterion. A promising dimension is the need for autonomy, which increases with age and which is correlated to social isolation and other individual drawbacks. Thus, focusing on autonomy as a guideline for developing products and services that support people in maintaining or regaining their independence is a viable approach to developing innovation for the silver market, hence "silver products." In this chapter, we present four cases from different industry settings where silver products were developed that help users to sustain or regain autonomy in combination with different functions (e.g., hearing, continence, vision). We present different approaches to technological and functional complexity and newness in these innovation projects, and depict related approaches to marketing and market research.

Introduction

The accelerated aging of many populations and the demographic shift are expected to have major implications for innovation management and new product development across all industries. Products and services need to be either adapted or newly developed to better respond to the changing needs and demands of an aging population (cf. e.g., [1, 2]). Even though many useful practical recommendations can be derived for product development from the work on transgenerational design (see Chap. 9 in this book), universal design (see Chap. 8 in this book), and design for inclusivity [3], the lack of research on innovation management, research and development, and new product development for the aging society is surprising.

In the course of this chapter, we aim to contribute to further closing this gap. We present concepts of how to systematically approach silver markets as a starting

F. Kohlbacher and C. Herstatt (eds.), *The Silver Market Phenomenon*,
DOI 10.1007/978-3-642-14338-0_1, © Springer-Verlag Berlin Heidelberg 2011

point to develop innovations for seniors. To underpin this, we use an explanatory multiple case study approach, and present how firms in very different industrial contexts have created "silver innovations." In the cases presented, a particular need turned out to be the starting point for developing all innovative solutions to silver clients. We observed autonomy – the capacity of a person to freely decide and run her own life as independent as possible – to be core, and the most important, common denominator of all these projects.

Competing in the Silver Market

Strategies of Market Development

Aging customers represent risks as well as opportunities for companies. Both stem from changing needs and means which accompany aging. Companies who want to leverage the business potential of an aging clientele – the "silver market" – consequently need to adapt their innovation-related work. This will typically affect their market research, product development/design, and product delivery, including service. Companies firstly need to clearly understand and define their market space, and align their innovation strategy accordingly.

Obviously there is no one best approach, and previous research in Japan has identified a variety of strategies for competing in the silver market [4]:

– Innovation strategies that aim at developing and marketing products and services especially for elderly people (unique solutions)
– Innovation strategies that aim at adapting products and services especially for the elderly (extended solutions)
– Innovation strategies that aim at developing ageless/age-neutral products and services that offer value to elderly people while also attracting younger customers, or focus on connecting and integrating different generations (universal solutions)

The benefit of these strategies corresponds with the context of the clientele and the firm. In the following, we focus on developing unique and extended solutions for silver customers. Figure 1.1 relates these strategies to each other in combination with age.

The Need for Autonomy

Serving the "Silver Market" as a whole seems to be economically infeasible for many reasons. Therefore, companies innovating products and services for seniors, need first to segment this market and then to identify the most attractive business opportunities based on solid market research. Such an approach seems necessary

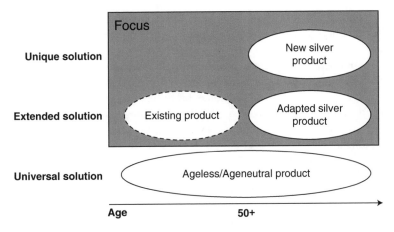

Fig. 1.1 Strategies of silver market development (own depiction)

and effective, since the opposite, unfocussed approach – considering the whole silver market, i.e., all 50+ people – will not lead to differentiated product/service offerings corresponding to age-specific needs. Why? Aging is a multidimensional process (e.g., [5, 6]), and chronological age by itself is not a sufficient segmentation variable. Customer needs diverge with age, leading to highly heterogeneous distributions of consumer preferences (e.g., [7]). For this reason, looking for the one distinct variable that differentiates all people above the age of 49, for example, from all other consumers is likely to fail.

Obviously, a promising avenue for developing unique and distinct solutions for seniors leading to improved or new products and services is to address needs that are related to physical and psychological aging of people and become manifest in phenomena such as constricted viewing, loss of hearing or decline in working memory [8]. Such physical handicaps are the domain of gerontology and related research. Becoming dependant on others is a frequent consequence of physical and psychological handicaps. We argue that most people would like to prevent this, and therefore a common aspiration which human beings share is to stay autonomous and independent throughout their life course [9]. Autonomy, which originated from the Greek "autonoma" (*auto* stands for self, *nomos* means law), can be defined as the capacity of a person to freely decide and run his or her own life as independently as possible (cf. [10]).

Typically, with growing age functional capabilities of humans begin to decline, and by this individual autonomy is reduced. These effects of normal aging are not to be confounded with pathological effects which originate from diseases [11]. This differentiation, however, is more of an analytical nature, since the two effects cannot be distinguished clearly in practice, and both influence autonomy of individuals negatively [12].

The described negative side-effects of aging go hand in hand with becoming more and more dependent, since aging people cannot perform tasks they used to do in daily living [13]. Decreasing sensory abilities complicate the use of products, e.g., opening of bottles, reading displays; lower cognitive capabilities inhibit the fast consumption and processing of data, e.g., comprehension of speech, using interfaces [8].

A commonly used measure to determine individual autonomy is to scale to what extent a certain individual can care for himself/herself in daily living. The activities of daily living (ADL) construct includes basic functions such as eating, drinking, getting up, etc. [14]. The instrumental ADL is extended to more complex and social activities like preparation of food, shopping, and housekeeping [12, 15].

The concept of autonomy is closely related to successful aging, a term introduced by Rowe and Kahn [11]. They claim that successful aging is not only influenced by physiological factors, but also needs to include sociopsychological aspects. Rowe and Khan [16] describe low probability of disease or disability, high cognitive and physical function capacity, and active engagement with life as antecedents to successful aging. We cannot discuss the many facets and views of the constructs here [17], but find strong support for the argument that autonomy is a sine qua non condition for successful aging [9].

Not all, but a major share of aging people will be affected differently by losing their physical and cognitive possibilities. Depending on their individual constitution, values, and temperament, as well as other personal characteristics, people will suffer differently from these emerging deficiencies. The need for maintaining or regaining autonomy is dependent on the individual constitution, too. Consequently, different patterns of aging on the one hand and experiencing the need for autonomy on the other can emerge. The most likely pattern correlates with physical capability [18], and combines decreasing autonomy with growing age (see Fig. 1.2). Autonomy-enhancing solutions can fill the gap between the menacing lower state of autonomy and the preceding, original state, at least for some time. Providing solutions to delay the loss of autonomy may also catch the attention of younger consumers, since they exhibit higher degrees of aging anxiety and fear dependence,

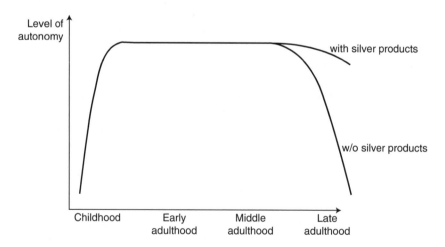

Fig. 1.2 Individual autonomy throughout life stages (own depiction)

more than those who are aging already [19]. As a consequence, firms can serve specific needs today but also build reputation and customer retention in younger customers whose needs will materialize in the future.

From the perspective of a firm that investigates opportunities to innovate for aging people, this observation may lead to attractive, entrepreneurial opportunities. If, in a given market, this firm additionally does not find appropriate solutions corresponding to unmet needs for realizing independence, this observation can become an entry point for an innovation project [20].

In addition to the positive effects of individually satisfying the need for autonomy, other positive effects may occur, including social welfare effects (cf. also Chap. 17 in this book).

We consider autonomy to be a preference throughout all population groups that gains growing importance with age.

In the course of this chapter, we will present case evidence from firms that focus on products that help to maintain individual independence.

Product Design for Autonomy

To support our argument, we now present four case studies to exemplify how companies can develop innovative solutions to help older consumers to maintain and/or enhance their autonomy. These cases stem from very different industrial contexts in the B2C world.

Our first case describes a recent development project in the area of tissue strengthening implants by Johnson and Johnson Medical (Germany), where the starting question was to what extent existing products of a certain business unit were affected by an aging clientele. During the course of the project, the focus moved to the field of weakening tissue structures and the resulting risk of incontinence in higher age. Incontinence was confirmed already to be a severe problem for millions of aged people, which heavily affects the autonomy of these individuals. This was the starting point for developing a product concept that was based on the known mesh technology and aims at tightening the ureter when pressure in the abdominal area increases.

The second case describes development work by Emporia (Austria) in connection with communication devices for aged people. Over a number of years, Emporia has been developing mobile phones for senior users. As seniors are often not used to the fancy design and complicated menu navigation, they are dependent on the help of others in order to use a mobile phone. Emporia has early recognized this need and develops solutions with highly usable design and flattened functionalities adapted to the physical and mental capabilities of aged people. To deliver these functionalities, Emporia´s R&D heavily interacts with typical users, testing each development step with silver customers.

The third case describes the development of an age-friendly notebook by a leading consumer electronics firm in Japan, Fujitsu. The "Raku Raku notebook" (raku = easy) is a PC for silver customers developed by Fujitsu. It draws from the product concept of the "Raku Raku Phone," which was a huge success in Japan and won seniors with easy-to-use interface and less complex functions. In November 2008, Fujitsu came out with the "Raku Raku PC," targeted at silver beginners. Two models are available, a desktop and a laptop version. Both are equipped with an easy-to-use keyboard, mouse and menu using touch-screen technology, so that older people using a PC for the first time can easily understand it. The letters and icons of the menu are 25% larger than on the usual ones. The most often used and vowel keys are marked by colors and function keys such as the space key have the Japanese function written on them. When turning the Raku Raku PC on, the menu shows the most important programs such as e-mail or internet. In addition, Fujitsu offers a home installation service and the Raku Raku PC Help Line, a customer support, which is free for the first year of product usage.

Our fourth and last case presented here, is the Robot Suit HAL (Hybrid Assistive Limb), which has been developed by University of Tsukuba Professor Sankai. This device helps handicapped and elderly people to move their limbs as well as workers to carry heavy weights by wearing a "cyborg" type robotic suit. HAL enhances and strengthens the limb motion of human bodies by detecting the weak bioelectrical signal through the body from the brain which generates the nerve signal to control the musculoskeletal system. The system of HAL captures nerve signals via moto-neuron through a sensor attached on the skin of the wearer. Based on the signals obtained, the power unit is controlled to move the joint in sync with the wearer's muscle movement, enabling to support the wearer's daily activities. The product was launched onto the market in 2009 by the university spin-off Cyberdyne Corporation, with seed money from a major Japanese corporation, Daiwa House.

Comparing the four cases presented here, we find both common factors and differences in terms of the technological as well as the marketing approach.

On the technological side, one has to differentiate between technology and functionality and their corresponding complexities. Whereas "a function is an attribute to the product, substantive technology is the knowledge by which the product is created" [21]. In our cases, the degree of technological newness included to provide solutions can be regarded as varying from relatively low-tech to high-tech. One example draws on technologies that are well-understood and have been implemented before in combination with other products (J&J); others include new technologies which have been developed partly for other applications first (Emporia and Fujitsu) and then transferred. In one case, the technology has been proprietarily developed for silver solutions (i.e., the Hal-suit).

Furthermore we observe that in addition to the different levels of technological newness and complexity, the product offerings also differ in the functional complexity they exhibit from the perspective of the user. In some cases this functional complexity is lower than in comparable products offered to the "mainstream market," due to fewer usage options being provided (Emporia and Fujitsu). In one case (Hal-suit), totally new functions are being offered, which have never been combined in a product before. Again, in another case functionality remains unaltered, but is being offered to a new target clientele corresponding to their needs (J&J).

When companies develop totally new and complex technologies as the core of their autonomy supporting solutions or silver products, it seems mandatory to provide usage functions with a minimum of complexity for the user. This is, for example, one of the major challenges for the Hal-suit project: To deliver a user-friendly product despite the high technical complexity.

Transferring from either known or new technologies, our case companies needed to build up specific capabilities with regard to either technology or market or both.

In order to understand the market, close interaction with potential users of their products in an appropriate and empathic way is needed. By appropriate we mean that the companies had to choose the best available approach to best understand the needs of their target clientele, by either talking, interviewing, observing or combining all approaches in different environments (e.g., customer clinics).

Looking only at the four cases here already shows the magnitude of approaches to delivering useful solutions to the silver market. Creating silver products, like any other solutions for clients, asks for a high degree of empathy and the willingness to devote substantial resources to understand the specific customer situation. Table 1.1 summarizes the most important findings from the case studies.

With regard to market research as a first, essential activity in new product development, all projects were based on a common ground: it is important to empathize with silver customers (cf. [3, 22]), who are on the verge of losing their autonomy, and take their (latent) needs into consideration. However, we found differences in the cases in terms of the approach towards market research methodology. If minor cognitive or psychological restrictions are the reasons for decreasing autonomy, direct qualitative market research such as interviewing the silver customer is still possible and promising; with lowered mental and sensual abilities, ethnography and observation in real-world situations are more promising, because the observer will gain a deeper understanding of the use context, and this knowledge could very likely not be explained by the persons in focus. If physical constraints affect the independence of silver customers, indirect techniques such as using an age simulation suit (cf. [23]) or integrating medical experts may be an alternative to more complex, direct methods. However, these decisions are not either–or choices, and each approach should be complemented by other methods for validation (multi-method approach). Especially in the case of medical innovation, a combination of methods seems inevitable in order to match medical experts' and users' needs.

Need-Driven Versus Age-Specific

With regard to the silver market and age-specific segmentation, it is important to note that successful new products oriented to the needs for autonomy are not exclusively restricted to the use of the elderly. In this respect, these products may offer value for other consumers who are restricted in their senses, cognition, or movement control, or prefer easy-to-use products. In these cases, an ageless

Table 1.1 Summary of cases

Case	Johnson & Johnson Medical	Emporia	Fujitsu	Hal Robot Suit
Product	Urogenital implants	Cell phone	PC	Robot Suit
Customer focus/ autonomy restraining factor	Customer has to use incontinence products such as pads or diapers	Customer has problems with regular phone menu navigation and comprehending the interface	Customer has problems with regular PC menu navigation and comprehending the interface	Customer has problems in moving his/ her limbs and/or lifting heavy objects
Autonomy enhancing effect (examples)	Customer regains continence can move freely, and does not feel stigmatized	Phone can be used by the senior directly without help from others, by simple interface. In addition, phone allows seniors to stay in contact with family and friends and avoid isolation	Using the PC supports older people in staying connected with and using services and functions being offered via Internet. Remote service supports senior user when problems occur	User can lift heavy objects, and muscles are supported while moving
Product innovation	New	Adapted	Adapted	New
Technological newness	Existing technology base transferred	Existing technology base transferred, combined with partly new technology (e.g., noise control)	Existing technology base transferred	New technology (e.g., sensory, triggers, etc.)
Market research	Netnography patient surveys, medical lead users	Focus groups	Prototype testing with users within the target group of clientele	User clinics

marketing strategy (cf. [24]) should be pursued. A supporting example is the Raku Raku Phone: originally developed for older people, this cell phone with enhanced usability and universal design features did not only appeal to older consumers. This led to the development of new versions targeting a much broader clientele including young and old users. Another case in point is the Robot Suit HAL, which has many potential applications beyond the silver market. It can be used by heavy-duty workers in factories or care givers who have to lift patients, and it can also be employed for rehabilitation and entertainment purposes for example. Indeed, it is actually not necessarily a senior product per se.

In the medical industry, for example, a more subtle approach has to be chosen in combination with many products, because customers often feel high levels of stigmatization related to their specific situation and physical/mental condition. Here, an open communication strategy seems often not possible or even counter-productive. Therefore, firms should better communicate to opinion leaders (word-of-mouth effects) or sponsor events first. But, even if the satisfaction of the need for autonomy seems to be a promising strategy for companies that aim at the silver market, the means for reaching product success depend on the reasons for the loss of autonomy and the severity of the consumers' condition.

We find that the need for autonomy can be seen as an overarching segmentation criterion when it comes to the development of products aiming especially at the silver market. Yet there are two distinct, implicational aspects of autonomy-enhancing products. The first, direct effect is connected to the use of the product itself: products need to be engineered in a way that they can be used independently, i.e., without help from others. This requirement is closely connected with questions of usability and product design. The second aspect reaches further, and is related to a more comprehensive perspective that takes the product functions, product environment and related services into account: products should help users to keep their autonomy as long as possible. Products meeting this requirement enable seniors to maintain their mobility, freedom of choice and social participation. As opposed to the first aspect of autonomy, which helps seniors to use products independently, the second layer supports silver customers in maintaining and sustaining their autonomy and living their life independently from other aiders or supporters, offering high quality of life.

Summary and Conclusion

Aging societies and customers apparently ask companies across all industries to respond to the expectations and demands of the changing clientele with improved or new solutions. But looking more closely at the phenomenon and its possible impacts from the perspective of the firm, many issues need to be resolved, e.g., how to segment the "Silver Market," where to start (adapting existing solutions versus developing new ones), how to approach and integrate customers for the purpose of design, etc. Although many useful practical recommendations can be derived for product development from related work on transgenerational design, universal design, and design for inclusivity, a big gap in the areas of innovation management, research and development and new product development for older customers exists.

One way to approach the silver market without explicitly excluding younger customers is to focus on autonomy, representing an important synonym for a good life, disappearing in a more or less continuous manner over the life cycle of a human being. Offering solutions that will allow people to maintain autonomy and to use products and services in an autonomous manner seems to be a promising avenue for firms in all kinds of industries. Therefore, it can be perceived as a boundary-spanning argument and a common denominator for starting development initiatives leading to innovations targeting the silver market.

Actual and potential applications seem to be immense, and comprise a large variety of products and services in uncountable applications, industries and sectors. Taking the needs and wants of older consumers seriously, and developing new products and services that really cater to their demands, not only offers attractive profit opportunities in a time of shrinking youth segments, but additionally benefits older people and their consumer welfare. At the same time, it may attract the attention of younger customers looking for functionally less complex products and designs and in that way prepares future customers by signaling a firm's preparedness to respond to gradually diminishing autonomy, which seems to be unpreventable for all of us.

In contrast to employing age or other direct age-related constructs as segmentation criteria, the need for autonomy will become relevant in each person's life sooner or later. Thus, it can be regarded as an important and common denominator of divergent needs emerging with age, and serve as a guideline for silver product development.

References

1. F. Kohlbacher, C.C. Hang, Disruptive innovations in a new market reality: Evidence from the greying market. Paper presented in R&D Management Conference, Vienna, June 2009
2. F. Kohlbacher, C. Herstatt, "Silver product" development: The reality of R&D firms in Japan. Paper presented in R&D Management Conference, Vienna, June 2009
3. R. Coleman, C. Lebbon, J. Myerson, Design and empathy, in *Inclusive design: Design for the whole population*, ed. by P.J. Clarkson, R. Coleman, S. Keates, C. Lebbon (Springer, Berlin, 2003). p. 478
4. C. Herstatt, F. Kohlbacher, Innovation strategies for the silver market. Paper presented in International Association for Management of Technology Conference, Dubai, Oct 2008
5. V.L. Bengtson, M. Silverstein, N. Putney, *Handbook of Theories of Aging* (Springer, Berlin, 2008)
6. G.P. Moschis, *Gerontographics: Life-stage Segmentation for Marketing Strategy Development* (Quorum Books, Westport, 1996)
7. G.P. Moschis, *Marketing Strategies for the Mature Market* (Quorum Books, Westport, 1994)
8. A.D. Fisk, W.A. Rogers, N. Charness, S.J. Czaja, J. Sharit, *Designing for Older Adults: Principles and Creative Human Factors Approaches* (CRC, Boca Raton, 2009)
9. E. Rubio, A. Lazaro, A. Sanchez-Sanchez, Social participation and independence in activities of daily living: a cross sectional study. BMC Geriatr. **9**, 26 (2009)
10. I. Randers, A.C. Mattiasson, Autonomy and integrity: upholding older adult patients' dignity. J. Adv. Nurs. **45**, 63–71 (2003)
11. J.W. Rowe, R.L. Kahn, Human aging: usual and successful. Science **237**, 143 (1987)
12. E. Hoffmann, S. Menning, T. Schelhase, Demografische Perspektiven zum Altern und zum Alter, in *Gesundheit und Krankheit im Alter*, ed. by K. Böhm, C. Tesch-Römer (Robert Koch-Institut, Berlin, 2009)
13. P. Raina, M. Wong, H. Massfeller, The relationship between sensory impairment and functional independence among elderly. BMC Geriatr. **4**, 3 (2004)
14. S. Katz, A.B. Ford, R.W. Moskowitz, B.A. Jackson, M.W. Jaffe, Studies of illness in the aged: the index of ADL: a standardized measure of biological and psychosocial function. JAMA **185**, 914 (1963)

15. M.P. Lawton, E.M. Brody, Assessment of older people: self-maintaining and instrumental activities of daily living. Gerontologist **9**, 179 (1969)
16. J.W. Rowe, R.L. Kahn, Successful aging. Gerontologist **37**, 433 (1997)
17. A.B. Ford, M.R. Haug, K.C. Stange, A.D. Gaines, L.S. Noelker, P.K. Jones, Sustained personal autonomy: a measure of successful aging. J. Aging Health **12**, 470 (2000)
18. D. Kuh, A life course approach to healthy aging, frailty, and capability. J. Gerontol. A Biol. Sci. Med. Sci. **62**, 717 (2007)
19. S.M. Lynch, Measurement and prediction of aging anxiety. Res. Aging **22**, 533 (2000)
20. S. Shane, S. Venkataraman, The promise of entrepreneurship as a field of research. Acad. Manage. Rev. **25**, 217–226 (2000)
21. B. Kogut, U. Zander, Knowledge of the firm, combinative capabilities, and the replication of technology. Org. Sci. **3**, 383–397 (1992)
22. D. McDonagh, Do it until it hurts! Empathic design research. Des. Principles Pract. **2**, 103–110 (2008)
23. C. Cardoso, J. Clarkson, User Simulation in Product Evaluation, in *Design for Inclusivity: A Practical Guide to Accessible, Innovative and User-centered Design*, ed. by R. Coleman, J. Clarkson, H. Dong, J. Cassim (Gower, Aldershot, 2007). pp. XX, 246 S
24. D.B. Wolfe, R.E. Snyder, *Ageless Marketing: Strategies for Reaching the Hearts & Minds of the New Customer Majority* (Kaplan, New York, 2003)

Chapter 2
Silver Age Innovators: A New Approach to Old Users

Britt Östlund

Abstract When designing innovations for the silver age, it is not sufficient to discover old people's needs only. In addition, one also has to discover old peoples' new roles as consumers, citizens and innovators. Since these are people who until recently have been given few opportunities to make their voices heard, there is a need for methods that identify their needs and demands. More importantly, we need to study and use methods that reveal the sources of innovations behind their expressed problems and lifelong habits as users of technology. Three attempts to identify old people's needs and demands by involving them in the design process are presented, drawn from design projects implemented in Sweden from 2005 to 2009. One project explores how the furniture market can be opened to new segments of older consumers. Another project concerns the development of services. The third project links older people's lifelong habit of watching TV to the development of communication via the television medium. The results were analyzed from two points of view: How do we recognise a need that can be explored in design? When discovered, how do we know that this is a worthwhile need to explore? The first attempt shows that older people can present needs as active users with expressed and specific demands; the second attempt shows that older users can have a need to support the solution to problems which are not yet expressed and activated; and the third attempt shows them as users with latent needs that originate from their lifelong experiences, and needs to keep up with daily routines.

Introduction

This chapter deals with older people as innovators; specifically, the way older people's experiences are important for innovations and design in general. Many view ageing populations as constituting a growing segment with specific needs, and understand ageing as a process having no value for any other age group other than their own. With the exception of the concept of "design for all" and "universal

F. Kohlbacher and C. Herstatt (eds.), *The Silver Market Phenomenon*,
DOI 10.1007/978-3-642-14338-0_2, © Springer-Verlag Berlin Heidelberg 2011

design" it is rare for older people to be described as resources having value to people of all ages. Old people are defined by factors such as age, social loss, physical impairment and technical illiteracy, and ascribed roles as patients, care receivers, users of assistive technologies and subject to other measures, while other kinds of experiences and competences have been neglected. Far too little attention has been focused on older people's capacity for innovation, and on how their life experience can contribute to the development and redevelopment of products and technologies. However, it is insufficient to simply talk about old people or to categorize them in accordance with what we already assume. We need to talk *with* them.

I will describe three different ways to explore old people's needs and demands, based on how accessible they are. The conclusions are drawn from projects to promote and develop products and services for older consumers in Sweden during 2005–2009. One of the main reasons why their experiences are of topical importance is that modern ageing presents new demands. In addition, older generations wish to make their voices heard not only as patients or care receivers but also as citizens and consumers. Another reason is that we actually lack sufficient knowledge when developing innovations. We know enough to continue in the direction of the arrow, but this knowledge is insufficient for creating new markets. At best, present trajectories reinforce already existing markets and existing images of older people.

Often, the interpretation of their preferences does not rest with the elderly themselves, but with those who exercise care for the elderly. A stereotype is that older people are unfamiliar with or even fearful of new technologies. It is easy to forget that their long experiences with technical change and technological development make them the most experienced technology users in society today. While they may not know about the very latest innovations, they definitely have lived with and experienced many innovations that they have had to consider and make decisions about [1]. There is a gap between what we *think* they want on one hand, and what they actually ask for or how they want to be treated on the other. Consequently, innovations for the silver age will require a different approach than simply projecting the needs of older persons. Rather, silver age innovations must be based on discovering how older persons function in their new roles as consumers, citizens and innovators.

Old People and Innovations

By "innovations" I mean new ways of doing things in methods, products or services. When something innovative is fairly defined, the design process takes off. This chapter deals with both the innovation process and the design process. Usually old people, as well as people in general, have been allowed to step in at certain stages predefined by engineers, designers or researchers. A design process can consist of three stages: preparatory work with an analysis of a problem; second, synthesis and visualization creating a prototype which is tested and modified; and third, evaluation with follow-up of the results. Most often, the second phase is where users get the chance to influence the process by being test persons. It is well-known that users in general can be a significant source of innovation [2, 3]. When it comes to old people's role in the design process, unfortunately that is not the case. What then is the point in letting them contribute more substantially?

The value of integrating life-experienced people into the design process is that their experiences, needs, and knowledge of them correspond to the demands put on successful innovation and design processes. According to innovation researchers such as Michael Porter, successful innovation processes are characterized by customers or users who present intractable problems, have high requirements, offer resistance, but still have the patience to stay on [4]. This is exactly what older people can contribute, as they are life-experienced, pragmatic and trustworthy. A growing selection of creative examples can be found such as the experience automat developed in Japan in cooperation between designers at Kyushu University and the company RICOH. The automat is used to find relevant experiences among recently retired colleagues when the company establishes new plants. A younger colleague involved in plant design should always accompany an older colleague.

When the ageing and design programme became a priority at the Institution for Design Sciences at Lund University in Sweden 2004, the main aim was to understand the expectations of today's older generations, and develop methods that avoided stereotypes. The cooperation with companies and public health care organizations made it possible to apply our results, and contribute to the development of products and services.

When the outcome and implementation process was analyzed, we were able to observe different stages of awareness among the users and the possibility of supporting older persons' articulation of their needs and demands. To identify these needs and demands requires different methods and a time span not usually found in most innovation studies. Older persons have demands and needs that are quite observable, but they can also have what I call "inactive" or "latent" needs that can be revealed only by using specific methods. Thus, we get a third question, namely how can they participate? What methods are available to realize the ambition that innovations should be user-driven?

The methods used in these projects differ according to the users' awareness of their needs, i.e., their ability to express their demands and desires. In addition to interviews and focus groups, it is not always possible to obtain the needs or desires we are looking for as something independent of the individual who is the carrier. The only way to explore these needs and desires is to involve older persons in the innovation or design process. The concept "sticky information" suggest that it is not always possible to separate needs from the owner, and gives a taste of how closely the user and the knowledge of their needs can be related [5].

Another prerequisite is the fact that older people are divided into different segments. Consequently, their needs cannot be generalized to fit the needs of all the elderly population. They constitute a heterogeneous group, which also applies to their demands and preferences. However, the way they are culturally defined gives them experiences of ageing in modern society that sometimes overshadow their differences. Some of these experiences have a bearing on them as consumers, such as the experience of being retired and excluded from the possibility to catch up with technological developments, societal discrimination in general, generational values shaped by certain events, and the experience of being the oldest [1, 6].

Users with Active Needs in the PLUS Furniture Project

The development of the Swedish wood processing and furniture industry with user-oriented and competitive PLUS products was a project conducted between 2008 and 2010. The aim was to explore the demands of a new ageing population market segment by testing defined PLUS values in furniture: functionality, elegance and durability. The project was conducted by the Department of Design Sciences at Lund University and the Engineering Department at Linköping University in cooperation with seven Swedish furniture producers: Lammhults, Swedese, Nelo, Allinwood, Stolab, NC Möbler, and OH Sjögren. The project managers were Britt Östlund and Elisabeth Dalholm Hornyanzsky. Thirty persons were involved, between 57 and 87 years old. The main outcome was the identification of user requirement specifications for the companies that could be used in meeting the needs and demands of the new market segment of older consumers.

The purpose of the project was to respond to the apparent lack of a specific product serving what was an obvious demand. The aim of the project was to develop criteria for a product group of furniture serving older consumers. The idea actually was raised by a furniture dealer who observed that he had met a new group of consumers for whom he did not have an appropriate selection of furniture. Earlier, the situation was that when someone came into the store to buy furniture for the elderly, it was a person from a retirement home which would act on older persons' behalf. The furniture that was designed for older people was usually functional, but not particularly attractive. It was certainly not the sort of furniture that you wanted in your home.

Today, older individuals are coming directly into stores by themselves to purchase furniture for their own homes. They are also known as being in the third age, unlike those in the fourth age, who are elderly with a need for daily care [7]. When third age consumers enter furniture stores they cannot find what they are looking for. Considering their lifelong experience with being furniture users, the PLUS furniture project decided to provide the woodfurniture industry with criteria that have a bearing on three aspects: functionality, elegance and durability.

Expressed Demands To Be Designed

To get the most realistic picture as possible, the researchers chose subjects who were about to move from their present home to something smaller or to senior housing. The methods used to identify demands were pretty much straightforward. Focus group interviews were followed up by individual interviews with people already living in a kind of retirement home. In order to visualize the demands, and make them more relevant for design and production, two visualizations took place and some mock-ups were developed. One company also built its own prototype that was tested at a furniture fair. Moreover, the companies were asked to pick out a number of chairs that they assumed already had PLUS values. These chairs were tested and commented upon by the sample of users [8, 9].

The older persons studied were identified as relevant users because they were on their way to change their furniture at home and identified what they were actually looking for to be a problem. The results from this project are now being followed up by the companies, who will integrate the PLUS criteria into their designs for new products or into the development of already existing products.

The results of these studies have led to an understanding of how users experience potential PLUS values in chairs – functionality, elegance and durability. These values are supposed to work as leading demands coming from a new segment in the market, and help companies to formulate their own more specific description characteristics, i.e., user requirement specifications in terms that they can use in their continuing efforts to develop PLUS furniture.

Users with Not Yet Activated Needs Looking for Support

The project Business Solutions for Local Support in the Third Age was carried out during the period 2005–2007. The goal of this project was to explore the needs and demands for services among people in the third age who wanted to remain living in their own neighborhood despite growing old. The project was established by the Department of Design Sciences at Lund University in cooperation with the Swedish Church, the parish of Adolf Fredrik in the city of Stockholm. The project manager was Britt Östlund. One hundred and five persons 60–99 years old were involved in interviews during 2005. Twenty-one women 63–88 years old participated in this project during 2006 and 2007, which identified the need for new services for people in the third age.

The main outcome was the development of a model revealing that existing services mainly focus on the needs of the fourth age, and was heavily influenced by donors' service perspective, and the alternative characteristics of services asked for by people in the third age.

The most challenging way to grasp old people's needs and demands is to enable those who have knowledge and experience not yet expressed – inactive needs. Not that the users themselves are inactive as opposed to active; it is that their needs and demands that are not yet activated. Like those with active needs, old persons have a need for support for something they want to do or realize in their lives, but it is not necessarily specified. Their needs are expressed in terms of problems rather than as a demand for specific products or services. At the same time, they are more pragmatic than they were earlier in life. The challenge when taking on users with inactive needs occurs when addressing actions to solve their problems or giving them the tools to do that. Older persons are on the edge of articulating their demands, and need a push to go forward.

The purpose of one project that we undertook in the city of Stockholm in the period 2005–2008 was to develop services appropriate to retired persons belonging to the Church of Sweden in the parish of Adolf Fredrik. It was pretty obvious to the church board that the old people in the parish were no longer attracted to the same activities they were one or two generations ago.

Demands To Be Realized

The project therefore needed to find out what the older people who wanted to participate in the project actually wanted to do, and what they lacked support for; and then it had to develop this specific support. The sample was again active people in the third age. The method used was research circles, which is a method open to active participation and which explicitly strives to change social practice [10]. Research circles are driven by the participants' will to achieve something, and includes a research interest to create both a new structure and the systematic development of knowledge. The strong emphasis on participation is in contrast to approaches aimed at group interventions to relieve loneliness or at training profes- sionals to do things for older people [11]. The research circle instead involves doing things with them.

The research circles started by giving the participants the opportunity to describe the life they wanted to live in old age, the extent to which they wanted to increase their capacity, and what they were prepared to do themselves to improve their situation. The results revealed one main theme: living on my own terms – when housing for old people does not exist or is not attractive, what can we do then? The group decided to increase their social networks in the neighborhood in order to continue as residents in spite of ageing. But what kind of services could be developed from the tax-funded welfare system or from the commercial market that the older persons in the group were not able to satisfy by themselves?

Missing Markets

The result of their investigations identified a gap between the services their older neighbours were offered and the services they really needed. In fact, they have to live with the fact that they are categorized according to obsolete stereotypes of ageing, and have to cope with meeting their own demands by combining different solutions such as municipally-financed home help service, the private sector, the black market and assistance coming from relatives and friends. They realized that it was not the old people's needs, but rather the service provider's priorities that governed the supply of help they could receive. Moreover, they concluded that the services available today primarily address people with fourth age needs who chiefly require help with household chores, not with services in general.

The type of service requested can be explained in terms of time and competence, not focusing on action but on time. Services for older people, for example in the form of help in the household, are usually packaged for any form of action involved. This segment asked for the possibility to buy time and use it optionally. One reason is that they often do not want to hand over the entire execution to someone else but be involved themselves. One example is the need to be helped to carry down the laundry to the laundry room, but to sort the laundry and choose the laundry programme themselves. The results also suggest the need for the public care sector to re-evaluate what they actually supply and better assess changes in demand. In addition, today people in the third age do not accept being passive recipients of services. They are ready to self-organize until they enter the fourth age.

To conclude, the research circles are, in spite of them being time-consuming, a way to discover hidden demands and to activate consumers. The worthwhile discovery in this project concerns services. Society provides services mainly built around the needs we have in the fourth age, and is heavily influenced by donors' service perspective. The third agers' demand for services is characterized by the need for continued independence and to be allowed to choose what they want help with. They are more pragmatic and more comfortable than before, and happy to let things go which in the past they took great pride in doing. In the third age, the user of a service wants to be the same person who decides about how that service is delivered, and to pay the service providers delivering the service or technical support systems. In the fourth age, the decisions and payment provision are often handed over to someone else to take care of.

Users with Latent Needs

The project: New Networks for Modern Ageing ran through 2008 and 2009 with the aim of supporting social networks for older people through interactive communication via their own TV through the use of mobile radio networks. The project was a joint adventure between Inview Inc. and the Department of Design Sciences at Lund University, where the new possibilities for technological convergence interacted with 10 years of research about old people's TV viewing.

The project took into consideration both the changing requirements of participation among the elderly, and the technological developments that now make it possible to develop interactive TV. Thirteen persons between 54 and 82 years old tested the prototype "ippi" at home, and contributed to the design process and the demarcation of future consumers. The result consists of a modified and improved product and knowledge of the usefulness of ippi problems for the owners, and the target group among the elderly that should be best helped by ippi. The result indicated a general benefit to those who watch much television as well as those who combine ippi with the Internet and mobile telephony.

Innovation should focus on the old as well as the new. Lifelong habits are often not regarded as being innovative because the development of products and services for old consumers most often emphasizes novelties and revolutionary technologies. There is a window of opportunity to search for evolutionary innovations, however, based on learning from existing habits, including the use of technology deeply rooted in everyday routines. Many needs that can shape technology which were previously undisclosed can be recognized when users are granted priority in interpreting and defining their needs and can be more actively involved in defining them. A key element in this discovery process depends on a competence to identify patterns in daily life. These patterns consist of many years of well-established and integrated habits and routines. The fact is that research about the use of technology in everyday life teaches us very clearly that lifelong habits affect the way we approach new technologies. Not least, technologies are part of the constitution of everyday life, and as such are embedded into social relations and into experiences of safety and familiarity.

In one of the projects, old people's lifelong habit of TV viewing was discovered as a source for innovations. Statistics show that old people watch TV to a greater extent than any other age group, and that TV viewing in the fourth age tends to be more individualized compared to earlier in life [12–14]. As such, TV viewing makes a significant contribution to the capacity to cope with disengagement in old age, and can be used as a way to promote communication and wellbeing [15]. Considering the extensive TV viewing among older people and TV viewing as a lifelong habit, why take a detour by relying only on mobile phones or the Internet to offer older people the opportunity to communicate more effectively? Why not build directly on everyday use of TV?

Evolutionary Innovations

Well, one company actually made use of TV as a more interactive communication opportunity. They developed a patent which allows the possibility of communication between a mobile telephone and a TV, or between the Internet and a TV. The name of the solution is ippi. With the help of a remote control, ippi makes it possible to communicate asynchronously by sending pictures or voice messages to and from the TV set at home. One question was whether familiarity with the TV, "the TV as metaphor," could serve as a resource for promoting new technologies and developing services for old people.

We assumed that it could, and the extent to which it could proved to be confirmed beyond our expectations. Being able to watch the TV screen reduced the uncertainty for the participants and facilitated the initial use of the ippi. A simple installation required that each participant simply attach a SCART connector to the TV and plug the ippi into an outlet in the wall; this contributed even more to increasing the desire to try the ippi. Most likely, initial difficulties in installation or use can quickly reduce users' motivation. This experiment shows that the absence of complications related to the installation of users decreased uncertainty about the new application.

But while the TV metaphor worked for attempting and wanting to try out the ippi, it did not contribute primarily to using the ippi on a daily basis. Rather, it was the access to a social context or a social network that determined the extent of usage. Consequently, the use of ippi, as in any other communication technology, was dependent on a social context. The use of ippi was also tied to daily user patterns that can be of use in developing innovations. Identifying such usages depended on the competence of trained researchers in being able to identify habits and routines, as these phenomena are fairly invisible when integrated in everyday life, and taken for granted as a part of life. The ability to locate these patterns is also based on the fact that technology is used and shaped in social contexts.

Three Types of Needs

A summary of these attempts to involve old people as users in design processes points to the fact that needs can be visible, hidden and even latent. The first attempt shows that older people can present specific demands in an active way. This needs to be interpreted as *active needs*, as they create a movement forward, but without a method of support.

As the second attempt shows, however, need can appear as problems as well as preferences or desires, which reminds us of the fact that just because a need is not formulated does not mean that a need does not exist. In the second attempt, older users have a need of support when solving problems which is not yet expressed and activated. As such, the needs are *not yet activated*. With appropriate support, older users can make their voice heard, and activate their needs to create innovative approaches and open new markets. This approach might be even more important considering the fact that the expectations among older people today regarding how they would like to spend the latter part of their life are changing. Modern ageing populations will hardly match stereotypes of what old people might need or prefer.

The third attempt shows older persons as users with *latent needs* that originate from their lifelong experiences, and the need to keep up with daily routines. Latent needs are dependent on someone else to see what experience they are charged with, and what habits and routines can be developed into services or products. Table 2.1 provides an overview over various user requirements and needs which are described, how they appear, and suggested methods for identifying them. Active needs are expressed as a demand for a specific product and service, and are characterized by the fact that there is a lack of supply of these products or services. However, general preferences or complaints or other kind of general comments (for example that "technology is a bad thing") should not be mixed up with what is worthwhile to explore as an actual need. Of course, a specific demand can be

Table 2.1 Three kinds of needs defined in terms of needs as active, not yet activated or latent, the way they appear, what should not be mixed up with needs worthwhile to explore, and suggested methods to reveal active, not yet activated and latent needs

	Active needs	Not yet activated needs	Latent needs
Expression	Demand for specific products or services	Need for support or social change	Charged with user experiences
How needs appear	Lack of supply	The presence of problems	Need for continuation of established habits and routines
False or incomplete ways to identify needs	General preferences	General complaints	Claims of lack of needs or experiences
Suggested methods to reveal needs	Surveys, focus groups and interviews	Research circles for social action	Scientifically trained personnel doing field work

waiting at the end of that road, but this is another process and much more time-consuming to identify, and the comments made by older persons on the surface should not be confused with their specific demands. While specific demands can be fairly demarcated, the suggested methods are pretty much straightforward. Focus groups are a good way both to broaden and limit the scope, followed by the use of surveys or interviews with closed or open-ended questions as well as interviews. Inactive needs are characterized by a need for support for something that the users want to do in life. This is most often associated with what needs to be changed, such as prejudices against old people that prevent them from being active citizens. Inactive needs are often expressed as problems rather than as needs or demands. However, focusing only on older persons' general complaints about things will not be sufficient for identifying the architecture of needs. Instead, you have to look at the will to engage in an active way to improve an actual life situation. For this reason, research circles are suggested as a method that encourages social action. Latent need users, on the other hand, require consent from the users but not necessarily an active engagement. They are walking containers, with mental mappings and experiences that are a goldmine for researchers, able to reveal habits and routines that can lead to innovations and make learning curves less steep.

There is still a lack of knowledge about the growing silver age market, which suffers from stereotypes where ageing is associated with something obsolete rather than with innovations. No company wants to be associated with decline. Discovering old people as innovators might be one way of increasing the business value of life experience. So, how possible is it to realise the suggested methods for market-dependent companies and entrepreneurs? It is true that identifying and developing user-driven products might seem to be time-consuming. On the other hand, older users get a lot out of projects that identify their needs, and often want to participate in such projects over an ongoing period. Entrepreneurs and innovators having technical knowledge should also consider fund-raising together with academics and problem owners, since it is well-known today that innovation systems are not a result of isolated initiatives but of networks and cooperation linking various kinds of knowledge.

Summary and Conclusions

To conclude, this chapter suggests that exploring old people's needs and demands is about defining the appropriate method. Old people's needs are not absent just because they are not visible. Expressed demands are easy to identify, but also problems and hidden abilities can become sources of innovations. The first attempt presented in this chapter shows that older people can present specific demands in an active way, interpreted as *active needs* in demand for new PLUS criteria for furniture. However, as the second attempt shows, needs can appear as problems as well as preferences or desires for not yet existing services. As such the needs are *not yet activated*. The third attempt shows them as users with a *latent need* hidden in lifelong experiences such as TV viewing. The discovery of latent needs is dependent on someone who has an eye for hidden patterns and routines that can be developed into services or products. Applying this discovery process can contribute to the development of new markets which might emancipate old people to become active consumers and citizens, and also contribute to the development of innovations in general. Not least, a new approach to old users will contribute new business opportunities for industry.

References

1. B. Östlund, Design Paradigms and Misunderstood Technology: The Case of Older Users, in *Young Technologies in Old Hands – An International View on Senior Citizen's Utilization of ICT*, ed. by B. Jeager (DJØF Publishing, Copenhagen, 2005)
2. C. Raasch, C. Herstatt, P. Lock, The dynamics of user innovation: Drivers and impediments of innovation activities. Int. J. Innovat. Manage. **12**(3), 377–398 (2008)
3. C. Herstatt, E. von Hippel, From experience: Developing new product concepts via the lead user method. J. Product Innov. Manage. **9**(3), 213–222 (1992)
4. M.E. Porter, *The Competitive Advantage of Nations* (Free Press, New York, USA, 1998)
5. E. von Hippel, *Democratizing Innovation* (MIT, Cambridge, MA, USA, 2005)
6. B.S. Turner, Ageing and Generational Conflicts: a reply to Sarah Erwin. Br. J. Sociol. **49**(2), 299–304 (1998). London School of Economics, London
7. P. Laslett, *A Fresh Map of Life. The Emergence of the Third Age* (Harvard University Press, Cambridge, MA, USA, 1991)
8. O. Jonsson, Hur kan personer i "den tredje åldern" involveras i projektet PLUS-produkter för att skapa ny kunskap och bättre design av möbler? [How to involve people in "the third age" in the project PLUS-products to improve knowledge and design of furnitures?] Examination paper, Karlstad University Sweden, 2009
9. O. Jonsson, E. Dahlbom, L. Sperling, Användares upplevelser av Plusvärden hos sittmöbler. [Users' experiences of plus values implemented into furniture]. Project Report (Department of Design Sciences, Lund University, Sweden, 2010)

10. B. Östlund, The revival of research circles: to meet the needs of modern ageing and the third age. Educ. Gerontol. **34**(4), 255–266 (2008)
11. K.H. Pitkala, L. Blomquist, P. Routasalo, M. Saarenheimo, E. Karvinen, U. Oikarinen, T. Mantyranta, Leading groups of older people: A description and evaluation of the education of professionals. Educ. Gerontol. **30**, 821–833 (2004)
12. J.D. Robinson, T. Skill, Media usage patterns and portrayals of the elderly, in *Handbook of Communication and Aging Research*, ed. by J.F. Nussbaum, J. Coupland (Lawrence Erlbaum Associates, New Jersey, USA, 1995), pp. 359–91
13. G. Häggblom-Kronlöf, U. Sonn, Interests that occupy 86-year-old persons living at home: associations with functional ability, self-rated health and sociodemographic characteristics. Aust. Occup. Ther. **J53**, 196–204 (2005)
14. Nordicom (2005) www.nordicom.gu.se/common/stat_xls/690_5520_daily_reach_sex_age_2004. xls. Accessed 22 Jan 2009
15. B. Östlund, Watching television in later life: a deeper understanding of TV viewing in the homes of old people and in geriatric care contexts. Scand. J. Caring Sci. **23**(4), 623–825 (2009)

Chapter 3
Disabled Persons as Lead Users for Silver Market Customers

Pia Helminen

Abstract It is important to understand user needs when developing new products. User-centered design provides tools for learning about the user needs in question, but studying only the target market customers may result in constricted need data because of the functional fixedness of these customers. The lead user approach, on the other hand, aims to learn from the lead users of a certain target group in order to find better solutions for the needs in the target market. In this chapter, I show through a study on mobile phones how disabled persons can be seen as lead users when developing products for silver market customers. I also present methods for exploring the needs and solutions that disabled users possess.

Introduction

The customers of the so-called silver market are people who are often beginning to suffer from deterioration in their eyesight, hearing, or mobility. Product development has traditionally concentrated on developing products for the general, able-bodied public. It should not be forgotten that up to 25% of the population in industrialized countries are older people or people with a disability, most of them in the silver market. As the target market of most of the products, such as mobile phones, is virtually all consumers, this means that the aging population should not be shrugged aside, as it continues to fill an ever-increasing part of the target market.

I first introduce the concepts of user-centered design, user innovation, and lead users. Then I show through a study on mobile phone user interfaces that disabled persons can be seen as lead users, when developing products for the silver market. The study also shows how methods like photo-diary and contextual inquiry can be used in order to better understand the needs of silver market customers.

F. Kohlbacher and C. Herstatt (eds.), *The Silver Market Phenomenon*,
DOI 10.1007/978-3-642-14338-0_3, © Springer-Verlag Berlin Heidelberg 2011

User-Centered Design and Lead Users

It is common understanding among designers and product developers that user needs have to be taken into account when developing a product. The roots of user-centered design are in the military industry. In World War II it was found that the performance of technology can be improved if attention is paid to the ergonomic requirements of those who use the technology. The goal of user-centered design is to transfer user needs into product specifications, and thus ensure the satisfaction of the future customers. What is common in all user-centered design methods is that they provide the designer with information that he or she can use when designing the product. *The role of the user is to be purely an information source for the designer*, who then hopefully is able to innovate.

User innovation means innovation carried out specifically by users. Users are individual consumers or companies that expect to benefit from using a product or a service, whereas manufacturers expect to benefit from selling a product or a service. Traditionally, users have been seen as passive consumers who just consume the products that manufacturers develop. In reality, users have always made modifications to products when needed. In fact, when users need something badly and there is no solution in the market, they will generate a solution by themselves – they will innovate.

Often, user innovation is confused with user-centered design. The user-centered design approach offers a variety of methods for user needs assessment: interviewing (group, open, structural, etc.), contextual inquiry [1], probing [2], observing, etc. All of these methods help the designer learn about the needs of the targeted user. Thus, the company first learns about user needs and then develops a responsive product to fill that need. Even if the user has developed some type of solution to his/her need, companies very often overlook the user's solution and only register the need. The main difference between user innovation and user-centered design is who carries out the actual innovation. *In user-centered design the innovator is the designer who works in a company. In user innovation it is the user himself.*

Users innovate because they have to, and they benefit directly from the innovation they develop. Users do not care how the need is filled as long as it is. Companies on the other hand need to struggle with many things other than the optimal solution: product portfolios, strategy, manufacturing capability, etc. Users can come up with the most creative solution, because they are searching for the best possible *functional* solution to their own problem.

To better grasp the concept of user innovation, von Hippel [3] developed the term *lead user*. These are the users that companies need to find in order to benefit from user innovation. In order to understand what lead users are, we need to understand what diffusion is. Rogers's [4, 5] ideas on diffusion are well-known. He talks about diffusion of new ideas through a society, and the fact that a considerable time lag exists from the introduction of a new idea to its widespread adoption. The main elements in the diffusion of new ideas are (1) an innovation that is (2) communicated through certain channels, (3) over time, (4) among the members of a social system. In spite of the fact that the communication of most innovations involves a time lag, there is a certain inevitability in their diffusion. Most attempts to prevent innovation diffusion over an extended period of time have failed. For instance, the Chinese were unsuccessful in their attempt to maintain sole knowledge of gunpowder. And today, the secret of the nuclear bomb is no longer a secret [4–6].

According to the diffusion model, an innovation is completely diffused when it has been adopted by 100% of the members of the social group to which it has been introduced. Rogers divides the adopters into five categories: innovators (the first 2.5% to adopt), early adopters (13.5%), early majority (34%), late majority (34%), and laggards (the final 16% to adopt) [4].

The theory of lead users relies on the idea that there is always somebody who has the need first, and that the rest of the marketplace will have the need later. As all new things diffuse through a society over time, there are always users whose present needs foreshadow general demand [6]. Von Hippel defines lead users of a novel or enhanced product, process, or service as those displaying two characteristics with respect to it:

1. Lead users face needs that will be general in a marketplace – but face them months or years before the bulk of that marketplace encounters them.
2. Lead users are positioned to benefit significantly by obtaining a solution to those needs [3].

According to the first lead user characteristic, the "ahead on an important market trend" variable, there are users who experience new needs and are prepared to generate innovations that substantially differ from existing market offers. The second characteristic, the "expected benefits" variable reflects the possibility of the users initiating the development of a new solution if the solution would bring them significant benefit [7, 8]. In other words, lead users are well ahead of market trends and have needs that go far beyond those of the average user [9].

It is important to distinguish lead users from the categories defined by Rogers. *Lead users act solely on their needs*, whereas Rogers's innovators and early adopters are driven by their interest in the new technology. In other words, as stated by von Hippel [10]: "Note that lead users are not the same as early adopters of an innovation. They are typically ahead of the entire adoption curve in that they experience needs before any responsive commercial products exist – and therefore often develop their own solutions." See Fig. 3.1.

Classical research on problem-solving shows that it may be inhibited by the functional fixedness of solution objects [11]. This means that if we examine users that are already familiar with the product, we might find them not able to generate new ideas for its use. They are functionally fixed and then not able to think out of the box. If a person is asked to perform a task that requires the use of a wire, he is less likely to unbend a paper clip if he is given the clip attached to papers than if he sees the clip loose. Or, for example, a screwdriver is designed for handling screws but as it is long and sharp, it could also be used as a crowbar or a chisel.

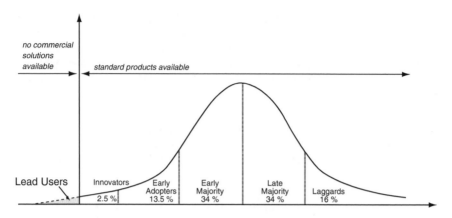

Fig. 3.1 Lead users' position on a market trend compared to Rogers's diffusion curve

In user-centered design, we take a look at the targeted customers. The problem with the targeted customers is that however well we study them, they are going to be functionally fixed and therefore not able to reveal information that enables us to create breakthroughs. *Lack of functional fixedness makes lead users very appealing to product development*, i.e., lead users do not base their views on existing products but on their needs. As Lilien et al. state: "In contrast, lead users would seem to be better situated in this regard – they 'live in the future' relative to representative target-market users, experiencing today what representative users will experience months or years later" [12].

Who are lead users, then? A lead user is often somebody who is trying to improve their way of working, rather than consciously trying to invent. Like the developer of World Wide Web Tim Berners-Lee says: "It was something I needed in my work." Berners-Lee wanted simply to solve a problem that was hindering his efforts as a consulting software engineer at CERN, the European particle-physics laboratory in Geneva. Mainly to become more efficient, he developed a system that provided easy-to-follow links between documents stored on a number of different computer systems and created by different groups [13].

Very often lead users will have already invented solutions to meet their needs. This is particularly true among highly technical user communities, such as those in the medical or scientific fields [14–16]. Also, innovations in sporting equipment are often developed by lead users. Shah [17] shows that innovations in skateboarding, snowboarding, and windsurfing have typically been developed by a few early expert participants in those sports. The idea for the heart rate monitor was originated by a Finnish professor, Seppo Säynäjäkangas, in the early 1970s. He enjoyed cross-country skiing, and he started wondering what methods could be used to monitor the development of his condition. The Finnish Ski Association soon became interested in the idea and started developing a prototype with Säynäjäkangas. Later this invention was utilized by all competitive athletes, and nowadays the heart rate monitor has diffused to serve a big part of the population who enjoy recreational sports. Also, the energy bar is a user innovation. It was invented by an Olympic marathoner, who cooked up the first PowerBar in his kitchen.

Lead users can also be found among those who function in harsh conditions, such as aerospace or the military, for example.

When 3M, a diversified technology company, was trying to develop cheaper and more effective infection control in the area of surgical drapes,[1] they gathered information outside the target market, in order to find lead users. They traveled to hospitals in Malaysia, Indonesia, South Korea, and India, and learned how people in less than ideal environments attempt to keep infections from spreading in the operating room. They interviewed veterinarians who had great success keeping infection rates low despite cost constraints and the fact that their patients were covered with hair and did not bathe. They interviewed Hollywood makeup artists who had learned effective ways to apply nonirritating, easy-to-remove materials to skin, which is important to the design of infection control materials. With the help of these lead users, 3M was able to create three new product-line concepts [9].

In the following study I show that disabled persons can be lead users for able-bodied users, and especially for the silver market customers.

Disabled Persons as Lead Users in Mobile Phone Design

The purpose of this study was to (1) investigate if disabled persons could be seen as lead users in mobile phone user interface design, and (2) to evaluate the suitability of the selected research methods on the examined user groups.

Traditionally, mainstream consumer product design has not explicitly considered the needs of older or disabled people. Instead, their needs have been considered in the design of niche products, e.g., disability aids, providing separate and also stigmatizing solutions for these user groups. Yet in many ordinary circumstances we all suffer from a "situational disability": When there is no light, we cannot use our eyesight, for example. When there is a lot of noise, we are not able to hear. When driving a car, we should not use our hands for anything other than driving nor look away from the road. Moments of situational disability are even more common among the silver market users.

I argue that if a mobile phone user interface is designed based on the user needs of the target market (i.e., the majority of consumers, who are people that hear and see well), we end up leaving out everyday situations, where the use of eyesight and hearing is limited or completely prevented. Yet, it is a significant advantage for a mobile phone to work well in all possible situations. I suggest that if a mobile phone user interface was designed based on the needs of disabled persons, the special disability situations would be covered as well.

---

[1]Surgical drapes are thin adhesive-backed plastic films that are stuck to a patient's skin at the site of surgical incision, prior to surgery. Surgeons cut directly through these films during an operation.

In this study I investigated whether the needs of a disabled user in an "ordinary" situation correspond to the needs of an "ordinary" user in a special situation. In other words, are specifications derived from an actual disability equal to those derived from a situational disability? Three members of three different groups of mobile phone users were studied and compared: deaf, blind, and "ordinary users" who see and hear well. The methods that were used in the study are *photo-diary* and *contextual inquiry* combined with an *open-ended discussion*. Contextual inquiry was used for learning about users needs. Photo-diary and open-ended discussion provided information not only on user needs but also on the leading edge behavior of the disabled persons. The methodology of the study is presented in detail in the appendix.

I will present the results of the study on how disabled persons can be lead users for silver market customers, firstly by showing the comparison between the user needs of the disabled users and the ordinary users (situationally disabled users), and secondly, by showing examples of the leading-edge behavior of the disabled users, and how they indeed face needs that the ordinary public, and especially the silver market customers, may encounter. I will also show some design guidelines for visually and hearing-impaired users. These guidelines apply not only to completely blind and deaf users but also to users with milder impairments that are common among silver market customers.

User Needs of Disabled Users Versus Ordinary Users

Photo-diaries documented the course of the participant's day, and the objects and devices that had been used during the day. The photographs taken by the blind participants turned out well. Only aiming at the target was slightly inaccurate, but it did not impede recognition of the photographed object (see Fig. 3.2). The contextual inquiry and open-ended discussion were able to widen the understanding of the actual user needs of each participant.

All ordinary users articulated situations when use of mobile phones is difficult because of not being able to hear well: urban noise, rock festival, library (when the

Fig. 3.2 Photographs taken by a blind person

Table 3.1 Ability to perform given tasks (situationally blind vs. blind)

Task	Situationally blind (complete darkness)			Blind		
	Ordinary 1	Ordinary 2	Ordinary 3	Blind 1 *no TALKS*	Blind 2 *TALKS*	Blind 3 *TALKS*
Can he find the silent phone, when not holding it, and make a call?	No	No	No	No	No	No
Can he find the ringing phone, when not holding it, and answer the call?	Yes	Yes	Yes	Yes	Yes	Yes
Keypad locked, can he unlock it and make a call?	Yes[a]	Yes[b]	No[c]	Yes[b]	Yes[d]	Yes[d]
Keypad unlocked, can he make a call?	Yes[e]	Yes[e]	Yes[e]	Yes[f]	Yes	Yes
Keypad unlocked, can he send a text message?	Yes[e]	Yes[e]	Yes[e]	Yes[f]	Yes	Yes

[a]Pressing one determinate key lights the screen and makes the instructions to unlock the screen visible. *User knows the determinate key by heart*
[b]Pressing two determinate keys is needed to unlock the keypad. The screen is not lit until unlocked, i.e., the instructions to unlock the screen not visible. *User knows the determinate keys by heart*
[c]Pressing two determinate keys is needed to unlock the keypad. The screen is not lit until unlocked, i.e., the instructions to unlock the screen not visible. *User does not know the determinate keys by heart*
[d]*TALKS* speaks out the instructions to unlock the screen
[e]The screen is lit
[f]*User knows the menu structure and keys by heart*

phone should be silent and no speaking is allowed). Speaking on the phone when walking in the city center was found difficult and uncomfortable since it is not possible to clearly hear the voice on the other end. In noisy environments you cannot talk on the phone and you cannot hear the phone ring.

Two blind participants have TALKS[2] speech output software on their mobile phones. It speaks out the words and letters that are shown on the screen. The third participant is not a TALKS user, but uses the mobile phone just by touch. She has a limited access to mobile phone functions since she has to memorize the menu structure.

Both blind and situationally blind users performed equally in given tasks (see Table 3.1). None of the users were able to find a silent phone if it was placed in an unknown location, but if the phone was ringing, they found it easily guided by the sound.

Some phones require pressing two determinate keys to unlock the keypad. The screen of the phones will not be lit until the keypad is unlocked, i.e., the instructions

---

[2]SpeechPAK TALKS converts the display text of a cellular handset into highly intelligible speech, making the device completely accessible for blind and visually impaired people. SpeechPAK TALKS runs on Symbian-powered mobile phones to speech-enable contact names, callerID, text messages, help files, and other screen content.

to unlock the keypad that are shown on the screen cannot be seen. In order to unlock the keypad without instructions, one must remember the correct key combination by heart. One situationally blind and two blind users did not remember the combination. These two blind users were, however, able to listen to the instructions on the screen through TALKS and were then able to successfully unlock the keypad, where as the situationally blind user was not. In other words, the blind users had found a solution to their need by installing TALKS on the mobile phone.

One ordinary user drives a lot and uses a hands-free holder for the mobile phone in the car. He finds it very difficult to drive and simultaneously hit the right buttons when phone is placed in the holder. This problem is very similar to the one of unlocking the keypad in the dark.

Also, deaf and situationally deaf users performed equally in given tasks (see Table 3.2).

All users talked about the importance of a good keypad. None of the ordinary users were satisfied with their current keypad. One ordinary user hoped for a keypad with good tactility that would enable the use of it without watching. She also wanted to wear a protective cover on the mobile phone but found using the keypad difficult through the cover. She uses the protective cover on the phone not only in order to protect the phone but also in order to get a better grip when digging out the phone from a bag without looking. Two blind users had found a solution to their tactility need: They had modified the keypad by adding a small "lump" on the 5-key or all keys in order to make the keypad more tactile.

What is found is that the needs that ordinary (situationally disabled) users face in special situations are similar to those of disabled users in ordinary situations.

Table 3.2 Ability to perform given tasks (situationally deaf vs. deaf)

Task	Situationally deaf (noisy environment)			Deaf		
	Ordinary 1	Ordinary 2	Ordinary 3	Deaf 1	Deaf 2	Deaf 3
Can he find the ringing phone, if not holding it?	No	Yes[a]	No	No	No	No
Incoming call, can he find the phone, if the phone placed in a pocket or a handbag? (phone vibrating)	No	Yes	Yes	Yes	Yes	Yes
Incoming text message, can he find the phone, if the phone in pocket or handbag? (phone vibrating)	No	Yes	Yes	Yes	Yes	Yes
Can he make a call...	Yes	Yes	Yes	Yes	Yes	Yes
...and communicate the message?	Yes[b]	No[c]	No[c]	No	No	No
Can he send a text message?	Yes	Yes	Yes	Yes	Yes	Yes

[a]User notices the blinking light on the screen

[b]User notices when the call is answered, and then speaks out the message on the phone

[c]User does not notice when the call is answered. User speaks out the message on the unanswered phone

Leading-Edge Behavior of Disabled Users

It was found that disabled persons experience needs that ordinary users may also experience, and that in many cases they have already obtained solutions to those needs. There are examples of solutions the disabled users have found that have later become general among ordinary users. There were also several examples of solutions currently used by disabled users that may become common in the future.

Deaf users rely heavily on text messages, and in Europe they have, in fact, adopted text messaging much earlier than the ordinary public. This, however, requires writing in a language other than native, which for the deaf is sign language. One deaf user sends her husband photos of products from stores, in order to avoid time-consuming text messaging. For ordinary users this would in many cases be more efficient than trying to describe something using words. Today, many online news services in fact offer readers a possibility to send in photo and video messages on accidents and other news-worthy incidents – after all "a picture is worth a thousand words."

One blind participant still actively uses Memona Plus (see Fig. 3.3) for making notes. Memona Plus is a pocket-sized electronic, portable Braille note-taker that weighs 180 g and can be connected to a PC or to a mobile phone. The storing capacity is 30 A4 pages. The written texts can be checked sign by sign through the inbuilt digitized speech output. The notes can be stored as different files and they can easily be transferred to a PC. Short voice messages can be recorded through the inbuilt microphone. Memona Plus also tells the time and date. The predecessor of Memona Plus was Memona (introduced in 1992), which had a smaller storing capacity and no voice message recording. The first personal digital assistants (PDAs) had practically the same functions. One of the first was Palm Pilot that came to market in 1996, 4 years later than Memona.

One blind user actively uses Navicore Personal[3] navigation software through TALKS, as he is not able to see the map on the phone screen. Although Navicore

Fig. 3.3 Memona Plus

[3]Navicore Personal is a software application that is installed on the mobile phone by memory card, and used together with an external Bluetooth GPS-receiver (http://www.navicore.fi/).

was designed to be used when driving, he uses it for personal navigation when walking. Separate navigation systems especially designed for car use tend to have a speech output option for exactly the same reason, i.e., not being able to look at the map when driving.

To compensate for the missing possibility to make calls, deaf users have been using MSN messenger[4] service on the internet for years. Nowadays, MSN messenger and the like have also been adopted by the general public. The next step, from using the messenger service with a webcam, is making two-way video calls, which two deaf users already do on their clamshell phone that has two cameras: one on the outer side and one on the same as the screen (inner side).

The majority of current mobile phone users have not yet started using two-way video calls or even sending one-way video messages. There are several reasons why video calls and messages may become popular among all users.[5] In the modern world we live in, families and friends often live geographically far away from each other. By making two-way video calls instead of phone calls, grandparents could stay in tighter contact with their grandchildren, for example. A parent would be able to show the other parent the first steps of their child as he or she is taking them. Instead of sending a holiday text message stating it is sunny and the beach is beautiful, one could send a video message actually showing it. Also, working life has become more dispersed over the years and people spend more and more time on business trips. Video conferencing is used but it requires special equipment, which makes organizing such a conference complicated. A two-way video call could be established right then and there, whenever needed.

The deaf users also indicated that there should be a small light source integrated in the phone. Otherwise it is not possible to make two-way video calls or send one-way video messages in the dark. That naturally would apply for all users.

Two blind users had installed TALKS on their mobile phones, but all users would clearly benefit from the possibility of switching to speech output when in the dark or driving a car, for example. Most silver market customers need special reading glasses for being able to see clearly at a short distance, so when the glasses are not available, a speech output function would help.

One visually impaired participant described a problem considering routing when outdoors. He is able to notice signboards but not able to see what is written on them. He suggested image recognition as a solution to this problem: User would take a photo of the signboard and have TALKS read out the text. This would be a handy tool for anybody visiting a foreign country. Before departing for a trip, one would just download a suitable dictionary on the mobile phone. For silver market customers with deteriorating eye sight, image recognition on the mobile phone would be really practical.

---

[4]Internet messaging service by Microsoft (http://messenger.msn.com/).

[5]This study was carried out in 2005. Now (February 2010) video messages and video calls have become popular in Japan and in some parts of Europe.

An everyday problem that blind people face is trying to locate objects. One blind user suggested that in order to stop worrying about keys, the mobile phone could be used to lock and unlock the home door. That would clearly help everybody, as we all seem to be carrying more and more objects every day, and especially silver market customers who suffer from memory disorders.

These multiple examples show that the disabled users do indeed exhibit leading-edge behavior in adapting and developing new communication aids.

Critical Attributes for Visually Impaired Users

Examining altogether six blind or visually impaired users gave information on attributes that are critical for these users to be able to successfully use a mobile phone. These guidelines apply well not only to blind users, but also to users with the milder visual impairment common for silver market customers.

Good keypad is essential. Since blind users are not able to perceive the keys visually, they need to rely on the tactile feeling of the keypad. There are a few attributes that define a good keypad:

- Keys need to be separate from each other. When the keys are clearly separate from each other, it is easy to know when your finger is on a key.
- Good tactile response when pressing a key. The sensation of "click" signals the user that a key has in fact been pressed. A feather-touch switch, for example, is not a good choice.
- Keys in straight rows, no strange arrangements, such as U-shape. If keys are not arranged in straight rows and columns, it is not easy to know which key is which. In a U-shaped arrangement, for example, when you go to the left from the 5-key, you can accidentally end up on the 7-key instead of the 4-key.
- Tactile cue on the 5-key. To facilitate the positioning of fingers on the keypad, there should be a tactile cue on the 5-key. The cue needs to be on the key, not beside or below the key like in some phone models.
- Surface of the key not slippery. For better touch, the keys should not be slippery. A rubber-like surface, for example, was preferred by the research participants.

Not many changing functions on one key was a common wish. If one key has changing functions depending on what is shown on the screen, the use of the keypad becomes complicated for users who cannot see the information shown on the screen. Softkeys[6] like the NAVI-key,[7] for example, was mentioned as problematic.

---

[6]A multifunction key usually positioned beneath the mobile phone display with the corresponding textual or graphical function label shown on the display [18].

[7]Navi™-key: Nokia's one-soft key interaction style; first applied in the Nokia 3110 phone model [18].

If the user gets lost, there must be a way to easily *climb back up the menu structure and start over*. In many phones this is done through pressing the cancel button for a few seconds.

For visually impaired users that are not using speech output software like TALKS, a *logical menu structure* is essential. When you are not able to see the screen, you must be able to create a mental model of the menu structure.

Critical Attributes for Hearing-Impaired Users

Since a mobile phone interface relies heavily on visual information, there are not as clear critical attributes for hearing-impaired users as there are for visually impaired users. As long as the interaction with the mobile phone is based on text, symbols, or images, a hearing-impaired user is able to use the phone. For two-way communication, deaf users can apply two-way video calls.

For hearing-aid users, an inductive loop set[8] is essential. Even with severe hearing impairment, the use of an inductive loop set enables calling on a mobile phone. Without the loop set, the user would have to rely on the use of text-messages only.

Summary and Conclusion

The customers for any product are not alike, but they differ in their capability to perform tasks on and interface with the product. The importance of taking user needs into account when developing new products is nowadays common knowledge. To be able to satisfy the needs of a market where – mainly due to the aging population – user needs have become increasingly heterogeneous, concepts like "universal design" (USA and Japan), "design for all" (Europe), and "inclusive design" (UK) have been developed. In addition, more labeling concepts such as "design for disability," have come up. All of these concepts fall under the umbrella of user-centered design, where the user needs are indeed considered but where the designer of the solution is an engineer. The lead user approach, in contrast, sees lead users as a source of possible solutions.

This study shows that the user needs of situationally disabled users, i.e., ordinary users in special situations, overlap with the needs of disabled users in ordinary situations. In addition, several examples of leading-edge behavior in disabled users

---

[8]All hearing aids support the induction loop technology. When the hearing aid is on the T-mode, it captures the signal supplied from the loop.

were found. When we look at the data gathered through this study in reference to von Hippel's definition of lead users, we find that the second lead user characteristic clearly applies to disabled users: disabled users surely benefit significantly by obtaining a solution to their needs. As for the first characteristic, there are examples showing that disabled users have found solutions such as text messages that have later become common among all users. There seems to be a similar trend in two-way video calling. This suggests that *disabled users can be seen as lead users* when developing products – in this case mobile phone user interfaces – for the ordinary public who undergo moments of situational disability.

The aging customers of the silver market often suffer from deterioration of eyesight and/or hearing. They, in fact, are even more often situationally disabled than the younger and more able-bodied customers, which means that many products, such as mobile phones, are more difficult for them to use.

As explained earlier, user-centered design concentrates on gathering user needs from the targeted customers, but the targeted customers may be functionally fixed and not able to give us information that could help develop breakthrough products. The targeted customers are seldom able to articulate the latent needs behind their fixedness. For an aging customer, this can be even more so, because deteriorating eyesight, for example, might be a delicate matter for them. Therefore it is possible that they are less willing to expose their actual, everyday needs, when approached by a designer.

In this study, only visually and hearing-impaired users were examined as possible lead users. The aging population suffers not only from visual and hearing impairments but also from deterioration of mobility. I assume that if the user needs of persons with a physical disability were examined, we would get a similar result.

The study also showed that the selected methods were applicable for studying deaf and blind users. Photo-diary was found to be an effective and easy method for self-documentation, also when studying blind users. No other equipment is needed for documentation, as long as the photos are later gone through in a separate discussion. No major difficulties occurred in carrying out the contextual inquiry and open-ended discussion.

When working with visually and hearing-impaired users, the designer should remember the role of language in interaction. Common language means fluent and more personal communication. Sign language is the native language of the congenitally deaf. For a blind person it is easier to contact the designer by e-mail or by phone, since he or she can do it in their native language. The deaf participants can feel uncomfortable and perhaps even shy about sending a written message. It should not be presupposed that a deaf person can fluently write in the predominant language. Having to book a sign language interpreter makes scheduling more complicated and the meetings a little less personal.

This study concentrated on the mobile phone user interfaces, but this approach can easily be transferred to any other products. I recommend that when developing products for the customers of the silver market, disabled persons should be seen as lead users and therefore as a valuable source of not only user need data, but also as a source of possible solutions.

Appendix: Overview of the Study

Three members of three different groups of mobile phone users were studied and compared: deaf, blind, and "ordinary users" who see and hear well. Deaf and blind groups were selected to represent disabled persons, because of the clear definition of these groups, and the fact that it was rather easy to access these groups. Blind and deaf persons were contacted through several associations and societies, such as Finnish Federation of the Visually Impaired and Finnish Association of the Deaf, and through personal contacts. The three deaf persons were deaf since birth. Two of the blind participants were congenitally blind, and one had lost his eyesight in adulthood.

The methods used were *photo-diary* based on a theme, and *contextual inquiry* combined with an *open-ended discussion* (further details are given below). Contextual inquiry was used for learning about users needs. Photo-diary and open-ended discussion provided information both on user needs but also on the leading-edge behavior of the disabled persons.

Photo-diary and self-photography have been used in various disciplines. Gaver et al. [2] included a disposable camera in the cultural probes package when studying the elderly, and Brown et al. [19] used photo-diary followed by semistructured interviews to capture information on working life.

Contextual inquiry is a field data-gathering technique developed by Beyer and Holtzblatt [1]. The most basic requirement of contextual inquiry is the principle of context. Staying in context enables the interviewer to gather ongoing experience rather than summary experience, and concrete data rather than abstract data. Gathering data on an ongoing experience means that the interviewer is present when work is being done. If a person is asked a question, the answers tend to be summarized, for it is very difficult to go into detail and describe exactly what happened. The job of the interviewer is to recognize the actual work structure, which arises out of details of mundane work actions. In order to discover concrete data instead of abstract data it is very important to talk in concrete terms. When the customer says "generally I do this" or "usually..." the interviewer must pull the customer back to a real experience. To gather concrete data you need to ask questions like "what did you do last time" instead of "what do you do usually."

Contextual inquiry helps us to understand the real environment people live in and work in, and it reveals their needs within that environment. It uncovers what people really do and how they define what is actually valuable to them [20].

There were two meetings with every participant. The first meeting was a short 30-min meeting where participants were given the photo-diary assignment. Approximately 2 weeks later in the second meeting the contextual inquiry and the open-ended discussion were carried out. At the same time, the photo-diary results were talked through and used as inspiration in the discussion. An outside interpreter took part in the meetings with the deaf participants.

The study was piloted with one ordinary user. The pilot revealed that in the photo-diary assignment, the use of flash on the disposable camera was a bit

Table 3.3 List of participants and their mobile phones

User	Sex	Age	Mobile phones
Blind 1	Female	34	Nokia 8310 (personal), Nokia 1100 (personal)
Blind 2	Female	58	Nokia 3660 (personal)
Blind 3[a]	Male	36	Nokia 6600 (personal)
Deaf 1	Male	25	Nokia 6100 (personal), SonyEricsson Z1010 (personal), Nokia 6600 (work)
Deaf 2	Male	33	Nokia 9110 (personal), SonyEricsson Z1010 (personal), Nokia 6310i (personal), Nokia 9110 (work)
Deaf 3	Female	28	Nokia 6820 (personal)
Ordinary (pilot)	Female	27	Nokia 3510 (personal)
Ordinary 1	Male	29	Siemens ST60 (personal)
Ordinary 2	Female	30	Nokia 6600 (personal)
Ordinary 3	Male	60	Nokia 9210i (personal, work), Nokia 6230 (personal, work)
Severe visual impairment	Male	43	Nokia 6600 (personal, work)
Severe visual impairment	Male	37	Nokia 6600 (personal, work)
Severe visual and hearing impairment	Male	57	Nokia 9300 (personal) + Nokia LPS-4 inductive loop set

[a]Not congenitally blind. Not able to read braille

complicated. This problem was addressed by giving the participants step-by-step instructions on the use of the disposable camera. The tasks to be performed by ordinary users in special situations were shaped during the pilot study.

In addition to the nine participants presented above, two open-ended interviews were carried out. The first interview included two persons who have progressively lost a major part of their eyesight in adulthood. The second interview included one person who had a similar visual disability but who also suffered from a severe hearing impairment. Two of these persons were found through personal contacts. One was a volunteer found through a society of the visually impaired. The purpose of these interviews was to gain a wider perspective on disability in general, since these persons had literally seen both worlds. In addition, all three had tried out a variety of mobile communication devices. All participants are listed in Table 3.3.

Photo-Diary

The photo-diary assignment consisted of a disposable camera and a stamped return envelope. Instructions on how to use the camera were given verbally in the first meeting, and also on paper or by e-mail depending on the person's choice. The theme of the photo-diary was to take a picture of "everything you use for communication, or use for receiving or transmitting information." Some general examples were given:

- If you read a newspaper, take a picture of the newspaper
- If you listen to the radio, take a picture of the radio

- If you check the temperature, take a picture of the thermometer
- If you use a mobile phone, take a picture of the mobile phone

The time frame within which the photo-diary was supposed to be carried out was one day, starting from waking up in the morning until going to sleep in the evening. The participants could choose the day themselves (see pictures in Fig. 3.4).

The blind participants were advised in practice on how to use the disposable camera. Since the pilot study had showed that there might be problems with the flash when using a disposable camera, step-by-step instructions were given to all participants on paper or by e-mail.

No additional equipment was required, just the disposable camera.

It was possible to take 28 pictures with the camera, but participants were advised not to worry, if at the end of the day they had taken only ten photos. The important thing was to document all possible things and equipment that were used according to the given theme. After finishing the photo-diary, the camera was to be sent back to me (within 2 weeks) in the stamped return envelope, in order for me to develop the pictures.

Contextual Inquiry and Open-Ended Discussion

In the second meeting, the pictures taken in the photo-diary assignment were discussed one-by-one. The participant explained the meaning of each picture in the order they were taken. Each object in the pictures was discussed in detail: how many times it was used during the day, why, and for which purposes.

Fig. 3.4 Photo-diary pictures

The use of mobile phone was discussed following the principles of contextual inquiry: What have you done with your mobile phone today? Show me how you do it. What devices have you used this week? For which purposes? Why? Show me.

The disabled users were observed when using their own mobile phones in their ordinary environment, such as home or work environment.

The ordinary users were observed when using their mobile phones in special situations that included complete darkness, and a noisy environment. These special situations were created in the participant's home. Complete darkness was achieved in a walk-in closet or in a bathroom. A noisy environment was created by using an industrial hearing protector headset that included total noise-canceling and an FM radio. This way, all sounds from surrounding environment were blocked out and replaced with music. To assure total canceling of surrounding sounds, disposable foam ear plugs were used under the headset.

The special situations were chosen to be such that really simulate a possible everyday disability situation. Therefore, the "situational blindness" was not simulated by concealing user's eyes. It is highly unlikely that a person ends up in a situation where their eyes are concealed, but it is possible that eyesight is limited by lack of light.

In these special situations the ordinary users were asked to perform basic tasks, such as calling, receiving a call, sending a text message, and receiving one. The starting point of the tasks varied: the mobile phone was to be found in the pocket, in the bag, or in the surroundings in proximity of the user. The use of mobile devices was studied also in the ordinary environment in the same manner as was done with the disabled users.

After going through the pictures of the photo-diary, and the contextual inquiry, the participants widely expressed their views on their current mobile devices, their expectations, and desires. They told about problems they have faced, and shared their visions on what kind of devices they would like to use and how.

References

1. H. Beyer, K. Holtzblatt, *Contextual Design: Defining Customer-Centered Systems* (Morgan Kaufmann, San Francisco, 1998)
2. B. Gaver, T. Dunne, E. Pacenti, Interactions **6**(1), 21–29 (1999)
3. E. von Hippel, Manage. Sci. **32**(7), 791–805 (1986)
4. E.M. Rogers, *Diffusion of Innovations*, 4th edn. (Free, New York, 1995)
5. E.M. Rogers, *Diffusion of Innovations* (Free, New York, 1962)
6. E.M. Rogers, F. Shoemaker, *Communication of Innovations: A Cross-Cultural Approach* (Free, New York, 1971)
7. E. von Hippel, *The Sources of Innovation* (Oxford University Press, New York, 1988)
8. E. von Hippel, *Democratizing Innovation* (MIT, Cambridge, MA, 2005)
9. E. von Hippel, S. Thomke, M. Sonnack, Harvard Bus. Rev. **77**(5), 47–57 (1999)
10. E. von Hippel, *Horizontal Innovation Networks – By and For Users*. Working Paper No. 4366–02, Sloan School of Management, Massachusetts Institute of Technology, Cambridge, MA, 2002

11. K. Duncker, Psychol. Monogr. **58**(5), 270 (1945)
12. G.L. Lilien, P.D. Morrison, K. Searls, M. Sonnack, E. von Hippel, Manage. Sci. **48**(8), 1042–1059 (2002)
13. H. Brody, Technol. Rev. **99**(5), 32 (1996)
14. C. Lettl, Technol. Health Care **13**(3), 169–183 (2005)
15. C. Lettl, C. Herstatt, H.G. Gemuenden, R&D Manage. **36**(3), 251–272 (2006)
16. C. Lüthje, *Proceedings of the 32nd EMAC Conference* (Glasgow, UK, 2003)
17. S. Shah, *Sources and Patterns of Innovation in a Consumer Products Field: Innovations in Sporting Equipment.* Working Paper No. 4105, Sloan School of Management, Massachusetts Institute of Technology, Cambridge, MA, 2000
18. H. Kiljander, *Evolution and Usability of Mobile Phone Interaction Styles* (Helsinki University of Technology, Publications in Telecommunications Software and Multimedia, Espoo, Finland, 2004)
19. B.A.T. Brown, A.J. Sellen, K.P. O'Hara, *Proceedings of the SIGCHI Conference on Human Factors in Computing Systems* (ACM, New York, 2000), p. 438
20. M. Kuniavsky, *Observing the User Experience: A Practitioner's Guide to User Research* (Morgan Kaufmann, San Francisco, CA, 2003)

Chapter 4
Integration of the Elderly into the Design Process

Karin Schmidt-Ruhland and Mathias Knigge

Abstract With demographic change looming in the background there has been an ever greater need for products and aids for the growing target group of elderly people. Previous methods and ideas in the areas of product development and design have not proven to be good enough to develop attractive and helpful solutions that meet the wishes and needs of this age group.

New approaches and product concepts have been developed in the *sentha* research project. *sentha* stands for "seniorengerechte Technik im häuslichen Alltag" (Everyday Technology for Senior Households). Working in this interdisciplinary research project are designers from the Berlin University of the Arts in cooperation with the Technical Universities of Berlin and Cottbus, as well as the Berlin Institute for Social Research.

The goal was to develop products and services for an increasingly aging society so that seniors can maintain their independence in daily life as long as possible.

At the Institute for Product and Process Design (Prof. Achim Heine) of the Berlin University of the Arts, designers Karin Schmidt-Ruhland and Mathias Knigge have been working on the development and positioning of senior-friendly products and services. In their projects they have focused on specific wishes and needs of elderly people without limiting themselves in form and function solely to this one target group. The article elucidates the specific design approach as regards this user group and the methods for integrating elderly people, and shows a selection of designs that have been realized in the *sentha* project.

Introduction

Demographic change poses an enormous challenge for product manufacturers and service providers because conventional offers do not always meet the demands of elderly people, who complain about lack of user-friendliness and being overtaxed. For many needs and requirements at this age, there are no offers at all.

F. Kohlbacher and C. Herstatt (eds.), *The Silver Market Phenomenon*,
DOI 10.1007/978-3-642-14338-0_4, © Springer-Verlag Berlin Heidelberg 2011

Until now, solutions for this target group have been found from the field of aid provision for handicapped persons. However, the methods and ideas in product development and design are not sufficient for providing helpful and attractive solutions. One essential reason for this is the lack of empathy, especially on the part of young developers dealing with elderly to very old consumers [1].

Therein lies a great chance for manufacturers, commerce, and service providers in the development of such user-oriented solutions. Equipped with innovative quality features, the solutions for such a financially strong target group range from being interesting to being necessary, in order to allow people to become old with the greatest amount of self-determination possible in their own homes [2].

This is where the research project *sentha* has its starting point for developing new approaches and product concepts. *sentha* is the German abbreviation equivalent to Everyday Technology for Senior Households (see Abstract above).

Against the background of a steadily growing share of elderly people in the total population, together with a great increase in life expectancy, the project has researched products and services that in the future can enable people to lead their lives as independently as possible in old age.

This field, which in the meantime has become important, hardly received any attention in the past and the usual senior-friendly solutions were rejected by elderly users because these solutions obviously originated from handicapped and rehabilitation technology. Consequently, innovative products should be developed that are of interest for all ages in the sense of a "design for all" concept, but that especially offer elderly people more safety and comfort in their everyday home life [3].

The group of researchers selected an integrative and interdisciplinary approach for this plan, financed by the Germany Research Society (Deutsche Forschungsgemeinschaft – DFG) for over 6 years:

- *Integrative* through the strong orientation and integration of elderly people in the development processes, within which user- and product-related questions were combined. A senior citizen advisory council was available, which was continuously integrated into the work.
- *Interdisciplinary* through the integration of the most diverse competencies, which made a synthesis of disciplinary perspectives possible.

Members of the joint research group included designers from the field of industrial design, scientists from the Technical Universities of Berlin and Cottbus, and the Berlin Institute for Social Research. As a result, experts were available for the joint work from the fields of social sciences and manpower studies, design, construction engineering, as well as biomedical and communications technology.

Particular importance was placed on the partial project for design. Here methods were developed and practiced with which the wishes and needs of elderly people could be recognized and taken into account in the development process. Furthermore, prototypical designs were worked out in the project that showed what future solutions for elderly users could look like without limiting the form and function solely to this one target group.

The main point of departure was a specific design approach.

How the Discipline of Design Views Itself Within the *sentha* Project

For us, product formation and design do not simply mean the design of the form/ shape. "With design" means that we are not only dealing with the product "in itself", but that the design is always embedded in cultural and social interrelations. This integrates the dealings with "things" with an understanding of the target group – in this case the senior citizens. We have thus abandoned the traditional fixation of designers on objects. We understand design as an integral concept in which complex social, economic, and cultural contexts for the design process are also reflected. This is the understanding of design we have pursued as part of *sentha*.

Of course, this does not exclude "making things beautiful", something we placed a great deal of value on as part of *sentha*. In addition, concentrating exclusively on shape and form is an understanding of design that we at the Berlin University of the Arts view as being too limited. For us, design is a comprehensive phenomenon and a multilayered process in dealing with things and technical systems. Everyday culture, consumer habits, life styles, and thus also the pluralization of life styles and corresponding product worlds, are all embedded in the goal of design [4].

In this respect, we have had an interdisciplinary orientation per se: always with a view toward neighboring fields, disciplines, and the formulation of questions about our actual task, namely the final design of the objects.

This implies a holistic, interdisciplinary approach. Instead of designing the results of the other disciplines at the end, it was always important for us in the research project to start as a whole and to be correspondingly integrated in all work steps.

Specifically, this means that we have expanded the narrow questions, in contrast to other disciplines which cooperated in the *sentha* research project, which always had very concrete questions and concrete work steps. For example, we were not only concerned with the optimized, senior-friendly design of a video recorder, but also always included the importance of video and television in general, the viewing habits of senior citizens, etc. in our work.

Senior-Friendly Product Design: Going Beyond Stigmatizing Aids

From the very beginning, we concerned ourselves with the question of how one can find and develop a new product language that is less stigmatizing and transcends the marginalizing form language of senior-friendly products. Therefore, what does a product and its adequate marketing strategy (catchword: image) have to look like so that it fulfills the needs of senior citizens but is not recognized and decoded at first sight as "a product for old people". The age which the majority of people over 60 feel lies 10–15 years under their calendar age [5], while at the same time bodily limitations are felt as a sign of age but are especially perceived in other people [6].

If the things that elderly people need in the sense of aids can be made hip and trendy, then the design of these things has to be changed to such a degree that they look normal, and that is then design in the narrower sense. Thus, design also means "making something beautiful" in a specific, nonstigmatizing manner.

In this connection, it was an important concept for us to keep the subject open. This meant that we not only had aids for seniors in mind, but also did not focus exclusively on elderly people. We thus developed sponsorship models in which we observed and consulted elderly people. In this way, ideas for new products emerged. It was, however, central to our approach toward senior-friendly design always to keep in mind that the results were just as usable and appropriate for other people, i.e., that the elderly people were only an indicator of the deficits in their everyday home lives, but product design was intended to stretch beyond this specific target group and its handicaps.

The partial project for design did not focus only on a certain age group, this is connected with our general understanding of design: for a designer, every product is an aid because there are many, many things people generally cannot do. Consequently, they make use of different aids in order to be able to do something. They cannot open a tin can with their mouth or their fingers, which is why we have can openers. They cannot fly, which is why we have airplanes. It is not possible to carry very heavy loads, consequently there are cranes. From the time of birth there are aids. In this respect, every person is a "disabled person" and design has to a certain extent developed prostheses for everyone. This perspective is assuredly not new since Sigmund Freud in the 1920s characterized the bodily inadequate human being as a "prosthesis god" [7]. This perspective, however, was particularly important as part of *sentha*. Even if the project naturally focused on elderly persons and their situational needs, we were always concerned with overcoming the problem-centered view toward seniors in the sense of "handicapped people." We succeeded in our concept because we expanded our view to all of society, because that which can provide relief to elderly people can also be helpful and useful for younger people [8]. In the area of "senior-friendly products" there are very many things that not only elderly people want to have, but that in principle are of interest for many. There are many things that can be done without any problem but you ask yourself again and again: why am I actually doing this?

Why am I dragging this out so tediously? Is not there any better solution? Even a 40-year-old's back hurts when he has to carry something laboriously. That is why we decided to open up the subject. We have always said: "these are simply aids." We never spoke of specific aids for seniors. This approach helped us to view the problematic matter of age as a quite normal problematic matter. Therefore, we were able to work against the cultural marginalization of seniors. At the same time, we were able in our ideas and through age-transcending design to overcome the stigmatization through product design. This understanding also found expression of course in the form and design of senior-friendly helpers in everyday home life – senior-friendly does not mean senior-specific, but means an aid for seniors and others.

Design as an Empirical–Experimental Process

The well-known procedure in other disciplines consists of establishing hypotheses beforehand to be verified or negated. This is connected very closely with the actual formulation of questions or way of looking at a problem. However, it can become more difficult to open up toward phenomena or knowledge that have not been drawn up within the research approach. Such an approach is relatively closed toward new, surprising, previously unthought-of influential factors and questions. Therein lies the strength of our approach: quite consciously we take the naïve point of view exploratorily and experimentally: "I will now pretend that I do not know anything and as if I had no premonition or hypothesis and then look and see what kinds of answers I get to my questions".

There are different methodical approaches in the design process, which we have worked out and quite consciously employed in project work at the Berlin University of the Arts. These techniques and methods were conceived and tested especially in the expert group of Prof. Hans (Nick) Roericht [9]. For example, in exercises such as "Jumping into the matter," products are created, without any previous research, directly on the basis of our own experiences and influences. In the "Unconventional thinker exercise" completely diverse objects are combined: fusion as design methodology. In the *sentha* projects with the title "…lifting and aging" the characteristics of things were changed, i.e., young becomes old and vice versa. Here, primarily formal and esthetic aspects and social placement are investigated, questioned, and altered. The result is products and visualizations that are stimuli for further creative approaches in product development. "Design has a great deal of room for improvised use of its methods and can take over or reject methods or also cut its specific occurrences to its own use. . ... Since design is not obliged to produce accurate depictions of reality it can experiment in a way which would not be tolerated in other sciences" [10].

That design works empirically–experimentally means in concrete terms that we basically combine scientific survey and analysis methods with rather artistic–experimental methods. This means that the participatory observation and qualitative social research, the hermeneutic interpretation – whereby understanding certain processes or phenomena play just as an important role in our approach as experiments and association – observation, interviews, scientific analysis, and experiments are interlocked [4].

We are dealing here with a multistage, cyclical research process in dialog form rather than a stringent linear one. The point of departure was taking stock. What products are there at present for elderly people? How functional and senior-friendly are these offers really? What image is used in advertising to stage-manage and communicate these products?

With this knowledge we then turned to elderly people.

Participatory Observation

The situation in the everyday home life is such that the sequence of most household actions is performed routinely and proceeds unconsciously. Who really thinks about why he makes coffee in such a way or why he makes certain hand movements when taking a shower? Formulated in another way: especially in everyday home life, many things take place unconsciously and unreflectively. Consequently, they can only be partially opened to analysis in linguistic terms. You can only reflect upon things and give information when you take note of them yourself.

The rest remains uninvestigated "tacit knowledge," know-how that one has, but cannot reflect upon because it has already become such an obvious matter that one no longer thinks about it, indeed, it no longer even strikes one as special know-how.

With this background for our research, participatory observation for *sentha* acquired a quite fundamental importance. Participatory observation has the advantage of being sensitive even for unreflective, habitual, everyday actions. It is thus no accident that participatory observation is regarded as the "royal road" in field research because it is also in a position to train one's sights on things that cannot be explored by linguistic–interrogative methods such as interviews and group discussions. Whoever can take part in routine everyday processes as a sensitive observer sees more as a rule than the observed person can communicate in an ensuing talk. Participatory observation is thus, unlike an interview, a very usable and sensitive instrument for researching everyday life. Motions and hand movements, which go on in a perfectly routine manner, can especially be a point of departure for one's work. Here, for example, is such a trick from the everyday life of an elderly person: a screwed-in light bulb as a darning mushroom that is illuminated from within because elderly people can no longer see well in dim light. You often experience people who are very forgetful and stick post-its on their door when they go out. These are small things, which are not even noticed by the source person and which people do not even talk about. These are unreflective routine actions that are carried out completely unconsciously. You can only perceive them when you deliberately look at them. Only then can you ask specific questions.

This was deliberately practiced with students. "Digital stage-managing" was the title of a project in which, by observing the users on location, we got an idea of how elderly persons deal with things that surround them. What things are important and what is the relationship to them? The resulting relationship was to be produced and recorded in a picture, an intensified observation. In the illustrated example, the love of an old married couple for books and reading was the theme. Intensive research and close cooperation with the seniors preceded the photos (Figs. 4.1 and 4.2).

The project "Who rests gets rusty" about the search for and finding of short-term resting spots dealt with exact observation and not just of elderly people, but in particular of what surrounds us. It dealt with places where people hang around, take a break, and put aside their cares. Using a camera, we looked for, observed, and recorded places. The result of good observation is the draft "The bench" (Fig. 4.3) by Andreas Bergmann. The beginning of the draft is: "many visitors and curious

Fig. 4.1 Breakfast at the Gorisch's

Fig. 4.2 ... and at night they like to have a second helping

onlookers at Berlin construction sites and construction site fences". The motto was that the barrier fence became a kind of bench for lingering and resting. In doing so, the needs and wishes of not only elderly people were taken up. The work was given an award in a competition by the Deutsche Bank [11].

The Dialog: Participative Principle of Our Research

From the beginning of the project, the dialog principle was a fundamental matter of concern in our research. As in modern ethnology (in which the research objects are increasingly integrated into the research process), by commenting on one's own

Fig. 4.3 The bench

interviews or on the concrete research results, we thus wanted to actively involve the seniors in the research process. This means that the research objects, i.e., the seniors, became subjects who consequently became the experts of our research. In several dialog phases the seniors in a so-called senior council followed, discussed, checked, and commented on our work steps in the *sentha* project. From the very beginning, we integrated our user group not only through questioning and partici-patory observation, but especially through sponsorship models and joint trial and error. The members of the senior council were also involved right from the beginning of the project (Figs. 4.4 and 4.5). They were, so to speak, motivated to play along and thus had the possibility of discovering their own needs in the design and production processes. Every student picked up the theme directly on location in the form of sponsorship models and looked for solutions together with the users. By means of this direct contact to later users it was possible to come up with user typologies in order to vary use and production characteristics, e.g., according to age, sex, educational level, culture, etc.

This integration and consideration of the user leads to consideration of the needs of the greatest possible group of addressees through the designer in the sense of "inclusive design" [12]. This happens by integrating the needs of groups that have so far been excluded from consideration, e.g., because of their age, their handicap, or on the basis of changing technologies or work structures. Thus, the exclusion of special user groups in events and actions is prevented.

Roger Coleman describes this by using the example of a train journey in which many questions are asked; for example, in the beginning by obtaining information about a selected destination, about advice, orientation, transportation, and comfort up to the final destination. The trip by train can thus be seen as a chain of individual products and services, the availability of which is only as strong as the weakest link in this chain. In order to reach one's destination, all areas have to be available to everyone. Therefore, we have to illuminate the process and design the weakest links in such a way that they are manageable for everyone.

Fig. 4.4 Participation I: discussion in the packing project

Fig. 4.5 Participation II: discussion at a table with seniors

If you look at the action from one particular point and then build a chain of the most diverse possibilities, then a great deal of design leeway is evident: both the focusing on detailed solutions as well as the conceptual opening of the point of departure. Design can therefore begin at any point [13].

Empathy: The Foundation for the Designs in the Sense of the Later User

How can I put myself in the position of the later user, or how do the individual small steps of an action become clear to me? In order to answer these questions, we in the *sentha* project have attempted in the most diverse places to "feel into" the user group of elderly people. We looked for and invented exercises, methods, and aids that give a feeling of how one feels in certain situations or how detailed certain actions in the course of everyday life actually are. These methods help in the analysis of products and in describing the requirement specifications.

The actual sequence of actions, e.g., a series of single photos of washing in the morning, was recorded in the project "My wonderful bathroom – new bathtubs for old users." Every activity was written down in a log book and subsequently analyzed (Fig. 4.6).

In the project "Handicapping, speculating, and manipulating with senses" we, together with the students, experimentally pushed an empathetic approach into the forefront. What would happen if a sense was dropped or was added?

What does it mean when someone can no longer sit or stand up or if one's hand shakes? In this respect we are dealing with experimental designs in order to experience these feelings on our own bodies. The task was then to "conceive of a tool with which one's own and other's senses can be weakened, strengthened, shifted, channeled, expanded, limited, exchanged, and instrumentalized".

The photos show a few examples of experimental designs such as the "brush feet" for an unsteady gait, "gaping straight ahead" for tunnel vision, or the "ax in the nape of the neck" for the stooped-over gait. This series of experiments has been further developed for the permanent exhibition "Man" in the Hygiene Museum in Dresden, and are exhibits that visitors can try out [14] (Fig. 4.7).

Interdisciplinarity: Stimuli Through the Disciplines Involved in the Research Project

Both in the projects with students and in the dialog with seniors we dealt with a reciprocal feedback process: a briefing for the students was formulated from the subject area. The young male and female designers then developed concrete ideas and innovative solutions, which in turn were incorporated into the *sentha* research project and discussed with the seniors. This ping-pong effect is very important especially because new impulses can be generated through the feedback of others, from the outside, which in the end constitutes innovation and creativity. Without this opening we would have argued, thought, and developed ideas within our own closed horizons, and surely less interesting ideas would have originated [15].

This expresses a very fundamental catchword: interdisciplinarity. One could indeed say that the project interrelationships of *sentha*, consisting of labor and

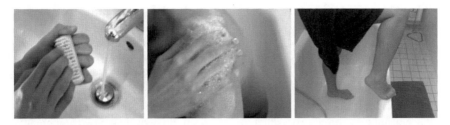

Fig. 4.6 Washing photo sequence

Fig. 4.7 Handicapping photo sequence. Examples: Berit, Michael, Harald

social scientists, construction and communication engineers, and biomedical doctors, and including the senior and industrial council, have already genuinely taken into account the way designers see themselves. As part of the design process, a designer in the end always makes eclectic use of the level of knowledge of other disciplines – from the psychology of perception, to the cultural sciences and the engineering sciences. Consequently, the interdisciplinary approach belongs to the way designers see themselves and it practically goes without saying that we have ourselves profited from the interdisciplinary nature of the research project.

A concrete example of this interdisciplinary cooperation is the joint project "Designing crosswise." Within the period of a week, from Monday to Friday, we gave ourselves the concrete task of "Senior-friendly technology in everyday home life."

We had four archetypical products – an iron, knives and forks, a bottle of mineral water, and an electrical outlet – that we wanted to optimize for senior-friendliness with respect to previously defined product qualities: more demanding, safer, simpler, and more entertaining. We then set up teams of two consisting of a labor scientist and a designer who were supposed to reflect upon the archetypes and translate them into a specific product quality. Each day the teams moved on to the next product in order to improve its product quality. This means that the product quality of every archetype was further developed by every team. On the last day, all products were presented. Needless to say, the project included discussions, differences of opinion, and a transfer of knowledge between the labor scientists and the designers. What does "safer" actually mean? Why does it have to be "more demanding" for elderly people at all? What do we mean when we speak of "simpler"?

We also understand interdisciplinarity in a further sense: all perspectives and results do not always have to be integrated into a harmonious, interdisciplinary whole. Much would surely be lost if one had to limit oneself to a very small common denominator. This means that we comprehend interdisciplinarity not in the sense that texts and ideas that point in different directions are argued over in a different way and disparate thoughts are formulated in order to be swirled together in a kind of cerebral blender. It is more the idea (exactly because of this polyphony) of acquiring new stimuli from other voices: to simultaneously see two or more ways of looking at things, to be able to think about things and then come up again with new ideas. In the end something arises out of this mixture of different texts and thoughts, a point of knowledge or innovation, which could not have developed in any single discipline.

In this respect you can establish a cross-connection to the association so important for male and female designers, namely, everything that can stimulate the mind, release ideas associatively, and give new impulses can serve the design process. Knowledge and information from neighboring or even distant disciplines can have a stimulating effect and provide new impulses.

This supports our fundamental point of view, namely, that research and design always take place in a dialog, associative and as partners.

Product Development

This section introduces some exemplary designs from projects that originated at the Institute for Product and Process Design at the Berlin University of the Arts as part of our research project. The aim of the design work was to develop products and services that support people's independent living in everyday home life and that do not use any kind of stigmatizing senior-specific product language.

As long as an object is used, so goes the hypothesis, there will be people who make functional inadequacy the driving force of their attempts to improve it [16].

That is how we proceeded in our design projects with expanding the questions and considering the products in their context [17]. Similarly, we focused on user habits and actions, especially of the age group we set our sights on. In addition, there are analogies and the consideration of other sequences of action.

In addition to observation, participation, and the empathetic approach to understanding processes and phenomena, experimentation, and association play for us just as important a role, so that all levels interlock in an integral project: observation, interviews, scientific analysis, association, and experiments.

An example of such a design comes from the project "Living longer – transformation in living areas", a case in which the kitchen cutting board meets a work bench. A kitchen cutting board that facilitates work in the kitchen was developed here in an analogy to other work steps and locations.

First of all, the different "tools" are hidden in the work surface and are used in the work steps when needed, i.e., they reduce complexity. The principle of the guillotine shears from a paper or metal workshop is integrated in the design, and the rings on the top of old kitchen stoves are given new functions. For example, a mixing bowl can be lowered, and stirring with one hand becomes possible. There are many such situations, be it when making a telephone call, carrying a child in your arm, or when there is not sufficient strength in the other arm.

By means of such tools, support for the motor movements of the hands is provided and the exertion of force for these actions is minimized.

The design "Upside down" by Nicolas Möbius and Karen Olze has received several awards in the "My way" competition and in the "Life dreams" competition by IF Hannover (Industrie Forum Design Hannover). In the meantime, the work has been integrated into the collection of the kitchen appliance producer Alno (Fig. 4.8).

The title of the project "Living longer" stood for the demographic change in our society. The greater life expectancy and the desire for independence in old age require new products as well as new ways to use them. Here concepts and products for living areas have been developed that meet the demands of elderly persons. Design solutions were sought in which form and function are attractive to a wide circle of users. The reading cushion "Time to read" by Lucie Grünzig and Sandra Hirsch is an example. It is a symbiosis of static and textile elements, which makes extended reading more pleasant. The book support with pull-out reading lamp can be integrated into the cushion with a one-hand movement (Fig. 4.9). The weight of

Fig. 4.8 Kitchen photo sequence

Fig. 4.9 Cushion

the book is reduced and the reader can then sit in a relaxed position. Reading in bed becomes more comfortable for young and old.

Diploma theses have also been written on this research subject in addition to the projects, for example, "My first Sony – investigations on the subject of easy operation" by Christoph Eberle [18].

The fundamental thought was the fact that, with every new device, people often reach the point where their initial curiosity and pleasure with their new possession turns into helplessness. Thick instruction manuals, incomprehensible symbols on the operating panel, and numerous multifunctional switches and pushbuttons frustrate the first-time user. As a rule, they are finally satisfied when they can manage to handle some of the functions. Sometimes the device disappears back into the cardboard box. The users often think the fault lies with them. Again and again you hear the remark; "I am probably too stupid to do it."

One result of this diploma thesis was to redesign an answering machine (Fig. 4.10) with new, unconventional and easier operating elements [18].

One important aspect of the research project was to motivate and promote up-and-coming designers, which was also the trigger for launching a professional competition for young male and female designers. The "Alternative products for a new elderly generation" competition was offered twice within the project.

The question posed was: what should technical products and devices look like that meet the needs of elderly people and are at the same time also attractive for many age groups? Students and recent graduates majoring in design and architecture were asked to develop new products and concepts. Even minimal products were submitted and received awards, for example, the "A-Button" by Antonia Roth, which can be threaded through button holes more easily because of its formal design, or concepts such as "Newspapers for listening" by Harald Kollwitz (Figs. 4.11 and 4.12).

The concept provides for more social integration of elderly people in daily life, but also offers other target groups interesting uses. That is why newspaper articles are provided with individual barcodes. With the aid of a device you can call up an article and the publishing firm can load it as an audio file onto the device. The user

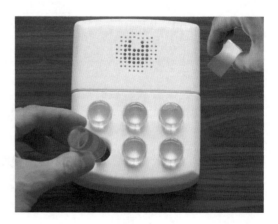

Fig. 4.10 Answering machine

Fig. 4.11   The A-button

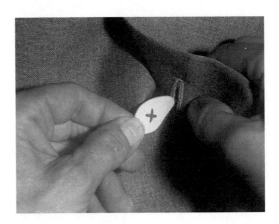

Fig. 4.12   Listening to newspapers

Table 4.1 Overview of the articles presented in the *sentha* project

Title	Contents	Result
Image – age in images and the image of age	Analysis of the age image as depicted in advertising (print media)	• Images do not correspond to the self-image of elderly people • They do not feel they are being taken seriously • They think depictions are exaggerated (positive/ negative) • Elderly prefer realistic images; like to see themselves pictured as part of different generations • They have a high regard for positive values such as knowledge, experience, affluence
Small helpers – product range and sales channels in the market for seniors	Analysis of products developed especially for seniors with regard to design, functionality, and evaluation of the attendant sales channels	• The design of many products is slipshod or old-fashioned and does not appeal to elderly people • The solution to a deficiency is almost always in the foreground, lack of positive reasons to buy the product • Sales structures or forms of presentation do not correspond to the wishes or the needs of elderly people
Digital productions – stories of aging and of things	Photo project in which stereotypical ideas of age are countered by the self-image of elderly people	• Research of biographies, life circumstances and objects used • Photographic production on the basis of discovered "histories"
Who rests gets rusty – on the search for and finding of short-term parking spots	Design of products for public spaces for resting, relaxing, or putting aside one's cares	"The bench" – The construction site fence as chance to sit down
My wonderful bathroom – new bathtubs for old users	New design solutions for bathrooms that provide support and take user habits into consideration	"Sea saw" – bathtub and shower in one
Handicapping – speculating and manipulating with senses	Design of "tools" in order to make aging capable of being experienced and comprehended	• Different "tools" that simulate and represent individual aspects, e.g., hearing, seeing, feeling, smelling, moving • Taking the representation of change and positive changes into consideration, not just the deficiencies
	Interdisciplinary cooperative exercise between engineers	• Definition of age demands (product quality, how

(*continued*)

Table 4.1 (continued)

Title	Contents	Result
Designing crosswise – I'll do it... for elderly people	and designers. Joint redesigning of daily objects	convenient, safe, self-explanatory, etc.) • Design of numerous variations (Products such as electrical outlets, scissors, bags, etc.)
Living longer – changes in living areas	Design of new solutions for living areas that allow adaptive methods of use	"Time to read" – comfortable book support with integrated reading lamp "Upside-down" – aids for daily action sequences in the kitchen "Upset" – chairs and sofas as aids in getting up
My first Sony – investigation on the subject of "easy operation"	Study on elderly-friendly operating panels and sequences	"My first Sony" – an answering machine with intuitive operation and tactile interface
Alternatives – products for a new elderly generation	Design competition with the goal of enthusing up-and-coming designers for the subject and to offer a platform for good designs	"A-Button" – a button that you can close with one hand "Footwear" – shoe with spring mechanism that you can put on and take off without bending over "Listening to newspapers" – barcodes are scanned under newspaper articles and the corresponding article is read aloud via the internet

can then listen to the selected spoken text using headphones. This is not only advantageous for people who can no longer see well, but also when one's attention is distracted, such as when driving [19].

Summary and Conclusion

In conclusion, we can state that the *sentha* project approach has proven to be worthwhile. With the aid of a multistaged, cyclical (not linear) process and the intensive integration of elderly users, solutions could be found that stood up to the demands of universal design as well as our own demands on design.

In addition to participatory observation, the fundamental elements in this process are the participatory elements such as user tests of the hypotheses, which produced important feedback from the seniors' trial actions. With this help we were able to optimize, complement, and further develop our own ideas.

The research project clearly confirmed that elderly people did not like products that were developed solely for the "elderly" or for "seniors." They preferred "solutions for everyone" and exactly that is possible by taking into consideration the wishes and needs of the older user group in the process described in the beginning. At the same time product attractiveness has to be achieved, which is also of interest to other target groups. Therefore, emphasis should be placed on the combination of good design and additional product advantages.

A very important task in the research project was putting the subject in the curricula of the Design Department at the University of the Arts in Berlin. The inclusion of this subject in courses can sensitize the younger generation to the needs of the elderly. The theme "Design for the elderly," as illustrated in the examples above, can be integrated in an attractive and lasting manner by means of interesting project work and by involving the "elderly person" user group in the process. In this way new areas were and are being established and designers trained who are specialized in products for elderly people and, as experts, will help in the future to reduce present deficits in product development.

We see a very large need for participatory approaches in the future, such as user tests in order to check products for their "demographic steadfastness" and to work out suggestions for optimization. Only in this way can producers and service providers make positive use of the challenges posed by demographic change. In doing so, the innovative potential of such approaches should not be underestimated since new concepts in the future, which will be of great interest to a wide target group, can arise with the user-centered occupation with existing solutions (Table 4.1).

References

1. M. Knigge, J. Hofmann, *Auf dem Prüfstand der Senioren – Alternde Kunden fordern Unternehmen auf allen Ebenen* (DB Research, Frankfurt am Main, 2003)
2. K. Bastuck, N. Keil, *Wachstumschance Senioren – Potenziale seniorengerechter Produkte* (Rölfs MC Partner, Frankfurt am Main, 2004)
3. W. Friesdorf, A. Heine (eds.), *Sentha – seniorengerechte Technik im häuslichen Alltag – Ein Forschungsbericht mit integriertem Roman* (Springer, Heidelberg, 2007)
4. K. Schmidt-Ruhland, M. Knigge, in *Third International Conference on Gerontechnology*, München, 10–13 Oktober 1999
5. J. Smith, P.B. Baltes, in *Altern aus psychologischer Perspektive: Trends und Profile im hohen Alter*, ed. by K.U. Mayer, P.B. Baltes. (Die Berliner Altersstudie Berlin, Akademie-Verlag, Berlin), pp. 221–250
6. W.C. Thomas, The expectation gap and the stereotype of the stereotype: images of old people. Gerontologist **21**(4), 402–407 (1981)
7. S. Freud, *Das Unbehagen in der Kultur* (Internationaler Psychoanalytischer Verlag Erstdruck, Wien, 1930)
8. R. Coleman, *Design Für Die Zukunft* (Köln, DuMont, 1997)
9. H. Roericht, die Lehre an der hdk/udk berlin 1972–2002, http://www.roericht.de/_ID_IV/index.html. Accessed Jan 2008
10. R. Rickenberg, *Wörterbuch Design*, in *Entwurfsmethoden*, ed. by M. Erlhoff, T. Marshall (Birkhäuser, Basel, 2008), p. 128

11. Deutsche Bank (Hrsg.) (ed.), *Internationaler Design-Wettbewerb* (Die Deutsche Bank für die deutsche Bank, Katalog Frankfurt am Main, 1999). Selbstverlag
12. R. Coleman, S. Keates, P.J. Clarkson, C. Lebbon, *Inclusive Design, Design for the Whole Population* (Springer, Berlin, 2002)
13. R. Coleman, *Living Longer – The New Context for Design* (Design Council, London, 2001)
14. K. Weining, *Deutsches Hygiene-Museum Dresden* (München, Prestel, 2005)
15. A. Peine, H.-L. Diene, Living Old Age, in *Defining a Common Framework of Objectives – A New Methodological Focus for Developing Senior Household Technology (L'Occidente e la modernizzazione)*, ed. by A. Guerci, S. Consigliere (Erga Edizioni, Genoa, 2002)
16. G. Basalla, *Messer, Gabel, Reissverschluss*, in *Die Evolution der Gebrauchsgegenstände*, ed. by H. Petroski (Birkhäuser, Basel, 1994)
17. L. Burckhardt, *Die Kinder fressen ihre Revolution* (Köln, DuMont, 1985)
18. Ch Eberle, *My First Sony, Diplomarbeit, Institut für Produkt- und Prozessgestaltung* (Universität der Künste, Berlin, 2003)
19. Universität der Künste Berlin (ed.), *Alternativen – Produkte für eine neue alte Generation* (Ausstellungskatalog, Berlin, 2001)

Chapter 5
Leveraging Disruptive Innovations for the Silver Market

Florian Kohlbacher and Chang Chieh Hang

Abstract Some researchers have proposed that the silver market might be an ideal field of application for disruptive technologies and innovation, and that there are important business opportunities in this market segment that could be leveraged through them. This chapter builds and extends on this research (a) by analyzing how changes in the external reality of the firm can create new opportunities for the development of disruptive innovations and how R&D has to grasp and react to these changes, and (b) by analyzing the important role of disruptive innovations in aging societies. This chapter aims to contribute to the stream of research on the front-end question of technology creation and the area of purposeful R&D to create disruptive technologies. R&D should consciously match these with potential markets in order to accelerate the pace of business growth through disruptive innovations by investigating R&D efforts for disruptive innovations catering to the needs of the emerging market segment of the so-called silver market. The chapter also contributes to the knowledge of analyzing disruptive potential in R&D activities, and adds to efforts to clarify the concept of disruptive innovations in general. Finally, we also aim to give recommendations to practitioners such as R&D and product managers.

Introduction

The demographic challenge requires innovative responses from politics, business and society. Drucker [1, 2] has even identified (changing) demographics as one of the sources of innovation opportunities. In a more general sense, it has been argued that the increasing importance of changes in the environment has to be embraced by R&D management research and practice [3], and that – when looking "more closely at environmental and structural factors" – "there are many neglected influences in previous research that are relevant for the front end of innovation" ([4]: 488). The demographic shift has already spurred the emergence of a new area of technologies,

F. Kohlbacher and C. Herstatt (eds.), *The Silver Market Phenomenon*,
DOI 10.1007/978-3-642-14338-0_5, © Springer-Verlag Berlin Heidelberg 2011

namely gero(n)technologies (e.g., [5]), but as of yet, this but touches the tip of the iceberg of the needs and wants of aging consumers [6].

Some researchers have proposed that the silver market might be an ideal field of application for disruptive technologies and innovation, and that there are important business opportunities in this market segment that could be leveraged through them [7]. This chapter builds and extends on this research (a) by analyzing how changes in the external reality of the firm can create new opportunities for the development of disruptive innovations and how R&D has to grasp and react to these changes, and (b) by analyzing the important role of disruptive innovations in aging societies. For this purpose, this chapter will look into both low-end and new market disruptions. Due to the lack of previous research, our approach is rather theory-building than theory-testing, and combines conceptual development with explorative empirical research. Indeed, our theoretical reasoning is illustrated by a number of explanatory cases of disruptive innovations for the silver market in both Japan and India.

This chapter aims to contribute to the stream of research on the front-end question of technology creation and the area of purposeful R&D to create disruptive technologies. R&D should consciously match these with potential markets in order to accelerate the pace of business growth through disruptive innovations by investigating R&D efforts for disruptive innovations catering to the needs of the emerging market segment of the so-called silver market. The chapter also contributes to the knowledge of analyzing disruptive potential in R&D activities (cf. also [8]), and adds to efforts to clarify the concept of disruptive innovations in general (e.g., [9]). Finally, we also aim to give recommendations to practitioners such as R&D and product managers.

Disruptive Innovations

The theoretical framework of this chapter is based on Christensen's concept of disruptive technologies and disruptive innovation [10–13]. Under the disruptive innovation framework, Christensen differentiates sustaining innovation and disruptive innovation based on technological performance and market segmentation [10, 12]. In sustaining innovation, technologies are developed to help companies sustain their growth in the existing or established marketplace to ensure market growth and domination. The focus is on improving the performance of current products or services. Disruptive innovations occur once in a while when new technologies are available which have lower performance initially but may be attractive to certain markets owing to some features which are not valued by the established marketplace. As they typically under-perform the established products in the mainstream market when introduced, they are largely ignored by the incumbents. The technologies are typically cheaper, simpler and frequently more convenient to use; and are applied by entrepreneurial firms to create products at the low-end or new products in a new market. Once they establish a foothold in the low-end or new market, their performance could continue to improve over time toward meeting the performance requirement of mainstream customers. When the mainstream customers switch from the existing products, such technologies/innovations would disrupt the established players and create a new dominant design [14].

In short, the disruptive innovation theory points to situations in which new organizations can use relatively simple, convenient, low-cost innovations to create growth and triumph over powerful incumbents [10, 12, 13]. The theory holds that existing companies have a high probability of beating entrant attackers when the contest is about sustaining innovations. But established companies almost always lose to attackers armed with disruptive innovations. Figure 5.1 illustrates the disruptive innovation theory.

Note that disruptive innovations introduce a new value proposition, as they either create new markets or reshape existing markets [13]. This is why we can distinguish two types of disruptive innovations: low-end and new-market. The first type is good-enough performance and low-price innovation, serving in existing, low-end markets [14]. These low-end disruptive innovations can occur when existing products or services are "too good" and hence overpriced relative to the

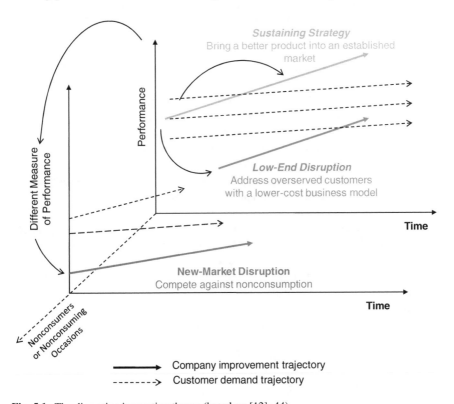

Fig. 5.1 The disruptive innovation theory (based on [12]: 44)

value existing customers can use [13]. The second type is good-enough performance and low-price innovation, serving in new markets [14]. These new-market disruptive innovations can occur when characteristics of existing products limit the number of potential consumers, or force consumption to take place in inconvenient, centralized settings; in short, they bring consumption to "nonconsumers" or "nonconsuming contexts" [13]. Successful new-market disruptive innovations follow two patterns: either (1) they introduce a relatively simple, affordable product or service that increases access and ability by making it easier for customers who historically lacked the money or skills to get important jobs done, or (2) they help customers do more easily and effectively what they were already trying to get done, instead of forcing them to change behavior or adopt new priorities [13]. It is important to note, however, that many disruptions are dual-focused, i.e., both new-market and low-end approaches could be used together [12]. As a matter of fact, it is rather difficult to find pure low-end disruptive innovations, and many of them are new-market creations.

With the attractiveness of disruptive innovations and the maturing of research on the theory, some attention has recently been paid to the front-end question of technology creation [15]. Indeed, Christensen's framework focuses on the role of business models, leadership, marketing and the commercialization process of new products from disruptive technologies, without further deliberating on the technological aspect of disruptive innovation. One new research track [15] has therefore been proposed in the area of purposeful R&D, to create disruptive technologies and then consciously match them with potential markets in order to accelerate the pace of business growth through disruptive innovations. We propose here that the silver market might be an ideal field of application for such an approach. Before moving on to the detailed discussion of disruptive innovation and the silver market, we shall define the term disruptive technology, following Yu and Hang [17]: "disruptive technologies are technologies which enable a product to have features suitable for it to be used in conjunction with the new business model that altogether leads to disruptive innovation".

In sum, Christensen's concept of disruptive technologies and disruptive innovation [10, 16] has raised the attention of academic scholars and business practitioners alike. While the literature has addressed many aspects of disruptive innovation from business model innovation and organizational management perspectives, discussions of the R&D processes behind disruptive innovations and technologies and their purposeful creations are still scarce (cf., e.g., [17]). Indeed, Christensen's framework focuses on the role of business models, leadership, marketing and the commercialization process of new products from disruptive technologies, without further deliberating on the technological aspect of disruptive innovation. But with the attractiveness of disruptive innovations and the maturing of research on the theory, some attention has recently been paid to the front-end question of technology creation and the area of purposeful R&D to create disruptive technologies and then consciously match them with potential markets in order to accelerate the pace of business growth through disruptive innovations [15, 18].

Disruptive Innovations for the Silver Market

Demographic changes have led to an increased life-span over which products and services are demanded and consumed. However, these products may be generic/universal, in the sense that they are demanded and consumed – more or less – independent of age. It might just be the case that there is a higher demand, because elderly people – such as retired baby boomers for example – may have sufficient time and affluence to consume. Indeed, there are customers who have not had the money, time, etc. to use/consume certain products and services. In this case, the disruption usually does not come from completely new products but from adapted existing products with new benefits such as convenience, customization, or lower prices. Another implication of the demographic shift is that changing conditions in people's life and health give birth to new, unprecedented needs and wants. People go through different stages in their life course, and have to adapt to changing life conditions in the form of life event experiences that create physical, social and emotional demands and circumstances [19, 20]. This means that products and services need to be adapted or newly developed to respond to changing needs and demands.

Building on Christensen's framework described above, we propose the following two potential applications of disruption in the context of the silver market. Note that – as was mentioned above – in reality most disruptive innovations are dual-focus, combining new-market and low-end approaches.

1. Low-end disruption: there are customers at the low end of the market who would be happy to purchase a product with less (but good enough) performance if they could get it at a lower price. Indeed, older consumers and workers are often overburdened by complex products, and find it too difficult to use technology.
2. New-market disruption: there are customers who have not had the money, time etc. to use/consume certain products and services. In addition, changing conditions in people's life and health give birth to new, unprecedented needs and wants. Products and services for the silver market have to help potential customers get a job done that they have always been trying to get done – but have not yet been able to do in a simple, convenient and/or affordable way.

In summary, disruptive innovations for the silver market are expected to mainly target nonconsumption, and help to support and enrich elder people's life and work. We will now discuss each of these disruptions in turn.

Low-End Disruption

With scientific progress advancing at an unprecedented pace, the second half of the twentieth century and the beginning of the twenty-first century have experienced enormous advances in all kinds of technological fields. This has opened possibilities for ever sophisticated products and functions, high speed and performance. Whereas innovators, adopters and lead users have usually been quite swift in adopting new technologies and innovations [21–24], experience tells us that elderly people often tend to be laggards or even absolute nonconsumers, as they reject new technologies and innovations as too difficult and complicated to understand and use (note that Rogers ([22]: 288), however, in his theory of the diffusion of innovations, assumed that age would not affect the adoption of innovations, i.e., that earlier adopters are no different from later adopters in age). A case in point is mobile phones for example. Most mobile phones nowadays have a wide range of functions – camera, games, internet connection, etc. – that go far beyond the functionality of simply making phone calls. In addition, the size of keys and characters on screens gets smaller and smaller, making them difficult to use for elderly people with impaired vision [25]. Low-end disruptive innovations – which by definition are good-enough performance and low-price innovations serving in existing, low-end markets – would offer two major benefits here. First of all, the good-enough performance aspect would help to solve the problem of overly high complexity and unnecessarily elevated performance, but instead focus on the core value proposition of the product or service. This supposedly would make the new technology/innovation for the first time available for consumption to elderly people. The second benefit comes from the low-price aspect, which supposedly further lowers the financial burden to purchase/consume, especially in the case of often risk-averse elder consumers. Note that this good-enough performance – easy-and-safe-to-use – and low-cost advantage also becomes increasingly important for the B2B sector as the workforce of organizations is also aging. Older workers and employees progressively will need appropriately designed and easy-and-safe-to-use machinery and equipment.

New-Market Disruption

In the case of new-market disruptions, it is important to compete against nonconsumption rather than to compete against consumption [13]. In the case of the silver market, we can think of two basic scenarios where consumers could be turned from nonconsumption to consumption. First, in many cases of new-market disruptions for the silver market, there was no market and consequently no consumption because of two reasons. First, people lacked the time and money to consume certain products and services they wanted. When they were still working, they were too busy, were trying to accumulate wealth, support their children, build a house, etc. All of these have restricted their temporal and financial resources. The life-span after retirement used to be rather short and accumulated wealth scarce, and thus there was not much leeway for consumption. Now, with high life-expectancy and good financial conditions, unprecedented needs and wants emerge and can be satisfied for the first time. Second, also because the life-span after retirement used to be rather short and because elderly people were usually supported by their children and/or other relatives, the need for supportive devices, universal design products, "gerontechnologies" and the like was not that urgent. With elderly people living longer and longer, and becoming ever more dependent on themselves, a new market for these kind of supportive devices and services emerges. In this case, there had actually been consumption; however a nonmarket one, as people consumed the "services" through their relatives and friends. New products and services from the market now (partly) compete against this consumption.

Second, changing conditions in people's life and health give birth to new, unprecedented needs and wants. This is especially obvious in the areas of supportive and medical devices and other so-called "gerontechnologies" (technologies to support geriatrics), products with universal design, and services – e.g., financial services, insurance, etc. – especially adapted to the needs of the elderly. These products and services need to be designed especially for the particular needs and wants of elderly people [26, 27]. Obviously, many of the existing products and services do not attend to the specific needs and wants of the elderly. Here again, new-market disruptive innovations could be leveraged to bring consumption to "nonconsumers" or "nonconsuming contexts."

Dual-Focus Disruption

As was mentioned above, in reality most disruptive innovations are dual-focus, using both new-market and low-end approaches. This means that they target both overshot customers with less complexity, performance, functionality in traditional terms of measurement and/or lower-cost business models, as well as nonconsumption, i.e., those customers who have never used such a product because they perceived it as too complex, difficult-to-use and/or expensive. Since some customers in the silver market are looking for easy-to-use, good enough performance and others – who are financially not so well-off due to a lack of savings and small pensions for example – looking for cheaper deals (with good enough performance), dual-focus disruptive innovations have the potential to reach both of these types of gray consumers.

Examples/Cases

One example of a disruptive innovation for elderly consumers in the cell phone market is NTT Docomo's "Raku-Raku" (Easy-Easy) phone, with its strong emphasis on usability, including easy-to-read fonts, keys, and functions. Mobile phone carrier NTT Docomo had it developed by a supplier and brought it onto the Japanese market for the first time in 1999. In 2009, the sixth generation of the Raku-Raku phone was introduced, boasting accumulative sales of more than 17 million handsets since its initial market introduction. The Raku-Raku phone family consists of different models, starting from the simple "basic" version and featuring also more sophisticated models with GPS, video telephony and other advanced functions. However, all models share the strong focus on usability. In late 2008, Fujitsu introduced the Raku-Raku PC for senior citizens, which is also designed to be easy to use. Indeed, the notebook and PC versions are both specifically designed to make computing easier for the senior population or any novice computer user: letters on the keyboard are enlarged for easier viewing, vowels and often-used letters are color-coded for easy identification, a "one-touch button" located above the keyboard lets users change the screen resolution, open FAQ software, control volume with a single touch, commonly used functions such as the Internet and email are easily accessible via a special menu, and preinstalled Internet search software supports users who struggle with character input by enabling them to progress through a search by clicking the mouse. The notebook and the PC come with a 1-year service bundle, which offers users a special hotline with guidance and remote inspection of the PC/notebook. Both the Raku-Raku phone and the PC/notebook target overshot/overburdened customers as well as nonconsumption.

Another interesting example is Nintendo's new game console Wii. The disruptive innovation is the new controller which can detect and transmit the movements of the players directly into virtual reality and thus leads to an absolutely new experience of video game playing. As is typical for disruptive innovations, the new technology still underperforms the competitors' products in terms of speed and screen resolution. Nevertheless, it has successfully disrupted the market and given Nintendo a great lead over Sony and Microsoft. In addition, Wii has helped Nintendo to tap into new customer segments and compete against nonconsumption, especially as far as women and elderly people are concerned. In a strict sense, we could argue that in creating the Wii, Nintendo augmented a sustaining innovation with a disruptive feature so that the product still also appeals to their existent, mainstream customers. Moreover, Wii is really transgenerational and enables a whole family or people of all ages to enjoy the game together and jointly. It is a success story of transgenerational design, ageless marketing and disruptive innovation at the same time.

In the field of transportation, electric bikes like those offered by Ampere Vehicles Pvt. Ltd in India is an example of a transgenerational disruptive innovation. In comparison with traditional motorbikes, the speed is lower (less than 40 km/h) and it is thus safer and easier to ride. The e-bikes are affordable (similar capital cost to gasoline motor-bikes, but electricity bill is 1/10 of fuel cost), and in the case of the three-wheeler model the stability offered improves both safety and convenience, especially for elderly people. Ampere Vehicles hopes to apply the technology also to motorized wheelchairs, and thus lower the price for them substantially. With its e-bikes, Ampere Vehicles targets both the youth market segment and elderly citizens and disabled people. In the latter case, the products are mass-customized to fit the individual needs of the driver.

Finally, in the field of gerontechnology, the mental commitment robot Paro is a case in point. Mental commitment robots are developed to interact with human beings, and to make them feel emotionally attached to the robots. Rather than

Product	Type of disruption	Targeted performance of the product	Targeted customers or market application (competes against...)
Raku-raku phone and Raku-raku PC/notebook	Dual-focus (low-end and new-market)	Fewer complex functions, but better performance in simplicity, convenience and usability	Overshot customers and nonconsumption
Nintendo Wii	New-market	Less powerful processor and graphics performance, but better performance in usability, intuitiveness, feeling/fun and easier to play for beginners/non-hardcore gamers	Focus on nonconsumption
Paro	New-market	Cannot replace a real animal on all dimensions, but good enough functions for the purpose of therapy, plus increased safety, no sanitary issues	Focus on nonconsumption
Electric bikes	Dual=focus (low-end and new-market)	Not as fast and powerful as real motorbikes, but good enough to get from A to B for short distances, plus increased safety and stability	Overshot customers and non-consumption

Fig. 5.2 Case comparisons (*Source*: authors' own illustration)

using objective measures, these robots trigger more subjective evaluations, evoking psychological impressions such as "cuteness" and comfort. Mental commitment robots are designed to provide three types of effects: psychological, such as relaxation and motivation, physiological, such as improvement in vital signs, and social effects, such as instigating communication among inpatients and caregivers. Paro was developed at the National Institute of Advanced Industrial Science and Technology in Japan and is modeled after a baby harp seal. It is covered with soft artificial fur to make people feel comfortable, as if they were touching a real animal. Research indicates that Paro has positive effects – psychologically, physiologically and socially – on elderly people in nursing homes, especially those affected by dementia [28, 29]. Paro is selling successfully in Japan as well as other countries. The cost is reasonable (at least for institutions, but there is also a rental service for individuals) and the features good enough. It competes against nonconsumption. It cannot compete with a real animal, but it can be used in hospitals, nursing homes, etc. It is transgenerational (it is also used in pediatric therapy and educational institutions for children, for example), and it does not try to fully emulate a real animal (i.e., it only emulates the functions necessary for the therapy, like reactions to patting, etc., but it does not walk, etc.). In comparison with art therapy, music therapy and animal therapy – all of which require well-trained therapists, and in the case of animal therapy safety and sanitation are issues – and learning therapy – which requires patient effort for continuation – as well as pharmaceutical treatment – which has side-effects – robot therapy using

Paro is safe, convenient, and does not require special skills, places, or other tools [28, 29]. In the case of therapy, Paro is a new-market disruption. However, Paro is also used as a substitute for pets by elderly couples in Japan. Here, the disruptive innovation is dual-focus, as it targets both those customers overshot/overburdened by a real pet, as well as those who may keep a "pet" (i.e., Paro) for the first time as real pets were too cumbersome for them to keep or were not allowed in their mansion/apartment, etc.

All of the examples/cases that we have looked at in this section are basically dual-focus disruptions that potentially could target the low end of the market as well as creating a new market. However, the focus of most of them can probably be seen as lying on the new-market side, targeting nonconsumption. Overall, this seems to be the most viable approach in disruptive innovations for the silver market. Many elderly customers in the silver market are experienced consumers and are often apprehensive of low-end products. Hence good design, affordable pricing, ease-of-use are essential features. In addition, the strategy of augmenting a sustaining innovation with a disruptive feature, as we have seen in the Wii case, could be a new, viable pattern of disruptive innovation for the silver market. Figure 5.2 shows a case comparison along different dimensions.

Summary and Conclusion

Our research shows that (1) changes in the external reality – e.g., demographics – of the firm can create new opportunities for the development of disruptive innovations, (2) the silver market is an excellent field of application for low-end disruptions, as elderly customers will increasingly demand just good-enough performance – easy-and-safe-to-use – and affordable products and services, (3) the silver market is an excellent field of application for new-market disruptions, as elderly customers will increasingly demand new products and services they had not demanded or had not been able to demand before, (4) the silver market is an excellent field of application for both low-end and new-market disruptions, (5) in practice, most of the disruptive innovations for the silver market will be dual-focus, with a bias for new-market applications, (6) transgenerational and ageless products and services (solutions) are an excellent field of application for disruptive innovations, as elderly customers will increasingly be interested in consuming the same products and services as other age groups, and will increasingly demand to consume them jointly with other age groups, and (7) R&D has to grasp and react to this new market reality by adapting its processes and activities, in order to leverage the potential of disruptive innovations and technologies for aging societies.

Christensen's theory of disruptive innovation is a powerful framework for analyzing innovation and industry change. In this chapter, we have applied the theory to the emerging silver market phenomenon as an implication of the shift in demographics around the world. As we have shown, there are important business opportunities in this market segment that could be leveraged through disruptive technologies and innovation. We argue that this would actually benefit companies and customers alike. Firms should be careful not to exclude those customers at the bottom of the innovation pyramid, not only because – as is the case with many baby boomers – the fortune at the bottom of this pyramid is enormous, but also because of corporate social responsibility, as they can benefit both individuals and societies with "gerontechnologies" and related products and services. Indeed, the need to pay attention to potential adverse social (and other) side-effects of disruptive technologies has been pointed out recently [30]. Analogically, we would like to emphasize the potential positive social side-effects of disruptive innovations, and urge more research on this important topic.

The above discussion indicates strong needs for further research, both academic and company-based. The goal of such research should be to look at and analyze major stages in the development process of disruptive innovations for the silver market, including the purposeful creation of suitable disruptive technologies. These stages are reiterative and can be overlapping, and basically consist of:

1. Market research/investigations: how can the – often latent or not yet existing – needs and wants of elderly people be identified?
2. Product development: how does the product development process for disruptive innovations work? How can (potential) customers be integrated into the development process? How should R&D be planned to accelerate the development of suitable disruptive technologies for this market?
3. Business model creation/marketing: how can profitable business models be developed for disruptive innovations? How can the silver market effectively be targeted? How does "silver" marketing work?
4. Transgenerational design and ageless marketing: how can transgenerational design and ageless marketing be effectively developed and leveraged for disruptive innovations? How do they differ from age-related solutions?

As pointed out above, Christensen's research has so far focused mainly on the business model of disruptive innovations, and taken the technology/ product as given. Future research needs to crack open the black box of the disruptive innovation process and shed some light on how disruptive innovations for the silver market evolve and can deliberately and actively be developed and managed. In addition, a redefinition and reconceptualization of the distinction between low-end and new-market disruptions may be in order. As we have shown, most of the examples from the silver market were the new-market type. Consumers may be interested in low-end in the sense of simplicity, affordability and ease-of-use, but probably not in the sense of lower-quality, cheap-looking products. This means that firms had better position them as new-market disruptive innovations. Design and appearance might play an important role here, a topic that has not really been looked at in connection with disruptive innovations. Of course, all this may also depend on the market in question, i.e., there are supposedly big differences, for example, between emerging markets like China and India and more mature markets like Japan. This means that while the overall approach may basically be the same in most markets, fine-tuning based on detailed market research will be necessary in each individual market.

References

1. P.F. Drucker, The discipline of innovation. Harv. Bus. Rev. **63**, 67–72 (1985)
2. P.F. Drucker, *Innovation and Entrepreneurship: Practice and Principles* (HarperCollins, New York, 1985)
3. J. Butler, New Challenges for R&D Management, in *Bringing Technology and Innovation into the Boardroom: Strategy, Innovation and Competences for Business Value European Institute for Technology and Innovation Management* (Palgrave Macmillan, Basingstoke, 2004), pp. 269–291
4. S. Bröring, L.M. Cloutier, J. Leker, The front end of innovation in an era of industry convergence: evidence from nutraceuticals and functional foods. R&D Manage. **36**, 487–498 (2006)
5. D.C. Burdick, S. Kwon, *Gerotechnology: Research and Practice in Technology and Aging* (Springer, New York, 2004)
6. F. Kohlbacher, C. Herstatt, 'Silver Products' Development: The Reality of R&D in Firms in Japan. Paper presented in the R&D management conference 2009, Vienna, Austria, 2009
7. F. Kohlbacher, C.C. Hang, Disruptive Innovations and the Graying Market. Proceedings of the 2007 IEEE international conference on industrial engineering and engineering management (IEEM), Singapore, 2007, pp. 1915–1919
8. S. Hüsig, C. Hipp, M. Dowling, Analysing disruptive potential: the case of wireless local area network and mobile communications network companies. R&D Manage. **35**, 17–35 (2005)
9. C. Markides, Disruptive innovation: In need of better theory. J. Prod. Innov. Manage. **23**, 19–25 (2006)
10. C.M. Christensen, *The Innovator's Dilemma: When New Technologies Cause Great Firms to Fail* (Harvard Business School Press, Boston, 1997)
11. C.M. Christensen, M.W. Johnson, D.K. Rigby, Foundations for growth: How to identify and build disruptive new businesses. MIT Sloan Manage. Rev. **43**, 22–31 (2002)
12. C.M. Christensen, M.E. Raynor, *The Innovator's Solution: Creating and Sustaining Successful Growth* (Harvard Business School Press, Boston, 2003)
13. C.M. Christensen, S.D. Anthony, E.A. Roth, *Seeing What's Next: Using the Theories of Innovation to Predict Industry Change* (Harvard Business School Press, Boston, 2004)
14. C.C. Hang, K. Neo, K. Chai, Discontinuous Technological Innovations: A Review of Its Categorization. Paper presented in 2006 IEEE international conference on management of innovation and technology, vol. 1, 2006, pp. 253–257
15. C.C. Hang, K. Chai, Creating Technologies for Disruptive Innovation: An R&D Goal. Keynote speech paper at ISMOT 2007, Hangzhou, 2007
16. C.M. Christensen, The ongoing process of building a theory of disruption. J. Prod. Innov. Manage. **23**, 39–55 (2006)
17. D. Yu, C.C. Hang, Creating Candidate Technologies for Disruptive Innovation: A case study approach. Paper presented in proceedings of the IEEE ICMIT conference, Bangkok, 2008, pp. 65–70
18. C.C. Hang, D. Yu, K. Chai, An Exploratory Study on Understanding the Technological Dimension in Disruptive Innovation. Paper presented in Proceedings of ISMOT, Hangzhou, 2007
19. H.R. Moody, *Aging: Concepts and Controversies, 4th edn* (Sage, Thousand Oaks, CA, 2002)
20. G.P. Moschis, Life course perspectives on consumer behavior. J. Acad. Market. Sci. **35**, 295–307 (2007)
21. C. Lüthje, C. Herstatt, The lead user method: an outline of empirical findings and issues for future research. R&D Manage. **34**, 553–568 (2004)
22. E.M. Rogers, *Diffusion of innovations, 5th edn* (Free, New York, 2003)
23. E. von Hippel, Lead users: A source of novel product concepts. Manage. Sci. **32**, 791–806 (1986)
24. E. von Hippel, *Democratizing Innovation* (MIT, Cambridge, 2006)

25. T. Irie, K. Matsunaga, Y. Nagano, Universal design activities for mobile phone: Raku Raku PHONE. Fujitsu Sci. Tech. J. **41**, 78–85 (2005)
26. W.C. Mann, *Smart Technology for Aging, Disability, and Independence: The State of the Science* (Wiley, Hoboken, 2005)
27. J.J. Pirkl, *Transgenerational Design: Products for an Aging Population* (Van Nostrand Reinhold, New York, 1994)
28. K. Wada, T. Shibata, Living with seal robots – its sociopsychological and physiological influences on the elderly at a care house. IEEE Trans. Robot. **23**, 972–980 (2007)
29. K. Wada, T. Shibata, T. Musha, S. Kimura, Robot therapy of elders affected by dementia. IEEE Eng. Med. Biol. Mag. **27**, 53–60 (2008)
30. J.K. Hall, M.J.C. Martin, Disruptive technologies, stakeholders and the innovation value-added chain: a framework for evaluating radical technology development. R&D Manage. **35**, 273–284 (2005)

Chapter 6
Gerontechnology for a Super-Aged Society

Ryoko Fukuda

Abstract Various rapidly developed technologies are supporting the daily lives of younger users, but have left older adults behind. However, in a super-aged society, technologies could (and should) contribute to helping older adults maintain independent lives. The chapter introduces "gerontechnology," which means the study of technology and aging, for the improvement of the daily functioning of the elderly. Through such means as behavior observation, eye tracking, and the subjective evaluation of participants in a daily situation, the difficulties older adults encounter in using technologies are clarified, and products aimed at the elderly are designed and produced based on the obtained data. More empirical studies are still required to verify the effectivity of products aimed at the elderly. At the same time, efforts should be made to help more people become familiar with gerontechnology.

Introduction

Japanese society has aged rapidly and has now become a "super-aged" society. Parallel to the rapid growth of an older population, various technologies have been developed at high speed (in support of the era of rapid economic growth of Japan). Modern high technologies have been developed aimed mainly at younger users by younger developers. Both hardware and software were therefore developed to accommodate the functions and needs of younger adults. However, such technologies are frequently not so useful for older adults, as the needs and functions of older adults are different from those of younger adults. For instance, most younger adults have no problem using a mobile phone, whereas older adults often experience great difficulties: small buttons that are difficult to press, a small display that is hard to look at and read, a ring tone that is hard to hear, and menus that are very complicated and difficult to operate. Due to these difficulties, many older adults still shy away from mobile phones. It is hard to imagine that older adults over 90 use high technologies such as computers without experiencing any difficulties. Put bluntly, current technologies leave older people behind.

F. Kohlbacher and C. Herstatt (eds.), *The Silver Market Phenomenon*,
DOI 10.1007/978-3-642-14338-0_6, © Springer-Verlag Berlin Heidelberg 2011

This phenomenon is common in most developed countries. Although the speed of aging and that of technology development in other countries are different from those in Japan, many older adults in these countries likewise have great difficulties in using modern technology products. Technologies are developed to support human beings and improve our lives, and this should also be true for older adults. The development of technical products that take into consideration the needs of older adults is one of the most important tasks in our highly aged society, a task that can be addressed using gerontechnology.

What Is Gerontechnology?

"Gerontechnology" is a composite word combining gerontology and technology, which means the study of technology and aging for the improvement of the daily functioning of the elderly [1]. Since the term "gerontechnology" was coined by Jan Graafmans in 1989, many studies have been carried out with the help of older participants and respondents.

Gerontechnology covers very wide areas of research. Technology and aging here encompass terms such as research, design, manufacturing, and marketing [2]. Studies in gerontechnology can be divided into several groups. The first group tries to clarify the characteristics of older adults and the difficulties derived from these characteristics. Understanding the differences between younger and older adults helps us know how to show consideration to the decline in functions experienced by older adults. The second group includes studies on products or environments aimed at older adults. Based on data from studies in the first group, products aimed at older adults compensate for age-related declines in abilities and enhance the functions of older adults. Through observations of older adults using such products, their effectivity is verified. Technologies and training that prevent age-related declines in functioning are also investigated in gerontechnology. For the elderly whose functions have unfortunately declined and become impaired to the extent that some care is required, support technologies both for care-receivers and care-givers should be provided.

It remains unclear why many older adults still face difficulties in using technologies, given that gerontechnology is aimed at improving the daily functioning of the elderly. One reason may be that many problems still remain for older adults. Gerontechnology is a new research area, and experiments with and surveys on older adults sometimes require more effort than is the case with young participants. Recruitment of older participants is difficult, because younger researchers have no connection with the older population in general. It takes also more time to have participants understand their tasks in experiments or surveys. In addition, one supposes that gerontechnology is still largely unknown, both for older and younger adults. In fact, most of the students attending the author's lecture on gerontechnology as well as older participants in the author's experiments were not aware of the term "gerontechnology." In order to make readers of this book more aware of gerontechnology, this chapter introduces some topics on research works in geron-technology, mainly aimed at promoting "healthy" or "independent" older adults.

Age-Related Decline

Studies aimed at identifying the differences between younger and older adults in daily situations show declines in various functions through the aging process [3, 4]. Basic knowledge about age-related declines in functioning has already been shared in gerontology and summarized in various other books [5–8]. Key findings on age-related changes in perceptual, cognitive, and movement control factors show that with regard to sensory and perceptional functions, taste and smell show age-related declines, and perceptual thresholds for temperature and vibration are increased. Auditory declines are especially common for high-frequency sounds. Visual acuity declines, glare becomes more problematic, dark adaptation slows, breadth of visual field decreases, visual processing speed slows, and perceptual flexibility declines. With regard to cognition, a decline in working memory is generally more obvious than in semantic, prospective, and procedural memories. Older adults are slower and less successful at acquiring new procedures compared to younger adults. Selective attention and dynamic attention both show age-related declines. The rate of information processing is slowed if a task is complicated, and the perfor-mance of older adults in coordinating multiple tasks is worse than in younger adults. Spatial cognition declines with age, whereas language comprehension remains intact, unless inferences are required and working memory is overloaded. With regard to movement control, older adults respond more slowly, and move less precisely and with greater variability than younger adults [5].

Sometimes quantitative data regarding age-related decline are needed in the design process. The data provided in Steenbekkers and van Beijsterveldt (1998) are one good example of a set of data for designing products for older adults [9]. In addition, ISO/TR 22411 "Ergonomics data and guidelines for the application of ISO/IEC Guide 71 to products and services to address the needs of older persons and persons with disabilities" also provides plenty of base data for design guide-lines [10].

The problem is that the above-mentioned data were mainly collected in a controlled laboratory setting. In gerontechnology, however, it is essential to clarify to what extent age-related declines are observed as well as their influence on the behavior of the elderly in a daily situation. In order to develop a variety of technologies and products designed in consideration of older adults, experiments that take this into account are required. Below, difficulties encountered by older adults with regard to home appliances and information and communication tech-nology (ICT) are discussed from a gerontechnological aspect, based on experi-ments. Ideas to diminish the difficulties that are already implemented in commercial products will also be introduced.

Gerontechnology for Home Appliances

Modern home appliances are now highly developed and offer various "useful" functions. This tendency is especially strong in Japan. Home appliances with "additional" "useful" functions, such as microwave ovens which offer huge variety of cooking menus, washing machines with disinfection function, or rice cookers with voice guidance, are made by Japanese companies. However, such home appliances are frequently difficult to use for older adults. The more menus there are, the more buttons there are. As space for buttons on a device is limited, the size of each button decreases. From a gerontechnological perspective, a minimal required button size and spacing between them, in consideration of the physical functions of older adults, needs to be agreed upon. Likewise, the force required to depress a button should not exceed that which can be applied by an older adult; and so as to give effective feedback, a minimal required force to feel a tactile response should be considered. The legibility of text or symbol on each button and display should be secured by adjusting the contrast, luminance level, font size and typeface to suit the visual functions of older adults. Recommendations for each element have already been provided based on experimental studies [11, 12].

With regard to highly developed home appliances, difficulties with the associated software are more critical than the above-mentioned difficulties with hardware. The problem is related to the selection of menus and the sequence of task accomplishment. If they are different from the mental model of users, it leads to confusion. As experimental studies on this aspect [13] are not frequently undertaken, the behavior of older adults in such a setting was analyzed using a simulated user interface for a rice cooker [14]. The rice cooker is one of the most common home appliances in Japan, and is used by many older adults. The modern rice cooker even has menus for baking cakes and making yogurt, so users need to select the appropriate cooking menu from of a large array of menus. In the experiment, participants were asked to select a particular rice cooking menu and set the timer using four interfaces. During task accomplishment, the participants' eye movement and behavior were recorded. At the same time, physiological measurements were taken to evaluate stress objectively. The results clearly showed that similar-looking buttons caused confusion among older users. In the trial, using the interface that including a "menu" button and a "course" button, many participants looked at first one and then the other of these two buttons several times. When the participants were comparing these two buttons, their galvanic skin response (GSR), which was employed as a stress index, increased. In interviews after these trials, participants said they were confused by the two buttons being similar. It was unclear for them which button should be used to select a specific rice cooking menu. Participants were also confused when they pressed a button and the rice cooker interface gave a feedback different from that the participants had expected. These problems were related to cognitive functions, and they could be discovered only in the context of use.

Even in the case of a simple home appliance, it is still difficult to show its functionality. In another experiment, the behavior of older adults using a blood pressure monitor was observed [15]. The blood pressure monitor tested was of a type that requires that users need only insert their arm into a cuff for correct monitoring, as the device provided support to maintain a proper posture for monitoring. In use, the device requires that users first open the cuff by pressing a button, and then insert their arm into the cuff. In the experiment, many participants tried to insert their arm into the device without opening the cuff, and they were confused with the problems they then encountered. The reason was that when the participants looked at the device, there was no indication that the cuff needed to be opened, and they did not see a button that would prompt them to do so, so they immediately tried to insert their arm into the cuff, unaware that it needed to be opened first. Although the button to open the cuff was colored orange and was distinctive, it was positioned on the opposite side of the device from the user, so that it was hard to find in the context of use. On the other hand, the "power" button and "measure" button were very large and easy to find, and the large display provided good legibility, and these features helped older participants during the trials.

These two studies show the importance of observation of older adults in the context of use. By means of experimental studies that investigate usage from information perception to action, the difficulties encountered by older adults can be comprehended as a whole.

Gerontechnology for ICT Products

Speaking generally, the current generation of older adults has great difficulty using ICT products, as many of them started to use such technological products after retirement. ICT products are far more complex than home appliances. A mobile phone offers not only a verbal communication function, but also messaging or e-mailing, a Web browser, camera, music player, television, scheduler, address list, etc. At the same time, the body is made compact for ease of carrying. The smaller the mobile phone's body, the smaller the screen and buttons. As with home appliances, there exist difficulties with hardware – which is critical for older users. The multifunctionality of mobile phones leads to another difficulty for older adults: they cannot find the function they desire. As the number of buttons that can be installed is limited, each button functions differently according to context. In addition, the key to understand how buttons function is displayed on a small screen, and it is hard to read and understand.

As older adults tend to use only a limited number of functions, mobile phones providing verbal communication only came to the Japanese market a few years ago, and they were successful in sales. "Tu-ka-S," which was one of such simple mobile phones, had top sales among all models of Tu-ka (Japanese mobile phone provider) for 1 year. Recently, demand from older adults for popular mobile phone features such as e-mail and a camera have increased. To meet these demands, mobile phones that enable easy access to frequently used functions were developed. In consideration of older adults, some of them have a pedometer function. In another model, battery-charging information is sent to a server, so that the user's family can remotely monitor the user by checking the battery-charging history. These types of mobile phones, designed with older adults in mind, have sold well for a long time – especially to older adults. These types of mobile phones have created a niche segment for themselves within the mobile phone market.

Another solution for difficulties with small buttons and complicated functions is the introduction of the touch screen. Since the iPhone was thrown into the market, the introduction of the touch screen to mobile phones has been accelerated. A touch screen displays only the buttons necessary in each context, so that an adequate individual button size is ensured, and difficulties in locating the required button are reduced. However, the fact that a touch screen provides no tactile feedback may cause other difficulties for older adults. As the haptic function of older adults declines, further consideration is required to confirm whether mobile phones equipped with a touch screen are really useful for older adults.

The use of computers by older adults is gradually increasing. However, difficulties with operating the keyboard and mouse, looking at visual information such as text and icons on the computer display, and using application software still keep older adults away from computers. Difficulties with keyboards are related to problems in distinguishing the keys. Keyboards with large labels on the tops of keys or differently colored keys help to distinguish keys. With regard to the mouse, older adults have problems with understanding the relationship between the movement of the mouse on a desk or table and the movement of the mouse cursor on the display. In order to solve this problem, gain of mouse should be accommodated to functionality of forearm or hand of older users. Similarly to the case of mobile phones, the introduction of a touch screen is also effective here because elements on the display can be pointed at directly using the finger. Since Windows 7 appeared on the market, the number of computers equipped with touch screens has increased. One of them is Fujitsu's "RakuRaku PC" (see Chap. 1 in this book). In addition to a touch screen, keys are labeled with large characters or symbols and colored differently for easy identification, "one-touch keys" to access frequently used functions are provided, and a mouse with differently colored buttons and whose form fits to the hand show the consideration given to hardware. In terms of software, various efforts have been made to make applications easy to use. Frequently used functions are brought together in a special menu. Individual functions are represented by a large button, so that touching or clicking on them is easy. For easy input, in addition to a conventional screen keyboard based on QWERTY keyboard layout, a screen keyboard arranged in order of Japanese kana characters is provided. A support service is also offered, so that older adults can use computers free from any anxiety.

Along with home appliances and ICT products, a verification of the effectiveness of technologies aimed at the elderly is frequently discussed in relation to mobility and transport, health and home care, housing, etc. In recent years, there has been a focus on robotics that support older adults, or games enhancing physical or mental aspects of older adults.

Existing Products Aimed at the Elderly in Japan

As shown by the above-mentioned examples, generally speaking, products designed for the elderly should be easy to see, hear, operate, and understand [5]. More detailed points of consideration for seven different fields with regard to sensory, cognitive, and physical functions and allergy are summarized in ISO/IEC Guide 71 "Guide-lines for standards developers to address the needs of older persons and persons with disabilities" [16]. The already-mentioned ISO/TR 22411 "Ergonomics data and guidelines for the application of ISO/IEC Guide 71 to products and services to address the needs of older persons and persons with disabilities" also provides design guidelines based on data, which is provided in the same technical report [10]. ISO/IEC Guide 71 is translated into Japanese (JIS Z 8071), and 26 separate JIS standards with regard to elderly and disabled persons have already been published (as of September 27, 2010). The product areas here are consumer products, packaging and receptacles, clothes, housing appliances, public restrooms, vending machines, visual signs and displays, braille signs and tactile guide maps, and information/communication equipment, software and services.

Products particularly tailored for the elderly are frequently called "universal design" or "barrier-free" products in Japan. As the "barrier-free" concept mainly concerns impaired people, "universal design" is misunderstood as a similar concept to "barrier-free" by many people. Based on the JIS standards mentioned above, a wide range of packages, ICT, and building elements such as toilets, have been produced. However, they are produced not solely designed for older adults, but also for physically impaired people. Therefore, the needs of "healthy" elderly users in particular are not well fulfilled. It is assumed that information about such products is not sufficiently provided to the elderly. Although there are some databases on products targeting the elderly in Japan (e.g., Accessible Design Foundation of Japan, Welfare Channel, and Home Care and Rehabilitation Exhibition), most of the elderly are still unfamiliar with the use of databases, so that they have a minimal chance of accessing such information. In addition, it is unclear whether these products are appropriate for the elderly. What do elderly people think about such products, and what kind of needs do they have? Answers to these questions need to be addressed in order to develop products that truly cater to the needs of the elderly.

Do Older Adults Really Need "Elderly-Aimed" Products?

As mentioned above, many studies have shown that special consideration with respect to older adults is required for the development of technologies and products. In addition, many products that take older adults into consideration have been produced. However, a report on products aimed at the elderly, which was published in 2004 by the Japanese Ministry of Economy Trade and Industry, showed that only a small percentage of elderly respondents intended using such products, and gave the reasons why they found such products unnecessary [17]. This begs the question: do older adults really need "elderly-aiming" products?

The author can respond affirmatively to that question, based on a questionnaire [18]. Respondents were asked about 18 products designed for the elderly: how important they found the individual features of those products, whether they had known about the products, would they like to use or purchase the products, etc. The results showed that most of the products were unfamiliar to the elderly – except a washing machine and a mobile phone without e-mail or any other Internet functions which were frequently advertised on television. On the other hand, an interest in or willingness to use such products among older adults was confirmed. In fact, when the author introduced such products to older adults, many reacted positively to them, saying: "I didn't know there was such a useful product! Where can I get this?" This means that more information needs to be provided to older adults.

As an information resource, information provided by friends, sales clerks in stores, or members of the community, and articles in newspapers and magazines were preferred over advertisements on television or on the Internet. Television commercials can be a trigger to make people aware of products, but more detailed information needs to be given, either by person-to-person communication, or in print media. Databases would be efficient in providing comprehensive information about such products, but at present they are not familiar information resources for older adults, being more useful for today's younger adults and the older adults of the future.

Required features were different among products. For instance, a cordless vacuum cleaner was regarded as good because its weight was light, so that it did not require too much strength to operate it, and there was no danger of tripping over a cord. In the case of cellular phones, legibility of the display and audibility of the caller's voice were the most important factors among the respondents, whereas video call or reading mail aloud functions were less important to them. These results suggest that the features that facilitate the use of essential or the "original" functions of a product are important for older adults. Overall, features that secure understandability, operability, legibility, and audibility were regarded as important. Features reducing the power required or "additional" functions were less important to the elderly.

Further research is required to determine which functions are really needed by the elderly, and then to design products so that such essential functions can be incorporated.

Needs of Older Adults Identified Through Trial Use of Products

The above-mentioned survey shows what older adults thought about elderly-aiming products. However, a questionnaire-based survey has limitations with regard to reality: in order to answer questions, respondents must imagine what they would think when they actually use the product. If the product had been available at the time of answering questions, practical needs could be extracted more easily. In addition, if brochures of products had been available, a real purchase process could have been simulated.

The author examined information acquisition from a product brochure and trial use by using a "just-insert" blood pressure monitor and a "easy-to-listen-to" radio, both designed for older adults [15, 18]. The needs of the elderly were investigated by evaluating the importance of each product feature in the same way as in the above-mentioned survey. In addition, the eye movement and behavior of the participants were observed, as the participants' thoughts can be reflected in these data. In this way, the needs of the participants were also objectively investigated.

In the subjective evaluation, we confirmed some differences in the participants' evaluation of the product before and after the trial use. From the product brochure, we obtained only the information that the manufacturer of the product wanted to provide. Eye-tracking data showed that descriptions of such recommended features attracted the attention of participants. However, most participants had difficulty using the blood pressure monitor or the radio. This was directly reflected in the subjective evaluation conducted after the trial. The importance of the features in those effects was not clearly confirmed and declined after the trial. On the other hand, features that facilitated the use of these devices were regarded as more important than before the trial. User experience made elderly users aware of their real needs. These experiments suggested that products aimed at the elderly should facilitate use of their essential functions. Additional features can be regarded as important only when the basic requirement is fulfilled. This result is similar to the result from the questionnaire mentioned earlier.

Generally, the most important features for the elderly are those that enhance sensory functions, such as legibility and audibility; features that enhance physical functions, such as operability; and features that enhance cognitive functions, such as understandability. However, in order to consider concrete implementation, it is essential to understand what is really required in the field. The difference in subjective evaluation before and after the trial also highlights the importance of trials. Each product should be evaluated through trial use with regard to the place where the product is used, the person who uses the product, and the purpose of using the product.

As users become familiar with a product, their impression changes on acquiring experience [19], so it is also recommended that a trial period be offered. A trial use, which was accomplished in these studies, was the first trial for participants. Therefore, user evaluation could change through continued use of products. The problems of users can be classified into two groups: problems related to user in-experience, and those that persist after users acquire experience. The latter are regarded as essential problems, which need to be solved.

To date, sufficient data are not available on the preference and behavior of the elderly in daily life situations. Further experimental studies must be conducted in order to clarify how elderly users perceive information from the outside, how they think about the perceived information, and how they behave after processing the required information. The needs and requirements of older adults should be defined on the basis of such data, and applied to the design of products that are truly designed for the elderly.

Summary and Conclusion

The essential role of technologies is to help human beings. In general, it is said that the elderly do not like modern technologies. Actually, elderly people are interested in modern technologies. Due to lack of consideration of age-related decline, current modern technologies are not sufficiently usable by the elderly, so elderly people do not try to use those technologies. In order to solve this problem, gerontechnology is needed.

Gerontechnology is aimed at improving the daily functioning of the elderly through technologies. For that to happen, it is important to understand declines in abilities caused by aging in various aspects, and to discuss how such declines can be prevented, compensated, and supported by the application of technologies. The research works introduced in this chapter suggested that products aimed at the elderly should be designed in such a way that their basic functions can be used with ease. Even functions that compensate for human characteristics showing age-related decline should be designed carefully so that their use does not lead to any further difficulty. In order to accurately understand the needs of users, it is recommended that not only a simple paper questionnaire be conducted, but also that a combination of a questionnaire and observation of user behavior during trial use should be implemented. Without knowing the elderly, elderly-aiming technologies cannot be produced.

Gerontechnology is a rather young research area, and unanswered questions regarding technologies for older adults still remain. Further collection of behavior data concerning older adults using technologies in daily context is strongly required. There are many older adults who are interested in modern technologies. We should make every effort to encourage participation of older adults in experimental studies in gerontechnology. In addition to experimental data, we can hear opinions directly from the elderly, which can also be considered in development of various technologies.

In addition, a subject that needs to be discussed is how to provide information about gerontechnology to older adults. Currently, elderly people know very little about gerontechnology. The elderly who heard about gerontechnology were convinced by its importance and showed great interests. Some elderly people have even asked where such technological products aimed at the elderly were available. Technologies and products backed with the data obtained in gerontechnology will certainly be accepted by the elderly, so that silver market will be activated.

References

1. H. Bouma, Gerontechnology: Making Technology Relevant for the Elderly, in *Gerontechnology*, ed. by H. Bouma, J.A.M. Graafmans (IOS, Amsterdam, 1992), pp. 1–5
2. J. Graafmans, V. Taipale, in *Gerontechnology: A sustainable investment in the future*, ed. by J. Graafmans, V. Taipale, N. Charness (IOS, Amsterdam, 1998), pp. 3–6
3. S.J. Czaja, N. Charness, A.D. Fisk, C. Hertzog, S.N. Nair, W.A. Rogers, J. Sharit, Factors predicting the use of technology: findings from the Center for Research and Education on Aging and Technology Enhancement (CREATE). Psychol. Aging **21**, 333–352 (2006)
4. W. Kosnik, L. Winslow, D. Kline, K. Rasinski, R. Sekuler, Visual changes in daily life throughout adulthood. J. Gerontol. Psychol. Sci. **43**(3), 63–70 (1988)
5. A.D. Fisk, W.A. Rogers, N. Charness, S.J. Czaja, J. Sharit, *Designing for Older Adults: Principles and Creative Human Factors Approaches*, 2nd edn. (CRC, Boca Raton, FL, 2009)
6. J.L. Fozard, S. Gordon-Salant, Changes in vision and hearing with aging, in *Handbook of the Psychology of Aging*, ed. by J.E. Birren, K.W. Schaie, 5th edn. (Academic, Burlington, MA, 2001), pp. 241–266
7. C.J. Ketcham, G.E. Stelmach, Movement Control in the Older Adults, in *Technology for Adaptive Aging*, ed. by R.W. Pew, S.B. van Hemel (The National Academies Press, Washington, D.C., 2004), pp. 64–92
8. K.W. Schaie, Cognitive Aging, in *Technology for Adaptive Aging*, ed. by R.W. Pew, S.B. van Hemel (The National Academies Press, Washington, D. C., 2004), pp. 43–63
9. L.P.A. Steenbekkers, C.E.M. van Beijsterveldt, *Design-Relevant Characteristics of Ageing Users* (Delft University Press, Delft, 1998)
10. ISO/TR Standard 22411, *Ergonomics data and guidelines for the application of ISO/IEC Guide 71 to products and services to address the needs of older persons and persons with disabilities*, 2008
11. K. Kurakata, K. Sagawa, Development and standardization of accessible design technologies that address the needs of senior citizens. Synthesiology **1**(1), 15–23 (2008)
12. K. Sagawa, Age-related luminance and span of categorical colours for designing visual signs for older people. Paper presented in proceedings of AIC 2003 Bangkok: Color communication and management, Bangkok, 4–6 Aug 2003, pp. 431–435
13. M. Ziefle, S. Bay, How older adults meet complexity: Aging effects on the usability of different mobile phones. Behav. Inform. Technol. **24**(5), 375–389 (2005)
14. R. Fukuda, Difficulties in use of "high-tech" home appliances for older users – Experimental consideration based on behavior analysis, eye tracking, and physiological measurement during use of rice cookers. Keio SFC J. **9**(2), 51–62 (2010)
15. R. Fukuda, Analysis of elderly's needs and difficulties in use of a blood pressure monitor based on eye tracking, behavior observation, and subjective evaluation. Trans. Jpn. Soc. Kansei Eng. **8**(2), 307–312 (2009)
16. ISO/IEC Guide 71, *Guidelines for standards developers to address the needs of older persons and persons with disabilities*, 2001
17. Japanese Ministry of Economy Trade and Industry, *Report on Industrial Infrastructure for Promotion of Senior-Aiming Industry* (METI, Tokyo, 2004)
18. R. Fukuda, Needs of the elderly regarding products designed for their use: A gerontechnological view. Paper presented in Proceedings of the 13th IEEE international symposium on consumer electronics (ISCE 2009), pp. 378–381
19. R. Fukuda, Influence of User Experience on Affectiveness, in *Human–Computer Interaction, Part III, HCII2009, LNCS 5612*, ed. by J.A. Jacko (Springer, Berlin, 2009), pp. 615–620

Chapter 7
Designing for Everyone, One Person at a Time

Deana McDonagh and Dan Formosa

Abstract Products that surround us have a profound impact upon our lives. When they empower us to complete daily tasks with ease, speed, and dignity they contribute to our well-being and independence. When they generate negative experiences, they can strip us of dignity and erode our independence. Many companies confuse age with ability, which can diminish the value of the final product. This chapter discusses two techniques that address ability by adding empathy to the design process. *Real People* targets specific individuals. *Empathic Modeling* simulates physical challenges that designers can experience for themselves.

Introduction

The products that we surround ourselves with impact our daily experiences – affecting our perception of ourselves, the world around us, and our personal independence [1]. Design influences all aspects of our lives, including our ability to perform basic tasks related to things such as mobilization, personal hygiene and communications. We relate to products on both rational and emotional levels [2]. Each day, people are forced to work with products that are poorly conceived and poorly designed. As a result, we see people avoiding the task, adapting in some way, or modifying the products themselves. In a sense, they are participating in the creative process by developing workarounds to solve problems of daily living. In effect, they have to adapt to their material landscape rather than have their needs accommodated.

Many companies are looking to develop products and services that address these basic human needs and abilities, from a sense of social responsibility and for the opportunity to gain a competitive edge. Toward both goals, older consumers can be a viable, lucrative target market. A problem with discussions about design and older consumers is that the topic often carries two assumptions: one, that older consumers are all impaired, and two, that younger consumers are not. In corporate language,

F. Kohlbacher and C. Herstatt (eds.), *The Silver Market Phenomenon*,
DOI 10.1007/978-3-642-14338-0_7, © Springer-Verlag Berlin Heidelberg 2011

the word "age" is commonly confused with "ability." This unfortunately can undermine efforts to design for *real* people in the *real* world. Stereotypes can be detrimental to the goal. In America for instance, in actual number there are almost as many younger people with arthritis as older people. There are also, of course, many nonarthritic older consumers. Older *and* younger people are diverse groups that defy simplistic categorizations, gross assumptions or generalizations.

As Pirkl (Chap. 9, p. XX) puts it so concisely:

Young people grow old
Disabled people grow old
Young people can be disabled
Old people can be disabled

When a product development team approaches the topic of ability correctly, opportunities for innovative products and services abound. This chapter on design is not about *aging*. It is about *empathy*.

Empathy is:

... our intuitive ability to identify with other people's thoughts and feelings – their motivations, emotional and mental models, values, priorities, preferences and inner conflicts. [3]

We will discuss techniques that help product and service development teams find solutions that can work for everyone, accommodating people spanning a wide range of abilities and ages. This practice is often referred to as Inclusive Design and Universal Design [4, 5]. In our approach, the key is not to understand market segments, as has been traditional practice for targeting consumers, but to understand the person. In order to design for everyone, our approach is about understanding individuals through empathic design research.

To this goal we discuss two techniques that have been helping product development teams get to know people better: *Real People* and *Empathic Modeling*. *Real People* [6] is based on the idea that, while companies think in terms of sizable target markets, those target groups are composed of individuals. Designing for a small number of real people can be insightful, and difficult – much more of a challenge than designing for a cumulative "average." *Empathic Modeling* [7] serves a similar purpose. It encompasses a range of techniques that allow a member of a design team to experience products or services in the way another individual may experience them. We acknowledge that there are many ways in which a person may carry out any particular task [8]. As product developers, we have much to learn from the diverse ways in which users engage with products and environments. That individual may have physical challenges or situational conditions beyond the typical experience of the team member. Altering a body or the environment to simulate a specific difficulty can help the team understand and solve for the challenge. Importantly, we will discuss both techniques with the underlying principle that it is often better to think in terms of ability than age.

Ability, Not Age

In creating a product or service, a marketing group will often define an average person, a person that represents a wide group or subgroup within a population. Age, gender, family life, work life and other factors are tightly defined. Along with the definition of average comes a tendency to oversimplify – a "target consumer" profile is often distilled down to a single PowerPoint slide.

This simple definition of an average consumer can underestimate the diversity of real people, the complexity of the problem at hand, and even the varied needs of any one individual. The ultimate result can be a product or service that falls short of its potential. Any one person can be complex unto him or herself. A large group of people, of course, will be even more complex.

Designers need to focus on that diversity, considering everybody. This is a real and difficult challenge. The goal is not necessarily to design a single product that suits everyone. The goal is to make products, technologies and services available to everyone. Designing for a well-defined average can exclude people. A common practice that may be even worse is to design for an aspirational person, an ideal. The tendency for companies to do this can be traced to some fundamental differences between marketing and design. While there may be reasons to create marketing materials portraying an aspirational image – a perfect cook, athlete, singer, parent or whatever – design is not marketing. *Designing* products or services, to be used by real people, requires a reality-based approach.

Failure to do so can have dire consequences. In cases where the products we create exclude people with specific physical challenges, it is not just a bad business decision – it becomes discrimination. It is the social responsibility of companies to ensure everyone benefits from design and technology, not just make them available to a few. This is also a good business move, since products and services that attract a wider audience result in increased sales – and, of course, lessens the chances of negative impressions of that product or service. Of course there are many products and services that, justifiably, target older consumers. But the automatic assumption that older equals impaired, and that younger equals healthy, defies reality. That is why it is critical to employ techniques that respond to real people, real situations and real needs.

Design Is About the Experience, Not the Object

A study conducted by Smart Design in the mid-2000s [9] showed that, in the US, the meaning of the word "design" is changing. People are associating design not with a physical product or aesthetics, but with the *experience* of using a product. "Great design" does more than meet expectations. To qualify as great, products need to exceed expectations. People expect products to work. When they do, it is good but not exceptional. Excitement about a product or service relies on it being better than anticipated. In our experience, the ability of a product or service to excel, and to have real impact on real people, is more important than ever before. Achieving this requires that we understand not just people or situations "in the middle," but also people at the extremes.

Design research only started to emerge as routine practice in the late 1970s.[1] Today, relatively few designers have training in design research. Yet they practice or utilize it routinely. While design research should encompass many aspects of user experiences, many efforts are limited to ethnographic research, which in turn can be reduced to short, opinion-taking sessions. These efforts often forgo issues such as biomechanics, ergonomics and usability, which are specialized topics important for design groups to understand, but are not always within the scope of a marketing-funded research project.

Historically, a typical product design process was a linear activity, design followed by engineering, then tooling, manufacturing and production. Each activity was completed before the project progressed to the next activity. User input was sought late in the product development process, relying on the product designer to be the voice of the consumer in the early phases. User input was acquired only after much of a concept's refinement had occurred, near the end of the design process (refer to *A* in Fig. 7.1 Design Process and User Input) [10]. With the advent of the more user-centered approaches of Universal Design (refer to *B*), users became a more integral part of the process. We advocate that design is too important to leave to designers alone, and integrating the user at the beginning of the process offers more benefits to all, including the mainstream user (refer to *C*).

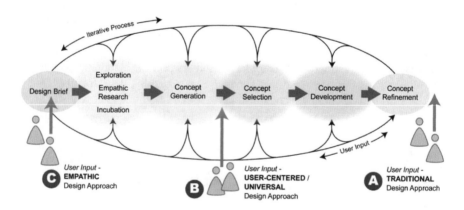

Fig. 7.1 Design process and user input (McDonagh et al. [10])

---

[1]There are earlier examples of interest in the topic. For instance, designer Henry Dreyfuss' 1955 Designing for People and 1960 Measure of Man compiled government databases on anthropometric sizes of men and women for use in product design.

Real People

Not only are people diverse – any one person can find him or herself in diverse situations. In past projects, we have found that the rejection of an average person or stereotype as a target, replaced with an understanding of individual needs of many people, has led to innovation. It has therefore been our approach to reject the notion of "average" or "ideal" and consider the spectrum.

Understanding real people will lead to real-world performance. Getting this right allows new products and services to come to the attention of many, quickly. The concept behind the *Real People* approach [6] is simple: find a workable, small number of people who your team would like to accommodate with the product or service being developed, and design it for them. The number of people could be six or more – as long as it is kept to a manageable number.

Typically, we receive two immediate responses to this approach (1) "We cannot design our product or service for just a few people!," and (2) "How do we choose the people?" First, you will find that it is actually difficult to design something that fits into the lives of six to twelve people. In comparison, designing for an imaginary persona or average is easy. The distilled average does not complain. Responses to new products or services, when presented to a large group of people as in typical practice, culminate in "average" scores. Findings report that people *tend* to prefer (or not prefer) various options. From this, the team eventually chooses a direction. This approach is rarely a method for detecting the weak signals that can lead to meaningful innovations. Designing for a group average can dilute our responses to true individual needs and points of view, and therefore dilute the final outcome.

In contrast, it is much more challenging to succeed with a small number of individuals, who through the course of a project the design team has come to know, and who can become very articulate and vocal about their personal needs and situations. Attempting to deliver a design that accommodates even a small group of individuals is not easy. Remember that "accommodate" is a minimum requirement. A great product needs to exceed expectations, not just meet them. Remember also that if your team has traditionally defined an average consumer, or a persona as the target, that definition is actually just one person. One made-up person. Based on presentations the authors have seen prepared by product development groups in the past, it is often an imaginary person that seems to like everything the product development team creates.

For the second question, "how do you choose the people?" – you can certainly be strategic and choose a cross-section of consumers. However, we also challenge design teams to choose *any* people that they would consider to be in their target group, because these are, in fact, people you want to impress. If that is accomplished (and you may find that much more difficult than you think), add more people to the group. The other goal of this method is to get to personally know the people, introduce them to the project at the beginning, and work closely with them throughout the duration of the project. Rather than "test subjects" they become adjunct members of the design team. This is not exactly cocreation (ideas may come completely from the design team) but it is a continuous reality-check that can significantly change the course of thinking by the team.

Another positive effect – we have found in other projects that team members refer to consumers as a faceless "they." As in "I think *they* will be able to use this feature successfully if we design it this way." When designing for real people, the team incurs more empathy. Team discussions become much more personal and warm. For instance "I think Carl will be able to use this successfully, but what about Lindsay?" The team then has the advantage of calling Lindsay to come in to discuss this issue with the team or to try it out. This develops a closer and more in-depth understanding.

We have applied this approach to a wide range of projects. Here is an example applied to an extreme case of universal design. UCB Celltech, a pharmaceutical company headquartered in Brussels, developed a medication called Cimzia for use by people with rheumatoid arthritis. Cimzia is to be administered by self-injection, at home. Disposable syringes have been available for decades and have become commodity items. While they may be well-engineered, they are not well-designed, even for people without arthritis. Sharp corners and protrusions on plastic parts do not fit the hand well for anyone, but as we witnessed, were especially problematic for patients with rheumatoid arthritis. People in this group can have greatly reduced strength and can be extremely sensitive to pressure in the finger joints – especially on a "bad arthritis day." The Cimzia Prefilled Syringe is the first syringe designed for use by people with arthritis (Figs. 7.2 and 7.3).

To carry out the project, UCB Celltech partnered with OXO[2] to bring brand recognition and design expertise. Unlike osteoarthritis, associated with older adults, rheumatoid arthritis can strike at any age. The new syringe needed to fit into a wide range of lifestyles. From the outset, our design team set its goal not simply on the design of a new syringe, but on a larger picture of improving patient compliance through the creation of a more positive experience. It was critical for our team to consider the mechanism of rheumatoid arthritis, underlying biomechanics, and the effect of rheumatoid arthritis on patients' abilities to self-inject. It was also important to understand the social context in which the medication is used – its affect on an individual patient's lifestyle and psyche.

While our design team worked with more than fifty patients throughout the course of the project, we worked with six patients very closely. We saw Janet unable to effectively hold a traditional syringe and push the plunger, while less-affected Dave applied enough force to break it. Every step in the process, from uncapping the needle (uncapping can result in accidental needle sticks) through injection and disposal, was examined. Things that worked for an "average" patient did not work for everyone. Things that worked for some of our worst-case patients did not work for our less-affected patients. Some of our stronger patients had poor

---

[2]OXO's Good Grips line of kitchen tools were designed by Smart Design to address the needs of everyone, including people with arthritis. They have become closely associated with the concept of Universal Design, design for everyone.

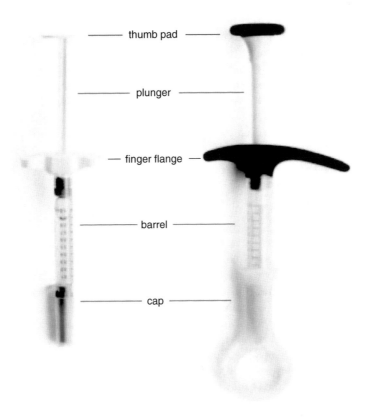

Fig. 7.2 Traditional syringe and the Cimzia prefilled syringe

Fig. 7.3 Uncapping the
Cimzia prefilled syringe

vision – also a factor affecting successful injection. By paying personal attention and accommodating the needs of each individual in our group, we stretched further than we would if we had we focused on an average patient, or a disembodied range of users. Every weak signal detected was addressed, for the good of all patients. While larger groups of patients were consulted at various points in the project, our core group of six patients was invaluable in providing insight and inspiration for the design team. As a result, the design of the Cimzia Prefilled Syringe allows patients to exert 48% more force on the plunger, allowing a wide range of patients with weakened hands and fingers to self-inject.

Empathic Modeling

Effective designers recognize they cannot rely solely on their own experiences (e.g., background, physical abilities, education) in the development of new products. Their ability to create successful products is enhanced through gaining empathy with users. Empathic design research deepens the designer's understanding. Intangibles such as feelings, emotions, dreams, aspirations, and fears can provide the designer with critical cues, triggers and inspiration that provide the essence of more balanced functional and suprafunctional products (e.g., iPod, Mac Air laptop). Using empathic methods such as ethnography, empathic modeling (e.g., able-bodied designers using wheel chairs and/or restricting their mobility or handgrip dexterity), and shadowing, designers gather a range of textual, verbal, and visual data. The incubation period that follows provides designers with opportunity to reflect, imagining a design solution that refines, develops and/or matures what already exists. It enables designers to develop new ways of seeing, thinking, and experiencing as they generate more visionary ideas and concepts. Empathic design research builds on the synergy of individuals developing relationships [11] and is the essence of qualitative design research [3]. Designers can combine this qualitative research with more traditional objective research data (e.g., marketing, socio-economic and anthropometric) to fuel their creativity, develop inspired products, and ensure more relevant design outcomes.

For many professions, empathy may not be critical, but designers need to acknowledge their own boundaries of understanding and knowledge. Use of empathic design research methods is a key factor in "expanding the designer's empathic horizon" [6, 8, 11], and provides designers more relevant data and creative product outcomes. Empathic design research has resulted in the success of many commercial products.

With the shift away from generalizing users and a move towards developing more empathy with users, empathic modeling can provide valuable insight (Fig. 7.4). Design is less about generating products and more about creating positive experiences for users. With this in mind, our future designers need to be fluent in traditional design skills (e.g., drawing, model-making) as well as research skills (e.g., empathic modeling, shadowing, cultural probes [12, 13]).

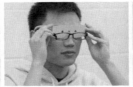

Fig. 7.4 Designers carrying out empathic modeling to help them understand a range of disabilities

As an effective product does not develop within a vacuum, an effective designer needs to become connected with the user, the use environment and culture to ensure the product is received, used and that a lasting user–product bond is made. This activity begins to change how the designers relate to users who may be different from themselves.

After conducting empathic modeling in the design studio and also in more naturalistic environments (e.g., shopping centers, restaurants), the designers' feedback can be extremely positive, from the perspective of them not focusing on specific disabilities or impairments, but concentrating on exploring *new* ways of doing everyday tasks. This shift in thinking, from there only being one way to perform a task to the many possibilities of users engaging with products differently and performing tasks based on their abilities and skills, positively shapes the way designers perceive their audience.

Discussion

Focusing on real people rather than the average person has been invaluable in developing products that accommodate everyone. The biggest challenges in implementation may come not from carrying out these methods of thinking, but in convincing product development teams to break away from past research practices. Because design needs to address diversity, the reduction of consumers to a single average person, or series of homogenized personas, limits design's view. Therefore we are seeing that small numbers of real people, as well as first-hand simulations, can help a design team innovate by uncovering real needs and opportunities.

Summary and Conclusion

We are entering an era in which consumers require fewer products, but products with more personal meaning. For products and services to be effective, design decision-making processes need to be based on "authentic" understanding of the user. This can be realized by focusing on the real needs of real people. Empathy can play a significant role in ensuring more intuitive design outcomes, as the designer feels more in-tune with the target user. Design can tangibly contribute to enhancing a person's high quality of life, sense of empowerment, independence and well-being. Designing products or services to be used by real people requires a reality-based approach. It is time to design for *real* people, *real* situations and *real* needs.

References

1. L.H. Campbell, D. McDonagh, Visual narrative research methods as performance in industrial design education. Qual. Inq. **15**, 587–606 (2009)
2. J. Chapman, *Emotionally Durable Design: Objects, Experiences and Empathy* (Earthscan, London, 2005)
3. D. Formosa, The six real people. Paper presented in the proceedings of the international association of societies of design research, Coex, Seoul, Korea. Korean Society of Design Science [CDROM], Kyunggi-do, 2009
4. W. Lidwell, K. Holden, J. Butler, *Universal Principles of Design: 115 Ways to Enhance Usability, Influence Perception, Increase Appeal, Make Better Design Decisions, and Teach Through Design* (Rockport, Beverly, MA, 2010)
5. J. Fulton Suri, Empathic Design: Informed and Inspired by Other People's Experience, in *Empathic Design: User Experience in Product Design*, ed. by I. Koskinen, K. Battarbee, T. Mattelmäki (IT, Finland, 2003)
6. D. McDonagh, Do it until it hurts! Empathic design research. Des. Princ. Pract. **2**(3), 103–109 (2008)
7. N. Hansen, C. Philo, The normality of doing things differently: Bodies, spaces and disability geography. Tijdschrift voor Economische en Sociale Geografie **98**(4), 493–506 (2007)
8. D. Formosa, D. McDonagh, I wasn't that comfortable anyway (in design-system-evolution). Paper presented in the proceedings of the 6th international conference of the European academy of design, EAD06, Bremen, Germany, 29–31 Mar 2005
9. D. McDonagh, J. Thomas, S. Chen, J. He, Y.S. Hong, Y. Kim, Z. Zhang, F. Pena-Mora, Empathic Design Research: Disability + Relevant Research. Design Connexity. Paper presented in the 8th European academy of design international conference, The Robert Gordon University, Aberdeen, Scotland, 1–3 April 2009, pp. 310–315
10. M.L. Khuri, Working in emotion in educational interwork dialogue. Int. J. Intercult. Relat. **28**, 595–612 (2004)
11. H. Denton, D. McDonagh, Using focus groups to support the designer in the evaluation of existing products: A case study. Des. J. **2**(2), 20–31 (1999)
12. B. Laurel (ed.), *Design Research: Methods and Perspectives* (Massachusetts Institute of Technology, London, 2003)
13. J. Clarkson, R. Coleman, S. Keates, C. Lebbon, *Inclusive Design: Design for the Whole Population* (Springer, London, 2003)

Chapter 8
Universal Design: Innovations for All Ages

Oliver Gassmann and Gerrit Reepmeyer

Abstract Demographics require companies to abandon the concept of solely targeting young customers. They need to create new products that are attractive to both younger and older customers. The key to success is Universal Design. Products that follow the principles of Universal Design do not separate but integrate customer groups, and they substantially increase a company's target markets. This chapter not only highlights the economic potential of Universal Design, it also shows how Universal Design can be implemented within any corporation. A successful implementation needs to (a) define a suitable Universal Design strategy, (b) establish adequate processes within the firm, (c) design the products right, and (d) market the products appropriately to customers. The chapter concludes by illustrating attractive areas for universally designed innovations.

Introduction

The demographic time bomb is ticking: the society of most western economies is getting older every day. However, while the "Generation 50+" turns out to be one of the most attractive target groups for many companies, the term "aging" itself is controversially discussed. It is still fairly prevalent that everybody will become old, but no one wants to be old. But this antiquated perception of age has become outdated itself. The "new" elderly generation is much more vital, has a higher purchasing power and increasingly loves to experiment with new products compared to "older" elderly generations. This is not very surprising if it is considered that today's 50+ generation grew up under totally different circumstances from the traditionally known "older generation." Today's 50- to 65-year-olds grew up in a cultural environment with Rock "n" Roll, Elvis Presley, and The Beatles. They identify themselves with people such as Tina Turner, Robert Redford, Sean Connery, or Mick Jagger. It is simple but true: someone who was 26 years old in 1968 is 65-years old today.

F. Kohlbacher and C. Herstatt (eds.), *The Silver Market Phenomenon*,
DOI 10.1007/978-3-642-14338-0_8, © Springer-Verlag Berlin Heidelberg 2011

Despite this development, many companies still have not launched appropriate initiatives that intentionally include this fairly new and fast-growing market segment of people over 50 years of age into product planning and development activities. Research by the Arizona State University has shown that only 12 out of 125 Fortune 500 companies mention on their websites that they proactively consider the specific needs of the elderly in their product strategy. Upon request, only two of these companies were able to provide more detailed information about these initiatives.

Our explorative study in 2003 with 105 companies in 11 different industries showed similar results. Eighty-five percent of companies considered it important to align product offerings with demographic developments. However, only 29% of respondents have proactively thought about opportunities to launch the respective initiatives. Only around 20% of companies have conducted or even read market research reports discussing the potential of demographic change. This negligence has serious consequences, because companies miss out on real opportunities. The survey asked companies who already offered age-friendly products about the products' performance. Seventy percent of the respondents confirmed that they were very satisfied with this type of product diversification, and that these products were successful on the market. Fifty-nine percent of all companies expected that age-friendly products would lead to at least average if not above-average growth. Only 2% believed that age-friendly products would lead to growth rates below average (see Fig. 8.1). This study is of explorative character, and needs further research with larger samples in different regions.

In addition to the lack of awareness among companies, the amount of research on the economic potential of demographic change is fairly limited as well. The only available studies relate to customer segmentation approaches and to defining the needs and special demands of older consumers [1–3]. Hupp [4] observed the decision-making of older people, whereas Trocchia and Janda [5] analyzed Internet usage of senior users. Szmigin and Carrigan [6] looked at the societal construction of aging and the resulting self-perception of the elderly. Wolfe [7] has taken this approach a step further and analyzed the thought structures of the elderly. Silvers [8] did research about marketing-relevant events for people of older age, and Bristol [9] analyzed the impact of the "endorser age" on the value of brands. All authors collectively came to the conclusion that a focus on only younger customer generations is wrong [4, 10–13]. Some other researchers analyzed advertising and sales concepts targeting the elderly as well as the role of older customers in advertising and commercials [12, 14, 15]. In addition, there are some studies available that analyze the consumer behavior of older customers. Lazer [16] was one of the first researchers who observed the purchasing power and consumer acceptance of seniors. Hock and Bader [17] have built upon this approach and analyzed the purchasing and consumer behavior of the 55+ generation.

Most companies are still overwhelmed with the opportunities and corresponding challenges of demographic developments. Some companies have tried to address older customers by offering products that are particularly declared and promoted as products for the elderly. However, developing products especially for seniors has

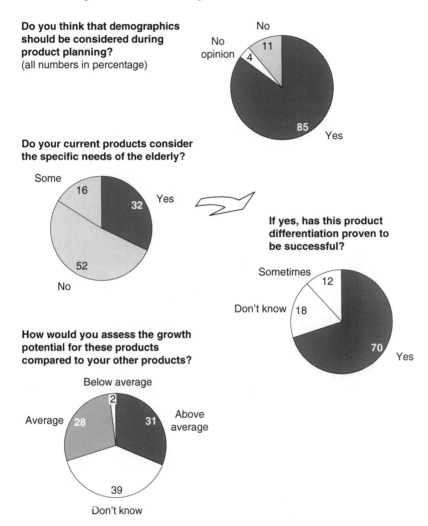

Fig. 8.1 Many companies consider demographic developments to be important for their product offerings, but only a few companies have launched corresponding initiatives: the potential of age-friendly products seems to be significant

not shown to be effective in addressing these customers. As most of the people over 50 are still physically fit and vital, they prefer to buy their products in the same locations as younger generations. They do not want to be separated from younger and healthier generations by shopping for products that have a connotation "for seniors."

This leaves companies with no other choice than developing products and services independent of the customers' age. These products and services need to combine the product requirements (logic, complexity, dimensions, functions, handling) with the special capabilities of the elderly (sensory and cognitive capabilities, mental agility, physical condition, technical experience). Successful innovations follow the motto: "Creating products for younger generations excludes the elderly. Creating products for all ages, however, includes all generations – young and old."

The Potential of Universal Design

In this context, innovation management has recently started to become engaged with the new paradigm of "Universal Design." Universally designed products are attractive to all customers, independent of their age. Universal Design integrates. It does not differentiate between disabled, normal, old, and young. Universal products take into account the needs and requirements of all possible users and customers. Therefore, Universal Design conceptually represents a standard, not an exception. Universal Design intentionally avoids highlighting the users' and customers' different capabilities. A 30-year-old would not buy a car that has been developed for a 60-year-old. However, the 60-year-old would not buy this car either. By offering products that are independent of their users' age, companies can eventually maximize their possible target customers.

The Center for Universal Design at North Carolina State University in the United States is one of the pioneers in promoting Universal Design as a product standard. The Center has come up with principles for universally designed products. These principles have found broad acceptance in product development around the world. Table 8.1 provides a brief overview of the seven Universal Design Principles. The application of all principles ensures a universal product design that is truly independent of the customers' age.

The origins of Universal Design date back to the early 1950s. Because of the high number of veterans of World War II, the public has slowly developed an interest in the needs of disabled people and people who cannot live a normal, regular life due to physical impairments. Many people were either directly affected by disability or knew someone in their immediate social environment who was disabled due to the consequences of the war. It was during these times that efforts were made to develop products that were designed to take disabled people's needs into account. However, those products were usually designed and declared as "products for the disabled." In addition to a lack of esthetics in design, the prices were comparatively high as well.

It took another couple of years (it was only after the end of the Vietnam War in the mid-1970s) for the first laws to come into effect that constituted favoring situations and environments for people with disabilities. The USA introduced the "American Disability Act" in 1990, and the UK passed the "Disability Discrimination Act" in 1995. Only in 1998 did the first real tangible benefits for people who were physically challenged become evident with the introduction of "Section 508" of the "Workforce Investment Act." This section states that public contracts may only be issued to companies that design their products in a way that they can be also

Table 8.1 The seven Universal Design principles (source: The Center for Universal Design)

Principle	Explanation
1. Equitable use	The design is useful and marketable to people with diverse abilities *Guidelines* (a) Provide the same means of use for all users: identical whenever possible; equivalent when not (b) Avoid segregating or stigmatizing any users (c) Provisions for privacy, security, and safety should be equally available to all users (d) Make the design appealing to all users
2. Flexibility in use	The design accommodates a wide range of individual preferences and abilities *Guidelines* (a) Provide choice in methods of use (b) Accommodate right- or left-handed access and use (c) Facilitate the user's accuracy and precision (d) Provide adaptability to the user's pace
3. Simple and intuitive use	Use of the design is easy to understand, regardless of the user's experience, knowledge, language skills, or current concentration level *Guidelines* (a) Eliminate unnecessary complexity (b) Be consistent with user expectations and intuition (c) Accommodate a wide range of literacy and language skills (d) Arrange information consistent with its importance (e) Provide effective prompting and feedback during and after task completion
4. Perceptible information	The design communicates necessary information effectively to the user, regardless of ambient conditions or the user's sensory abilities *Guidelines* (a) Use different modes (pictorial, verbal, tactile) for redundant presentation of essential information (b) Provide adequate contrast between essential information and its surroundings (c) Maximize "legibility" of essential information (d) Differentiate elements in ways that can be described (i.e., make it easy to give instructions or directions) (e) Provide compatibility with a variety of techniques or devices used by people with sensory limitations
5. Tolerance for error	The design minimizes hazards and the adverse consequences of accidental or unintended actions *Guidelines* (a) Arrange elements to minimize hazards and errors: most used elements, most accessible; hazardous elements eliminated, isolated, or shielded (b) Provide warnings of hazards and errors (c) Provide fail-safe features (d) Discourage unconscious action in tasks that require vigilance
6. Low physical effort	The design can be used efficiently and comfortably and with a minimum of fatigue *Guidelines* (a) Allow user to maintain a neutral body position (b) Use reasonable operating forces (c) Minimize repetitive actions (d) Minimize sustained physical effort

(*continued*)

Table 8.1 (continued)

Principle	Explanation
7. Size/space for approach/use	Appropriate size and space is provided for approach, reach, manipulation, and use regardless of user's body size, posture, or mobility *Guidelines* (a) Provide a clear line of sight to important elements for any seated or standing user (b) Make reach to all components comfortable for any seated or standing user (c) Accommodate variations in hand and grip size (d) Provide adequate space for the use of assistive devices or personal assistance

used by disabled customers. The advantage of this act was that it left a lot of freedom to companies to decide what actions they prefer to take in order to achieve this goal – and if they intend to achieve it at all.

Many countries in Europe have also adopted the principle of caring about people with disabilities. For example, the European Union declared the year 2003 as the "Year of People with Disabilities." In this context, the EU launched a big initiative to fund research projects focusing on issues related to Universal Design.

Despite the clear governmental mandate, however, industry still has little experience when it comes to Universal Design. The tasks and costs are frequently considered to be still unknown, and many companies have not yet responded to this trend. Only a few examples exist that show the real tangible benefits of Universal Design, but this number is growing. Sometimes, other notations are used for the concept of age-independent design, such as transgenerational design. However, the idea behind all those initiatives remains the same – to create products and applications that can be used by all customers, independent of their age or physical and mental conditions.

It does not always take a lot of effort and energy to come up with a universally designed pathway to impact. The company Whirlpool, for example, might serve as a good case in this context. A few years ago, Whirlpool (one of the world's leaders in appliances, especially washing machines) received an unusual amount of letters and complaints from their customers indicating that the company's products were hard to understand and use. As a response, Whirlpool conducted a few smaller modifications, such as placing an easily understandable manual with large letters right underneath the cover of the machine. While the older customers did not send any complaints to Whirlpool any more, the younger customers did not complain either. In addition, the younger customers were indifferent towards the new design. Thus, Whirlpool was able to make only small adjustments to its current product, but was able to increase the group of satisfied customers quite substantially, which is right at the heart of the meaning of the concept of Universal Design.

Implementing Universal Design Within the Corporation

Define a Suitable Strategy

Anchoring the concept of Universal Design in the product strategy is the first step towards a successful implementation of Universal Design. Top management has to make clear how strategic initiatives should be conceptualized and implemented. The following questions need to be addressed:

- Should Universal Design be implemented within the entire company, certain business units, or only some selected product lines or groups?
- What resources and competencies are necessary, and how can the company's own core competencies best be leveraged?
- What are the potential applications and what is their market potential?

A successfully implemented Universal Design strategy defines how the company intends to position itself toward its stakeholders, what message the company wants to promulgate, and what products and services it should offer. Every company can rely upon three generic strategies to define its degree of implementation of Universal Design (see Fig. 8.2):

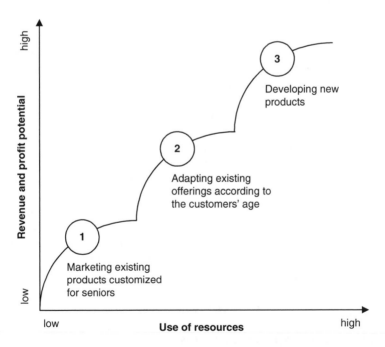

Fig. 8.2 Universal Design can be implemented in the corporate strategy in multiple ways and can have different scopes [18]

1. *Marketing existing products customized for seniors.* This strategy simply relies upon redirecting the company's marketing concept. The yet-neglected target group of the elderly will intentionally be integrated into the marketing of existing products and services. However, existing products and services are usually not adapted accordingly. The company only changes its way of communicating and addressing the possibly new customers in order to attract older customers.
2. *Adapting existing offerings according to the customers' age.* This strategy systematically analyzes all existing products and services and determines if they fulfill the Universal Design requirements. If some products or services do not meet these criteria, the company can try to come up with possible adaptations in order to make the products and services more attractive for the elderly.
3. *Developing new products.* This strategy includes the development of entirely new products and services that strictly follow all Universal Design principles, from ideation to market introduction. The elderly are proactively included during product development phases in order to ensure adherence to Universal Design standards.

The first strategy entails fairly low market risks. Small changes in product marketing may lead to comparatively quick market success. The strategy's implications on sales and profit may be limited, however.

The second strategy requires more resources. The higher effort, however, will most likely lead to greater leaps in revenues and profits because this strategy indeed offers more attractive products and services for the older generation, in addition to an age-friendly marketing. The increased attractiveness of the products and services is usually based upon an improved design of the interfaces between the product and the user (i.e., the technology and the older customer). Good examples are telephones with enlarged number keys as well as high-resolution and high-contrast digital displays.

The third strategy is characterized by the highest development and market risks. It also requires the largest amount of resources. Due to comparatively longer lead times in development, this strategy will usually increase sales and profits with a slight delay. By contrast, these products and services are most appropriately suited to include satisfying the needs of the elderly as they proactively include their opinions and perspectives.

These three strategies are not mutually exclusive. They can be applied in parallel, and they are applicable in a broad range of industries ranging from high-tech to consumer goods. The textile and fashion company Betty Barclay, for example, has broadened its product offering – purposely including the elderly – and has achieved great success since then. While most textile and fashion companies in Germany have posted declining revenues and profits, Betty Barclay, however, was able to present an increase of sales in 2003 of 1.6%. The average Betty Barclay customer is 39 years of age or older.

Another example of a company that has radically shifted its strategy a couple of years ago, and now primarily, but not exclusively, offers products that target the market of the elderly is the Swiss company Synthes-Stratec. Initially, the company produced high-quality Swiss watches. The company's engineers were experimenting with new materials, with the objective of discovering nonmagnetic alloys that are resistant to shocks and corrosion. Today, these alloys are still used in well-known brands such as Rolex or IWC. The company's management recognized that these new alloys were applicable not only in watches but in a couple of other market segments that were characterized by high growth rates. Because of that, the company engaged in cooperation with the Association for Osteosynthesis. This cooperation represented the company's entrance into prosthetics, a market segment that primarily, but not exclusively, includes older customers. In the following years, Synthes-Stratec has substantially changed gears, and now focuses on prosthetics. Today, the company is world leader in osteosynthesis and generates revenues of more than CHF 1.5 billion.

In most instances, small changes in the company's product strategy are sufficient to make products and services attractive and applicable to users of all ages. While all age groups will benefit from these adjustments, it is most often the group of the elderly that benefits the most. Whereas younger users are usually able to adapt to new circumstances and new situations, older users usually do not have these capabilities. That is the reason why they appreciate universally designed products the most.

Establish Adequate Processes

In order to identify and define processes that permit the implementation of Universal Design strategies, a closer look at the older customers' specific capabilities and abilities has proven to be a very effective first step. Physical and mental capabilities usually worsen with old age. Many age-related medical conditions lead to the fact that sensory capabilities and velocity-related activities decline. Vision usually starts to deteriorate at an age of around 40. The eye's abilities relating to contrast and colors are usually impaired by then. Starting at around 60 years of age, more severe constraints frequently occur. Hearing impairment usually starts at an age of around 60, the same age at which muscular strength usually starts declining as well. For example, a 60-year-old has on average 15–35% less muscular strength than a 20-year-old. In addition, problems of the joints usually occur. Taking all these factors into account, many researchers in gerontology have come to the general belief that people beyond their mid-1960s face considerable multimorbidity issues [2, 19, 20]. However, studies have shown that substantial losses of physical fitness only correlate for people with an average age of over 85.

In addition to physical capabilities, the mental capabilities of older customers also face significant challenges. For example, older people tend to rely too much on their previous experiences. Due to their life experience, older people usually have accumulated highly specific knowledge systems: the part of their intelligence that is based on experience is usually fairly high. As a result, older people tend to assign new information to familiar schemes and thinking [21, 22]. Therefore, the ability to understand novel technologies and functional principles usually declines with increasing age. However, this should not be confused with generally lower intelligence. Only the "fluid" intelligence, i.e., the intelligence that is used to process new and complex information (also referred to as comprehensive power), is lower for people of older age [23]. The "crystallized" intelligence, by contrast, which contains factual knowledge and relies on capabilities acquired during the course of a person's lifetime, rarely declines with old age. Moreover, the crystallized intelligence can even partly compensate for the declining fluid intelligence in older people.

Considering the situation of many older people, the main problem of product development becomes clear: in many cases, fairly young engineers, designers, and marketing experts are creating products that are expected to be purchased by the elderly. Simply because of the difference in age, they have never been exposed to the special physical and mental challenges that most of their customers are facing. They usually know the perspectives and opinions of younger customer generations quite well, but they mostly lack the knowledge and empathy to grasp and understand the special capabilities and needs of older customer generations. A successful implementation of Universal Design therefore always requires merging of the innovative products' features with the special capabilities and abilities of the older consumers (see Fig. 8.3).

In order to make it happen that the product's requirements and features match the customers' physical and mental capabilities, three generally accepted strategies can be applied to address this challenge:

1. *Checklists for product features.* Multiple groups of researchers (including the Center for Universal Design in the USA) have already developed guidelines that describe the characteristics of age-friendly products and services. Companies can use these guidelines to identify potential for improvement of their current product and service offerings. However, they should keep in mind that concrete design implications can usually not be generalized. Every product or service design needs to be handled as an individual case.
2. *Deficit simulation.* Besides theoretically elaborating the needs and capabilities of older customers, physically experiencing these challenges is an even more powerful tool for really understanding the special issues related to serving the elderly. The company Meyer-Hentschel Management Consulting has developed an "Age Explorer" that uses glasses, headsets, weights, and other tools to simulate the physical and cognitive capabilities of older people. If a younger designer or engineer uses the "Age Explorer," his or her own capabilities are literally reduced, and the "Age Explorer" allows them to have the same experience using products and services that the older customers would have. That way, the deficits of old age can be made recognizable and experienceable.
3. *Participative design.* Participative design describes a method that directly includes elderly customers in product development activities, ideally from idea generation to final market testing. This allows giving a voice to older customers and lets them articulate their needs and expectations. In addition, the designers also get a much closer understanding of the older people's opinions

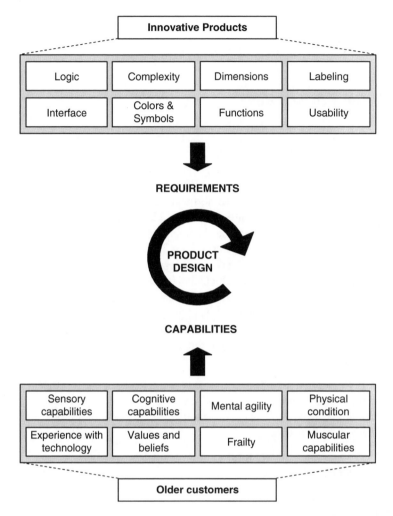

Fig. 8.3 Successful product development under the Universal Design paradigm matches the requirements of the innovative products with the abilities of older customers

and perspectives. Companies could proactively employ older people in their R&D departments in order to allow for participative design. A well-balanced mix of young and old designers and engineers seems to be a promising approach to a successful implementation of Universal Design product strategies.

The needs and requirements of customers can only be appropriately considered during the product development process if the customers that actually use the product are included in the product development process. In addition, the capabilities of the users need to comply with the requirements of the product. Only under these conditions will innovations be adopted and actually used. Products fulfill the requirements of Universal Design if all of these aspects are taken into account and, simultaneously, the younger customer groups are not excluded or scared away by the product's design. If these conditions are met, the product has the best prerequisites for becoming a market success.

Design the Products Right

The product's design and interface with the user is becoming particularly important. If a customer uses a product for the first time, this usage should be a success. Particularly, studies among the elderly have shown that first-time use is highly predictive of a product's success [24]. While the technology adoption and implementation theory of Rogers [25] came to the conclusion that early adopters are usually neither older nor younger than late adopters, the fact that age has no relevance on technology adoption has been critically discussed by many researchers. Rogers [25] himself has noted in this context that there is inconsistent evidence about the relationship of age and innovativeness. Martinez et al. [26] have come to the conclusion that the likelihood of customers being among the early adopters of certain household appliances declines with increasing age.

However, Wahl and Mollenkopf [27] have shown that there is converging evidence that older adults are neither "enemies" of technology nor uncritical users of technological innovations. The authors suggest two dimensions of attitudes among the elderly:

- Cognitive–rational aspects of technology (e.g., "technological progress is necessary and therefore one has to accept some inevitable disadvantages")
- Emotional–affective aspects of technology (e.g., "technology is more a threat than a benefit to people")

The combination of these attitudes has resulted in four types of older people's relation to technology, namely:

1. Positive advocates
2. Rationally adapting
3. Skeptical and ambivalent
4. Critical and reserved

A survey among 1,417 older people has shown that all four types are distributed roughly equally among the sample (see Fig. 8.4). It is interesting to note that the study revealed that there were no significant gender differences within the four types of older people.

Market the Products Appropriately

After developing and designing a new product that follows Universal Design principles, companies need to introduce the product to the market appropriately.

Fig. 8.4 Different types of technology acceptance [27]

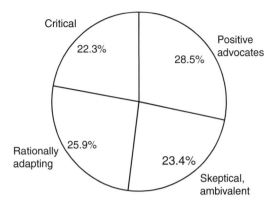

The field of "senior marketing" has found fairly broad resonance in research so far. Most experts usually differentiate between two marketing concepts:

- Integration marketing: target younger and older customers comprehensively; however, explicitly take older customers' needs into account.
- Modern senior marketing: target only the elderly specifically with a specially designed marketing program.

In the context of Universal Design, both approaches are acceptable. Although the actual product development has been done universally, marketing the products does not necessarily have to follow the same comprehensive approach. A targeted marketing approach to sell universally designed products might work better in some industries or environments. This segmented approach might even create an increase in the overall number of targeted customers.

However, differentiating the elderly into "young" and "old" elderly should be avoided. Successful marketing for seniors uses a high level of individualization. For example, a 50-year-old has other needs and a totally different purchasing behavior to a 75-year-old. In particular, the new group of elderly stemming from the Baby Boomer generation is expected to be very demanding when it comes to individualized and customized products and services.

In addition, every Universal Design strategy should take into consideration that older customers expect both an intensive and competent consultation while they make their purchase decision, as well as fast customer service after they have made the purchasing decision, and in the situation that there are additional questions concerning shortcomings of the product. Experienced sales support and consultation is therefore critical to success. Older customers will only become loyal long-term customers if they find both.

Thus, while necessary, it is not sufficient to simply sell age-friendly or age-adjusted products. The product's application by the customer needs to be accompanied by the company as well, and therefore should be included in the company's marketing approach. In particular, a well structured and aligned after-sales approach may allow success to be achieved quickly. A simple phone call to check if the older customer is happy with the product, if it meets his or her expectations, and/or if it may cause any problems during usage, could significantly increase customer satisfaction.

After-sales service also allows for substantial improvements in customer loyalty as older customers seem to value this type of service. Even if this type of consultation is time-consuming, it is a key success factor in selling a product to an older customer, and it is often regarded as a requirement for a successful sale. The right design of an innovative product for an older customer always depends on the company's understanding of the user's behavior in the context of his/her capabilities and opportunities. If the use of a product asks for a higher sophistication than the user has to offer, it is the product that is responsible for its nonusage, not the user.

Summary and Conclusion

Market success of innovations is defined simply neither by technology determinism nor by the pure existence of customer needs. Only the interconnection of both technologies and market needs substantially increases the economic success of an invention. When discussing the potential of Universal Design, companies frequently ask which products or bundles of products represent the highest potential for innovation. In order to derive and identify attractive areas for innovation, the intersection between novel technologies, markets, customers, and applications needs to be analyzed in greater detail. The largest potential for innovation is right at the intersection between technologies and markets where both merge in a well-balanced proportion. Figure 8.5 represents this intersection of specific customer needs of the 50+ generation and a couple of selected gerontechnologies (i.e., technologies that can be applied specifically to improve the day-to-day life of the elderly). The objective of gerontechnologies is to provide older people with the opportunity to live and experience an "active aging."

In general, innovative solutions targeting the elderly can be found everywhere, because every industry is principally affected by demographic developments – some industries more, some less. Industries that offer products that are preferably consumed by older customers offer, of course, the highest potential for innovation. However, industries that have a broad customer profile and target all age groups can also benefit substantially from applying Universal Design principles. It can be assumed that the areas for innovation in Fig. 8.5 are characterized by a comparatively high innovation potential due to their strong technology affinity. Apart from the innovation areas in Fig. 8.5, there are additional sectors that might benefit from the demographic development. However, they usually depend less on innovative technologies. Examples of these "soft" innovation areas include financial services, religion and esotericism, gero-transcendence, culture, and traditions.

In summary, the importance of demographic change needs one high-level issue to be addressed: the awareness and sensitivity around the potential, chances, and

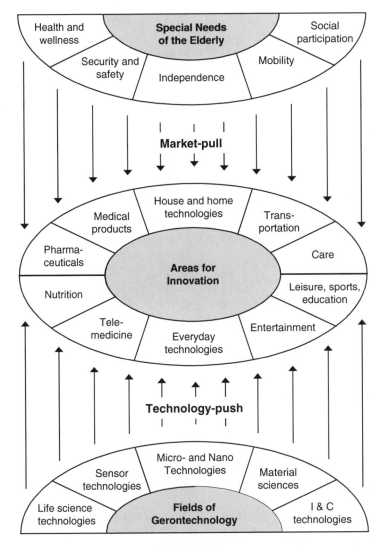

Fig. 8.5 Attractive areas with a high potential for innovation emerge where markets meet technologies

opportunities that arise from demographic change need to be taken into account not only by politicians and society, but also by leaders in the corporate world. Products and services that include older generations but do not exclude younger generations have a high value for society, and therefore for companies. Only if the mindset of all stakeholders fully grasps the meritorious character of age-friendly products is it possible to find the necessary reforms in society and business that address one of the most pressing challenges of the future – demographics.

References

1. B.O. Brünner, *Die Zielgruppe Senioren – eine Analyse* (Peter Lang, Frankfurt, 1997)
2. B. Kölzer, *Senioren als Zielgruppe: Kundenorientierung im Handel* (Deutscher Universitäts-Verlag, Wiesbaden, 1995)
3. G.P. Moschis, E. Lee, A. Mathur, J. Consum. Mark. **14**(4/5), S282–S293 (1997)
4. O. Hupp, *Seniorenmarketing: Informations- und Entscheidungsverhalten älterer Konsumenten* (Kovaè, Hamburg, 1999)
5. P.J. Trocchia, S. Janda, J. Consum. Mark. **17**(6/7), S605–S616 (2000)
6. I. Szmigin, M. Carrigan, Psychol. Mark. **18**(10), S1091 (2001)
7. D.B. Wolfe, J. Consum. Mark. **14**(4/5), S294–S302 (1997)
8. C. Silvers, J. Consum. Mark. **14**(4/5), S303 (1997)
9. T. Bristol, J. Curr. Issues Res. Advert. **18**(2), S59 (1996)
10. M.K. Dychtwald, J. Consum. Mark. **14**(4/5), S271 (1997)
11. C. Krieb, A. Reidl, *Seniorenmarketing – So erreichen Sie die Zielgruppe der Zukunft* (Moderne Industrie, Landsberg am Lech, 2001)
12. H.G. Lewis, *Seniorenmarketing – Die besten Werbe- und Verkaufskonzepte* (Moderne Industrie, Landsberg am Lech, 1997)
13. G. Meyer-Hentschel, *Handbuch Senioren-Marketing: Erfolgsstrategien aus der Praxis* (Meyer-Hentschel Management Consulting, Dt. Fachverlag, Frankfurt a.M., 2000)
14. M. Carrigan, I. Szmigin, Bus. Ethics. Eur. Rev. **9**(1), S42 (2000)
15. J. Nielson, K. Curry, J. Consum. Mark. **14**(4/5), S310 (1997)
16. W. Lazer, J. Consum. Mark. **3**(3), S23 (1986)
17. E.-M. Hock, B. Bader, in *Fachbericht für Marketing*, vol. 2001/3, ed. by C. Belz, T. Tomczak, T. Rudolph (Thexis, St. Gallen, 2001)
18. O. Gassmann, G. Reepmeyer, Wachstumsmarkt Alter, *Innovationen für die Zielgruppe 50+* (Hanser, München, 2006)
19. C. Krieb, A. Reidl, *Senioren-Marketing – so erreichen Sie die Zielgruppe der Zukunft* (Ueberreuter, Wien, 1999)
20. H. Meyer-Hentschel, G. Meyer-Hentschel, *Das goldene Marktsegment: Produkt und Ladengestaltung für den Seniorenmarkt* (Dt. Fachverlag, Frankfurt a.M., 1991)
21. T. Hess, in *Aging and Semantic Influences on Memory*, ed. by T.M. Hess (Amsterdam, North-Holland), p. S93 (1990)
22. G.E. Rice, M.A. Okun, J. Gerontol. Psychol. Sci. **49**, S119 (1994)
23. M. Yom, T. Wilhelm, D. Beger, Planung und Analyse **28**(6), S22–S25 (2001)
24. T.W. King, *Assistive Technology: Essential Human Factors* (Allyn & Bacon, Boston, MA, 1999)
25. E.M. Rogers, *Diffusion of Innovations*, 5th edn. (Free, New York, 2003)
26. E. Martinez, Y. Polo, C. Flavián, J. Consum. Mark. **15**(4), S323 (1998)
27. H.-W. Wahl, H. Mollenkopf, in *Impact of Everyday Technology in the Home Environment on Older Adults' Quality of Life*, ed. by N. Charness, K.W. Schaie (Springer, New York, 2003)

Chapter 9
Transgenerational Design: A Heart Transplant for Housing

J.J. Pirkl

Abstract Time and circumstances reshape one's expectations and priorities. Responding to his past research and the realities of the aging process, the author describes why and how he designed and built the first fully accessible house aimed directly at Baby Boomers and beyond. The project offers a vehicle for broadening consumer awareness of, and increasing the demand for, "transgenerational" housing and household products. This uniquely innovative design neutralizes many restrictive effects of aging, accidents, illness or chronic conditions. It also demonstrates that attractive transgenerational houses can be designed to promote, provide, and extend independent living, remove barriers, offer wider options, supply greater choices, and enhance the quality of life for all – the young, the old, the able, the disabled – without penalty to any group.

Introduction

Forty-five years ago, I led one of three design teams that developed the General Motors *Futurama* exhibit at the 1964 New York World's Fair. Our assignment was to envision the "world of tomorrow" that would demonstrate how knowledge could be used to span the new challenges of time, distance, and environment.

Futurama transported 70,000 visitors a day on an imaginative three-dimensional panoramic adventure to experience technology's future possibilities on a global and cosmic scale. They witnessed the moon's exploration, polar ice cap mining, undersea oil drilling, atomic-powered submarine transportation, laser beam tree harvesting, remote control desert farming, and highways connecting remote residential communities. The climax was a ride through a "city of tomorrow" punctuated with sleek high-rise buildings, covered "moving sidewalks," "containerized" freight terminals, and "automated parking facilities," all laced by expansive ribbons of "automatic highway lanes" [1].

The experience convinced us that future "dream cars," "kitchens of tomorrow," and robotic household products would pamper our every whim and extend our

F. Kohlbacher and C. Herstatt (eds.), *The Silver Market Phenomenon*,
DOI 10.1007/978-3-642-14338-0_9, © Springer-Verlag Berlin Heidelberg 2011

pursuit of happiness into an ageless future. The thought of growing old and retiring never entered our minds.

But, time and circumstances reshape and reorder one's expectations and priorities. As a young designer, I never confronted the fragility of ability or longevity – or the probability of acquiring a physical or sensory impairment – until my mother's stroke underscored the frustrating lack of supporting environments and products. A decade ago, after several bouts of medical repairs, my wife and I began to experience similar environmental frustrations and recognized our own growing need for a new kind of supportive housing.

Looking back, I cannot point to any particular time where I began to morph into an aging senior. But here I am, along with hundreds of millions like me, who have also experienced. or will experience, the physical and sensory effects of discriminating environmental challenges.

I am now living in that "world of tomorrow." I have enjoyed owning a "dream car" or two, and discovered retirement in my 60s. And I am still exploring new challenges, this time, age-related design projects having a "transgenerational" focus.

An Emerging Design Challenge

A quiet revolution is taking place – the world's population is aging. Never before has our planet contained so many older people, or such a large percentage of them. Throughout the world today, there are more people aged 65 and older than the populations of France, Germany, Japan, and Russia combined [2]. Thirty-six million Americans are aged 65 and older, a number larger than the combined populations of New York, London, and Moscow. Twenty-five years ago, Japan was the youngest society in the world. Today, it is the oldest [3]. In one generation, the life expectancy of Japanese people has already increased by more than 30% with the number of older people expanding from 15 to 25% by 2025 [4].

Still, the numbers continue to grow. Fifty million American Baby Boomers, the driving force behind yesterday's youth culture, are aging toward retirement. Many will experience periods of illness, accidents, and normal declines in their physical and sensory abilities while, at the same time, trying to balance the needs of their children with those of their aging parents.

In the decade ahead, according to the National Association of Home Builders (NAHB), Boomers will be the fastest growing segment of the home-buying public. Clearly, this is an emerging market for "transgenerational" housing and household products that respond to their changing needs. And, while this realization has attracted the attention of forward-thinking manufacturers and homebuilders, many others fail to accept the challenge of developing and offering alternative choices within today's housing, retirement community, and elder care markets.

In his book *Age Power*, Dychtwald [5] observes: "aging is not something that begins on one's 65th birthday. Rather, all of the choices we make regarding how we care for ourselves, how we manage our lives and even how we think about our futures, shape who we ultimately become in our later years. It [is] obvious that many of the painful, punishing challenges of old age could be prevented if informed choices were made earlier in life."

Builders and manufacturers, aware of the exploding aging Baby Boomer population and the effect that their informed choices will have on sales, increasingly speak in terms of "universal" and "transgenerational" design. However, Bauer [6] suggests that "mainstream companies are sometimes fearful of the term 'universal design' because they interpret these words to mean that a product must satisfy persons of every level of ability." Feeheley [7] concurs, asserting that "the term Universal Design has not lived up to or inspired people to its promise...having become associated with a design movement that targets only the aged and the handicapped."

As a result, transgenerational design is emerging as the favored terminology for housing and household products that offer informed aging Baby Boomers a new generation of attractive, accommodating choices.

Why Transgenerational Design

A Matter of Terminology

We do not see much in the popular press about transgenerational design, nor hear it being discussed at cocktail parties. Yet an increasing number of astute global manufacturers and research organizations are embracing the transgenerational design concept, recognizing its competitive advantage for attracting the attention – and collective buying power – of the exploding aging market. Researchers such as Leahy [8] have "found it beneficial to speak of transgenerational design (TD) rather than universal design (UD) when making presentations to company executives" because "TD piques the interest of corporations trying to tap into the aging Baby Boomer market."

It is unfortunate, however, that those who benefit the most from the application are those who know the least about it. Yet, when confronted with an example, most people immediately recognize the benefits. When introduced to a new transgenerational product or environment, the accommodating design helps transcend the frustration of a painful impairment or disability. Such designs promote graceful aging, soften the impact of the aging process, extend independent living, and enhance the quality of life for all – the young, the old, the able, the disabled. In short, the designs *sympathize* rather than *stigmatize*.

Let me further clarify the issue.

Transgenerational design is *not* about producing more cynical elderly housing, homes for the aged, or adult retirement communities that provide only bland code-compliant environments outfitted with such adaptive add-ons as grab bars, ramps, and raised toilet seats that reek with medical, aging, and institutional connotations.

It *is* about designing *all* residential environments and household products to be attractive and accommodating to the widest possible spectrum of those who would use them – the young, the old, the able, the disabled. And it does so by integrating human-sensitive architecture, living spaces, appliances, fixtures, products, and communications designed for safety, comfort, convenience, beauty, accessibility, clean-ability, adjust-ability, ease of use, and bodily fit. These are all transgenerational features that neutralize the effects of age and disability.

We call it transgenerational design because it bridges the generations by making products and environments compatible with those physical and sensory impairments associated with human aging, and which limit major activities of daily living [9].

I coined the term in 1986 conducting a research project at Syracuse University with gerontologist Anna L. Babic under a grant from the US Department of Health and Human Services. Our published guidelines and strategies for designing transgenerational products were the first to accommodate one's changing limitations in vision, hearing, touch, dexterity, and mobility that lead to impairments and disabilities [10].

It is a mistake, however, to inseparably link age with disabilities and impairments. While most physical and sensory limitations do occur in older people, we tend to forget that one does not have to be old to acquire them. Indeed, they can, and do, occur during our younger years. And because they do, transgenerational design extends its supporting benefits to those temporary disabilities that most of us acquire throughout our lives: falls, sprains, burns, broken bones, and even pregnancy, which limit our activities and curtail our independence. Consider, in the USA today:

- Some 49 million people, of all ages, have some form of disability; 35 million are under age 65 [11].
- Over 46 million Americans, of all ages, suffer from arthritis. It is the leading cause of disability among Americans aged 15 and older, limiting activities for over seven million individuals [12].
- Problems related to stiffness or paralysis affect five million households, including about 60% of all elderly households.
- Falls are the second leading cause of unintentional deaths, accounting for 50% of all injury deaths [13].

In the light of such statistics, should not a kitchen, bath, laundry, patio, or even a garage or a thermostat, be as readily and easily used by a child with a sprained ankle, a Baby Boomer with heart disease, an octogenarian with a broken hip, or a pregnant 20-something housewife with an arthritic spine? We think they should.

A fair question would be: what kind of housing will extend independence and improve the quality of life for all who use them – young or old, able or disabled? My answer is, transgenerational housing, which:

- Bridges the transitions across life's stages
- Responds to the widest range of individual differences and abilities

- Offers a variety of ways to accomplish one's activities of daily living
- Provides an opportunity to maintain one's dignity and sense of self-worth
- Enables personal and social interaction, and intergenerational relationships

This is why transgenerational design is so important. A transgenerational house accomplishes each by removing barriers, promoting and extending independent living, providing wider options, offering greater choices, and enhancing the quality of life for all, and at no group's expense.

The Transgenerational Paradigm

As an industrial designer, I look at a house as a product, albeit a very large product. But, whether a product is large or small, people of all ages and abilities desire, buy, and use a product based on a blend of three perceived consumer value categories: humanics, esthetics, and technics. I call them the "HAT" values of transgenerational design (see Fig. 9.1).

- Humanics refers to the humane aspects of a product's value. Is the product safe and easy to use or operate? Is it comfortable? Does it fit one's body? Does it accommodate different age groups or physical and sensory abilities? Without humanics, a product lacks the values of safety, comfort, convenience, accommodation, ease of use, and ergonomic fit, regardless of its esthetics and technics values.
- Esthetics denotes the visual/sensory aspects of a product's value. Is the product attractive? Does its form, color, texture, and sound reflect one's taste? Does it

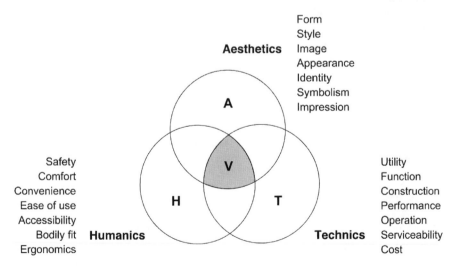

Fig. 9.1 Primary product design value categories

symbolize one's group, clique, or coterie? Does its appearance reflect the product's function? Without esthetics, a product may be unattractive, ugly, intimidating, discriminating, or demeaning, regardless of its humanics and technics values.

- Technics deals with the technological aspects of the product's value. Does it perform its intended function? How is the product constructed? How effective is its operation? Is it affordable? Can it be repaired or serviced? Without technics, a product cannot work, function, operate, perform, or be repaired, regardless of its esthetics and humanics values.

The design of our 2,700 ft^2 transgenerational house – its concept, plan, furnishings, appliances, materials, lighting, and attention to details – is a seamless blend of each HAT value category articulated in the design program. The following case study may offer additional insight.

The Transgenerational House: A Case Study

Project Goals

We began our experimental transgenerational house project by establishing a guiding set of three achievable goals:

1. Demonstrate that accommodating "accessible" housing can be attractive, appealing, and desirable to the widest spectrum of people.
2. Stimulate consumer interest by informing the general public about the advantages that transgenerational design can bring to housing, interior environments, and household products.
3. Communicate the competitive advantages of transgenerational design to the home building, remodeling, and household product industries.

The Design Program

Before beginning the design phase of the project, we prepared a 12-page design program setting down our needs, desires, and requirements – our "wish list." It included such objectives as:

- Provide safety, comfort, convenience, beauty, accessibility, and easy use for the widest diversity of potential users.
- Create an attractive, upbeat, contemporary design that appeals to young as well as older residents.
- Create an esthetic blend of structure, open floor plan, and large glass openings with "universal" access.

- Produce a passive solar structure with low-maintenance, utilizing energy-efficient and environmentally sensitive materials.
- Design the kitchen, dining, and living room as one flowing flexible space that accentuates the site's dramatic mountain views.
- Develop a wheelchair-friendly plan that reduces the need to bend, squat, lift, or stand for long periods of time.

The program also included an extensive room-by-room inventory of our "value" needs. In addition to the usual grab bars, lever door handles, extra wide doors, and level thresholds, our list also included such specific items as:

- Keyless entry locks
- Movable partitions and sliding panels
- Radiant heating sympathetic to legs and feet
- Multilevel counters and work surfaces
- Curb-less, dual-use showers with adjustable seating
- Sustainable materials such as cork and bamboo flooring
- Adjustable-height bathroom vanities
- Extended bathtub deck for easy transfer
- Easy-to-reach, side-mounted bathtub controls
- Flexible-use, indoor and outdoor spaces
- Sliding pocket doors to eliminate wheelchair interference
- Multiple 5-ft diameter wheelchair turnabouts
- Internet, entertainment, and communication systems
- Remote security, medical, and environmental control systems
- Higher electrical outlets and lower light switches
- Remote controls for operating high window blinds
- Level no-step thresholds

The Site

We selected a site in a new residential community called Sundance Mesa, located about halfway between Albuquerque and Santa Fe, New Mexico. The site had an elevated plateau with magnificent views of the Sandia Mountains to the southeast and a sweeping horizon of mesas and plains to the west, across and beyond the Rio Grande. To the north, a natural rolling expanse of foothills offered freedom to stroll, hike, or walk a dog. A small arroyo cut diagonally across the lot, supporting a variety of southwestern vegetation – chemise, purple sage, juniper, and four-wing salt-bush.

We also selected the site because it challenged accepted principles of accessibility – it was not a flat lot. "Why," we thought, "should one be limited to flat lots when building a house accessible to all?" Building on the site's elevated plateau, however, was not without design problems. We located the driveway along the edge of the site, bridging an arroyo and raising the grade gradually to the parking apron and garage. Thus, the car became the elevating conveyance from street level to house level, providing equal access to all without using ramps. Our plan integrated the house with the site's natural contours and existing landscape. It also preserved most of the site's natural environment – another of our early design priorities.

The Plan

The plan of the house evolved from numerous schematic layouts in which we explored our desire to:

- Capture the site's dramatic views of the Sandia Mountains and the Rio Grande valley
- Provide a private, walled courtyard "oasis" accessible directly from all major living areas
- Produce a dramatic visual and functional interplay of both indoor and outdoor spaces
- Utilize natural, "green" sustainable materials
- Achieve single-level wheelchair accessibility throughout

We accomplished our objectives by positioning and integrating four function-defining activity zones:

- *Zone A* contains the "public" areas: the main entry, kitchen and laundry, and the living/dining areas that access an outdoor dining patio and the private courtyard.
- *Zone B* includes a library/media/activity room, which overlooks the courtyard and links the "public" and "private" areas. An adjacent guest bedroom has a connecting guest bath, which is also accessed from the connecting tiled hallway. Guests access the courtyard from a door opposite the guest bathroom.
- *Zone C* contains the "private" areas. The master bedroom suite, with direct access to the courtyard and exercise pool, contains a fully accessible master bath. The office/studio opens onto its own private courtyard. The nearby utility/storage room offers an expedient transition from house to garage.
- *Zone D* encloses the private courtyard "oasis" conveniently accessed from each of the other zones. Upon entering the courtyard, wide sidewalks direct one past raised flower and herb beds to the solar-heated, self-cleaning exercise pool.

All indoor and outdoor spaces are equipped with lever door handles, level thresholds, nonslip floors and walkways, and multiple 5-ft diameter, 360° turning circles to accommodate wheelchair users (see Fig. 9.2).

Green Design

In addition to applying the tenets of universal and transgenerational design, we also applied such green and environmentally sustainable principles as:

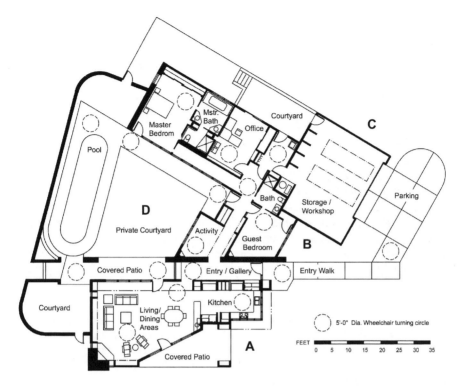

Fig. 9.2 Plan of the transgenerational house. Such green principles save health, energy, and resources. They help simplify the activities of daily living and contribute to the mutually inclusive objectives of both universal and transgenerational design

- Design for energy efficiency
- Utilize renewable energy
- Optimize use of materials
- Install water-efficient, low-maintenance landscaping
- Design for durability and low maintenance
- Plan for future reuse and adaptability
- Avoid materials that give off gas pollutants
- Utilize renewable materials like cork and bamboo flooring

Tour the Transgenerational House

Our experimental transgenerational house project provides an informative case study meant to spark discussion, initiate innovation, offer alternate solutions, increase public awareness, and generate market demand. The tour begins at the entry and proceeds through the four activity zones, focusing on the most innovative solutions.

Zone A

Entry: One approaches the house – set on a raised acre with southwestern vegetation – by climbing a steadily rising, curved driveway to the parking apron. Approaching the door, a wide level walkway, flanked by natural vegetation, leads directly to the weather-protected entry. A full-length sidelight permits residents to view visitors before opening the door.

A raised recessed platform adjacent to the entry provides a convenient, protected spot to set down packages or groceries. A 5-ft diameter wheelchair turn-around area provides ample maneuverability while unlocking and opening the front door, which is fitted with an optional keyless lock (see Fig. 9.3).

Once inside, a handy pass-thru counter provides a convenient place to set down grocery bags and packages intended for the adjacent kitchen. Below it, a convenient seating *banco* with storage drawers offers a place to remove hiking boots, gloves, etc. A 5-ft wide, slip-resistant tiled floor stretches from the entry to a ceiling-high window at the end of the hallway, extending one' view into the courtyard and framing a view of the mesa beyond.

Kitchen: The window-wrapped kitchen features a resilient cork floor and multi-level work surfaces designed to ease body pain from bending or standing. The line of windows follows the counter tops around the corner, offering a panoramic view of the mountains. Horizontal mini-blinds moderate the natural light while, outside, an exterior overhang keeps out direct sunlight. Indirect cove and task lighting supplement the kitchen' central skylight.

All base cabinets are raised 8 in. instead of the usual 4 in., making cleaning easier and minimizing the need to bend or squat. Cabinets and drawers open with D-pulls or hand cutouts and are designed with slide-out storage shelves, pantry units, and towel racks. The multiheight countertops offer fingertip-grasping edges designed for steadying or, if in a wheelchair, pulling closer to the counter. The sink cabinet's doors and floor are easily removed, permitting clear knee space for easy

Fig. 9.3 Entry view from the parking apron

wheelchair access. A trash-recycling drawer pulls out and separates trash into four easily accessed bins with self-closing lids.

A rolling trolley locks onto the countertop's finger lip-edge detail, offering the option of temporarily reconfiguring the countertop layout. It is also useful as a serving cart, or for transporting items within the kitchen, or throughout the house or patio. It docks conveniently within a cabinet cavity when not in use. A stack of display cabinets, appearing to be fixed, pull out individually, revealing a hidden storage area behind the shelf's vertical display panel.

The under-counter dishwasher is also raised 8 in. This permits easier loading and unloading. Its countertop, used as the pass-through from the entry to the kitchen, doubles as a work surface. The easy-to-reach built-in microwave and convection ovens are installed at convenient heights. The shallow side-by-side refrigerator, with in-the-door water and ice dispensers, offers cooling and freezer access to users of different sizes and reach abilities.

Laundry: The raised, front-loading washer and dryer are conveniently located at the edge of the kitchen within a matching set of cabinets. Their proximity allows cooking and laundry chores to be carried out simultaneously. (The utility room in Zone C, which contains a utility sink, is also plumbed to accept the washer and dryer as an alternate location.) The appliances' solid-surface cabinet top provides a convenient place for sorting and folding clothes.

An adjacent drawer-mounted ironing board folds out at sitting height to accommodate both chair and wheelchair users. Laundry and ironing supplies can be stored in one of the nearby hidden display/storage areas. The kitchen's rolling trolley is also useful for transporting clothes and supplies to and from other rooms.

Living/Dining Area: High ceilings and bamboo flooring set a "natural" theme for the area's light-filled flowing spaces. Translucent floor-to-ceiling roll-up window blinds fill the bright open space with soft natural light. Privacy, light control, and height adjustment are controlled remotely.

In the far corner, a raised remote-controlled gas-fired fireplace, flanked by thin vertical windows, offers a wide, chair-height hearth for sitting or wheelchair transfer. Recessed walls, fitted with easy-access cabinets and bookcases, provide overhead glare-free lighting for hanging artwork.

The area's generous maneuvering space also offers raised electrical outlets (18 in.) and lower light switches (42 in.), which reduce bending and reaching. Two 3-ft wide glass-paneled doors open onto two wheelchair-accessible outdoor areas: a dining patio with a gas barbeque hook-up and the central courtyard located in Zone D. "Easy-to-use" thermostats offer oversize, high-contrast, three-dimensional numerals with tactile feedback for those with sensory or tactile impairments.

Zone B

Library/Media/Activity Room: A wide, slip-resistant tile walkway extends from the entry hall, through the area, and connects with Zone C. To the left, resilient cork flooring extends to a row of desk-high windows that look out onto the central courtyard "oasis." To the right, recessed cabinets and shelves provide easy access to storage cabinets, shelves, and books. Recessed lighting complements the natural light controlled by the windows' adjustable blinds. A vertical pane of nonglare translucent glass diffuses the corner's built-in fluorescent light.

Guest Bedroom: The room's angled wall offers alternative furniture arrangements. The floor covering is commercial-grade, no-pad, low-pile carpeting, which provides easy-rolling wheelchair travel. Remote controlled, translucent floor-to-ceiling window blinds provide privacy and light control. The corner's built-in fluorescent light, diffused with a vertical pane of nonglare translucent glass, echoes the one in the library.

The room's 3-ft wide door has an 18-in. frosted glass sidelight, which permits natural light to enter from the adjacent courtyard. It also offers additional space for a person in a wheelchair to grasp the handle and pull the door open. A well-lit closet provides adjustable height shelves and clothes rack. An identical door with side-light, directly across the walkway from the guest bedroom, offers access to the central patio and exercise pool.

Guest Bathroom: The guest bath serves both the public spaces and the guest bedroom. Twin 3-ft wide sliding pocket doors provide easy wheelchair access and maneuverability from either the guest bedroom or the connecting walkway. A skylight delivers diffused natural light for glare-free illumination.

The slip-resistant tile floor provides clear 5-ft diameter wheelchair turnabouts for easy access and transfer to the raised, off-the-floor, wall-hung water closet. The wall-mounted fingertip flusher can be removed, providing access to an in-wall water tank and flush mechanism. Blue-accented stainless steel sidewall grab bars offer added safety and transfer assistance. Motion sensors control lights and fans.

The one-piece fiberglass roll-in shower is equipped with grab bars, an adjustable-height showerhead and hand spray, and an adjustable fold-down seat. An overhead built-in light provides glare-free lighting.

An off-the-floor vanity with a recessed front and a single-lever faucet adjusts in height to accommodate a chair, a wheelchair, or people of any height. Its one-piece solid surface top with integral basin has grasping fingertip edges. A row of incandescent bulbs above the medicine cabinet provides even illumination for makeup or shaving.

Zone C

Master Bedroom: One approaches the master bedroom through a wide tiled passageway flanked on one side by a floor-to-ceiling, south-facing window-wall that borders the central courtyard. A roof overhang and translucent window shades shield the summer sun, keeping the floor and opposite wall in cool shadow. During the winter months the low-angled sunlight heats the floor and the adobe trombe wall, providing sustainable solar heat.

One enters the bedroom through a 3-ft wide sliding pocket door onto an expanse of bamboo flooring. A no-threshold glass-paneled door at the end of the window-wall opens into the central courtyard, permitting wheelchair access to the exercise pool.

At the opposite end of the room, four side-by-side sliding mirrored doors enclose a deep wall-wide closet system with fully adjustable clothes racks, shelves, and drawer units. Overhead recessed lighting provides glare-free illumination. A nearby set of narrow recessed shelves extends from floor to ceiling, offering a convenient place for books, photos, and mementos.

Master Bathroom: The bamboo floor of the master bedroom flows into the master bath, through a 3-ft sliding pocket door, which visually joins the two areas. The tub and vanity units encircle an open 5-ft diameter turnabout, affording easy wheelchair maneuverability.

The whirlpool tub is centered within a wide 17-in. high wall-to-wall surface for sitting or wheelchair transfer. A narrow shelf above the surrounding grab bars provides a short reach for bath items, plus added safety and stability for all ages and abilities. Side-mounted controls and a retracting hand-held showerhead offer easy water temperature and spray adjustment prior to and after entry.

Off-the-floor twin corner vanities adjust to accommodate users of any height; the mirrored medicine cabinets feature diffused sidelights. A 3-ft wide sliding pocket door, located between the two vanities, leads past pull-out drawer and storage units into a "wet room" containing the shower and water closet.

The no-slip, roll-in shower offers an adjustable-height fold-up seat and an adjustable hand-held showerhead. Stainless steel grab bars provide additional safety and security. The shower's glass door can be removed if additional maneuverability is required, utilizing the room's "wet room" function. The raised, wall-hung off-the-floor water closet makes floor cleaning easy, while stainless steel grab bars and a wall-hung telephone provide additional safety and convenience. Like the guest bath, motion sensors control lights and fans, and a skylight provides diffused natural daylight.

Zone D

The house wraps around a walled central courtyard and exercise pool, underscoring the advantage of indoor and outdoor living in the semiarid climate of New Mexico. Accessed by level thresholds, the area is wheelchair-accessible throughout. The raised flowerbeds and herb gardens offer the benefits of no-bend gardening. Wide level walkways, with 5-ft diameter turnabouts at each end, lead to and surround the self-cleaning lap pool. Sitting, dining, and entertaining areas are positioned beneath the roof overhangs in the courtyard and the patio adjacent to the dining area. The 5-ft high wall provides privacy, while offering dramatic views of the mesas and the western horizon beyond the Rio Grande.

Summary and Conclusion

It is time to explore better ways to design for the needs of a transgenerational population. Achieving results, however, requires us to reconceptualize our association of age with disability. In reality:

- Young people grow old
- Disabled people grow old
- Young people can be disabled
- Old people can be disabled

Such understanding can help to change the prevailing mindset from one of *compliance* to one of *assistance*. Conventional practice suggests that "accessible" housing is best achieved through laws, statutes, standards, codes, or regulations.

History, however, clearly reveals the limitations of this approach. It takes more than just complying with mandated principles and dimensioned templates to achieve genuine transgenerational environments and products. Code compliance, while important, only addresses the *functional*, *utilitarian*, and *liability* aspects of accommodation. It does not address the environmental "HAT" values that help define our humanity, individuality, dignity, and self-worth.

As innovative examples of transgenerational designs begin to emerge, attract attention, stimulate sales, and create demand, the competition for a share of this swelling market will cause discerning designers, builders, and manufacturers to respond with an ever-increasing flow of attractive and desirable transgenerational designs.

I have learned that the best kind of design requires not simply the ability to envision a direction, not simply the courage to take an unpopular one, but also the belief that perseverance is essential for transforming rigid attitudes. There is no limit to what can be accomplished when everyone genuinely has a stake in the outcome and in achieving the possibilities.

Working – and aging – together, we can help provide a "heart transplant" for housing and live in the "world of tomorrow" that we collectively envision.

References

1. General Motors, Futurama, New York World's Fair, 1964–65. Visitor handout booklet (General Motors Corporation, Detroit, 1964)
2. US Bureau of the Census, Table no. 1334. Population by Country: 1980 to 2000. *Statistical Abstract of the United States: 1997*, 117th edn. (US Bureau of the Census, Washington, DC, 1997)
3. P.G. Peterson, *Gray Dawn: How the Coming Age Wave Will Transform America and the World* (Random House, New York, 1999)
4. K. Bole, *Graying Japan poses golden opportunity*. San Francisco Business Times, 16 Dec 1996

5. K. Dychtwald, *Age Power: How the 21st Century Will be Ruled by the New Old* (Tarcher/ Putnam, New York, 1996)
6. S.M. Bauer, Invisible no longer: Newsletters June 2005. The Family Center on Technology and Disability (June 2005), http://www.fctd.info/resources/newsletters/displayNews letter. php?newsletterID=10022. Accessed 20 Dec 2007
7. T. Feeheley, PROTEUS web site. Transgenerational design (2007), http://www.proteusde-sign.com/transgenerational_design.aspx. Accessed 20 Dec 2007
8. J.A. Leahy, Transgenerational design and product differentiators in product development (2004), http://t2rerc.buffalo.edu/pubs/conference/fulltext_2004_leahy_2.htm. Accessed 20 Dec 2007
9. J.J. Pirkl, *Transgenerational Design: Products for an Aging Population* (Wiley, New York, 1994)
10. J.J. Pirkl, A.L. Babic, *Guidelines and Strategies for Designing Transgenerational Products* (Copley, Acton, MA, 1988)
11. US Bureau of the Census, *Statistical Abstract of the United States: 1195*, 115th edn. (US Bureau of the Census, Washington, DC, 1995)
12. Arthritis Foundation. Arthritis facts (2007), http://www.arthritis.org/facts.php. Accessed 6 Sep 2007
13. National Safety Council, What are the odds of dying? (2006), http://www.nsc.org/mem/educ/ slips.htm. Accessed 6 Sep 2007

Chapter 10
Service Innovation: Towards Designing New Business Models for Aging Societies

Patrick Reinmoeller

Abstract The aging of industrialized countries, led by Japan, requires firms to fundamentally rethink their business models. Firms active in Japan have to reconsider how to deal with unprecedented demographic change, which alters the resources available, to satisfy the shifting demand. Throughout the supply chain, aging of human talent and retirement requires firms to anticipate and prevent the negative effects of losing knowledge and skills. Adjusting the supply chain, developing new products, and/or augmenting products with services to target the silver market may offer short-term benefits but are not enough to sustain success. Firms need to develop and implement new business models leveraging service innovation to meet the needs in aging societies. Examples of service innovations and the case study of Seven-Eleven Japan and Yamato Transports' shared business model innovation illustrate how companies can seize the opportunities to create and capture more value in aging societies.

Introduction

Large-scale environmental changes and rivalry increase the volatility and uncertainty for companies [1]. Climate change, political instability, or shifts in the demographics such as the mass retirement of baby boomers in Japan and other aging societies (including the industrialized countries) all question organizational strategies and shake the foundations of corporations. By 2020, one retiree's pension in Japan, Germany, the UK, and France will rely on only two workers: a drop from three and a half in 2000. The successful one-child policy of Chinese administrations, intended to limit the growth of China's population, is expected to have unintended consequences including the rapid aging of China. These changes will affect societies, economies, and companies. Often highly disruptive, these changes lead to dwindling demand for companies' offerings, loss of knowledge through retirement and competitive hiring, and lack of quality supply. However, these changes also offer opportunities to develop new products and services, to conquer

F. Kohlbacher and C. Herstatt (eds.), *The Silver Market Phenomenon*,
DOI 10.1007/978-3-642-14338-0_10, © Springer-Verlag Berlin Heidelberg 2011

new markets, and to add more value to existing offerings. Opportunities are for the well-prepared; companies need to anticipate such large-scale shifts and embrace emerging opportunities in advance.

Japan lives in the future of the West. Japan is now the largest and richest emerging silver market. In other words, Japan may well be the lead silver market that allows for learning. The research, development, and design efforts of Japanese firms and foreign firms in Japan today may generate and even foreshadow superior products, service, and public design for decades to come. Unfortunately, many existing offerings are not able to satisfy the needs of aging societies; many products were designed for young segments and services are often accessories to tangible products. Better services not only need to make hardware usable, they also need to create new business opportunities by delivering value in a changing market. Today's organizations are designed to procure, produce, and promote products for the society of baby boomers. The future of aging societies demands different products and services and the organizations able to create these. Adapting to the requirements of the aging society can be done most effectively with business model innovation. While other chapters define the silver market, describe the shifts the leading economies are experiencing, and show how they influence company performance, this chapter focuses on the creation of new business models that are aligned to the emerging reality of silver markets.

Aging Societies and Business Issues

The size, financial volume, and sophistication of demand in the silver market offer opportunities for businesses capable of adjusting. The notion that advancing age in society poses a threat only to industrialized countries is illusory. How China's rapid development and the one-child policy contribute to this society's graying has been mentioned before. Industrial success has so far reduced birth rates in most industrialized nations and it seems not implausible that India will also succumb to this effect with enduring economic growth. While the scale of this global phenomenon, especially in areas such as healthcare and social support, focuses much attention, it should not be forgotten that the retiring generation of baby boomers is the richest generation of retirees ever in the USA, Europe, and especially in Japan. McKinsey reports the disposable income of baby boomers in the USA to be 40% higher compared to the previous generation. The opportunity measured in terms of size of the market and financial resourcefulness is unrivaled. At the same time, however, these relatively wealthy consumers are financially not ready to retire and after the Lehman Shock are even more concerned about their future. In other words, the large demand for new offerings in financial services or social care waits to be served. Current supply often does not satisfy the sophisticated demand of these retirees who have seen their expectations rise over a lifetime and have become used to rising standards of living. This generation, having adapted to post-war, cold-war, and post-cold war times, is flexible and demanding. This offers large opportunities for firms able to create offerings that meet the needs in this silver market. Growing income disparity in Japan is linked to these generational differences. While older generations still benefit from more generous employment contracts, members of younger generations often work part-time without lucrative salaries and benefits. Companies able to develop new business models are poised to seize the opportunities if they address the silver market's new demand for financial wealth and security, a safe and adventurous life, healthy but not boring personal experiences, social activities, or opportunities to generate income after retirement.

Why Service Innovation in Japan Matters

The business potential of the silver market suggests that companies pay attention to the seismic shift. The potential for disruption of existing businesses and the challenges related to the sophisticated demand in the silver market require firms to innovate. However, product innovation alone is not enough. Exploring some of the opportunities for companies capable of adjusting to the silver society, this chapter focuses on service innovation and why it matters. The broader economic development, the characteristics of demand in the silver market, and the scarcity of research show that our knowledge on developing new business models focused on services needs to grow.

Service Economies

Of late, the economy of each developed country becomes progressively more dominated by services [2]. The GDP in advanced nations has grown over recent decades, mainly driven by growth in services, which are now the most important sector in all OECD economies. Since 1987 the share of services in advanced economies frequently exceeds 60% or even 70% of total GDP [3]. In times of resource scarcity and the importance of China as location of choice for many a manufacturer, it is often overlooked that not only India's service industries are growing rapidly. China's service sector had already reached 40% in 2005 and it continues to grow. Service innovation and growth in the service sector have driven the economic advances in recent decades'. However, a recent study by the OECD [4] suggests that in order to enhance overall economic growth in the future, improving the performance of the services sector is crucial. Growth is driven by factors such as globalization and innovation. Services innovation is an important driver for significant growth. In 2001, investment in R&D aiming at service innovation was as high as 40% of all business R&D in countries such as Norway, Australia, and Denmark; service industries in Japan and Germany have shares of less than 10% of business R&D. Service innovation is needed to rekindle growth in advanced countries and prolong growth in countries that still rely on manufacturing.

Aging Markets Worldwide

Japan's aging society leads the way for other industrialized countries. We consider the characteristics of the silver market in the context of the world's demographic development. The global drama of senescence begins with the growth of world population; the population of 6.5 billion people today is expected to reach 9.1 billion in 2050. India is facing a baby boom. India's population will be the largest in 2050 with 1.628 billion compared with today's 1.104 billion. The average African mother will continue to give birth to more than five children. At the same time, the picture in the industrialized countries could not be more different. There, fertility rates are declining: Italy, Germany, Japan, and Korea watch their populations shrink. Improvements in living conditions together with better health care result in unprecedented longevity for large segments in these societies. This exacerbates the problem of seniority. The large population of senior people has to rely on fewer people to provide the basis for increasing living standards.

Looking at the net effect on global demographics, the percentage of elderly people aged 65+ stands today at 7.4%. At an elderly person level of 7%, societies are said to be aging; at 14% they are called aged societies. The world will be aged in 2040. By 2050, the forecasts see even more elderly: a group as strong as 16.1%. By then, 320 million elderly people will live in the developed countries and 1.14 billion in the developing countries.

Paying attention to the Japanese silver market is especially important because Japan's society is aging quickly, ahead of other countries. The general Japanese population peaked in 2006 [5]. In rural areas such as Shimane prefecture on the East Sea, from where young adults have long left for jobs in the cities, the population today has 26.7% aged 65 and above. Japan's population now has 19% seniors aged 65 and above. More than a million Japanese citizens are older than 90, twice as many as in 1996. Japan has 23,000 centenarians today. By 2050, about 40% of Japan's population will be over 65-years old. These elderly people want to maintain or even improve the high quality of their life. Firms in Japan need to learn – quickly – how to serve the elderly population, and how to maintain the younger generations needed to rekindle growth of the Japanese economy and society.

Service Innovation

Innovation

Reviewing the academic literature, one finds much theoretical and empirical research that describes, explains, and offers guidelines for the development of efficient supply chains and new products. Being an important area of innovation, developing new products is by far not the only area in which innovation is needed. However, research on service innovation is still rare. Services are intangible and their production and consumption is often simultaneous. These commonly accepted characteristics of services make managing for new services more challenging than managing for new products. This has resulted in many offerings where services are tied to products and are often bundled with hardware. Packaged in this way, services appear more manageable but these add-on services, such as maintenance or repair activities, often remain limited by the link to a physical product. Important as these activities may be, in focusing on them companies forgo the potential of more fundamental service innovation.

In recent research on innovation, three important themes have emerged that go beyond the development of products:

1. Academics have devoted much attention to specific functions, mainly management of technology and of research and development. Aiming to understand productivity increases of basic and applied research, many articles develop and test ideas on how management of technology and R&D is linked to performance, often measured by patents registered.
2. Management of knowledge, especially tacit knowledge to foster product innovation, has been a particularly rich area since the mid-1990s [6]. Creating knowledge individually or in small teams and disseminating it across units and organizations explains the successes of leading firms in industries such as the automotive, electronics, or optical and mechanical equipment industries.
3. Open innovation (as a new approach to tap into external resources) has received much attention under the labels of inclusive or outside innovation [7–9]. Linked to entrepreneurship and new business development is the creation and integration of new venture and start-ups as the test-beds for new services and new kinds of organization, in order to develop ideas quickly by interacting with markets.

In what follows I shall focus on the way companies renew their capabilities and organize for ambidexterity [10–13], i.e., develop new business models by integrating and coordinating specialized activities and creating new services.

Services

In silver markets the importance of services is increased because service innovation has the potential to create value and meet the requirements of sophisticated and wealthy customers who experience disadvantage and constraints coming with age. Services, according to Zeithaml et al. [14] are "deeds, processes and performances"[1] to satisfy customers [15, 16], either as supporting good products and/or as the process for making these products good. Service is defined as a process of

---

[1]Lists of services include wholesale and retail trade, transportation and warehousing, information, finance, insurance, professional, scientific, and technical, management of companies, administrative and support, education, healthcare and social assistance, arts, entertainment and recreation, accommodation and food services, or public administration (e.g., US Bureau of Census).

more or less intangible activities that often take place in interactions between the customer and service employees or artifacts, aimed at adding value for customers. The nonphysical character of services hinders product and price comparisons [17]. Consumers cannot easily analyze the cost–value ratio given that the products are invisible and service quality is assessed based on their experience of the service (customer satisfaction). Customers use key components to judge a company's service [18], such as physical facilities, equipment, personnel and communication materials, as well as intangibles such as reliability, responsiveness, assurance, and empathy.

Without including the level of integration with products, Välikangas and Lehtinen [19] categorize three types of services, which they term generic, specialized, and customized services. Generic services are categorized as basic services in which the focus lies on low price. Specialized services require resources or skills to create a superior or unique performance vis-à-vis competitors. Customized services are strategic services. New business models can include service innovations of the three types, with different emphasis on key components. Often service innovations are hybrids of the three at different levels of integration with products.

Changing Business Models with Service Innovations

The term "business model" is defined in different ways [20]. In particular, the proliferation of information and communications technologies in the last 20 years has led to a broad discussion of the choice of the right business models [21–24]. Magretta [25] argues that a good business model stays important to every successful organization, whether it is an established player or a new venture. The foremost objective of a business model is to abstract the business [26] and to organize a firm to serve its customers in an effective way [27]. Amit and Zott [28] define a business model as the structure, the design of transaction content, and governance as ways to create value while exploiting business opportunities.

We extend and clarify in two ways. First, better business models are systems that exploit opportunities and create value by using the intertwined and complementary nature of tangible and intangible elements. Raising the importance of services beyond the level of repair and maintenance to a vital element of the total offering, services can help differentiate more forcefully and to renew firms. Consider how Dell established itself as a leading computer retailer by developing customer service delivered by telephone marketing, complementing its system of low-cost assembly [29]. Second, better business models expand dynamically by interacting with customers and business partners. The dynamic expansion is opportunity-driven and resource-driven. Opportunities and resources reveal themselves in interaction. The business model allows new opportunities and resources to be integrated, and helps to exploit them with existing resources. Amazon.com illustrates this point well. The online site's ability to generate recommendations is one of the most important marketing and sales instruments, and it was developed by

Amazon to enhance its basic proposition in the business of selling books. Multiple ways of offering suggestions to customers of the bookstore today drive not only book sales but also allowed Amazon to more quickly raise the profile of its ventures into other categories.

Being a vital part of a company's business model and service, innovation is an effective way to create and develop new business models that withstand disruption by seismic shifts. Consider how Apple Computer has changed by designing its new business model by service innovation. Apple Computer's business model was based on selling computer hardware and earning a premium on computer software. Since the introduction of the iPod, Apple has entered the market space of portable music. The service innovation that brought about the new business model is linked to making the vast archives of the music industry searchable online with Apple's easy-to-use interface and expanding this into the online retail business iTunes. Apple now benefits from low margins on content because the music sales drive hardware sales. The dynamic expansion of its business since the introduction of the iPod into movies, with the launch of the iPhone into communications, and the iPad into publishing, shows how service innovation together with the complementary elements of its business model allow for exploration and exploitation of new opportunities.

Designing and Implementing Service Innovation

Designing and implementing service innovation has helped outstanding Japanese companies to develop new business models to meet the demand of silver markets. The cases presented below are based on empirical research conducted in Japan since 2005. Interviews, field observation, and archival research yielded a rich database from which the following illustrations of service innovation were selected. The cases show how service innovation enabled successful business model design and how two Japanese companies lead in satisfying the needs of the silver market.

Seven-Eleven Japan (SEJ) is the franchise system of convenience stores known also in other countries. Yamato Transport's Takkyubin (YTT) is a small-lot haulage service, which is less known abroad but illustrates clearly how important service innovations can be in creating value for senior segments in the market. As will be explained later, SEJ and YTT enhance the utility of each other's offering in a subsidiary of SEJ called Seven-Meal Service (7Meal).

Seven-Eleven Japan

SEJ is the largest convenience store franchise operator in Japan. Concentrating with more than 12,750 stores in the larger metropolitan areas of Japan, SEJ has seen sales and profits grow for decades. SEJ's vision to adapt to changing customer needs led

Seven-Eleven from introducing the concept of a convenience store in Japan to becoming one of the most admired firms in Japan. Initially licensing the Seven-Eleven brand and system, SEJ has over time succeeded in outshining the original owner of the concept. SEJ's continuous service innovation has turned the operator of convenience stores into an infrastructure platform supportive of the Japanese life-style. Four points explain how SEJ continuously innovates: from product to service orientation, network of stores, assortment, and item-by-item stock management:

1. Seven-Eleven's brand name and practice emphasizes long opening hours, i.e., a store that opens early, stays open until late and sells convenience items. SEJ has emphasized the idea that adaptive capability is what underpins its success. Consequently, service innovations such as extending into financial services or online business have become successful service elements of a strengthened business model.
2. SEJ's extensive network of stores is accessible to large parts of the population. In metropolitan areas people live within walking distance of the next convenience store. In the popular press, this omnipresence has led to comparing SEJ's stores to private storage rooms for customers, e.g., powder room, kitchen, and refrigerator. Taken for granted to such an extent, the stores fulfill the needs of many who are not willing to stock a product at home or drive to a hypermarket.
3. Seven-Eleven has over the years developed a system that allows it to offer a standard group of basic offerings that are an important part of the assortment. These include, for instance, cosmetics, newspapers and magazines, snacks and beverages, and fresh bread and rice dishes. Besides these taken-for-granted products that can be found in all shops, SEJ developed a system to develop differentiated assortments so as to adapt to the local demand even at a single store. Location and demographics are important in shaping the demand. Shops close to schools, for example, carry different items from shops close to office buildings. Stores in areas where many families reside have different offerings from stores in areas where more elderly people live. Other dimensions also matter: monitoring weather changes, SEJ's headquarters offer locally specific weather forecasts to help in adapting the assortment in time. New product development also benefits a lot from SEJ's awareness of local differences, which is a source of new ideas.
4. Item by item stock-keeping, together with sophisticated logistics, enables SEJ to avoid running out of stock. Local employees place orders based on the hypothesis (location-specific demand forecasts for items). These hypotheses are immediately tested by objective data available from the company's point-of-sales systems. Avoiding overstocking and opportunity loss are key elements in gaining trust, increasing reliability, and in enticing customers into trying some new offering.

Seven-Eleven's emphasis on offerings and service innovations have turned a retailer into a taken-for-granted institution providing services such as selling theater tickets, postal services, and financial services. Accessible, innovative, and reliable, the stores are a supportive platform, especially for elderly customers, because the small-scale "mom-and-pop" and neighborhood retailers are quickly disappearing. In the silver market, convenience stores fulfill important functions as they help seniors to manage their own lives and postpone the need of some for senior homes and caretakers.

Yamato Transport's Takkyubin

YTT service innovation has changed what haulage means in Japan. The YTT delivery comprises haulage of parcels, packages, suitcases for travelers, and also golf bags, clubs, or skis. Originally, haulage had been a packages service for mainly corporate customers. After years of striving to become a company that would transport any quantity to anywhere in Japan, Masao Ogura, who was the president of Yamato between 1971 and 1987, reconsidered the strategy [30]. The insight that Yamato and its customers might be better off if the firm offered only a focused service triggered a series of changes that created YTT and helped the company to regain profitability and reputation.

In January 1976, YTT inaugurated the home-to-home service with a distribution network that was modeled on the hub and spoke system of airlines. Satisfying demand from households required that Yamato's office network would expand. Tokyo and its surrounding prefectures were covered with a next-day delivery service. If a truck was to go to a household, ¥500 were surcharged. Initially, YTT chose liquor shops as Yamato's agents for drop-off and pick-up because of their presence in every town. Today, SEJ has become a powerful partner.

The business model behind YTT's service innovation helped to charge standardized prices and to generate cash immediately (cash payment). Two years later the fundamental change toward the new business model became apparent when YTT withdrew from large-lot haulage and unattractive haulage contracts to concentrate on small-lot haulage. Five years after the start YTT broke even.

Four important points need to be made, i.e., delivery network, service standardization, next-day delivery, and improving quality:

1. YTT's delivery network covers Japan, which allows easy drop-off and pick-up at all locations. This service greatly increases the value YTT provides to customers.
2. Large simplification of package sizes, delivery rhythms, and prices made sending and receiving by YTT much easier for customers. YTT's house-to-house haulage system increases the ease with which citizens, especially seniors, can send and receive parcels.
3. Since 1981, YTT has increased the area in which it guarantees next-day delivery and introduced on-time delivery to satisfy the customers' need to have parcels delivered when they are at home and not when they are absent. YTT's service

innovation was so successful that the number of 150 million parcels delivered in 1984 exceeded that of the Japanese postal system.
4. Improving quality was an important part of the new business model design. YTT developed an excellent reputation for customer service and quality of delivery, despite the time pressure on delivery staff. YTT also increased its appeal further by the introduction of haulage of chilled cargoes introduced in 1988.

YTT's emphasis on service innovations has turned haulage from a service for corporations into a service for families and individuals to help their haulage needs. Today YTT has become a taken-for-granted institution providing services indispensable in large metropolitan areas where traveling with luggage is difficult or where quick delivery is needed. In the silver market, YTT fulfills important functions in helping seniors to manage their haulage needs.

Seven Meal Service

SEJ sells and YTT delivers goods. These complementary services of SEJ and YTT are now being taken beyond this evident link of firms in retail and logistics. The development from the first relationship to 7Meal, a new subsidiary of SEJ, is evidence of a dynamically expanding business model that has been jointly constructed by two companies.

Selling a wide variety of about 200 meals and submeals daily through catalogs, its website, and the Seven-Eleven chain of convenience stores, 7Meal also offers home delivery of the preordered meals. SEJ's skills and experience with fresh food sold in its stores were instrumental in developing 7Meal practices. This first-hand experience helped to gain a first understanding of what kind of meals may be needed at which price levels. Allying with YTT helped to solve the issue of affordable yet high quality transport. Interacting with customers and business partners, SEJ and YTT together exploit new opportunities and develop new capabilities to increase the value added by their service innovation, i.e., a for-profit, large-scale meal delivery service that includes the silver market as a key target segment. In what follows I illustrate how 7Meal exploits opportunities in the silver market and creates value by leveraging the complementary skills and capabilities of SEJ and YTT.

The alliance between SEJ and YTT was initially centered on the SEJ stores serving as pick-up and drop-off points and complementing YTT's haulage system. Patrons leave their parcel so that YTT staff will pick it up and bring it to its destination, or the recipient may pick it up at any local store. This contributes to Seven-Eleven's taken-for-grantedness in everyday life in Japan, or to put it differently it has become an institution. SEJ serves an assortment of prepackaged, often perishable, goods. Since 1988 YTT has offered Cool Takkyubin, the service of chilled cargo haulage, which enabled customers to send any products found at the convenience store and more to locations all over Japan. Having thus extended its capabilities, YTT's skills and know-how opened new opportunities for SEJ with the delivery of freshly prepared or on-demand merchandise. SEJ could now start thinking of selling and delivering fresh snacks anytime, or proper meals and submeals (courses) for breakfast, lunch, and dinner.

In August 2000, SEJ established Seven Meal Service, a subsidiary focusing on home delivery of food and meals, which started services in September 2000 in the Tokyo metropolitan area. Since starting the service, 7Meal has been expanding the area covered by its service over 7 years. In summer 2007 Hokkaido was finally included in the coverage area, effectively completing full coverage of Japan. 7Meal had to address three main obstacles that made rapid extension of coverage difficult: variety, freshness and price. Learning from interaction with customers and slowly rolling out its business, 7Meal overcame the obstacles by building volume, cooperation, and affordable quality.

Successful meal services need to offer enough *variety* to guarantee being able to satisfy heavy users. Variety has two dimensions that increase costs considerably: increasing the choice on each given day increases the cost of new product development and production while at the same time it also reduces the sales of each specific dish (diminishing the benefit from scale economies, given stable demand). Variation over time means that 7Meals cannot enjoy cost benefits of repetition, and this increases the cost of new product development. In 2000, when 7Meal started operations, SEJ operated only about 8,000 stores in Japan. In 2010 it operates more than 12,750 in Japan and 37,496 worldwide. The increase of almost 50% of stores in Japan helped SEJ to improve the economics of its supply chain.

Freshness of meals requires efficient production and delivery appropriate for the nature of the meals. Increasing economies of scale and learning increase SEJ's ability to reduce the production-related costs. Chilled transport, especially in the warm and hot seasons or southern areas, is a critical capability only offered by YTT. This ability complements SEJ's business model design for 7Meal. Delivery of perishable meals to the home is costly. Allying itself with YTT, 7Meal is able to benefit from YTT's extensive service network and SEJ's shared history of a successful cooperation. The transport costs for each 7Meal delivery of ¥200 are charged in addition to the cost of the products, which range from approximately ¥500 to ¥2,000. 7Meal offers its customers the choice between front-door deliveries by YTT or pick-up at a designated SEJ convenience store.

Meals services need to be affordable and may not compromise on quality. Building up the scale of operations over 7 years, the price–quality ratio has been upgraded continuously. 7Meal chose an alliance with YTT for reasons of quality and price. The longstanding cooperation between SEJ and YTT reassured SEJ that YTT would conduct deliveries professionally at highest quality levels. YTT offers to deliver a single meal for about ¥200 to the doorstep of a customer, which is much lower than the comparable delivery price for a parcel. Today 7Meals has more than 200,000 users, more than 50% of the patrons being seniors aged over 60. The other half chooses the service because of lack of time or because of preference. About half of the users pick up their meals at a close-by location. The number is somewhat smaller for the senior customers; however, many also choose the pick-up option because they enjoy the flexibility and also the social interaction with staff. Walking to the store, looking around and interacting with SEJ staff offers them an opportunity to complement their meals with other products and to overcome isolation by having a chat with the sales clerk.

Summary and Conclusion

Having shown how the aging of societies increases the need for service innovation and renewal of business models, this chapter has explained how service innovation can help to change business models for the special case of Japan, the country that precedes all industrialized societies on the journey to senescence. Japan's companies are among the first to feel the changes in the demand for services and supply in the workforce related to the demographic changes that are occurring. Developing the notion of business models in the literature, I extend the concept by emphasizing service innovation as a means to better explore and exploit the opportunities of the silver market. Introducing the dynamics of new business model development as driven by service innovation, this chapter shows how interaction with customers (SEJ and YTT) and with business partners (Seven Meal Service) expands the range of what is possible and – over time – the skills and capabilities needed to seize emerging opportunities.

Japan is a showcase for how societies change and its demographic changes antecede those in other markets. Such a lead market offers the attentive observer key lessons to be learned. Researchers seeking to build theory that better explains how innovation happens and how it matters need to focus more on the service economy in such markets. Dynamic capabilities and ambidextrous systems are suggested to be the result of continued infusion of tacit knowledge. It is not well understood precisely how this upgrading of dynamic capabilities and innovation through informal, intangible, and implicit knowledge happens. The questions of "where do dynamic capabilities come from?" and "how do they emerge from tacit knowledge" have set the agenda for more empirical research.

Four lessons seem to be especially useful for decision-makers in business and governmental organizations, i.e., infrastructure and tacit knowledge, ambidextrous systems, innovation as strategy, and private solutions for public issues:

1. The importance of infrastructure to exploit opportunities in aging societies is shown. Lower mobility of seniors leads to more efforts to provide services and goods at home or at convenient locations nearby. However, retail outlets or car parks alone do not satisfy the new demand. Accumulating tacit knowledge over time through interaction with customers and partners in the supply chain is indispensable for innovation and renewal. The shop clerks at SEJ and the drivers of delivery trucks at YTT become invested in their regional network and highly attuned to the needs and behavior of "their" customers. While companies need to think how they can tap the tacit knowledge of stakeholders, regional government

or country leadership needs to pay attention to what is happening in the leading silver market to learn from success and to avoid failure.

2. The widespread networks of SEJ's convenience stores and the YTT haulage system are two models for companies in industrialized countries because they show how one business model manages the paradox of pursuing localization and customization without the need to sacrifice scale. Exploring the new and emergent needs of customers helps the companies to offer more value. Ensuring that volumes remain sufficiently large so that the benefits of economies of scale accrue to both firms, they successfully integrate scale and variety.

3. SEJ and YTT illustrate how the quest for innovation is the core of their strategy. The continuous expansion of their range of ideas and businesses shows the strong growth orientation. The complementary services and the hardware platform allow tacit knowledge and insights to lead the business model to renewal.

4. Government intervention to solve societal problems can sometimes be flawed; often it is less efficient than market-based solutions. Yet, market-based solutions often seek profits more than the public good. This chapter shows how profit-oriented firms can renew and expand their business models and at the same time provide the organizational basis for one aspect of taking care of the elderly.

These four lessons learned seem useful for individual companies but also for regions or countries that also face the arrival of the silver market. Infusing tacit knowledge into organizational systems can enable firms to overcome paradox, i.e., to become ambidextrous, and succeed in contributing to the solution of societal issues by introducing new services and business model innovation.

References

1. R.A. D'Aveni, *Hypercompetition: Managing the Dynamics of Strategic Manoeuvring* (Free, New York, 1994)
2. D. Iacobucci, Services: What do we know and where shall we go? A view from Marketing, Advances in Services Marketing and Management, **7**, 1–96 (1998)
3. OECD, *The Service Economy, Science Technology Industry Business Policy Forum Series* (OECD, Paris, 2001)
4. A. Woefl, *The Service Economy in OECD Countries*, OECD Science, Technology and Industry Working Papers, 2005/3 (OECD, Paris, 2005)
5. Ministry of Internal Affairs and Communications, *Statistical Handbook of Japan* (Statistics Bureau, Tokyo, 2007)
6. I. Nonaka, H. Takeuchi, *The Knowledge-Creating Company: How Japanese Companies Create the Dynamics of Innovation* (Oxford University Press, New York, 1995)
7. H. Chesborough, *Open Innovation: The New Imperative for Creating and Profiting from Technology* (Harvard Business School Press, Cambridge, MA, 2003)
8. E. von Hippel, Innovation by user communities: Learning from open-source software. MIT Sloan Manage. J. **42**(4), 82 (2001)
9. P. Seybold, *Outside Innovation* (Collins, New York, 2006)
10. K.M. Eisenhardt, J.A. Martin, Dynamic capabilities: What are they? Strateg. Manage. J. **21**, 1105–1121 (2000)

11. C. O'Reilly, M. Tushman, *Ambidexterity as a Dynamic Capability: Resolving the Innovator's Dilemma*. Stanford Graduate School of Business, Research Paper Series, No. 1963 (2007)
12. P. Reinmoeller, *Ambidextrous Organization* (Routledge, London, 2011 in press)
13. D. Teece, G. Pisano, A. Shuen, Dynamic capabilities and strategic management. Strateg. Manage. J. **18**, 509–533 (1997)
14. V.A. Zeithaml, M.J. Bitner, D.D. Gremler, *Services Marketing: Integrating Customer Focus Across the Firm* (McGraw-Hill Irwin, New York, 2006)
15. C. Grönroos, A service quality model and its marketing implications. Eur. J. Mark. **18**, 36–44 (1984)
16. C. Grönroos, Strategic management and marketing in service sector. Manag. Serv. Qual. **11**, 150–152 (2001)
17. L. Berry, M.S. Yadav, Capture and communicate value in the pricing of services. Sloan Manage. Rev. **37**, 41–51 (1996)
18. L.L. Berry, V.A. Zeithaml, A. Parasuraman, Five imperatives for improving service quality. Sloan Manage. Rev. **31**(4), 29–38 (1990)
19. L. Välikangas, U. Lehtinen, Strategic types of services and international marketing. Int. J. Serv. Ind. Manage. **5**, 72–84 (1994)
20. M. Morris, M. Schindehutte, J. Richardson, J. Allen, Is the business model a useful strategic concept? Conceptual, theoretical, and empirical insights. J. Small Bus. Strategy **17**, 27–50 (2006)
21. R.E.S. Boulton, B.D. Libert, S.M. Samek, A business model for the new economy. J. Bus. Strategy **21**, 29–35 (2000)
22. K. Chaharbaghi, C. Fendt, R. Willis, Meaning, legitimacy and impact of business models in fast moving environments. Manage. Decis. **41**, 372–382 (2003)
23. S. Forge, Business models for the computer industry for the next decade. Futures **25**(9), 923–948 (1993)
24. S. Shafer, H.J. Smith, J. Linder, The power of business models. Bus. Horiz. **48**, 199–207 (2005)
25. J. Magretta, Why Business Models Matter. Harv. Bus. Rev. **80**(5), 86–92 (2002)
26. J.A. Zackman, *Concepts of the Framework for Enterprise Architecture* (Zackam International, Los Angeles, 1996)
27. D.W. Mitchell, C.B. Coles, Building better business models, Leader to Leader, Summer **29**, 12–17 (2003)
28. R. Amit, C. Zott, Strateg. Manage. J. **22**, 493 (2001)
29. K.L. Kraemer, J. Dedrick, S. Yamashiro, Refining and extending the business model with information technology: Dell Computer Corporation. Inf. Soc. **16**, 5–21 (2000)
30. M. Ogura, Delivering the Goods: Entrepreneurship and Innovation in a Japanese Corporation, translated by David S. Noble, Tokyo: International House of Japan (2004)

Part II
Marketing for the Silver Market

Chapter 11
Current Strategies in the Retail Industry for Best-Agers

Gunnar Arnold and Stephanie Krancioch

Abstract In view of the current demographic transformation, the retail trade faces a clear challenge to reconsider its existing concepts, and to include older target groups in its marketing planning to an increased degree. In this chapter, we will look first at the factor of location, one of the central success factors in the retail trade. Next, we will examine the preferences of German best-agers for certain types of businesses, such as shops close to home rather than out-of-town malls. We then proceed to discuss the effects of changed customer needs for the design of the assortments and of packaging resulting from the customer's decreasing physical capabilities. We will present examples from the daily practice of the trade. In conclusion, we will provide a brief overview of foreseeable trends in the retail trade.

The Retail Trade in the Face of Demographic Change

An adjustment to the needs of older customers is necessary in the retail trade, since this area has, in some respects, a great need to catch up with developments, and because the potential of the best-agers is being underestimated. This very heterogeneous target group includes people over 50 years of age with different socio-demographic characteristics, value orientations, leisure-time activities, and consumer preferences. It must always be considered that, regardless of the particular leisure preferences, interests, or consumption habits of older people, they share the basic wish to supply themselves via retail shopping as long as they are physically able to do so. The spending power of the German best-agers is also attractive. Those aged 50–59 spent about €24,000 per capita in the retail trade during 2005. The 60+ generation had €20,000 per annum to spend, giving them €1,000 more purchasing power, on average, than the target groups through age 49.

The demographic impact on retail trade substantially affects such matters as decisions on the location of commercial establishments. The demands of older target groups with regard to convenience and comfort in shopping absolutely

F. Kohlbacher and C. Herstatt (eds.), *The Silver Market Phenomenon*,
DOI 10.1007/978-3-642-14338-0_11, © Springer-Verlag Berlin Heidelberg 2011

coincide with those of younger target groups. Purchase outlets must be accessible, and designed in such a way that the consumers feel good there [1].

The specific wishes and needs of older customers for the retail trade include (see p. 58 in [2]):

- Entry at ground level or by elevator
- Safe place to put shopping carts
- No turnstiles
- Wide corridors and short distances in markets
- Shallower shopping carts that are easier to push
- Help when shopping, personal contact, and opportunities for social contact
- Clear identification of sections at eye-level
- Products always located at the same place
- Easily legible price labels
- Pricing on items, not on shelves
- Magnifying glasses at the shelves
- Less depth in freezers and refrigerators
- No need to bend down or reach up
- Small portions and light packaging
- Less technology (e.g., bottle-return machines)
- Places to rest
- Standing supports at cash registers; less hectic atmosphere there
- Possibility to leave items in shopping carts during checkout
- Packaging help and delivery service; installation of equipment
- Easily legible sales slips
- Convenient transportation of purchased items to the car

Effects on Location and Types of Business

Scientific examinations by the Institute for Trade Research at the University of Cologne (IFH) and by BBDO Sales GmbH confirm that two-thirds (67%) of those aged 50–89 in Germany usually shop near home. More than half (52%) often shop in pedestrian shopping districts in city centers. Conveniently located out-of-town mall sites with good connections to transportation are frequented by 41% of those surveyed; shopping centers achieved 39% (cf. Table 11.1).

Table 11.1 Locations frequented [3]

Where do you frequently shop?	Proportion of persons surveyed (%)	Close-to-home and ... (%)	Close-to-home, but not ... (%)
Close to home	67	–	–
Inner-city pedestrian district	52	39	28
Convenient out-of-town malls	41	30	37
Shopping center	39	29	38

$n = 1,370$ (multiple answers/rounded)

Even if older consumers frequently shop within walking distance and in city centers (39%), in malls outside of town (30%), and in shopping centers (29%), a significant difference is still apparent between the frequency of shopping close to home versus that at more remote locations.

Of those surveyed, 29% shop close to home, but avoid inner-city pedestrian districts; 37% shop close to home, but not in out-of-town malls; and 38% shop close to home, but not in shopping centers.

With regard to single age groups in the 50–89 range, it turns out that close-to-home locations for shops enjoy high market acceptance values in all groups (cf. Table 11.2). Although the willingness to shop in out-of-town malls increases slightly among those aged 50–69, it drops again noticeably among 70-year-olds. The 70–89 age group prefers to do its shopping close to home. All in all, it can be stated that older consumers prefer to shop within walking distance of home, and patronize inner-city pedestrian shopping districts, shopping centers, and out-of-town malls ever less frequently with advancing age [3].

In order to meet the demand of easy accessibility, the location of a market must be chosen so that it has an optimum connection to public transportation and to the road network. Customers want to shop near their place of residence or their workplace, and find the products they need quickly.

Up to the mid-1990s, the retail trade still pursued the concept of targeted steering of customers, forcing them to first walk past products of irregular demand (such as textiles, magazines, and CDs) before crossing the drinks and preserved-foods section and finally reaching the fresh-foods section.

Today, there has been a change in attitude in that respect. In order to stimulate the customers to spontaneous purchases in specialty-store centers for example, clothing stores were purposely placed in various locations. Here, customers actually consumed up to a third more than they had planned. Overall, however, drops in sales volume were registered, since consumers shifted to other shopping centers that offered greater convenience. Thus, a self-service market would have to be designed so that it would be up to the customer to decide in which order s/he wished to visit various sections. For specialty-store centers, such a reorganization could mean, for example, grouping several retailers that supply irregularly required products. Thus, clothing stores oriented toward different price levels could be located directly adjacent to one another. The establishment of a discount store and a drugstore in the immediate vicinity of a self-service department store would

Table 11.2 Location preference, by age group [3]

Preferred locations				
Age	Close to home (%)	Convenient out-of-town malls (%)	Shopping centers (%)	Pedestrian shopping districts (%)
50–59 years ($n = 561$)	67	42	43	57
60–69 years ($n = 450$)	69	46	43	58
70–79 years ($n = 234$)	63	38	31	39
80–89 years ($n = 53$)	70	26	13	38
Values rounded				

enable customers to obtain all their regularly required products without moving long distances [1].

The location decisions of retailers are usually closely connected to the selected type of business. The preferences of consumers for certain types of business must therefore also be included in considerations. Figure 11.1 shows that over 50-year-olds most frequently shop at discount stores (82.1%) and at supermarkets (80.2%). Of those surveyed by the IFH, 60.4% frequently shop at department stores, while 42% stated specialty stores. In that survey, 25% described themselves as frequent customers of mail-order houses, 17.1% stated that they often made use of home-delivery, and no less than 13.8% frequently shopped on the Internet (cf. Fig. 11.1). Overall, the best-agers prefer types of business that supply their daily needs and are typically located close to their residences. Other business types, which are more likely to provide for long-term requirements, are less frequently visited.

It should be noted with regard to particular age groups that those aged 50–69 like to shop in department stores and specialty stores, but that this frequency drops considerably among customers over 70. The trend of ever-fewer people frequenting various types of business is also shown in Table 11.3. This suggests strongly that best-agers also shop ever less frequently in supermarkets and discount stores with advancing age. Moreover, it is evident that home services are used mainly by the 70–79 age group. The 50–59 age group, however, like to shop on the Internet and by mail order (cf. Table 11.3).

These descriptions strongly suggest that locations near residential areas are likely to gain in significance again in the future [4]. Particularly, markets with small floor space stand a good chance of becoming close-to-home suppliers, and will be able to score points with personal contact, good counseling, and friendly service [5]. Already, a trend by discount stores to move away from the periphery

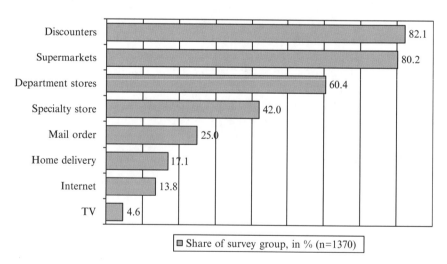

Fig. 11.1 Types of business frequented (50 to 89-year-olds) [3]

Table 11.3 Business form preferences, by age [3]

Preferred business types							
Age	Supermarkets (%)	Discounters (%)	Department stores (%)	Specialty stores (%)	Home delivery (%)	Catalog/ mail order (%)	Internet (%)
50–59 years (n = 561)	80	84	62	40	18	31	23
60–69 years (n = 450)	81	84	65	47	15	20	8
70–79 years (n = 234)	85	78	59	73	20	21	5
80–89 years (n = 53)	74	72	40	28	15	19	0

Values rounded

and towards close-to-home and inner-city locations can be observed. Shopping centers too are being increasingly located in city centers [4].

The Consequences for Assortment Structuring and Packaging Design

In addition to location selection and store design, there is another problem involving the products in the market itself. Here, the packaging is often a problem for older customers, as all senses (such as sight and touch) deteriorate with age, as do motor skills and strength [6]. Viewed in this light, packaging is often not user-friendly [7]. A study by the European Association of Carton and Cartonboard Manufacturers (ProCarton) confirms that only 19% of the over-60s are very satisfied with the packaging of products. On the other hand, 83% of older customers stated that, for them, packaging is the decisive factor in purchasing [8]. Packaging can thus become an indicator for the success or failure of a product at the point of sale [2]. To attain a maximum level of comfort for the customer, the first thing should be to provide smaller packaging. A 10-kg package of detergent, while it may be an advantage for a family, is often a problem for older customers, since they may not be able to transport it home due to physical restrictions [7]. Another problem is too-complicated sealing mechanisms, which make it difficult to take the product out [2]. It is therefore not surprising that 36% of the more mature customers surveyed state that they would not repeat the purchase of a product if they could not open it comfortably [9].

The visual design is also very important. Thus, matted packaging is recommended to avoid a dazzling effect. An appropriately large type-face should be used for marking, due to deteriorating eyesight, and the color selection should avoid using blue and green, which older people can easily confuse [2]. Older consumers in particular include many diabetics, for whom the information on ingredients on the packaging must be easily recognizable. For this reason the following statements should be present:

- Exact price
- Expiration date
- Composition
- Method of application (dosage, preparation)
- Warnings for certain target groups (people suffering from allergies)
- Safety regulations and disposal instructions
- Information about manufacturer and origin

Unfortunately, this information is often entirely lacking, or only available in English, which can cause a problem for people whose native language is not English. Due to bad packaging design, mistaken purchases often occur. This true not only for older customers, but also for younger ones, who are often pressed for time [7].

For this reason, the folding box manufacturer Edelmann has developed a number of packing solutions to meet these new requirements. From the point of view of the manufacturer, these involve particularly understandable instructions for opening and closing mechanisms, legible names and information, and contrasting backgrounds. Under the brand name CEasy, various innovative packaging types are now provided, including sliding packaging with recessed grips, column-shaped packaging with large flaps to be grasped, or folding boxes with opening aids (cf. Fig. 11.2) [8].

Moreover, the packing design is closely connected to the assortment selection, since here too certain characteristics can be determined for the older target groups. For example, not only are the small packet sizes already mentioned advantageous here, but also organic products have a high value [7]. This was also confirmed by a

Fig. 11.2 Packaging solutions by the Edelmann company [10]

survey by TNS Infratest. A high affinity for organic products was ascertained, precisely among people over 50 years of age [11]. This is due mainly to cultural, religious, and idealistic values. The consumer behavior of persons with this characteristic combination of values is regarded as extremely demanding. A high-quality diet is of great importance for them. The great confidence of this target group in the organic-food quality label is also due to this factor [11].

Due to the low price sensitivity of the best-agers, there is great leeway in brand choice from a marketing point of view, particularly as regards trade brands. According to a current survey by KMPG, trade brands are enjoying ever-greater market acceptance, and are no longer to be found only in the lower price segment. On the contrary, given the largely similar assortment in the food retail trade for example, they can serve as a mark of distinction [12]. In addition, the convenience aspect of the products is very important for older people. A former professional woman who used to reach automatically for the frozen-food rack will continue to do so in old age. For that reason, the per capita consumption of frozen food more than doubled between 1983 and 2003 (cf. Fig. 11.3). This convenience boom thus also represents a great potential for the retail trade [13].

But, convenience alone is not enough for the older target group. A healthy diet is very important to them. The high value they place on maintaining their health is confirmed by surveys conducted by the Allensbach Institute, a polling agency. Older people in the 60–69 age group are the leaders here (cf. Fig. 11.4).

Convenience and staying healthy have long stopped being a contradiction [12]. In that sense, it is not surprising that best-agers prefer products such as dairy products and local products which contain many additional vitamins and vital substances. Thus, health and functional foods offer good growth opportunities for the retail trade. In 2005, the sales volume of such products as fluoridated table salt, wellness waters, and probiotic dairy products grew strongly, with an increase of 16.8%. These growth rates were reached both due to the successful introduction of new products and due to the discount stores. Particularly among the best-agers, the

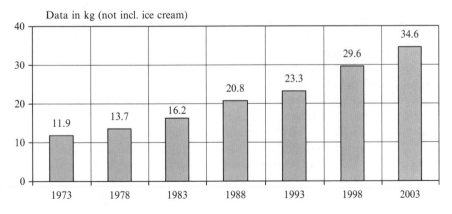

Fig. 11.3 Consumption of frozen food [13]

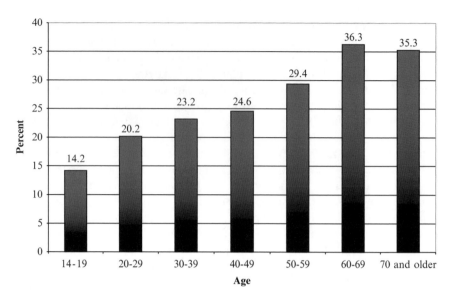

Fig. 11.4 People particularly concerned about their health [14]

use frequency of products in the health and functional foods segment is growing. This circumstance reflects the value they place on a healthy, high-quality diet, with price playing a relatively subordinate role [15].

Implementation and Trends

Retailers are increasingly orienting themselves toward the needs of the older target groups, and are developing innovative concepts. In addition to the Swiss Coop and a Globus supermarket in Saarbrücken [4], the Austrian Adeg retail chain assumed a pioneering role in 2003 with the opening of *Aktiv Markt 50plus* stores. The parent company Edeka, too, followed that good example and, by 2009, had opened fifty stores subtitled *Supermarket of the Generations* in Germany. The Metro Group is testing special concepts on the best-agers in the *future store* of the Galeria Kaufhof, and the mail-order house Otto is providing special assortments in its catalogs. Bus tours from all over Germany are bringing customers to Germany's first *seniors department store* in Großräschen in Lusatia. Additional stores on a franchise basis are planned [16]. The Tengelmann Group has entered this new territory as well, with its Kaiser's *Generation Market* in Berlin which has increased its turnover by 50% since its opening in 2006. During selection of the location, it was ensured that approximately 57% of the population in the intake area were 50 years old or older. The share of single budgets is 56%, hence also above the national average. The market is to appeal to young and old target groups alike, but is to particularly take the needs of the older target groups into account. A good overview and good orientation are achieved by means of numerous signs identifying product groups, and colored product illustrations. The fresh-foods and dry-goods areas have been broken down both by design elements and by color-coding of the nonslip floor coverings. Good legibility is a priority in price and product information. There are numerous magnifying glasses on the shelves for fine print on the items, and also on the shopping carts, which are provided with integrated seats. Numerous bells are placed in the extra-wide walks, with which an employee can be called to certain places in the supermarket for questions and support (Fig. 11.5).

A pleasant shopping atmosphere was created by the remodeling of the facility and the lighting concepts for each of the sections. In addition to these individual services, the "Kaiser's Meeting Point" was established directly opposite the bakery. In this separate area, customers can enjoy coffee and cake, and socialize in a relaxed atmosphere. Moreover, a comfortable seating corner, a massage couch, an information monitor and Internet access are available. An additional special feature is the small and single packaging marked "for the small household," since older customers and singles have specifically asked for that [17]. Following this successful example, the British supermarket Tesco plans to open a similarly designed store. Therefore, they sent elderly people to Berlin in order to investigate how it operates [18]. The gourmet division of a warehouse in Frankfurt even spares its older customers the annoying repacking process at the cash register. With the aid of *Scanny*, a mobile scanner terminal, the customers enter the prices themselves, and

Shopping cart with seat

Magnifying glass on shopping cart

Massage couch in the "Kaiser's meeting point"   Product identification "for the small household"

Fig. 11.5 Kaiser's "Generation Market" in Berlin [17]

are rewarded with a bonus book, which reminds many of trading-stamp booklets. On weekends moreover, a packing service and delivery to the car is provided [2]. Several studies indeed confirm that standing in line at the cash register is the greatest annoyance for customers [19]. The cash register area is normally marked by jams, customer stress, and impatience. The introduction of new technical solutions is an attempt being undertaken in many places to remove this sore spot in the conventional supermarket in a manner advantageous to all customers [20].

Summary and Conclusion

In order to be successful in the best-agers segment, the retail trade has to provide well-accessible locations and a convenient store layout. The assortment and packaging should address the specific target group needs. It thus also offers good prospects for other industries, like the food and packaging industry. Distinctive features and additional income could be created through special services and offers, with an additional benefit. If the retail trade fulfills all these needs it can also develop a higher attraction for younger target groups. This is because they are not at all put off by all these adaptations but, quite the opposite, they appreciate them too.

Nonetheless, only a few established service products in Germany have to date been able to demonstrate promise for the future. US retail chains provide not only an inviting ambiance, but also products targeted to older customers, in the marketing of fruits and vegetables. These include special product-friendly packaging, complete with health tips, for example. "Meal solutions" too are an area in which the German retail trade has some catching up to do. The integration of ready-to-eat products into the supermarket assortment holds added value potential and an opportunity to set oneself apart from the discount stores [21]. Marketing campaigns on such topics as cooking, health, regional, or seasonal products, and special offers for older target groups, could contribute to such a counter-positioning of supermarkets and close-to-home stores [20]. In step with the needs of the older generation, the significance of service and counseling-oriented products for the retail trade will tend to increase [1].

References

1. B. Schoofs, Immobilien und Finanzierung **19**, 662 (2006)
2. A. Reidl, Neue Verpackung **5**, 54 (2006)
3. M. Preißner, A. Knob, Handel im Fokus **2**, 101 (2006)
4. D. Rees, Lebensmittelzeitung **38**, 58 (2000)
5. Wellness- und Energy Boom (Wellness and energy boom). *Rundschau für den Lebensmittelhandel* **3**, 36 (2007)
6. C. Krieb, A. Reidl, *Seniorenmarketing – so erreichen Sie die Zielgruppe der Zukunft (Seniors marketing – how to reach the target group of the future)* (Ueberreuter, Vienna/Frankfurt, 1999)
7. M. Hens, *Professionelle Ladengestaltung für 50plus Kunden (Professional store design for 50plus customers)* (BBE-Verlag, Cologne, 2006)

8. Die Best Agers im Fokus der Verpackungsentwicklung (Best-agers in the focus of packaging developments). *Neue Verpackung* **6**, 36 (2007)
9. H. Krost, Lebensmittelzeitung **39**, 68 (2004)
10. Edelmann Group, *CEasy, die Generation 50plus* (*CEasy, the 50plus generation*) (Edelmann Group, Heidenheim, 2007)
11. TNS Infratest, *Semiometrie – Die Zielgruppe für Biolebensmittel* (*Semiometrie, the target group for organic food*) (TNS Infratest, Bielefeld, 2007)
12. T. Kreimer, M. Gerling, *Status quo und Perspektiven im deutschen Lebensmitteleinzelhandel 2006 (Status quo and prospects in the German food retail trade 2006)* (KPMG, Berlin, 2006)
13. SevenOne Media, *TrendReport – Die Anti-Aging Gesellschaft* (*Trend report: the anti-aging society*) (SevenOne Media, Unterföhring, 2005)
14. Institut für Demoskopie Allensbach, *Allensbacher Markt- und Werbeträgeranalyse (Allensbach Market and Advertising Media Analysis)* (Institut für Demoskopie Allensbach, Allensbach, 2003)
15. Health and functional food. *Lebensmittel Prax.* **24**, 40 (2006)
16. M. Martell, *Handel entdeckt über 50-Jährige* (*The retail trade discovers the over-50-year-olds*). http://www.stuttgarter-zeitung.de/stz/page/detail.php/1273025, 2007. Accessed 11 June 2008
17. Kaiser's Tengelmann, Press release: *1. Kaiser's "Generationen-Markt" in Berlin!* (*1st Kaiser's Generation Market in Berlin!*) (Kaiser's Tengelmann, Viersen, 2006)
18. P. Sims, Tesco reveals Britain's first 'pensioner-friendly' supermarket – with magnifying glasses and seats on trolleys. www.dailymail.co.uk/news/article-1050195/Tesco-reveals-Britains-pensioner-friendly-supermarket–magnifying-glasses-seats-trolleys.html, 2008. Accessed 20 Feb 2010
19. I. Kober, Regal **2**, 112 (2006)
20. Verschlafen wir nicht den Zug der Zeit (Let's not oversleep and miss the train of our time!). *Regal* **2**, 3 (2006)
21. S. Biester, Lebensmittelzeitung **21**, 32 (2007)

Chapter 12
Silver Pricing: Satisfying Needs Is Not Enough – Balancing Value Delivery and Value Extraction Is Key

Stefan Lippert

Abstract At first glance, the silver market provides a highly lucrative opportunity for businesses willing and able to meet the needs of Japan's senior generation. International and domestic players have been pursuing these new opportunities in the last few years. Thoroughly understanding the needs of the silver generation is a key to capitalizing on it. However, this is just one side of the value coin. A need is not the same as demand, and demand is not the same as profitable business. To turn a profit, you have to balance value delivery and value extraction. Value delivery is relatively easy: it requires market research, appropriate products and services, and an effective distribution system. Value extraction is difficult: you need to set and implement the right prices across products, regions, and channels. A marketing strategy based solely on demographic and socioeconomic data, customer needs, and buying power is simplistic, misleading, and in some cases dangerous. Capitalizing on the silver market requires a systematic approach to developing and profitably selling products and services tailored to the older generation. It takes a solid understanding of customer requirements, value-to-customer, ability and willingness to pay, price elasticities, and revenue and profit functions. The best way to achieve this is by means of a professional pricing process covering and connecting pricing strategy, price setting, and price implementation.

Introduction

Japan's Silver Market: At First Glance, a Highly Attractive Opportunity

The rapidly aging population in Japan poses an unprecedented challenge to marketing. For many decades, marketers concentrated on consumers aged between 15 and 40. In some cases, such as in the premium automotive market, private banking, real estate, luxury goods, leisure, and healthcare, the age groups of 40–50 and 50–60

F. Kohlbacher and C. Herstatt (eds.), *The Silver Market Phenomenon*,
DOI 10.1007/978-3-642-14338-0_12, © Springer-Verlag Berlin Heidelberg 2011

also played a role. The silver market is widely understood to start with the 60+ age group, which is mostly uncharted territory from a marketing perspective. There are three reasons why Japan's silver market is so attractive:

1. *Size*: Today, 22.6% of the Japanese population is 65 or over. If the current demographic trends (low birthrate, rising longevity) continue, this figure will almost double to 40% by 2055. Over the same period, Japan's population is expected to drop by 30% to less than 90 million, after peaking near 128 million in 2005. These facts are having a huge impact on business. Both the supply side and the demand side are affected. On the supply side, the main challenge is a dramatic shortage of labor. The latest government forecast suggests there will be 1.3 workers per senior citizen in the 2050s, down from 3.3 in 2005. On the demand side, the overall domestic market will shrink significantly (30 million fewer people by 2055), *but the size of the silver segment will markedly increase – from currently 26 million to 36 million people by 2055*. Between 2012 and 2014 alone, the number of elderly people will increase by one million every year, since most baby boomers will turn 65 then. By 2015, senior citizens will account for 26% of the population. The "super-aged" society, in which one in four people is 65 years or older, will arrive in less than 10 years [1].

2. *Purchasing power*: In spite of the demographic challenge, Japan will most likely maintain its position as a global economic powerhouse. Current economic research suggests that, even in 2050, Japan will be number five in a global GDP ranking, behind the USA, China, the EU and India.[1] The country's high level of wealth will be distributed among fewer people, and the elderly will have the lion's share of the assets. The key facts and figures are:

   • The total amount of retirement benefits the baby boomers are entitled to during the period 2007–2009 is estimated to amount to ¥50 trillion.
   • The 6.8 million boomers account for 5.4% of the population, but they hold total financial assets worth ¥130 trillion, or 10% of the total financial assets held by individuals. If retirement benefits are included, the latter figure increases to 14%.
   • Elderly households have more financial assets than other generations. On average, households comprising people aged between 60 and 70 are worth ¥17 million. Households of people aged 70 and over are worth ¥15 million; households of people aged 50–69 are worth ¥11.5 million [2].

3. *Value change*: Older generations of the past diligently saved their money to enable the next generation to receive a good education. They also saved money to balance out the expenses connected with caring for grandparents and older

---

[1]Japan Center for Economic Research 2007 (ranking based on 2000 purchasing power parity, in US$). Most recent research indicates that the group of the "old, poor and sick" might indeed become the majority of the silver market; see F. Kohlbacher and A. Weihrauch: Silbermarktphäno-men "revisited": Goldene Gelegenheit oder rostige Realität?, in: Japan Markt 8/2009, pp. 13–15.

family members living at home. This behavior is now changing drastically. The baby boomers no longer expect their few children, who often live and work farther away, to care for them in their advanced years. On the other hand, they also feel less disposed to save for the younger generation. Leading financial institutes such as JP Morgan, Goldman Sachs, and Nomura Securities believe that the demographic change in the coming years will be advantageous for Japan's economic growth. This conviction is strengthened by the fact that senior citizens spend substantially more than other age groups. Retirees draw on their savings (as they do in the USA), while workers over 60-years old accrue hardly any savings. This trend is spreading. In 2000, retirees spent about 15% more than they received in retirement. Their expenditures are now 29% higher than their income. These figures are also reflected in consumer spending: Japan's senior citizens consume more than the younger generation, with average per capita expenditure increasing clearly until the age of 70 [3].

At first glance, the silver market provides a highly lucrative opportunity for businesses willing and able to meet the needs of Japan's senior generation. International and domestic players have been pursuing these new opportunities in the last few years.

Consider HSBC, which has decided to tap into the premium retail banking market. The bank targets the upper middle class, especially baby boomers receiving their retirement benefits and looking for good advice on how to invest the money properly.

Allianz Group and other international players have entered the Japanese life insurance market by selling variable annuity (VA) products primarily to the older generation; the Japanese VA market skyrocketed from less than US$1 billion in assets in 2000 to over US$50 billion until the economic crisis of 2008 hit.

Nomura Securities sells an investment fund that pays out dividends six times a year, when seniors get no payment from the public pension system, which pays only every other month. The fund raised ¥660 billion in the first year.

MUFJ Trust&Banking focuses on developing will and inheritance operations. Customers pay sign-up and annual management fees, and the bank takes a percentage of the will's value upon its execution. The bank plans to broaden the service into a conduit for selling private banking services. The bank had about 20,400 wills under contract as of March 2008, about one third of the total number of bank-deposited wills and inheritance arrangements in Japan (61,000, roughly 54% higher than in 2003, according to the Trust Companies Association of Japan).

International investors have acquired a large number of golf courses, restructured them, and established new companies (e.g., Accordia Golf). Domestic companies focus on opportunities in the leisure, travel, fitness, wellness, education, entertainment, and real estate sectors, to name just a few. In particular, the healthcare market provides attractive opportunities. Healthcare costs have reached 8% of the Japanese GDP, compared with 4.4% in 1965. More than 40% of healthcare costs are related to patients aged 70 or above. Further massive growth in the healthcare market is expected, given the demographic shift and the low level of per capita health spending (about half of the US level) [4]. On the B2B side, companies providing solutions for the shrinking workforce (e.g., automation, robotics) are likely to profit from the demographic change.

It's Worth a Second Glance: Value Delivery and Value Extraction

Thoroughly understanding the needs of the silver generation is a key to capitalizing on it. We call this *value delivery*. However, this is just one side of the value coin. The other side is that *business is about making money, not just satisfying needs. A need is not the same as demand, and demand is not the same as profitable business. To turn a profit, you have to balance value delivery and value extraction.* Value delivery is relatively easy: it requires market research, appropriate products and services, and an effective distribution system. Value extraction is difficult: you need to set and implement the right prices across products, regions, and channels. A few real-life cases of silver market-related businesses in Japan illustrate this:

- You have read about the interest of retiring boomers in cultural travel and want to set up a conveniently located travel agency focusing on premium vacation tours. Assuming that you are able to address your target segment: What is the convenience and advice worth to your potential customers? Are they really willing to pay more for convenience and advice if the same trip is offered at a lower price over the web? Or, do they use your services and end up booking electronically? What kind of pricing levels, structures, and fencing mechanisms does it take to prevent this?
- You want to offer advice on financial planning to retirees and sell products accordingly. Market research has uncovered a huge need, and you have read the reports of investment banks that tend to indicate the same. Yet, you realize that it is by no means clear whether this need is actually backed by a sufficient willingness to pay. Can you compete with incumbents that offer low-level consultation for free? Apart from consultation, which features of your product (e.g., a lifecycle investment fund) really matter to your customers? How much are they willing to pay for them? Does your brand influence the buying decision? How would demand react if you change prices by 2.5, 5, or 10%?
- You make premium household goods. Your Japanese chief marketer recommends changing product specifications in order to better meet the needs of senior customers. In particular, handling and design should be modified. You like the idea, but you realize that this increases the costs of R&D, production, and handling. You ask your marketer about the possibility of charging a higher price that reflects the additional costs, but you hear that this would be difficult. You realize that the silver market wants specific products, but does not want to pay more for them. Is the assessment given by your marketer accurate? How much would sales decline if you actually charge a higher price? What would be the overall impact on revenue and profit?

The silver market story sounds good, but it's not so easily cracked. Before venturing into the uncharted territory of the silver market, you should have a clear, profound understanding of both the ability and the willingness to pay.

The *ability to pay* may be affected in the long term by a reduction in savings and wealth due to a shrinking and aging population. A recent study suggests that the continuous increase in the standard of living in the post-war period will come to an end. Regardless of further GDP growth, savings will decline to almost zero over the next 20 years. The decline in the savings rate has a direct impact on wealth and economic growth. If new savings dry up, less wealth is created, and, consequently, dramatically less money is available to be spent. In concrete terms, financial wealth in Japan is projected to fall slightly from 2003 to 2024, after increasing by 5.5% a year from 1975 to 2003. Hence, if effective counter-measures (such as a broad shift towards higher-yielding asset classes or massively increased productivity) are not taken, the wealth of the average Japanese household in 2024 will be more or less the same as it was in the mid-1990s [5].[2]

However, this gloomy long-term perspective must not be mixed up with the short- and mid-term outlook. Here, the question is not whether enough money is available but how to extract it. Uncertainties stem particularly from the fact that the elderly face a long and unprecedented retirement period of about 18 years (men) and 23 years (women) after turning 65. Are they really big spenders, in spite of the weaknesses of the public pension system and the lack of family support? These questions boil down to the issue of *willingness to pay*.

Understanding Willingness to Pay: The Key to Smart Profit Growth in the Silver Market

Of the three factors of the profit equation – price, units sold, and costs – price is the most effective profit driver. In the silver market, the role of intelligent pricing cannot be exaggerated because a needs-based view still prevails. Understanding

---

[2]The study argues that the decline in savings is driven by three main factors. Firstly, retired households will outnumber households in their prime saving years, so savings rates will naturally decline. The prime savers ratio – the number of households in their prime saving years (aged 30–50) divided by the number of elderly households (aged 65 and above) – has been below one since the mid-1980s. Secondly, the generational saving behavior has changed. The young generation saves less than the older generations have. This is particularly true for the generation born in the 1960s and 1970s, which has been moving into the prime saving years since 1990. These households have higher disposable incomes than earlier generations, but they also spend more. Thirdly, Japanese households traditionally build wealth through new savings rather than asset appreciation. Recent data indicate a slight shift towards asset classes with higher yields (e.g., mutual funds and life insurance products), but eye-catching media reports on Japanese housewives pursuing "carry trades" must not divert from the fact that low-yielding bank deposits still account for more than 50% of household assets. It is unlikely that the basic investment pattern, which is deeply rooted in a specific risk culture and the painful experience of stock market and real estate crashes in the 1990s, will change significantly over the next 10 or 20 years [5, 6].

your silver customer's needs and developing products and services accordingly is necessary for successful sales, but it is not sufficient to make sure you turn a profit.

Serving the silver market can entail higher sales costs and stricter customer protection requirements. Consider the financial services sector. The new Japanese investor protection law, which took effect in fall 2007, requires banks to overhaul their practices of selling investment trusts (mutual funds) and other risk products to elderly customers. To avoid disciplinary action from the regulator, banks had already set up internal rules on how to deal with customers in their 70s or 80s. For example, SMBC requires that customers aged 70+ be accompanied by a family member when purchasing a variable annuity, while MUFG states it explains the risks involved in complex financial products at least twice to customers over 70. Banks also plan to increase their after-sales services by, for example, visiting elderly customers to explain the performance of investment products or inviting them to investment conferences [7]. All these activities cost money, and the question the bank (or insurance company) has to answer is whether the return on these activities is sufficiently high.

Further, silver pricing has to factor in the specific value structure and peculiarities of the target group. Consider variable annuities, an investment-linked, rather complex life insurance product, which is bought mostly by customers aged 60+ in Japan. Variable annuities have been a booming product in the overall shrinking Japanese life insurance market (until the Lehman shock, it is currently [March 2010] uncertain whether and when the market will take off again). Competition has been fierce and the shelf space provided by the bank assurance channel is rather limited. To be successful in the challenging market, it takes – apart from a rigorous financial risk assessment on the actuarial side – an exact quantitative analysis of the product features from the perspective of the Japanese seniors: Which features do they really appreciate and how much are they willing to pay for them? Figure 12.1 exemplifies the differing value perception of the same age group in two countries.

Investment security, for example, plays a high role for German customers, whereas Singaporeans prefer products that offer an option to withdraw money flexibly and high returns. Translated into willingness-to-pay, it becomes clear that these two markets require tailored, very different products to profitably meet the specific value structures. A one-size-fits-all approach does not work. It is a no-brainer to say that these value structures are deeply rooted in mental and cultural history. It is less clear why international companies still tend to neglect the specific value structure of their Japanese customers.

Whether or not age-based price discrimination is possible depends on the given business situation (sector, product group, intensity of regulation, etc.). In non- or less-regulated sectors such as travel, age-based discounting has become quite common in Japan; in particular, train tickets and vacation packages are sold with certain age-based discounts. In financial services, Kabu.com, a leading online brokerage, launched a commission discount program in 2006 for investors aged 50–60. According to the company, about 30% of its customers are aged 50 or over. In 2009, the electronics retailer Bic Camera began offering a new service package, Raku Raku Anshin Pack, that includes delivery and set-up of PCs for customers

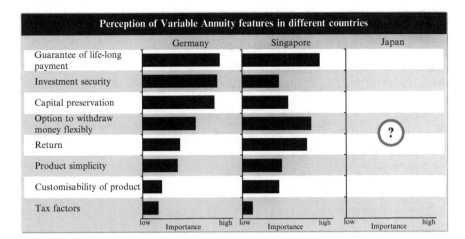

Fig. 12.1 Value perception differs largely between countries

over 60. The service also includes unlimited tech support over the telephone. Normally, such a combination would cost ¥21,000, but for silver customers, the service sells for ¥9,800, a steep discount of more than 50%. At PC Depot, a similar package targeted at the silver generation comes at a discount of 20%.

However, the goal of silver pricing cannot be discounting. Discounts boost units sold rather than profits. In fixed cost-based businesses such as software, pharmaceuticals, or securities order processing, higher units sold translate quite directly into higher total profits, but in businesses with high variable costs (e.g., manufacturing automobiles, mobile phones, or TV flat screens) discounts destroy margins and, in most cases, total profits. The goal of silver pricing is to make sure you get what you deserve. This requires an accurate understanding of the actual willingness to pay, the price–response function, the revenue function, and the profit function:

- How much are our silver customers going to pay for the product/service offered to them?
- How will demand shift if we change price levels or structures?
- What is the optimal price level/structure in order to maximize our revenues?
- What is the optimal price level/structure in order to maximize our profits?

To get the right answers to these critical questions, a well-structured pricing process is the key. If there are no clear, convincing answers, any business plan based upon silver needs is based on guessing and benevolence rather than on profit orientation.

Price Is the Primary Profit Driver

Assume a bank sells its silver market-oriented account package for ¥10,000 and its sales volume is one million units. The variable costs per unit (sales, back office processing, etc.) are ¥8,000, resulting in a contribution margin of ¥2,000 per unit.

A 10% improvement in...   **... leads to a profit increase of...**

	Profit Driver		Profit (Yen)		
	Old	New	Old	New	
Price (monthly account fee)	10,000	11,000	1.0 b	2.0 b	100%
Variable unit cost	8000	7200	1.0 b	1.8 b	80%
Sales volume	1 m	1.1 m	1.0 b	1.2 b	20%
Fixed cost	1.0 b	0.9 b	1.0 b	1.1 b	10%

To be read as follows: **A 10% price improvement brings the price up to 11,000 Yen. Everything else unchanged, this increases profit by 100% to 2.0 billionYen.**

Fig. 12.2 Impact of profit drivers

The bank's fixed costs are ¥1 billion. In this situation, the bank earns a profit of ¥1 billion [= (¥10,000–8,000) per unit × 1 million units − ¥1 billion fixed costs]. How does each of the four profit drivers – price, variable costs, volume, and fixed costs – change profit when improved by 10%?

A 10% increase in price (¥10,000 to ¥11,000) leads (*ceteris paribus*) to a profit increase of 100%, from ¥1 billion to ¥2 billion. The effect of the other profit drivers is clearly lower. A 10% improvement of variable costs, volume, and fixed costs (*ceteris paribus*) would yield a profit increase of 80, 20, and 10% respectively. This simple yet typical example undermines the key role of pricing. This is especially true in situations where unit margins are low (Fig. 12.2).

To facilitate the decision of whether to raise or lower prices, Fig. 12.3 shows the impact of price changes depending on different cost–income ratios. The percentages given in the tables indicate how much volume has to be gained (price reduction) or can be lost (price increase) in order to keep the cost–income ratio constant. The silver marketer should change a price only if the expected effect on volume is higher/lower than the given percentages. For example: at a cost–income ratio of 0.75, a price reduction of 10% increases profit only if a volume increase of 67% or more is expected. A 10% increase in price increases profit only if the volume decrease is less than 29%.

Increased margins stimulated by professional pricing immediately increase profit and do not require expensive upfront investments or severance payments. Relative to cost-cutting, price optimization offers three opportunities: it gains time, avoids additional upfront expenses, and has a stronger impact on profit. So, the crucial question is: how can these profit potentials be leveraged effectively?

Price Reduction in %	Cost-Income-Ratio*												
	0.95	0.90	0.85	0.80	0.75	0.70	0.65	0.60	0.55	0.50	0.45	0.40	0.35
	Increase of Volume in % to keep Contribution Margin constant												
2.0	67	25	15	11	8.7	7.1	6.1	5.3	4.7	4.2	3.8	3.4	3.2
3.0	150	43	25	18	14	11	9.4	8.1	7.1	6.4	5.8	5.3	4.8
4.0	400	67	36	25	19	15	13	11	9.8	8.7	7.8	7.1	6.6
5.0		100	50	33	25	20	17	14	13	11	10	9.1	8.3
7.5		300	100	60	43	33	27	23	20	18	16	14	13
10.0			200	100	67	50	40	33	29	25	22	20	18.2
15.0				300	150	100	75	60	50	43	38	33	30
30.0							600	300	200	150	120	100	86
40.0									800	400	267	200	160

Price Increase in %	Cost-Income-Ratio**												
	0.95	0.90	0.85	0.80	0.75	0.70	0.65	0.60	0.55	0.50	0.45	0.40	0.35
	Decrease of Volume in % to keep Contribution Margin constant												
2.0	29	17	12	9.1	7.4	6.3	5.4	4.8	4.3	3.8	3.5	3.2	3
3.0	38	23	17	13	11	9.1	7.9	7	6.3	5.7	5.2	4.8	4.4
4.0	44	29	21	17	14	12	10	9.1	8.2	7.4	6.8	6.3	5.8
5.0	50	33	25	20	17	14	13	11	10	9.1	8.3	7.7	7.1
7.5	60	43	33	27	23	20	18	16	14	13	12	11	10
10.0	67	50	40	33	29	25	22	20	18	17	15.0	14	13
15.0	75	60	50	43	38	33	30	27	25	23	21	20	19
30.0	86	75	67	60	55	50	46	43	40	38	35	33	32
40.0	89	80	73	67	62	57	53	50	47	44	42	40	38

* reads: At a price reduction of 10% and a cost-income-ratio of 0.75, an increase in volume of 67% is required to keep contribution margin constant.

** reads: At a price increase of 10% and a cost income-ratio of 0.75, volume can decrease by 29% to keep contribution margin constant.

Fig. 12.3 Decision table for price reductions and price increases

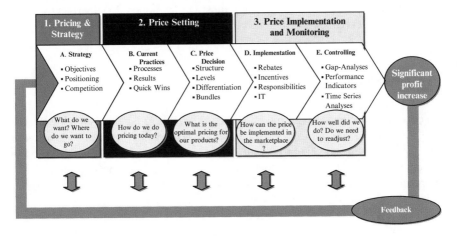

Fig. 12.4 Five phases of the pricing process

Pricing Process

"Simple" price increases are risky and mostly do not result in the projected effects. Just increasing existing prices or ordering sales staff to negotiate higher prices with silver customers will fail. Silver marketers must use an effective pricing process. A pricing process is a system of organizational rules, guidelines, and measures intended to determine, manage, and implement prices. When companies offer a large number of products, or prices are negotiated for each transaction, pricing processes are crucial. However, due to the high number of necessary price decisions, the effort involved in each decision has to be limited. Precisely defined processes are required to determine and implement prices and thereby garner optimal yields (Fig. 12.4).

A professional pricing process usually includes five basic steps: strategy, analysis, decision, implementation, and monitoring.

Pricing Strategy

The pricing strategy and vision should be developed well before the new product (or service) is launched. Typically the strategy is formulated in the early stages of product development, when there is already a clear concept and fixed specifications. The product managers in particular are responsible for creating the guidelines and framework for future pricing within the product strategy. The pricing strategy must involve a clear strategy for the market entry (skimming or penetration), premium potentials, lifecycle aspects, and regional differentiation where necessary and possible. Likewise, the pricing strategy must be developed for other new aspects such as parts, services, equipment, etc.

Price Analysis

To develop a pricing strategy and optimize prices, it is critical that all relevant data be collected and the right analyses be applied. These steps are basic elements of pricing processes and should be well-structured and considered as standard. The information regarding the strategic triangle – silver customers, products, and competitors – must be complete to ensure that pricing is performed correctly using all relevant data. Among the typical questions to be answered are: How successful are today's pricing processes? Which data and information is necessary for an optimal pricing decision? Which methods are used? How important is the price in the purchase decision process? How do the competitive situation and price–value relationships look from the silver customers' perspective?

Price Decision

The price decision determines the optimal price and is subsequently confirmed by the decision-makers. It is clear that all parties involved in the price decision must understand which price is being analyzed (list price, discounted price, transaction price, with/without VAT, etc.), for which product, in which configuration, and for which channel and/or region.

The value-based approach to pricing comes into play here. Cost-plus and competition-based pricing provide a certain range, but are not directly interrelated with the silver customer's buying decision. For example, the baby boomer couple looking for a brain-training video game do not care about the development and distribution costs of the software vendor. Neither are silver customers willing or able to compare the highly complex price–product architectures of competing medical insurance products. However, they know what they want and what they are willing to pay. Hence the best way to conduct silver pricing is to consider customer requirements, value-to-customer, and the customers' willingness to pay. To understand and quantify these factors, indirect, multivariate methods deliver the most accurate results. A particularly powerful approach is conjoint measurement. A conjoint measurement exercise basically simulates the real buying decision with real customers (through focus groups or telephone/web-based interviews). Because the customer has to indicate preferences for realistic price–product configurations, the pitfalls of direct, price-oriented methods are avoided. The buying decision is always a trade-off between the value the product delivers and the price. The most sophisticated versions of conjoint measurement are adaptive, i.e., the computer generates realistic product/price pair comparisons based on the previous answers. After 20 or 30 of these pair comparisons, the value structure of the individual customer is sufficiently understood. The relative utilities of the key attributes can be compared and the willingness-to-pay for different levels of each attribute and for the entire product can be calculated. By aggregating preference patterns, distinctive customer segments emerge. Such a value-based segmentation is extremely effective when it comes to designing new products and services for the silver market.

Further, up- and cross-selling potentials need to be taken into account. *Upselling*: what is the optimal price gap between a standard and a premium product in order to optimize total profits? *Cross-selling*: how would silver customers react to bundling offers? This field provides tremendous opportunities for smart silver marketers, especially in sectors in which convenience plays a larger role. For example, a car package that includes an easy-entry option as well as an insurance package pinpointed to the needs of the older generation (e.g., including travel repatriation insurance) might be an attractive offering. The same holds true in the insurance sector, where various policy types (e.g., health and life insurance) can be sold at a package price, profiting from extremely low additional sales costs.

Price Implementation

After determining optimal price levels and structures, implementation is key. It calls for a functioning organization, process/goal-oriented organization, effective IT systems, and clever incentive systems for both sales people and customers.

Pricing organization, especially in Japan, is an often overlooked success factor. A professional pricing organization has to set the framework for successful pricing processes. This involves clear responsibilities, availability of relevant information, and a structured feedback system to enable lessons to be learned from the past.

Clear responsibilities are the cornerstone of all pricing issues. In many cases responsibilities are not clearly defined. They vary for different pricing tasks and between divisions. Quite often, responsibility is borne by a group rather than a single individual.

There has to be a clear process owner for all relevant processes within price management. This process owner is responsible for the timely and correct execution of the process as well as for the involvement of relevant experts and the outcome of the process. As an important side effect, the responsible person can be easily identified by the company's employees who are not involved in the process in question.

The existence of a pricing department facilitates (but does not guarantee) the development of a formalized pricing process. A more important factor seems to be a direct link to senior management and good awareness at that level of the importance of pricing. If pricing is conducted decentrally, clear guidelines and monitoring are necessary.

Monitoring

Monitoring is an essential element in pricing to increase profitability. The implementation of the prices has to be checked continuously and adjusted if necessary. Daily statistics and transaction price studies support the checking and adjusting tasks by identifying negative price developments. This information also serves as input data for the initial pricing step. Key questions to be answered are: Which prices have been achieved in the market? How did prices, revenues and profits develop? Where and why have target prices not been reached?

Summary and Conclusion

The silver market offers tremendous potential, but it also harbors a lot of uncertainties and potential pitfalls. A business strategy based solely on demographic and socioeconomic data, customer needs and buying power is simplistic, misleading, and in some cases dangerous. This is even true for top-notch Western companies, whose Japanese ventures recently failed: Vodafone, Carrefour, Prêt à Manger, eBay and, in the 1980s, IKEA, to name just a few. Of course there are specific reasons in each of these cases – wrong hiring decisions on country manager level, lack of suitable sites in order to gain scale advantages and concessions from Japanese suppliers, insufficient will to invest in Japan-specific product design and infrastructure, roll-out of an American-centric service model, etc. But all of them "suffered from rather serious lapses of judgment, employed flawed strategies and demonstrated a lack of understanding in regard to both the dynamics of the market to which they had come, and the highly particular demands of the Japanese consumer" [8].

Note that most of these businesses focused on the younger generation, which has been thoroughly studied by marketers for decades. The uncharted territory of the silver market bears a significantly higher risk of failing. Capitalizing on this market, with its specific value structure and peculiarities, requires a systematic approach to developing and profitably selling products and services tailored to the older generation. Specifically, it takes a clear, solid understanding of customer requirements, value-to-customer, willingness to pay, price elasticities, and revenue and profit functions to be successful in this attractive, but also difficult market. The best way to achieve this is by means of a well-structured, professional pricing process covering and connecting pricing strategy, price setting, and price implementation.

References

1. Cabinet Office, *White paper on aging society* (Government of Japan, Tokyo, 2007)
2. Dai-Ichi Life Research Institute, *Following the first baby-boom generation's money: where the savings of the elderly go*, (Dai-Ichi Life Research Institute, Tokyo, 2005)
3. Financial Times, Deutschland, 4 June 2005
4. Japan Times, 4 Oct 2007
5. McKinsey Global Institute, *The coming demographic deficit: how aging populations will reduce global savings* (McKinsey and Company, Chicago, 2005)
6. B.P. Bosworth, R.C. Bryant, G. Burtless, *The impact of aging on financial markets and the economy: a survey* (Brookings Institution, Washington DC, 2004)
7. The Nikkei Weekly, 1 Oct 2007, p. 12
8. G. Lane, *Failed businesses in Japan*, Japan Inc 7/2007, p. 6

Chapter 13
Changing Consumer Values and Behavior in Japan: Adaptation of Keio Department Store, Shinjuku

Nozomi Enomoto

Abstract Japan has been the most aged society in the world since the early 1990s. Retailers in Japan now face various changes in the business environment – including demographic change, economic globalization, development of information technology, and changes in consumer values and behavior. Consumer values and behavior in Japan reflect a characteristic transition in the retail sector, in which department stores have been a major force. The Keio Department Store Co. Ltd (Keio Department Store Co. Ltd. runs two department stores, and sales at Keio Department Store, Shinjuku accounts for nearly 90% of their revenue) in Shinjuku has been gearing its business toward seniors since the mid-1990s. The purpose of this study is to examine how an organization adapts to a changing business environment by exploring Keio Department Store, Shinjuku as a case of a senior-focused retailer, extracting factors that are important in tailoring business practices.

Introduction

Learning from Western department stores, Japanese department stores have developed in their socioeconomic and cultural characteristics since their introduction in 1904, and held a dominant position in the retail sector in Japan for many years. However, when Japan entered a period of slow economic growth after the first oil crises in 1973, department stores experienced diminished sales. This revealed an inherent weakness of traditional department stores, and they seemed incapable of responding to changes in the competitive environment and to changing consumer values and behavior, particularly after the 1980s. Further, the shortsighted downsizing of merchandising efforts in the wake of plummeting sales after the 1991 collapse of Japan's bubble economy served only to make the department stores even more ill-equipped to attract customers during tough times.

Given such circumstances, Keio Department Store, Shinjuku (Keio) reached a turning point, combined with a fierce battle with a new Takashimaya department store in Shinjuku in 1996. Keio's strategic innovation in adapting to a changing business environment was to differentiate itself by making seniors its target

F. Kohlbacher and C. Herstatt (eds.), *The Silver Market Phenomenon*,
DOI 10.1007/978-3-642-14338-0_13, © Springer-Verlag Berlin Heidelberg 2011

demographic. To analyze Keio's external environment, the changing business environment, along with consumer values and behavior, will be explored in the following sections from the perspective of factors in the change and transition of the retail sector in Japan.

Mechanism and Factors in Changing Values and Lifestyle

Japan's current dynamic social environment, combined with economic globalization and the development of information technology, largely influences the diversification of people's lifestyles and values. With constant access to new information and knowledge, people become more tolerant toward different ways of thinking. The infiltration of the Internet and other information technology into everyday life has not only diversified people's lifestyles and values but also their personal relations and communication styles. Between 1997 and 2006, the number of Internet users increased from 11.55 million to 87.54 million, and the user diffusion rate jumped from 9.2 to 68.5% ([1], p. 28). In today's society, family members live far away from one another for educational or employment reasons. The number of Japanese students studying abroad, for example, increased from 14,297 to 82,925 between 1985 and 2004 [2]. Likewise, the number of foreign students in Japan increased from 10,428 to 121,812 between 1983 and 2005 [2]. Such exposure to a new social environment increases individuals' drive to seek out new information and pursue their own styles; in the past, such information was conventionally limited, and mostly received in a passive manner.

Weakened demand for traditions or customs is one indication of the diversification of values and lifestyles. People now enjoy their own time in their own way and value leisure time a great deal, but this was not always the case in the past. Valuing personal leisure time has influenced people's perspectives on conventional marriage, for example. Along with the increase in marriages later in life, the number of unmarried people in their 20s and early 30s has been increasing dramatically. The percentage of single people increased from 18 to 54% between 1970 and 2000, with more than half of all women in their late 20s unmarried. In addition, the percentage of unmarried men in their late 30s increased from 12 to 43% during the same period. Because people still tend to have children after marriage in Japan, the decline in the marriage rate has led to a decline in the birth rate [3].

The enactment of laws and regulations can also be a factor that influences demographic change and values and lifestyle diversification. For example, the Equal Employment Opportunity Law, enacted in 1985, encourages women to be economically independent. When women pursue careers and their work is incompatible with childcare, fewer women have children. In terms of the declining birth rate, the gradual downward tendency continued into the late 1980s, and the rate hit its lowest postwar record of 1.29 live births per woman in 2003. The number of children born per year was about two million in the first half of the 1970s, but decreased to around 1.1 million in 2006 [3].

Other environmental factors that influence changes in values and lifestyles are the spread of epidemics – such as avian flu and tainted food – along with natural or man-made disasters that result in greater concern for disease prevention and security. This heightened concern promotes consumer demand for safer, healthier food and other health-related goods. These factors drive changing values and lifestyles, as only a few examples of the mechanisms to be explored in how the diversification of values and lifestyles affects – and is affected by – ever-changing natural and social environments. Although it would be difficult to specify factors that influence consumer values and behavior and analyze their degree of importance, it is crucial to accept the viewpoint that values, lifestyles, and changing natural and social environments mutually influence one another, particularly for long-term assumptions about the business environment.

Figure 13.1 shows the mechanism of change, and the key factors that interact with one another in society, lifestyle, and values.

Transition of Department Stores and the Retail Sector in Japan

Consumer values and behavior in Japan generally reflect the characteristic transition in the retail sector. In the early post-war period, consumer demand was almost exclusively for daily necessities. However, the demand picture changed as

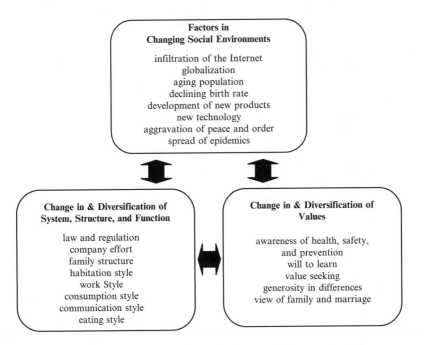

Fig. 13.1 Mechanism of change and key factors that interact with one another in Japan
Source: author's figure

production and distribution of consumer goods increased and retail formats transformed. The growth in consumer demand allowed the growth of new retail formats ([4], p. 38). The department store was the first retail format, and played an important role in the development of the retail sector in Japan. In the following sections, the transitions of department stores and the retail sector will be explored from the perspective of the changing external business environment.

Early Stage of Department Store Development

The prewar distribution system in Japan – characterized by a multilayered, complex system with a surplus number of small-scale retailers in relation to population – was often blamed for structural weakness, low effectiveness, and high distribution costs compared with that of Europe and the United States ([5], p. 4). Therefore, the introduction and the development of the department store had a great impact on distribution and retail businesses. Learning from Western department stores, the long-standing Mitsukoshi Gofuku-ten (Mitsukoshi Mercer Store) declared itself a "department store" in 1904, named itself Mitsukoshi Department Store, and targeted wealth in its early stages. After Mitsukoshi's reorganization, other major dry goods stores – including Matuzakaya, Takashimaya, and Daimaru – followed ([6], pp. 27–28). Compared with other small retailers, the department stores were characterized by size and the wide selection of the latest high-grade goods ([7], p. 2).

However, the Great Kanto Earthquake in 1923 was an historic turning point for the department stores ([4], p. 18). The existing department stores in Tokyo began gearing their business toward seeking popularization and expansion of their customer base. As Jinbo cited from the histories of some major department stores, one of the main reasons for this change in direction was to fulfill a market need at the time. Most general retail stores had been destroyed by fire and the department stores that were quickly able to restore operations played a role in supplying daily necessities to the public ([6], pp. 28–29).

In addition, a new type of department store – selling necessities such as food and household goods, with capital from the private railway companies – emerged in the late 1920s at the start of suburban rail services. As competition among department stores intensified, friction arose between the department stores and the small- and medium-sized retailers. As a result, the Department Store Law was passed in 1937, and control over the department stores was strengthened ([6], p. 30).

Dynamic Change in Retail Formats with Economic Growth

With the economic boom that followed the Korean War, Japan enjoyed unprecedented prosperity from the mid-1950s to the early 1970s. Its prewar retailing system, consisting of a few powerful department stores and countless small- and medium-sized retailers, revived. Despite the fact that the Department Store Law, originally enacted with the aim of ensuring business opportunities for small- and medium-sized retailers, was reintroduced in 1956 ([4], p. 38), the department stores remained remarkably competitive until the early 1970s. The number of railway-station department stores, for example, increased rapidly from the 1950s to the mid-1960s, along with growth of the suburban population ([6], p. 32).

With rapid economic growth, a standardized mass popularized consumption market appeared, and large-scale retail businesses developed during the 1960s. These new retail formats formed the base of the modern distribution establishments (e.g., large-scale household-appliance specialty stores), that did not have affiliated conventional distribution channels, along with chain stores. The outstanding development of chain stores, particularly general superstores, shook the nationwide retail sector, and sales volume of the superstore segment surpassed that of the department stores in 1972 ([8], p. 59).

The first oil crisis in 1973 led Japan into a recession. At the same time, enactment of the Large-Scale Retail Store Law in 1973 hardened distribution and retail systems, affecting the rapid growth of the superstore segment. Instead, the popular consumption market disintegrated into many market segments, and the retail sector became more diverse. The number of retailers whose business activities targeted specific parts of the subdivided consumption market increased rapidly. Further, with the growth in personal automobile ownership, the radius of shopping expanded. Large roadside specialty stores dealing in such items as toys and menswear appeared, along with suburban shopping centers. Convenience stores opened in the mid-1970s and later developed with multifunctional services, including ATMs and home delivery ([9], pp. 75–81). At the same time, general superstores and department stores adopted a market segmentation strategy and sought differentiation and identity. Thus, new retail formats and the innovations in traditional business appeared one after another during the 1970s.

Falling into Functional Insufficiency

Through the 1970s, 1980s, and 1990s, Japanese department stores had sluggish sales, except for a short-lived recovery between 1986 and 1991 – the days of the bubble economy. The weaknesses of Japanese department stores during this time were revealed in their functions and systems: their multifunctional structure included features such as cultural exhibitions, theaters, special displays, playgrounds, and restaurants to attract customers. While "multifunctional" became characteristic of a Japanese department store, it caused malfunctions ([10], p. 61). Another important characteristic of Japanese department stores that should be pointed out is an outsourcing system of merchandising, using temporary sales staff. The system was introduced by an apparel wholesaler to gain competitiveness in 1953. The system was mutually beneficial for avoiding the risk of absorbing losses from unsold goods, and knowledgeable salespersons were sent to the department stores. Looking at this risk reduction, the system spread among department stores across the country, and department stores saw sales grow until the early 1970s ([6], pp. 39–40). However, this system ultimately resulted in a weakness in department stores in the area of their own managerial capabilities and lack of integrated management – and, above all, limited room for creating differentiation and innovations.

The weakened integrated management capability of these retailers was evidenced by their practices after a protracted recession and the collapse of the bubble economy in the early 1990s. To cut costs, conventional functions and merchandising were reduced and externalized during this restructuring period. Departments such as women's apparel and medical supplies were expanded while furniture, household appliances, and sporting goods were eliminated. For example, sales of women's clothing rose from 21.5 to 25.3% of the total sales volume in Japanese department stores between 1991 and 2001, whereas sales from furniture fell from 6.0 to 2.7% ([11], p. 9).

In addition, many large specialty retailers – including Bic Camera, Yodobashi Camera, Best Denki, and Otsuka Furniture – opened concessions within department stores. Urban department stores such as Kyoto Kintetsu, Shinjuku Mitsukoshi, and Sukiyabashi Hankyu converted parts of their buildings for such tenant use ([10], p. 62). Such measures further reduced the effectiveness of department stores' management and innovation. In addition, they created similar merchandise selections and compromised a store's unique characteristics. Thus, while strong administrative management capability was required for Japanese department stores, the reforms narrowed the management range by externalizing merchandise dealings. In other words, Japanese department stores diverged from their originality of functions and innovations. The department stores' resulting inertia made them incapable of responding to changes in the competitive environment and to changing consumer values and behavior after the 1980s.[1]

Changing Consumer Values and Behavior

Consumer demand was commonly for daily necessities as it was in the early postwar period. However, this changed with the increased production and distribution of consumer goods. When Japan experienced rapid economic growth for a period of about 20 years starting in 1955, the demand for daily necessities was met, and people moved on to fulfilling special needs ([4], p. 33). However, consumer values and behavior at that stage were still characterized as conformist, largely due

---

[1]Sales from the non-core business of among department stores continued to expand. One of the outstanding movements can be seen in Nikkei's forecast in February 2010 that Takashimaya's non-core business income, mostly supported by real estate business, accounts for 71.8% of its consolidated income, 32.4 points up from the previous February [12].

to the appearance of a standardized, large-scale, popularized consumption market accompanied by the development of a mass-targeted retail sector.

When the postwar economic boom ended with the first oil crisis in 1973, many consumers became more selective and started seeking individual lifestyles. At the same time, the popular consumption market fragmented into numerous segments. The remarkable tendencies seen in the early 1980s included a differentiated quality-of-life orientation, fashion orientation, and smart consumption. The various combinations of these orientations made for extreme diversity ([5], pp. 13–14).

Younger people respect diversity more than traditional ways. These trends reverse for both men and women in their 40s. Views of marriage are today becoming liberalized, drifting away from the traditional mindset that "one should get married" ([13], p. 10). The number of households with no children is increasing, and more people live alone. This is also true among seniors. However, more consumers accept word-of-mouth as a reliable opinion, via Internet and communication with family and friends ([13], p. 13).

Different approaches and research studies have revealed certain trends in consumer' values and behavior. For example, consumers enjoy more relaxation services in their free time, and they pursue lifestyles and consumption patterns that attach great importance to their individuality. Accordingly, consciousness in terms of collecting and searching for information about lifestyles has increased. "The cheaper, the better," a dominant sentiment in the 1970s, is no longer the most important issue for consumers ([14], pp. 9–10).

Japanese consumers have traditionally been described as displaying "bipolarization": a high-grade orientation toward buying goods regardless of the price, and price-oriented to buying inexpensive goods without being particular. Shiozaki's research group suggests a new framework for analysis of current consumers' behavioral patterns. By setting high and low prices on the vertical axis, and setting stronger and weaker particularities about things toward the right and left on the horizontal axis, consumers' behavioral patterns can be classified into four styles: high-grade seeker, convenience seeker regardless of price, reasonable-price seeker of particular things, and price seeker (i.e., "the cheaper, the better") ([14], pp. 15–18). The increased number of Internet users reveals that customers enjoy a social environment which makes it easy for them to search for information. Also, even when divided into the four categories, individuals change their inclination depending on items and occasions. Although the percentage and absolute number of people in each group are not shown, the obvious trend is toward diverse consumer values and behavior, with more careful consideration of purchases by way of searching and collecting reliable information.

Even among seniors, their consumption styles tend to "involve caring about the reputation or comments from other people about the product" or to "examine whether a price is reasonable for good quality." For example, in research conducted in 2000, 2003, and 2006, the numbers of male and female consumers who considered the validity of price and quality increased. Likewise, the number of seniors who are particular about what they want is also increasing, especially among males ([15], pp. 24–25).

According to research performed by the Bank of Japan, the individual propensity to consume is strong even among youths, and has been particularly remarkable among seniors in recent years. The factors in seniors' consumption trends could be structural factors of demographic change, such as the aging population, changes in consumer values and company efforts, and the introduction of the nursing-care insurance system. Generally, the propensity to consume decreases from youth to middle age, and then increases with age. Taking a long-term view of the propensity to consume, a cohort analysis was also applied in order to break down the propensity into the age effect, the generation effect, and the period effect. As a result, it has been confirmed that the change in the composition of the aging population steadily increases the overall propensity among that population to consume ([16], pp. 11–18).

In terms of changing lifestyles, seniors who have more financial security want to "enjoy life." Businesses view "active seniors" who can afford to buy as an important target group. A trend in a "tertiary industry activity index" shows that travel agencies, fitness clubs, and bars are experiencing high growth rates. Expanding distribution channels for consumption include convenience stores, drugstores, specialty stores, and shopping malls, as well as TV and online shopping. However, a study from Nomura Research Institute clearly shows that seniors are more inclined to go the way of one-stop shopping (purchasing as many items as possible at one store) than are consumers of other generations, and the radius of consumption for seniors is smaller [7]. This means that distant and large-sized stores are not appropriate for frequent patronage by seniors.

Thus, Japanese consumer values and behavior are, in general, becoming more diverse and increasingly oriented toward quality of life in terms of health, safety, and relaxation than they were in the 1960s. They are also more selective and wary of value-oriented consumption. All of these trends can be seen among consumers regardless of their generation, except in a physical domain such as consumption radius.

Case Study: Keio Department Store, Shinjuku

Keio Department Store, Shinjuku, a subsidiary of Keio Electric Railway Company, opened in 1964. It is located at Shinjuku Station, which, serving ten railway and subway lines, is the busiest station in Japan. In addition, Shinjuku is the country's most competitive area for department stores in terms of number of commercial facilities, restaurants, and crowded offices. It is home to several major department stores.

At Keio, customers over 50 years of age account for about 70% of sales, and the constituent percentage of seniors is higher than at other department stores. Pioneering among department stores in Japan, Keio has its own customer membership system, giving members discounts or vouchers depending on the amount of installment savings, for example, over the course of 12 months. Customers who were in their 20s or 30s when the store opened are now in their 50s or 60s. As for the number of member cardholders, according to the age groups of Keio Department Store, Shinjuku customers in 2004, 55–57 is the highest 3-year bracket, and the majority are in their 50s and 60s. Most of those who purchase are in their 50s, 60s, or 70s. The growth rate is particularly marked among people in their 40s and 50s. People in their 50s and 60s purchase the most, and 73% of sales in 2004 were to those 50 or over [17].

Subdividing Senior Customers into Even Smaller Categories

When business apparel and clothing for the younger generations led women's consumption, merchandise for middle-aged or senior people was normally grouped together with full-line and full-targeted selections. However, at Keio, analysis of its customer data and studies of other research results revealed clearer characteristics and trends regarding its senior female customers, and led to subdivision into even smaller groups, corresponding to the diverse values and characteristics of its senior customers: over 65, 55–64, and 40–54 for senior people, and another category for people under 40.

Keio views the first group (over 65), the prewar generation, as having a tendency for sound consumption and a mindset for saving. They do buy new things and enjoy casual opportunities for postwar values, but still need a reason for consumption. Keio appeals to their style with an intellectual, innovative image.

The second senior group (55–64), the first baby boomer generation, shares values with the younger generation. They have information from overseas and an interest in traveling and leisure. They are authenticity-oriented but still conservative. People of this generation pay more attention to their private lives than the older generation, and are not like eager beavers devoting their lives to work. This group still values individuality and word-of-mouth information from family and friends. This leads to a great deal of consumption power. Their interest in anti- and healthy-aging products is also very high. Keio believes that nice-looking, good-quality materials are important to this generation. They also appeal to the younger generation's consciousness in an international sense.

The third senior group (40–54), the post-baby boomers, is a strategically targeted generation. They do not hesitate to buy expensive, brand-name items with an international and youthful style. In fact, individual consumption unit price is higher than that paid by customers in their 60s, according to Keio's data.

Then there are the junior baby boomers, who are below 40 and go for young career fashion. Thus, Keio has developed a clear concept of generational characteristics. However, this subdivision of seniors is a subgroup within a classification, and characteristics of these divisions overlap and remain invisible.

Keio's incremental renovation in the fall of 2006 concentrated on the second, third, and fourth floors as a part of a 5-year renovation project (2003–2007). The following shows the arrangement of Keio's customer categories and relevant selections on each floor during the renovation.

Subdivision of Customer Category

- Category A: Prewar generation
- Category B: Baby boomer generation (the most important target)
- Category C: Post-baby boomer generation (a strategic target)
- Category D: Junior baby boomer generation

Targeted Categories and Women's Apparel Floor Layout: The Second, Third, and Fourth Floors

- Fourth floor: Most targeted category is A (plus categories B, C, and D as A's daughters)
- Third floor: Most targeted categories are B and C (plus categories A and D)
- Second floor: Most targeted category is D (plus categories B, C, and A as D's mothers)

In the women's sections (from the second to the fourth floor), the department store rearranged the fourth floor in 1995, making it easier for customers in their 50s and 60s to navigate. For example, based on Keio's customer survey data analysis, travel was the highest-ranking purchase motive. Keio has taken its customers' consumption habits and tastes into account and applied them to a substantiality of selection, price range, and, above all, quality customer service. As a result, sales on the fourth floor increased by 7.8% from 1995 to 2005.

The renovation on the fourth floor was aimed at improving satisfaction among existing customers. To avoid alienating them with a new and unfamiliar layout while intensifying its youthful image, the floor layout was kept intact. The image has been changed most daringly on the renovated third floor, which Keio considers important, as it is supported by a wide range of generations. The purpose of that renovation was to expand the brands supported by the strategic target (the post-baby boomers) and to boost sales and increase migration by the most important target, the baby boomer generation (Category B). As a result, sales on the third floor increased by 20%, and sales on the fourth floor achieved 10% growth, according to data from 20 days after the renovation in September ([18], pp. 74–77).

Selections

Consistent with its diverse values, Keio has some items designed just for seniors (e.g., women's clothes, with subdivisions in terms of sizes, colors, and designs).

Keio has also developed its own original brand for seniors. For example, Keio has achieved the top sales in Japan for its sweaters. In 2007, its sales from April to September increased by 7% from 2001. Bathing-suit sales increased by 15% in the 3 years after it shifted the selection from seasonal to sport swimsuits for year-round purchases in 2002 ([19], p. 14).

After the women's hat corner was revised in 1998, it also became a big profit maker, with 300 million yen annual turnover, the top sales in Japan for hats. Keio enlarged its selection by marketing hats as a method of sun protection and for covering hair in a fashionable way. In 1995, Keio established the walking shoes corner, which was the first of its kind among department stores in Japan. For a customer who has foot trouble, Keio is easy to access from the station. Keio's selections also correspond to different types of feet. All of these selections are based on the top-ranked values among its customers (e.g., leisure, health, relaxation, and safety). For sports shoes, counter sales in 2006 increased by 80% from 2001, and sales from April to September 2007 increased by 85% over 2001 levels. Additionally, in 2006, sales at the town walking-shoes corner from April to September increased by 40% from the first half of 2001 and 47% in 2007 from 2001. These are also the country's top sales in this kind of section [17]. Figure 13.2 shows sales in the store and on the fourth floor at Keio Department Store, Shinjuku.

Following the collapse of the bubble economy, private consumption gradually recovered after the fall of 1993 and then increased from late 1996 to early 1997, accompanied by front-loading expansion of spending prior to the consumption-tax hike from 3% to 5% in April 1997 [20]. Accordingly, Keio sees the decline of 1997 as the aftermath of the expansion of consumption in the previous year. The decline

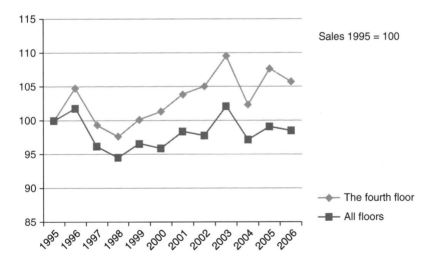

Fig. 13.2 Sales at Keio Department Store, Shinjuku
Source: Keio Department Store Co. Ltd.

in 2004 is reaction to "the baseball team championship sale" of 2003 and full-scale remodeling construction. Typically, railway companies in Japan nowadays hold businesses in sectors such as transportation, real estate, retail, travel, and leisure. However, some railway companies used to own baseball teams in the hopes of transporting fans to and from stadiums, thus adding value to the route. Not as many railway companies in Japan today own professional baseball teams, as compared with the 1960s. Hanshin Electric Railway Co., owner of the Hanshin Tigers, is one of the few that still do. Keio Corporation, which is a railway company, does not own a baseball team. However, because of its collaborative relationship with Hanshin Department Store, whose parent company is Hanshin Electric Railway Co., it holds a sale when the Hanshin Tigers reach the championships.

Sales growth for 2003 and 2005 was exceptional because of the baseball championship sales carried out in those years. In particular, in 2003 the Hanshin Tigers won for the first time in 18 years, which created a social phenomenon involving a wide range of people cheering the team across the country. Over 120,000 people flooded into the store on the first day of the sale. The usual number is about 70,000 a day. Interestingly, the influence of these sales appeared in the middle and senior age groups which came to the fourth floor, showing a conspicuously strong reaction to the sale.

For Quality Communications and Accurate Marketing

One of the characteristics of Japanese consumers that Chen pointed out is that they are among the most demanding in the world regarding service and quality: complete fitness, absolute freshness of produce, swiftness of delivery, and so forth ([21], p. 234). Additionally, Japanese consumers have close relationships with their small neighborhood shops, and such shops offer an important opportunity for socializing. Likewise, department stores offer a similar function as centers of social life and have close relationships with customers. Therefore, Japanese shops and stores in general are highly service-oriented and make the needs of their customers their top priority ([21], p. 228). One research result showed that seniors react less to trends and advertisements ([22], pp. 52–53). Accordingly, based on Keio's research, word-of-mouth is the most reliable information source for both Keio and its customers, particularly seniors. Therefore, quality customer service becomes especially important when its customers with diverse values rely on word of mouth. To improve customer service and communication, Keio Department Store, Shinjuku provides full-scale training, conferring qualifications of Service Advisors on those who complete the training, and increased the number of Shopping Advisors (from 34 to 64) and of Color Advisors (from 21 to 45) in 2007. Keio plans to increase these numbers further in the coming years.

Keio Department Store, Shinjuku strives to understand the changes in consumer values and behavior, and to apply them to its marketing arrangements based on knowledge and information analysis. According to an analysis of consumers in general and of Keio's in particular, more seniors want to enjoy life, and they are shifting to a more casual, health-conscious, and beauty-conscious approach to life. One example of Keio's arrangement for these senior customers is that half of the women's clothing floor is arranged by item so that customers can choose clothes according to price, size, and color lines by themselves, not brand. To meet with the increasing consumer values in "things for killing time" (such as trips, events, or cultural pursuits, which are increasing in popularity in department stores), what Keio focuses on is the stated values and purposes of its customers (e.g., merchandise to relax or for a trip). Playground equipment and sporting goods, which were once reduced along with other merchandising systems during restructuring after the collapse of the bubble economy, have returned to Keio, creating three-generational shopping. Thus, Keio's strategy is not to create new values or trends but to realize its own customers' needs, anticipating what customers want and need. It integrates hypotheses and verifications from analysis based on collected information through communications with some of its 70,000 daily customers. Therefore, its renovation is carried out according to a 5- or 10-year plan.

All of these efforts in merchandise arrangement are consistent with making effective use of information systems, which became a drive to promote Keio's senior-targeted marketing. Keio introduced a data warehouse information system in 1996, around the time when it started to gear its business toward seniors. Through cross-analysis of customer and merchandise information data, according to Hoksaka, a director of sale planning at Keio Department Store Co. Ltd., the introduction of a new data warehouse netted positive results in caring, for example, about the characteristics of each customer, about when, which target, and what kind of direct mail should be sent, and about the results of and feedbacks of measures taken based on data analysis. In fact, Keio was introduced as an advanced case of data warehouse introduction at an international conference hosted by a users' group in October 2009 [23].

After Being Dragged into an Economic Recession

After the first edition of the book was published, economic recession and financial crisis placed department stores nationwide in an even worse situation; it was particularly severe in those department stores with low responsiveness to the changing business environment. Sales of existing department stores have been below the previous year 13 years in a row in 2009 [24]. Poor sales are obvious in areas dealing with expensive items, such as watches and jewels, and clothing targeting the younger generation. In addition, newly emerging fashionable low-price women's clothing megastores, such as UNIQLO and H&M, drew younger customers from department stores. The nationwide department store sales in 2008 fell below that of the previous year, accounting for 95% of the total 227 department stores surveyed. Top-ranked seller Mitsukoshi Tokyo (−6.1%), second-ranked Isetan Shinjuku Head (−6.6%), and sixth-ranked Takashimaya Tokyo Head (−7.9%) in 2008 were among those that experienced serious sales declines from the previous year [25]. Keio Department Store, Shinjuku faced the same problem. Figure 13.3 shows the store sales after 2006, setting 1995 sales as 100.

However, when looking at the fourth floor of the store, the decline is less compared with all floors and other item categories except for food. The floor is strategically arranged to target seniors. Table 13.1 shows the sales decrease in 2008 as compared to 2007 in the case of Keio Department Store, Shinjuku.

Although the results of Keio's senior-targeted marketing challenges were not remarkable in 2008, with steady effort Keio Department Store opened its first satellite outlet, in September 2009, in a new shopping mall, Mitsui Shopping Park LaLaport Shin-Misato [26]. The satellite outlet is a new business format for Keio, along with an original senior-targeted marketing policy. News and TV media reported about the satellite outlet, and Keio's senior-targeted marketing policy is spreading among consumers and becoming a strength of the department store.

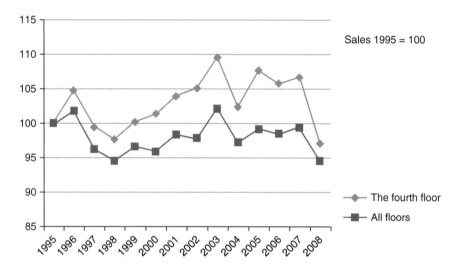

Fig. 13.3 Updated Sales at Keio Department Store Shinjuku (see Fig. 13.2)
Source: Keio Department Store Co. Ltd

Table 13.1 The sales decrease in 2008 as compared to 2007 at Keio Department Store, Shinjuku		
Total		−5.2%
Clothes		−7.7%
Food		+2.7%
Expensive items (art works, jewels, watches, etc.)		−14.6%
The 4th floor		−4.9%

Source: Keio Department Store Co. Ltd

Discussion

The Keio Department Store, Shinjuku effectively offers a case study that details the ways in which an organization adapts to a changing business environment by revealing the measures that its management took in order to differentiate it from its competitors.

In the early stages of their inception, department stores in Japan targeted wealthy consumers. They later became more popular and turned to high-class luxury selections and multifunctionality, took on concession tenants, and installed amusement facilities. They have maintained an important position among retailers, and have impacted Japan's complicated distribution system since the first department store opened in 1904. However, sales have been affected by changes in the business environment, including market changes evidenced by the entry of new competitors, regulatory developments, the emergence of new retail formats, changes in consumer values and behavior, and, particularly, the recent, extensive economic recession.

Keio faced severe challenges, particularly in 1996, when a powerful new competitor opened a department store in the same keenly competitive part of Shinjuku, Tokyo. Keio's challenge was to overcome sluggish business and successfully employ a new, more diverse strategy that targeted seniors in the face of market changes with respect to the competitors' new business activities, demographic transition toward a rapidly aging society, and consumer values and behavior.

Innovations exhibited by Keio's competitors include rapid and drastic transformations to the retail format. The South Building of Shinjuku Mitsukoshi was rented out to Otsuka Kagu, a furniture retailer, in 1999. The interior annex HALC of Odakyu Department Store has been tenant-occupied by BIC Camera since 2002, following the poor performance of furniture sales in that space ([11], p. 29). Shinjuku Mitsukoshi reinvented itself as a miscellaneous-goods specialty shop called Shinjuku Mitsukoshi Alcott in 2005. Moreover, in April 2008, Mitsukoshi and Isetan merged and created Japan's largest department store group by integrating operations under a joint holding company named Mitsukoshi Isetan Holdings.

In contrast, Keio's attempts reveal a unique approach that focused on internal improvement rather than external exploitation. More specifically, Keio focuses on existing customers rather than tapping new shoppers, recognizing and valuing its intrinsic resources and properties. Keio arranged for three-generation consumption in the 1960s, instead of highlighting the newest top luxury world-brand fashion, as seen at Isetan and Shinjuku Takashimaya, and applied a longer-term, incremental renovation project. As a result, Keio's "unchanged innovation" turned out to be a substantial distinction from other department stores.

Keio differentiates itself from department stores that present luxurious imported and high-priced goods through (1) a classification system that addresses the senior generation brackets, (2) detailed efforts to offer small quantities of an array of reasonably-priced casual and fashionable items, and (3) making the Baby Boomer Generation its consumer focus and the post-baby boomer generation a strategically targeted secondary bracket.

Keio's decisions on how it should escape from its financial predicament and correct its track with a new senior-targeted strategy was its evolutionary attempt to review and establish its customers as its cornerstone. The measures that Keio took to cope with the changing environment and diversification of its consumer values reflected an analysis of consumption trends based on customer data from its membership and from comments voiced daily in the store. In effect, these pools of data contributed to the creation of hypotheses, strategies, and verification of theories to meet customer needs.

Naturally, reliable information is supplied to both customers and Keio through customer service offerings, which simultaneously supports hypothetical scenarios.

Thus, the examination of Keio's efforts to operate in its severe business environment demonstrates three remarkable yet basic strategies: clarification of its target customers, consistent review of individual customer wants, and an application of knowledge and information to its marketing arrangements. For these strategies, Keio targets senior customers, using analysis of customer data, application of assumptions and inspection, and continuous information-gathering to keep consumption trends in perspective. One of these attempts is the physical layout of the store's theme-relevant product assortments, on the hypothesis that travel, leisure, health, and safety are essential considerations. In addition, the layout of each floor and allocation of the whole building are based on the hypothetical action scenario that more senior customers prefer a one-stop shopping approach and a wider radius in the building's interior. Such approaches are Keio's strong points in achieving consumption among three generations.

Keio's practice can be effective against the weakness of department stores of limited flexibility, which has surfaced since the late 1970s, particularly in the face of a changing market and consumers' vacillating values and behavior. It can also be effective against a lack of integrated managerial capability, which has become apparent since the early 1990s. With clear vision and precise targeting of customers, one may expect increased centripetal force that leads to integrated management. Also, improvement in service quality evidenced by an effort to provide a qualification system for its full-time sales staff instead of outsourcing underscores secure responsiveness to customers' needs and, consequently, flexibility in addressing their changing values and behavior. The important thing is to logically integrate all innovations and efforts once a target is identified.

The store's potential for an effective senior-marketing strategy is evidenced by its move to open a first satellite outlet that offers an original arrangement of merchandise, despite the present economic recession.

Summary and Conclusion

This study evaluates the ways in which an organization adapts to a changing business environment by examining the Keio Department Store, Shinjuku. Keio presents an example of a senior-focused retailer, and the factors that are vital in tailoring corporate practices to a changing business environment. When making long-term assumptions regarding the business environment, it is particularly crucial to analyze a retailer's strategies by taking into account how consumer values, lifestyles, and changing natural and social environments mutually influence each another. While diversification of Japanese consumer values and behavior, which reflects the transition of the retail sector, is presented as a major factor of change in the business environment, department stores' weaknesses, which are common, in integrated management practices and innovation limit their capability to respond to changes in the competitive environment.

In order for Keio to challenge its powerful new competitors, it also had to adapt to changes in the business environment. Accordingly, Keio's key internal innovations consisted of efforts to improve the quality of service and communication by identifying the values and traits of its existing customers from a long-term perspective. Some of Keio's strategies were the opposite of the approach that its competitors were taking, and resulted in distinctive operation in terms of store size, resources, speed, degree, innovative approaches, and the scope of target, price, and assortment. Specifically, its medium size, conventional resources, senior-targeted approach that considered patronage by three generations, substantial merchandise selection at reasonable prices, long-term incremental changes, and invisible innovation each developed out of its efforts. In addition, these strategies and efforts are logically interwoven and integrated as a whole. Thus, at Keio, a clear vision of targeting customers and its logically integrated strategies increased centripetal force. Therefore, Keio obtained the flexibility to adapt to the changing external competitive business environment, including consumers' diverse values and behavior.

Appendix

Japan became an "aging society" in 1970 and an "aged society" in 1994. At present, it is the most aged society in the world. However, both the public and private sectors in Japan are still underdeveloped in terms of provisions for an era of an aged society. A case study was conducted to examine the ability of organizations to cope with the changing business environment, particularly the retailers' adaptability to the needs of an aged society.

The study case was selected from among 30 retailers. Each exhibited shifts toward a niche business and quality service improvements, based on a positioning map generated by an analysis of small- and medium-sized enterprises which was conducted by a financial research institute ([27], pp. 71–80).

With a scenario that met the selection criteria of an organization that (1) was already catering to a core clientele of seniors, (2) recognizes internal and external aspects of the business environment, and (3) has implemented innovation, this case study involved the following aspects and research methods:

- A comprehensive analysis and interpretation of changing business environments from socioeconomic and cultural perspectives, primarily obtained from government statistics and interpretations, with additional research data acquired from advertising and financial research institutes.
- An exploration of conventional business practices in the retail sector, along with changes in the business environment, with research references on marketing, the retail sector, and department stores.
- An examination of the effectiveness and adaptability of internal functions and systems to external changes in the business environment, as evidenced by a case study of one department store.
- Face-to-face and telephone interviews and online communication with the following individuals between late October 2007 and January 2008: Sachiko Shindo, Senior Manager, Public Relations Department, Keio Department Store Co. Ltd., and Yoko Yasuda, Deputy General Manager, Marketing and Sales Promotion Officer, Takashimaya Co.
- Follow-up telephone interviews and online communication in February 2010 with Sachiko Shindo, Keio Department Store Co. Ltd.
- Field studies on store layout, selections, customers, services, and communication of the following department stores between August 2007 and January 2008: Isetan (Shinjuku), Keio Department Store (Shinjuku), Mitukoshi (Nihonbashi), Odakyu Department Store (Shinjuku), Seibu Department Store (Ikebukuro), Takashimaya (Nihonbashi), Tobu Department Store (Ikebukuro).
- Data analyses provided by Keio Department Store Co. Ltd.

References

1. Ministry of Internal Affairs and Communications, White Paper. Information & communication statistics database, 2007
2. Ministry of Education, Culture, Sports, Science and Technology, Japan (2008) http://www.mext.go.jp/b_menu/shingi/chukyo/chukyo4/019/gijiroku/08011108/004.pdf#search=1806676464. Accessed 17 Feb 2010
3. National Institute of Population and Social Security Research (2008) http://www.ipss.go.jp/syoushika/, http://www.ipss.go.jp/syoushika/seisaku/html/a2.htm. Accessed 18 Jan 2008
4. H. Meyer-Ohle, *Innovation and Dynamics in Japanese Retailing: From Techniques to Formats to Systems* (Palgrave Macmillan, New York, 2003)
5. M. Miura, *Introduction, in Nihon ryûtsû sangyô-shi* (Dobun-kan, Tokyo, 2002)
6. M. Jinbo, *Hyakkaten no Nihon-teki tenkai to mâkettyingu, in Nihon ryûtsû sangyô-shi* (Dôbun-kan, Tokyo, 2002)
7. H. Takei, K.-I. Kudo, T. Miyata, Y. Ito, *Adaptive Strategies for Japan's Retail Industry Facing a Turning Point: Rebuilding Corporate Strength to Respond to Change with Agility.* NRI papers, no 110 (Nomura Research Institute, Tokyo, 2006)
8. K. Tateno, Sûpâ no Nihon-teki tenkai to mâketyingu, in *Nihon ryûtsû sangyô-shi* (Dôbun-kan, Tokyo, 2002)
9. H. Kim, *Konbiniensu-sutoa no Nihon-teki tenkai to mâkettyingu, in Nihon ryûtsû sangyô-shi* (Dôbun-kan, Tokyo, 2002)
10. K. Miyazoe, *J. Market. Distribut.* Ryûtsû Kenkyû. 61 (2005)

11. Y. Asakura, A. Ôhara, *Zenkoku hyakkaten no tempo senrhyaku* (Dôyu-kan, Tokyo, 2003)
12. Nihon Keizai Shinbun, morning edition, 17 Feb 2010
13. Nomura Research Institute, Seikatusha ichiman-nin ni miru nihonjin no kachikan, shôhikôdô no henka [Changes in Japanese values and consumption behaviors as seen in 10,000 questionnaires] (2004) http://www.nri.co.jp/news/2003/031215/031215.pdf. Accessed 15 Feb 2010
14. J. Shiozaki, H. Nitto, N. Kawazu, *Daisan no shôhi sutairu [The Third Consumption Style]* (Nomura Research Institute, Tokyo, 2005)
15. J. Shiozaki, *Taishû-ka suru "IT shôhi."* *Chiteki Shisan Sôzô* (Nomura Research Institute, Tokyo, 2007)
16. Bank of Japan, *Why Has Japanese Private Consumption Remained Firm?* (Research and Statistics Department, Japan, 2006)
17. Nikkei Sangyô Shôhi Kenkyûsho, 2007-nen ritaia dankai shijô o nerae (from Nikkei shôhi keizai seminar 29 January). Nikkei Shôhi Mainingu, 2006
18. Seni Torendo [Fabric Trend], Nov–Dec. Tôre Keiei Kenkyû-sho, 2006
19. SC Japan Today, *Kenshô 2007-nen mondai. Shin-shijô to naruka dankaisedai mâketto* [Is the baby-boomer generation creating new markets?] (Nihon Shoppingu Centâ Kyôkai, Tokyo, 2006)
20. Bank of Japan, Monthly report of recent economic and financial developments (The Bank's View, Bank of Japan, Japan, 1998). http://www.boj.or.jp/en/type/release/teiki/gp/gp9812.htm. Accessed 25 Feb 2010
21. M. Chen, The Japanese distribution system in transition, in *Asian management systems: Chinese, Japanese, and Korean styles of business*, chap 19, 2nd edn. (International Thomson Business Press, London, 2004)
22. M. Sugihara, *Chiiki ni okeru jinkô-kôreika to kôreisha no seikatsu-ishiki: Takasaki-shi shigaichi-riyô-kôreisha ni taisuru mensetsu chôsa.* Chiiki seisaku kenkyu. Takasaki Keizai Daigaku Chiiki-seisaku Gakkai, vol 6, no 4, 2004
23. It media Co. http://www.itmedia.co.jp/enterprise/articles/0910/27/news016.html. Accessed 19 Feb 2010
24. Nikkei Ryutsu Shinbun p. 5, 12 Feb 2010
25. Nihon Keizai Shinbun, morning edition, 12 Aug 2009
26. Keio Co. http://www.keio.co.jp/company/stockholder/business_report/pdf/2009cyukan_ir.pdf. Accessed 25 Jan 201
27. Chûshô Kôko, *Shinia shijô ni chûmokusuru chushôkigyô no Senryaku to kadai* [Strategies and challenges of small- and medium-sized enterprises in the senior market], Chûshô Kôko report no 2004–3 (Chûshôkigyô Kinyûkôko Sôgô Kenkyûsho, Tokyo, 2005)

Chapter 14
Bargain Hunting Belongers and Positive Pioneers: Key Silver Market Segments in the UK

Lynn Sudbury and Peter Simcock

Abstract Although the importance of older consumers to marketers is well-documented, there exists a relative paucity of UK-based empirical studies into the attitudes, values, and behaviours of these consumers. Moreover, silver consumers are often treated as a homogeneous mass. Based on an extensive survey into a range of socio-demographic, health and physical, socio-psychological, psychographic, and behavioural variables amongst adults aged between 50 and 79 years ($n = 650$), this study confirms that the older consumer market is not homogeneous. Rather, analysis of the data leads to the first comprehensive segmentation model of the older consumer market in the UK. This chapter profiles two of the major segments to emerge from this analysis, which differ considerably from each other on a range of variables, including consumer behaviours. The marketing implications for targeting these different segments are discussed.

Introduction

The UK is ranked 17th out of 192 countries in terms of its proportion of people aged 60 and over in relation to the population as a whole [1]. Life expectancy in the UK is now 81.5 years for females and 77 years for males [2]. Although retirement age in the UK is 60 or 65 and the median age is currently 39 [2], consensus among gerontologists (e.g. English Longitudinal Study of Ageing), policy makers (e.g. new ISA limits), charities (e.g. Age Concern), academics [3] and practitioners (e.g. SilverSurfers.net, SAGA) has resulted in age 50 becoming the inclusion point for studies, policies and target markets. The addition of Baby Boomers (born 1947–1964) to this group has resulted in the emergence of a market potentially comprising over 20 million people in the UK [4].

Increases in longevity, coupled with better nutrition and advances in healthcare, have led to some evidence to suggest *healthy* life expectancy in the UK is increasing at least as quickly as life expectancy [5]. Moreover, there are also groups, particularly amongst the baby boomers, who shaped modern marketing [6], as

F. Kohlbacher and C. Herstatt (eds.), *The Silver Market Phenomenon*,
DOI 10.1007/978-3-642-14338-0_14, © Springer-Verlag Berlin Heidelberg 2011

business was forced to focus on an ever expanding market of young, affluent consumers with markedly different wants and needs from preceding generations. The consumption patterns established in their youth continue into their maturity. UK consumers aged between 50 and 64 years are amongst the highest spenders on hairdressing and beauty treatments, insurance, foreign vacations, alcoholic drinks (particularly wine), household appliances, new cars, ladies' clothes, and a range of grocery products from cakes and biscuits to fresh fruit and vegetables [7]. Despite the clear opportunities to be found in this market, practitioners are still reluctant to target older adults [8]. One possible reason for this reluctance is a lack of valid and reliable research on which to base marketing strategies.

Silver Market Segmentation

Grouping all silver consumers into one age-based category may result in business overlooking crucial segments of this important market. Indeed, Moschis [9] asserts that no other consumer market justifies segmentation more than older consumers, because as people age they become more dissimilar with respect to lifestyles, needs, and consumption habits. The USA leads the way in silver market segmentation models, and from early studies that tended to be based on chronological age, several more sophisticated segmentation methods have emerged. These include Towle and Martin's [10] six segments based on buying styles, personality traits, self-concept measures and demographic variables; Lumpkin et al.'s [11] model based on different shopping orientations towards apparel and some lifestyle factors; a six segment model based on lifestyle dimensions [12]; Leventhal's [13] model that takes into consideration factors such as buying power, marital status, and health; and finally the most comprehensive segmentation model of older Americans, the Geronto-graphics method proposed by George Moschis and his colleagues at the Centre for Mature Consumer Studies at Georgia State University [9]. Gerontographics is based on a variety of social, psychological, and biophysical variables, which offers four distinctive segments. The one drawback to these general models is that few demographic differences between segments can be identified, and, as Ostroff [14] notes, the best and most useful profiles of older consumer segments integrate a wide variety of variables, including demographic data.

There is another group of American models which are based on specific product categories. These include Morgan and Levy's [15] segments for health products and food; five segments for over the counter drugs [16]; and four segments for apparel shopping [17]. Two studies also offer ways of segmenting the travel and tourism market for older consumers [18, 19]. Although all are no doubt useful in particular circumstances, the obvious limitation of these models is that they are based on specific product categories, and thus cannot be extended beyond those categories.

In contrast to America, the UK is marked by a paucity of silver segmentation studies. Indeed, only one academic study exists, where Tynan and Drayton [20] identified a potentially important segment known as "Methuselahs". The date of this study and subsequent cohort effects means the applicability of this model is likely to be of limited value in segmenting today's seniors.

Based therefore on the obvious need for a current, comprehensive, empirically based segmentation model of the silver market in the UK, the study detailed here aimed to provide a segmentation model to help guide practical marketing strategies. Included in this study are socio-demographic data pertaining to chronological and self-perceived age, work status, income bands, marital status, and progeny; lifestyle issues including health, exercise, social and leisure activities, and media usage; and a battery of existing scales relating to social gerontology and psychographic, psycho-social, and consumer behaviours. (Full details of the precise methodology used, including the actual scales utilised and the data analysis methods are available from the authors on request.) A self-administered questionnaire was sent to an age-quota sample, resulting in a usable sample size of 650 adults aged 50–79 years (mean age 62 years), that mirrors the UK age demographic of this sector of the population.

Five segments emerged, which differ significantly on a range of variables. A profile of two very different segments, which between them account for over two-thirds of the silver market in the UK, now follows.

Positive Pioneers (30%)

This is the youngest segment in terms of both chronological and cognitive age, with an average age of 56 and 46 years respectively. It is relatively affluent, despite having the fewest empty nests, with more than one in four still having grown-up children living at home, and more than half have young grandchildren. Unsurprisingly, then, they also have the most frequent contact with their families than any other segment. Despite their relatively young age, only half rate their health as good, suggesting some minor health problems in this segment. More than half enjoy energetic activities, a further third is moderately active, and they take the most holidays abroad. This segment can be accessed through magazines and the internet, but have the lowest levels of radio consumption.

As their name suggests, positive pioneers are by far the most venturesome (i.e. willing to try new brands), and display far greater market maven tendencies (i.e. have a high propensity to share market and shopping information) than any other segment identified in this research. They also have the most positive attitudes towards marketing and consumerism, display relatively high levels of materialism, have positive attitudes towards credit, and are not particularly price-conscious although they are still unsure about senior discounts.

Bargain Hunting Belongers (38%)

This is the oldest cluster, with a mean chronological age of 70, and an average self-perceived age of 61. Bargain hunting belongers are the least affluent segment with the vast majority now retired. Despite its older age, this group still feels relatively healthy. However, in terms of hobbies and pastimes, they are the least physically active of all older consumers. Their media consumption profile reveals that they are the highest consumers of television, relatively high consumers of radio, newspapers and magazines, but have the lowest internet usage.

Despite being the oldest, they are by no means the most nostalgic. Fun and enjoyment is their least important value; this group places greater importance on a sense of belonging than any other. Perhaps this is why they see their friends more frequently than any other segment. They are also close to their families. They display moderate or average scores across the range of psychosocial factors, although this group displays the lowest levels of negative effect – perhaps suggesting an element of "stiff upper lip".

Although this segment is only moderately materialistic and moderately venturesome, it displays above-average market maven tendencies, and has relatively positive attitudes toward marketing and consumerism. Probably due to their restricted incomes, this group enjoys a bargain, in that it is highly price-conscious and displays the most positive attitudes toward senior discounts. It is also less averse to credit than several of the other segments.

Benefits of the Model

This segmentation model confirms that senior UK consumers are not all the same. Rather, five groups can be identified, which differ considerably on a range of important criteria. The model has a number of advantages. First, it is not based on speculation or conjecture, but rather is the result of the largest known empirical study into the consumer behaviour of older adults in the UK. Second, it is comprehensive in that it utilises a wide range of biophysical, sociological, and psychological variables, all of which have been shown to be particularly relevant to older adults in the gerontology literature. Thus, the model has a sound theoretical basis. Moreover, its use of additional socio-demographic, media usage, and consumer behaviour variables means it is useful to the marketing practitioner. Third, the segments presented here are not limited to a specific product or product category. Finally, the model meets the criteria for effective segmentation, as suggested by [21] in that the resulting segments are measurable, accessible, substantial, and differentiable.

Additionally, the model has a number of advantages over existing silver segmentation methods discussed earlier in this paper. First, it is more comprehensive than the models proposed by Towle and Martin [10, 12], both of which had smaller sample sizes and utilised fewer consumer behaviour, psychographic, socio-demographic, health and media usage measures than the present study. Importantly, both studies used chronological age only, with no attempt to measure cognitive age. Despite these differences, there appears to be some overlap between them (viz. "active retirees" with "bargain-hunting belongers"; and "young and secures" with "positive pioneers"). The final general model, Moschis's [9] gerontographics, employed a much larger sample size than that of the present study, measured cognitive as well as chronological age, but used slightly fewer (136 against 165) measures of biophysical, psychological and social ageing, psychographics and consumer behaviour. However, given the much more comprehensive nature of Moschis's study, it is surprising that there is only one instance of overlapping segments ("ailing outgoers" with "bargain-hunting belongers") between the two models. This might be due to the fact that different variables were measured in the two studies, or that there are fundamental attitudinal and consumer behaviour differences between older adults in the USA and the UK.

Managerial Implications and Applications

Identifying discrete segments provides firms that wish to target older consumers with a starting point for a range of marketing decisions. Product policy should differ between segments based on differences in cognitive age, marital status, health and fitness, and income. For example, the cognitively young and relatively energetic positive pioneers take more vacations outside of the UK, and enjoy better health than the cognitively older bargain hunting belongers. Thus it makes sense to target the first segment with active pastimes, overseas vacations and perhaps even adventure holidays, whereas the second segment would seem a natural target for UK vacations, more leisurely pastimes, and mobility and dexterity aids.

Equally, pricing policy should be informed by the insights provided, which relate not only to income, but also to price consciousness, attitudes toward credit, and senior discounts. In the past, far too much of the trade literature, in particular, has stressed the differences between younger and older adults relating to price consciousness instead of exploring the differences within the older consumer market, as presented here. For example, bargain hunting belongers, despite being the oldest (both chronologically and cognitively) and least affluent segment, are not averse to credit, as is commonly assumed. Thus, although they might have the lowest disposable incomes in the older market, they should not necessarily be automatically excluded as a target for more expensive purchases, as it may be possible to offer them the right type of credit and allow them to spread the cost.

Traditional assumptions regarding senior discounts also need revising in the light of this research. As might be expected, bargain hunting belongers have highly positive attitudes to senior discounts. Consumers in this segment are the most likely to be retired empty-nesters, and the vast majority are grandparents with their oldest grandchild at the landmark age of 18. Thus, their positive attitudes towards age-based sales promotions are to be expected, given that they have a host of other reminders that they are no longer young. They have begun to accept the discounts offered to them, and are more likely to take advantage of as many senior promotions as possible; indeed, they sometimes seem to feel that price discounts based on seniority are rewards they have earned.

In contrast, marketers cannot assume that the cognitively young and more affluent positive pioneers will all have negative attitudes towards senior discounts and promotions that, by definition, undermine their youthful self-image. Rather, this segment is unsure about, but not completely averse to, such age-based discounts. This segment needs to be targeted carefully, and might prefer such offers via mail, telephone or, given that they are the highest users of the internet, on-line senior discounts are appropriate. This way, the effects on their young self-perceived age will be minimised, as they do not have to admit to being old enough for such discounts in public.

Targeting, positioning, and advertising strategies can also be improved by using the wide range of information pertaining to cognitive age, values, attitudes, and psychographic details provided for the two segments. For example, a sense of belonging is of crucial importance to bargain hunting belongers, thus the need to portray older models in social settings in advertising campaigns is very important for this segment, although less so for positive pioneers. Furthermore, for increased effectiveness and efficiency, media strategies need to be tailored. Bargain hunting belongers are best reached using television and print media, whereas positive pioneers – although relatively heavy consumers of television – might more cost-effectively be reached via the internet.

Finally, the fact that the proposed model is not product- or industry-specific, providing many advantages over alternative segmentation models proffered in the past, does mean that it may not be appropriate for all product categories, and bespoke marketing research will still be needed for in-depth understanding of attitudes and behaviours toward certain products and marketing practises. Nevertheless, it provides some insight into the many facets of opinions, attitudes, and perceptions among older UK consumers, previously unavailable to marketing practitioners.

Summary and Conclusion

This chapter has provided an overview of the largest known empirical study into older consumers in the UK. The study comprised a quota-sample of 650 adults aged 50–79, and used a battery of variables based on the major dimensions of ageing, and behavioural variables previously shown to be pertinent to older adults in the gerontology and marketing literature. Five distinct segments emerged, two of which are profiled here. The model overcomes many of the limitations of previous segmentation studies pertaining to older adults, and also fills a research gap noted by several previous researchers in that a variety of different types of age are utilised. The research confirms that the silver market in the UK is not homogeneous, and the model meets the criteria for effective segmentation in that the resulting segments are measurable, accessible, substantial, and differentiable. The model has practical implications for targeting silver consumers.

References

1. United Nations Department of Economic and Social Affairs, Population Division, *World Population Ageing 2007* (United Nations Department of Economic and Social Affairs, Population Division, NY, USA, 2007)
2. Office for National Statistics, *Social Trends* (Government Publications, London, 2009)
3. L. Sudbury, P. Simcock, Understanding older consumers through cognitive age and the list of values: A UK perspective. Psychol. Mark. **26**(1), 22–38 (2009)
4. Employers Forum on Age. *Age information and research* (2009). http://www.efa.org.uk/
5. Academy of Medical Sciences, *Rejuvenating Ageing Research* (2009). http://ac medsci.ac.uk/p.99html
6. K.E. Thompson, N.S. Thompson, *Advertising to Older Consumers: Theory into Practice.* Paper presented at the Academy of Marketing Conference, Kingston University, 2007
7. Office for National Statistics, *Family Spending – A Report on the Expenditure and Food Survey* (Government Publications, London, 2008)
8. P. Simcock, L. Sudbury, The invisible majority? Older models in UK television advertising. Int. J. Advertising **25**(1), 87–106 (2006)
9. G.P. Moschis, Gerontographics: A scientific approach toanalyzing and targeting the mature market. J. Consum. Mark. **10**(3), 43–53 (1993)
10. J.G. Towle, C. R. Martin, The elderly consumer: One segment or many? Adv. Consum. Res. **3**, 463–468 (1976)
11. J.R. Lumpkin, B.A. Greenberg, J.L. Goldstucker, Marketplace needs of the elderly: Determinant attributes and store choice. J. Retail. **61**(2), 75–105 (1985)
12. P. Sorce, P.R. Tyler, L.M. Loomis, Lifestyles of older Americans. J. Consum. Mark. **6**(3), 53–63 (1989)
13. R.C. Leventhall, The aging consumer: What's all the fuss about anyway? J. Consum. Mark. **8**(1), 29–34 (1991)
14. J. Ostroff, *Successful Marketing to the 50+ Consumer* (Prentice-Hall, New Jersey, 1989)
15. C.M. Morgan, D.J. Levy, *Segmenting the Mature Market* (Probus, Chicago, 1993)
16. B. Oates, L. Shufeldt, B. Vaught, A psychographic study of the elderly and retail store attributes. J. Consum. Mark. **13**(6), 14–27 (1996)
17. D. Mumel, J. Prodnik, Grey consumers are all the same, they even dress the same – myth or reality? J. Fashion Mark. Manag. **9**(4), 434–49 (2005)
18. E.M. Lieux, P.A. Weaver, K.W. McCleary, Lodging preferences of the senior tourism market. Ann. Tour. Res. **21**(4), 712–28 (1993)
19. M.C. Sellick, Discovery, connection, nostalgia: Key travel motives within the senior market. J. Travel Tour. Mark. **17**(1), 55–71 (2004)
20. A.C. Tynan, J. Drayton, The Methuselah market. J. Mark. Manag. **1**(1), 75–85 (1985)
21. P. Kotler, G. Armstrong, *Principles of Marketing* (Pearson, New Jersey, 2004)

Chapter 15
Grey Power: Developing Older Customer Strategies

Sue Tempest, Christopher Barnatt, and Christine Coupland

Abstract This chapter explores the increasing importance of "grey power" in the labor market and the marketplace. To fully understand grey market potential, companies need to develop an understanding of individual older customers and their broader social contexts in terms of both their varying immediate household compositions, and their intergenerational relationships. In this chapter we first challenge stereotypes and then introduce a model of older-person segmentation. The frame of analysis is then extended beyond the individual older customer in order to assess the range of "future households" in which the old will increasingly play a key role when purchasing decisions are being made. We provide a wealth/health segmentation for firms seeking to develop older customer strategies, and supplement this with a categorization of future households and the issues raised by intergenerational dynamics. This is then used to challenge false assumptions about older household compositions in the twenty-first century. In turn, this provides a segmentation of the old as workers and as customers in a variety of social contexts, which we hope offers some useful tools for companies seeking to capitalize on grey power now and into the future.

Introduction

In June 2007, YouTube asked 79-year-old web celebrity "Geriatric 1927" to provide the launch video for their UK website. A month later, NASA set up a panel of retired engineers from its Lunar Module Reliability and Maintainability team to provide advice to current employees charged with returning a man to the moon by 2020. And, 2 months after that, on 23 September the US Department of Labor celebrated its fifth National Employ Older Workers Week. As demonstrated throughout this book, as population aging continues to increase, so the "old" are increasingly being recognized as icons of consumer power, a source of key knowledge, and vital labor force participants.

F. Kohlbacher and C. Herstatt (eds.), *The Silver Market Phenomenon*,
DOI 10.1007/978-3-642-14338-0_15, © Springer-Verlag Berlin Heidelberg 2011

This chapter explores the increasing importance of "grey power" initially in the labor market, but more significantly in the marketplace. In doing so, it first challenges stereotypes and then reasserts a model of older-person segmentation of potential value to companies seeking to most successfully market their products and services. The frame of analysis is then further extended beyond the individual older customer in order to assess the range of "future households" in which the old will increasingly play a key role when purchasing decisions are being made.

Older Workers

As people live longer, rigid work retirement distinctions are becoming untenable. The world's elderly population is projected to rise from 0.5 billion in 2000 to two billion by 2050 [1]. Across Europe, the median age of the population is projected to rise from 37 in 2002 to 52 by 2050. In the US, 27% of the population will be aged over 60 by 2050, including a forecast of one million centenarians [1]. Emerging economies will be affected by population aging too. By 2030, more than twice as many people over 65 will reside in developing countries as in the developed world [2]. More people are also living to be centenarians. Research into centenarian longevity suggests that if you have been healthy you live longer, and even amongst this very old cohort, 30% have no significant deterioration in their thinking ability [3].

Widespread increases in longevity and in lifelong health necessitate a reappraisal of the work/retirement distinction and a revisiting of our stereotypes of older workers [4]. Older workers (those aged 50+) are sometimes perceived as unable to adapt to change, unable to learn new techniques and skills, and reluctant to embrace new technologies [5]. This can even become a self-fulfilling prophecy if older workers mentally and emotionally disengage from the workforce. Indeed, there is the danger that older people themselves internalize this socially constructed stereotyping and "discriminate against themselves" by not coming forward for training or promotion [6].

Governments are concerned about the low participation rates of older people in the workforce. This has manifested itself in concern about dependency ratios between the economically active and the economically inactive. Governments also have good reason to be concerned. Evidence suggests that many older workers are leaving the labor force on an involuntary basis. For example, OECD statistics for 2005 for the UK show employment rates for those aged 15–64 as 80.5% for men and 67.9% for women; whereas for the population aged 55–64 employment rates fell to 65.7% for men and 48.2% for women [7]. Age discrimination is the most commonly experienced form of discrimination, with 23% of people reporting experiencing it in some form [8]. Older workers are particularly at risk from restructuring, being passed over for promotion or being excluded from development and training [7]. In Europe, this has promoted a focus on equal opportunities and age discrimination legislation, as has been in place in the USA for many years. Companies too are becoming concerned about demographic changes, with a "war for talent" emerging as the proportion of younger people in the population in developed countries continues to fall. This has prompted debate about the optimal role and deployment of older workers. Organizations such as IBM, Bosch and NASA have developed initiatives to encourage knowledge sharing across generations, such as "reengaging" retirees on specific projects, or encouraging intergenerational learning [9]. All this implies that there is a growing recognition that long-held stereotypes of older workers are unhelpful and increasingly redundant [4].

As a first step in challenging stereotypes, we would suggest a need to recognize the increasing diversity of older workers on the basis of both their wealth and their health. This concept is supported by an ongoing study by the US National Council on Aging which suggests that decisions about when to retire will in future be influenced primarily by accumulated savings and health decline [10]. Figure 15.1 illustrates our resultant categorization of older workers into the four quadrants of a wealth/health segmentation matrix.

In the bottom left quadrant of the wealth/health segmentation matrix, we see that older people in most difficulties are those who experience poor health and who face financial insecurity. These individuals have a restricted ability to work, and are

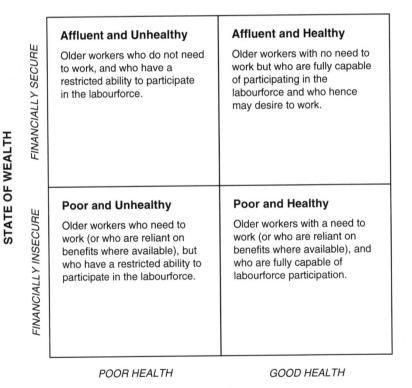

Fig. 15.1 The older worker wealth/health segmentation matrix

likely to be dependent on benefits where available. Research shows that workers with poor health generally retire earlier than those with good health [11]. Such individuals can find themselves in a vicious circle where health and wealth spiral downwards, because affluence provides access to better housing, diet, and lifestyle which also contribute to health [10].

In the top left quadrant of the wealth/health segmentation matrix sit older people who have poor health but coupled with financial security. These individuals may not need to work, but may still have a desire to continue to do so on in order to remain socially and/or mentally active. Such workers may need technical or other support in order to remain employed. Alternatively, poor health may act as a push factor to self-employment for this older worker category [11].

In the top right quadrant of the wealth/health segmentation matrix are older people who enjoy both good health and who are financially secure. These individuals can afford to retire but may also choose to continue to work, perhaps on reduced hours and most likely on their own terms. This most fortunate group of older people is likely to have enjoyed high levels of professional success, making them valuable human capital. Workers with valuable knowledge are increasingly being viewed as "customers" by employing organizations. Indeed, it has been suggested that "the most talented workers are the most sophisticated consumers, looking for the best-tailored employee deals" [9].

Finally in the lower right quadrant of the wealth/health segmentation matrix sit older people enjoying good health but who are financially insecure. These people are hence both able to work, and need to do so if benefits are either unavailable or viewed as insufficient for a reasonable quality of life. Such workers are likely to be able to participate in the labor force until conventional retirement ages and possibly beyond if circumstances permit.

As our older worker wealth/health segmentation matrix helps to highlight, a diversity of health and affluence amongst older workers necessitates a move away from a single stereotype of older workers. In turn, this will necessitate more customized employment practices if firms are to make the best use of their older human capital. In the UK, this is also starting to happen, with companies such as Asda, IBM, Capital One, and B&Q developing targeted retention policies and innovative retirement solutions for older workers.

Older Workers as Older Customers

An acceptance that older workers may be usefully segmented on an axis of wealth and health is no longer as radical or unusual a proposition as it was. It is therefore surprising that many companies seem to have forgotten that the collective word for the workers in any economy is "customers," and that any useful categorization of older workers therefore ought in parallel to drive a similar categorization of older customers.

Much of the existing marketing literature highlights the challenge of segmenting older customers on the basis of their heterogeneity and the fact that aging does not take away an individual's unique personality. However, whilst respecting the diversity of the individual, we would argue that it is increasingly useful to understand older people as customers by keeping in mind their parallel categorization as older workers on a wealth/health basis. We hence propose an extension of Fig. 15.1 that results in an older customer wealth/health segmentation matrix, as illustrated in Fig. 15.2.

Before considering the specific implications of the segmentation of older customers as Fig. 15.2, it is worth highlighting the importance of understanding the economic influence of the old, as well as alternative models for older customer segmentation. In the USA, people aged over 50 account for nearly half of the market share for housing, food, transportation and health. The older consumer is growing in number and economic might, and yet most firms continue to market to and design for younger people [12].

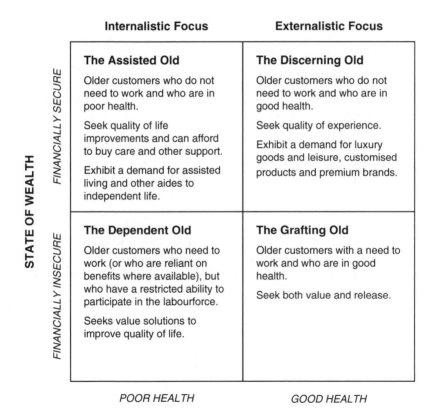

Fig. 15.2 The older customer wealth/health segmentation matrix

Those companies that are capitalizing on grey market opportunities are also proving highly successful. For example Saga – a UK firm specializing in leisure and services for older people, with a strap line "doing things properly" that is especially reassuring in a more anxious, post credit-crunch world – has reported a tenfold increase in the past 13 years in trekking trips booked to Nepal by older travelers (mostly aged 60–79), coupled with a surge in interest in activity holidays by mature travelers [13]. And it is not just the younger old who offer market potential. A study of centenarians in a nursing home chain found that 27% liked to watch MTV music channel, 15% played video games, and 4% knew how to use an iPod [3]. Nor are the opportunities of maturing market places confined to the obvious markets of financial services, leisure and recreation, health and consumer products. In 2008, a 91-year-old became the oldest person to be awarded a PhD from Cambridge University [14]. Unexpected applications of existing products may also apply to mature customers. For example, the Nintendo Wii is being used to provide physiotherapy for older people. This of course all suggests that writing off the older consumer *at any age* or in any market may be a grave mistake.

Firms have been accused of ignoring older consumers for a number of reasons. One argument is that marketers are not fully aware of the potential of the grey market. However, this argument seems increasingly untenable given the growing media coverage being given to demographic aging globally. Alternative explanations of firms' lack of responsiveness to mature customers include older people not being categorized as a separate segment, older people being misunderstood, with misconceptions remaining about their beliefs and lifestyle [15], and older people being considered so heterogeneous that this raises challenges about how best to consider the older consumer [16].

It is known that differences of character do not change significantly with age. This means that there will be much diversity in the aging population [17], in turn making segmentation of older customers potentially challenging. Many of those seeking useful ways to categorize segments of the older population have therefore tended to subdivide the old on the simple basis of age [16] or cohorts born in a similar era who arguably share similar attitudes and beliefs. However, such approaches can be a crude indicator of attitudes, interests and capabilities. We argue that the most useful forms of older customer segmentation need initially at least to consider the wealth and/or health factors increasingly accepted as key to the segmentation of older workers.

Internalistic Versus Externalistic Older Customers

The wealth/health segmentation matrix as presented in Fig. 15.2 subdivides older customers into four categories – the dependent old, assisted old, discerning old and grafting old – which can, we believe, be effectively targeted or otherwise by specific retailers, manufacturers, and service providers. In the figure we have also chosen to highlight how those older customers in poorer health are likely to have a more internalistic focus as customers, whereas those enjoying better health are likely to be more externalistic in their market approach.

Older consumers prefer to spend on experiences rather than physical goods [18]. However, for less healthy individuals the focus becomes more internalistically focused upon living better and the maintenance of their remaining health. We of course need to be wary of portraying the older customer market too negatively as, in practice, being old does not necessarily equate with poor health. For example, in the USA only 5% of the mature market (those 55+) are in nursing homes, and only 12% have a chronic illness [19]. However, changes in health such as issues of mobility, sight, or hearing can change an individual's product and service needs [12].

For companies, the customers in the top "financially secure" boxes of our grid inevitably offer the most potentially lucrative business opportunities. The *discerning old* have high customer power, being both financially secure and healthy. For this group, life is for living as long as possible. They seek quality of experience and aesthetics via high quality design and brand differentiation. This externalistic focus is captured by research carried out by a specialist holiday firm Activities Abroad that revealed that older people enjoy activity holidays because they broaden their horizons, take them beyond their comfort zone, and enable the development of new social contacts [13]. In terms of aesthetics, the rise of demand for designer glasses by design leaders such as Armani and Gucci to make older people look better [20] shows design and image remain key to older people with externalistic outlooks.

The *assisted old* are financially secure but less healthy. This segment may suffer faculty decline (such as variations in sight or hearing) or chronic illnesses. This group of customers is primarily focused on quality of life improvements via products or services. They will seek quality care and technological innovations to ease the impact of their conditions and facilitate independence. They will also seek functionality rather than aesthetics, and have the resources to purchase well-designed products and services. The assisted living industry (offering round the clock services from laundry services to take-out gourmet meals and doctors who make house calls) is a rapidly growing industry in the USA [20].

Within the bottom two segments of our wealth/health segmentation matrix, the less affluent old will be most concerned with value but can again be usefully separated into older customers with either an internalistic or externalistic focus based on health. Being financially insecure, the *grafting old* will not have high levels of disposable income, and if they are still working may lack much spare time. However, as they are healthy they will still seek externalistic leisure opportunities that offer value for money. The Asda supermarket chain in the UK (owned by Wal-Mart) now offers older workers, often on relatively low wages as shop assistants, "Benidorm leave" so that older workers can leave the UK to spend the winter in Spain. In terms of reasonably priced beauty products, Unilever has used its Dove brand to develop ProAge, a range of beauty products for women over 50. Part of the marketing of this range rests on promoting attitudinal change in society that "beauty has no age limit" rather than age as "an imperfection that needs to be corrected" [21].

Finally, in the bottom left quadrant of Fig. 15.2, the *dependent old* are those older customers likely to be reliant on benefits and the state due to their financial insecurity and restricted ability to work. There may be opportunities for niche providers of value products and gadgets to assist these individuals and improve their independence. In the United States, AOL the interactive services company has partnered with the National Council of Aging to launch an online service to provide older Americans with one-stop access to federal and state benefits information. This online service covers nearly a thousand programs that span financial assistance, healthcare, nutrition, energy, legal, and transport services [22]. However, this category of older customer is in danger of being ignored by many companies, due to their inability to be able to afford private care services or expensive aids. This said, opportunities will still increasingly exist to sell budget health products, as well as value products designed for ease of use by those with restricted dexterity, sight or mobility, to this large but cash-poor older customer segment.

The Older Customer Challenge

All firms need to start thinking about where their target customer groups are on the older customer wealth/segmentation matrix today, and where they will be in the relatively near future. To some extent, this will be influenced by firms' actions as employers of older workers. In seeking to develop their relationships with older customers, firms need to reflect more on their diverse needs, and on the position of their products and services in meeting those needs.

There is also thankfully at least some evidence that a few firms are starting to think about their product and service offerings on the lines we have discussed. Age-inclusive or age-neutral design is one way of ensuring older people have access to more products and services. One firm taking notice of the needs of older workers in the design of its offerings is Fidelity Investments. The company has been observing how older people use web sites as a key customer interface, and has sought to improve ease of navigation of its online offering for older customers as a result. Improvements have included larger text and links that are more obviously clickable [12]. Another company targeting the needs of older customers is OXO International. This was founded to develop the "Good Grips" line of kitchen gadgets in collaboration with Smart Design (a New York based industrial design firm) that would be easier to grip, twist, and squeeze but at the same time be stylish in design. The firm embraces universal design principles to produce over 350 products that appeal to a wide range of customers beyond the aging customer [12]. Food companies and pharmaceutical firms are developing "functional foods" with medical benefits to help manage diabetes, arthritis, and heart disease. GE has a vision of "early health" whereby healthcare of the future will offer earlier presymptomatic diagnosis and disease prevention. GE and Intel have an alliance to market and develop home-based health technologies that will target fall prevention, medication compliance, sleep apnea, cardiovascular disease, diabetes and personal wellness monitoring supported by an online interface to enable doctors to manage care remotely. The market for telehealth and home health monitoring is predicted to grow to $7.7 billion by 2012 [23].

Some technology companies are additionally starting to respond to the needs of internalistic older customers for functionality, whilst also trying to meet the demands for stylish aesthetics exhibited by more externalistic older customers. For example, a lightweight hearing aid is being developed by a Danish firm that weighs less than a butterfly, fits invisibly into the ear, and can be programmed to enhance the clarity of speech in noisy environments [20].

All of these developments mentioned above potentially signal what will almost certainly have to become a growing trend for a blurring of the boundaries between the healthcare sector and all other industries in product design. What the above examples indicate is that more *product* development intended to assist in targeting older customers is today focused on meeting the internalistic needs of older customers with poor health. On the other side of our wealth/health segmentation matrix, service offerings, such as Saga holidays, are being developed successfully for the externalistic, healthy old. However, what is *not* happening is the development and/or redesign of products for the healthy old who nevertheless struggle to punch small buttons and read tiny text on tiny screens. The first companies in particular that mass-market phones, televisions and computers designed for older customers rather than teenagers are likely to do very well indeed!

Older Customers in Context

We would hope that our proposed wealth/health segmentation will be of value to companies trying to develop their older customer strategies. However, we would also contend that any segmentation of older customers at an individual level at best provides just a partial understanding of their market potential and position. This is because any model reliant on individual segmentation detaches its consumers from their social context.

To fully understand the grey markets of today and tomorrow, companies need to develop an understanding of the broader social contexts of older people in terms of both their varying immediate household compositions and their intergenerational relationships. Both of these factors are largely neglected in much of the literature on aging at present. However, only by considering the broader social context of the older customer in focus will firms be able to develop informed strategies for achieving competitive advantage in grey markets. The following section therefore provides a categorization of future households, and examines the intergenerational dynamics and challenges faced by countries with an aging population.

The Future Household

Many products and services are purchased and used in a family context where there are competing priorities. As populations age, the nature of households is also shifting. As people live longer and the traditional nuclear family gives way to the evolving blended family, a more diverse range of households in part populated by older people emerges. More complex generational mixes within households raise issues for firms of who the product/service is designed for, and with what category of customer does the spending decision reside?

We would suggest that the broad household types where older people are likely to play an influential role in purchasing decisions are as follows:

- *Pensioners with pensioners*: In such households, older people reside with other older people. This is usually the family unit of the older married couple or cohabitees, who are often empty nesters whose children have grown up and left home. Increasingly, such household units are likely to be populated by single-sex partnerships, or older friends possibly of the same sex, or older relatives living together. Much of the marketing to older people to date has tended to focus on the older married couple as the stereotypical older household where such decisions are shared, if compromised. The discerning old within this household have been encouraged by leisure firms recently to "spend the kids' inheritance" by enjoying their old age by prioritizing their lifestyle over those of their children.

- *Pensioners in isolation*: This is the household of the widowed, divorced, or never-married older person. Such households are characterized by older people living in isolation. Such individuals may have a wide network of friends and family, although their ability to maintain contact with them may be influenced by health and wealth considerations. Such households will be characterized by individualistic purchasing needs and decisions, and segmented quite precisely by our older worker wealth/health segmentation matrix.

- *Pensioners with parents*: Older people living with very old dependent parents. As the very old increase as a proportion of the population, there is an increasing group of those aged 50+ whose parents are still alive. The less affluent old or those who can afford domestic assistance may wish their relatives to remain at home. However, even in the care home we may see changing household dynamics. Indeed, Henderson [20] contends that: "It's no longer out of the question to find parents and children living together in the same nursing home." In such households, the needs of the younger old and the assisted or dependent old need simultaneous consideration by firms.

- *Pensioners with teenagers*: This household type is becoming more common due to a delay in starting families, as well as blended families bringing together children from existing and previous relationships. People of traditionally pensionable age may hence increasingly find themselves living with teenagers, dependent students or young adults. This will pose some interesting questions for companies, and not least those marketing domestic products. For example, in pensioner-with-teenager households, who will the kettle and the telephone be designed for?!

As the last point above signals, as more households include older people, companies will need to increasingly think about who is actually going to use the products or services they are developing. Market opportunities may exist aimed at those growing numbers of families where two, three and in some cases even four generations of needs coexist under one roof.

One approach will be to adopt a strategy of "universal design" whereby products are developed that work for people with differing physical capabilities and so benefit the population as a whole. For example, the Whirlpool Duet clothes washer and dryer is built on a pedestal that provides storage and minimizes bending when loading and emptying the machine. The enlarged door and angled basket also make use easier for all users, old and young [24].

In the workplace, as older workers become older customers, employers also need to be aware of the more diverse permutations of mature households in workplace planning. For example, research into attitudes and practices towards older workers in Scotland revealed a general attitude by employers that "as older employees were free from family commitments they could work more hours and be more flexible" [6]. Such an attitude is clearly based on a false assumption of older household compositions in the twenty-first century, where older people increasingly are themselves caring for older parents and/or younger children. Left unchallenged, such false beliefs could undermine the feasibility of both a firm's HR strategy and its business models.

The Intergenerational Agenda: From Savers to Spenders to Debtors

The final thrust of the argument is that intergenerational exchanges should not be forgotten in considering grey market potential. Rather ironically, whilst many firms have been slow to see the opportunities of an aging population, there are some signs in the media that some organizations are beginning to pursue a heralded "gold-rush" by exploiting grey markets at the very point when the opportunities may have reached a tipping point in the West. In business and strategy, timing is everything. We know from the segmentation literature that life cohorts differ in their attitudes to consumption and saving. What has received less attention is how these differences in life cohort attitudes combine to impact upon intergenerational wealth and exchange. Intergenerational exchange is largely ignored by the current literature on grey market potential, as policy-makers have focused on short-term political objectives. However, intergenerational exchange is nevertheless a vital consideration for firms developing grey business strategies, if their business plans are to be realized.

For example, in the West, the generation that experienced either the depression and/or post-war austerity witnessed widespread hardship first-hand and remained financially cautious thereafter. This generation became *savers* who were advised "never a lender or a borrower be." This generation sought to live within their financial limits, and such caution encouraged them to save to build capital for themselves and their families. For working people, many aspired to be the home owners in their families for the first time. For this generation, dying with a legacy in terms of a house or assets to pass to their children was a mark of lifetime achievement. Indeed, if we go back to 1997, 75% of mature consumers carried no debt [17]. However, in more recent years the dominance of the older savers generation is starting to give way to the *spenders*.

Baby boomers (those born between 1946 and 1964) and onwards are generally affluent because they have enjoyed a post-war boom period of relatively high employment (taking aside cyclical swings), and because many inherited or are likely to inherit from the savers. The attitude of this generation is "we have never had it so good and we are going to enjoy it." However, the high levels of conspicuous consumption by many of those currently employed, the spenders, to which much of the grey marketing is currently aimed, conceals the fact that this generation is stoking up problems for the next generation that may undermine the grey markets of the future. This generation prides itself on spending the kids' inheritance whilst benefiting from final salary pensions schemes. This generation's only legacy may be dying in debt, leaving the kids to effectively inherit the mortgage or the credit card bill.

The generations currently entering the workforce face very different prospects. In a knowledge economy, a greater proportion of this generation are remaining in higher education for longer, and starting work later, with possible stark consequences given the intergenerational legacy they will inherit. They are more likely to begin their employment with higher levels of debt, and are less likely to enjoy final salary pensions. Intergenerational dynamics suggest that this generation will be less able to rely on inheritance from the spending generation. The next generation are more likely to be *debtors* as they have more debts at the start of life, and are less likely to inherit or have their own equity to release as home ownership becomes harder. This will be due to house price inflation or devalued equity, as baby boomers cash in their housing equity over the coming years to sustain their consumption, thereby shifting the balance of property supply and demand.

Clearly, intergenerational issues are culturally relative. However, in developing strategy globally for grey markets, firms need to bear in mind the specific intergenerational dynamics at play in the countries they are targeting their products and services at, if they are to fully understand future households and the forces that shape them. This requires looking at the West and monitoring the intergenerational issues in the rapidly developing economies of Asia and Latin America longer-term. HSBC, which promotes itself as "the world's local bank," has produced a range of reports that provide detailed information on the changing nature of aging societies, families, and retirement in key global markets, which highlight the strategic importance of understanding household and intergenerational issues for product and market development.

Summary and Conclusion

In this chapter, we have extended the debates about older people and business strategy in three ways. Firstly, we have provided a basis for rethinking the segmentation of older workers as older customers, and for segmenting both older workers and older customers based on a wealth/health segmentation matrix. Secondly, we have extended consideration of grey market potential beyond thinking of older workers and customers in isolation, by suggesting that older customers in particular need to be at least in part considered within the context of their household setting and its wider needs. Finally, we have signaled how firms need to be wary of merely jumping on the emergent "grey gold-rush" bandwagon without first taking into account intergenerational dynamics in planning their longer-term silver strategies.

Whilst our research is based in a Western framework, we would argue that our wealth/health segmentation matrix and subsequent consideration of older worker/ older customer profiling on a household basis, as well as intergenerational dynamics, are of direct relevance to those planning grey strategies in all countries. The household compositions in which the old reside, as well as intergenerational dynamics factors, will clearly to some extent be different and potentially unique across different nations. This will require differing approaches to grey strategy development in different countries. However, our key point of recognizing household compositions and intergenerational dynamics as key factors in grey strategy development offers universal application.

Older people are not all the same and will never meaningfully be able to be categorized as such. However, to conclude from this fairly obvious proposition that the old as workers, let alone as customers, cannot be usefully segmented is inaccurate. We live in a world in which the young as a generation do not have to think because marketeers and the media do it for them. And, provided that these marketeers and the media convince the young that they are different from all other generations, the young seem fairly happy to accept this.

Unfortunately for marketeers and the media, the old are not such an easy sell. They have several things on their side, not least including experience, wisdom, and in many cases degrees of affliction in terms of health, dexterity and mobility which will lead them to base their decisions as customers on far more personal and practical considerations than the young. This said, we believe that these personal and practical considerations in large part stem from the wealth/health status of the individual, before being shaped by their domestic household context and the broader behavior of their generational grouping. Taking these factors into account as we have herein, some sensible segmentations of the old as workers and as customers do therefore become realistic and reliable, and beyond this, useful as tools for companies seeking to capitalize on grey power now and into the future.

References

1. United Nations. Demographic and Social Statistics. http://unstats.un.org/unsd/demographic/. Accessed 15 Aug 2008
2. P. Hewitt, Global aging and the rise of the developing world. The Geneva Pap. Risk Insurance, **27**(4), 477–485 (2002)
3. T. Allen-Mills, 100 not out. Sunday Times 17 June, 20 (2007)

4. S. Tempest, C. Barnatt, C. Coupland, Grey advantage: New strategies for the old. Long Range Plann. **35**(5), 475–492 (2002)
5. W.C.K. Chiu, A.W. Chan, E. Snape, T. Redman, Hum. Relat. **54**(5), 629–661 (2001)
6. W. Loretto, P. White, Hum. Resour. Manage. J. **16**(3), 313–330 (2007)
7. W. Loretto, S. Vickerstaff, P. White (eds.), *The Future for Older Workers: New Perspectives* (The Policy Press, Bristol, 2009)
8. Age Concern. www.ageconcern.org.uk/AgeConcern/job-losses-release-210109.asp. Accessed 14 Nov 2009
9. M. Leibold, S. Voepel, *Managing the Aging Workforce: Challenges and Solutions* (Wiley, Germany, 2006), p. 213
10. N. Cutler, J. Financ. Serv. Professionals **55**(2), 52 (2001)
11. J.M. Zissimpoulos, L.A. Karoly, Labour Econ. **14**, 269 (2007)
12. C. Pak, A. Kambil, Over 50 and ready to shop: serving the aging consumer. J. Bus. Strateg. **27**(6), 18–28 (2006)
13. J. Knight, A husky sled? Well, that's one way for Grandad to broaden his horizons. The Times 15 Sept, 2 (2007)
14. W. Longbottom, 91-year-old war veteran becomes oldest person to collect PhD from Cambridge University, Daily Mail, 19.07.2008
15. A. Alexander, IRI study shatters baby boomer shopping myths; September 11, vol. 4, p. 49 (2006). http://www.drugstorenews.com
16. R. Ahmad, Int. J. Mark. Res. **44**(3), 337 (2002)
17. R.C. Leventhal, J. Consum. Mark. **14**(4), 276–281 (1997)
18. G. Moschis, C. Folkman Curasi, D. Bellenger, Cornell Hotel Restaur. Admin. Q. **44**(4), 51 (2003)
19. P. Weisz, Brandweek **37**(4), 28 (1996)
20. C. Henderson, The Futurist **Nov**, 19 (1998)
21. Unilever 'Beauty has no age limit'. http://www.unilever.com/brands/hygieneandwelbeing/beautyandstyle/articles/beautyhasnoagelimit.aspx. (Accessed 30 Sep 2010)
22. AOL Time Warner, AOL announces first ever on-line service to provide older Americans with one-stop access to federal and state benefits (2010), www.timewarner.com/corp/newsroom/pr/0,20812,668786,00.html/28.01.10
23. GE, GE and Intel team up on home health (2010) www.gereports.com/ge-and-intel-team-up-on-home-health-tech/29/01/10
24. T. Purdum, The age of design: baby boomers serve as the common denominator for consumer durables manufacturers, August, 2002. http://www.industryweek.com. Accessed 11 June 2008

Chapter 16
Catering to Older Consumers' Customer Service Needs

Simone Pettigrew

Abstract Older consumers have distinct customer service preferences that can constitute a source of competitive advantage for forward-thinking marketers who seek to attract this large and relatively affluent segment. This chapter focuses on the supermarket, financial planning, and healthcare industries to demonstrate the importance of providing personalized attention to allow for the older person's deteriorating physical and cognitive abilities and shrinking social networks. In particular, emphasis is placed on the need to allow older customers to form meaningful relationships with service staff. This strategy has implications for the recruitment, training, and retention of staff members who are able to demonstrate genuine concern for the welfare of the older consumer.

Introduction

Aging brings with it a range of physiological changes that have consequences for individuals' marketplace behaviors. Of particular interest in this chapter are the implications of these changes on older consumers' service needs. While suppliers of goods and services have typically focused on the physical adaptations of their products and premises that are required for their older customers, less attention has been given to the personal interaction elements of the exchange process. This chapter will show that older consumers can have distinct service preferences and that these have implications for suppliers wishing to differentiate themselves in the marketplace by offering superior customer service to their older clientele. Customer service is defined as those aspects of service that support the provision of the company's core products. The personal interaction that occurs in the exchange process is a primary component of customer service.

A brief account of the primary age-related physiological and social changes is provided below, followed by the findings of a large Australian study on seniors' service preferences and a discussion of the implications of these changes for

F. Kohlbacher and C. Herstatt (eds.), *The Silver Market Phenomenon*,
DOI 10.1007/978-3-642-14338-0_16, © Springer-Verlag Berlin Heidelberg 2011

marketers wishing to deliver high levels of customer service to the large and growing cohort of older consumers.

Functional Changes

Age-related physical deterioration is an inevitable aspect of the aging process. While individuals experience this deterioration to a greater or lesser degree depending on their genetic inheritance and lifestyles, there are certain physical changes that are generally to be expected with age. For example, most people begin to notice vision impairment in their 40s and 50s. This reflects a gradual thickening and hardening of the lens and a shrinking of the pupil that in combination make it more difficult to focus the eyes [1]. Increasing hearing loss is also very common with age. Hearing impairment is of particular concern for cognitive function because it is associated with reductions in functional intelligence, especially memory [2].

Physical mobility also tends to reduce with age, largely due to decreasing muscle mass and muscular strength [3]. Reductions in mobility are particularly problematic when they result in falls as many older people suffer permanent disabilities, or even death, as a consequence of falling. Partially as a result of their smaller stature, women tend to experience greater losses of strength and mobility with age [4].

Along with these functional changes come alterations in cognitive processing. Slower processing occurs as the neural pathways to the brain deteriorate with age [2]. The outcome is that at any point in time the older person has less attentional capacity to direct at any particular stimuli and it becomes more demanding to perform the same mental tasks that used to be less challenging. As a result, new information is more difficult to assimilate, especially when it involves unfamiliar stimuli. For this reason, where new information contradicts previously learned information the older person is more likely to fail to change existing beliefs [5]. In addition, it becomes more difficult for older people to recall the source of information, which may make them more susceptible to repetitious advertising [6].

Social Changes

The physical and psychological changes discussed above have effects on individuals' social status. Deteriorating mobility, vision, and hearing shrink the older person's circle of regular contacts and make it difficult to establish new relationships. In addition, the likelihood of the death of a spouse and close friends increases with age, so older people are more likely than younger people to live alone and to have smaller social networks [7]. As a result of these factors, the incidence of loneliness increases with age. Loneliness can trigger depression in the older person, a trend that is particularly common among older women [8]. Reflecting the close relationship between mental and physical health, depression tends to be more severe amongst those experiencing lower levels of perceived physical health [9]. Depression is thus directly associated with deteriorating physical health as well as indirectly through the relationship between physical health and loneliness because failing health makes socializing more difficult. The physiological changes that occur with age can therefore impact significantly on an individual's frame of mind and his or her ability to interact effectively with others.

Understanding the Older Consumer

These functional and social aspects of aging are likely to influence individuals' attitudes to products and their subsequent purchase decisions [10]. The bulk of marketing research that has focused on older consumers has concentrated on their product-related attitudes and how these are manifest in purchase behaviors. Less research has been directed at analyzing how these attitudes have changed over time as a result of changing physical and social characteristics. Studies are typically cross-sectional in design and as such identify variations between current cohorts but not variation within cohorts over time. The latter remains an area of untapped potential in understanding how age-related physical and social changes impact upon older consumers' preferences and choices. This will become increasingly important in the future as later cohorts of seniors can be expected to behave differently from current cohorts because of their very different life experiences [11].

Studies of older consumers' consumption behaviors have also tended to focus primarily on specific product categories, product attributes, and advertising effectiveness. For example, research has examined older consumers' attitudes to products as diverse as apparel, cars, meat products, and financial services. Packaging as a product attribute has also received attention because of the difficulties older consumers can face when coping with "senior-proof" wrapping [12].

Across most studies involving the senior segment, older consumers have been found to be similar to younger consumers in most respects. Any differences are usually in degree rather than in nature. For instance, seniors can exhibit higher levels of store loyalty [13], and tend to have somewhat smaller brand repertoires [14–16]. Compared to younger consumers they tend to exhibit greater avoidance of self-service technology [17, 18], and they have been found to be less price-sensitive and to have higher quality expectations [19, 20]. Older consumers are reported to be more appreciative of emotional advertisements than younger consumers, especially when the advertisements feature nostalgia appeals [21, 22].

With this emphasis on products and promotion, less empirical attention has been given to the customer service aspects of seniors' consumption experiences. While the literature on aging consumers contains many assertions relating to customer service (e.g., the importance of recruitment and retention of older sales staff, avoiding condescension in interactions, and offering seniors' discounts carefully to prevent causing offense [12, 20, 23, 24]), these recommendations are usually unsupported with empirical data and instead reflect intuitive assessments made on the basis of the likely needs of those who experience the functional and social changes associated with the aging process. Those studies that have explicitly addressed customer service aspects of the older consumer's shopping experience usually do so as merely one element of the consumption process and as a consequence report limited results relating specifically to customer service. One common finding among these studies is that assistance from staff is especially appreciated by older consumers [25].

Although studies of seniors' customer service preferences are largely neglected in marketing research, the health literature offers some insights on this subject as substantial work has been done on older patients' experiences when receiving medical services. In particular, the nursing literature provides numerous accounts of the physiological and social requirements of older patients and how these translate into specific needs in a service provision context [26–28]. These studies have emphasized the need to focus on older people as a specific group with specific needs, to be responsive and empathetic to older people's individual requirements, and to actively work to reduce the confusion that may occur during the various stages of the decision-making process as a result of slower cognitive processing or illness [29].

Due to the lack of empirical data relating to older consumers and their customer service preferences, most of our understanding in this area comes from studies conducted in service contexts as these exchange processes typically contain a high degree of human interaction. The health and financial services sectors tend to have been examined the most in terms of older consumers as many of their products cater specifically for this segment. There are lessons to be learned from this research, although future work that focuses on seniors' customer service expectations and preferences is needed to fill the current gap in the literature that relates to the kinds of personal interaction and other forms of customer service that are most valued and appreciated by older consumers. The section to follow outlines the results of a major Australian study into seniors' perceptions of what would constitute a "senior-friendly" business (see [30] for background details). This project identified those aspects of the service experience that were considered most important and relevant to a broad range of seniors across multiple industries.

Age-Friendly Service Providers

The Age Friendly Guidelines Project was undertaken by the Positive Aging Foundation of Australia under the sponsorship of the then Western Australian Department for Community Development, Seniors Interests. The main objective of the project was to provide managers with guidance on how to make their businesses more senior-friendly. The research focused on Australians aged 50 years and older, and involved more than 30 focus groups and two telephone surveys ($n = 1,300, n = 505$). The first phase of the study, which comprised the bulk of the focus groups and the larger survey, identified those industries that were viewed by older consumers to be most important to their general welfare and therefore those for which it would be most beneficial to adopt age-friendly customer service strategies. These industries were found to be supermarkets, financial services, and the health sector (primarily general practitioners and hospitals). Those aspects of service delivery considered to be especially important to older customers in these industries were then explored in the remaining focus groups and the smaller of the two surveys. The results of this project offer important insights for marketers in these and other industries that target the growing senior segment. While the results are of specific relevance to Australian marketers, the tendency for most research relating to senior consumers to be conducted in the USA and the UK means that any research conducted outside these contexts has the potential to add deeper insight into the international phenomenon of aging consumers.

Supermarkets

Grocery stores are a form of retail outlet that continues to be frequently patronized by consumers in their later years. Shopping for groceries is a relatively physical pastime that requires some degree of strength and agility on the part of the shopper. For this reason, previous research has identified a range of issues relating to the layout of the store and surrounding areas. For example, parking access, availability of seating, and store temperature have been noted as especially important to older shoppers [31–33]. Service considerations such as waiting times at checkouts and attitudes of service staff have also been highlighted [11, 34, 35].

The Australian research supported these priorities and highlighted the importance of customer service elements such as the demeanor and availability of service staff, assistance in locating products, and the provision of multiple delivery options to cater for different physical abilities [36, 37]. Of most importance was the ability of staff members to interact pleasantly with older customers. Almost all (99%) of older Australians surveyed noted this to be either an important or very important aspect of visiting a supermarket. Reflecting the recognized role of shopping in facilitating social interactions for isolated older people [38, 39], focus group participants commented on their desire for "real" interactions with store employees rather than parroted, superficial greetings that they assume are the result of the training that service staff members have received. While recognizing that there is little opportunity for in-depth conversations, the participants felt that it is reasonable to expect staff to look them in the eye when greeting them and engage in friendly small talk while processing their items through the checkout.

Reflecting the physical limitations often faced by older consumers, 90% of the survey respondents felt it is important or very important for staff members to be readily available to provide assistance with product location. Some suggested that supermarkets could hire a "hospitality person" who could be given the prime role of assisting older customers. They felt that such supermarkets would be much more attractive to seniors compared to regular supermarkets that they found to be uncaring and focused on profits at the expense of customer service.

For many older people, walking around a supermarket can be physically exhausting. This discomfort is exacerbated when it is necessary to search for items that have been moved or that are being purchased for the first time. Focus group participants discussed the need to do just one trip around the supermarket without needing to return to previously visited aisles to search for particular items. They noted that it is often very difficult to find staff to assist with information about the location of items or to pass down items from high shelves. The tendency for older people to be shorter than younger people means that they can be disadvantaged when shelves are built to cater to average height customers. Of major concern was the danger of falling while reaching up to high shelves. Deep freezers were also viewed as posing a significant physical challenge, with some focus group participants speaking with fear of falling into freezers and not being able to right themselves. They were concerned about both their physical safety and dignity in such circumstances. The provision of additional staff dedicated to ensuring the welfare of older shoppers by assisting with product location and product access would allow enhanced customer service to compensate for the physical aspects of the store that can present real hardship for the aged.

The availability of multiple delivery options was considered important or very important by 82% of the survey respondents. These options included drive-through and home delivery services that would reduce the need for older shoppers to manage heavy bags of groceries. While not averse to being charged for home delivery services, those stores that provided this service on a complimentary basis were considered to be especially senior-friendly.

Financial Planners

The financial planning sector is of increasing importance around the world due to governments' realization that the aging of the population is resulting in the need for older people to become self-financing rather than reliant on the state for retirement income. In the Australian context, older consumers are particularly attractive to financial planners as those 55 years of age and older earn around 25% of the nation's disposable income while controlling almost 40% of the nation's wealth [40]. This combination of income and assets makes them the most financially powerful segment in the marketplace. Not only are financial planners very interested in older consumers, but seniors are also typically very interested in financial services because of the need to carefully manage their income over the remainder of their lives. In theory, this should mean that the two parties view each other as providing mutually beneficial interaction, but this is not always the case. The technical nature of the information that needs to be conveyed between financial planners and their clients can make it difficult to achieve effective communication. This means that financial planners need to possess good interpersonal skills and to be sensitized to the perceptual abilities and limitations of their clients. In particular, the meaning of complex terminology needs to be conveyed in such a way as to maximize comprehension. Financial planners need to be capable of assisting clients to visualize themselves in the future so they can picture themselves benefiting from the delayed gratification that is typically necessary in sound financial planning [41].

This necessary reliance on clients' cognitive skills means that financial planners should consider the effects of age-related limitations on individuals' abilities to perceive stimuli and process information. Kennet et al.'s [42] US study of financial planners and their approaches to the mature market found a strong focus among planners on the development and promotion of financial products that are useful to this segment but a general lack of appreciation of the specific service needs of older clients. Kennet et al.'s recommendations included strategies to cater for both the physical and social changes experienced by older clients. For example, they suggested using larger font sizes in documents, providing suitable access into and within the building, offering home delivery of documents, training staff to be aware and understanding of older clients' needs, and hiring older staff to liaise with older clients.

These recommendations were supported by the Australian research [43, 44], which again highlighted the customer service aspects of interactions with company personnel. Of primary importance to the respondents was the quality of the relationship formed between the client and the financial planner. Ninety-six percent of respondents rated it important or very important to develop a working relationship with their financial planner that was characterized by mutual trust and the preservation of the client's dignity. Focus group participants traded horror stories of those who had fallen victim to unethical financial planners and as a result had been financially disadvantaged. They wanted to feel confident that their financial planner had their best interests at heart as this would prevent the same happening to them.

Also of concern was financial planners' ability to determine the appropriate amount of information to deliver to clients and the manner in which it was to be conveyed. Ninety-four percent of the survey respondents rated this aspect of customer service as important or very important. Flexibility in communication style was described as an essential attribute of a financial planner because of the varying knowledge levels and intellectual capacities of different clients. It was suggested that financial planners should be ready to provide information in both graphical and written form to allow individuals with different learning styles to have their communication needs accommodated. This flexibility should be provided in a considerate fashion as the focus group participants were adamant that older clients should not be treated with condescension simply because they lack a detailed understanding of financial planning principles.

Health Sector

The aging of the world's population has enormous implications for the healthcare sector. As a consequence of this demographic trend and the long-standing acknowledgement of the importance of customer service in the health industry, the customer service needs of older patients have been the subject of greater attention than has been the case in other industries.

Health services are of particular importance to older people as usage of these services increases significantly with age. The Australian Bureau of Statistics estimates that per-person health expenditure is four times greater amongst those aged 65 years and older than in younger age groups [45]. The degree of dependence of older people on healthcare services is illustrated by the fact that, over a 2-week period, almost 40% of Australians aged 65 and older will have visited a doctor [46].

General Practitioners

Healthcare customers of all ages are known to be particularly concerned with the quality of the personal interaction skills of their medical practitioners [26, 47]. Older patients are no exception, and past research has identified the relationship between doctor and patient as one of the most important criteria used by older patients to assess their satisfaction with their doctor [31]. It appears likely that patients use their perceptions of a doctor's bedside manner as a proxy for quality of care because of their inability to assess the technical quality of the care received [48, 49]. This highlights the need for medical practitioners to ensure that they are meeting patients' relationship needs as this is likely to influence their perceptions of the quality of care and therefore their intention to comply with medication prescriptions and other behavioral recommendations [47].

The Australian research supported the emphasis in the literature on the relationship that is formed between doctor and patient [50, 51]. Ninety-seven percent of survey respondents rated a caring bedside manner and good communication skills as important or very important in their interactions with general practitioners (GPs). Many of the conditions that older patients need to discuss with their doctors can be embarrassing and difficult to articulate. A compassionate demeanor was considered essential to allow full disclosure of symptoms. One aspect of a caring bedside manner that was considered particularly critical was the time taken by doctors to genuinely listen to patients' concerns (94% agreement). The focus group participants described feeling rushed by the short appointment times typically allocated per patient. For some, this resulted in them feeling flustered and unable to focus their thoughts, which prevented them from communicating effectively with the doctor. This problem was exacerbated when patients considered their symptoms or condition to be demeaning or embarrassing.

A further aspect of customer service that was considered important by the study participants was the appropriate provision of information. Ninety-seven percent felt that doctors should make the effort to ensure that the information they provide relating to medications is readily understood by their older patients. Especially when unwell, older people can experience difficulties in assimilating and retaining information. Focus group participants noted that they preferred their doctor to write down medication instructions or details about their condition as this prevents them from getting confused or forgetting the information by the time they get home. Similarly, 90% wanted clear information concerning the costs of the services provided and any rebates that may be available to seniors. Eighty percent wanted to be given estimates of waiting times upon arrival, as even just sitting in a waiting room can be an onerous task for an older person who is feeling unwell. Knowing the length of the wait ahead of them allows older patients to mentally prepare themselves for the delay or make alternative arrangements if the wait is going to be too long for them to tolerate.

Hospitals

The findings relating to hospitals were similar to those for GPs in that trusting relationships with carers were a high priority [52]. Relationships with nurses appeared to take priority over relationships with doctors in a hospital context as patients have much greater contact with nursing staff over the duration of their hospitalization. Inpatients are in a highly dependent state and as a consequence they can feel very vulnerable and desirous of empathy from those attending to their physical needs. The focus group participants expressed preference for staff members who introduce themselves, refer to the patient by name, exhibit a compassionate and friendly demeanor, and make patients feel at ease in potentially awkward or embarrassing situations. These findings mirror the outcomes of other studies of older patients' hospital experiences, where being recognized and treated with dignity were found to be primary factors influencing satisfaction [27, 53, 54].

Preference was also exhibited for staff members who take the time to get to know patients, at least a little. While acknowledging the many demands on health-workers' time and the stresses associated with working in a hospital environment, the focus group participants expressed a desire for staff to demonstrate an unhurried demeanor and to take the time to ensure they were familiar with the older patient's condition. Seniors often take multiple medications so it is important for staff to be aware of possible negative consequences of combining different medications. This awareness only occurs when members of staff take the time to familiarize themselves with the patient's medical history.

The customer service experience in a hospital commences at admission, making this an important interaction for the older patient who is likely to be nervous and experiencing pain. It was suggested that the admissions process could be improved in many hospitals to prevent seniors from waiting for long periods. In particular, it was noted that the same information was often required at both hospital admission and ward admission, suggesting that the information collection process could be streamlined to prevent this duplication.

Implications for Service Delivery

Existing knowledge of the physical and social changes associated with aging and the consumer studies profiled above provide insight into the customer service preferences of older consumers. These preferences can be effectively accommodated by marketers who appreciate the value of the senior segment and make this group a specific focus of their strategising. The aspect of customer service that appears to be most valued by older consumers is a genuine understanding of and concern for their individual needs. Older consumers appreciate those providers who take the time to get to know them as individuals and demonstrate sincere concern for their welfare. In this sense, seniors do not differ from other segments other than that the need for individual consideration is of a more profound nature because it partly stems from the age-related physical and social changes being experienced. Deteriorating sensory perception and cognitive processing abilities require information inputs and other forms of communication to be tailored to the specific needs of the older person. Similarly, the growing isolation that often accompanies older age can result in the need for more personalized interactions to compensate for shrinking social networks.

The provision of more tailored and personal service may appear at first glance to be a costly and resource-intensive burden on firms. However, as the large segment of baby boomers continues to enter the senior segment and experience the physical and social changes associated with the aging process, it will increasingly be in marketers' interests to ensure their offerings are senior-friendly in every way possible. In addition, achieving high levels of differentiated customer service will serve marketers well in their efforts to attract other segments that also prioritize this element of the exchange process. The relative affluence of newer cohorts of seniors will facilitate this increase in service standards by permitting higher costs to be passed on to those older consumers who are willing to pay higher prices for superior service.

The preference among seniors for service staff who exhibit sincerity and a genuine concern for their needs has implications for employee recruitment, training, and retention. Staff members will need to be selected according to their ability to demonstrate empathy with older customers. To some degree, this may require the recruitment of older workers who are capable of empathizing with the needs of seniors. Customer service training will need to cover aspects such as appropriate ways of addressing older people, appropriate physical and verbal demeanor, ways to preserve the customer's dignity, the determination of how and when to render physical assistance, and the prevention of long waiting times. In some industries it would also be beneficial to provide service staff with specific instructions about the most effective ways to convey information, such as in which circumstances information should be provided verbally or in writing, and when to use pictures. Employee retention is also important as it will allow older customers to build relationships with those members of staff with whom they regularly come into contact.

Summary and Conclusion

Marketers wishing to target older consumers need to understand the strong desire among members of this segment for individualized attention. Personalized interactions are especially important to older consumers because of their deteriorating physical and cognitive abilities and their growing social isolation. Reductions in mobility, sight, and hearing leave the older person vulnerable in many consumption situations where physical adeptness is required to locate, compare, select, and carry products. Similarly, shrinking social networks can make the older person overly reliant on interactions with the providers of goods and services to obtain human contact. There is thus an opportunity for organizations to differentiate their marketplace offerings through superior customer service that recognizes and caters to older consumers' need for greater levels of physical assistance and a heightened desire to form personal relationships with those from whom they regularly purchase goods and services. Customer service targeted at the older consumer would be therefore ideally characterized by friendly but respectful interactions, the provision of physical assistance where needed, and the pacing of information to suit the customer's processing needs. Such an approach can provide a source of differentiation that is valued by older consumers and is also likely to be attractive to members of other segments that prioritize high quality service.

Given the noted similarities between the results of the Australian studies described above and those conducted in other countries and in other industries, it appears that the customer service recommendations provided here would be applicable to numerous other cultural and product contexts. The universal nature of the aging process and the resulting implications for marketplace behaviors suggest that marketers everywhere would be well served to consider how their customer service processes can be better geared to the changing physical and social needs of aging consumers.

References

1. C. Stuen, E.E. Faye, Generations **27**(1), 8 (2003)
2. H. Wahl, V. Heyl, Generations **27**(1), 39 (2003)
3. M.J. Daley, W.L. Spinks, Sports Med. **29**(1), 1 (2000)
4. M.M. Samson, I. Meeuwsen, A. Crowe, J. Dessens, S.A. Duursma, H. Verhaar, Age Aging **29**, 235 (2000)
5. G.E. Rice, M.A. Okun, J. Geronotol. **49**(3), 119 (1994)
6. C. Yoon, G. Laurent, R. Gonzales, A.H. Gutchess, T. Hedden, R. Lambert-Pandraud et al., Mark. Lett. **16**(3/4), 429 (2005)
7. M. Bondevik, A. Skogstad, West. J. Nurs. Res. **20**(3), 325 (1998)
8. P. Tiikkainen, R.L. Heikkinen, Aging Ment. Health **9**(6), 526 (2005)
9. F.M. Alpass, S. Neville, Aging Ment. Health **7**(3), 212 (2003)
10. C. Cole, G. Laurent, A. Drolet, J. Ebert, A. Gutchess, R. Lambert-Pandraud, E. Mullet, M.I. Norton, E. Peters, Market. Lett. **19**, 355 (2008)

11. G.P. Moschis, *Marketing to Older Consumers* (Quorum Books, Westport, CT, USA, 1992)
12. S. Fairley, G.P. Moschis, H.M. Meyers, A. Thiesfeldt, Brandweek **38**(30), 24 (1997)
13. N.J. Miller, K. Soyoung, J. Small Bus. Manage. **37**(4), 1 (1999)
14. H. Evanschitzky, D.M. Woisetschläger, Adv. Consum. Res. **35**, 630 (2008)
15. P.G. Patterson, J. Serv. Mark. **21**(2), 112 (2007)
16. M.D. Uncles, A.S.C. Ehrenberg, J. Advert. Res. **30**(4), 19 (1990)
17. D.H. Dean, Manag. Serv. Qual. **18**(3), 225 (2008)
18. F. Simon, J-C. Usunier, Int. J. Res. Mark. **24**, 163 (2007)
19. G.P. Moschis, A. Mathur, Mark. Manage. **2**(2), 40 (1993)
20. H.N. Tongren, J. Consum. Aff. **22**(1), 136 (1988)
21. T.S. Gruca, C.D. Schewe, Mark. Res. **4**(3), 18 (1992)
22. P. Williams, A. Drolet, J. Consum. Res. **32**, 343 (2005)
23. J. Johnson-Hillery, J. Kang, W-J. Tuan, Int. J. Retail Distrib. Manage. **25**(4), 126 (1997)
24. K. Tepper, J. Consum. Res. **20**, 503 (1994)
25. C. Pak, A. Kambil, J. Bus. Strateg. **27**(6), 18 (2006)
26. M.R. Bowers, J.E. Swan, W.F. Koehler, Health Care Manage. Rev. **19**(4), 49 (1994)
27. T. Koch, C. Webb, A.M. Williams, J. Clin. Nurs. **4**(3), 185 (1995)
28. M. Rantz, N.K. Davis, R.A. Tapp, J. Nurs. Care Qual. **9**(3), 1 (1995)
29. J.N. Doucette, Nurs. Manage. **34**(11), 26 (2003)
30. Positive Aging Foundation of Australia. The age friendly guidelines project (Positive Aging Foundation of Australia, Perth 2002) http://www.community.wa.gov.au/NR/rdonlyres/5C473211-F8E6-42FA-9C98-8492435B1351/0/DCDRPTAgefriendlyguidelines200309.pdf. Accessed 11 Jun 2008
31. M. Morrison, T. Murphy, C. Nalder, Health Mark. Q. **20**(3), 3 (2004)
32. G.P. Moschis, Am. Demograph. **18**(9), 44 (1996)
33. B. Oates, L. Shufeldt, B. Vaught, J. Consum. Mark. **13**(6), 14 (1996)
34. D.R. Goodwin, R.E. McElwee, Int. Rev. Retail Distrib. Consum. Res. **9**(4), 403 (1999)
35. C. Hare, Int. J. Retail Distrib. Manage. **31**(5), 244 (2003)
36. S. Pettigrew, K. Mizerski, R. Donovan, Australas. J. Aging **23**(3), 142 (2004)
37. S. Pettigrew, K. Mizerski, R. Donovan, J. Consum. Mark. **22**(6), 306 (2005)
38. H. Myers, M. Lumbers, J. Consum. Mark. **25**(2), 294 (2008)
39. L.C. Wilson, A. Alexander, M. Lumbers, Int. J. Retail Distrib. Manage. **32**(2), 109 (2004)
40. Access Economics, *Population Aging and the Economy* (Commonwealth of Australia, Canberra, 2001)
41. P.T. Gibbs, Eur. J. Mark. **32**(11/12), 993 (1998)
42. P.A. Kennet, G.P. Moschis, D.N. Bellenger, J. Serv. Mark. **9**(2), 62 (1995)
43. S. Pettigrew, K. Mizerski, R. Donovan, J. Financ. Serv. Mark. **7**(4), 341 (2003)
44. S. Pettigrew, K. Mizerski, R. Donovan, Australas. J. Aging **23**(3), 144 (2004)
45. Australian Bureau of Statistics, *Australian social trends 1999 – Health – Health Status: Health of Older People* (Australian Bureau of Statistics, Canberra, 2002)
46. Australian Bureau of Statistics, *The Health of Older People, Australia* (Australian Bureau of Australia, Canberra, 2004)
47. D.H. Thom, B. Campbell, J. Fam. Pract. **44**(2), 169 (1997)
48. E. Babakus, W.G. Mangold, Health Serv. Res. **26**(6), 767 (1992)
49. M. Peyrot, P.D. Cooper, D. Schnapf, J. Health Care Mark. **13**(1), 24 (1993)
50. S. Pettigrew, K. Mizerski, R. Donovan, Australas. J. Aging **23**(3), 146 (2004)
51. S. Pettigrew, K. Mizerski, R. Donovan, Aust. J. Prim. Health **11**(3), 38 (2005)
52. S. Pettigrew, Aust. J. Prim. Health **12**(3), 52 (2006)
53. I. Ekman, B. Lindman, A. Norberg, Heart Lung **28**(3), 203 (1999)
54. C.S. Jacelon, Qual. Health Res. **13**(4), 543 (2003)

Chapter 17
Business Strategies for Enhancing Quality of Life in the Later Years

George Moschis and Simone Pettigrew

Abstract As the earth's population ages, businesses globally need to become more attuned to the needs of older consumers. This chapter emphasizes the importance of understanding the factors that enhance well-being in later life, and suggests strategies that can be adopted by marketers to assist consumers achieve this objective. This emphasis on developing strategies that enhance well-being entails a change in philosophy, involving a more holistic approach to marketing that focuses on both profits and enhancing consumer well-being.

Introduction

The aging of the world's population suggests that businesses will be dealing with increasingly larger numbers of older consumers. Of course, you may ask: "Why is it important to understand the well-being of older consumers?" We show that such knowledge has important implications for businesses. Our main premise for a focus on well-being in later life is that consumers can develop and even adopt habits at earlier stages in life that promote satisfaction in their later years. In this context, businesses can help consumers improve their well-being across the lifespan. This emphasis entails a change in philosophy that involves a more holistic approach to marketing that focuses on both profits and enhancing consumer well-being.

This chapter proposes strategies that businesses can use to assist consumers to age well. The first section focuses on factors that contribute to enhanced well-being in later life, including a discussion of the ideal characteristics of the empowered older consumer. Once these factors have been presented (based on previous research), the second section of the chapter focuses on strategies that should be implemented by businesses to (a) empower older consumers and (b) prepare younger adults for enhanced well-being in later life.

F. Kohlbacher and C. Herstatt (eds.), *The Silver Market Phenomenon*,
DOI 10.1007/978-3-642-14338-0_17, © Springer-Verlag Berlin Heidelberg 2011

Factors that Enhance Well-Being in Later Life

The concepts of "life satisfaction" and "well-being" have received a great deal of attention in the social sciences. As a result, we have learned much about the many factors that contribute to happiness in later stages of life. For example, some widely researched determinants of life satisfaction uncovered by previous studies include physical and emotional health, independent living, spirituality, employment, social relationships, and a wide variety of psychological states (e.g., stress, optimism, self-esteem) [1]. Relationships between consumption-related activities and life satisfaction have been largely ignored. We know little about how consumption activities, skills, and knowledge acquired at earlier stages in life affect the older person's consumption activities, and how such activities contribute to the older person's well-being.

A review of present knowledge derived from several disciplines, including marketing, gerontology, and several areas of social science, suggests that life satisfaction and well-being in later life are a matter of choices people make at earlier stages in life. These observations suggest that the individual has a great deal of control over his or her life, especially when it comes to addressing issues of living longer and better [2]. Knowing the factors that contribute to enhanced well-being in later life can help one make choices during the life course that would adequately prepare the person to meet these needs when they arise. Because much has already been written on the effects of nonconsumption factors on the person's well-being, our discussion here focuses on understanding the relationships between well-being and consumption-related thoughts and actions. Specifically, we present research on the effects of people's choices relating to healthcare, finances, and select discretionary and nondiscretionary consumption activities, and how these choices influence their well-being in later life.

Choices Affecting Physical and Emotional Health

Health is the most important ingredient in a person's happiness and well-being. Concerns with health intensify in later life as people experience an increasing number of ailments associated with aging. Health usually becomes the number one concern in people's life after they experience a life-threatening event such as a stroke. The thought of possible deterioration of health in later life reminds people, especially those with inadequate financial resources, that they might become a burden on others. In one of our national surveys at the Center for Mature Consumer Studies, we found that 62% of baby boomers and three-fourths of their parents worry to some extent about a devastating physical impairment [1].

The good news is that the future state of our health is controllable to a great extent, and so is the number of years we are going to live within the human life span. This holds true even for people of very old age. The choices we make daily affect our present and future state of health, longevity and well-being in general. People have much control over the things they do to their bodies, including what they eat and their participation in physical activity. When the effects of exercising are assessed in the context of functional aging, the available knowledge suggests that moderate and regular exercise deters aging and increases longevity. Bed-ridden nursing home residents (some in their 90s) were able to function independently after researchers at Tuft's University put them through a resistance (weight) training program. Similarly, we know of cases where people in their early 60s entered a nursing home with heart problems and by exercising were not only able to overcome their frailties, but ran marathons in their 80s [3]. Exercise promotes hormonal growth, strengthens the immune system, and helps the body function more efficiently. It is perhaps the single most important controllable activity that has the greatest benefits, even more than dieting, according to scientists at the National Institute on Aging who have been studying longevity issues for years.

While developing a healthy body through exercise and diet is important in deterring and reversing aging, perhaps of greater importance in efforts to affect life span is the ability to enhance emotional health. The evidence in support of mind–body effects is overwhelming. For example, stress can be the cause of several fatal health conditions and between 60 and 80% of the symptoms requiring a visit to the doctor. Emotional health means (a) the absence of negative feelings that can affect physical health, such as stress, anxiety, self-pity (low self-esteem), and depression, and (b) the presence of positive feelings such as optimism, high self-esteem, zest, and purpose for living. As our research at the Center for Mature Consumer Studies shows, people whose state of mind is characterized by aversive rather than positive feelings also tend to have more health problems that may shorten their lives. In contrast, positive feelings such as optimism and a favorable opinion of oneself promote good mental health.

Financial Assets

While good health is a necessary condition for longevity, it is not sufficient for optimum well-being in later life. Financial resources also seem to affect a person's overall life satisfaction. However, according to the findings of several dozen studies in western countries, having wealth accumulation as the ultimate goal does not make you happier and it may even have negative effects on the person's well-being. But if you have the right attitude about money, managing it properly to accomplish multiple life goals, wealth can have beneficial effects on one's life satisfaction and well-being. Having adequate financial resources contributes to life satisfaction in four important ways. First, one does not worry about not having enough money in later life and therefore becoming a financial burden on other family members. Both baby boomers and their parents are becoming increasingly aware of the "costs" of increasing longevity. Those who have not saved enough for retirement, especially the baby boomers, are concerned with the quality of life in their retirement years, while their parents who have more assets are concerned with outliving their savings and becoming financially dependent on others. Such financial concerns undermine a person's emotional well-being.

A second reason why adequate financial resources enhance life satisfaction is because they enable people to do things they enjoy the most, and keep them from having to engage in undesirable activities or lifestyles. We know that everyone wants to have fun in later life, but lack of money and having to work indefinitely because of limited financial resources are constraints to a desirable lifestyle in retirement. Third, having adequate financial resources allows a person to gain better control over his/her environment, including people, thus enhancing feelings of self-worth and well-being. Similarly, people who can afford to help family members financially or buy gifts for them have greater control over their relatives' present and future actions.

Finally, money can buy peace of mind over and above the fear of becoming a burden on loved ones. If well-being is enhanced not only by getting or having things that give us pleasure but also by eliminating or reducing aversive feelings, then money can help reduce such feelings and enhance a person's quality of life. Many of the things people worry about are controllable to the extent that they have the money to pay for them. For example, people lose sleep over things such as personal and home safety, health, and having to do daily chores. People with adequate resources are less likely to be concerned with such things because they can make changes to reduce these concerns, such as moving to a safer neighborhood, receiving proper health-care services, and paying for at-home chores and care-giving services (such as cleaning and meal preparation). As our research at the Center for Mature Consumer Studies reveals, people in lower socioeconomic classes experience greater levels of anxiety about such things.

Discretionary Consumption Activities

The third source of life satisfaction is the way a person chooses to live his or her life – one's lifestyle. People appear to be happier when they engage in activities that give them a sense of control over their bodies and their environment. Diet and physical fitness programs allow us to exercise control over our bodies. Similarly, the ability to buy and consume certain products reflects a sense of control over our emotions because such activities help us "medicate" adverse feelings such as depression and boredom. As we found in one of our studies, some people indicated greater life satisfaction as a result of their starting of diet and exercise programs. A busy lifestyle that includes participation in a wide variety of activities, especially activities that involve social contact, such as attending adult education classes and volunteering, appears to enhance a person's life satisfaction. Engagement in such activities gives a person a sense of accomplishment and control over his/her environment, both of which are promoted through the enactment of various roles, such as the role of a student, volunteer, or worker.

The lifestyles of people in mid-life and beyond include a heavy dose of leisure time and activities. Preoccupation with self-indulgence declines with age, but regardless of age those most preoccupied are people who have fewer economic resources. For most people in middle and later years in life, fun often involves learning to do new things, such as taking on a new hobby or attending a class. At the Center for Mature Consumer Studies we found that eight in ten baby boomers and six in ten of their parents want to learn how to do new things.

Access to Information

The most frustrating thing in the lives of many mature adults is getting helpful information on a variety of things. However, a lack of ability to obtain useful information does not appear to be a matter of availability or accessibility to sources. Instead, this frustration is partly due to a lack of perceived credibility of the sources of information and partly as a result of the person's inability to use the available information.

In sum, consumption-related actions that contribute to the older person's well-being include making the right decisions on how to care for one's body and mind, building up financial resources, ability to engage in activities that are fun and self-enhancing, and possessing skills that help one make sound purchasing decisions. Deficiencies in these areas appear to create aversive feelings that undermine the older person's satisfaction with life.

How Businesses Can Enhance Consumer Well-Being

While the need for people to take control of their lives and plan for a longer and fulfilling life is recognized, the challenge facing those interested in enhancing older adults' well-being lies primarily in getting people at every stage of life to modify their consumption habits. The basic premise for developing guidelines for well-being in later life is that people are interested and willing to *act now, regardless of age*. They need to be willing to take steps to build the resources related to consumption that promote and enhance the person's quality of life throughout their life course.

In this section, we develop recommendations aimed at enhancing consumer well-being of both younger and older people, we discuss how businesses can help enhance people's well-being and their profits in the process, and we provide guidelines to businesses to help promote such lifestyles and enhance consumer welfare.

The general theme that emerges from the findings of the studies presented in the previous sections is that people can be more in control of their well-being and life in general than they think they can. This suggests the need for developing strategies that extend life and increase life satisfaction. It also suggests the need for a life-long commitment to these strategies. We can place the strategies for increasing well-being that are appropriate for any stage in life into two broad categories (a) strategies that can help enhance one's quality of life, and (b) strategies that help one avoid experiences that impair quality of life.

The information presented suggests several consumption-related strategies relevant to the first category. These include:

- Developing habits that promote preventive health care, especially in regard to potential health problems one might "inherit" from one's parents.
- Building up adequate financial resources to use in later life.
- Developing interest in several areas and consumption habits that promote an active lifestyle.
- Learning to pursue educational activities that promote empowerment and learning new skills that would enable one to be competitive in the labor market.
- Developing hobbies and interests in consumption activities that are mentally challenging and immune to physical aging.

On the other hand, strategies that help one avoid the adverse effects of life events and circumstances that deter longevity and well-being include:

- Preparing for the assumption of care-giving responsibilities for older relatives, and for consumer decisions one would need to make on their behalf.
- Learning to avoid consumption activities that have the potential of becoming compulsive and physically, emotionally, and financially destructive.
- Developing consumer skills and knowledge related to a wide variety of consumer decisions, and learning to detect deceptive business practices.

Businesses that develop goods and services that assist consumers in enacting these proactive and preventive strategies will be well placed to take advantage of the burgeoning market of older consumers. In particular, businesses need to communicate effectively with members of this segment to explain how their product offerings can assist them achieve a long and happy life.

The information that we have presented suggests the desirability of targeting young people to help them prepare for later life while also helping older adults live better lives. While these two approaches are not necessarily mutually exclusive, their implementation and effectiveness depends on the person's stage in life.

Helping Younger Customers Prepare for Later Life

The earlier consumers begin implementing strategies for well-being, the easier it is for them to stick to them and the greater their effectiveness. Pharmaceutical companies, physicians, and insurance companies should encourage consumers to practice preventive health care, in part by pricing preventive measures within reach. This encouragement can also include (a) acknowledging patients' health problems and the high probability of experiencing particular ailments, (b) understanding the patterns and sequence of the development of these illnesses, and (c) proactively sharing the information with the patient and his/her family. Again, health care providers, including insurance companies, can have a significant impact on their "customers" by encouraging frequent check-ups and engagement in activities or behaviors that are likely to deter or prolong the appearances of these health problems. Here again, a marketer can help consumers perform "personal audits" by including checklists on websites, in product packaging, and in print advertising. With respect to social marketing, the underlying marketing message should aim to help consumers understand that exercising should be an obligatory activity like eating and working, rather than a discretionary activity such as television viewing.

There are numerous implications for financial services organizations. In particular, they should segment this market to carefully target the right services and messages, depending on the needs and resources of the segment. They should educate consumers at different stages in life who are not proficient in investing by assessing their goals for later life and helping them understand the various reasons for saving. They should also explain the types of financial instruments which are most likely to help them achieve their goals and that will contribute to a more comfortable life during their retirement years.

Enhancing Older Consumers' Quality of Life

Information about the needs, mindsets, lifestyles, and consumption habits of older consumers can form the bases for strategy. Specifically, effective business strategy should result in greater customer satisfaction, enhance the well-being of mature consumers, and generate more profits for those companies capable of serving the needs of these customers. While these strategic recommendations are likely to be effective when trying to reach consumers of any generation, they are likely to be more effective when marketing to the older than to the younger generation of mature consumers.

Companies that understand the mindset of their customers who have recently experienced or are about to make transitions into new roles or life stages are likely to be in a better position to satisfy their older customers' needs, and thereby profit by doing so. In addition, marketers who wish to attract new customers from among those who use competing products may want to appeal to those who have recently experienced or are about to experience major life transitions (e.g., retirement, widowhood) because consumers are most likely to develop new needs during such transitions. Life-changing events present marketing opportunities as people buy products and services that ease transition and accommodate change. As consumers try to adjust to life changes, they are likely to reevaluate their consumption priorities, and needs for specific products and brands may develop or be intensified. Whether changes in consumption activities reflect efforts to cope with stressful changes or stress-free responses to change, marketers who understand the circumstances that make people prone to change might be in a better position to attract new customers and to preserve their existing customer base.

Several studies which we conducted at the Center for Mature Consumer Studies, and published in various academic journals from 1996 to the date of the publication of this book, suggest that stress is one of the mechanisms that link life-changing events to changes in consumption patterns. It is therefore imperative that businesses that market to people who have recently experienced life-changing events understand that they are dealing with consumers under stress. The opportunity lies in alleviating consumers' anxiety, not merely in offering products suited to their new needs. In addition, they need to do this in a sensitive way. For example, upon loss of her spouse a widow might expect her service providers (e.g., doctors, bankers, lawyers) to provide emotional support in addition to basic services. Marketers who understand the emotional consequences of the life-changing event are likely to gain a stronger base of loyal customers.

This approach presents opportunities for classes in stress management, websites that help people cope with stress, books on stress management, and positioning products as stress relievers. Although there are pharmaceuticals on the market that are designed to help deal with stress, smart product developers and marketers will also look at positioning products such as lounge chairs, herbal teas, milk and soy products, decaffeinated beverages, and services such as vacations and health clubs as stress relievers. Marketing messages can help consumers develop coping strategies that enable them to effectively deal with a stressor and solve the problem that creates negative feelings.

The way mature consumers think, feel, and act their age affects their responses to products and retail offerings in general. Marketers need to understand that because a person is of a certain age, he or she may not necessarily think like another person of the same age; they need to be sensitive to the differences in their customers' mindsets about their age and aging in general.

There may be a main message here for marketing communications: rather than poking fun at people in mid- and late life, advertisers may want to promote positive images which leave viewers feeling uplifted. They are more likely to respond to product messages that leave them feeling in control of their lives rather than to messages that make them feel like bumbling fools who are the butt of jokes.

Health and wellness professionals have numerous opportunities to be part of the solution by stepping up their efforts to identify the signs and symptoms of depression, and to encourage clients and support their efforts to seek help. Health care services that can enhance the older person's emotional well-being, such as psychotherapy, are likely to increase in demand as the population ages and an increasing number of people become aware of their benefits.

Summary and Conclusion

How we age has much to do with the decisions we make earlier in life. Our choices of goods and services throughout the lifespan will go some way towards determining the quantity and quality of life we experience. In particular, the choices we make early in life in relation to caring for our health, accumulating financial resources, and engaging in activities that enhance physical and emotional well-being will have a substantial impact on how we live during our later years. Life satisfaction is adversely affected where these elements are deficient.

Population aging represents a unique opportunity for marketers to develop goods and services that assist consumers in achieving favorable outcomes as they age. This process involves developing strategies that have a positive impact on quality of life and strategies that assist consumers to avoid experiences that are detrimental to their present and future quality of life. The former can include developing products designed to stimulate the mind in engaging and varying ways, whether these be goods (e.g., games, software, and books) or services (e.g., educational television programs and skill development classes). The latter could include the provision of information relating to financial planning or deceptive business practices.

Understanding the role transitions experienced in later life and how these influence consumption patterns is an important part of developing effective marketing strategies. Also essential is an appreciation of the various pathways to a happy and healthy later life and how these can be enhanced through the design, distribution, and promotion of products that can assist consumers accumulate the physical and mental resources they require to age well. Through such efforts, marketers have an important role to play in optimizing well-being in aging societies while simultaneously building and sustaining profitable businesses.

References

1. G.P. Moschis, A. Mathur, *Baby Boomers and Their Parents: Surprising Findings About Their Lifestyles, Mindsets, and Well-Being* (Paramount Books, Ithaca, NY, USA, 2007)
2. J.W. Rowe, R.L. Kahn, *Successful Aging* (Pantheon Books, New York, NY, USA, 1998)
3. G.P. Moschis, *Marketing to Older Consumers* (Quorum Books, Westport, CT, USA, 1992)

Chapter 18
Silver Advertising: Older People in Japanese TV Ads

Michael Prieler, Florian Kohlbacher, Shigeru Hagiwara, and Akie Arima

Abstract Choosing the right models and portraying them appropriately are crucial tasks in marketing management and advertising creation. The way older television viewers feel represented by a company has an influence on the overall company image and purchase intentions. This chapter reports that despite a strong increase in older people in Japanese television advertisements between 1997 and 2007 there is still an under-representation of older people. This is especially the case for older women. These findings are in accordance with extant research from different parts of the world. However, our study also finds that, when represented, older models are overwhelmingly depicted in major roles. Overall, our study not only adds a Japanese perspective, but is also the first one that compares two periods in time. In terms of product categories we found finance/insurance and real estate/housing to feature the largest number of older people. Finally, results from a survey of Japanese consumers give further insight into the phenomenon of older people in Japanese TV ads and how Japanese think about them. Even though our content analysis had revealed a strong under-representation of older people, the consumer survey shows that TV ads are not seen as showing too few older models, and the vast majority of respondents refuted the idea that they did not want to see older people in television advertising. Implications for advertising research and practice are discussed.

Introduction

Choosing the right models and portraying them appropriately are crucial tasks in marketing management and advertising creation. The way older television viewers feel represented by a company has an influence on the overall company image and purchase intentions [1]. Research has revealed potential negative effects of consumers' comparisons with models in advertisements [2] and shown that advertisements, which consumers find congruent with their self-concept, are more effective in terms of brand preference and purchase intention [3]. Therefore, it is an important

F. Kohlbacher and C. Herstatt (eds.), *The Silver Market Phenomenon*,
DOI 10.1007/978-3-642-14338-0_18, © Springer-Verlag Berlin Heidelberg 2011

question in the marketing context how and with which models older people are addressed adequately and this even has implications for corporate social responsibility (CSR). It is thus no surprise that there are a substantial number of studies on the representation of older people in television commercials around the world (see Prieler et al. [4] for a detailed overview).

This chapter focuses on the use of older people[1] in Japanese TV commercials,[2] how they are represented, how far these representations reflect the realities of Japanese society, and what reasons there might be for possible differences. We look at Japan as it is the most mature market in terms of population aging in the world and despite this fact is still under-researched in the field of mature marketing. This chapter is structured as follows. We first discuss the representation of older people in Japanese TV commercials. Then we analyze how using older people is connected with products targeted at them, and for which product categories they are used in advertisements. These results are discussed and placed in a global context in order to determine if our findings are special for Japan or similar in different parts of the world. Finally, we present results from a survey on the opinion about older people in Japanese television advertising and conclude that, in contrast to findings from previous studies, respondents have positive attitudes towards older models in television advertisements.

The Representation of Older People

One finding of our content analysis is an unequal age distribution within commercials featuring people[3] (see Table 18.1). The 15–34 age group clearly dominates, followed by the 35–49 age group. Age groups 50–64 and 65+ are only minimally

Table 18.1 Age distribution in Japanese commercials and population census

Year of TV ads/census	0–14 years % (n)	15–34 years % (n)	35–49 years % (n)	50–64 years % (n)	65 + years % (n)
TV Ads 1997[a]	19.3 (238)	66.3 (820)	37.9 (469)	13.7 (169)	4.6 (57)
TV Ads 2007[b]	19.8 (242)	64.2 (783)	39.3 (480)	21.4 (261)	6.1 (74)
Census 1995[c]	16.0	28.2	21.9	19.4	14.6
Census 2005[c]	13.8	25.1	19.3	21.7	20.2

[a]Number of all ads with people = 1,236. Different age groups in one commercial possible
[b]Number of all ads with people = 1,220. Different age groups in one commercial possible
[c]Percentages of the census are based on Ministry of Internal Affairs and Communications [5, 6]

---

[1]In accordance with Japanese advertising agencies we define "older people" in this chapter as 50 years and older.

[2]This research on older people in Japanese television advertising is part of a larger research project. We would like to thank the Yoshida Hideo Memorial Foundation for supporting this project.

[3]As opposed to those not featuring any people at all.

present in Japanese commercials. The same is true for the age group 0–14. It is striking that the distribution in 1997 and 2007 is overall very similar. However, there is one major exception, namely the age group 50–64, which increased by 56.2% from 13.7% to 21.4% Also, the 65+ age group increased by 32.6%. These increases must certainly be explained in the context of the growing interest in the silver market over the last years. This is especially true for the age group 50–64, which has become a major target group in Japan.

These results already tell us a great deal about the changes between 1997 and 2007 as well as about what age groups are preferred in Japanese commercials. A comparison with the population census gives better insight into a possible under- or over-representation of age groups (see Table 18.1).[4] There are some clearly visible findings: the age groups 15–34 and 35–49 are overrepresented, and the age group 65+, which actually increased even more in the census than in the TV ads (namely by 38.4%), is under-represented in Japanese TV advertisements.

Male Versus Female Ratio

There are proportional differences between males and females within different age groups (see Fig. 18.1). Whereas for the 1–14 age group there are only slightly more

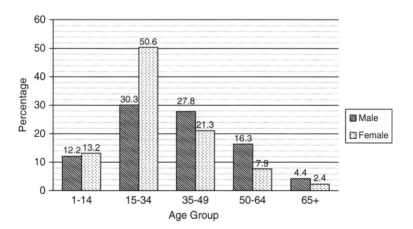

Fig. 18.1 Age (The male/female ratio does not include infants, since their sex could not always be determined) and sex distribution in Japanese commercials, 2007 (Percentage of commercials featuring males and females within all commercials featuring people ($N = 1,220$) – male and female and different age groups together in one commercial possible [4])

---

[4]The age distribution in the 2005 census and the 2007 TV commercials are not perfectly comparable since the TV ads amount to more than 100% (due to the fact that different age groups can coexist in one commercial).

females ($n = 161$) than males ($n = 149$) in the 2007 TV commercials, in the 15–34 age group females ($n = 617$) clearly outnumber males ($n = 370$). The situation, however, changes drastically after the age of 35, when males ($n = 339$) start dominating Japanese commercials and females ($n = 260$) become subordinate. This is especially pronounced in the age group 50–64, where males are featured ($n = 199$) twice as often as females ($n = 96$). The same is true for the age group 65+, where males ($n = 54$) again clearly outnumber females ($n = 29$). This is even more noteworthy considering the fact that in Japanese society older females actually outnumber older males. This is the case with the 50+ age group, where the number of females exceeds males at a ratio of 1.18:1, and also with the 65+ age group, where females outnumber males at a ratio of 1.36:1 (based on Ministry of Internal Affairs and Communications [6]).

The overall percentages between 1997 and 2007 are rather similar, so the results from 1997 will not be displayed here. In terms of older people, however, it is worth mentioning that the number of males strongly increased, whereas the number of females decreased. The number of females in the 50–64 age bracket increased slightly (from 5.8%/$n = 72$ to 7.9%/$n = 96$), which does not match the growth of appearances by males of the same age (from 9.0%/$n = 111$ to 16.3%/$n = 199$). Similarly, the number of females aged 65 and over decreased (from 2.8%/$n = 35$ to 2.4%/$n = 29$), whereas the number of their male counterparts increased (from 2.9%/ $n = 36$ to 4.4%/$n = 54$). This led to a lower number of females in all commercials featuring older people. The fact that the number of older females decreased from 1997 to 2007 runs against the overall trend of more older people appearing in Japanese TV commercials, and necessitates further investigation [7].

The Role of Older People

Even though older people are under-represented, it is important to ask what their role in television advertisements actually is. Do they play a major role, a minor/ supporting role, or are they shown in the background? In 1997, 69.2 % ($n = 144$) of commercials with older people show them in major roles, a similar percentage to 2007 (69.9%, $n = 214$). Minor roles accounted for 35.1 % ($n = 73$) in 1997 and for 34.6 % ($n = 106$) in 2007. In the background older people appeared less often in both years: in 1997 25.5% ($n = 53$) and in 2007 only 11.4% ($n = 35$). These results suggest that, although older people are under-represented, when they are used in advertisements they are mostly shown in major roles and therefore as important.

Product Categories

The following product categories have an extremely high percentage of older people: real estate/housing, distribution/retailing, finance/insurance, and apparel/

Table 18.2 Percentage of older people represented within each product category

1997		2007	
CMs featuring 50–64 age group % (n)	CMs featuring 65+ age group % (n)	CMs featuring 50–64 age group % (n)	CMs featuring 65+ age group % (n)
Real estate/housing 35.1 (13)	Distribution/ retailing 13.7 (10)	Finance/insurance 41.7 (20)	Apparel/Fashion, Accessories/ personal items 15.8 (6)
Apparel/fashion, accessories/ personal items 21.2 (7)	Real estate/ housing 10.8 (4)	Distribution/ retailing 38.8 (26)	Materials 11.1 (1)
Finance/insurance 19.0 (12)	Foods/beverages 6.4 (19)	Real estate/ housing 31.3 (15)	Precision instruments/ office supplies 9.8 (4)

fashion or accessories/personal items (see Table 18.2). In contrast, commercials for the product categories household products, publications, and automobiles use relatively few or no older people.

The number of older people in advertisements, however, does not say anything about how many advertisements are actually targeted at older people. Older people as a target group could only be clearly and objectively identified if this was indicated in the ad through a statement, or else through the fact that other age groups cannot use the product, such as diapers for the elderly, hearing aids, products for dentures, and wrinkle creams. This led to extremely few commercials that could be clearly identified as targeting the age group 50–64 (3 for 1997, 9 for 2007), as well as the age group 65+ (10 for 1997, 13 for 2007) within all commercials.

Opinions About Older People in TV Ads

We surveyed Japanese people aged 15–65 on their opinion about older people in television advertisements. Results were mixed with responses clustering in the middle. For the question whether there are too few older people in advertising, there is a slight tendency in the responses that this is not the case. In other words, most respondents do not feel that older people are under-represented in Japanese television advertising, which was shown in our content analysis, or do not perceive it to exist. The question whether the number of commercials targeted at older people increased was affirmed by the majority of the respondents (45.1%). This shows that our respondents are also aware of the changing situation in the world of Japanese television advertisements with its increasing usage of older people. Finally, the majority of the respondents (62.9%) deny that they do not want to see any commercials with older people. This result is evidence that advertising agencies might want to include a larger number of older people in the future. Interestingly, however, a higher percentage of older people than younger people agree with this statement. Older people, therefore, either do not want to see older people or think that the number shown in television commercials is already sufficient.

Discussion

Overall, we found a general under-representation of older people, especially older females, a gradual increase in older people featured in advertising, and an emphasis on the real estate/housing and finance/insurance product categories. In addition, our survey shows that some of our results from the content analysis might have different effects and are differently perceived than anticipated.

Nearly all previous research reports an under-representation of older people in television commercials [4, 8–10]. In our research, this was true for the 50–64 age group in 1997 (13.7% in TV ads vs. 19.4% in the census) as well as for the 65+ age group in 1997 (4.6% vs. 14.6%) and in 2007 (6.1% vs. 20.2%). At first glance, the under-representation of older people in a country traditionally regarded as having respect for the elderly seems like a contradiction. However, even if Japanese society still holds special respect for the elderly, this may have no connection with the number of older people appearing in Japanese commercials. Respect for the elderly is not the same as regarding older people as ideals of beauty (and commercials are a world of "beautiful" people). Nevertheless, respect for the elderly could create a more positive/important representation of older people, as could be seen in the roles in which older people were represented. In contrast to most previous studies in other countries [11, 12], where older people were overwhelmingly shown in minor or background roles, this study found older people predominantly in major roles [13]. The only other country where a similar phenomenon was observed is Korea [8, 14], a country quite similar to Japan in many aspects of its cultural heritage. Despite these cultural similarities, this phenomenon in both countries might be explained by the high number of celebrity appearances in these countries' commercials (more than 50% of commercials) [15, 16].

One reason for the under-representation of older people in advertising might be that older people identify themselves with people who are actually 5–10 years younger [17, 18]. This leads to a use of younger models in advertising, even when targeting older people. In fact, existing research findings suggest that older people do not necessarily want to be targeted with older people but with models 10 years younger than their actual age [19]; i.e., with models of their cognitive age rather than their chronological age. This is why it has been argued that, in advertising, the use of "cognitive-age congruent" models or spokespersons should prove fertile as a consumer's self-perceived age interacts with the perceived age of the model or spokesperson seen in an ad, and can subsequently influence the response to the advertising message [20, 21]. This is also supported by our survey results that a larger number of older than younger people prefer not to see older models in TV advertisements.

Additionally, some research shows that advertising agencies commonly believe that older models alienate younger consumers [19, 22]. It is assumed and partly shown in some studies [23] that younger people are not interested in products advertised by older people, so their use in advertisements for products for other age groups might be limited. In contrast to these findings, our survey has shown that it is not the case that (young) people reject older models in television advertisements.

Although older people are still under-represented, the number of older models clearly increased from 1997 to 2007. This increase was so pronounced that it was also realized by the respondents of our survey. One reason for the increase in older people in Japanese television advertising might be the growing interest of companies and advertising agencies in the 50+ age group, which includes the Japanese baby boomer generation (*dankai sedai*). It seems no coincidence that it is precisely this age group that strongly increased between 1997 and 2007. Using older people in advertising is only one way to target older consumers, as confirmed by our interviews with several Japanese advertising agencies. It can be assumed that there are various commercials not depicting older people while still trying to target them as customers.

Although this chapter is mostly concerned with the marketing side of the representation of older people in Japanese commercials, one final aspect should also be mentioned. As in the previous literature [9, 10], we too found an under-representation of older females. This result refers to a general image of (older) women in society and especially in the media. More than men, it is women who have to look young and beautiful. Naturally, advertisements are not the creator of such images, but they also reflect social trends, and also reinforce and shape them. Western researchers usually refer to a type of sexism that celebrates younger females and ignores older ones [11]. This interpretation seems also highly probable in the Japanese context where research has confirmed a preference in commercials for young and beautiful women [24].

In terms of product categories, real estate/housing and finance/insurance especially proved to show a high number of older models. Both product categories target older people in Japan. Older people are especially targeted for reforming their existing home or even buying a new (additional) one. Advertisements for finance/insurance for older people are not as common in many other countries, but in Japan a large number of insurance companies especially target older people who want to explore new options or want to improve the conditions of their current insurance.

Summary and Conclusion

This chapter has confirmed results from previous research, such as the under-representation of older people and the even more pronounced under-representation of older females. At the same time, it has also contributed new results. Our project is the first English language study on Japan, and it is also the first study worldwide that compares two time periods, i.e., 1997 and 2007. This has led to new and interesting results, such as our observation that the number of older models in TV commercials increased over the decade between 1997 and 2007. In addition, we could also show that the under-representation of older people must be seen in context. On the one hand, older people are (when represented) shown in major roles, which indicates their overall importance. On the other hand, consumers do not seem to recognize this under-representation, as shown by our survey, and thus such under-representations might not lead to any negative effect on the consumption side.

There have been substantial changes during the last 10 years in Japan, especially in terms of the number of older models featured. Japanese advertising agencies seem to have understood that older people have become an important market segment, and have adapted to the new situation. However, there are still several areas that remain to be changed. This includes the under-representation of older people in general, especially those older than 64. The under-representation of older women has not only remained unchanged, but has become even more pronounced. This is an area that should be rethought by advertising agencies in the future, considering the fact that (older) women are major consumers in Japan. This is not just a simple issue of numbers, but – as indicated in the introduction – a distorted representation of older people that might in the end come back to the companies and their image. After all, the importance of older people for the economy will increase during the coming years, not only in Japan, but in many countries around the globe. As a result, advertising researchers and practitioners are well advised to deal with this topic more carefully and more systematically.

Appendix

Content Analysis of TV Commercials

Our research sample was based on a commercial database that includes all advertisements broadcast in the Greater Tokyo Area since 1996. In order to produce a valid sample, a systematic sample of 28 days with an equal distribution of weekdays over 2 full years (1997 and 2007) was established. This led to 1,495 commercials in 1997 and 1,477 commercials in 2007: 2,972 commercials in total. Out of these commercials, 1,236 of the 1997 commercials included people; in 2007, 1,220 commercials included people.

Consumer Survey

A research grant by the Yoshida Hideo Memorial Foundation allowed us to participate in an annual omnibus-survey on consumer life and advertising in Japan. This survey was conducted in June 2008 in Greater Tokyo Area among Japanese people between 15 and 65 years, and yielded 720 usable responses.

References

1. T.A. Festervand, J.R. Lumpkin, Curr. Issues Res. Advert. **8**(2), 203 (1985)
2. M.L. Richins, J. Consum. Res. **18**(1), 71 (1991)
3. J.W. Hong, G.M. Zinkhan, Psychol. Mark. **12**(1), 53 (1995)
4. M. Prieler, F. Kohlbacher, S. Hagiwara, A. Arima, Keio Commun. Rev. **31**, 5 (2009)
5. Ministry of Internal Affairs and Communications, Census 1995. http://www.stat.go.jp/english/data/kokusei/1995/1513.htm
6. Ministry of Internal Affairs and Communications, Census 2005. http://www.e-stat.go.jp/SG1/estat/ListE.do?bid=000001005118&cycode=0
7. M. Prieler, F. Kohlbacher, S. Hagiwara, A. Arima, *Gendered Portrayals of Older People in Japanese Television Advertising* (DIJ Working Paper 09/2. Tokyo, 2009)
8. B. Lee, B.-C. Kim, S. Han, Int. J. Aging Hum. Dev. **64**(4), 279 (2006)
9. M.M. Lee, B. Carpenter, L.S. Meyers, J. Aging Stud. **21**, 23 (2007)
10. P. Simcock, L. Sudbury, Int. J. Advert. **25**(1), 87 (2006)
11. A. Roy, J. Harwood, J. Appl. Commun. Res. **25**(1), 39 (1997)
12. L.E. Swayne, A.J. Greco, J. Advert. **16**(1), 47 (1987)
13. S. Hagiwara, M. Prieler, F. Kohlbacher, A. Arima, Media Commun. **59**, 113 (2009)
14. F.S. Ong, H.K. Chang, J. Bus. Policy Res. **4**(2), 1 (2009)
15. S.M. Choi, W.-N. Lee, H.-J. Kim, J. Advert. **34**(2), 85 (2005)
16. M. Prieler, F. Kohlbacher, S. Hagiwara, A. Arima, Keio Commun. Rev. **32**, 5 (2010)
17. N. Stephens, J. Advert. **20**(4), 37 (1991)
18. S. Yamasaki, *"Toshigata shinia" māketto wo nerae! [Targeting the "Urban Type Senior" Market!]* (Nihon Keizai Shimbunsha, Tokyo, 2005)
19. A.J. Greco, J. Consum. Mark. **6**(1), 37 (1989)
20. C. Chang, J. Advert. **37**(3), 19 (2008)
21. S. van Auken, T.E. Barry, Asia Pac. J. Mark. Logistics **21**(3), 315 (2009)
22. I. Szmigin, M. Carrigan, J. Prod. Brand Manag. **9**(2), 128 (2000)
23. M.B. Mazis, D.J. Ringold, E.S. Perry, D.W. Denman, J. Mark. **56**, 22 (1992)
24. A. Arima, Sex Roles **49**(1/2), 81 (2003)

Chapter 19
Advertising Agencies: The Most Calcified Part of the Process

Chuck Nyren

Abstract Today's advertising industry needs a minor revolution. Talented men and women in their 40s, 50s, and 60s must to be brought into the fold if you want to target the Silver Market. This includes copywriters, graphic artists, producers, video directors, and creative directors. If you plan on implementing a marketing strategy that includes Baby Boomers as a primary, secondary, or tertiary market, and you turn it over to only people in their 20s and 30s, you will forfeit the natural sensibilities required to generate vital campaigns.

Introduction

You can analyze marketing fodder all day and night, read countless books about marketing to Baby Boomers, attend advertising and marketing conventions around the world, and soak up everything all the experts have to say. But the bottom line is this: if the right people aren't in the right jobs, what happens is what happens in all arenas of business – failure and mediocrity.

And the reverse is true. If you had a product or service for late teens and twentysomethings, and you walked into your advertising agency and your creative team was made up of *only* people in their 50s and 60s – I would imagine that you would be very, very worried.

For over 5 years I've been writing, consulting, and speaking about advertising to Baby Boomers. Before long, I realized that most follow-up questions from readers, clients, and conference attendees required answers soaked in history. Queries were usually variations of "Why do ad agencies and the media marginalize and ignore the 50+ market?" or "Why does my agency tell me that there is no need to target people over 50? That they buy products anyway?"

The answer to all is that most agencies are not interested in nor equipped to produce vital, successful campaigns targeting this demographic. Here's why:

F. Kohlbacher and C. Herstatt (eds.), *The Silver Market Phenomenon*,
DOI 10.1007/978-3-642-14338-0_19, © Springer-Verlag Berlin Heidelberg 2011

A Very Brief History of Advertising Creatives in the United States

From the late 1800s until World War I (WWI) just about anybody could leap into advertising if they had the nerve, the verve, and a talent for persuasion. The industry was spread out geographically, culturally, ethnically. While there were advertising agencies large and small, many companies created their own ads, mostly using agencies for what is today known as media planning.

The expansion of railroads made it possible to haul consumer products and magazines/periodicals nationwide – and market nationwide. By the late 1910s advertising was becoming a very big business.

The war put a damper on this growth – but afterwards, as the USA hurriedly switched from a wartime to a consumer economy, companies garnered huge excesses of earned income. The most attractive and reasoned way to spend much of this money was on advertising [1]. Large agencies benefited because they were equipped for major campaigns.

As was the case in most businesses, the power eventually ended up in the hands of white, Protestant, Ivy-League educated men. Ethnic, cultural, and religious diversity was soon frowned upon. If you were Jewish, Catholic, Irish, or Italian you did your best to play it down or hide it. Women were also marginalized.

Also, to protect itself, industry headquarters settled in New York City. This was the beginning of what we refer to literally, and now metaphorically, as "Madison Avenue."

The cultural zeitgeist of the post-WWI era was "be rich," so it didn't hurt that advertising was being created by people who had a good shot at realizing this dream. It is simple common sense that the best advertising is done by people who advertise to themselves.

The 1920s was also the first time a young generation was niche-targeted. Naturally, young copywriters and art directors were assigned these accounts.

There were a few powerful, talented women. One was Helen Landsdowne, recruited by Stanley Resor, president of J. Walter Thompson's Cincinnati office. Soon, they married.

After a move to New York and a reorganization of JWT, Stanley Resor was named president, and Helen Resor quickly became one of the top copywriters in the industry. *This was a woman spearheading campaigns targeting women.* If not something new, it certainly wasn't common. Some say that Helen Resor was the primary reason JWT grew to be the largest advertising agency in the world (and it continued to be for the next 30 years).

But during her decades at JWT, Helen Landsdowne Resor was "on paper" merely the head copywriter for many major accounts, although she often presented and pitched to major clients. Business propriety did not permit a woman to be an executive.

Throughout the Great Depression and WWII, the advertising zeitgeist glorified the middle class. It was bad taste to "be rich." Along with radio and a flood of inexpensive magazines, average Americans were the heroes and heroines. Smart advertising agencies added to their stables, searching and finding talented individuals with more varied, down-to-earth backgrounds.

As in the 1920s, women were still marginalized. A few couldn't be held down. A good example was Jean Wade Rindlaub of BBDO. Her campaigns for Campbell Soup and General Mills spoke directly to mothers and the middle class, and her wartime ads for Community Silver (This is for keeps), portraying wives and mothers saying goodbye to their husbands and sons, were the "pin-ups" for those at home during the war. Ms. Rindlaub also created what was considered the preeminent research department in the industry, considered to be the prototype of what are now focus groups.

It wasn't until after WWII that Jean Wade Rindlaub attained V.P. status. And, it wasn't until the mid 1950s that Ms. Rindlaub was appointed to BBDO's Board of Directors, the first woman on a board of a major advertising agency.

The post-WWII era brought more changes to the advertising industry. The zeitgeist shifted from extolling middle-class values to glorifying upper-mobility, a "keep up with the Joneses" mentality.

While its roots date back to the 1920s, the 1950s also brought about a messy revolution in methodology. Hard-sell, fact-based scientific advertising collided with creative, soft-sell approaches. The best advertising was often a queasy but effective melding of the two.

Here and there, Jews, Catholics, and women began to be "officially" accepted in powerful positions. Below is a handful of the most productive and influential creatives in the early 1950s through the middle 1960s. All are on the list of the top *Advertising Age*'s 100 advertising people of the twentieth century (with their positions on the list noted):

Bill Bernbach (#1) was the first enormously successful and openly Jewish advertising creative in 30 years, spearheading campaigns for Orbach's Department Store, Volkswagen, Avis Car Rental, Life Cereal, and many others. Quotes from Bill Bernbach:

> Advertising isn't a science, it's persuasion. And persuasion is an art.
> Research can trap you in the past.
> Logic and over-analysis can immobilize and sterilize an idea. It's like love – the more you analyze it, the faster it disappears.

Leo Burnett (#3) was a Midwesterner copywriter and creative director who only later in his career migrated to Madison Avenue. During the 1950s and 1960s, he and his people created icons that are still recognized today, including The Jolly Green Giant, Tony the Tiger, The Pillsbury Doughboy, and Charlie the Tuna.

David Ogilvy (#4) is still considered by many to be the greatest copywriter of all time. During his heyday, Mr. Ogilvy boosted the branding of companies like Hathaway Shirts, Shell Oil, Sears, KLM, American Express, IBM, Schweppes tonic, Rolls-Royce, and Pepperidge Farm. Quotes from Mr. Ogilvy:

> I notice increasing reluctance on the part of marketing executives to use judgment; they are coming to rely too much on research, and they use it as a drunkard uses a lamp post: for support rather than for illumination.

> Much of the messy advertising you see on television today is the product of committees.
> Committees can criticize advertisements, but they should never be allowed to create them.

Rosser Reeves (#5) believed in thorough research, and codified the Unique Sales Proposition (USP), a technique of focusing on the distinctive qualities of a product. His campaigns included "M&Ms melt in your mouth, not in your hand." A quote from Rosser Reeves:

> Let's say you have $1,000,000 tied up in your little company and suddenly your advertising isn't working and sales are going down. And everything depends on it. Your future depends on it, your family depends on it...Now, what do you want from me? Fine writing? Or do you want to see the goddamned sales curve stop moving down and start moving up?

Shirley Polykoff (#24) hid that she was Jewish for most of her career. As the sole woman copywriter at Foote, Cone & Belding, Ms. Polykoff was tossed the Clairol account. She came up with *"Does she... or doesn't she? Only her hairdresser knows for sure,"* and *"Is it true blondes have more fun?"* Sales of Clairol products quadrupled. Ms. Polykoff scoffed at research, and wrote from the gut.

Bernice Fitz-Gibbon (#62) was the ad manager at Macy's, Wanamakers and Gimbels. With her unique, classy copywriting and creative direction, Ms. Gitz-Gibbon was the highest-paid women in advertising in the middle 1950s.

The 1960s cultural revolution, with Baby Boomers and the youngest of the Silent Generation coming of age, had a profound effect on the industry. Doors were now open to all ethnicities, cultures, and backgrounds. Women flourished. It didn't matter who you were as long as you had the moxie, the talent. The grip that Madison Avenue had on the industry loosened. Large, medium, and small agencies were almost indistinguishable in terms of quality of output.

With the rise of multinationals during the following two decades, advertising became a truly global phenomenon. Great campaigns were now coming out of the Midwest, the West in the USA, and around the world. For the first time, a "golden age" of advertising (in the 1980s) blossomed in another country, England.

But, as with each era of advertising, there was a blind spot, a prejudice. Along with the openness of the 1960s came a new primary zeitgeist: "be young." This was fine through the 1980s. The largest market was Baby Boomers (give or take a few years), and advertising agencies were actively recruiting and handing over power and influence to creatives in their 20s. After all (if I may repeat myself for the umpteenth time), the best advertising is done by people who advertise to themselves. Why wouldn't you hire young people to create campaigns for young people? They instinctively know their market.

Ad agencies pre-1960s, while often excluding minorities and women, always had a good age mix. *This was their diversity.* While creative departments usually skewed young, they weren't made up exclusively, or even primarily, of young people.

During my presentations, the slide that always elicits gasps is the one where I slowly reveal the ages of the top creatives mentioned earlier. I say, "Many advertising historians consider the most productive phases of their careers as being between the early 1950s to the late 1960s. How old were they in the middle of their whirlwind creative periods – in 1960?"

- Bill Bernbach: 49
- David Ogilvy: 49
- Rosser Reeves: 50
- Shirley Polykoff: 52
- Bernice Fitz-Gibbon: 66
- Leo Burnett: 68

Remember: this was in the *middle* of their creative periods. Much more was to come from them. In fact, for some their most successful work was produced in the latter half of their careers. And, they surrounded themselves with people of all ages. A quote from Rosser Reeves when he was 52-years old:

> No, I don't think a 68-year-old copywriter can write with the kids. That he's as creative. That he's as fresh. But he may be a better surgeon. His ad may not be quite as fresh and glowing as the Madison Avenue fraternity would like to see it be, and yet he might write an ad that will produce five times the sales. And that's the name of the game, isn't it?

You can argue the points Mr. Reeve's puts forth. But what astounds most people about the quote is the fact that up until the 1970s there *were* 68-year-old creatives actively involved in advertising. Ask someone today about older versus younger advertising creatives, and the quote would have to begin, "*No, I don't think a 38-year-old copywriter can write with the kids. . . .*"

Mr. Reeves retired from the business when he was 55-years old. It was the talk of Madison Avenue at the time. There were arguments and speculations about why he did so. Many wondered why someone would retire from advertising at such a young age.

Today, things are a bit different:

> The advertising industry is notoriously associated with young people, crazy ideas, wild parties, and general excessiveness. The average age in the industry is way below 30... Advertising agencies are in the business of creativity. They are also in the business of managing human perceptions. It's therefore interesting that although many tactics are employed to ensure creativity, agencies have traditionally not cottoned on to the fact that a more diverse workforce, inclusive of nondiscriminatory age policies, poses the potential for greater competitive advantage. (Paula Sartini) [2]

The problem is that this zeitgeist hasn't changed. It's still "be young." The advertising industry is not at all "cutting-edge," but behind the times. This is especially counterproductive now that we have complex market segmentations and new ways of reaching and targeting consumers.

From *The Business Case for Diversity* [3]:

> . . . An increasing number of European companies are adopting diversity and equality strategies, not only for ethical and legal reasons but also for the business benefits they are expected to deliver. Among the most important of these benefits are a wider pool of high quality workers, greater innovation, and enhanced marketing opportunities (The European Commission Directorate-General for Employment).

An excerpt from my book, *Advertising to Baby Boomers* [4]:

Today's advertising industry needs a minor revolution. Talented men and women in their 40s and 50s must be brought back into the fold if you want to reach Baby Boomers. This includes account executives, copywriters, graphic artists, producers, directors, creative directors. If you plan on implementing a marketing strategy that includes Baby Boomers as a primary, secondary, or tertiary market, and you turn it over to a different generation of advertising professionals, you will forfeit the natural sensibilities required to generate vital campaigns.

Truth is, you can analyze marketing fodder all day and night, read countless books about marketing to Baby Boomers, attend advertising and marketing conventions around the world, and soak up everything all the experts have to say.

But the bottom line is this: If the right people aren't in the right jobs – well, you know what happens. What happens is what happens in all arenas of business: failure and (sometimes even worse) mediocrity.

But my advertising agency says that people over 50 buy products anyway...

Sure "they" do. But do they buy *your* product instead of the competition's? Advertising agencies write off *your potential target market* because they don't know how to advertise to Baby Boomers anymore than I know how to reach a teenager or young adult who wriggles and zigzags around in his or her chair, punching, skidding, and spastically rattling something I believe is referred to as a *joystick*. (Chuck Nyren)

Not too long after the second edition paperback was released, Rance Crain, publisher of *Advertising Age*, penned some columns that mirrored much of what I had been saying for years. Two excerpts:

From *Boomer Boon* [5]:

... The ad business is woefully out of touch with baby-boomer buying power. Young ad people think older people are stuck in their ways, so it's a waste of money to try to get them to change brands...a prime-time TV show with most of its viewers in the 34-to-49 range can get 30% more per ad minute than one that caters to people 55 and older. Yet consumers age 50 and up already spend more than $1.7 trillion on goods and services a year...

Agencies like to think of themselves as the last bastion of creativity, but they're in many ways the most calcified part of the process. Enlightened clients are beginning to realize this resistance to change is holding them back; the next step is to bypass their agencies' counsel.[1] (Rance Crain)

From *You Know Who's Boss – Consumers* [6]:

... It makes all the sense in the world for ad makers (both clients and agencies) to be well-stocked with people who understand consumers, whether young people who fathom the mysteries of cyberspace, a good mixture of people who reflect the ethnic and cultural diversity of our country, and, yes, even older people who understand the vitality and buying power of the great gorge of baby boomers overtaking our land.

If the ad business is serious about regaining control of its brands, it must first understand that the "boss" is not just a 35-year-old white American. He or she is older, black, Asian or Hispanic... (Rance Crain)

As I write this, an email pops into my inbox. It's not much different to ones I receive every week. Excerpts:

---

[1]Italics are mine.

> I know you are onto something regarding the Baby Boomer business. I have enclosed a resume, and wonder if there is a way for existing ad agencies to embrace this potential, or do you see starting an ad agency devoted to baby boomers exclusively?
>
> I have been thinking about it, and no doubt there are a lot of other boomers who (a) see age discrimination and/or (b) wonder why the largest advertisers or agencies are not "getting it."
>
> I have submitted my resume to the top 100 ad agencies and I have received not a word. The people I know basically tell me that the agencies are looking only for young people.

This gentleman's resume (he's a graphic artist/creative director) is impressive. It includes well-known and successful national and international campaigns from 15, 20, and 30 years ago. He has the sensibility required to reach the 50+ market because he was advertising to this same market when they were in their 20s and 30s. He is one of them. He instinctively knows what their concerns are, and how to reach them now that they have matured.

But no agency wants him.

Advertising Today: Is It Only the Experienced, Older Creatives that Agencies Need to Bring into the Fold?

One other presentation slide of mine usually shocks. I talk a bit about David Ogilvy: "How old was David Ogilvy was when he wrote his first ad?" Remember, many consider him to be the greatest copywriter of all time. He is #4 on *Ad Age*'s list of the "Greatest people in advertising in the twentieth century." Many would rate him #1.

"So how old was he? Was he a child genius? Thirteen? Sixteen? Eighteen? Twenty-one?"

The answer: David Ogilvy wrote his first ad when he was *39-years old*. He spent the next 25 years actively involved in creating advertising campaigns, and another 20 involved in an executive capacity.

Here is a revolutionary thought: Agencies should also be searching for people in their 40s, 50s, and 60s who have never worked in advertising.

In the recently published book *Old Masters and Young Geniuses*, David Galenson analyzes the creative productivity of famous artists from all fields [7]:

> Experimental innovators work by trial and error, and arrive at their major contributions gradually, late in life. In contrast, conceptual innovators make sudden breakthroughs by formulating new ideas, usually at an early age. Galenson shows why such artists as Michelangelo, Rembrandt, Cézanne, Jackson Pollock, Virginia Woolf, Robert Frost, and Alfred Hitchcock were experimental old masters, and why Vermeer, van Gogh, Picasso, Herman Melville, James Joyce, Sylvia Plath, and Orson Welles were conceptual young geniuses.[2]

Baby Boomers are finishing up the first part of their lives, and many are ready to pursue new careers. They are going back to school, learning new skills, finally

---

[2]http://www.davidgalenson.com/, excerpt from the publisher's book description.

following their dreams. The largest age demographic for new entrepreneurs is Baby Boomers (and a bit older). They feel as if they are beginning exciting, innovative, productive lives. There are scores of books and literally hundreds of articles about "second career" Baby Boomers. I'll cite two:

> From *Boomers Embark on New Midlife Careers* [8]:
> According to author Marc Freedman, these (Baby Boomers) are part of a revolution that may change the nature of work and retirement in the USA – people who, instead of fading from the workforce in midlife, are embarking on second careers. "Instead of the freedom from work, they are searching for the freedom to work; instead of saving for a secure retirement, they are underwriting a new career," Freedman writes in his new book, *Encore* [9]. (Teresa Mears)
>
> From *Baby boomers make seasoned PROs* [10]:
> They were America's very first mass advertising market and a public relations officer's dream: nearly 78 million baby boomers who have come of age with radio and television. As children, they were the first consumers of breakfast cereals and baby foods. As adults, they were the biggest trendsetters in the country. But, as they started to outgrow the 18–49 year old age bracket, they are now creating a new frontier as some of the country's most established and seasoned public relations officers (PROs)... Smart PR firms are now opting to break the age-old PR model... Slick firms are now beginning to comprehend that seasoned professionals with good business backgrounds will storm the PR market. Not only do these respected practitioners treat reporters and editors with the respect that is due them, but they also have the ability to provide them with services in a fast yet professional manner.
>
> It is this ability of the baby boomers to strategize that defines their well-advanced intellectual status, making them one of the best options in the PR industry. With their skillful ability to implement those strategies, they are known to all and sundry as the great PR practitioners. Keep in mind that executives love to have someone alongside them strategizing and managing their organizations so that they come out as winners in the marketplace. (Anna D. Banks)

But how many advertising agencies are willing to hire novices in their 40s, 50s, or 60s? You could come in with some great writing – perhaps from a different field, and/or be fresh out of "going back to college" after taking advertising courses, or be a brilliant graphic artist with a distinguished career who has never worked in advertising....

And you'll be politely shown the door.

How many Baby Boomers, ones who've always wanted to do something creative and have a secret desire to get into advertising, are opening up their own ad agencies? I doubt any would even consider it. Three decades into his career, David Ogilvy sent a memo to his staff [11]:

> Will Any Agency Hire This Man?
> He is 38, and unemployed. He dropped out of college. He has been a cook, a salesman, a diplomatist and a farmer. He knows nothing about marketing and has never written any copy. He professes to be interested in advertising as a career (at the age of 38!) and is ready to go to work... I doubt if any American agency will hire him.

David Ogilvy was writing about himself.

Three Successful Campaigns, And A Possible Backlash

Pressured by CMOs and a few forward-thinking folks in advertising agencies, things are changing. The 50+ market is now on the radar.

Unfortunately, 50+ creatives aren't. Most campaigns targeting Baby Boomers are clumsy and ineffective, as they take turns waving 1960s Peace Symbols while bedding moldy, psychedelic music, or portray people over 50 as smiling, vapid, mindless pod people only interested in making sure they don't have to pee while playing golf or sunning themselves at the beach, or assume that Boomers are so technologically incompetent that when confronted with a computer they press a blank piece of paper to the screen in order to "print."

However, three recent campaigns are top-notch, and take opposite approaches in reaching their target market. All succeed. The Dove Pro Age campaign has a diverse history. Hatched from the Dove Real Beauty campaign created and incubated in Europe and the USA, it consists of aesthetic, commercially viable photographs of nude women over 50. On the surface, it's pure creativity, with no facts or research.

Or so it seems.

The Crest Pro-Health toothpaste ad, at first glance, appears to be simple and dull: a picture of the product package and two columns of health and beauty benefits (but mostly health). One list refers to Crest Pro-Health, the other (with less checkmarks) to "regular toothpaste." It's pure fact-based, hard-sell advertising with no creativity or emotional connection with the target market.

Or so it seems.

Why has the Dove Pro·Age campaign been so successful? Simply because of its outrageousness in daring to promote its product by using nude women over 50? It is much better than that.

Although it may appear to be purely "creative," this campaign is steeped in research. For Baby Boomer women (and a bit older), after 40 is better than before 40.

While there has always been a small percentage of women who bloomed in their later years, for Boomers it has become a generational ethos. Again, there have been major studies, scores of articles, and a handful of books on this subject. A good one is *Primetime Women: How to Win the Hearts, Minds, and Business of Boomer Big Spenders* by Marti Barletta (Kaplan Business, 2007).

Here are some excerpts from my book, *Advertising to Baby Boomers* [4]:

Contrary to popular myth, Baby Boomers do not believe that they are still teenagers or young adults...

Boomers are slyly redefining what it means to be the ages they are. Included in this new definition are some youthful attitudes, but the real change is that instead of winding down, many are winding up...

There is a big difference between thinking you are younger than you are, and not thinking that you are old. This "night and day" distinction may confuse many pundits, but it does not confuse most Boomers...

Baby Boomers do not want to be twenty again, or thirty again. They want to feel as good as they possibly can for the ages they are. They do not want to be marketed and advertised to as if they were young adults or thirty-somethings...

In fact, Baby Boom women are the real age revolutionaries. Many are feeling very empowered, very alive, and ready to take on the world. While they could do without some of the wrinkles and some of the aches, ask most women over 40 if they would like to live their 20s and 30s all over again, and they'll say, "No thanks. I'm happier and more productive now than I have ever been."...

So if an advertising agency tells you "when you target 19-to-35-year-olds, you likewise reach Baby Boomers," they are sadly out of touch with one of the largest and certainly the richest market segment today...

The second and even more important reason for this campaign's success has to do with the major two people involved in its creation and development: Shelly Lazarus (b. 1947) and Annie Leibovitz (b. 1949). Ms. Lazarus is Chief Executive for Ogilvy & Mather Worldwide (the agency that created the campaign), and has a reputation as a hands-on CEO (especially with this campaign, from what I've heard). Ms. Leibovitz has had and is having such a long and varied career that it's hard to sum it up without going on for pages. While she's much, much more, Ms. Leibovitz can certainly be described as the quintessential Baby Boomer creative.

Let's talk reality: You may not be able to find a comparable Shelly Lazarus to spearhead your campaign. You might not be able to afford Annie Leibovitz as your artistic director. But, if you are targeting women over 50, don't you think it might be a bright idea to find and hire people with similar business and creative sensibilities as Ms. Lazarus and Ms. Leibovitz?

During my presentations, I toss up a slide with some quotes and pictures from an article in *Advertising Age* – and up a hypothetical situation, playing it out as only a middle-aged wannabe ham actor can. With my tongue in my cheek towards the end, I say:

Here's a speech I liked hearing about, reported in *Advertising Age* by Lisa Sanders, from the mouth of Euro RSCG Worldwide's David Jones (age 38):
From *Ignore the Research and Trust Your Gut* [12]:
Taking a "swipe at the research and pre-testing industry," Mr. Jones next exhorted listeners to stop asking permission. Drawing on a "truth" from British comedian Vic Reeves that "96.2% of all statistics are made up," Mr. Jones, also a Brit, argued that some of the most well-liked ads aren't based on research or focus-group results. Instead they rely on a creative director's gut instinct of what consumers will like. He cited Procter and Gamble's effort for Charmin toilet tissue created by Euro rival Publicis Worldwide that riffs off of the many euphemisms for elimination. "Publicis took a risk, and did it without a bit of research," he said.

And, by way of reinforcing the previous point, his last bit of advice was for creatives to "trust your gut." Advertising is changing fast, and to not take a risk is risky, even though it's scary to take a risk. (Lisa Sanders)

No argument from me. I love it.

But there is one big problem. When targeting Baby Boomers you have to have the right guts around to trust. That'd be 50+ creative guts.

It wouldn't be too bright to trust my gut to come up with a campaign for a product aimed at twentysomethings. My gut would tell me, "... Ummm ... ummm ... Wait! I got it! I got it! We get some twentysomething guy or gal or both an' spike their hair an' give'em tattoos and put rings in their noses an' iPods on their heads an' bed some hip-hop music an' have'em hold up the product! Yeah! They'll buy it! They'll buy it!"

It's fine to champion creatives and their guts and call this a "risk" – but are agencies prepared to take the common sense "risk" of hiring creatives with the best guts to trust when targeting specific demographics?

Saatchi & Saatchi, an agency famous for attempting to create "love" for their clients' products, went against their own grain with Crest Pro-Health toothpaste. On the surface it's hackneyed USP (unique sales proposition) – factual and direct, with no emotional connection. You might likewise think that such a nonevasive, noncreative campaign wouldn't have much impact anymore, but:

> Three months after its debut, Crest Pro-Health could be the most successful US toothpaste launch in the last decade... The study found two-thirds of Pro-Health buyers normally use other non-Crest brands of toothpaste, including nearly 25% who said they used Colgate Total, Crest's main rival... Pro-Health's secret? Targeting the needs of consumers who put a premium on the healthcare aspects of their toothpaste... Those who had seen Pro-Health ads were 40–50% more likely to buy it. (C. von Hoffman) [13]

No big surprise to me. About 6 months before the campaign was launched, I read about Crest coming out with a toothpaste – and targeting Baby Boomers. While they won't admit that they are (who wants to target old people?), this is it. And 2 years before that, I wrote this in the 2005 edition of my book [4]:

> Here's an example of the way Madison Avenue wants you to think: For years, pre-teens and young teenagers never paid any attention to toothpaste ads. But for the last decade or so, toothpaste has been developed, manufactured, and marketed to kids and teenagers. Forty-odd years ago toothpaste was marketed to adults only. Crest began targeting parents, claiming fewer cavities for kids with Crest, implying smaller dentist bills.
> Did we, as children, care? Not really.
> However, if you watch toothpaste ads today, you would think that people brush their teeth up until their early thirties and then all of sudden they magically turn seventy and buy only denture cream. (I guess in Madison Avenue's alternative universe, this is why all senior citizens lose their teeth. They haven't brushed in 40 years.)...
> So what toothpaste should I buy? Anybody have any ideas? I have a trillion dollars in the bank, and 300 billion to spend as I please. And I'm sauntering around the dental care aisle, hands in my pockets, jingling a few million in loose change, looking up and down, side to side, and I'm not sure *what* I'm going to buy.
> As advertising agencies have told you, I'm going to *buy something*. I guess it doesn't matter to you whether I buy *your* product or not, because I'll buy something...
> Here's an alternative universe you might consider. And it wouldn't be such a bad one for me, either:
> Hmmm. What's *this* toothpaste? I think I've heard about it. Saw a commercial, read an ad about it. The person in the ad was around my age. She talked a bit about dental care, a bit about gums, about teeth, how to keep them healthy and strong. She had a nice smile, but not one that blinded me, sending me stumbling, feeling my way to the bathroom for the Visine. And the box doesn't look like it's an ornament for a science fiction Christmas tree. Maybe I'll buy it. (Chuck Nyren)

There is more: While it might not seem to be a visceral campaign, it resonates with Baby Boomers because these are the types of ads we saw as children. However, *it's not a retro campaign*. Saatchi & Saatchi did not try to turn it into something old, with 1950s fonts and layout. The background is metallic blue, the design fresh and modern. It's simple, factual, contemporary. It tells us what we want to know.

These two campaigns are successful because both use creativity and research. It's simply their styles and approaches have a different mix. How about a Dove Pro Age ad with a picture of their product and a list of ingredients and benefits? Or, for Crest Pro-Health – naked Baby Boomers brushing their teeth?

I think not. Good jobs by both agencies.

The most recent successful campaign targeting Baby Boomers is for Kimberly-Clark's Depend brand:

> Adult underwear no longer being given the silent treatment [14] The new TV commercials have ordinary boomer men and women engaged in some unscripted banter about the differences between the two sexes, such as whether men or women make better drivers and which sex actually rules the world ... The TV spots are carefully crafted to appeal to boomers who, if they don't use Depends themselves, may be caregivers for parents who do.

The creative is lots of fun. No surprise, since the spots were directed by Academy Award-winning filmmaker Errol Morris (born 1948). A Boomer directing Boomers. The principals are entertaining, loose, attractive.

What upsets me about this campaign is not the campaign itself. It's wonderful, effective. But why couldn't it have been a campaign for a new car? Laundry soap? Baked Beans? Gender-specific razors? Aluminum foil? A smart phone? Anything but some age-related malady.

Then there is this:

Use only as directed [15] ... Take one night last week, chosen at random, when NBC Nightly News aired 17 commercials during its 30-min broadcast. Of those 17 spots, 12 were for (in order): Zyrtec, an over-the-counter allergy medication; Citrucel Fiber Supplement With Calcium; Advil PM, a combination pain reliever and sleep aid; Transitions prescription eyeglass lenses ("healthy sight in every light"); Spiriva HandiHaler, for use by COPD (chronic obstructive pulmonary disease) sufferers; the cholesterol-lowering properties of Cheerios; Bayer aspirin and its heart-attack prevention benefits; Omnaris nasal spray, a prescription allergy medication; Just For Men hair coloring (let's help graying old Dad get a date!); Boniva, which helps reverse bone loss in postmenopausal women, most notably actress Sally Field; ThermaCare heat wraps, for relief of muscle and joint pain; and Pepcid Complete, a heartburn and acid reflux remedy.

The Backlash: If every time someone over fifty sees a commercial targeting them and it's always for an age-related product or service, pretty soon their eyes will glaze over, they'll get itchy and grumpy.

The Real Issue: Marketing and advertising folks grasping the fact that Boomers will be buying billions (trillions?) of dollars worth of *non-age* related products for the next 20-odd years. If you target this group for toothpaste, computers, clothes, food, nail polish, sporting equipment, toenail clippers – anything at all (almost), and you do it with respect and finesse, they will appreciate and consider your product.

And looking at the big picture: Let's hope that ad agencies will see these Depend spots and realize they're missing out not hiring people over 50 to create campaigns for just about any product or service.

Boomer Brains

With all the high-tech advances over the last 10 years come new ways to measure how the brain works. *Science News* and *New York Times* talk about studies of older and younger older brains.

From *Aging Brain Shifts Gears to Emotional Advantage* [16]:
Advancing age heralds a growth in emotional stability accompanied by a neural transition to increased control over negative emotions and greater accessibility of positive emotions ... A brain area needed for conscious thought, the medial prefrontal cortex, primarily influences these emotional reactions in older adults. . . In contrast, people under age 50 experience negative emotions more easily than they do positive ones. These younger adults' emotion-related activity centers on the amygdala, a brain structure previously implicated in automatic fear responses... This gradual reorganization of the brain's emotion system may result from older folk responding to accumulating personal experiences by increasingly looking for meaning in life. (Bruce Bower)
Older Brain Really May Be a Wiser Brain [17]:
When older people can no longer remember names at a cocktail party, they tend to think that their brainpower is declining. But a growing number of studies suggest that this assumption is often wrong. Instead, the research finds, the aging brain is simply taking in more data and trying to sift through a clutter of information, often to its long-term benefit.
How to Train the Aging Brain [18]
Over the past several years, scientists have looked deeper into how brains age and confirmed that they continue to develop through and beyond middle age ... The brain, as it traverses middle age, gets better at recognizing the central idea, the big picture. If kept in good shape, the brain can continue to build pathways that help its owner recognize patterns and, as a consequence, see significance and even solutions much faster than a young person can. These recent studies about the differences in age-related brain functions give advertisers more reasons to put pressure on agencies to hire a diversity of creatives.

Summary and Conclusion

The way a product or service is perceived by a creative, and then presented to potential consumers, is the essence of successful advertising. *A diversity of creatives – and creative diversity. That's how to reach the 50+ market.*

In countries and markets where the population is homogeneous, age diversity is an even more important ingredient.

References

1. S. Fox, *The Mirror Makers: A History of American Advertising and Its Creators* (University of Illinois Press, Chicago, 2007)
2. P. Sartini, *Managing age diversity in the advertising industry.* MarketingWeb.com, 4 Sep 2006
3. Directorate-General for Employment, Social Affairs and Equal Opportunities, *The Business Case for Diversity: Good Practices in the Workplace* (European Commission, Luxembourg, 2005)
4. C. Nyren, *Advertising to baby boomers* (Paramount Market Books, Ithaca, NY, USA, 2005)
5. R. Crain, *Boomer boon,* Advertising Age, 2 Apr 2007
6. R. Crain, *You know who's boss – consumers.* Advertising Age, 30 Apr 2007
7. D. Galenson, *Old Masters and Young Geniuses* (Princeton University Press, Princeton, USA, 2005)
8. T. Mears, *Boomers embark on new midlife careers.* Miami Herald, 11 Aug 2007
9. M. Freedman, *Encore, Finding Work that Matters in the Second Half of Life* (Public Affairs, NY, USA, 2007)
10. A.D. Banks, *Baby boomers make seasoned PROs.* American Chronicle, 29 July 2007
11. Ogilvy & Mather Agency, *David Ogilvy – Biography* (Ogilvy and Mather, Manhattan, 2000). http://www.ogilvy.com/history/media/biography.pdf. Accessed 13 June 2008
12. L. Sanders, *Ignore the research and trust your gut,* Advertising Age, 2 Nov 2006
13. C. von Hoffman, *Crest Pro-Health toothpaste launch has P& G smiling.* Brandweek, 23 Oct 2006
14. Bob Moos, *Adult underwear no longer being given the silent treatment,* Dallas Morning News, 23 May 2009
15. Joseph P. Kahn, *Use only as directed,* Boston Globe, 6 Apr 2009
16. B. Bower, Older but mellower: aging brain shifts gears to emotional advantage. Sci. News **169**(25), 24 (June 2006)
17. Sara Reistad-Long, *Older brain really may be a wiser brain,* New York Times, 20 May 2008
18. Barbara Strauch, *How to train the aging brain,* New York Times, 29 Dec 2009

Chapter 20
The Importance of Web 2.0 to the 50-Plus

Dick Stroud

Abstract What is the importance of Web 2.0 for older people? This paper answers this question and provides suggestions for how organizations can use Web 2.0 to improve their online interactions with the older market. The chapter analyses the differences between the historical way that websites have been created and used and the opportunities and dangers of using Web 2.0 technologies. Social networking and Web video are the two best known applications of Web 2.0 and are discussed in detail. The author shows that whilst both these applications are associated with young people they are intrinsically "age-neutral" and are equally appropriate to older Web users. The chapter describes how social networking and Web video are likely to develop and the resulting implications upon the channel strategy of organizations targeting the older Web user.

Introduction

There can be little doubt that Web 2.0 has been the "hot" Web topic of the past few years. Strangely, for something that has attracted so much attention, it remains an ethereal and ill-defined subject. For many organizations the subtleties of Web 1.0 provide enough of a challenge without grappling with the complexity of the next phase of evolution.

When all of the jargon and hype is stripped away from Web 2.0 we find a combination of exciting new ways for organizations to do the thing that should be central to their Web strategy – understanding and communicating with their users.

A question that is rarely asked and almost never answered is: "What is the importance of Web 2.0 for older people"? This paper redresses this absence of discussion, and provides practical suggestions for how organizations can use Web 2.0 to improve their online interactions with the older market.

F. Kohlbacher and C. Herstatt (eds.), *The Silver Market Phenomenon*,
DOI 10.1007/978-3-642-14338-0_20, © Springer-Verlag Berlin Heidelberg 2011

What Is Web 2.0?

Most people agree that the term Web 2.0 entered the public domain following the first O'Reilly Media Web 2.0 conference in 2004. This is the only fact concerning Web 2.0 that is agreed upon. Since 2004 there have been numerous definitions and propositions about its role and importance.

In an attempt to add clarity to the debate, Tim O'Reilly produced the following definition [1]: "Web 2.0 is the business revolution in the computer industry caused by the move to the internet as platform, and an attempt to understand the rules for success on that new platform."

Whilst this definition is eloquent and brief, it lacks the specifics required for organizations to understand and apply Web 2.0 within their own, online environment.

The easiest way of understanding Web 2.0 is by contrasting it with Web 1.0, its predecessor. Much of the work involved in creating this definition has been done by Fidelity Finance [2]. To understand the difference between the two generations of websites, it is helpful to separate the Web into two components.

The first component is the website's *architecture*. These are the tools and techniques used to create the site. Secondly, there is the *application* of the site (i.e., the value it adds to the individual and/or organization). It is particularly important to separate websites into these two components when analyzing how they are used by older people.

The Differences Between Web 1.0 and Web 2.0

Summaries of the features involved in the architecture and applications of the two generations of websites are shown in Tables 20.1 and 20.2. This analysis illustrates the features that differentiate Web 2.0 from older sites. The following section considers the age-neutrality aspects of this new generation of websites.

Is Web 2.0 Age-Neutral?

The use of the term "age-neutral," in the context of marketing, was first used by the author Stroud [3] when describing marketing campaigns targeting consumers with a wide spectrum of ages.

When evaluating marketing creative channels and enabling technologies (such as the Web) it is vital to understand if they have the power to engage both young and old alike or are limited to a narrow age group.

The Web usability Guru, Jakob Nielsen, has firm views about the usability issues involved with Web 2.0 sites. His views are particularly important because a website's

Table 20.1 Website architecture that typifies the two generations

Architecture feature	Implication
Web 1.0	
Predominately HTML code	The formatting language of the website is old and was created for non-commercial applications
Hard coded static links	The linkage between regions of the website is "hard-wired" when the site is created
Single path through the content	The design of the site limits the user to a predetermined number of navigation routes
Limited customization	Most sites are unable to react to the user's specific requirements
Multimedia is an "add-on"	Functionality enabling users to experience audio and video content are an adjunct, not an integral part of the website
Web 2.0	
Inherently multimedia	Video and audio are incorporated into the fabric of the website
Interface adapts to the user	The interface reacts to the different behavior of individual users
Fewer links, more actionable elements (i.e., sliders, tabs, menus and widgets)	There are multiple design techniques to enable site navigation
Created using multiple technologies (AJAX, Flex, Flash)	Websites are constructed using an array of technologies (i.e., AJAX enables designers to update parts of a page without the whole page reloading)

Table 20.2 Website applications that typify the two generations

Application feature	Implication
Web 1.0	
The website user passively consumes content	Users have little opportunity to respond and add value to the information provided by the website
Single communications channel between the user and the website	The application's value is limited by the information provided by the website owner
Web 2.0	
Users create, refine and share content	The website "user" can contribute information, thereby increasing the value of the site's content
A community rather than solitary experience	Applications are not limited to the interaction between the site and a single user
The scope of the application is extended by integrating data from multiple sources. This is known often called a "mashup"	The functionality of the application is not limited to the resources of the site owner

usability is particularly important in determining effectiveness with older people. The following are three of his major concerns about Web 2.0 [4]:

- *Complex interfaces can confuse the user*. This conclusion is best illustrated by the way that AJAX, one of new Web 2.0 development tools, enables part of a web page to be updated rather loading an entirely new page. Whilst this means the transaction is faster, it risks confusing users who may be puzzled or unaware of what is happening. Nielsen tested 100 AJAX-created e-commerce sites and found that shoppers often didn't notice when their shopping carts were updated. This is not an intrinsic fault of the technology but a result of the way it is being implemented.

- *Few people contribute content.* The most famous example of user-contributed content is Amazon's book reviews, launched at the beginning of the Web era (1996). Web 2.0 has resulted in making it much easier and less costly for websites to incorporate content-sharing features. Just because sites have this facility doesn't mean it will be used. This has resulted in many websites with sparsely populated user-content areas that have limited value. What should be a user benefit can result in confusion.
- *Brand confusion caused by mashups.* Websites containing multiple sources of information (e.g., Google maps and BBC news) can result in the site's brand identity becoming diluted. More importantly, the aggregation of multiple services can degrade the quality of the site's usability because "mashed" services are unlikely to have the same quality of usability as the host site.

Many of Nielsen's concerns are about the poor and indiscriminate use of Web 2.0 features. Anything that degrades the usability of websites and makes them more complicated to use will cause older people problems.

Both Nielsen [5] and Fidelity [6] have researched the effect of aging on the speed and error rate when older people use websites. A summation of their conclusions is illustrated in Fig. 20.1. This shows that a 65-year-old is likely to take 60% longer and make 50% more errors than a younger person of equivalent Internet experience.

Because of the small sample sizes and the difficulty in comparing individuals of equivalent Internet experience, this linear relationship should be taken as a guide rather than an absolute rule. There is no doubt that age-related cognitive decline

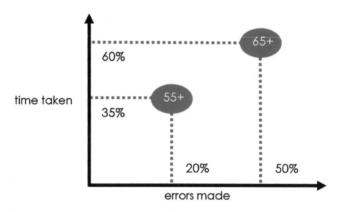

Fig. 20.1 The relationship between the time taken to use a website and the number of errors made and the age of the user

results in older people, even those with extensive Web experience, making more errors and taking longer to navigate sites.

So what is the answer to the question: "Is Web 2.0 age-neutral"?

The Web *applications* that people use are determined by their lifestyle and background, not their age (i.e., they are age-neutral). This is further discussed in Sects. "Social Networking" and "Summary and Conclusion."

The way designers are currently using the new generation of Web 2.0 tools is having a negative impact on the usability of websites, which has a disproportionate impact on older people. This means that the *architecture* of Web 2.0 is not age-neutral. There are no intrinsic reasons why this should be the case. It results from a lack of knowledge and concern that Web designers have for the results of physiological aging on website usability.

The following two sections of this paper consider the two most important and highest profile applications that Web 2.0 has enabled and how they relate to older people.

Social Networking

Whenever the term Web 2.0 is mentioned you can be certain that the phrase "social networking" will not be far behind.

Social networking has many similarities with the early days of texting (SMS), when adults were amazed as to why young people spent so much of their time keying messages into their mobile phones. The same bemusement exists about the ability of MySpace and Facebook to attract vast numbers of visitors. These two sites had 170 million unique visitors (in the US) in January 2010 [7]. Table 20.3 contains the URLs and a brief description of all of the websites mentioned in this section.

The ability of social networking sites to generate these huge volumes of Web traffic is proof of their popularity. But, there is a hard business rationale to these sites. Rupert Murdoch, somebody who avoided investing in Web companies during the dot.com era, was so convinced of their importance that he purchased MySpace. This company entered the Japanese market in November 2007. Microsoft is also convinced of social networking's business potential, as demonstrated by its purchase of a stake in Facebook.

Like all things related to Web 2.0, social networking has numerous definitions. The most useful way of explaining what it is and what it does, is by detailing its components of functionality. This is done in Table 20.4, using a set of definitions originally proposed by Danah Boyd [8].

The overarching thing about social networks is that their success is dependent on the willingness of their members to contribute and communicate. The website owner establishes the style of the network, provides the functionality, originates the content and sets the rules. But, it is the members' continuing levels of activity that determine the network's continuing success.

Table 20.3 Descriptions and URLs of the websites discussed in this section

Web site description	Web site URL
A major social networking site that was created for students in US universities and is now available to all users in multiple geographies	www.facebook.com
A major social networking site that was acquired by Rupert Murdoch's News Corporation and is available to all users in multiple geographies	www.myspace.com
A social networking site founded in the USA and now available in multiple geographies. The site is targeted at teenagers and young adults	www.bebo.com
The largest global online employment website	www.monster.com
Venture funded US social networking site targeted at Baby Boomers	www.eons.com
Social networking site and portal for US grandparents	www.grandparents.com
US Web site, with imbedded social networking functionality, which is used for locating individuals providing in-home care and support services	www.care.com
A UK portal site targeted at the 50-plus	www.funkyfogey.com
A UK site providing a free service allowing people to create and maintain a memorial website for deceased family and friends	www.gonetoosoon.co.uk
A UK portal website providing services and products for grandparents	www.begrand.net
Part of the John Lewis group. The first UK supermarket web site that uses elements of social networking functionality	www.waitrose.com
The largest Japanese social networking site	www.mixi.jp
Mobage-town is a mobile phone portal providing games, avatars and social networking aimed at young Japanese people	www.mbga.jp
Twitter is a social networking website providing a micro-blogging service that enables its users to send and receive text-based posts of up to 140 characters (called Tweets)	www.twitter.com

Table 20.4 The main components of a social networking website

Social networking component	Purpose
Profiles	Profiles are pages that enable individuals to describe themselves in terms of their age, sex, location, interests and a host of other variables. The profile might also contain rich content such as photographs, sound and video
Network of contacts	After joining a social network site users can identify and contact other members This might involve assigning contacts "privileges" for the types of content they can exchange
Messaging	Most social network sites also have a mechanism for users to send messages and append content to their friends' profiles. For registered members of the network this can become a replacement for e-mail
Content Sharing	This might be as simple as exchanging messages and textual content. More probably, it also involves the ability to add to the site photos and videos. Increasingly it also includes the facilities for network users to construct their own blogs and wikis
Add-value content	Increasingly social networking sites are partnering with providers of content and widgets (modules of computer code) to enrich users profiles

"Fogeys Flock to Facebook" was the title of an article in the August 2007 edition of Business Week [9]. This is an amusing way of describing the evolution of social networking websites to become age-neutral. The media has historically portrayed Facebook and MySpace as the playground of teenagers and young adults. Contrary to this popular belief, the largest age group for both sites is 35–54 year olds. The majority of Facebook users in the US are over 35 years old.

Only those who believe the 50-plus group to be homogeneous and technophobic would be surprised by these numbers. The relationship between a person's age and their use of the Internet is complicated. For instance, as a group the 50-plus has the lowest level of Internet use. This is true in Europe, Japan and the USA.

But, if Internet uptake is analyzed by socio-economic class, a more complicated and less age-related picture emerges [10]. In the UK, the average 55–64 year old, in the AB class group, uses the Internet more than all ages in groups C2DE. There is only a few percentage points difference between all ages of C1s and the older group. Only 16% of the over-65 year olds are connected to the Internet, but those who are spend more time online than any other age group.

Entrepreneurs in the USA have realized the business potential of social networking sites aimed at an older market. Jeff Taylor, the founder of Monster.com, has launched eons.com, a Facebook equivalent for the 50-plus sector. This site has stimulated a torrent of new Baby Boomer social networking sites, all trying to capture the spending power of the 76 million Boomers in the USA.

The notable lack of success of these "generic" sites is that the user's age is the only thing that connects them to the other members. Lifestyle is a far better factor for grouping people together than their age. A more interesting and sustainable business model is where social networking is used as an enabler, not as the site's primary purpose. Grandparents.com is an example of this new breed of site which contains social networking functionality that makes life easier for the grandparent. Another example is Care.com, which uses social networking to improve the process of locating care support resources.

The UK has a few examples of sites using forums and networking designed for the 50-plus market. Saga and 50connect.com have the highest number of visitors, followed by a raft of much smaller companies such as Funkeyfogey, Gonetoosoon and BeGrand. More interesting than these age-specific sites is the way that major online brands, with significant numbers of older customers, are starting to use networking functionality. Waitrose, one of the UK's largest supermarkets, recently relaunched its website containing forums, scrapbooks and profiles, all the functionality found on a social networking website.

In Japan, Mixi is the leading personal portal and social-networking destination. The company was started in 1999 as an employment job site targeted at the young. In 2006 the company was floated and in July 2007 was valued at $2 billion.

According to the Japan Times [11], in May 2009 Mixi announced its financial results and forecast a fall in profits of 15% from the previous year. This is the first drop in profits since the company went public. In addition, its growth in the number of page views and members has been slowing.

In response to these problems the company is opening its PC and mobile platform to third-party developers and new applications, following Facebook's strategy.

Mixi has 17 million users, a high percentage of whom are active, with the majority accessing the website from their mobile phones. The majority of Mixi users are women. Nearly 90% of the website's users are under the age of 40 years old.

"If you want to engage with young people in Japan, you've got to have a mobile presence," says Forrester Research senior analyst Jonathan Browne [10]. For this reason, the new social networking competitors entering the Japanese market are mobile rather than PC-centric. Websites such as "Mobage-town" (mobile gaming town) rely totally on mobile access.

This doesn't mean that older people will only use PCs to access the site. The use of mobiles by older people is very high and will be further stimulated by the launch of new phone handsets, designed for older people (e.g., NTT DoCoMo new handset with a large, high-definition screen and large buttons). The smartphone, in particular Apple's iPhone, will stimulate mobile access to all types of social networking sites.

How Is Social Networking Likely To Develop?

The following are some of the other ways that social networking is likely to develop in Japan and other countries:

- *It will become a commodity application.* The great majority of the 50-plus market will use social networking functionality and be oblivious to the fact. Unlike the current crop of age-centric sites, the real volume adoption will result from the network being part of an interest/industry/company/activity website. It is likely that most large, Web-literate companies in retail, travel, healthcare, and consumer electronics are already considering how to use social networking to increase eye-fall and the networking effect of their Web presence.
- *There will be pressure to make the networks "open."* Facebook, MySpace and Mixi are all "walled gardens." This means that communications between users and access to information is restricted to members. This is very different from the "open" nature of e-mail and the Web. Companies are starting to create more open and accessible platforms, allowing personal data to be shared with other networks and making it easier to interface with other Web service providers. For example, Facebook makes its member profiles available to search engines so that nonmembers can find out who has a profile on the site.
- *It will be easier and cheaper to acquire social networking functionality.* The first generation of social networking sites were bespoke and expensive to create. This is changing. New generations of Web software companies are providing inexpensive tools that enable new sites to be created and companies to embed social networking into their existing Web platforms. The main companies providing these tools are Affinity Circles, Social Platform, Joomla and Ning.

- *Social networking is limited by the finite time users can "socialize."* It is a statement of the obvious, but there is a limit to the number of social networks a person, of any age, can join and the time they can spend online. There has undoubtedly been a "fashion" element to explain the success of MySpace, Facebook and Mixi. The demand created by the trendiness of online socializing is transient and will transfer to the next "cool" technology innovation. AOL learnt this lesson when it was forced to sell Bebo, within 24 months of purchase, for a fraction of the 850 million purchase price.

Whatever way that social networking develops, its lasting success depends on delivering real benefits to customers, irrespective of their age.

Twitter is the development that has already had a significant impact on the world of social networking and yet is still evolving. It is a mystery to many older people why anybody should want to continually write and read messages of up to 140 characters in length.

In 2009 the number of Twitter users in the US was 12 million and forecast to grow to 18 million in 2010, the majority of them being female.

According to Pew Internet [12] approximately 10% of US Internet users aged 45–64 years old use Twitter. The median age of US users is 31 years, and the fastest growing demographic is the 50-plus. A major reason for Twitter's success has been the attractiveness of the application to both consumers and organizations.

Web Video

The head of creative at Avenue A | Razorfish, the largest interactive agency in the USA, believes Web video is the most exciting of the new digital technologies. Why is this?

In the same way that GIF and JPG images added richness to plain text, so video provides a new dimension to the Web's ability to communicate and entertain. Even though we have just begun the Web video revolution, the magnitude of its impact on the Internet is already staggering. Approximately half of all Internet traffic currently consists of TV shows, YouTube clips and Web animations. Within the next 24 months, video could account for 90% of all Internet traffic.

Why the Rules of Web Video Have Changed

A combination of technology developments has made the creation and viewing of Web video a mass market experience.

Firstly, the costs of video cameras and software to create and edit video have plummeted. Al Gore's Oscar-winning global warming crisis documentary, *An*

Inconvenient Truth, was created using standard Apple Keynote and editing software and with a video camera costing less than $4,000. The production team needed to produce most Web videos has shrunk to just two people – one person to act as the journalist/interviewer and the other as the cameraman/editor.

The second development is the widespread availability of broadband. There is now a worldwide audience of 420 million subscribers who can access the Internet at broadband speeds.

According to the OECD [13], Japan has the second highest number of broadband subscribers (31 million) behind the USA. The demand for Web video and broadband access are now in a virtuous circle whereby broadband take-up is driven by the desire to view video, which in turns increases the audiences and supply of video material.

Finally, the costs and simplicity of the key determinants of Web video's success have radically improved:

- *Hosting*. There are over 100 websites providing free video hosting services, double the number at the beginning of 2007. YouTube, by far the largest, contains over 100 million video clips. Aside from the USA, Japan represents YouTube's largest user base. During 2007, Sony launched a video-sharing service in Japan called eyeVio, enabling users to upload and distribute their own videos. Although Sony is considering launching eyeVio outside Japan, for now it is focusing on the Japanese market. Whilst YouTube has the worldwide coverage, the Sony service has some unique features. The most important is the high quality of the video that is "near DVD quality" and far superior to that of YouTube.

Searching. Google is evolving its video search capability with the development of "universal search." This will process all content, including video, images, news, and websites, and then present a single, integrated set of search results.

Viewing. Adobe's Flash player has become the default software used by the main Web hosting companies, including YouTube and MySpace. Adobe estimate that 99% of the world's developed markets can view Flash Player content. This means that the vast majority of PCs have the software to play video.

Web Video Is Age-Neutral

Organizations must avoid pigeon-holing Web video as being a niche activity that is only used by the young and is nothing to do with older people. The fact that the average YouTube user in the USA is not a teenager but a 39-year-old proves this point.

Table 20.5 shows the US breakdown of Web video users by age. There is a surprisingly small variation in the penetration of video use across the whole age spectrum. There will be country differences in this age profile but there are no reasons why Web video consumption will not become age-neutral in all geographies.

Table 20.5 Demographic profile of US Internet users who used Web video

Age range	Percentage of age group who have viewed online video
12–17	70
18–24	74
25–34	74
35–54	71
55+	64

Source: ComScore Video Metrix April 2009

The Challenges of Web Video for Organizations

Arguably, Web video is causing the most significant changes to the way websites are designed and used than any other development since the Web's creation. The following guidelines are intended to assist organizations in adapting to this revolution:

- Web video is a reality, it is not going away! Organizations need to plan for its use, in order to ensure consumers' time is spent watching video associated with their brands and marketing campaigns – not those of their competitors.

Web video should only be used for applications where it adds significant value compared with other communications media. The temptation of treating video as "eye candy" and indiscriminately sprinkling it around the website must be resisted.

The same quality standards must be applied to Web video as to any other communications technique. The novelty value of Web video will only last a short time and may already have passed. Poor quality video will then be ignored or will annoy Web users.

Web video requires script-writing not copy-writing skills. In any 2-h feature film script there are normally only about 8,000 words of dialog. That means that in a 2 min video you would have fewer than 150 spoken words.

Judging the effectiveness of Web video requires more than simple website analytics because the video will be viewed from multiple sources, other than the website. The video can be distributed as part of an e-mail campaign, pushed through RSS feeds and viewed via YouTube and Sony's eyeVio.

The ownership of the Web video's intellectual property must be understood. As YouTube is discovering, it is very difficult to stop people loading and displaying video material they do not own. If a company's Web video uses music and actors then there might, almost certainly will, be copyright implications. The same applies if the video is sourced from a marketplace site such as Mochila and Brightcove. Web video adds an extra burden on organizations to ensure their content is legal.

How Is Web Video Likely To Develop?

Web video is undergoing a phase of rapid evolution that is creating new and exciting opportunities. Unfortunately, most organizations are finding it difficult to respond to these new possibilities. The following are the developments that can be expected during the coming year:

- Web video will become high definition (HD) video. Adobe's latest version of Flash Player and Intel new chips are both optimized for HD viewing. Japanese users of eyeVio can already see the potential of high-grade video.

A new generation of websites is emerging that are primarily video-based, with text as a supporting medium. The limitation of only using video within the "video box" will disappear as it evolves to become the core of the website.

The mobile will be equally important, if not more so, as the device through which people consume video. The hugely successful Smartphone mobile, in particular the Apple iPhone, provides an easy-to-use device to view video media.

2010 was probably the year when Web video reached the tipping point and became a website necessity and not just an optional extra.

Summary and Conclusion

These conclusions are not specific to any country or region. The market leaders in social networking, Facebook and MySpace, both originated in the USA but have evolved to become global businesses with operations in Europe, Australasia and Japan.

Social networking sites, dedicated to the 50-plus, first started in the USA but all major countries now have their indigenous versions. Web video has followed the same evolution path with the US-originated YouTube remaining the largest company but with look-alikes across the globe.

The power of Web 2.0 to expand the range of applications and functionality of websites is as important to older audiences as to any other age group. Web 2.0 enables users to experience a richness of the content and sophistication of Web applications far beyond the scope of those delivered by Web 1.0 technologies. Unfortunately, there is a negative side that we are only just beginning to understand. The same tools that enable these new applications can also create websites that are harder and more complicated for older people to use.

Web video and social networking are currently perceived as separate applications but will evolve to become an integral part of the fabric of websites. Both applications are intrinsically age-neutral. Web video will have the greatest impact on the way websites are designed, because of its power to explain complex, visual and emotive issues. The balance of content that is displayed in video format, compared to text and imagery, will continually increase.

The people responsible for the construction and operations of these new Web 2.0 sites, in particular Web designers, need to understand the way that physiological aging changes the way older people interact with these applications. Unless this occurs, the ability of Web 2.0 to enrich and simplify the older person's Web experience will have the opposite outcome. Just when the challenge of designing age neutral Web 2.0 websites is being understood, there is a new group of technologies for marketers and designers to master. HTML5 and Apps, like Web 2.0, have the potential to deliver radically new age neutral functionality. Like Web 2.0, however, these technologies have the associated risk of antagonising and alienating older people.

References

1. T. O'Reilly, *Web 2.0 Compact Definition: Trying Again* (2006). http://radar.oreilly.com/archives/2006/12/web_20_compact.html. Accessed 2 Jan 2008
2. A. Chadwick-Dias, M. Bergel, T. Tullis, in *Senior Surfers 2.0: A Re-Examination of the Older Web User and the Dynamic Web*. Universal Access in Human Computer Interaction. Coping with Diversity (Springer, Berlin, 2007), p. 868, doi 10.1007/978-3-540-73279-2_97
3. D. Stroud, *The 50-Plus Market: Why the Future Is Age-Neutral When it Comes to Marketing and Branding Strategies* (Kogan Page, London, 2006), ISBN-10: 074944939X
4. J. Nielsen, *Web 2.0 Can be Dangerous...* (2007). http://www.useit.com/alertbox/web-2.html. Accessed 2 Jan 2008
5. J. Nielsen, *Web Usability for Senior Citizens* (Nielsen Norman Group, Fremont, 2002) http://www.nngroup.com/reports/seniors/. Accessed 13 Jun 2008
6. T. Tullis, Older Adults and the Web: Lessons Learned from Eye-Tracking, in *Universal Access in Human Computer Interaction. Coping with Diversity* (Springer, Berlin, 2007), p. 1030, doi 10.1007/978-3-540-73279-2_115
7. Comscore, *Social Networking 2010*. http://www.clickz.com/3636504. Accessed 1 Mar 2010
8. D. Boyd, N. Ellison, Social network sites: Definition, history, and scholarship. J. Comp. Mediated Commun. **13**(1), 11 (2007). http://jcmc.indiana.edu/vol13/issue1/boyd.ellison.html. Accessed 10 Jan 2008
9. A. Ricadela, *BusinessWeek*, 6 Aug 2007. http://www.businessweek.com/technology/content/aug2007/tc2007085_051788.htm. Accessed 2 Jan 2008
10. R. Worcester, *Just Who Does the Internet Reach?* (Ipsos, London, 2007). http://www.ipsos-mori.com/content/just-who-does-the-internet-reach.ashx. Accessed 13 Jun 2008
11. Mixi faces challenges as competition grows, The Japan Times, 24 June 2009. http://search.japantimes.co.jp/cgi-bin/nc20090624a2.html. Accessed 1 Mar 2010
12. Pew Internet, *Twitter and Status Updating*, Fall 2009. http://www.pewinternet.org/~/media//Files/Reports/2009/PIP_Twitter_Fall_2009web.pdf. Accessed 1 May 2010
13. Directorate for Science, Technology and Industry, *OECD Broadband Statistics: Total Broadband Subscribers by Country* (Organisation for Economic Co-operation and Development, Paris, 2009). http://www.oecd.org/sti/ict/broadband. Accessed 1 Mar 2010

Part III
Industry Challenges and Solutions

Chapter 21
The Business of Aging: Ten Successful Strategies for a Diverse Market

Hiroyuki Murata

Abstract In Japan, in the last few years, an increasing number of enterprises have been focusing on developing new products and services for older adults or for the Baby Boomer generation. In most cases, these efforts failed. One of the reasons for this is that their visions are too narrow. Many enterprises consider the older adult market or the Boomer market as a single homogeneous iceberg. However, in a modern economy, it is not sufficient to say that the Boomers represent a large part of the market just by sheer numbers. The reason is that the nature of today's market is different from that of the past. This chapter gives readers the essence for correctly viewing the Baby Boomer market or Senior market, and insights to success in serving such markets in other countries.

Introduction

In Japan, in the last few years, an increasing number of enterprises have been focusing on developing new products and services for older adults or for the Baby Boomer generation. In most cases, these efforts failed. The reason why is that their visions are too narrow [1]. Many enterprises consider the older adult market or the Boomer generation as a single homogeneous iceberg. However, in a modern economy, it is not enough to say that the Boomers represent a large part of the market just by sheer numbers. The reason is that the nature of today's market is different from that of the past.

What are the key elements that affect the Boomers' buying decisions today? The answer will be different for each Boomer, but the following five types of changes are the main influences on their decision making (Fig. 21.1):

1. Physical changes due to aging
2. Changes in each individual's life stage
3. Changes in the life stage of their family
4. Changes in their tastes based on their generation
5. Changes in the time or fashion

F. Kohlbacher and C. Herstatt (eds.), *The Silver Market Phenomenon*,
DOI 10.1007/978-3-642-14338-0_21, © Springer-Verlag Berlin Heidelberg 2011

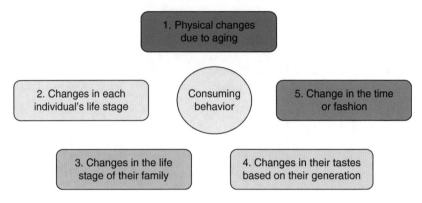

Fig. 21.1 Five key factors that influence the consuming behavior of the 50+

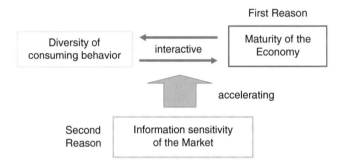

Fig. 21.2 Two reasons why the consuming behavior of the 50+ will be diverse in the modern age

There are, of course, other influential elements. Even so, it is easy to see how diversified the Boomers' decision-making processes are just by focusing on these five elements. Their actions as consumers will be as diverse as their decision-making processes. This is because those who are in their late 50s – the so-called "leading edge Boomers" – are more likely to be facing the five changes mentioned above than any other age group.

The impact of each influence is not the same for everyone. The importance of each factor will be different for each different product, service, or individual. The Boomers are so diversified as consumers that you can call the Boomers' market "an aggregate of diverse micromarkets." This is the most significant change in the nature of the Japanese Boomers' market since the time of high economic growth after WWII.

The behaviors of the Boomers as consumers are even more diverse in the modern day due to two additional factors (Fig. 21.2). The first factor is the maturity of the economy. As our standard of living increases, goods or products become superabundant. This superabundance gives us more choices, and increases our expectations and demands. Then, product providers try to provide customers with more products and increase our expectations even more. This interactive relation makes consumer behavior more diversified.

The other factor that has changed the nature of the market today is the emergence of the "information society." In Japan, as of 2002, broadband Internet cost just 18 cents per 100 Kbps, which is the least expensive in the world, while the USA with a cost of $2.86 per 100 Kbps was the most expensive among the developed countries (Fig. 21.3).

Due to this low cost, more than 50% of the people in their 50s in Japan today are users of the Internet. Also, more than 40% of the people in Japan in their 60s own a cell phone (Fig. 21.4). As access to information increases, so does consumer choice and consumer expectations. Thus, we are living in a time of economic maturity and

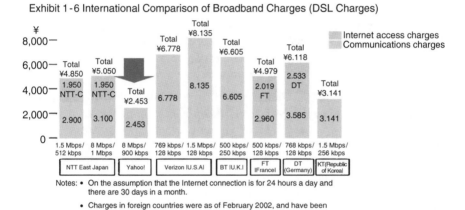

Fig. 21.3 Japan is the cheapest country in the world for Broadband access

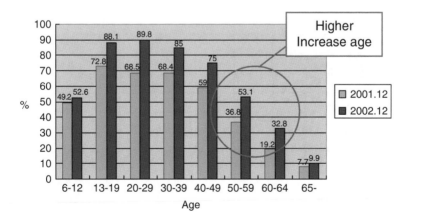

Fig. 21.4 Internet penetration ratio by age

of the information age market. These two phenomena are still progressing, and will continue to diversify the Boomers market even more.

Now, what do you do to respond to these challenges? You need to widen your vision towards the world of your target customers. You must have enough adaptability for a diverse market. These are the keys to success.

To understand adaptability for a diverse market, it is useful for Japanese to look at what's going on in the US market. This is because the USA is a more diverse country than Japan, and is expected to have more adaptability to the diversity. Some advanced business examples in the USA may give us insights as well as inspiration, since their market condition is very similar to ours. Although there are many differences between the two countries, we can see the following common characteristics in the modern economies of developed countries like the USA and Japan:

1. Demographic change due to aging of the population (Fig. 21.5)
2. Superabundance of goods
3. Shift from manufacturing industry to service industry
4. Increase of lifestyle-related diseases such as diabetes and obesity
5. Information technology becoming an everyday affair
6. Increase in free agents and changes in working style

Based on the above, we can see many similarities between the two countries. On the other hand, there are many differences, of course. Although there are some differences, both countries are becoming similar in terms of socio-economic development. Therefore, if we have a wider vision and an open mind to other countries, we can learn mutually and inspire creative strategies for the future.

The purpose of this chapter is to give readers the essence of how to perceive the Baby Boomer market or Senior market, and insights into success in serving such markets in your country. This chapter will show you the following ten strategies [2]:

- *Strategy 1*: Become a "Finder of FUDI." New FUDI (feelings of uneasiness, dissatisfaction, inconvenience) can be found with saturated markets.

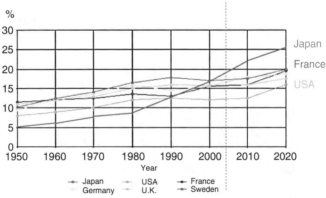

Fig. 21.5 Aging ratio (people 65+ to total population)

- *Strategy 2*: Become a "Need-Focused Merchandiser." The ways of service will shift from selling products to solving problems.
- *Strategy 3*: Become a "Aging-Friendly Stylist." The priority of the product will shift from function-oriented to style-oriented.
- *Strategy 4*: Become a "Refuge Temple" at the customer's home. The place for providing services will shift from the shop to the customer's home.
- *Strategy 5*: Become a "Private Concierge." Use high-tech to enable mass customization and maintain high quality.
- *Strategy 6*: Create a "Third Place" for retirees, a replacement for the workplace. The number of retirees who have no places to go everyday will increase.
- *Strategy 7*: Arrange "Intellectual Camp Experiences" in your services. Experience-learning will be more appealing for lifelong learning.
- *Strategy 8*: Become a "Knowledge Net Worker." "Nanocorps," own-sized mini-companies will increase and need sales support.
- *Strategy 9*: Use "Intellectual Tie" as the appeal of the service. Intellectual stimulation creates the chemical reaction and the attractiveness of a residential community.
- *Strategy 10*: Focus on "Loose-Tie-Big-Family." The border between individuals and groups will become blurred.

The goal of this chapter is to provide information on how to start a new business or improve existing business models. This chapter contains summaries of the ten strategies for success in serving older adults in a diverse market.

The primary focus of this chapter is the Japanese market. However, I believe it is useful for all readers in developed countries, even though it includes examples of companies only in the USA and Japan. This is because those have achieved success by implementing these strategies and can be transformed among the developed countries.

Strategy 1: Become a "Finder of FUDI" (Feelings of Uneasiness, Dissatisfaction, Inconvenience): New FUDI Can Be Found With Saturated Markets

You may think that most markets today are saturated. Are you sure that it is true? It is not, as a matter of fact. The fitness club market is a good example. In the 1990s, the growth of fitness clubs in the USA and Japan reached a plateau. Particularly in Japan, the aging of the population and the decline in the birthrate made it necessary for the fitness club industry to find a new market among older adults and/or the Boomer generation. This effort brought a certain amount of success, but the overall growth of new members seems to have reached a peak. Still, many traditional fitness clubs missed out on countless potential customers among these target generations.

The women-only fitness company called "Curves" proved this fact. Since its founding in Waco, Texas, in 1992, Curves has spread its franchises dramatically.

Curves now has more than 10,000 franchises all over the world, and represents nearly one-third of all fitness clubs. The average age of their members is 50, and most of them have never joined a fitness club before. Not surprisingly, there were millions of American women, particularly middle age or older women, who were not at all attracted to conventional fitness clubs. They did not want to be exposed to men when they were exercising to lose weight. They also did not like the impersonal atmosphere of traditional fitness clubs that were filled with machines. And they did not want to spend long periods of time "working out."

Curves has been successful because they resolved all these concerns by offering a new service that is totally different from the conventional fitness clubs. At Curves, women do not have to worry about men. The clubs are only for women. Curves developed their original training machines, which are easy to use for older women. And, they offer an exercise program that requires no more than 30 min to complete.

One other innovation introduced by Curves is to allow its customers to work out in a small group instead of exercising by themselves. Instead of having the exercise machines facing the wall, as in a traditional fitness club, the machines at Curves are arranged in a circle facing inwards, so the customers can see and interact with each other as they workout. These innovative ideas have made Curves enormously popular among women of many different ages.

This example shows that within any apparently saturated market, you can always find countless customers who are dissatisfied with existing goods and services. To identify their negative reactions (feelings of uneasiness, dissatisfaction, or inconvenience) is the first step. If you have ideas about how to satisfy these feelings, those ideas might turn into a new successful business.

If you examine the products and services that have sold well to the older adult market, you will find that many of them offer relief from some negative element in the existing market. In Japan, a medical insurance product called "Hairemasu (You Can Apply)" by Alico has been a big hit because it was the first life insurance that anyone who is 50 or older can buy. It gives older adults relief from their feelings of uneasiness about their financial security in the future when they get sick. Kao's cooking oil, "Kenko (Healthy) Econa," is said to be good for your health because the fat will not be stored in your body as much as with other oils. This product became a big hit among those who feel uneasy about their health, especially those who are worried about diabetes or hypertension.

The "Raku-Raku (easy-easy) Phone" by NTT DoCoMo, the biggest cell phone carrier in Japan, is a hidden best-selling product for older adults who did not like to use cell phones due to their small buttons and narrow displays. Raku-Raku Phone solved the inconvenience of cell phones for the older generation by redesigning their phones to be "aging-friendly."

In addition, Curves Japan was established in 2005 due to advocacy by the author. Curves Japan has opened over 640 stores nationwide in Japan during only the past two and half years. This means unbelievable success, and is clear evidence that my strategy is proven.

Strategy 2: Become a "Need-Focused Merchandiser": The Ways of Service Will Shift from Selling Products to Solving Problems

Consumers today have too many choices. Many older adults don't know how to make the best choices when they want to resolve their dissatisfaction. For example, where do you go when you have back pain problems?

"Relax the Back" is a US specialty store that is a one-stop solution for such people. Here is their core concept: provide customers with the means to avoid back and neck pain. If you walk into one of their stores, you will find beds, pillows, office chairs, and other products that are all designed to support or comfort your back. Their selection of products is based on the customers' needs and not on conventional product lines. This is the most remarkable characteristic of this store. You can call it a "theme store" designed for people with back problems. A back pain counselor is always available for consultation in their stores. You can also try their chairs or beds to see how they feel.

The stores are not trying to sell products. They are selling "the real experience of back pain relief" through using their products. And yet, they offer even more. They give out information on clinics or massage therapists with good reputations. If necessary, they will even give you information on products that they are not selling in their store. With their knowledge and advice, they have established their position as the back pain experts for their customers.

In Japan, The Hankyu Department Store in Umeda, Osaka opened a new relaxation and beauty zone for women called "Refre-Pit Ainee" in July, 2002. This is an area where you can find five different beauty treatments (massage, foot care etc), beauty salons, a make-up studio, a café, etc., which are all the name brands in each field. This place is extremely popular with women as a "one-stop-shop" for those who want to be pretty. All of the shops here provide services, not products.

One more characteristic is that their services are not selected by the "product-focus" (like women's clothing or men's clothing), but by the customer's "need-focus" (like wanting to be pretty or ecology-conscious). These examples show the increasing value of providing services based on the customers' needs around a single theme. The customers' needs are the basic focus, not the products.

Strategy 3: Become a "Aging-Friendly Stylist": The Priority of the Product Will Shift from Function-Oriented to Style-Oriented

As we get older, we may gradually lose our physical abilities, but we never lose our fashion sense. However, most clothing and other products designed for older adults is usually unfashionable and offers only a narrow selection. From now on, products for older consumers must have an elegant style to compensate for the inconvenience that is caused by the decline of physical abilities due to age. Products must evolve from the function-oriented to the style-oriented. However, when we talk about "a real style," we are not just talking about the superficial style such as the quality of materials or design. A product with a real style must have taken the users, older adults in this case, into consideration.

A good example of this strategy is an online store called "Gold Violin." Their walking stick does not look like something that people with a walking problem hold on to. It is designed as if it were a part of a woman's fashionable accessories, just like her shoes or her handbag. Another example of a product with a strong positive appeal is "Elderhostel," which provides learning adventures for people who are 55 and over. This age limit is not discrimination. It is a positive message that older people still have lots to learn through traveling filled with outdoor adventures.

In Japan, Wacoal, a women's underwear manufacturer, created two new brands, "La Vie Aisee" for women in their 40s or older and "Gra-P" for women in their 60s or older. "La Vie Aisee," is a line of fashionable underwear that is intended to be comfortable for women whose skin gets sensitive because of menopause. "Gra-P" offers a line of nicely designed underwear, with beautiful lace and other trimmings, where the material is carefully chosen so that it is elastic and comfortable for older women's shoulders and other parts of their bodies.

The product/service provider for older generations should be a smart "aging stylist" who can provide an elegant way to overcome the inconveniences of aging. Professional skill in merchandising is required, so that older adults can feel respect and consideration for their needs. If you study the products and services for older adults that have been successful in responding to their physical or psychological needs, you will feel the affection that merchandising people have for older adults. In other words, those who just try to sell products to older adults without feeling affection for them will not be successful. Never treat older people merely as consumers with lots of time and money and ignore their particular needs and interests.

The real wisdom of selling to older adults comes from having feelings of true affection, respect, and gratitude toward them. You'd better not try to tamper or use a trick. You just have to select what's best for your own parents or grandparents. The key is to make them happy.

Strategy 4: Become a "Refuge Temple" at the Customer's Home: The Place for Providing Services Will Shift from the Shop to the Customers' Home

"Husband for rent" is a new business that is popular in Moscow now. In a city with a high divorce rate, many women are living by themselves. The rented husbands do all kinds of manual labor such as furniture repair and so on for these single women.

In the USA, a similar service is offered by "Mr. Handyman." They do all kinds of odd jobs, mostly for older adults who are living by themselves. Their services include anything from carpentry to the cleaning of gutters. Other enterprises offered similar services before Mr. Handyman. But, most of them were small and fragmented businesses, and the quality of their services was often unreliable.

Mr. Handyman attempts to provide reliable, high-quality services as professionals. Specifically, they standardized their service menu, defining the content and the quality of each type of job with a clear price. They also equip their vans with the necessary tools and materials. Their staff visits their customers one by one, gaining their customers' trust through communication. With these efforts, they transformed this highly fragmented labor-intensive business into a new systematic service product that offers specific professional skills.

Although "Do It Yourself" is rooted in the American culture, many people give up such work as they get older. What they need then is not the "DIY shop" but the "DIY procurator service." In Japan, a new personal computer trouble-shooting service (Yokogawa Q&A) is becoming popular among older adults.

Now that broadband Internet service is available at low cost, an increasing number of older adults are using computers. However, they are not well-trained and have little understanding of the technologies, while new computer viruses and other problems keep appearing. As a result, the demand for a face-to-face computer support service is increasing.

Once you have gained the trust of your customers in this kind of business, you can get the advantage of calling on them frequently. It would be ideal to establish a stable relationship with the customers. Whenever they have a problem, you should be the "first person" that they wish to consult. In Japan, we call the function of this first person "Refuge Temple." The original meaning of the word is that the temple was the place that accepted refugees in olden days.

You should be the first "Refuge Temple" to be at their service. Since older adults with physical decline tend to stay at home, "Refuge Temple" must visit a customer's home. It is a good sign when the customers start to tell you about other problems, including problems that are not directly related to your business. This can increase your business opportunity.

Strategy 5: Become a "Private Concierge": Use High-Tech to Enable "Mass Customization" and Maintain High Quality

Many older adults wish to live independently in their own homes as long as possible. Even so, they often feel uneasy in their everyday life. Beacon Hill Village is a membership organization that offers essential services for older people living in this historic area of Boston, Massachusetts. They have been successful in understanding and meeting their customers' needs.

Beacon Hill is an eighteenth century upscale residential neighborhood near downtown Boston. About 14% of the area's 9,000 residents are 60 years old or older. Most of them do not wish to move out of this area even when they get quite old. "Village Concierge" is a popular service provided by Beacon Hill Village. A member can just call in and request services such as grocery shopping, transportation, cleaning, and other daily in-home services.

As the society is aging, the demand for concierge services will increase. Many older adults need services exclusively for them. However, it generally costs a lot to provide such time- and labor-intensive services. "Les Concierges" is a good example of how a business solves this cost problem. This San Francisco-based company provides individuals with the same kind of "concierge services" that high-class hotels offer their guests, such as access to hard-to-get tickets, restaurant reservations, etc. Their customers were initially limited to wealthy people, since the membership fee for these services cost a minimum of $3,540. In 1990, Les Concierges introduced a new business model. The company contracts with an employer and serves as a "private concierge" for its employees. The employer pays for the services that their employees receive. The services they provide vary from supporting an employee when a parent gets sick suddenly to arranging a family trip.

The structure of this business is similar to what we have in Japan, where an agent arranges reservations and other things for a company's employees to use the facilities and services that their company offers. The biggest difference, however, is that the "private concierge" offers truly customized services for each employee.

How can they do this? The combination of their highly trained professional staff and their own IT system makes it possible. They have built an IT system that can identify the possible needs of each customer based on all of their past service records. Thanks to this database of personal information, the staff of Les Concierges can communicate efficiently with each of the five million customers registered with them today.

In Japan, Suruga Bank claimed to be a "concierge bank," meaning that they will be the concierge for their customers by providing all kinds of financial services as well as support for their customers' everyday life. Specifically, they provide a service called "web concierge." Customers who have an account with them can see their account balance, the sum of their credit card payments, the balance of their loan, the sum of direct debits – all on one screen. And, you can make an inquiry by e-mail if necessary. While services such as this do offer confidence to the bank's customers, the bank will have to do more if it is to fully deliver its promise to provide true concierge-type services.

The combination of quality staff and the IT system has made it possible for service providers to turn a small-scale human-oriented "private concierge" business into a large-scale, highly profitable high-tech business. They have also succeeded in enlarging their market by popularizing the services that used to be limited to wealthy people.

Strategy 6: Create a "Third Place" for Retirees, a Replacement for the Workplace: The Number of Retirees Who Have No Places To Go Everyday Will Increase

Many older adults today do not consider themselves as "elderly people." As a result there are fewer people going to the so-called "elderly clubs" or "senior centers" both in Japan and the USA. Older adults do not like the elderly image of these places. On the other hand, many older adults who are retired do want to remain connected to society and are looking for a replacement for their workplace.

"Starbucks Coffee" became a big success with the concept of a "third place," which means neither home (the first place) nor workplace (the second place). "Mather Café Plus" in Chicago is a new type of café that is popular among this new type of older adults. "Mather Café Plus" is called the Starbucks for seniors.

What are the reasons for their success? They don't give you the impression that it is a place for "elderly people." At the same time, they offer many different programs and ideas to respond to the varied needs of older adults.

If you go in to a Mather Café Plus, you will find that they serve good quality drinks/foods at such reasonable prices that you can drop by regularly. The atmosphere of the café is rather stylish, not like a tacky elderly club at all. In a room next to the restaurant, they offer more than 40 different programs such as computer lessons and exercise classes where you can make new friends. Their staff looks after you with great hospitality, too. Even if you go there by yourself, they will talk with you or introduce you to other guests.

The remarkable point here is that they are not making money merely as a café for older adults. Their success comes from the structure that they have built. They offer a place for older adults to get together and meet other people. And then, their customers use many of the different activities that the cafe offers. Mather Café Plus offers other services as well. For example, they take suggestions from their guests for their menu. They also offer a free telephone counseling service that provides information of all sorts; they can recommend a handyman service or provide information about the cost of an in-house caregiver. This telephone service plays an important role in their business because the information from their customers helps them to understand the potential needs of older adults. And, this helps them improve the quality of their services for their customers.

In Japan, a Japanese-style public spa called "Super Sento (public bath)" is now a popular leisure spot in many cities in Japan. It is especially popular among older adults. For a fee of around ¥600 (US$5.75), you can enjoy about ten different types of baths (jet bath, herb bath, hot spring, outdoor stone bath, sauna, etc.). Outside the baths, there are other spaces such as a restaurant, a massage center, a barbershop, a Korean body scrubbing place etc. Super Sento has established a good business model of making profits from services other than the baths. Many older adults spend their time during the weekdays in this kind of spa, helping to increase the utilization rate of these places.

Strategy 7: Arrange "Intellectual Camp Experiences" in Your Services: "Experience-Learning" Will Be More Appealing for Lifelong Learning

Many older adults today are looking for an opportunity to enjoy learning something. Simple recreation is not enough. In today's service industry society, people seem to have more desk work than ever before. We have fewer and fewer opportunities to learn something interactively or experientially. As a result, education today is largely passive and learning tends to be a one-way process. If you can combine intellectual experiences with leisure services like traveling, you can offer exciting learning experiences that are differentiated from the usual leisure service providers.

For example, "Elderhostel" provides learning adventures to older Americans. Their program consists of not only the lectures in the classrooms, but also real experiences outside. Their programs are based on themes that stimulate the intellectual interests of older adults. For each group, Elderhostel provides a leader who will contribute in creating a friendly atmosphere, along with an opportunity to meet with people of similar interests. This is how they maintain the high rate of repeaters.

Another good example is "Senior Summer School." Those who would like to experience today's campus life can stay on a college or university campus for a couple of weeks. They can enjoy not only attending lectures but also exploring the area and making friends with other participants with similar interests. This program attracts many older adults who are tired of the typical sightseeing tours.

In Japan, there are now travel services like "Club Tourism" by Club Tourism Company or "Otona-no-Kyujitsu (Holidays for Adults)" by East Japan Railway Company that include opportunities for the participants to learn something through real outdoor experiences during their trips.

The participants are usually involved with the planning of the trip. The travel agency arranges their plan and sells the trips. The customers can experience what they want. This system works well for both parties. Any type of "intellectual camp experience" for older adults must have the following elements:

1. An opportunity to meet other people with similar interests
2. An opportunity to learn through real experiences along with lectures
3. A specialized topic with professional or academic content
4. A leader who is an expert on the topic and who will create a friendly atmosphere
5. A system that allows customers to plan their own programs
6. Activities that are not a physical burden for older adults
7. A reasonable price so that older adults can participate repeatedly

Another key to the success of this kind of program is that all the participants have similar levels of interests in the topic. It is important to give detailed information beforehand and explain about the program as much as possible to enable the participants to choose the right program for themselves.

Strategy 8: Become a "Knowledge Net Worker": "Nanocorps," Own-Sized Mini-Companies Will Increase and Need Sales Support

"Happy Retirement" used to be an ideal course of life, living the last stage of your life enjoying leisure on your savings. But times have changed. There are more people who wish to work even after their retirement [3]. In reality, it is often hard for a retired person to find a job. Instead, an increasing number of older adults/the Boomer generation are starting a "nanocorp" to earn an income by doing what they really want to do. A nanocorp is a small corporation usually with only one or two persons who are owners. In most cases they don't have sales people like more traditional corporations. So a new type of service has emerged to support the sales activities of nanocorps.

"Le Tip" is a membership business club where the members act as sales persons for one another. Almost all of the members are either individual "free agents" or owners of small businesses. In a weekly meeting, the members report their recent news, ask questions, exchange information, and make commitments to provide other members with access to clients. The club has strict rules to ensure that their activities are working effectively for their members' businesses. A strong spirit of mutual aid is consistently cultivated among the members.

Another outstanding example of a valuable support service for nanocorps is "High Tech Connect," a human resource agent that provides businesses that need outside help with access to a network of more than 1,500 independent consultants or nanocorps to meet their specific needs.

The trend of utilizing the manpower of the retired is getting bigger in Japan. There must be many people in Japan who wish to start a nanocorp. But, they are usually lack the ability to sell their services and need help to do this. The key to successfully supporting their sales activities is to have extensive knowledge about the background of the nanocorp owners so that agents can connect the people who need sales support with the people who look for solutions. I call this new type of function "Knowledge Net Worker." A Knowledge Net Worker must have the following conditions:

1. Deep background knowledge about the "people" who use the services
2. Extensive ability to identify qualities, trust, and coordination
3. Well-structured operation rules and clear benefits to users
4. A system in which each user can use each sales network mutually

One possible source for Knowledge Net Workers will be retired business executives. In Japan, a Japanese company called "Direct Force" helps nanocorps as an agent. Direct Force consists of retired executives from large corporations. Members of Direct Force work as consultants for a small business or as instructors at a university, etc. These retired people do not have to work to make a living, but they enjoy working in society, utilizing their ability and experiences.

Strategy 9: Use "Intellectual Tie" as the Appeal of the Service: Intellectual Stimulation Creates the Chemical Reaction and the Attractiveness of a Residential Community

Life expectancy is getting longer and our standard of living is getting higher. There are also much older adults than before who want to have intellectual stimulation after retirement. On the other hand, competition is getting more intense these days both in the senior housing market and in colleges/universities. If a college/university and a residential community for older adults can cooperate, they could provide a new type of experience that will appeal to older adults. We can expect to see an increase in intellectually connected retirement communities in the near future. Intellectual ties will play a more important role than family, geographical, or career connections.

Lasell Village is a college-linked residential community for older adults in Newton, Massachusetts. The Village, which is located on the campus of Lasell College, has a built-in educational component. Cooperation between the college and the community make it possible for the residents to study at the college. The older residents are allowed to use all the facilities of the college like the regular students and the faculty. The community also offers many chances for the older adults to study with young students of the college.

Learning is the best intellectual recreation. If you place it in the center of your living environment, you will have a number of advantages. As soon as Lasell Village opened, all 210 rooms were filled, with more than 110 people on the waiting list. The residents of Lasell Village are 83 years old on average. Very few of them are bedridden. Everyone is enjoying the life there, while the young students of the college appreciate having access to their advice and experience. There are still more people who would like to live in the village based on its reputation.

In Japan, the first implementation of the college-linked community was conducted in July, 2008 by the author's initiative. "Club Encourage Mikage," located in Mikage, an upscale residential area in Kobe, is operated through the partnership with Kansai University, one of the major private universities in Japan. It is 30 min away from the university campus. The facility provides 218 independent living units as well as 60 nursing care rooms. Every day the independent seniors are ferried by shuttle bus to school where they attend lessons on history, philosophy, and music alongside younger university students. By interacting with the students, the elderly are exposed to stimuli that will keep their minds active. I believe this project is one of the many creative solutions being designed in Japan to cope with its rapidly graying population.

As Confucius said, to learn and to practice is a joy of life. Using an intellectual tie is a key to differentiate a residential community for older adults. The following are the vital factors for this kind of housing product:

1. Allow residents to attend classes in cooperation with a college
2. Give residents the same access to college facilities as the students or the faculty
3. Offer as many opportunities as possible for the residents to meet with young students

Strategy 10: Focus on "Loose-Tie-Big-Family": The Border Between Individuals and Groups Will Become Blurred

As you get older, your biggest worry is often the safety of living independently by yourself. Many of those without children choose to live in a full-service Continuing Care Retirement Community (CCRC). But, many of those who have children choose to move near to them. In large cities, these days we see more and more examples of a new model of "loose-tie-big-family," Older parents and their children's families live separately but in the same neighborhood. They get together often and go out as a big family of three generations.

Another type of "big family" is emerging as the population ages. In retirement communities, many older adults who are in similar situations live together, supporting each other like a loosely connected big family. For example, in a CCRC in New Hampshire called "Kendal at Hanover," the residents have set up a nonprofit organization to participate in the planning and operation of the CCRC. They shape the structure of the community and the social, cultural, and intellectual life there. They determine all the management rules, how the residents get involved, how to cooperate with the local town, and all the other policies of management that are written down in a document.

One of the Japanese examples of a "loose-tie-big-family" is "Life House Tomodachi-Mura (Life House Friends Village)" in Nakaizu-cho, Shizuoka prefecture. Almost all the residents there are women who had been living by themselves. Most of them are in their 60s, all capable of living independently. The difference between this house and the usual apartment is that there are many spaces and facilities for common use. Here, you can live independently, respecting one another's privacy, while also enjoying other people's company through different activities. You will not feel the solitude or uneasiness of living by yourself, even when you get really old.

A similar example can be found in several other cities, such as "Denen Seikatsu-kan (Country Life Residence)" in Katsuura-cho, Chiba prefecture, "Co-operative House Shalom Tsukimino" in Yamato city, Kanagawa prefecture and a collective house for multigenerations called "Ashiya 17°C" in Ashiya city, Hyogo prefecture.

How can we maintain stable and friendly relationships in this new type of loose-tie big family? The key factor is whether the management can mix the individuals smoothly in a group. The management needs to do the following:

1. Establish rules to support a loosely connected big family
2. Build a system that enables each member to be involved in a loosely connected big family but also to have their privacy preserved
3. Coordinate the relationship between the local town and the loosely connected big family

Many people choose to live in a group to avoid the solitude of living by themselves. However, living with other people will bring its own problems and annoyances that you don't have when living by yourself. The ideal is to live with other people, respecting one another, being independent as an individual, and supporting one another whenever it's necessary. The mixing function of the individuals in a group will make it possible. In a loosely connected big family, each member will have an opportunity to learn from one another.

Summary and Conclusion

Many enterprises tend to look the older adult market or the Boomer market as a single homogeneous iceberg, due to the large numbers of population compared to other generations. In contrast, this chapter indicates that the nature of the Boomer or seniors market is "an aggregate of diverse micromarkets," which is different from those of the past. This chapter also describes what will form each diverse micromarket and what is necessary to adapt such diverse micromarkets by referencing advanced business examples in the USA and Japan.

Strategies 1–5 give you thoughts on adapting to the diverse consumer behaviors. Strategies 6–8 give you thoughts on adapting to the diverse ways of consuming time. Strategies 9 and 10 give you thoughts on adapting to the diverse ways of living.

Some readers may ask the following question: the ten strategies you offer are very interesting; however, sometimes we ask ourselves why should these be only specific to the elderly market? Wouldn't they work well with other age groups, too? Would it be possible to say that age-neutral or transgenerational approaches are best?

My answer to the question is "partly yes, partly no." If you say "age-neutral" or "ageless" market, it is too simplified. As I explained in the Introduction, our consuming behavior is very complicated. Age is one of the most important factors to consider; however, age does not always give us the whole information.

For example, in case of customers who joined Curves, the average age is around 50. But this does not mean women automatically come to Curves at age 50. Those who come to Curves are women who don't like traditional fitness clubs but want to reduce their weight, without men and saving time. What forms each diverse micromarket is "value," not age.

References

1. H. Murata, *Seven Paradigm Shifts in Thinking About the Business of Aging: Breaking the Barriers in a Diverse Market (in Japanese)* (Diamond Corporation, Tokyo, 2006)
2. H. Murata, *The Business of Aging: Ten Successful Strategies for a Diverse Market (in Japanese)* (Diamond Corporation, Tokyo, 2004)
3. H. Murata, *Retirement Moratorium: What Will the Not-retired Boomers Change? (in Japanese)* (Nikkei, Tokyo, 2007)

Chapter 22
The Age-Neutral Customer Journey

Removing the Barriers Between Brands and Silver Customers

Kim Walker

Abstract Nobody wants to feel old as a result of choosing or using a particular product or service. For this reason, age-based products and positionings will have limited appeal for mature consumers, particularly the aging baby boomer generation. These marketing-wise, life-experienced consumers will expect any purchase experience to be age-neutral. This will require just about every consumer business to make subtle or even radical changes to their product-development, marketing and after-sales approach. Changes that accommodate the relentless effects of physiological aging.

This chapter demonstrates why and how businesses and brands should become age-neutral. Using three distinct case studies, we introduce SilverAudit™, a unique process that measures and monitors age neutrality by applying 150 "experiences" of the customer journey against 15 identified "effects" of aging.

By making products, services and the entire customer experience "age-neutral" businesses can understand, measure, and ultimately remove the barriers between their products and services and mature customers, thereby unlocking the vast spending power of the "senior" markets.

Introduction

Perhaps the most common question in the mind of a corporate executive considering the impact of an aging consumer on their business is "where do I begin?" Sometimes they jump to erroneous conclusions about the need for dramatic changes or new product development, when in fact there's a simple, easy first step; that is, to understand how "age-friendly" the customer experience is, and what barriers may exist along the journey. This requires a systematic approach that tracks the journey relative to the physiological effects of age.

Through a rigorous method we can identify and remove barriers and spot opportunities for improvement. Covered extensively in his book, The 50-Plus Market [1], Dick Stroud [2] argues convincingly that the future is "age-neutral,"

F. Kohlbacher and C. Herstatt (eds.), *The Silver Market Phenomenon*,
DOI 10.1007/978-3-642-14338-0_22, © Springer-Verlag Berlin Heidelberg 2011

a concept he defines as "the practice of marketing theory minus the assumptions, hunches, stereotypes, pseudoscience and mysticism associated with aging and the age of consumers." The imperative for marketers to retain the swelling army of older customers while at the same time recruiting new users to brand usage means that they must reengineer their products, services and communications to remain accessible and relevant to all. That's why age-neutrality will become a marketing mandatory, and the reason why we created the SilverAudit™ [3] to help clients identify, measure and monitor it.

The Options for Business

"There is nothing more frightful than ignorance in action". Goethe

The evidence of demographic aging is so overwhelming, and covered in detail throughout this book, that "business as usual" is not an option for smart companies. In accepting this reality, the marketer is really left with only two options for action:

1. Develop new products and services to meet the needs of an older customer or
2. Adapt existing products and services to meet the changing needs of an older customer

Option 1. Develop New Products and Services To Meet the Needs of an Older Customer

No doubt this is an area of opportunity and where most minds immediately go when the subject of the silver market is raised. Retirement housing, assistive devices, special nutritional needs and the like will all provide opportunities for new products and services. But one must remember that limiting the business potential of the aging population to products for old people is like thinking only about baby diapers, toys and baby paraphernalia for all people under 30 years of age!

Another issue is that R&D costs and return on capital-employed considerations will often slow down the corporate decision process to venture into this market.

Option 2. Adapt Existing Products and Services To Meet the Changing Needs of an Older Customer

As will be explained shortly, most 50+ consumers don't want products that identify them by age. These consumers still eat, travel, entertain, educate and "grow," so the key is to understand what must be done to keep products and services relevant to consumers as they age. Understanding these needs and integrating them seamlessly into the offering is the basic definition of age-neutrality and will become an imperative for almost every consumer business.

In summary, while Option 1 is viable and important, Option 2 provides the greatest opportunities for companies and consumers alike.

The Principles of an Age-Neutral Business

The principles of age-neutrality govern (1) the product development and design: *Universal design* (covered in detail in chapter 8), (2) consideration of marketing: *Ageless marketing*, (3) sales and service: *Ageless sales and support*, and (4) communication with the customer: *Inclusive communications*. These are defined in Table 22.1.

While each is a vital component of the overall goal, we must be careful not to narrow our thinking and miss the forest for the trees.

An old ad-land expression goes; *"Advertising is the fastest way to kill a bad product."* In other words, if your product is unsuitable or uncompetitive, advertising and the resulting customer experience will magnify these weaknesses and kill the product. Similarly, a great product, well-marketed but with weak communications is destined to fail. For this reason, as we look at age-neutrality of business, we must not only look into the disciplines of product, marketing and communications, but most importantly we should take a holistic view across the entire consumer journey from product awareness through to postsale support.

Aging Consumers – Psychology + Physiology

Most older consumers have a split personality. One part of them doesn't want to be treated or considered as old, but another part wants companies to ensure that their products and services are equally useable by older people. This is the central challenge for marketers. Essentially, it's denial.

Table 22.1 The imperatives of age-neutrality

Universal design	Ageless marketing	Ageless sales and support	Inclusive communications
Products and services designed to accommodate the practical and emotional needs of young and old without an overt reference to either	Covers all aspects of marketing (i.e., packaging, point of sale, Web design etc)	Sales and service process, products and packages that make the buying process easier	Ensure that older consumers are not alienated by messages that are unnecessarily skewed old, young or ignored by media selection

Silver Group

European studies found that, on average, people over 50 think of themselves as 13 years younger than their real age [4]. In a SilverPoll [5] survey across key Asia Pacific markets in 2009, when asked: "how do you think and feel relative to your actual age" most said they felt younger than their real age. Top of the list were Japanese among whom more than 55% of people over 50 claim to feel 5–10 years younger than their age. This was followed by the Australians at 46% (Fig. 22.1). Basically, most people tend to deny the effects of physiological aging until they can no longer be disguised.

Because of this, marketers need to apply the principles of universal design in a way that does not signal that the brand user is "old." OXO [6] is an interesting case. Initially producing a range of kitchen utensils designed for arthritic hands, they now make a vast range of products with the same, easy-to-use principles in mind. Adults of all ages use them because they're functional and they look cool too!

The "new" 50+ consumers are working longer and are more mentally and physically active than previous generations of the same age and will respond positively to products and services that make them think, look or feel younger.

But while attitudes may remain young "forever," our physiological aging is unavoidable and does not discriminate between social groups. Whether it's the need for reading glasses (most common and annoying according to our research) [5], an old soccer injury starting to "play-up," forgetfulness, difficulty in hearing or simple lethargy, we all experience these effects to varying degrees, sooner or later.

Recent research from the USA suggests that the human body begins to age from as young as 27 years [7], so deny aging as we might, the unavoidable reality is that above the age of 45, everyone experiences some of the physical, cognitive or sensory effects of aging, and that as we grow older the incidence and intensity of these issues is likely to increase.

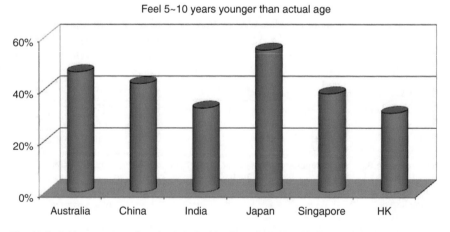

Fig. 22.1 Self-perception of age in Asia Pacific. SilverPoll of 170,000 respondents 50+. January 2009

So how can companies meet the needs of older consumers without making them "feel" older? They must reformulate their entire customer experience with an understanding of these physiological changes but make it appear as part of their normal offering – make the experience age-neutral, not age-defining.

Understanding these effects of aging and measuring the entire customer journey against them is the fundamental starting point to creating an age-neutral experience, and the key to remaining relevant (and in some cases unlocking the huge potential of) to the 50+ market, while remaining completely relevant and appealing to younger market segments.

The Customer Journey

To measure age-neutrality we must have a comprehensive understanding of two key influences; the customer journey (experiences) and the physiological effects of aging (effects) with an overall understanding of the psychology of aging. But where in the purchase cycle should we begin measuring these "experiences?"

For clues we should look at data from market research company Synovate [8] in Table 22.2. This quantifies what we instinctively know. Consumers make purchase decisions based on a multitude of influences, which affect them to different degrees at different stages of the journey. For example, "company-driven marketing" (39%), including all forms of paid advertising and promotion, and "past experience" (28%) have the greatest influence over consumers at the initial consideration stage. Word-of-mouth/online research (37%) and other subtle endorsements become influential during the "active evaluation" phase. While at the point of purchase, the store/agent/dealer interaction is critical (43%).

Table 22.2 The most influential touch points by stage of consumer decision journey, for competitors and new customers. Percentage of effectiveness

	The customers past experience	Company-driven marketing Advertising and promotions	Consumer-driven marketing Word of mouth, personal research	The experience with the store or agent
Awareness of the product	28	39	21	12
Actively consider purchasing the product	10	26	37	26
Purchase	5	22	31	43

Synovate PAX. Based on research conducted on German, Japanese, and US consumers across major consumer categories

Table 22.3 "Experiences" throughout the customer journey™

Communications	Online	Product	Retail	Phone sales/support
Advertising	Search	Design	Access	Sales
Creative	Help	Instructions	Ambience	After sales
Media	Website	Package	Amenities	Delivery
Direct mail	Shopping	Information	Cleanliness	Feedback and complaints
Events		Use	Comfort	
Sponsorships		Opening	Signage	
PR		Operating	Lighting	
Collateral		Closing	Point of sale	
		Pricing	Check-out	
		Warranty	Product location	
			Sales staff	
			Temperature	

SilverAudit™: Silver Group and Dick Stroud

What this means to us is that for a thorough assessment of the customer journey for any consumer, we must involve the touch points through the entire cycle of purchase.

In many cases, manufacturers will not be the retailers of their own products and while one may argue that this should be omitted from the assessment, to do so would be to fall into the trap of viewing the customer experience through corporate eyes rather than those of the consumer who may neither know nor care about the delineations of responsibility between manufacture, retail and after-sales service. If the audit provokes discussion between the respective corporate entities with the result that the customer experience is made more "age-neutral" surely this would be a positive outcome?

We have isolated the experiences or influences throughout the customer journey as shown in Table 22.3. Different products and services follow different paths to and beyond purchase however most will encounter a selection from these elements somewhere during the journey.

We also need to look holistically at the entire customer experience from initial awareness (word-of-mouth, marketing communications) through the phase of investigation (increasingly on-line via search engines and websites), then the journey to the physical store or a visit to the online store. Once purchased, it's getting the product "home" and using it. Finally, we need to consider after-sales: contacting the supplier to report an issue or make an enquiry. Each of these stages influences the customers' view of the brand or company.

The Effects of Aging

Until now, this assessment process could be applied irrespective of age. To some degree or other, we all follow a similar path in our journey through the consumption cycle. But what we need to do is filter this through the inevitable physiological effects of aging.

Table 22.4 15 effects of physiological aging™

Cognitive	Physical	Sensory
Issues that affect our ability to deal with information:	Cosmetic as well as skeletal changes that affect how we look and how we move:	The decline in sensitivity of our five senses:
Complexity	Dexterity	Eyesight
Comprehension	Digestion	Clarity
	Flexibility	Illumination
	Body	Hearing
	Peripheral	Filtering
	Hair	Volume
	Color	Smell
	Volume	Taste
	Menopause	Touch
	Skin	
	Pigmentation	
	Resilience	
	Strength	
	Weight and Size	

SilverAudit™: Silver Group and Dick Stroud

As they apply to the customer journey, SilverAudit™ identifies 15 effects of aging, shown in Table 22.4 and grouped under the headings of cognitive, physical and sensory effects.

Measuring and Monitoring Age-Neutrality

Most companies will evaluate the interplay of *some* of the physiological effects of aging with *some* of the ways they interact with the customer. It is very rare to find companies that systematically and regularly evaluate all points of the customer's journey for all types of physiological aging. This is mainly because there has been a lack of process to ensure this occurs. Yet conducting a detailed audit of the journey in this way will not only identify the areas where urgent action is needed, it will help establish benchmarks and best practices that companies can apply across their operations.

Helping business understand and remove potential barriers to the 50+ market is an issue for companies that apply equally in Asia Pacific, Europe and the US.

SilverAudit™ [3] has been developed by Silver Group [9], in collaboration with Dick Stroud [2]. The process uses an online tool to measure age-neutrality. It is capable of scoring the 150 experience touch-points against the 15 physiological effects of aging.

While not all experiences or effects will be relevant to all companies, it is theoretically necessary to measure 2,250 data points to provide a comprehensive view of a company's age-neutrality. The first task is to select the relevant combination of effect and experiences to ensure that the appropriate parameters are assessed and irrelevant ones removed. This is the "briefing phase" of the process and is followed by the "assessment phase" where we try to emulate the customer experience as closely as possible using a 5-point scoring system where 1 = unacceptable and 5 = perfect. We enter the scores into the online system together with comments and explanations where necessary (usually accompanied by pictures in the final report). Finally, we perform the "analysis and reporting phase" to examine the input data, assemble available reference to illustrate the issues then develop this into a concise, prioritized report of actions and recommendations.

Case Studies

The best way to understand the interaction between physiological aging and the customer journey is to look at three very different mini-case studies. We will assess the age-neutrality of a hotel, a home wireless phone and a simple toothbrush purchase experience.

In each instance, the audit begins with a search of the web and, in the case of the hotel, a call to the reservation office. Throughout the journey we remain critically mindful of the 15 effects so that each can be "scored" later when logged into the online tool. Scoring is done against a battery of questions prompting the particular issue. The 1–5 score is then recorded. Products or services that achieve an overall average index of 3.5 or more are considered to have achieved an acceptable level of age-neutrality, while a sustainable index of 4 should be the goal for businesses.

Because of client confidentiality we can't reveal the identity of the companies involved but we can use the output to show how the audit of physiological aging and customer touch-points provides a detailed analysis of what companies need to do to make themselves age-neutral.

Case 1: Hotel

A major hotel chain wanted to understand how better to connect with the lucrative older customers. Fig. 22.2 shows the SilverAudit™ output for the hotel website. Some of the key observations reflected in the scoring were:

- The website had just too many offers competing for the viewer's attention. This was distracting and made the page appear overly complex. Because of the clutter, hotlinks were too close together and could lead to mis-clicks among older users whose eye–mouse coordination may be lacking. Only half the site was visible on a standard screen without need to scroll down, and important information "below the fold" might be missed. [Navigation. Score = 3]

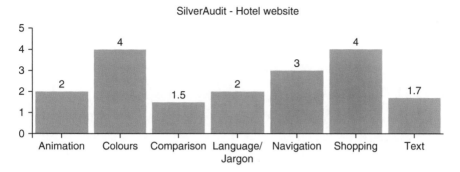

Fig. 22.2 The hotel website

- The main illustration was a series of animated (flash) photos of the property activated by a "mouse-over" action. This can be difficult for older users to manipulate. Better to have video or static, clickable screens to advance the slides. [Animation. Score = 2]
- The site had no type-increase (magnification) facility for older eyes. [Appearance. Score = 2.3]
- Details of specific rooms and rates were listed on separate pages but this required good memory skills to compare them. Better to have a side-by-side comparison feature. [Comparison. Score = 1.5]
- Although much of the site had good color contrast the visitor information page design used a graduated blue background. At times, the black type was placed against a dark blue background minimizing contrast and making it very difficult to read. [Text. Score = 1.7]
- General descriptive copy was long: a struggle, particularly for nonnative English speakers. The content should assume people know about the country of destination and focus on things to do within easy vicinity of the hotel – ideally, things of particular interest to older visitors, e.g., museums, art, music etc. [Language/jargon. Score = 2]

Figure 22.3 shows the output for the hotel room. On our journey from reception to the room, we noticed that the dull lighting in the elevator made the lift buttons very difficult to see until activated and illuminated. Furthermore, on arriving at the desired floor, the signage directing to the room was white lettering on clear perspex, mounted on a beige wall. Very difficult to see and to read. [Directional signage. Score = 1.5].

In the room, there were some obvious shortcomings. Older eyes need more illumination, so it was a major oversight that there were no bedside reading lights. The bedside lighting control device was hugely complex, and even needed a set of instructions on how to use it! The AV remote controls were also a source of confusion and required bothersome study. [Instructions. Score = 2].

The safe deposit box was located on the floor inside the wardrobe. Not only requiring body flexibility to access, but difficult to operate in the dim light.

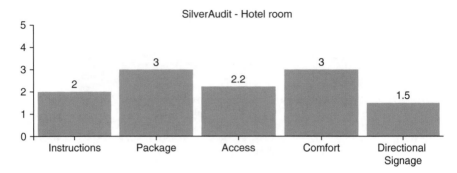

Fig. 22.3 The hotel room

The bathroom had no antislip treatment. While all faucets had easy-to-grip handles, the bathroom itself used a large knob, a nightmare for older hands. While the amenities were clearly labeled (a common complaint for those who don't wear glasses in the shower) once the top was removed, it required some strength and patience to squeeze out the contents. [Access. Score = 2.2].

Lessons Learned

Overall, the hotel customer journey earned a SilverAudit™ Index of 3.2, barely acceptable. The hotel had undergone some refurbishment under new management, but clearly the needs of older customers had been overlooked by the designers. The decline in the sense of sight means that lighting and signage becomes ever more important both in general areas, and elevators, and in the privacy of the room. Confusing lighting and AV controls need to be simplified and not require special study by the guest. Levered door handles and nonslip surfaces in bathrooms need to be adopted for hotels to be both age-friendly and safe.

Case 2: Home Cordless Phone

The next case is a home cordless phone from a leading global manufacturer. We chose to purchase this through one of the UK's premier supermarket chains and so we expected it to score highly, and it did.

But it wasn't perfect. The signage could be greatly improved, it should have provided rest seating and the product position on the shelves was not good. Overall, it is as good as one is likely to find.

Despite the fact that the product was from a well-known global brand, this case revealed how a company can take design very seriously (the pack is littered with the term "universal design"), but they failed badly in other areas.

For example, the instructions seemed to be written from the technical not the user's perspective. There was no hierarchy or logic to the information and too much confusing jargon was used. Anyone who has purchased a product from Apple will know that it is possible for technology companies to satisfy their lawyers and still deliver a consumer-friendly "product-opening" experience. Our other observations included:

- Instructions were more an explanation of the features (the sort of thing one needs to know prepurchase) rather than how to use the product – what we want to know postpurchase. Various elements in the box were overly technical and were out of sync with each other. [Instructions. Score: 1.7]
- The packaging was a confusing jumble of disconnected logos and facts. [Package. Score = 2.8]
- The website could be greatly improved through the removal of jargon and technical-speak. [Online. Score = 3.1]
- The online warranty support was sadly lacking. The customer service area was difficult to locate. The process to file a query and overall complexity of the warranty took over one week to resolve. [Warranty. Score = 1]

Lessons Learned

As is clearly evident from the analysis in Figs. 22.4 and 22.5, the basic product is fine, but the journey is let down because of the packaging and instructions.

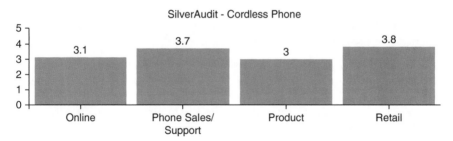

Fig. 22.4 The cordless phone – overall

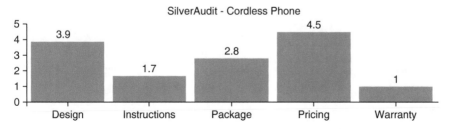

Fig. 22.5 The cordless phone – packaging and instructions

Based on product design and features alone, this product would probably be "best in class." Ironically, the changes needed to make this a truly age-neutral product are relatively minor and may, through the removal of unnecessary, confusing instructions and literature, actually save the company money in the long run! This example shows why a comprehensive audit of the full customer journey is important to help identify seemingly minor potential barriers to the market.

Case 3: Toothbrush

The third and final case relates to a toothbrush purchase from a leading consumer marketing company and purchased from a leading supermarket chain in Hong Kong. The summary output can be seen in Table 22.5, where the ultimate Silver-Audit™ Index Score was a miserable 1.8. One can also readily see from this summary table that the failings occurred across the board both in terms of the "customer experiences" and the "effects of aging."

Why such a poor result? First and foremost, the website was effectively useless for an older audience. It was clearly skewed to a younger market and had little in the way of practical information to help inform the decision. The flash, navigation, music and talent cues were exclusionary for an older audience. [Online. Score = 1.5].

The retail visit highlighted a number of other problems for older customers. In land-scarce Hong Kong, supermarkets have infamously narrow aisles but at this particular site they were made even more difficult to navigate because of POS stands and product bins randomly placed. Bilingual and poorly illuminated signs made it difficult to find the correct aisle. But that was the easy part! On arriving at the toothbrush section we encountered;

- A blinding array of choice with only subtle, hard-to-find differentiators to help people make informed choice. Interestingly, kiddies' toothbrushes were clearly identified.
- Products were displayed on shelves from the lowest to the highest, requiring effort and flexibility to reach and examine them.
- Packaging included tiny product diagrams and explanations – difficult to read or comprehend these overly complex product details. [Retail. Score = 2.1].

Table 22.5 SilverAudit™ summary output for the toothbrush showing a dismal total score of 1.8

	Cognitive	Physical	Sensory	
Communications	1.7	–	–	1.7
Online	1.5	–	–	1.5
Phone	1	–	–	1
Product	1.7	1.9	2.4	2
Retail	2	2.2	2	2.1
	1.6	2	2.3	1.8

© Silver Group

When the customer relations hotline was tested, we found that after entering a prolonged automated message system (which was "corporate" rather than "brand-specific" – a confusion in itself), we were ultimately informed the service was only open "from 9 in the morning to 5 in the evening." Not very customer friendly at all. [Phone Support. Score = 1].

Lessons Learned

If we look at the scores for this audit from the perspective of the physiological effects of aging, it is clear that the general confusion and overly complex purchase experience becomes apparent with low averaged scores for cognitive (1.6), sensory (2) and physical (2.3). Clearly there is work to be done to make this customer journey age-neutral.

Summary and Conclusion

Unlike generations before them, today's mature consumers are more likely to think and behave younger than their chronological age. Marketing to them on the basis of age is fraught with difficulty. But regardless of their attitudes and self-perceptions of age, physiological aging is relentless. To ensure these highly experienced consumers remain engaged with brands and businesses, the purchase journey must be age-neutral – not one which is optimized for younger people.

Physiological aging impacts all customer touch points, and these touch points need to be reassessed with regard to physiological aging.

The SilverAudit™ case studies highlight how even companies that are "best-in-class" make basic errors that create barriers between older customers and their products and services. Whether it's a hotel that overlooks the importance of better lighting and nonslip bathroom surfaces, a technology manufacturer that provides incomprehensible, complex user instructions or a toothbrush marketer that effectively "excludes" older users through most aspects of its customer experience, every company has something to learn.

Companies that fail to anticipate this basic human phenomenon and adjust their businesses accordingly risk shutting out a large, affluent and growing body of consumers: a body of consumers who have, throughout their lives, revolutionized businesses through their vocal rejection of seemingly discriminatory practices. If they sense this is an issue (and it will be) their voices will be heard! For all these reasons and more, making brands age-neutral is common sense. The world's first system to measure and monitor age-neutrality, SilverAudit™ was specifically designed to help businesses understand, measure, and ultimately remove the barriers between their products and services, and older customers.

By making products, services and the entire customer experience "age-neutral," businesses can unlock the vast spending power of the silver market and preempt their dissatisfaction.

References

1. The 50-Plus Market By Dick Stroud. http://www.the50plusmarket.com/index.htm
2. Dick Stroud. 20+30 Consulting. http://www.20plus30.com
3. SilverAudit™. http://www.silvergroup.asia/SilverAudit
4. Berlin Aging Study. University of Michigan and the Max Planck Institute for Human Development, Berlin. 516 people between the ages of 70 and 104
5. SilverPoll™. An online survey across 6 Asia Pacific countries between 23/12/2008 and 8/01/2009. 170,000 samples. http://www.silvergroup.asia/blog/SilverPoll-reveals-regional-differences.php
6. OXO. http://www.silvergroup.asia/blog/Profit-From-Design-For-Older-Users.php
7. When does age-related cognitive decline begin? Department of Psychology, University of Virginia. http://www.neurobiologyofaging.org/article/S0197-4580(09)00021-9/abstract
8. Synovate PAX tracks media, prosperity and influence in 11 countries across Asia Pacific and three countries in Latin America. http://www.synovate.com/pax/
9. Silver Group. http://www.silvergroup.asia

Chapter 23
The Discovery and Development of the Silver Market in Germany

Carolin Eitner, Peter Enste, Gerhard Naegele, and Verena Leve

Abstract In Germany, a paradigm shift is emerging in regard to the *silver economy* which is resulting in an increasing focus on the economic potential and the economic power of the elderly. Given the much increased buying power of the elderly, and the increased heterogeneity of consumption wishes and needs corresponding to the differentiation of old age, as well as the empirical evidence for an age-specific change in consumption requirements, it stands to reason to look for inherent stimulus to economic growth and employment by dint of new "age-sensitive" product ranges and services, and to promote their development and expansion. Today, in fact, the silver economy comprises products and services in very diverse and by no means only "social" market segments. In addition to the health economy, the silver economy affects such diverse sectors as mobility and IT. The following contribution provides an insight into the development of the silver economy in Germany and its future prospects.

Introduction

The challenges to society that accompany the demographic transition are currently being actively discussed in Germany. In the course of the debate, a paradigm shift is emerging with regard to the *silver economy* and, in particular, the development of products and services for ageing and old people, resulting in an increasing focus on the economic potential and the economic power of the elderly. While in the past, older people in the role of consumers were not regarded as a financially strong and free-spending target group by German providers of products and services, this perception has changed in the meantime. The days are long gone when the concept "silver market" was seen to pertain only to typical *seniors' products* or *seniors' services* such as geriatric agents, elderly care products or special recreational and touristic offers (for the elderly), which for the most part form part of the classic social services of public and independent non-profit organisations (i.e. especially of the local municipalities and of the charities). Today, in fact, the silver economy

F. Kohlbacher and C. Herstatt (eds.), *The Silver Market Phenomenon*,
DOI 10.1007/978-3-642-14338-0_23, © Springer-Verlag Berlin Heidelberg 2011

comprises products and services in very diverse and by no means only "social" market segments and, in addition to the health economy, affects such diverse sectors as mobility and IT.

This "new view" of older consumers is, in particular, related to manifold, empirically observable cohort effects or (behavioural) level increases, which can be perceived especially in the fields of income, educational background, vocational qualifications and social integration [1]. They simultaneously provide important links for the implementation of the likewise new ageing concept of *active ageing* [2], which is at present also experiencing a boom in Germany. The seniors of today have many potentials and resources which could be utilised to greater social and personal advantage than to date, e.g. in the labour market, in education, in volunteer service, in social and political participation, and precisely also in and by the economy. This is also one of the core messages of the "Fifth Report on the Elderly", and will also be taken up by the "Sixth Report on the Elderly" by the German Federal government, which deals with changes of images of old age [3].

This contribution provides an insight into the development of the silver economy in Germany, while taking into account the effects of the demographic ageing of the population. To this end, the income situation of seniors as well as their consumer needs and their consumer behaviour are discussed, in addition to the expected population development. By means of selected market segments, we will then outline how the development of the silver economy in Germany has already contributed and can continue to contribute to the enhancement of the quality of life and to the stronger integration of older people into society. Finally, we will point out further necessary developments in research and in practise regarding the silver economy in Germany.

Demographic Change

The constant increase in so-called further life expectancy, linked with the simultaneous constantly low birth rate, plays a fundamental role in the demographic ageing of the population. In 2008, the fertility rate was about 1.38 in Germany and therefore about one-third below the rate needed for the natural reproduction of the native population. Consequently, the number of older people is growing while the number of children is diminishing. In 1871, for example, the life expectancy of a newborn was below 40 years; this figure has continually risen in the course of the years to its present level of 77.2 years for a newborn boy and 82.4 years for a newborn girl. According to the available population projections, the life expectancy will continue to rise, and will reach 85 years for boys and almost 90 years for girls in 2060 [4].

In contrast, the birth rate is permanently low and will continue to be so. Thus, the number of births will decrease from its present level of approximately 685,000 to around 465,000 in the year 2060. This effect is merely slightly weakened by migration effects. Already since 2003 the German population has been diminishing, and a rapid decrease in the total population is expected. At present, Germany has around 82 million inhabitants; this figure will in all likelihood drop to approximately 65–70 million in 2060 [4].

These developments lead to profound changes in the population structure. In this connection, the so-called *triple ageing* plays a fundamental role (1) increase in the share of the elderly in the total population, (2) increase in the absolute number of older people, and (3) increase in the share and number of very old people (80+) [5, 6]. While approximately every fifth inhabitant of Germany was older than 65 in 2008, it is expected that by 2060 this will apply to every third inhabitant. At the same time, following the projections, the share of younger inhabitants below the age of 20 will fall from 19% (2008) to 15% in 2060. According to the data, the number of seniors (65 years and older) will increase from around 16.5 million at present to approximately 22 million in 2060, and approximately 14% (9 million) will be 80 years and older [4].

In the economic debate in particular, this demographic ageing of the population has been (and is in part even today) portrayed as a horror scenario (a threat to society). Besides negative implications for the social security systems and for the labour market [5], negative effects have been and are being conjured up, especially for the private demand for consumer goods and thus for growth and employment, most notably due to the declining number of consumers of private goods and services. Changes within phases of life, and therefore impacts on consumption patterns and demands of older people, have a close linkage to economic growth. The implied directness of the relation – fewer consumers, less consumption, declining employment and sagging growth – must, however, be rejected insofar as the private demand for consumer goods is strongly affected by the number of households and by the household structure. In this connection, one has to point to the fact that the number of one-person households has been growing for a long time, and will continue to do so. Moreover, one has to bear in mind that a restructuring or even expansion of the respective quantity and quality effects can also arise from changes in the consumer needs of the elderly reflected in the level and structure of their consumer goods demand [7, 8].

Income and Consumption of Older People in Germany

Until well into the 1980s, older people were regarded as a relatively low-income consumer group, whose consumer habits were therefore not studied in detail. This perception has changed significantly in the meantime. Numerous current studies confirm the trend that the income situation of older people in Germany as a whole has considerably improved in the past few years [3, 5]. However, the group of older people is quite heterogeneous in this respect: some seniors can still be economically active, while others have already retired. While the majority of the 50- to 59-year-olds probably still live in family households, or at least still have children to tend to, with increasing age most older people live in two-person or single-person house-holds [8]. On the one hand, there are many long-term unemployed seniors with only small pension rights, while on the other hand there is growing wealth, up to affluence, in old age [5]. Nonetheless, it holds true that the seniors of today are on average considerably better off than earlier cohorts [3].

Income Situation of Older People

The household income of older people in West Germany has risen markedly in the period between 1993 and 2003. If one compares the income situation of the 65+ age group with that of the under 50-year-olds, further trends become apparent. While the income of the elderly rose, the younger generation had to suffer losses of income. All in all, one can even detect a concentration of incomes in the middle and higher age groups [9]. The group of very old persons, which was in the past affected above average by old age poverty, also experienced noticeable income increases. In East Germany, the percentage increase in old age incomes in the same period was even greater due to the comparatively high wage rises and pension adjustments. Nonetheless, there is still a considerable gap between the available incomes in West and East Germany [9].

Consumer and Savings Behaviour of Older People

Expenditures with regard to private consumption in Germany amounted to around €1,341 billion in 2009. Compared to the expenditures in 2000 (€1,150 billion) an increase of 14% can be noticed for these years [10].

During recent years, the expenditures on private consumption in households with older persons (from 65 years onwards) rose far above average. In 2007, the 55–65 age group showed slightly above average in consumption, with €2,137 per month (compared to the national average of €2,067 per month). At the same time, this rise in consumption is markedly higher than the rise in income. In other words: the growth in consumption is effected at the expense of saving [9, 11].

On the basis of the findings of the sample survey on income and expenditure, it can be demonstrated that the spending for rent and energy increases with advancing age. While only 33% of the average household's expenditure is allotted to this factor, it accounts for 38% of the spending of the 70- to 80-year-olds and 43% of that of the over-80-year-olds. In comparison to younger age groups, the expenditure on health and body care as well as on recreation, entertainment and culture also continues to be above average. Of these cost factors, recreational and cultural services, as well as package tours, can be regarded as the most cost-intensive [4].

The Silver Economy in Germany

Why Is the Silver Economy Important as a New Socio-economic and Politico-economic Field of Activity?

The field of activity of the silver market in particular constitutes the starting-point for the economic aspirations and expectations connected with the demographic ageing of the population. These expectations, as it were, act as a "counterbalance" to the above-mentioned horror scenarios. Given the much increased buying power of the elderly, the increased heterogeneity of consumption wishes and needs corresponding to the differentiation of old age, as well as the empirical evidence for an age-specific change in consumption requirements, it stands to reason to look for inherent stimulus to economic growth and employment by dint of new "age-sensitive" product ranges and services, and to promote their development and expansion. Experts regard the silver economy as an important constructive "countermessage" to the macroeconomic horror scenarios. Today it is (as if it were evidence-based) assumed in Germany that the silver economy is a sector for the future that is worth discovering and developing, in the mutual interest of both the elderly and the different economic actors. There are expected to be win–win effects on both sides: an enhancement of the quality of life on the one hand, and the mobilisation of growth and the creation of new jobs on the other hand. The following reasons, amongst others, support this assumption [3, 8, 12, 13]:

- For a long time, the providers in the consumer goods and services markets paid little attention to older people as consumers; this was, inter alia, due to the largely negative connotations of the term "old age", as well as to the prevalent negative stereotypes on old age. However, the elderly are increasingly beginning to object to this.
- The present cohorts of older people are increasingly interested in private consumption, and for this purpose have a reserve at their disposal that is becoming scarcer and scarcer for other age groups, namely *time*.
- The elderly are an increasingly heterogeneous population group (differentiation of old age), and consequently also have correspondingly differentiated consumption wishes and needs, which can be met by a correspondingly differentiated range of products and services.
- The succeeding cohorts of older people have become both more demanding and more critical with regard to their quality notions and participation possibilities as customers.
- In addition to the wish for a good state of health and social integration, the desire for an enhancement of the quality of life, the maintenance of independence, and the promotion of individual safety are on the top of the individual preference scale of older people. The silver market concept offers good starting-points for all these fields.

- From an economic point of view, it is moreover significant that the number of old-age households is on the rise. For it must still be borne in mind that the private demand for consumer goods and services is not primarily guided by the number of persons but by the number of households. In other words, the demographically induced decreases in private demand due to the decline in population can be more than compensated for by a similar demographically, but also socio-structurally induced increase in small and especially one-person households (singularisation of old age).
- Although some economic sectors, which we will examine more closely later, have in the meantime developed good products and services that meet the special needs of the elderly (e.g. with regard to comfort, quality and manageability) it nevertheless holds true that most German enterprises have not yet actively discovered the silver economy as a strategic field of activity.

Only in recent years have political initiatives on the silver economy been established in Germany. In this respect we have to point to the exemplary role of North Rhine-Westphalia. In 1999, North Rhine-Westphalia was the first federal state to launch the federal initiative *Silver Economy*, with the objective of spurring on the development of seniors-oriented services and products. The aim was to improve the quality of life of the elderly, and in conjunction with this goal to promote employment opportunities [14]. Meanwhile, other federal states, regions and municipalities have followed this example, even though the setting of priorities with regard to content and the degree of the cross-actor co-operation vary strongly. Lower Saxony, Schleswig-Holstein, Mecklenburg Western-Pomerania, Rhineland-Palatinate, Bremen and Bavaria have to be mentioned here. On the regional and the municipal levels, there are several initiatives on the silver economy within the scope of local business development that are worth mentioning, e.g. in the cities of Hagen, Dortmund, Düsseldorf (all in North Rhine-Westphalia) or Mannheim (Baden-Wuerttemberg) [15]. The federal level was late to react. In 2008, the Federal Ministry of Family, Senior Citizens, Women and Youth and the Federal Ministry of Economy and Technology established an initiative called *Economic Factor Ageing* to stimulate companies to develop and implement innovative products and services for older persons. The initiative and its development is based on the findings of the "Fifth Report on the Situation of the Elderly" by the federal government, which focuses on the (economic) "potentials of old age for the economy and for society" and dedicates a chapter to the silver economy [3].

Economic Factor Ageing pursues two general aims: first, enhancing quality of life for senior citizens and second, strengthening economic growth and employment within the "silver market" [16]. To achieve these aims different activities are provided, e.g. economic information with regard to the silver market and related branches, close contacts to companies, associations and senior citizens' organisations, or events on silver economy issues. Also, in cooperation with the International Design Centre Berlin, *Economic Factor Ageing* presents a travelling exhibition of products of Universal Design. More than 50 products that improve quality of life for all ages are introduced.

Which Areas Comprise the Silver Economy?

All in all, the silver economy should not be regarded as an economic sector in itself but rather as a cross-section market, in which numerous industrial sectors are involved. The following economic segments can be attributed to it [3, 12, 13]:

- IT applications in inpatient and outpatient care
- Smart living, housing adaptations and supported living services, increasingly based on IT
- Promotion of independent living, likewise increasingly based on IT as well as on the municipal level
- Gerontologically relevant areas of the health economy, including medical technology and e-health, hearing and seeing aids technology, dental prosthetics and orthopaedics
- Education and culture (as it were in "response" to higher levels of education and more spare time)
- IT and media, in particular in conjunction with other market segments such as health, the promotion of independence, and security
- Service robotics, especially in combination with the promotion of independent living in the case of older people with severe health constraints
- Mobility and the promotion of mobility, e.g. car traffic safety
- Recreation, travel, culture, communication, and entertainment
- Fitness and wellness (in response to the higher health awareness particularly of the "younger old")
- Clothing and fashion (among other things, to document social integration)
- Services facilitating everyday life and other home services
- Insurance coverage, especially with regard to age-specific "risks"
- Financial services "sensitive to demography", especially in the area of capital protection, wealth maintenance and dissaving counselling

Only selected fields of activity of the silver economy will be examined in more detail.

Activity Field: Tourism

The conditions for the tourism sector to win new customers among the target group of the elderly are exceptionally good. After their withdrawal from the working force, older people in Germany have much spare time, and in most cases they also have the financial means to make the most of this time. The consumer behaviour of the elderly, moreover, shows that older people spend a large share of their income on travelling [17].

Today, about 30% of all holiday trips are made by people aged 60 years and more. It has to be assumed that the travel behaviour of future generations of seniors will intensify due to cohort related travel activities. If one looks at travel intensity,[1] 76% of the German population has at least taken one vacation in 2008 [18]. This is, compared to about 49% in 1972, a massive growth. This increase is also attributable to a disproportionate growth in travel intensity of older people. Nowadays, 77% of people aged 60–69 years and 65% of people aged 70 years and more take at least one trip per annum (1972: 41% and 30% respectively) [19, 20]. If one takes a closer look at household expenditures for package holiday costs, it can be seen that households with main income earners from 65 to 70 years spend about 4% or €75 (2007) of their consumption budget on package holidays. These expenditures are much higher compared to 2.6% or €55 (2007) on average for all households [11].

However, in the travel market too it is necessary to take into account the heterogeneity of the target group. The travel wishes of the elderly vary strongly, and depend on lifestyle, age, the degree of mobility, etc. Nonetheless, they have some characteristics in common that distinguish them from the travel preferences of younger people: good accessibility, a healthy climate, tranquillity, and guaranteed medical care at their holiday destinations are important prerequisites that older people increasingly expect when planning their holidays. On the whole, one can discern a trend to upmarket accommodation and to inland trips. Thus, for older people, Germany is an above-average popular travel destination. In 2007, 37% of the journeys of seniors in the age group 60–69 years were domestic; in the case of seniors in the age group 70–79 years this figure even amounted to 50% [19]. If older German people travel abroad, they prefer journeys to adjacent foreign countries or to southern European areas. Non-European goals only have a market share of 10% among the elderly, as compared to 15% in the total population [17].

A special trend that is becoming apparent in the field of tourism for the elderly is the combination of tourism and health promotion. This encompasses all offers that fall within the scope of preventive, health-promoting, wellness-oriented, rehabilitating, or curative tours, which are meeting with an increasingly great response from the elderly [17]. In order to be able to provide adequate offers for mobility-impaired persons and thus to cater for a further important target group, it is necessary to plan barrier-free, or low-barrier facilities.

Experience shows that both free-market and charity organisations operate in this market segment. Mixed organisational forms arising from the co-operation of welfare organisations and commercial tour operators have proved to be especially advantageous for the development and implementation of offers such as assisted holidays [21]. Thus, as in many areas of the silver economy, the joint and cooperative action of the involved regional and supraregional actors can be regarded as a success factor.

---

[1]Travel intensity defines the proportion of people (over 14 years in private households) within a population group that undertakes at least one journey of at least 5 days duration within a year.

Activity Field: Living

Living independently at home for as long as possible, even in the case of considerable physical and health impairments, or of seriously restricted mobility, is considered the top guiding maxim of old age policies and of care for the elderly in Germany. Foremost, one of the strongest wishes of the vast majority of older people is to live independently in their own home. Consequently, housing conditions and design are of considerable importance, and are highly connected to quality of life and social participation in old age. Barely 4% of the over-65-year-olds live in residential homes and the like. According to empirical findings, they only do so if they no longer have the possibility of living independently [5]. Even in the case of need for nursing care, most (approximately 68%) of the persons concerned stay in their own homes and are cared for there [22]. With its benefits catalogue, even the German statutory long-term care insurance is basically geared to the promotion and maintenance of independent living. From experience, however, the realisation of this goal becomes difficult if the concerned persons are very old and/or live on their own. In Germany, the so-called "singularisation of old age" is typical for around 40% of all the over-65-year-olds, of which 85% in turn are women [5].

According to representative population surveys, more than 80% of seniors indicate that they prefer to live in a normal flat. About 65% of the elderly are even prepared to put up with a move, even at advanced age, if the old flat no longer meets their wishes and requirements and if a suitable alternative (apart from residential homes) presents itself [23]. The great importance of independent living in old age also becomes evident from the fact that German seniors spend a large part (approximately 40%) of their income on housing. Furthermore, the share of the expenditure on housing has increased in the course of time [11].

On the whole, the housing conditions of seniors have markedly improved in Germany. Nowadays, standard equipment includes bathrooms with showers as well as central heating. There has likewise been a marked change in the structures of ownership. In 2007, around 50% of the elderly were flat or house owners. This is a remarkably rise compared with the previous decade (1994: 37.8%). The living space per household differs between rented and owned houses and flats. Today tenant households live on approximately 70 m^2, senior house owners can rely on a space of approximately 115 m^2 per household [24]. Due to the effects of demographic ageing and changing family structures, it is to be expected that the number of private seniors' households will continue to increase in future; this in particular holds good for single- and two-person households.

These trends pose new challenges, particularly for the building trade and the large housing industry companies. Much of the housing on offer is not senior-friendly and to complicate matters further, a good deal of the housing supply in the conurbations from the 1950s and 1960s can only be converted into senior-friendly living space with many restrictions [25]. Moreover, it has transpired that the creation of suitable living space for the elderly cannot only be limited to housing adaptations. Instead, the whole residential environment has to be incorporated into the planning concept: This includes, amongst others, the neighbourhood infrastructure, the connection to public transport and the provision of shopping facilities and other service offers.

This activity field holds much potential for the silver economy. Thus, for instance, the conversion of flats into senior-friendly living spaces opens up new fields of activity for crafts businesses. This economic sector already covers a broad spectrum of everyday products and services, and thus substantially contributes to an enhancement of the quality of life for all. Furthermore, the more than 970,000 craft businesses with almost 5 million employees and a turnover of approximately €511 billion (2008 figures) already fulfil important politico-economic and job-creating functions, which could be further enhanced by additional offers of silver economy products and services. In order to attract the target group of older people, it is also necessary to expand service and advisory service offers around the sales of the products and services. This does not necessitate an overall realignment of the business strategy but, at the most, an adjustment in various subdivisions. Generally speaking, one can distinguish three focal points:

- Qualification of employees, particularly in product designing, marketing and sales
- Networking and co-operation with possible partners (e.g. property developers and house building companies with housekeeping and nursing service providers)
- Marketing, especially also with respect to possible forms of financing

The following activity fields represent important starting points, especially for crafts businesses wishing to gear themselves to the seniors market:

- Housing adaptation: in addition to barrier-free adaptations, this also concerns the deployment of new, partly computer-assisted technologies, such as those used in the field of assisted living [25].
- Combination of adaptation measures with supplementary services, for example with regard to the renovation or refurbishment of living space. Here too, cross-sector networking of the individual service providers will be of vital importance in the future [26]. Networking not only enables service providers to improve the quality of their service by bundling several skills, but also allows them to reduce their organisational and planning costs and thus to improve their profitability [27]. In addition, it also facilitates a better acceptance among older customers by offering one-stop services.

The activity field living opens up new fields of opportunity in the personal services sector too, in particular as regards household-related services. Delivery services, maintenance services and the expansion of housekeeping services can be mentioned as examples of this. In this connection, meaningful co-operation with housing associations is also conceivable [26]. The activity field affords interesting starting points for the retail trade too (advisory and delivery services, mobility services, catering services) [6].

Despite the above-mentioned positive experiences, by far not all relevant trades are sufficiently sensitised to this issue, especially for the activity field of living. This is especially true for the field of information and entertainment technology.

Thus, the fastest growing group of internet users in Germany are older people. Numerous new chances and challenges arise from this development, not only for the electronic industry but for other providers too. Information platforms, internet trade or travel portals, for instance, are a few examples. The entertainment electronics industry can also profit from this new target group, as is shown by the high acceptance of brain-training software for games consoles in Germany.

Excursus: Computer-Aided Independent Living as a Central Future Field of the Silver Economy in Germany

Due to the demography-related strong growth in the number of very old people in need of help, experts see great development potential, particularly in IT-aided assisted living. The Enquete Commission on Care of the federal state of North Rhine-Westphalia distinguishes between six central areas of application [28]:

- General technology for the promotion of independent living in old age (such as rotatable hospital beds, easily manageable mobile phones, etc.).
- Mechanical household and mobility aids. This in particular concerns the equipment of the private households of older people with user-friendly domestic appliances as well as special technology, with which specific impairments can be compensated for, e.g. wheeled walkers or wheelchairs. In recent years, so-called service robots, such as the voice-controlled "Care-O-Bot" system, have attracted great attention.
- The utilisation of technology in connection with (age-adapted) housing adaptation. Amongst other things, this comprises measures of home automation that facilitate household management, e.g. self-adjusting blinds and blackout installations, and electrical equipment that automatically switches off in the case of malfunction. Modern computer technology even allows for "intelligent" housing (*smart homes* or *digital homes* and *accompanied living*). So far, the following technical application fields are discernible: safety, simplification of everyday life, home appliances, energy management, health promotion and communication [25].
- Technology-assisted health promotion and health control. These forms of help (also referred to as e-health or health-monitoring) are still to a large extent in the trial phase. They, for example, monitor the vital signs of typical high-risk patients, with the possibility of signalling the information to pertinent monitoring stations, or they monitor health-relevant behaviour patterns by, for instance, checking the intake of tablets and the sleeping habits. Furthermore, systems for the localisation of older patients suffering from dementia are in use.
- Technology-assisted communication. This technology is deployed in the stage shortly prior to the need for care. On the basis of home emergency call systems, the extended home emergency call system also offers additional help in the case of unexpected nursing problems, as well as everyday practical support and services. Latterly, it also includes communication offers. These extended home

emergency call systems can thus, all in all, be regarded as offers of activation and communication too.

- Tele-care: This term describes new forms of telematics-based care possibilities in the case of long illness and the need for care. They are mostly contemplated in connexion with other forms of intelligent household technologies and aids. Tele-care comprises the telecommunications-based long-distance support or care of patients or of persons in need of care in their private homes. The idea behind this is the "virtual" old age and nursing home that assures the quality of the home care by means of a support infrastructure, which can be operated both by mobile as well as by home telecommunications.

In recent years, projects dealing with IT-aided assisted living were initiated by German research facilities and institutes (e.g. Smart Senior, Fit4Age, Service4-Home). But of essential importance for the success of IT products in the field of assisted living and home care is quite probably the question of whether the German nursing care and health funds offer advantageous refunding possibilities (which is not the case so far). Many large housing societies, which are in charge of almost half of the private housing supply for older people, have, however, recognised the potential that an IT equipment of the flats of seniors holds for a longer independent life (and thus for longer-running lease contracts), and are currently already giving attention to the question of how to pass on possible additional costs via the lease prices.

Activity Field: Financial Services

The relationship between older people and finance management is in many ways ambivalent. On the one hand, the elderly are a, comparatively speaking, high-income and wealthy group. Financial assets of the older generation have grown significantly high compared to the younger generation in recent years. Seniors today own about 53% of the total assets. It is prognosticated that this figure will rise to two-thirds within a few years. On the other hand, it is unfortunately still common practise in the finance world to discriminate against older people or to put them at a disadvantage, e.g. within the scope of age limits for the granting of private loans. In order to make the most of the economic power of seniors, banks and insurance companies must therefore adapt themselves to the target group of the future in due time. Although a survey has revealed that the banks are aware of this trend, paradoxically only few of them offer age-based products [29].

Generally, financial services serve to make the income or assets available for expenditure, and to transfer them to where they are needed. They therefore play an important role in each stage of life, and can greatly contribute to the enhancement of the quality of life of people. In principle, the financial services perform the same function for the elderly as for all other age groups. But, as the financial services change their structures and their effects in the different phases of life, there are some age-related characteristics. The demand for credit is highest in the age bracket

25–35, while the highest savings rate can be observed in the age group above 35. This differentiation also holds good for the insurance industry. Depending on the age group, there are different risks that have to be covered by an insurance policy: accidents, unemployment, death or the need of care to name but a few.

The established criteria used for the evaluation of financial services also apply for the older customers of the banking and insurance industry. For one thing, the investment must be worthwhile, i.e. the interest rate has to be lucrative. Furthermore, the investment forms should be relatively safe, and it must be possible to exchange one product for another in a quick and simple procedure. The SALIS concept developed by the German Institute for Financial Services (iff) complements the financial services' classic triangle of influences (which takes into account the importance of yield, liquidity, and safety as assessment criteria of policyholders) by two further criteria for the analysis of financial offers, namely by *sustainabilitiy* or *social responsibility* and the *access* to financial services [30].

These criteria also coincide with the wishes and needs of older people regarding financial services. The factor *safety* plays a key role for older people: a survey of the German National Association of Senior Citizens' Organisations (BAGSO) shows, for example, that older people have a high degree of trust in their banks. This factor can, however, still be markedly improved by expanding the service and advisory functions. Moreover, older people prefer familiar and trustworthy staff members who can give them competent advice on their business matters. They are still sceptical towards online banking. Only 16% do their banking business via the internet [31].

The factor *rate of return* plays a minor role for most senior citizens, this is also reflected in their investment behaviour. Most older people would rather put money into a safe but relatively unprofitable savings account than choose a high-risk but potentially more profitable investment form (e.g. shares, property funds). Of much greater importance seems to be the criterion of short-term availability: products with a long maturity or long commitment periods tend to be rejected by the elderly. In the case of senior citizens, the criterion of accessibility must be explored from different angles. For one thing, their mobility is often restricted due to age-related physical impairments. This aspect plays an increasing role, especially in rural areas as many small bank branches there are closing. In this connexion, one has to consider other offers that continue to facilitate the access to finance (mobile branches, house calls etc.). Another aspect that falls within the scope of the subject *access* is age discrimination. While it is true that 95% of the older people polled in the above-mentioned BAGSO survey indicate that they have never been refused financial services on grounds of age, it is in fact often a different story when it comes to obtaining a loan. If older people are granted a loan, the terms and conditions of the loan are often much more unfavourable than those for younger people with a comparable asset situation [31].

If one has a closer look at the wishes and needs of older people, one can realise that the basic needs of older people with regard to classic financial services can often be met with the already existing products. Instead, it is all about optimising the already offered products and services for the silver market, e.g. shorter maturities, flexible payment models, "reverse mortgages" options. Also counselling and customer-oriented presentations of financial products and services are needed. Some banking and insurance companies start to offer more transparent counselling. They also begin to train their employees about the needs and requirements of senior clients. In addition to that, the Federal Ministry of Food, Agriculture and Consumer Protection initiated a campaign called "Quality Offensive Consumer Finances" in 2009, which includes, for example, a checklist and a consultation record for financial advice. This information particularly benefits older persons who need dissaving counselling rather than saving options.

In the silver economy (as well as elsewhere) it has proven to be of value to count on one-stop services, i.e. on services that bundle formerly single or partial services to a complete service package that can thus be tailored to the wishes and needs of the individual client.

Summary and Conclusion

This overview of the subject area "the economic power of older people" has shown that there is also great potential in sectors other than the classic health market for products and services that are sensitive to demographic change. There are already some sensible offers and approaches that have to be expanded, refined and, if need be, redeveloped in future. A critical synopsis of the experiences gained so far in the field of the silver economy leads to the following recommendations for a socio-politically sensible, and at the same time economically positive, further development of the silver market:

- Customer-oriented enhancement of the range of products as well as of services, and a differentiated market development
- Sensitisation and co-ordination of the actors
- Further development and increased deployment of senior marketing
- Provision for the consumer needs of poor older people
- Empowerment and a better representation of the interests of older consumers
- Dialogue-based product and services developement in dialogue with older people and designers
- Enhancement and expansion of the existing products and services
- Further development of user-friendly and seniors-oriented design
- Promotion of consumer protection for older people

As the experience in Germany has shown, the increasingly heterogeneous consumer group of the elderly shows an increasing interest in private consumption as well as differentiated consumption wishes and needs, which can be met by a correspondingly differentiated range of products and services. The silver market needs to be regarded as a strategic field of activity for social integration, the maintenance of independence, and the promotion of individual safety, and therefore for the enhancement of the quality of life of older people.

References

1. G. Naegele, Mitarbeit von J. Hilbert, V. Gerling, M. Weidekamp-Maicher, *Perspektiven einer produktiven Nutzung der "weichen" Folgen des Demographischen Wandels im Rahmen der Nationalen Nachhaltigkeitsstrategie*. Expertise, erstellt für das Bundeskanzleramt (FFG-Vervielfältigung, Dortmund, 2003)

2. A. Walker, in *The Principles and Potential of Active Ageing*, ed. by S. Pohlmann. Facing an Ageing World – Recommendations and Perspectives (Transfer, Regensburg, 2002), pp. 113–118

3. Bundesministerium für Familie, *Senioren, Frauen und Jugend, Fünfter Bericht zur Lage der älteren Generation in der Bundesrepublik Deutschland* (BMFSFJ, Berlin, 2006)

4. Statistisches Bundesamt, *Bevölkerung Deutschlands bis 2060 – 12. koordinierte Bevölkerungsvorausberechnung* (Statistisches Bundesamt, Wiesbaden, 2009)

5. G. Bäcker, G. Naegele, K. Hofemann, R. Bispinck, *Sozialpolitik und soziale Lage in Deutschland*, 4th edn., vol. 2 (VS, Wiesbaden, 2008)

6. C. Eitner, *Reaktionsfähigkeit des deutschen Einzelhandels auf den demografischen Wandel. Eine Analyse unter zielgruppen- und netzwerkspezifischen Gesichtspunkten* (Online-Publikation, Bochum, 2009)

7. Deutscher Bundestag, *Abschlussbericht der Bundestags-Enquete-Kommission "Demographischer Wandel"* (Zur Sache, Bonn, 2002)

8. V. Gerling, G. Naegele, K. Scharfenorth, Der private Konsum älterer Menschen. Sozialer Fortschritt **11**, 292–300 (2004)

9. Deutsches Institut für Wirtschaftsforschung, *Auswirkungen des demographischen Wandels auf die private Nachfrage nach Gütern und Dienstleistungen in Deutschland bis 2050* (DIW, Berlin, 2007)

10. Statistisches Bundesamt: *Deutsche Wirtschaft 2009* (Statistisches Bundesamt, Wiesbaden, 2010)

11. Statistisches Bundesamt, *Wirtschaftsrechnungen. Laufende Wirtschaftsrechnungen. Einnahmen und Ausgaben privater Haushalte 2007*, Fachserie 15 Reihe 1, (Statistisches Bundesamt, Wiesbaden, 2009)

12. R. Heinze, in *Der Demographische Wandel als Wirtschaftsmotor*, ed. by F. Schönberg, G. Naegele. Alter hat Zukunft (LIT, Münster, 2005), pp. 341–358

13. G. Naegele, J. Hilbert, Perspektiven der "Seniorenwirtschaft" – Anmerkungen zur Nutzung der "Wirtschaftskraft Alter". Theorie und Praxis der Sozialen Arbeit **3**, 12–18 (2003)

14. A. Roes, in *Die Landesinitiative Seniorenwirtschaft NRW*, ed. by F. Schönberg, G. Naegele. Alter hat Zukunft (LIT, Münster, 2005), pp. 359–374

15. H. Kooke, *Projekte und Initiativen in der Seniorenwirtschaft* (interne Veröffentlichung FFG, Dortmund, 2010)

16. Initiative "Wirtschaftsfaktor Alter". www.wirtschaftsfaktor-alter.de. Accessed 18 Feb 2010

17. Gesellschaft für Konsumforschung, *50plus* (GfK, Nürnberg 2002)

18. P. Aderhold, *Die Urlaubsreisen der Deutschen, Reiseanalyse RA 2009* (FUR Forschungsgemeinschaft Urlaub und Reisen e.V, Kiel, 2009)

19. B. Grimm, M. Lohmann, K. Heinsohn, C. Richter, D. Metzler, *Auswirkungen des demographischen Wandels auf den Tourismus und Schlussfolgerungen für die Tourismuspolitik* (Eine Studie im Auftrag des Bundesministeriums für Wirtschaft und Technologie, Berlin, 2009)

20. M. Lohmann, P. Aderhold, *Urlaubsreisetrends 2020. Die RATrendstudie – Entwicklung der touristischen Nachfrage der Deutschen* (Forschungsgemeinschaft Urlaub und Reisen e.V., Kiel, 2009)

21. G. Naegele, R. Heinze, J. Hilbert, A. Helmer-Denzel, *Seniorenwirtschaft in Deutschland – Tourismus und Wellness im Alter* (FFG-Veröffentlichung, Dortmund, 2006)

22. Statistisches Bundesamt, *Pflegestatistik 2007 Deutschlandergebnisse* (Statistisches Bundesamt, Wiesbaden, 2008a)

23. R. Heinze, V. Eichener, G. Naegele, M. Bucksteeg, M. Schauerte, *Neue Wohnung auch im Alter: Folgerungen aus dem demographischen Wandel für Wohnungspolitik und Wohnungswirtschaft* (Schader-Stiftung, Darmstadt, 1997)
24. Statistisches Bundesamt, *Mikrozensus – Zusatzerhebung 2006. Bautätigkeit und Wohnungen. Bestand und Struktur der Wohneinheiten, Wohnsituation der Haushalte*, Fachserie 5, Heft 1/2006 (Statistisches Bundesamt, Wiesbaden, 2008)
25. D. Wilde, A. Franke, *Die "silberne" Zukunft gestalten. Handlungsoptionen im demographischen Wandel am Beispiel innovativer Wohnformen für ältere Menschen* (Driesen, Berlin, 2006)
26. M. Cirkel, P. Enste, *Handwerk für Ältere Menschen* (FFG-Bericht, Dortmund, 2006)
27. A. Schilde, D. Salzig, C. Liedtke, *Unternehmenskooperation – was ist dran am neuen Zauberwort* (Institut für Klima, Umwelt, Energie, Wuppertal, 2002). http://www.wupperinst.org/uploads/tx_wibeitrag/ws26.pdf. Accessed 18 Feb 2010
28. Landtag Nordrhein–Westfalen (eds.), *Situation und Zukunft der Pflege in NRW. Bericht der Enquete Kommission des Landtages Nordrhein–Westfalen* (Eigenverlag, Düsseldorf, 2005)
29. R. Syre, Finanzindustrie – Weckruf "55 Plus". *Manager Magazine* May 31 2006
30. U. Reifner, in *Alter und Finanzdienstleistungen*, ed. by Deutsches Zentrum für Altersfragen. Produkte, Dienstleistungen und Verbraucherschutz für ältere Menschen (LIT, Berlin, 2006), pp. 283–348
31. B. Keck, *Die BAGSO Umfrage:"Ältere als Bankkunden"* (*The elderly as bank customers*) (German National Association of Senior Citizens' Organisations, BAGSO, Bonn, 2005). http://www.bagso.de/startaktuell+M534e265543e.html. Accessed 18 Feb 2010

Chapter 24
Japan's Population Aging and Silver Industries

Chikako Usui

Abstract The "aging problem" should not be viewed as an economic encumbrance. It is better viewed in the context of the robustness of the economy. Expansion of the carrying capacity of the active labor force, as well as active aging among older adults, will decrease the burden on society. This chapter draws out social and cultural implications of demographic changes in the context of Japan's transformation from a Fordist to post-Fordist economy. The distinction shifts attention to the social organization of technology-based service industries. The growing number of older persons and senior households means immense business opportunities for developing new solutions, products, and services. Older adults are potent consumers, willing and economically able to maintain independent living and a high quality of life. This chapter discusses a number of emerging silver industries, including housing and real estate, food, pets, robotics, senior care appliances, and the funeral market.

Introduction

The aging of the population in developed societies has taken on a kind of doomsday patina in many policy circles. It has brought foreboding and predictions of impending calamity. Yet the problem of population aging should not be viewed as operating in a static societal black box. The determination of the "aging problem" rests, in part, with the changing economic conditions in each country and the "carrying capacity" (productivity) of active workers. Relatively small increases in economic growth have the potential to substantially moderate the ill effects of demographic factors [1, 2]. Expansion of the carrying capacity of active as well as nonactive groups will decrease the burden for the dependent older population. In the twenty-first century, developed countries are shifting from a "Fordist" to "post-Fordist" economy with new levels of productive capacity. Any discussion of aging society must take this change in productive capacity into account [3, 4].

F. Kohlbacher and C. Herstatt (eds.), *The Silver Market Phenomenon*,
DOI 10.1007/978-3-642-14338-0_24, © Springer-Verlag Berlin Heidelberg 2011

The "aged dependency ratio" is a common measure for gauging the burden of the "dependent" population in an aging society. It is the number of actively working population divided by the number of "aged dependents" in the population. In 2009 older persons 65 years of age and older accounted for 23% of the total population in Japan. This translated to 2.8 workers supporting each older person By 2025 the figure is predicted to drop to two active workers for every aged dependent member [5]. Although the aged dependency ratio has become conventional in describing economic burden in an aging society, it is based on questionable assumptions. For example, the productivity and consumption patterns of different age groups are based on past patterns and are assumed to be static. On average, people of working age (aged 15–64) are considered productive and consumption-oriented, while the older population (aged 65 and over) is considered unproductive with relatively low incomes and low levels of consumption. In addition, policy-makers often focus exclusively on the denominator in the aged dependency ratio (i.e., older population) and look for solutions that reduce the burden of the aged dependents. The aged population is viewed in isolation and presumed to provide little or no contribution to society, while the active population is assumed to have a static carrying capacity with little change in their production or consumption patterns.

In contrast, this chapter presents a different set of views. First, demographics are an intrinsic part of the social organization of society. Historically, demographic patterns have been altered by socio-economic, technological, and political changes in society. Second, expansion of the productive and consumption capacities of either group will decrease the level of dependency for the same proportion of elderly. Third, productivity and consumption of any age group are more variable and dynamic than presently supposed. The logic that the working population will have to support the dependent population is based on assumptions of social organization and life cycle that characterized the Fordist economy of the twentieth century. In the twenty-first century, industrialized countries are shifting to a new logic of the post-Fordist economy.

"Fordist" refers to an industrial organization system associated with the Ford Motor Company in the early twentieth century [6, 7]. A Fordist economy is based on mass production and mass consumption, with products having relatively long life cycles. Worker skills, once acquired, also have relatively long life cycles. The auto, steel, and rubber industries are examples of the leading sectors in this type of industrial economy. In contrast, a post-Fordist economy is more oriented to the application of information technology. The economy is geared to the flexible production of selective goods and the consumption of a variety of goods. Goods and services have relatively short production life cycles, requiring continuous innovation. The computer software, telecommunications, and information-based service industries represent examples of the leading sectors of this type of economy.

The OECD [8] notes that a key to promoting the service sector is the diffusion of technology, and future increases in productivity can offset labor shortages in certain sectors. In other words, Japan's future hinges on whether new, post-Fordist growth industries will emerge and raise economic productivity and whether labor-market fluidity will accommodate these new industries. Some authors maintain that the key to sustaining a healthy economy is a continuous 2–3% economic growth rate [1, 2]. It is not the ratio of the working to dependent population but rather the economy's capacity that largely determines whether an aging population becomes a problem [2, 4, 9].

Japan's economy has considerable room for future productivity gains compared to other advanced nations, and it can produce more even though the labor force may shrink. Japan is ranked third among 24 countries in the labor productivity of the manufacturing sector, reaching $78,680 [8]. However, when the comparison was made for overall labor productivity among 30 OECD nations, Japan ($59,651) ranked nineteenth and the U.S. second ($83,683). Using different methods of calculations, Japan Center for Economic Research estimated Japan's productivity at 61% of that of the U.S. in 2007 [10].

Seniors as Consumers

There have been significant changes in living arrangements and lifestyles among older adults as well as changes in community structures. These multifaceted social changes involving household structures, intergenerational relations, and attitudes towards old age have given rise to business and industries called silver markets or mature markets. Today's older population is better off economically than other generations, creating a potent consumer market. Japan now has a larger number of older persons (aged 65 and older) than young persons (0–15 years of age), and the number of senior households without any nonsenior household members surpassed 9.5 million in 2009 [5]. Unlike their parents' generation that depended on their children's income and support in old age in coresidential arrangements, the current generation of older adults is healthy and places more emphasis on self-reliance and quality of life. They command a larger disposable income and national financial assets than their previous generations did. They are willing consumers of goods and services that promote independent living. Their concerns about living and dying have fueled the development of innovative products and services.

Silver markets involve the production of specialized goods and services in medical and health services and equipment, home care, real estate, construction, financial services, education and learning, food, cosmetics, travel, and entertainment. Innovations in telecommunications technology and equipment, telecare and telematics (both addressing new forms of health care deliveries), consumer electronics, robotics, and other high-tech engineering address new demands arising out of the social and cultural changes surrounding their living environments. There is a potential for active aging, which changes the current assumptions about the aged dependency ratio.

Senior households have large assets and are a key to the future expansion of the silver market. According to a national livelihood survey in 2002, the average per capita income of senior households (defined as those without anyone between the ages of 19 and 64) was 91% of the national average per person [5]. According to the

Internal Affairs Ministry's report in 2010, senior household spending rose by 1.2% while all other household spending decreased. The report highlighted that seniors are becoming a spending force [11]. In addition, the average financial assets held by senior households continue to increase, expanding the inheritance market [12]. Most personal financial assets and real estate are owned by seniors, and the transfer of assets to the next generation through inheritance will increase demands for new financial management services that involve more investment than savings which utilize personal financial assets. According to Nomura Research Institute, the number of heirs is expected to increase from 840,000 in 2007 to one million in 2015, and the total amount inherited such as real estate and financial assets will increase from ¥85 trillion in 2007 to ¥102 trillion in 2015. There are clear signs of generational shift in investment behaviors. For example, the baby boomers have active investment of financial assets and investment experience in stocks, mutual funds, and foreign currency deposits while their parents had relied on savings. The retirement of baby boomers will bring additional expansion of consumer markets in silver industries. Japanese baby boomers were born between 1947 and 1949; these roughly 6.8 million people account for 5.3% of the total population and hold even greater assets than the current generation of older persons. A Dentsu report (2006) indicates that direct spending by baby boomers prior to and after retirement will amount to ¥7.78 trillion ($70.7 billion), and the impact of this increased consumption will lead in the medium term to total economic outlays of ¥15.3 trillion ($139.3 billion) [13]. Of the ¥7.78 trillion in expected direct spending by baby boomers, the biggest outlays derive from house remodeling, real estate, and related sectors, yielding ¥4,092 billion ($37.2 billion) or 52.6% of the estimated consumption. The next largest category of estimated spending is hobby pursuits and education (¥1,196 billion or $10.9 billion). The third category is travel, with ¥1,116 billion ($10.1 billion). Purchase of durable goods, such as automobiles, is estimated at ¥404 billion ($3.7 billion) and purchase of financial products (e.g., stocks, bonds) at ¥675.5 billion ($6.1 billion) [13].

Emerging Silver Industries

Japan's demographic changes have important social consequences, affecting business in the emerging silver industries. We examine these issues in housing and real estate, food and food safety, pets, robotics, senior care appliances, and the funeral market.

Housing and Real Estate

According to JETRO [14], spending on housing and home renovation in 2005 was highest among the 65–69 age group, and this group spent twice as much as the 55–59 age group. Upgrading homes with seismic retrofitting, insulation, heating and ventilation, energy efficiency, security, and safety (barrier-free homes, wheel-chair accessibility) are the most popular types of renovation. Japan is the world leader in developing energy-efficient homes and accounts for nearly 50% of the total solar cell production in the world. The use of solar panels in homes has become popular and power companies purchase excess electricity generated from ordinary consumers [15]. Also, luxury home remodeling and vacation homes have attracted affluent seniors and are expected to increase with the retirement of baby boomers who have higher standards for comfort than the previous generation. Installation of home elevators, for example, is no longer out of reach for ordinary families.

Today's older adults tend toward "active aging" not just because they enjoy good health, but because they are the first generation willing and economically able to support themselves in old age. Post-material values such as quality of life and independent living have become important goals. A "quiet revolution" is taking place in their attitudes toward spending time and money [16]. Today's seniors are more willing to focus on their lives and spend money for their own independent lifestyles rather than saving for their children. This includes their preparation for long-term care.

The Japanese government facilitated the development of new living arrange-ments among seniors when it introduced the Long-Term Care Insurance (LTCI) (*kaigo hoken*) in 2000. In 2003 the government deregulated the industry to increase private-sector participation in nursing care sectors [17]. The government subsidizes much of the remodeling costs for seniors' homes, including the remodeling of disabled-access toilets and the installation of banisters, nonslip guides, and ramps, and the availability of LTCI has led to greater choices for older persons in private-sector facilities. In addition, there are affluent older persons willing to pay more for high-quality services and facilities that provide long-term care.

Food and Food Safety

Food accounts for 23% of expenditure by Japanese households [18]. For a popula-tion of 127 million, the Japanese food market is estimated at over $700 billion (compared to $1 trillion for a population of 300 million in the U.S.). Japan is the largest net importer of food products in the world, with the U.S. the leading supplier of agricultural products to Japan. Japanese consumers care a great deal about seasonal foods, freshness, and the esthetic appearance of food products, and the market for high-quality, safe food is booming [19]. They are eager to pay higher price for quality and convenience and are willing consumers of new niche products. Japanese consumers also set the standard for Asia in food products.

Japanese people are concerned with health and are more likely to seek dietary health through foods than through supplements. The aging population is driving a range of new trends in food markets. Due to the rapid growth in single-person and senior-couple households, mini-size packaging is popular. "Bulk" items and "super-size" products are no longer the standard [20]. Instead of low-priced products, older adults seek high-quality, high-priced, specialty products [18]. Market demands for ready-to-eat meals, take-out foods (including box lunches or *obento*), and food delivery services have sharply increased [19]. Shopping for food on TV, the Internet, and by mail-order has also expanded, aided by door-to-door home-delivery services (*takuhaibin* or *takkyubin*) [21].

"Nutraceutical" and organic foods are gaining larger market shares [18]. Nutraceutical foods (also called functional foods), claimed to have health benefits, make up a huge market in Japan: $27.1 billion in 2005 (compared to $22 billion in the U.S.).Examples of nutraceuticals are red wine as an antioxidant and an anticholesterolemic, broccoli as a cancer preventative, and soy and clover to improve arterial health in women. Some nutraceuticals are well-known, including gamma-linolenic acid, beta carotene, and anthocyanins. Food safety and traceability, freshness, and visual appeal are important features and food markets are integrating information technologies to improve food safety, including the use of devices that identify the origin and quality of products, such as the "protected designation of origin" (PDO) or "protected geographical indicator" (PGI), both developed by the European Union in 1992. Japanese consumers can trace back the food item by tagging products that can be read with a cell phone. Some local food producers have also included the pictures of themselves to provide reassurance to the consumer [21].

Specialty food stores based on the 7-Eleven business model, not Wal-Mart, are gaining appeal [19] as seniors find it more convenient to shop close to home rather than traveling farther away to discount stores offering a huge selection. Small and medium-sized retailers hold a large market share and are expected to dominate in the future. Convenience stores in rural towns with a large concentration of seniors are becoming senior-friendly stores, by changing the food menu to cater to older persons' taste, widening aisles, lowering shelves, enlarging price labels, installing blood pressure monitors, and stocking more goods for seniors [22].

Pets

Japanese people's attitudes toward pets have changed from "animals" to "family members" due to decline in family size, increase in the number of empty-nest households, and population aging. Following a recent but explosive pet boom, Japan now has more dogs and cats than children, over 13 million dogs in 2007 or an increase of 6.6 million in 10 years [23]. This market is assessed as a "trillion yen" ($9 billion) market and is expected to grow even larger. The popularity of pets has triggered vigorous demands in related industries, including pet food, books and magazines, pet insurance (for health/medical care), pet training and camps, grooming, pharmaceuticals (including vaccines, medicines and vitamin supplements), veterinary services, hotel and leisure services, and clothing. Unicharm PetCare Corporation, for example, is a producer of high-value, high-margin products and has become the largest Japanese-owned marketer of pet foods with over ¥30 billion

($255 million) in sales annually, entirely from domestic sales, targeting different consumers with small dogs, senior dogs, and overweight dogs [24].

The pet business has the potential to improve the quality of life among older adults [25]. Living with pets is known to improve the well-being of older adults because of benefits such as countering feelings of loneliness and provision of social interaction. Owning pets helps regulate the daily routines of elders, and pets induce more physical activities, help maintain emotional balance, and provide objects of affection, leisure opportunities, and extended circles of friendships.

Robotics

Rapid population aging, smaller family size, and declining work force have all led to a new robot revolution. According to the Ministry of Economy, Trade and Industry, the Japanese robot market is expected to grow to $55 billion by 2025, and three-quarters of this market would be for service robots [26]. Japan had an early romance with robots. Tetsuwan Atom (Iron Arm Atom or Astro Boy) began as a successful comic strip in the 1950s, followed by Tetsujin No. 28 in a 1963 television series, and Doraemon, a robotic cat. Doraemon was one of the most famous manga characters in the 1980s and became a cultural icon in Japan.

Japanese tendencies to anthropomorphize machines are critical to our understanding of their attitudes toward, and embrace of, new technology, including robots. Machines have become companions in everyday life whether they are office machines, factory robots, or automobile navigators. Tamagotchi (virtual/digital pets with morals and ethics), created in 1996, illustrate the scale of business and people's attitudes toward a mechanical pal. More than 13 million Tamagotchi were sold in less than a year. Between 1996 and 2007, some 37 versions of Tamagotchi were made and sold [27, 28].

Japan is "a kingdom of robots" [29]. Factories use over 410,000 robots, and Japan, a major exporter of robots, accounts for 60% of the world's supply, with an additional $4.4 billion worth of other robots. A robotic entertainment dog, AIBO, introduced by Sony in 1999, turned out to be Sony's biggest success in years [30]. AIBO is an autonomous robot integrated with a computer, vision system, and articulators. It is equipped with 100 voice commands and can learn and mature from interaction with its owner and the external environment. Owners enjoy teaching their robotic pets new behaviors. Priced at $2,500 each in 1999, all 3,000 units in Japan sold out in just 20 min, and 2,000 units sold in 4 days in the USA. Exceeding expectations, Sony provided 10,000 more AIBO units for sales in Japan, Europe, and the USA in late 1999 [30]. Other robots include NEC's R-100, a toddler-sized robot on wheels that can turn on the TV, send and receive email, and do a little entertainment. Mitsubishi, OMRON, and Matsushita have robot pets that send reminder messages for taking medications. These robots are linked to family members, hospitals, and community centers for monitoring via the Internet. They can fill a critical void at home in a society where an increasing number of seniors live alone.

Paro is a furry robotic baby seal, manufactured for alleviating stress and tensions for people with dementia in nursing homes. It provides amusement and comfort. In 2001 it was listed in the Guinness Book of Records as the "world's most therapeutic robot." Dr. Shibata Takenori, inventor of Paro, carried out trials in nursing homes and hospitals in Denmark, Italy, Japan, and Sweden. Paro looks like a harp seal pup and is 57 centimeters long, weighs 2.7 kg, and has a plump white body. It is equipped with sensors and responds to petting by fluttering its eyes and moving its flippers. Hand-attached eye lashes and hand-trimmed facial fur makes the face of each Paro unique. Danish nursing facilities will be equipped with 1,000 Paro by 2011 [31]. When sold as medical equipment, it is priced at ¥350,000 ($3,180).

Service robots will probably become part of everyday life in the near future and will make homes safer and assist in care giving. At present, service robots perform a wide variety of tasks such as cleaning, making coffee and serving tea, making the bed, and even feeding. A sophisticated type of service robot is the personal assistant robot. According to Research Horizon Magazine [32], the global market for personal robots is growing at 400% per year. Japanese companies are developing robots that can communicate better and incorporate sophisticated functions. A confluence of smart materials, low-cost, high-speed computing power, complex wireless communication systems, improvements in batteries, and continuing research on human–robot interactions (especially perception and reliability) are making this industry explosive. Over 100,000 visitors went to see service robots in just 4 days at the international robot exhibition held in Tokyo in November 2009, demonstrating rising interests in service robots [26]. For many Japanese, a robot will soon become as indispensible as a mobile phone.

Senior Care Appliances

The Sanyo Electric Company introduced its first robotic ultrasonic bath at the 1970 World Expo in Osaka. It was a full-body contraption for wash, clean, rinse, massage, and dry in 15 min. In 2004 Sanyo introduced a new elder care product, the human washing machine. According to a *New York Times* article [33], residents of nursing homes welcome the new technological help because the machines warm the whole body and protect their privacy. For staff members, it means less lifting of residents and physical burdens. The user sits in a chair that is rolled backward into place. The sides of the machine then close like a clamshell, forming an instant tub with the person's head sticking out the top. Shampooing and hair drying is done by hand. The human washing machine was developed by Mitsuru Haruyama, a businessman crippled by muscular dystrophy [33]. Another robotic bath introduced in Japan in 2008 is Avant's Santelubain 999 (sonic washing machine). Instead of showing upright, one lies down to get body shampoo and shower, heat and steam, and sound therapy [34].

Other examples that integrate modern technology include a robot suit, HAL (hybrid assistance limb) [35]. It was developed by engineering professors at

Tsukuba University. HAL is a computerized suit with sensors that weighs 22 lb and is belted to the waist. It helps people with mobility problems and became available for rent in 2008 for $2,200 a month [36]. HAL also assists people with a variety of daily activities of living, such as standing up from a chair, walking, climbing up and down stairs, and lifting objects. These devices and others in development will push Japanese sales of domestic robots to $14 billion in 2010 and $40 billion in 2025 from nearly $4 billion currently, according to the Japan Robot Association.

Although human washing machines cost almost $50,000 a unit – enough to pay a year's wages for two immigrant nurses – they save money in the long run and make care-giving tasks less labor-intensive. These practical applications of new technologies in care-giving offer promising solutions for the future. Fueling the demand are the decision by the government to push for home care and rehabilitation to promote more independent living among the elderly, rapid changes in family structure, and older adults' desire for independent living with a high quality of life.

Funerals

The industry is being transformed from religious ritual to a thriving death industry [37]. This industry is estimated at $1.7 billion, and the cost of funerals in Japan ranks among the highest in the world [38]. In 2006, the average cost of funerals ranged between ¥1.5 and ¥3 million ($15,000–$30,000).

Traditionally, funerals are organized by a neighborhood association and held in people's homes. However, due to changes in family structure and community networks, the use of packaged funeral services at franchised ceremonial halls has gained popularity. Hotels and railway companies have entered the market, further diversifying the types of services offered. These changes have also altered the pricing of funerals. It used to be socially improper to discuss the cost of funeral arrangements in advance. A 2005 study by Japan Fair Trade Commission found that 96% of the respondents were not given options in service and price when they made funeral arrangements. More recently, the industry began offering transparent pricing, and pricing has become competitive.

Japan's custom of ancestor veneration entails the continuity of family line and connections to family members. Family graves are the place where the dead are housed and remembered; graves are maintained and visited regularly. However, with falling fertility rates, increasing frequency of divorce, and increase in single-person households, people are concerned about their descendants' ability to care for the dead. In 1997, a movie entitled *Ohaka ga nai!* (I have no grave for myself) depicted modern grave-related problems (*haka mondai*) [39].

A variety of new businesses have emerged in response to *haka mondai*. Time of death has become a predictable event with the advancement of medical technology, enabling people to make funeral arrangements in advance. One prominent example is a permanent ritual care (*eitai kuyo*) in cemeteries. These graves are permanently cared for, usually for 33 years after death. Such care primarily targets people without successors or those who feel they could not expect ritual care from their children. A quick Internet search for *eitai kuyo* (written in Japanese) by the author of this paper found 265,000 sites providing information and/or such services. They advertize basic services for permanent ritual care as low as ¥10,000 ($100) per person in 2010.

Summary and Conclusion

In this chapter I have questioned demographic predictions of a societal catastrophe based on the aging of Japanese society. This popular view is based on a static view of the capacities of the population, economy, and institutions. Instead, this chapter has focused on the social aspects of demographic changes involving family structures, living arrangements, and the older generation's attitudes towards independent living and consumption. It has drawn out some business implications for the productivity-enhancing social and organizational changes in the context of the transformation from a Fordist to post-Fordist economy. The distinction between the Fordist and post-Fordist economies shifts our focus to the future expansion in the carrying capacity of technology-based service industries and consumption capacity of the older population. I have argued that the current and future generations of the older population tend towards active aging and are in a position to consume more than is currently assumed. Quality of life becomes an important goal in the post-Fordist economy, creating new demand for more selective goods and services. An increase in the older population creates demand for new industries in the silver industries and increases consumption. Population aging requires adjustments in markets, corporate practices, and government policies, but it should in no way be interpreted as the bankrupting of Japan's economy.

To illustrate elements of the transition from a Fordist to post-Fordist economy, this chapter has reviewed a number of emerging silver industries, including housing and real estate, food and food safety, pets, robotics, senior care appliances, and funerals. The robotics and senior care appliances markets are based on the intensive use of new information technologies, and demonstrate future improvements in quality of life among senior adults.

Significant attitudinal and behavioral changes among older adults have often been overlooked. The older Japanese population is healthy and is a vital resource to society as volunteers, care givers, childcare providers, and consumers. Goods and services that promote active and healthy aging as well as those that meet the needs of changing family structures are some of the key factors that will ensure the success of business in the Japanese market.

There are three lessons to be learned from this chapter. First, today's older population constitutes a distinctive and capable force affecting the Japanese economy and society. Second, the current generation of older persons has fueled demands for diverse goods and services as they tend toward an independent life-style and quality of life. Third, the demands for innovative goods and services are mediated by social and cultural sensitivities to the issues of living and dying.

As the first country to test innovative solutions in the silver market, Japanese experiences have several lessons for other countries. First, the social and cultural dimensions of aging should not be overlooked. Technological innovations and adaptations are modulated by social and cultural contexts of aging in any society. They condition the relationship between demographic changes and societal consequences. Japanese willingness to adapt to modern technological solutions described in this chapter is a good example. Second, Japan's experience shows the significance of generational and age-cohort changes that are a key to understanding new consumption trends. It is a common error to view each successive cohort of older persons as an unchanging, static group resistant to new ideas, products, or services. Third, the rising consumption capacity among the older population, and their desire to lead a healthy and active aging mean expanding new business opportunities. Japan provides an excellent testing ground for how new business can succeed.

References

1. J.C. Campbell, Population aging: hardly Japan's biggest problem. *The Demographic Dilemma: Japan's Aging Society*, Asia Program Special Report, No. 107 (Woodrow Wilson International Center for Scholars, Washington, DC, 2003), p. 10
2. J.H. Schulz, *Economics of Aging* (Auburn House, New York, 1995)
3. C. Usui, Int. House Jpn Bull. **21**(1), 42 (2001). Also published in Japanese as Kokusai Bunka Kaiho **12**(1), 54
4. C. Usui, in *The Demographic Dilemma: Japan's Aging Society,* Asia Program Special Report 107 (Woodrow Wilson International Center for Scholars, Washington, DC, 2003), p. 16
5. Y. Yamada, Aging in Japan. Japan Aging Research Center (June 2009). http://www.jarc.net/int/?p=271
6. D. Jaffee, *Organizational Theory* (McGraw-Hill, New York, 2001)
7. J. Myles, in *Beyond the Marketplace: Rethinking Economy and Society*, ed. by R. Frieland, A.F. Robertson (Aldine de Gruyter, New York, 1990), p. 271
8. OECD, Economic Survey of Japan 2006 (20 July 2006). http://www.ceri-sciences-po.org/archive/sept06/artoecd.pdf
9. International Institute for Applied Systems Analysis, in *Populations Aging, Pensions, and Health*, Options. vol Summer (International Institute for Applied Systems Analysis, A-2361 Laxenburg, Austria, 2003), p. 2, 6
10. R.Suzuki, Japan's Labor Productivity Only 61 percent of the United States. Japan Center for Economic Research, Staff Report (15 July 2007). http://www.jcer.or.jp/eng/pdf/kenho070602e.pdf
11. T. Inajima, Japan seniors weather wage slide and boost spending (Updated) (18 Feb 2010). http://www.businessweek.com/news/2010-02-18/japan-seniors-weather-wage-slide-and-boost-spending-correct-.html
12. Nomura Research Institute, Japan's Affluent and HNWI Markets Consisted of 903,000 Households and Amounted to 254 Trillion Yen in 2007, while its Inheritance Market will Expand to 102 Trillion yen by 2015 (1 Oct 2008). http://www.nri.co.jp/english/news/2008/081001.html

13. Dentsu Inc., Dentsu survey estimates the economic impact on consumption resulting from the retirement of baby boomers, News release by Dentsu Inc. Communications Division, No. 21-2006 (30 Mar 2006), http://www.dentsu.com/news/2006/pdf/2006021-0330.pdf

14. H. Nitta, Capitalizing on retirement of Japan's first baby-boomers. JETRO Japan Economic Report, April–May (2006). http://www.jetro.go.jp/en/reports/market/pdf/2006_18_u.pdf

15. Japan moving toward more efficient solar power. Japan Today (16 Dec 2004). http://www.ecomall.com/greenshopping/japansolar04.htm

16. PRNewswire Europe, This new generation of Japanese seniors is a consumer powerhouse (22 Mar 2010). http://www.prnewswire.co.uk/cgi/news/release?id=166835

17. JETRO, Attractive sectors: medical care – policy initiatives (January 15, 2010). http://www.jetro.go.jp/en/invest/attract/medical/medical_0909.pdf

18. Asia Pacific Trade Council, *Report of the Japan Market Advisory Group April 2007*, (APTC, British Columbia, 2007). http://www.asiapacifictradecouncil.ca/pdf/japan_report.pdf

19. J. Noguchi, Food business line. Japan Market Development Reports (USDA Foreign Agricultural Service GAIN Report), VII (3) (March 1–31) (Global Agriculture Information Network, Tokyo, 25 Apr 2007). http://www.fas.usda.gov/gainfiles/200611/146249483.pdf

20. Targeting the over 60s key to the Japanese market (7 Aug 2006). http://www.scoop.co.nz/stories/BU0608/S00140.htm

21. B. Harden, Japanese stores take convenience to a new level, Washington Post (8 Nov 2008). http://www.washingtonpost.com/wp-dyn/content/article/2008/11/07/AR2008110703512.html

22. AARP Global Network, *How Retailers Are Adapting Stores to Cater to Elderly Shoppers* (16 Sept 2009). https://www.aarpglobalnetwork.org/netzine/Industry%20News/Productsand-Services/Pages/Howretailersareadaptingstorestocatertoelderlyshoppers19367047.aspx

23. H. Tashiro, I. Rowley, Japan's pampered pet set, BusinessWeek (8 June 2007). http://www.businessweek.com/globalbiz/content/jun2007/gb20070608_699714.htm

24. M. Pehanich, Unicharm crashes in on trends, petfood industry (24 Sep 2008). http://www.petfoodindustry.com/ViewArticle.aspx?id=12636

25. L. Wood, B. Giles-Corti, M. Bulsara, The pet connection: pets as a conduit for social capital? Soc. Sci. Med. **61**, 1159 (2005). http://www.ncbi.nlm.nih.gov/sites/entrez?db=pubmed&uid=15970228&cmd=showdetailview&indexed=google

26. D. Lee, Japan sees its future in service robots, Asian Trends (18 Feb 2010). http://uniorb.com/ATREND/Japanwatch/servicerobot.htm

27. List of Tamagotchi Releases (January 15, 2010). http://en.wikipedia.org/wiki/List_of_Tamagotchi_releases

28. Tamagotchi. http://en.wikipedia.org/wiki/Tamagotchi

29. F.L. Schodt, *Inside the Robot Kingdom: Japan, Mechatronics, and the Coming Robotopia* (Kodansha International, Tokyo, 1988)

30. SONY, Press releases (25 Jan 2000). http://www.sony.net/SonyInfo/News/Press_Archive/200001/00-002E/

31. Trends in Japan, Cuddly Robot Comforts the Elderly (Sept 2009), http://web-japan.org/trends/09_sci-tech/sci090917.html

32. J. Sanders, From science to fiction to reality: personal robots emerge to improve quality of life at work, home and school. Research Horizons Magazine, Georgia Institute of Technology (8 June 2007). http://gtresearchnews.gatech.edu/newsrelease/personal_robotics.htm

33. J. Brooke, Japan seeks robotic help caring for the aged. New York Times (5 Mar 2004). http://www.nytimes.com/2004/03/05/international/asia/05JAPA.html?ex=1393822800&en=eb854fe2a4e6c9bd&ei=5007&partner=USERLAND

34. Automatic Human Washing Machine (14 Apr 2009). http://www.impactlab.com/2009/04/14/automatic-human-washing-machine/

35. Japan unveils "robot suit" that enhances human power. Space Daily (7 June 2005). http://www.spacedaily.com/news/robot-05zq.html

36. Y. Kageyama, Robot suit for rent in Japan to help people walk (7 Oct 2008). http://www.msnbc.msn.com/id/27066773/

37. A.L. Webb, Japan's dying industry. Newsweek International (23 Dec 2002), http://www.newsweek.com/id/66864. (Updated version 29 Oct 2007, http://www.newsweek.com/id/66864/output/print)
38. JETRO, Trends in the Japanese funeral industry. Japan Economic Monthly (Feb 2006). https://www.jetro.go.jp/en/reports/market/pdf/2006_13_p.pdf
39. J.W. Traphagan, J. Knight (eds.), *Demographic Change and the Family in Japan's Aging Society* (SUNY, Albany, 2003)

Chapter 25
India: Opportunities and Challenges of Demographic Transition

Suresh Paul Antony, P.C. Purwar, Neelam Kinra, and Janakiraman Moorthy

Abstract India is in the middle of its demographic transition. The 60-plus age group (elderly population) is projected to quadruple by 2050, while the 0–14 age group (child population) remains stagnant. India's population structure and distribution would then closely resemble that of nations currently with a high aging index. The high index, as seen now in nations like Russia and the UK, indicates that the elderly population is larger than the child population. Such changes in the size, structure, and distribution of the population will have implications for public policy as well as business. The Government of India has launched a slew of initiatives to meet this challenge. On the business front, many products and services have been launched that specifically target the elderly. However, there are many other products and services used by all age groups. These may have to be repositioned, if the motivations of the different age groups are not similar. Both from the angle of public policy and business, decision makers in India should closely examine the experience of nations with a high aging index, and respond to the challenges of demographic transition.

Introduction

The world is aging rapidly. The population median age has increased from 24 in 1950 to 27 in 2000, and is projected to increase to about 38 by the year 2050. The elderly[1] is the largest growing segment, growing five times faster than the total population. The elderly by 2050 would constitute 22% of the population from under 10% in 2000, and 8% in 1950 (see Table 25.1).

This chapter is based on the doctoral thesis of the first-named author, approved for award of the title "Fellow of the Indian Institute of Management Lucknow."

[1]We use the term "elderly" to refer to those aged 60-plus years.

F. Kohlbacher and C. Herstatt (eds.), *The Silver Market Phenomenon*,
DOI 10.1007/978-3-642-14338-0_25, © Springer-Verlag Berlin Heidelberg 2011

Table 25.1 Population aging by regions 1950–2050 [1]

Region	Year	Population distribution by age (%)			Median age (years)	Aging index
		0–14 years (child population)	15–59 years (working population)	60-plus years (elderly population)		
World	1950	34	58	8	24	24
	2000	30	60	10	27	33
	2010	27	62	11	29	41
	2050	20	58	22	38	112
More developed regions	1950	27	61	12	29	43
	2000	18	62	19	37	106
	2010	17	62	22	40	132
	2050	15	52	33	46	212
Less developed regions[a]	1950	37	56	6	22	17
	2000	33	59	8	24	23
	2010	29	62	9	27	30
	2050	20	59	20	37	99
Least developed regions	1950	41	54	5	20	13
	2000	43	53	5	18	12
	2010	40	55	5	20	13
	2050	27	62	11	29	41

[a]India's population parameters fall within those of the less developed regions

Population aging[2] worldwide will operate at varying levels of intensity, and in different time frames (see Table 25.1). In the more developed regions, the aging index will double to 212 in 2050. In the less developed regions (like India) and in the least developed regions it will quadruple to 99 and 41 respectively. The median age during the same 50-year period would rise from 37 to 46 in the more developed regions, from 24 to 37 in the less developed regions, and from 18 to 29 in the least developed regions. The aging index[3] in tandem, worldwide has increased from 24 in 1950 to 33 in 2000 and is expected to increase to 112 by 2050. This indicates that the younger population is shrinking. It also indicates that the population in the more developed regions has aged earlier, but the process has been accelerated in other regions of the world.

We examine in this chapter the facets of demographic change in India. We also discuss the strategic role of demographic analysis in market planning. Demographic change has two important implications for marketing – development of new products and services, and repositioning of existing products and services. Here we highlight some of the responses of marketers in India. Finally, we draw some lessons for countries in the early stages of demographic change.

---

[2]Population aging is the process by which older individuals become a proportionally larger share of the total population. At the root of population aging is demographic transition, the process by which mortality rates decline, followed by fertility declines [2].

[3]Aging index is the proportion of the elderly to the child population. An index higher than 100, would imply that the elderly population is larger than the child population [2].

The Indian Context

India has traditionally been a low-growth economy. However, it has shown signs of vibrancy over the last several years, and has been able to sustain high growth. Disparities in income levels that do exist, vary across states, and urban and rural markets. India has the world's largest middle class of 200 million, the top 20% of the population, which may also have high consumption levels. However, over a third of all consumer expenditure is by about 100 million people, the top 10% of the population. They could be classified as big-ticket buyers, and may be fuelling the growth in the economy. The penetration of "utility" goods is much higher than luxuries, comfort, and high-lifestyle commodities [3].

India, with the world's second largest elderly population, next only to China, is in the middle of its demographic transition [4] (also refer to Table 25.2). Its population parameters fall within those of the Less Developed Nations of the world (Table 25.1). The aging index is expected to rise to about 107 in 2050, from 14 in 1950 and 19 in 2000. At 38 by 2050, India's median age would equal the world's median age. Since the beginning of the twenty-first century, the elderly population in India has grown faster than the total population. This growth rate is expected to be sustained until 2050, for which projections are available. Despite this high growth rate, the elderly population numbered just about 20 million in 1950. However by 2000, while the total population trebled to over 1 billion, the elderly nearly quadrupled to 70 million. The working population has grown at much the same pace as the total population, while the child population has grown at a much slower pace (Table 25.2).

In the next 50 years, it is expected that while the total population and also the working population will increase by half, and the child population will not grow, the elderly population will again quadruple. The elderly at about 316 million would be larger than the child population at 294 million. The elderly would by then have become the second largest age group after the working population (Table 25.2). This indicates that the younger population in India is shrinking as well.

Table 25.2 India's aging population 1950–2050 [1]

Year	Population distribution by age[a]			Total	Median age (years)	Aging index
	0–14 years (child population)	15–59 years (working population)	60-plus years (elderly population)			
1950	139 (37)	212 (57)	20 (5)	372	21	14
2000	365 (35)	608 (58)	70 (7)	1,043	23	19
2010	374 (31)	749 (62)	92 (8)	1,214	25	24
2025	354 (25)	919 (64)	159 (11)	1,431	30	45
2050	294 (18)	1,004 (62)	316 (20)	1,614	38	107
Growth (1911–1950)	–	–	9 (74)	120 (48)		
Growth (1950–2000)	226 (162)	395 (186)	50 (248)	671 (180)		
Growth (2000–2050)	−71 (−19)	397 (65)	246 (352)	571 (55)		

[a]Figures in millions and percentage in parentheses

Within the country, however, there are variations. The proportion of elderly to the total population in rural areas is higher than that in urban areas. Kerala state in South India has the highest proportion of elderly to total population. The proportion of the elderly to the population is higher in the southern states, and relatively lower in the eastern and north-eastern region. It is also higher in Punjab, Haryana and Himachal Pradesh, which are economically better-off states, relatively. These states and also the southern states have done well on a number of socio-economic indicators, and have also been successful in bringing down their population growth rates. Among the poorest states, Orissa has a high proportion of elderly to total population. This regional pattern is more or less replicated in both rural and urban areas.

Moreover, there is a significant change of socio-economic circumstances for the elderly, with the breakdown of the traditional joint and extended family system [4]. The joint family as a traditional social unit took care of the elderly, sick, widows and orphans. The old age dependency ratio has seen a marginal increase between 1981 and 1991. Here again, there are variations. The dependency ratio[4] is somewhat higher for females than for the males, and much higher in the rural areas than in the urban areas. The higher ratio in rural areas may be explained by the migration of individuals in the working age population to urban areas.

India's population age distribution in 2000 closely resembles the distribution available in the less developed regions of the world. India's population by 2050, however, will more resemble the distribution seen today in the more developed regions (see Tables 25.1 and 25.2). This also indicates that the age structure of the population is changing.

This larger problem of aging has two critical concerns. Galbraith states: "The first is how the individual should respond to the mature years. The second is how the larger community, including the government, should respond to the needs of the old" [5]. Drucker [6] has noted that such demographic transition and changes in the population age distribution have far-reaching implications for retirement and pensions, housing, public policy, health care, labor markets, business, and marketing, among others. The fiscal gaps that are widening for instance in the USA, Europe, and Japan could become worse as the baby boomers[5] retire [8]. The Reserve Bank of India has proposed fiscal consolidation to combat the nation's deficit, which is expected to be aggravated by an aging population [9]. One illustration of the impact of population aging is the case of Kerala in India, where the pension bill grew more than the salary bill, and is causing nightmares [10].

At the public policy level, India has responded to the population aging, at least in recent times. Formulation of the National Policy on Older Persons [11] is a case

[4]The dependency ratio is expressed as the number of persons in the elderly population, per 100 persons in the working population.

[5]Baby boomers are those born post-war between 1946 and 1964 [7]; this definition is applicable to those born in the USA.

in point. The Government of India has launched the National Program for the Elderly [12], with a planned outlay of INR 4 billion[6] (US $100 million).

The Government launched the Senior Citizens Savings Scheme in 2004. The scheme offers higher differential rates of interest, and garnered over INR 80 billion (US $2 billion) in less than a year [13]. In the 6-month period ended Sep 2009, deposits garnered by the Department of Posts alone under this scheme, quadrupled to INR 30 billion (US $750 million) [14]. In a recent budget [12], the Government extended income tax concessions for investments made under this scheme. The objective is to offer safety and reasonable returns to this vulnerable group, which saw erosion in real incomes due to falling interest rates.

This has become critical to the welfare of the elderly as many of them, more so in the unorganized sectors of employment, do not enjoy pension benefits and depend on interest income derived from investment of retirement benefits. Moreover, social security measures in India are in a nascent stage.

Many financial institutions have responded to the needs of the elderly. HDFC Bank has, for instance, stipulated lower minimum balance requirements on savings accounts across rural and urban branches for the elderly [15]. Even though commercial banks have recently announced cuts in interest rates on term deposits, they continue to offer preferential rates to the elderly [16, 17].

The National Old Age Pension Scheme was introduced by the government in 1995 to address the issue of social security for the destitute. The rechristened Indira Gandhi National Old Age Pension Scheme enlarged its scope in 2007 to cover all the elderly below the poverty line. Some 16 million elderly, about 20% of India's elderly, would benefit [18]. In a recent union budget, the government allocated INR 34 billion (US $861 million) for this scheme [12].

Another related issue has been the lack of liquidity for the elderly. To own a home is a fundamental aspiration for the great majority of the Indian populace, and many manage to acquire one while in employment. Many of these acquisitions are funded by housing loans that are freely available. Late in the family life cycle, many families spend large sums on the education and marriage of children. Finally, after retirement, many are left with few options that give a steady stream of cash inflow. The Government of India has launched the Reverse Mortgage Scheme to provide financial income for the elderly who own homes, but who do not have sufficient income [19]. The government has further proposed that revenue streams received by senior citizens would not be treated as income for tax purposes [12]. Further, the National Housing Bank has recently launched a life-long reverse mortgage annuity facility for the elderly. This is an improvement on the earlier scheme, which had a 20-year limit on payments [20]. Central Bank of India, in a tie-up with Star Union Dai-chi Life Insurance has launched CENT Swabhiman Plus under this improved scheme [21, 22]. This would make the scheme much more attractive.

The government allocated INR 7 billion (US $175 million) for public health to focus, among others, on the national program for care of the elderly and their

---

[6]1 USD (US $) is worth about 40 INR (Indian Rupee).

rehabilitation [23]. During the eleventh plan period 2007–2012, the government proposes to set up two National Institutes of Aging with eight regional centers, in addition to a department of geriatric medicine with one center each in every state. Some private hospitals have already added geriatrics wings [24].

The impact of demographic transition on the structure and age distribution of our population will also impact consumer markets. We discuss this impact in the following section.

Demographic Analysis

Demographics explain 2/3rds of everything. They help predict which products will be in demand... (David K. Foot, Canadian demographer cited in [25], p. 188)

Demographics, the most important variable, describe and provide statistics that study population in terms of size,[7] structure and distribution.

Market Planning

Demographic analysis is the first step in market planning. Demographic trends are more reliable than other variables in the study of consumer behavior [25]. Demographic profiles are relatively straightforward, and a great deal of information is available on the various characteristics of various segments, for instance, the size and economic power of teenagers. Consumers buy products like many others of the same age group or life stage. They have many commonalities like shared values and cultural experiences [27]. But, responses to offers within age groups may differ [7, 28, 29]. While within-age-group differences may be large, between-age-group differences may equally be large and significant.

Demographic profiles are useful when we do not have enough knowledge about a market or when a market is evolving [25]. It lends itself relatively efficiently to media targeting, since data is available on the demographic characteristics of most media audiences [30].

When marketers need more insights than can be obtained from demographics, psychographics and personality variables help to identify, and define a segment. Demographic profiles are combined with other profiles like psychographics to form market segment descriptors. In such a sense, age is used as a proxy for other fundamental differences in consumer behavior [25, 31].

---

[7]Size is determined by fertility and birth rates, life expectancy and death rates, and migration, and refers to the number of individuals in our population. Structure describes the population in terms of variables like age and gender. Distribution refers to the geographic location of individuals in the population [26].

Demographic analysis also raises questions about macro-marketing, marketing from the society's point of view. Issues like consumer vulnerability and other consequences of marketing action become critical here. While the study of consumer behavior is focused mostly on micro issues, its roots are in macro-marketing [25].

As the population ages, demand for healthcare, nursing, retirement homes and such products and services targeted specifically at the elderly is bound to increase. While the share of the child population in the total population is shrinking, its importance may not decline. With small families becoming the norm, parents may be more able to spend on high-quality products and services.

The elderly or "young-again" market is a rapid growth segment worldwide (see Tables 25.1 and 25.2). Empty nests, more disposable income but fewer opportunities to spend, the luxury of time, and accumulated chronological age and experience characterize this segment [25]. On the flip side, rising inflation could cause a drop in real incomes.

It is clear that this demographic transition opens up opportunities as some age groups increase in size and economic power, and threats as others decline at least in size. We discuss the implications of this transition in the following section.

Marketing Implications of Demographic Change

Two important dimensions of the marketing implications are discussed here – new product and service development, and repositioning and branding strategies.

New Product and Service Development

If the needs of the elderly are not met in full, or only partially, and if the segment is substantial and profitable, marketers may choose to offer new products and services targeted specifically at the elderly. Offerings for instance could be refurbished and elderly-friendly bathrooms, special tour packages, cosmetics, healthcare, retirement homes, and pension funds. It would appear that marketers have responded well to this dimension.

A scientist at the Bangalore-based National Institute of Mental Health and Neuro Sciences (NIMHANS), for instance, has reportedly developed an herbal drug to arrest cognitive decline in the elderly [32]. A magazine for the elderly, *Harmony*, has been launched by Tina Ambani with India Today [33]. Four-seater electric cars called buggies, low-floor buses, buses with facilities for wheelchair-bound passengers, smart card-based bus passes for the elderly are some of the launches [34–36]. Housing is another area that has seen a slew of initiatives. A variety of projects catering to different economic levels have been launched across the country [37–39].

Many tour and hotel packages specifically targeted at the elderly have been launched [40, 41]. Leading tour operator Cox & Kings reports a rise in the number of foreign tour package bookings by the elderly [42]. Air India has recently announced a 20% discount on air fares for the elderly [43]. Informal discussions with financial services industry professionals indicate that the elderly form a growing and influential client base for such services as online share trading and mutual funds.

In-depth interviews with leading retailers of consumer durables in Lucknow[8] revealed that retailers were familiar with the demographic group of the elderly consumer. This had two nuances. Firstly, that the elderly were identified as a distinct segment, with differing motivations. Secondly, that the elderly were being seen visiting showrooms in sizeable numbers, and making purchase decisions jointly.

The question "What do senior citizens buy from your store?" elicited spontaneous responses: "Oh, they buy almost everything that younger persons buy." The assortment was as varied as refrigerators, air conditioners, microwave ovens, household furniture (including computer tables), relaxation products, toasters, and audio and video products. In addition to watches, jewelry, garments, sweetmeats, and gifts.

We were then interested to know whether younger consumers bought the same type of products. This question also drew insightful responses. For instance, in the Godrej store: "the elderly prefer the Storwel brand of almirahs,[9] and the younger the Slimline brand." Slimline is sleeker and sports a modern, sophisticated look. We could surmise that the elderly prefer Storwel, it being a retro and well-established brand. It is plausible that Slimline has chosen not to target the elderly. We do not know whether this is a well-deliberated dual brand strategy by Godrej to distance the two brands in an apparently age-neutral[10] product category.

Other product categories with similar age differences are dining tables and sofa sets. While the younger prefer tables with glass tops, the elderly prefer wooden tops. In sofa sets, the younger preference was for plushier, luxurious sets. We could gather that similar differences in preferences exist in the Titan range of watches. The Regalia and Royalle brands of watches, in the price range of INR 2,000–5,000 (US $125 to 313), were preferred by both the younger and the elderly. However, there appears to be a distinct preference by the elderly for the Nebula brand. The prices range from INR 21,000 to 80,000 (US $525–2,000). We do not know if they are being bought to be given away as gifts, as in the case of sweetmeats. Blackwell et al. [25] also note that the elderly make excellent prospects for luxury goods, travel-related products and services, and financial services.

---

[8]Lucknow is the capital city of Uttar Pradesh state in North India.

[9]Almirahs or cabinets are made of wood or metal. The Godrej range is made of metal. Almirahs are a must-have in every Indian home. They are used to store precious jewelry and garments.

[10]Product categories that are commonly used by all age groups are said to be age-neutral, like the common variants of toothpaste, or almirahs. In contrast, other product categories like adult diapers are age-specific.

There are also other product categories that are relatively new, such as cellular (mobile) telephones and digital cameras, and probably with a high degree of technology where surrogate decision-making is indicated. Many of these products are popular with the elderly. However, for instance to store phone numbers or to make decisions like renewals of service or purchase of instruments, the elderly rely on younger members of the family.

These insights are anecdotal, and need to be validated with rigorous research. It is, however, significant to note that at least the retailers seem to be aware of age-related differences in product preferences. However, a holistic and concerted strategy designed by the manufacturer is not evident as yet. For instance, we have not observed any special sale for the elderly, or signage that better accommodates the needs of the elderly.

Economic Times notes that the elderly are being targeted by marketers, but that understanding the requirements of the elderly is difficult [44]. This could imply that marketers are comfortable marketing products and services specifically used by the elderly like old-age homes. They might not have paid much attention, however, to understand their differing motivations, and so have not come to terms with marketing products and services in age-neutral categories. We discuss in the following section the need for repositioning in such categories.

Repositioning and Branding Strategies

The shrinking of the younger population "will change markets in fundamental ways. Growth in family formation has been the driving force of all domestic markets in the developed world" [45]. Marketers would then have to make significant reorientations. Loudon and Bitta [46] recount the case histories of companies like Walt Disney, Gerber, and Coca-Cola, which shifted focus from younger age groups to an older customer franchise. Such drastic reorientations were necessitated by the reality of a shrinking young population.

In India, Cadbury Dairy Milk as a brand has extended its customer franchise, from the traditional children segment to include youth. In a telephone interview, the company spokesperson suggested that Cadbury Dairy Milk was at present targeting the youth franchise. Its advertisements in recent times have featured as the brand spokesperson the film star, Amitabh Bachchan, considered a youth icon in India. It is remarkable that he is seen with graying hair and beard. An analysis of the advertisements for Cadbury Dairy Milk over the last few decades clearly indicates the transition that the brand has made from a child to an adult customer franchise. Many other advertisements also carry Amitabh Bachchan as the brand spokesperson. This also has to be viewed in the context of old-age stereotypes in society.

Household consumer expenditures will change significantly due to the varied product assortments demanded by different age groups. For instance, the elderly may spend more on over-the counter drugs and personal care products [46].

It is important to note that while the two age groups may share many assortments, its size may vary.

Products typically targeted at the younger consumer, such as chocolates, could be repositioned as an elderly consumer offering. The offering may thereafter become unattractive to the current younger customer franchise, if the elderly consumer were also to be targeted. This is a critical issue that cannot be glossed over, since for many marketers the younger customer franchise is the predominant segment being served currently.

Summary and Conclusion

Not many marketers are sure of the strategies to be employed [7]. Kennett [47] observes that, compared to other industries, the financial services industry is slow in implementing strategies targeted at the elderly. This may well be true of other industries as well. Moreover, the highly regulated nature of most services, like telecommunications, land and mobile telephony, and financial products may make it inherently difficult to vary services.

The younger age group presently accounts for a large share of consumer expenditure, and also receives a large share of marketing attention. With many product assortments shared by different age groups, marketers would have to examine whether products need to be repositioned for the elderly consumer. It then becomes critical to understand the motivations of elderly consumers. Given this demographic and marketing context, can the existing knowledge on behavioral responses be extended to elderly consumers? It is plausible that marketers lack knowledge and experience to develop a marketing strategy targeted at the elderly, more so for product and service assortments shared across different age groups.

It is plausible that many marketers, at least in India, are yet to come to terms with an aging population, it being a recent phenomenon. This age group has not been large enough to merit attention earlier – 20 million in 1950, 70 million in 2000, but projected to reach 316 million by 2050. The proportion is steadily increasing, and is estimated to reach 20% in 2050, larger than the child population (see Table 25.2). Their numbers have quadrupled over the last 50 years and are expected to more than quadruple again in the next 50. The total population, though, would increase only by half. Even worldwide, their numbers and proportions have not been large until now, more so in comparison with the younger age groups.

"Older" Indians may yet account for a quake in life-cycle spending patterns. Their spending is expected to rise faster than in any other age group, fuelled by a more educated and affluent generation entering senior citizen status [48]. However, it is to be recognized that not all older Indians may account for the quake.

Financial insecurity in old age is an area of concern that has been articulated in detail in the National Policy on Older Persons [11], and that also has implications for marketing. The situation has been exacerbated for a number of reasons: the growth of small and nuclear families, migration to urban areas, and the changing role of women in the workplace, among others. One-third of the population is below the poverty line, which is the bare minimum for subsistence. Another one-third is above it, but still belong to the lower income group. That leaves the middle class and upper income groups.

The National Policy on Older Persons [11] recognizes the fact that a large proportion of the elderly would be:

> ... middle and upper income groups, be economically better off, with some degree of financial security, have higher professional and educational qualifications, lead an active life in their 60s, and even first half of the 70s, and have a positive frame of mind looking for opportunities for a more active, creative and satisfying life.

It is comforting that the Government of India has affirmed to develop policy instruments for the elderly disadvantaged. As noted earlier, in the last few years several initiatives have been taken. Cumulatively, these could possibly have a cascading effect on consumer spending and open up hitherto unexplored markets – provide staples at affordable prices. The numbers at the bottom of the pyramid are huge, over 100 million by 2050. It is an opportunity and challenge that marketers in India cannot afford to miss.

Anticipating such trends is not enough. It is to be seen how society at large and marketers in particular will respond to the demographic transition. While some initiatives on the public policy front are clearly visible, concerted efforts are still needed to address the issue of aging in India, more so given the large inequalities in income levels, dependency ratios, and aging index, across regions and gender in particular. It will be instructive to share the experiences in particular with other nations in the less and least developed regions.

More importantly, the aging index in India by 2050 is expected to exceed 100, and the structure and distribution of her population would resemble nations like Russia, the UK and Ireland, and Sweden as seen today; these nations presently have an aging index higher than 100. It can be safely surmised that India is about 50 years behind such nations in demographic transition.

Therefore, from the perspective of both public policy and business, it would be expedient for countries in the early stages of demographic transition (like India) to closely look at the situation and experience of these nations. Secondly, measures should be put in place to meet the consequences of population aging.

References

1. United Nations. *World Population Prospects: The 2008 Revision* (*medium variant*) (Population Division, Department of Economic and Social Affairs, United Nations, Washington DC). http://esa.un.org/unpp. Accessed 15 Feb 2010
2. United Nations. *World Population Prospects: The 2004 Revision* (Population Division, Department of Economic and Social Affairs, United Nations, Washington DC, 2004). http://esa.un.org/unpp. Accessed 21 Jan 2006

3. Indicus Analytics. *The Size of the Indian Market: 2000 and Beyond – Final Report for Reebok India Limited* (Indicus Analytics, New Delhi, 2000). http://www.indicus.net/Home.aspx?id = Studies& submid = Consumer%20Economics%20%26%20Market& sr_no=10005. Accessed 10 Aug 2007

4. Planning Commission. *National Human Development Report 2001* (Government of India, New Delhi, 2002)

5. J.K. Galbraith. John Kenneth Galbraith's notes on aging. *Encyclopædia Britannica Online* (1999) http://search.eb.com/eb/article?tocId=9344838. Accessed 02 July 2005

6. P.F. Drucker, Population trends and management policy. Harvard Bus. Rev. **29**(5), 73–78 (1951)

7. G.P. Moschis, E. Lee, A. Mathur, Targeting the mature market: opportunities and challenges. J. Consum. Mark. **14**(4), 282–293 (1997)

8. P. Engardio, C. Matlack. Global aging. *Business Week Online*, 31 Jan 2005

9. Renewed focus on fiscal consolidation vital: RBI to meet the challenges arising from an aging population. *Financial Express,* 05 Oct 2004, p. 10

10. M.S. Varma, Pensions growth a nightmare. Financial Express **31**, 5 (2006)

11. Ministry of Social Justice and Empowerment. *National Policy on Older Persons* (Government of India, New Delhi, 1999) http://socialjustice.nic.in/social/sdcop/npop.pdf. Accessed 10 July 2007

12. P. Chidambaram, *Budget 2008–2009: Finance Minister, P Chidambaram's Speech Before the Parliament* (Ministry of Finance, Government of India, New Delhi, 2008)

13. Senior citizens' saving scheme proves a hit. *Economic Times*, 08 Apr 2005, p. 3

14. Post Office deposits surge on interest, safety scores: Total deposits have gone up by 32 percent in Apr–Sep 2009. *Business Line*, 12 Dec 2009, p. 1

15. HDFC Bank revises AQB requirements. *Economic Times,* 02 Feb 2010, p. 14

16. Karnataka Bank cuts deposit rates. *Business Line*, 30 Oct 2009, p. 6

17. Lakshmi Vilas Bank revises interest rates. *Financial Express*, 01 Oct 2009, p. 13

18. M. Singh. *PM Launches Indira Gandhi National Old Age Pension Scheme* (Prime Minister's Office, New Delhi, 2007). http://pmindia.nic.in/speech/content.asp?id=614. Accessed 19 Nov 2007

19. Aged can earn from property. *Business Standard*, 01 Mar 2007, p. 3

20. National Housing Bank launches life-long reverse mortgage annuity for senior citizens. *Financial Chronicle*, 29 Oct 2009, p. 3

21. Central Bank's reverse mortgage loan product offers life-time annuity: Tie-up with Star Union Dai-chi Life Insurance for CENT Swabhiman Plus. *Business Line*, 11 Dec 2009, p. 6

22. New reverse mortgage product unveiled by Central Bank of India in association with Star Union Dai-chi Life Insurance. *Economic Times*, 11 Dec 2009, p. 9

23. Centre allocates over Rs. 700 crore for public health. *Chronicle Pharmabiz*, 29 Mar 2007, p. 32

24. Manipal hospital adds geriatrics department. *Business Standard*, 26 Feb 2007, p. 5

25. R.D. Blackwell, P.W. Miniard, J.E. Engel, *Consumer Behavior*, 9th edn. (Thomson Asia, Singapore, 2002)

26. B.R. Lewis. Demographics, in *The Blackwell Encyclopedia of Management,* ed. by C.L. Cooper (Blackwell, Oxford, 2007)

27. M.R. Solomon, *Consumer Behavior: Buying, Having, and Being*, 5th edn. (Prentice-Hall of India, New Delhi, 2002)

28. G.P. Moschis, Marketing to older adults: an overview and assessment of present knowledge and practice. J. Consum. Mark. **8**(4), 33–41 (1991)

29. P.T. Sorce, P.R. Tyler, M.L. Loomis, Lifestyles of older Americans. J. Serv. Mark. **3**(4), 37–47 (1989)

30. C.D. Schewe, Marketing to our aging population: Responding to physiological changes. J. Consum. Mark. **5**(3), 61–73 (1988)

31. P.F. Bone, Identifying mature segments. J. Consum. Mark. **8**(4), 19–32 (1991)

32. Herbal drug to arrest cognitive decline. *Express Pharma Pulse*, 08 Oct 1998, p. 11
33. Harmony – a magazine for senior citizens launched by Tina Ambani, India Today group to distribute. *Insight Media* (14 Jun 2004)
34. BEST plans to buy 30 low-floor buses. *Auto Monitor*, 15 Nov 2004, p. 28
35. Buggy comes to aid of elderly, disabled. *Times of India*, 29 Apr 2007, p. 4
36. Bus transit systems: Update on recent initiatives – Mumbai. *Indian Infrastructure*, 31 Oct 2009, p. 64
37. Corsendonk hospitality arm extends to elderly in India. *Economic Times*, 25 May 2005, p. 8
38. LIC subsidiary plans to set up communes for senior citizens. *Times of India*, 05 Jul 2002, p. 13
39. LICHFL launches retirement village. *Realty Plus*, 30 Apr 2006, p. 14
40. Taj hotels unveils new package for the elderly. *Financial Express*, 05 Aug 2003, p. 4
41. TCI launches senior citizen holidays. *Express Travel & Tourism*, 31 Aug 2004, p. 13
42. The I and me consumer. *India Today*, 12 Jul 2004, p. 20
43. Air India senior citizen offer. *Financial Express*, 21 Nov 2009, p. 5
44. Urban–rural split impacts senior citizens. *Economic Times*, 13 Nov 2004, p. 1
45. P.F. Drucker. *The daily Drucker: 366 days of insight and motivation for getting the right things done*. (HarperCollins, New York, 2004)
46. D. Loudon, A.J. Della Bitta, *Consumer behavior: concepts and applications*, 3rd edn. (McGraw-Hill, New York, 1988)
47. P.A. Kennett, Marketing financial services to mature consumers. J. Serv. Mark. **9**(2), 62–72 (1995)
48. Euromonitor, *Consumer Lifestyles in India*, (Global Market Information Database) (Euromonitor, Singapore, 2004)

Chapter 26
Silver Markets and Business Customers: Opportunities for Industrial Markets?

Peter Mertens, Steve Russell, and Ines Steinke

Abstract Demographic change will pose distinct challenges for companies. The ratio of people over 65 years of age will rise in all triad countries. At the same time, the number of younger people, and thus recruits in all education levels, will drastically decline in Japan and Germany. In the USA, a shortage of highly skilled and educated workers is expected. The employment rate of aged people will therefore rise. Companies can react on many different levels. On the one hand, they can make it a business opportunity by developing and selling products and services that support older people. On the other hand, companies will have to cope with fewer younger workers. We discuss several ways to do this (1) to prevent loss of skills from retirement, (2) to accommodate older workers, and (3) to survive with fewer workers. These could lead to Business-to-Business (B2B) products and services that can help companies to solve the issues involved. We look at these possibilities in turn, and find that they each lead to ideas that have one or more of the following properties (1) they are actually Business-to-Consumer (B2C) products, (2) they are management or organizational solutions or services, and/or (3) their benefits are not specific to older workers but benefit all employees. Thus, we are led to the conclusion that the technical products best suited for the B2 Industry silver market will not be "silver-specific" products, but products "designed for all" with an emphasis on usability and problem solving.

Introduction

Demographic statistics show that the ratio of people over 65 to those under 65 will increase by a factor of two in all triad countries (Fig. 26.1).

This effect will have a severe impact on many parts of society. There will be challenges in the financing of retirement and health care, and there will be shifts in the purchasing behaviors of shifting consumer groups. In this chapter, however, we will concentrate on the impacts on companies. These impacts include a shortage of younger workers, and a shift towards a higher numbers of older workers. We will

F. Kohlbacher and C. Herstatt (eds.), *The Silver Market Phenomenon*,
DOI 10.1007/978-3-642-14338-0_26, © Springer-Verlag Berlin Heidelberg 2011

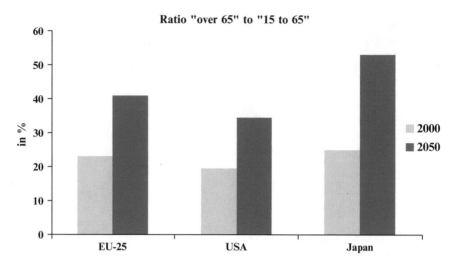

Fig. 26.1 Old-age dependency ratio; defined as the percentage of people aged 65 and over (retired) compared to people between 15 and 64 (working-age population) [1–3]

briefly summarize our conclusions on the consequences, and how these may lead to B2B (business-to-business) business opportunities. However, we first would like to take a more detailed look at the statistical data.

Although the forecast above requires assumptions on future birth rate statistics and migration, implications for companies with regard to their workforce are unambiguous, because the 20-year-olds to be hired in 20 years have already been born. A look at the age "pyramids" of Japan, Germany, and the USA tells an indisputable story.

In Japan, a very pronounced baby boom in the years after World War II led to a maximum population increase. This group is now going into mass retirement. Accordingly, one of the major concerns about demographic change in Japan is the retention of the knowledge and skills of these retiring baby boomers (see, for example, [4]). This situation is very similar in the USA.

In Japan, an additional effect can be seen: although the baby boomers had fewer children than their parents, their sheer number produced an "echo baby boom". However, the birthrate has kept declining, leading to an extremely low birthrate for echo baby boomers. The number of newborns is still shrinking, and in 2006 Japan saw the first year of negative population growth.

This effect is less pronounced in the USA and Germany. However, although the number of children in the USA seems to be more stable, companies there still report shortages of highly skilled and educated workers.

This can also be seen very strikingly in Japan, where we already see a decline of engineering students. From 2001 to 2006, this number declined from 463,000 to 425,000, a decline of more than 9% [5]. This is in spite of growing numbers of foreign students, especially from other Asian countries, accepted in engineering departments in Japan.

In Germany, the baby boom was later than in either Japan or the USA, so that some of the challenges treated here will become acute about 5–10 years later. However, it is forecast that when the population in Germany begins shrinking after around 2010, their labor force will shrink twice as fast [6, 7].

As a prosperous economy requires growth, this situation requires a solution. As the example of the USA shows, immigration and higher female participation in the workforce can be only partial solutions.

Therefore, in all countries mentioned, the employment rate of older workers is expected to rise. To get a feeling of the severity of the change, we offer some telling data [2, 8]:

- In the USA, more than 25% of the working-age population will have reached retirement age by 2010, resulting in a potential worker shortage of nearly 10 million people.
- The number of the total US workforce aged 55 or more will increase from 21.8 million in 2003 to 31 million in 2010, a growth rate four times faster than that of the overall workforce.
- In the European Union (EU), the number of elderly people (age 60+) will increase by almost 50% between 2005 and 2050. In absolute numbers this means around 151 million in 2005, around 198 million in 2025, and around 226 million in 2050 [2].
- The EU workforce with ages from 15 to 59 will shrink from 462 million in 2005 to 405 million in 2025, and down further to only 330 million in 2050.

Figure 26.2 shows that Japan and USA already have a quite high rate of employment of older workers. However, in the EU, an increase of this rate will be needed in order to tap the big potential of the additional older employees.

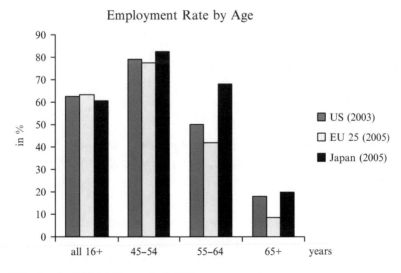

Fig. 26.2 Employment rate by age [1, 2, 8, 9]

The facts of demographic change pose both challenges and opportunities for companies. How companies can respond to these challenges is now a very active research field, and it has been treated in many publications, for example [10–13]. According to Mertens et al. [12], the challenges can be grouped in five categories:

1. Ensuring innovativeness
2. Retaining older workers and expertise
3. Accommodating older workers
4. Reducing company costs and risks
5. Other issues

The paper also contains a number of recommendations for company actions. This chapter aims at discussing business opportunities for companies arising from demographic change, but restricted to the B2B case. We see two broad categories of B2B business ideas that can be defined as:

1. Improving business success by supporting employees in older age groups.
2. Improving business success by helping companies cope with the challenges posed by demographic change.

We will address these two areas in turn.

B2B Business with Products Supporting Employees in Older Age Groups

This topic relates to products that older people use or are confronted with, or that are designed specifically with them in mind. Some of these products are not bought directly by these older persons, but instead by companies selling or catering to them. We briefly look at two major categories of this kind:

1. Components for products, where these products are ultimately bought and used by older people
2. Products for the healthcare and elderly care markets

Components for Products That are Sold to Customers: Where These Customers Use, Package, or Otherwise Resell These Products Ultimately to the Silver Market

In this first category, some examples are:

- Automotive components: As retired people become more numerous, and also much healthier than they used to be in most of the twentieth century, they will demand self-determined mobility and will use cars in much greater numbers than before. Still, on average, this customer group will have specific requirements to cope with diminishing eyesight, decreased flexibility in body movement, reduced ability to concentrate for long periods of time, etc. For this group of customers, car companies as well as automotive supplier companies are developing features and devices that make it easier and safer to use vehicles. Examples include seats and doors that make entry more comfortable, safety devices such as night vision enhancements, parking aids, distance radars, and signs and instruments in the car which are easy to see and interpret.

These components are usually developed by a supplier OEM (original equipment manufacturer) for the car company.

- Increasingly, older people will become accustomed to the lower costs and the higher convenience achieved with digital appliances. For instance, ATMs (automatic teller machines) and other digital public-use equipment (such as airline check-in machines, vending machines for tickets, and so on) have low or zero usage fees, yet they help to reduce the complexities and time burdens of banking and travel.

These consumer-support products are usually bought by businesses that are service providers. The service providers in turn often heavily influence the direction of further developments in conveniences.

So, both groups of examples, although they are B2B products, have the following characteristics in common:

- They are designed with a "silver" end user in mind. As such, when looking at end user requirements, market research, market acceptance, and so on, they should instead be treated like B2C products. This assertion is further supported by the need to extensively test these products for safety, utility, and usability with the intended customer group.
- The B2B customer has a lot of influence on the product design. In fact, this B2B firm is the customer that deals directly with the end customer.

Therefore such "OEM B2B products" cannot be viewed as a typical B2B business situation.

Another point of view would stress that many successful B2B companies emphasize that the best way to help improve the business of the industrial customers is to obtain an in-depth understanding of the end customer's needs. This puts us back into the B2C area, which is covered elsewhere in this book.

Products for the Health Care and Elderly Care Market

This market will be driven by the following demographic and scientific facts:

- The proportion of the world population over 65 will increase.
- The life expectancy will increase in all countries. The most dramatic increases of life expectancy, as well as number and relative proportion of older people, will happen in Asia, Africa, and South America.

- Age-related diseases such as Alzheimer's, Parkinson's, diabetes, many forms of cancer, and others, will increase.
- The health care systems in most developed countries are already financially stressed.
- Most people needing special care as elderly citizens will be living in poor or emerging economies, where health and elderly care is challenging even today.
- Dramatic progress in biology and medicine, using genomics, proteomics, and other technologies will extend life and health.

Today's hope is that with current technological developments, we will develop ways to substantially improve the health and care provided to elderly persons. The focus of efforts here lies in new treatment ideas, as well as efficiency improvements such as:

Preventive Medicine

- It is much better for the patient, and much more cost-effective, to prevent disease than to rely on remedial medicine. Promising ideas to do this include an increase of in vitro diagnostics and telemedicine, as well as novel testing and screening methods. For example, health officials in Scotland want to help prevent blindness resulting from diabetes by conducting special tests for all diabetes patients. Authorities are using software from Siemens to call the approximately 300,000 people in Scotland at risk into screening centers, and then to analyze the test results. In the centers, a screening of the ocular fundus enables doctors to detect alterations in the blood vessels of the eye very early. Such alterations can indicate, for example, calcification of the veins, which can be related to cardiovascular disease. In the eye, the veins are very small, so that changes can be detected very early. The images are automatically analyzed with image recognition software, which identifies alterations and classifies them for the use of doctors.
- Some examples following this approach are especially well suited for emerging economies, as portable, simplified devices for testing are being developed that take advantage of the growing availability of wireless communication in many countries. The availability of efficient, high-tech but affordable diagnostics can have an enormous impact, on both developed and on emerging economies.

Personalized Medicine

- Progress in medical science gives us hope that treatments based on the patient's personal genomic and proteomic make-up will allow more targeted treatments, which are more effective and also cheaper. Figure 26.3 shows an example. A combination of blood tests (in vitro diagnostics) and imaging technology (molecular imaging) enables personalized medicine (1) A fluid analysis is

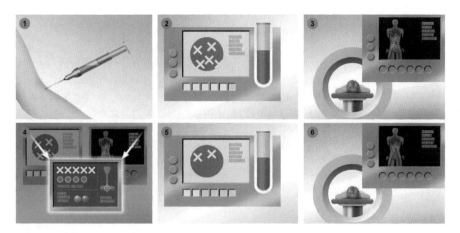

Fig. 26.3 Outline of tomorrow's molecular-based healthcare (1) fluid analysis, (2) in vitro tests, (3) PET/CT scan, (4) data integration, (5, 6) follow-up with in vitro and in vivo tests

performed, (2) in vitro tests indicate disease markers, (3) a PET/CT scan localizes and characterizes the abnormality, (4) data integration is carried out, and thanks to knowledge-based IT, doctors determine the ideal combination of medical treatment, and (5, 6) follow-up with in vitro and in vivo tests indicates steadily diminishing concentrations of disease biomarkers and shrinking tumors. This allows personal targeting of treatment, which promises not only to be more effective, but also helps to select very precisely which of the many (possibly very expensive) treatments is most promising. It therefore is both a promise of better treatment and of cost efficiency in health care.

- Healthcare IT. Today, in most hospitals, patient data are kept in many different forms and places: the manual patient file, X-ray photographs, letters and data kept in PCs, CT and NMR image files in computers, etc. The hospital personnel have to review these disparate sources and mentally combine them to form a state-of-the-art picture of the patient's situation. The combination of these disparate data sources across fields of medical specialty is supported by emerging approaches to computer-based collaboration, automatically translating field-specific terminologies, and focusing on the key issues in a particular patient's time-course of symptoms and treatments. Leveraging modern IT and communications technologies promises to dramatically improve efficiency in hospitals and health administration, in cost reductions for patient communication and monitoring, and in improving the quality of diagnosis and effectiveness of treatment. Today's healthcare IT enables the physician to pull together data from different examinations onto one PC in order to make a diagnosis. At the same time, the graphical nature of the presentation allows the physician to discuss diagnosis and treatment with the patient.

In conclusion, the health care and elderly care sectors will be strongly influenced by demographic change. We believe that companies providing solutions that aim at efficiency in healthcare will be successful providers for doctors, hospitals, health insurance agencies, and governments. Thus, the health care and elderly care markets are important opportunities for the B2B and B2G (Business to Government) market.

The driving characteristics of these markets will be determined by sheer numbers – demographic and financial – and scientific and technical progress mainly in biomedicine and information technology. These larger scale drivers will be far more important than any finer-grained personal characteristics of elderly consumers such as individual health history, exercise behavior, or budgeting and spending choices.

The assessment of business opportunities in these markets therefore requires a very specific approach, drawing heavily from a targeted knowledge of health care economics and biotechnology.

B2B Products for Helping Companies Cope with Demographic Change

To deal with this field, we suggest a division into three separate categories:

1. Prevention of the loss of skills from retiring workers
2. Accommodations for older workers
3. Survival strategies for business operations with fewer workers

We will analyze each of these categories in turn.

Prevention of the Loss of Skills from Retiring Workers

The area has been addressed in many publications [11–13]. The two principal action areas are:

• Delaying the time when employees retire
• Preparing for the fact that they will eventually leave

The first of these two has been addressed in detail in the publications cited above. They call foremost on companies to begin to implement a program addressing the special needs of older workers. The measures employed are, typically, human resources (HR) department-based management systems, incentive programs, and sustained training programs. For example, apart from the protected legal status sometimes afforded to older workers to discourage age discrimination, HR programs can reduce distracting business situations such as injuries and interemployee complaints. Also, by emphasizing the benefits and mandates for cooperativeness and respect, HR can lay the foundation for a more productive intergenerational set of contributors. Incentives for sales or production achievements can be accompanied, for instance, by recognition for teambuilding and idea sharing in social networks of contributors. As training technologies evolve, novel opportunities will arise for acquiring and recovering expertise – such as in virtual world simulations and game-like scenarios, or role-playing rehearsals of likely business situations.

These actions do not lead directly to B2B sales opportunities, with the exception of consulting and training to help companies set up their own programs.

The latter business opportunity, preparing for experienced employees to leave, will require both management solutions (for example, intergenerational teams) and technical solutions (for example, knowledge management). Here, we observe that many US and European authors, such as the ones cited above, stress that any solution must be embedded in the company culture, especially in its HR management processes.

For example, retaining knowledge when people leave a company can be best dealt with by transferring knowledge to younger workers. For this, it is necessary to have both a culture where sharing knowledge is encouraged, both for the experienced people to share with others, and also for the younger people to respect and appreciate receiving the information. The development of a more sharing office or manufacturing-line culture does not follow a simple prescriptive flowchart. Instead, managers have to be trained and specifically rewarded to make measurable progress in these interemployee interactions. Instituting the programs and progress metrics calls for skills derived from operations research and the social sciences, as well as a careful study of enhanced employee motivation in successful enterprises. Applying these findings as older employees retire, the entering groups of younger workers can thereby more fluidly integrate and absorb a larger portion of the possibly lost lessons and heuristic guidelines.

Next, since companies are subject to competitive pressure, to ensure cost efficiency of the knowledge transfer, a specific process should be in place [11, 12, 14].

Finally, the knowledge transfer process can be aided by knowledge management and training software and tools. Managing knowledge takes many forms, from better training manuals and search interfaces to contextually sensitive tools for ensuring company policy compliance and the focused application of previous business lessons learned. There are some simple recent approaches that show promise – such as end-user document and email tagging, mapping of common domain terminology dependencies (taxonomies and folksonomies), and visual connectivity-mapping for circles of friends and reliable information sources. It is often more important to know how to get a human-experience-contextualized answer through a small set of personal contacts than to try to look up an isolated fact in a vast words-only database. So, implementing and improving a set of know-how tools and methodologies will probably give significant competitive advantages to tomorrow's globally-contending firms.

Thus, the knowledge transfer process can be aided by knowledge-management and training software and tools. This is an approach that is especially favored by Japanese companies [15]. The emphasis on knowledge transfer is currently especially high in Japan because of the severity of the baby boomer mass retirement phenomenon.

In conclusion, helping companies prevent loss of skills from retirement provides B2B business opportunities for:

- Companies offering consulting and training for people and knowledge-retention programs
- Companies offering knowledge-management software and consulting

Obviously, these are niche opportunities rather than being capable of driving a large company's business.

Accommodations for Older Workers

Today's older workers are healthier and more motivated to continue working than those of 20 years ago. Today's 70-year-olds are in this manner more like yesterday's 60-year-olds.

Since there have always been employees aged between 60 and 65, they are not a new, unknown group in the workforce. Only the ratio of older to younger workers is changing. Consequently, we do not expect completely new product requirements, but rather a shift in the relative importance of requirements.

When looking at the literature cited above, it is a very wide field that addresses this area. Issues addressed include:

- The working environment
- The social working environment (intergenerational teams, travel, etc.)
- Payment schemes, insurance, and pension
- Work schedules: part time, retirement
- Health management
- Lifelong learning and training

All but the first of these issues require solutions in management and processes, focusing on the HR system of the particular company. Again, this leads to business ideas for specialized consulting companies, but not for companies dealing in technical products.

Learning and training are key factors for assisting older workers in their productivity and self-esteem. Solutions addressing this include knowledge management systems, which have already been discussed.

Working Environment

Older employees experience deterioration of physiological capabilities and to some extent cognitive abilities. Workplace design that takes account of an aging workforce has to address the specific needs of the elderly. Age-related constraints have to be compensated for in order to maintain the efficiency of work and accessibility of tools. It is necessary to design a work environment that makes allowances for the wide range of capabilities of the elderly.

Accessibility – defined as a product's capacity to be used by everyone, regardless of abilities or disabilities – is important at two levels:

- Older employees need an appropriate physical working environment
- Accessibility of hardware and software at the workplace has to be assured

Physical Working Environment

The major requirements and business opportunities for the design of an appropriate physical working environment come from the specific health-related needs of older workers and from various regulatory requirements. Considerations may address:

- Diminished visual or hearing acuity
- Diminished physical strength and endurance
- Higher risk of injury from repetitive work and mobility-related accidents
- Lower tolerance of heat, humidity and noise

Many of these issues can also be addressed by appropriate staffing, and by very simple measures such as:

- Good ventilation, air conditioning, and temperature control
- Increased illumination of the environment
- Availability of transport equipment (carts, shelves, cranes, etc.)
- Reduced ambient noise
- Increased levels of luminance contrast

Accessibility of Hardware and Software

The efficient use of tools for work by older employees requires appropriate human/system interactions. Besides sensory (visual, hearing, haptic) and fine motor skill restrictions, a design for an aging workforce has to also consider age-related cognitive changes. Not all facets of cognition deteriorate with age. Semantic memory, for instance, including factual knowledge, is not affected by age. Some older people actually show better performance in this respect than younger people [16]. Age-related impairments and capabilities do not apply to all elderly people to the same extent. They vary from person to person and may occur in different combinations. Examples of age-related cognitive changes are:

- Decrease in selective attention. Older people have more problems in filtering out irrelevant information [17].
- Decrease in working memory capabilities [18]. This involves short-term memory for temporarily storing and simultaneously managing information. It is required to accomplish complex cognitive tasks (comprehension, learning, reasoning).
- Divided attention, which allows completion of more than one task simultaneously (e.g., operating a machine and talking on the phone), decreases with age.
- Fluid intelligence (necessary for solving new problems), including information processing (abilities to differentiate, compare, classify), is reduced [19].
- Reaction times get longer.

Creation of work environments that are accessible to an older workforce starts with the analysis of user requirements and needs. This includes consideration of specific sensory, fine-motor, and cognitive capabilities as well as an analysis of the context of use in the daily work of older employees. Analyzing the usage context of interactive products includes looking at goals, workflows, task characteristics, equipment (hardware, software, materials), and the physical and social environment. The results of this analysis, supplemented by usability and accessibility standards, provide the basis for the definition of usability (including accessibility) goals. They are crucial for the subsequent design of the user interface. In the design process, use may be made of specific interaction technologies and recommendations that have proven to be supportive for elderly workers. Some examples:

- Multimodal user interfaces compensate for reduced sensory and/or fine motor abilities. For example, visual impairments can be compensated for by assistive audio technology such as providing audio output in addition to textual output. Voice recognition as an input mode might be a substitute for keyboard typing.
- To offset reduced working memory faculties, the interface should present a reasonably limited number of interaction options at any one time [20, 21]. Extended periods of time looking for information or possible user/system interactions should be avoided. The placement of visual cues in user interface design can reduce search time.
- Recommended means of counteracting reduced visual abilities are high-resolution computer monitors, high color contrasts, and minimal demands on peripheral vision [22].
- Cues such as specifically designed user interface elements can be used to facilitate the detection of task-critical information (e.g., indicating potential or actual hazards). Multimodality (using e.g., acoustic or haptic vibro-tactile cues) increases the effectiveness of cues. Cues lead to a change from selective to focused attention, which is, unlike selective attention, not age-related. Incorporation of such cues is also advisable because elderly people show reduced abilities regarding divided attention and fluid intelligence.
- To overcome reduced sensory-motor skills, different input modes to control a device can be offered (e.g., keyboard, mice, trackballs, head trackers, hand trackers, and voice).
- Individualization of the interface allows the interface to be adapted to the specific abilities and needs of the user. This may cover font size, selection of input and output devices, the speed and size of the pointer, the color and blink rate of the pointer, background and display colors, and the volume and speed of audio output.
- Personal preferences on one device at the workplace should be portable to other devices.
- Accessibility features should be easy to activate or deactivate.

In designing work tools suitable for older employees, consultancy by user interface experts at early stages of the planning of hardware and software is essential. This approach avoids the need for costly posterior adaptations. Existing workplaces should be evaluated. Usability tests of hardware and software focused on requirements analyses and usability/accessibility standards are fundamental to improving workplaces for an aging workforce.

Incorporating accessibility features and measures in the working environment supports effective task performance by elderly workers. The majority of accessibility features for the elderly also benefit younger employees. Needless to say, all of these measures would benefit all employees.

Another group of more specific ideas for enhancing the physical working environment is based on innovative solutions from the IT and automation areas:

- Automation products that allow workers to program in terms that are natural for their workplace, namely drawings, measurements, and metal-working processes. Figure 26.4 demonstrates one example. Workers do not have to program in programming languages, but can interact with the machine controls in terms of drawings, measurements, and metal-working processes, including simulation. This not only makes it easier to put in the desired work to be done on the workpiece, but also allows easier use of the experience older workers can bring to the workplace. In addition, the simulation allows one to check the results, again in a graphic form, leading to better quality of work results.
- Adaptive automation systems to prevent repetitive input and facilitate knowledge transfer: integrated knowledge management.
- Force-assist robots and other devices, and other task-automation equipment.
- Integrated PLM (product lifecycle management) software including engineering, design, manufacturing, and other areas, leading to improved working conditions in engineering and R&D (research and development).

On a closer look, all of these ideas will benefit not only the older workforce, but will improve working conditions and productivity for all employees. This echoes previous findings about barrier-free or universal design. For instance, the liftMatic oven is an example of design for all (Fig. 26.5). The design of the product takes into account the needs both of the elderly and of people with disabilities. It mounts on

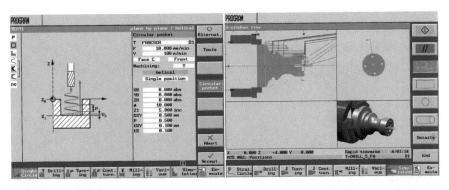

Fig. 26.4 Innovative graphical programming of machine tools, with examples from milling (*below left*) and turning (*below right*). The figure shows the use of these features when transferring knowledge from older to younger employees

Fig. 26.5 The liftMatic (Siemens) is an example of design for all

the wall like a cabinet. At the push of a button the entire oven floor can be moved up and down. The liftMatic is very easy to operate because it is filled from below, and food is always at eye level. The user can reach the cooked food from three sides and the controls are easy to reach. Illumination is optimal. The self-cleaning mechanism eliminates the need for cleaning inside the oven. The design of this product is appealing to all consumers.

In conclusion, accommodating older workers can lead to business ideas in:

- Consulting and knowledge management
- Working environments focusing on accessibility for the aging workforce (ease of use, design for all)

Survival Strategies for Business Operations with Fewer Workers

As said at the beginning, especially for those companies in Japan and in Western Europe, there will need to be a high degree of coping with fewer workers in their home bases, even when taking immigration into account. This will increase the demand for automation equipment and robotics in manufacturing, and will also increase demand for integrated PLM software to streamline the production process from development and design through to manufacturing, including design of manufacturing equipment and automation software.

This last approach will require a suite of software tools that enable a seamless integration of all those processes (Fig. 26.6). Modern PLM software allows for the production of a new product simultaneously with planning its future production. In a production site it will be very important to be able to simulate not only the production itself, but also the automation (to survive with fewer workers) and the ergonomics (to accommodate a growing percentage of older workers). Figure 26.7

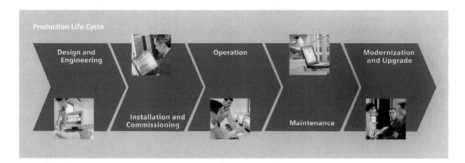

Fig. 26.6 Schematic view of the seamless integration from engineering through installation, commissioning, asset management and plant operation

Fig. 26.7 Simulation of production setup and environment

shows an example combining automation, ergonomics, and the human–machine interface (HMI) mentioned in the section on "Accommodations for Older Workers." The virtual production scenario can be optimized regarding automation, ergonomics, visualization, and HMI, and more. Thanks to simulation technology, the complex processes of a complete factory can be optimized and downtime can be drastically reduced. For experts in a given production operation, their experience can be readily brought into the physical environment even if they are at a location far from the actual work. The virtual production model can be shared using modern communications and visualization environments. This will allow seasoned workers to see clearly the current state of distant operations and problems, and thereby continue to apply their hard-earned production knowledge to an array of company workplaces.

Again, as in the section "Accommodations for Older Workers," we observe that these kinds of innovative products do not only help to accommodate older workers. They also benefit all of the other employees, and in this way they make sense as well for the younger demographic segments. Therefore, there will be multiple incentives for industry customers to use this equipment and software, independent of the Silver Market phenomenon.

Summary and Conclusion

In this chapter, we have analyzed whether the silver market phenomenon will lead to opportunities for business to provide business products and services.

The statistics tell us that the average age of citizens and employees will rise and lead to new requirements, for example in health care and for complex industrial products such as cars and ATMs. The statistics also indicate that the workforce will change, leading to a shortage of young, highly skilled workers, and a higher percentage of older workers.

We have analyzed these effects in turn. Putting it all together, we find several types of product ideas that can be addressed as being related to the silver market phenomenon. These examples fall roughly into five categories:

1. Supplying OEM companies that in turn serve the B2C silver market (as in automotive equipment, ATMs, ticket machines, etc.). This category is closely associated with B2C market ideas.
2. Products for the health and elderly care market. This is a very important issue. It has to be considered within the very different context of national health management systems and progress in medicine and biology.
3. Knowledge-management software and consulting. Business-critical know-how must be captured from retiring workers, and transferred efficiently to younger replacements. Also, familiarity with the aging population is needed and understanding their ways of thinking will be valuable. This familiarity can be promoted with specific knowledge-focused tools and targeted business-process

consulting. The increasingly knowledge-dependent marketplace will reward the increases in awareness of the aging consumers and the novel worker demands, and businesses that offer methods for improved knowledge utilization will also be rewarded. Knowledge-management advances driven by these issues will then help to promote a richer environment for corporate diversity and innovation in goods and services overall. This category is a specific answer to the silver market phenomenon, but will probably remain a niche market for specialized (and presumably mostly small) companies.

4. Automation equipment, including new possibilities of simulating production. This category is already a well-defined and big market, independent of the silver market phenomenon. Nevertheless it is supportive of the silver market/aging workforce, and is a major contribution for companies that have to cope with a shortage of workers.

5. Workplace products with an emphasis on ease of use and accessibility (design for all). The workplace products of this category have yielded examples such as user interfaces – universal design, adaptive automation, robotics and force-assist systems, learning and training systems, and knowledge management. All of these seem to benefit from a careful analysis of silver market requirements. However, this will not lead to completely new requirements, only to a higher emphasis on the usability issues. Thus, we expect that all users will benefit.

Category 5 comes closest to constitute a kind of B2B silver market. Thus, our summarizing conclusion is that the products best suited for the B2 Industry silver market will not be silver-specific products, but well-designed products with an emphasis on usability and problem solving, benefiting all sectors of the employee demographic.

References

1. Commission of the European Communities, *Confronting demographic change: a new solidarity between the generations*, Green Paper COM(2005) 94 (CEC, Brussels, 2005) http://ec.europa.eu/employment_social/news/2005/mar/comm2005–94_en.pdf. Accessed 16 Jun 2008
2. United Nations Population Division, Department of Economic and Social Affairs, Expert Group meeting on social and economic implications of changing population age structure, Mexico City, 31 Aug–2 Sept 2005, (UN Population Division, New York, 2005). http://www.un.org/esa/population/meetings/EGMPopAge/EGMPopAge.htm. Accessed 25 Feb 2010
3. Commission of the European Communities, *Demography Report 2008: Meeting Social Needs in an Ageing Society: Full Report plus Annexes* (Brussels 2008) http://ec.europa.eu/social/main.jsp?catId=611&langId=en. Accessed 25 Feb 2010
4. F. Kohlbacher, *Knowledge retention and HRM: insights from the "year 2007 problem" in Japan*, Paper presented at the Association of Japanese Business Studies (AJBS) conference, Indianapolis, June 2007
5. Japanese Ministry of Education, *Basic School Survey* (MEXT, Tokyo, 2007). http://www.mext.go.jp/b_menu/toukei/001/003/csv/tk1102.csv. Accessed 16 Jun 2008
6. Federal Statistical Office, *Germany's population by 2050*. Results of the 11th coordinated population projection (Statistisches Bundesamt, Wiesbaden, 2006). http://www.destatis.de/

jetspeed/portal/cms/Sites/destatis/Internet/EN/Content/Publikationen/SpecializedPublications/ Population/GermanyPopulation2050. Accessed 25 Feb 2010

7. J. Fuchs, D. Söhnlein, *Vorausschätzung der Erwerbsbevölkerung bis 2050*, IAB project no. 16/ 2005, (Institut für Arbeitsmarkt- und Berufsforschung, Nürnberg, 2005). http://doku.iab.de/ forschungsbericht/2005/fb1605.pdf. Accessed 25 Feb 2010

8. H. Wan, M. Sengupta, V.A. Velkoff, K.A. DeBarros, *US Census Bureau Current Population Report, 65+ in the United States: 2005* (US Government Printing Office, Washington, 2006), pp 23–209. http://www.census.gov/prod/2006pubs/p23-209.pdf. Accessed 25 Feb 2010

9. Japanese Statistics Bureau, *Annual report on the labour force survey* (Ministry of Internal affairs and Communications, Tokyo, 2005)

10. P.T. Beatty, M. Visser (eds.), *Thriving on an Aging Workforce: Strategies for Organizational and Systemic Change* (Krieger, Melbourne, FL, 2005)

11. D.W. DeLong, *Lost knowledge: confronting the threat of an aging workforce* (Oxford University Press, Oxford, 2004)

12. A. Kuebler, P. Mertens, S. Russell, R. Tevis, Enterprises face the aging demographic – some options to overcome demographic challenges in a multinational company. Int. J. Hum. Resour. Dev. Manag. **9**, 275–293 (2009)

13. M. Leibold, S.C. Voelpel, *Managing the Aging Workforce: Challenges and Solutions* (Wiley, New York, 2007)

14. Tennessee Valley Authority, *Knowledge retention: preventing knowledge from walking out the door* (TVA, Knoxville, 2006). http://www.tva.gov/knowledgeretention/pdf/overview.pdf. Accessed 25 Feb 2010

15. JARA (Japan Robot Association), 2007 Mass-retirement (I) and (II), *ROBOT* **2007/03** p. 1 ff, **2007/05** p. 1 ff

16. M. Martin, M. Kliegel, *Psychologische Grundlagen der Gerontologie* (Kohlhammer, Stuttgart, 2005)

17. W.A. Rogers, in *Attention and Aging*, ed. by D.C. Park, N. Schwarz Cognitive Aging: A Primer (Hove Psychology, Hove, 2000), pp. 57–73

18. F.I.M. Craik, Age-related changes in human memory, in *Cognitive aging: a primer* ed. by D. Park, N. Schwarz, (Hove Psychology, Hove, 2000), pp. 75–92

19. P.B. Baltes, U. Lindenberger, U.M. Staudinger, Die zwei Gesichter der Intelligenz im Alter. Spektrum der Wissenschaft **10**, 52–61 (1995)

20. A. Dickinson, R. Eisma, P. Gregor, *Challenging interfaces/redesigning users*. Proceedings of the 2003 conference on universal usability, Vancouver, 10–11 Nov 2003 (ACM, New York, 2003), pp. 61–68

21. C. Reynolds, S.J. Czaja, J. Sharit, Age and perceptions of usability on telephone menu systems, in *Proceedings of the Human Factors and Ergonomics Society 46th annual meeting*, Baltimore, 30 Sept–4 Oct 2002 (HFES, Santa Monica, 2002), pp. 175–179

22. F. Schieber, in *Human Factors and Aging: Identifying and Compensating for Age-Related Deficits in Sensory and Cognitive Function*, ed. by K.W. Schaie, N. Charness. Impact of Technology on Successful Aging (Springer, New York, 2003), pp. 5–99

Chapter 27
Business Opportunities in Personal Transportation: Traffic Safety for Older Adults

Kazutaka. Mitobe

Abstract Japanese society has many problems with regard to the aging population. This paper discusses safety changes in personal transportation for older adults. According to the statistics, the risk of traffic accidents among older adults is extremely high. In order to achieve traffic safety, it is important to address declining sensory and cognitive functions. We discuss three business opportunities aimed at reducing traffic accidents among elderly pedestrians: inspection technology, training technology, and assistive devices that compensate for cognitive functions. From the human factor study using virtual reality technology, the detailed situations of pedestrian traffic accidents become clear. Effective assistive technology can be developed based on risk factors for traffic accidents.

Introduction

The Akita prefecture is rapidly becoming an aging society in Japan. Medical care expenditures for the elderly, a shrinking number of working people, and increasing traffic accidents have emerged as social issues. Akita University has been studying the human factor in order to prevent traffic accidents. In this article, we discuss engineering techniques to enhance safe transportation for the elderly. Additionally, we describe business changes designed to address problems of personal transportation for older adults.

Automobiles are a popular means of personal transportation, but many older adults have to stop driving due to declining cognitive functions, to avoid the risk of traffic accidents. In general, the elderly are more aware of safety concerns than the younger generation. In 2004, traffic accidents caused over $55 billion of social loss in Japan [1].

In 2005, there were 78.8 million people with driver's licenses in Japan [2]. Adults over 65 accounted for 12.4%. Statistical predictions indicate that the number of older adults will approach 34 million in 2020 [3]. This creates a huge market for assistive technology. Currently, there is no assistive safety device that can compensate for the declining cognitive abilities of older drivers. Therefore, most

F. Kohlbacher and C. Herstatt (eds.), *The Silver Market Phenomenon*,
DOI 10.1007/978-3-642-14338-0_27, © Springer-Verlag Berlin Heidelberg 2011

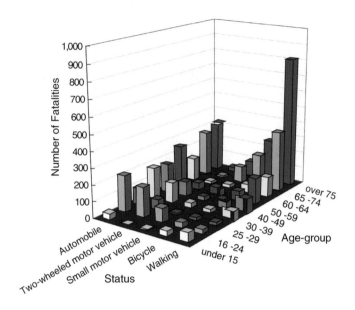

Fig. 27.1 Relationship between traffic fatalities, age group, and transportation devices

older drivers have to give up their licenses in favor of walking, which increases the risk of falling. Figure 27.1 shows the relationship between traffic fatalities, age group, and transportation devices [2]. Statistical data shows that older pedestrians account for the majority of fatalities. To reduce traffic accidents among the elderly, preventing pedestrian traffic is key.

In the latest study of human factors, one third of subjects displayed declining risk avoidance (capacity of balance, oversight, cognitive ability to assess speed, ability to estimate own speed etc.) [4–9]. Those declining functions might induce traffic accidents.

It is difficult to assist pedestrians using safety devices, because many people do not want to carry the devices. Currently, safety devices are mounted inside of vehicles and alert only the driver. However, devices that alert the pedestrian of traffic danger might be better able to reduce accidents.

Usually, the active safety devices on a car sound an alarm only to a driver. However, if the active safety devices can convey the danger of an approach of a car to a pedestrian in advance, it might be able to reduce traffic accidents of pedestrian. We named this concept to car-to-pedestrian friendly interaction system (CPFIS).

Transportation System for Older Adults

To reduce traffic fatalities among older adults, we propose a three-step strategy involving active safety technology, public transportation, and risk avoidance. The invention of active safety and assistive technology is key to boosting vehicle sales among the aging population.

Assistive Technology for Drivers

Active safety technology in Japan is not only useful for elderly drivers but also for other age groups. Table 27.1 presents active safety devices that are currently on the market. Assistive technology is divided into two types: stand-alone and cooperative. Standalone systems are self-contained devices, while cooperative systems can communicate with other vehicles and can be embedded in roads. Unfortunately, there are currently no available active safety devices that can assist with declining cognitive functions.

Electric Wheelchairs

Electric wheelchairs (maximum velocity 6 km/h) do not require a driver's license under Japanese law, and thus provide a useful form of transportation for older adults [16]. However, traffic accidents involving electric wheelchairs are increasing. In 2006, all fatalities and 60% of injuries resulting from electric wheelchairs involved older adults [17]. This shows that older adults are at risk of traffic accidents, even at low speeds such as for wheelchairs. Future electric wheelchairs should have sensors that can detect pedestrians and vehicles. Furthermore, wheelchairs should have an automatic warning system in order to establish a friendly interaction with automobiles and pedestrians.

Public Transportation

Community buses that are subsidized by the local government enhance convenience for older adults and handicapped persons. If more older adults use community buses, then the possibility of traffic accidents will decline. This administrative service functions effectively in downtown residential areas [18]. However, operation is difficult in local communities with dwindling populations.

Consideration of Transportation Systems for Older Adults

Providing a safe transportation system for older adults is important for preserving their quality of life. Public transportation is a good solution for older adults, but it is

Table 27.1 Active safety devices that are currently available	Intelligence	Technology
	Stand alone system	Lane-keeping system [9]
		Active headlights [10]
		Honda Night Vision [11, 12]
	Cooperative system	Intelligent transportation system [13]
		Advanced cruise-assist highway systems [14, 15]

inconvenient in local communities with dwindling populations. Many types of assistive technology for drivers have been developed, but it is generally difficult for older adults to deal with multiple information sources. The human interface that sends information to older adults is an important consideration. Technologies that can compensate for the decline of cognitive functions must be developed, but we must first determine which functions to compensate for.

Pedestrian Safety

Older adults without driver's licenses often choose walking as a method of personal transportation, which increases their risk of falling. Unlike drivers inside their vehicles, there are no steel shields to protect them from the physical impact of an accident. Older adults, who constitute 25% of the population, are a vital part of the local economy. Social participation by older adults is very important for revitalizing the economy. Therefore, ensuring the safety of older pedestrians is an important issue.

Assistive Technology for Older Pedestrians

Traffic safety depends on capturing the attention of both drivers and pedestrians (Table 27.2). Typical policies by the National Police Agency in Japan instruct older pedestrians to wear bright clothing or reflective stickers. A warning device to alert the pedestrian using a cellular phone, and vehicle navigation systems, have been developed but are not yet in practical use [19]. Full-time lighting devices have also been used to improve pedestrian visibility. Auditory cues, such as the sound of a car engine, can be helpful. Overall, however, there are few effective approaches to pedestrian safety in Japan. Thus, we propose the use of an active safety device, called the Car-to-Pedestrian Friendly Interaction System (CPFIS), to alert pedestrians to danger. Using a pedestrian simulator, we examine human factors in order to find the best method for CPFIS.

Table 27.2 Approach from a driver's side and a pedestrian's side for traffic accident prevention

Strategy	Measures
Alert for driver	Bright clothing for pedestrian
	Reflective sticker for pedestrian
	ITS with pedestrian's cellular phone [19]
Alert for pedestrian	Full-time lighting devices on a car
	Auditory cue of car's existence
	Car-to-Pedestrian Friendly Interaction System

Training System Using Virtual Reality

Virtual reality (VR) is a useful method for evaluating the cognitive abilities of older adults as well as the risk factors that induce pedestrian traffic accidents. The results can help us to develop a method that draws a pedestrian's attention to a vehicle.

Advantages of Using VR Technology

Table 27.3 summarizes the advantages of applying VR technology to prevent traffic accidents [20]. In cyberspace, it is possible to fully control time-varying environmental conditions such as visibility conditions, traffic environment, and the velocity of automobiles. VR techniques can reproduce traffic situations that are more likely to lead to accidents involving pedestrians, based on records of past accidents. This leads to a priori training by experience, enabling pedestrians to avoid accidents by their own efforts.

While it may seem to be a simple matter, sophisticated perception, recognition, and decision abilities are required in order to avoid accidents while crossing streets. One must notice approaching cars, estimate their speed, and act on the basis of an accurate understanding of one's own position relative to each car. This depends on one's own walking speed, under all weather conditions and times of day. If the motion of a subject can be measured during practice, it can be used as an indicator of various abilities needed to avoid accidents. There is a possibility of identifying recognition and physical functions that have been degraded due to aging without being noticed (screening). If a degraded ability is identified, then a cyberspace environment is used as a training device to complement the lowered ability (rehabilitation). Data on the relation between accidents and human motion that are accumulated in the above processes will help to analyze factors leading to traffic accidents that cannot be obtained directly from on-the-spot investigations.

Designing cars that operate in cyberspace will help to enhance pedestrian safety (human factor). In cyberspace, the visual and audio information presented to the subjects can be reproduced, and the recognition, decision, and action of the subject can be investigated. Furthermore, cyberspace can connect via a fiber-optic channel, allowing extension to a client-server remote inspection system with existing technology. Figure 27.2 shows the block diagram of an inspection system constructed with the pedestrian simulator system. The inspection system is composed of a video presentation unit, displaying the virtual traffic environment and measuring the

Table 27.3 Applications of VR techniques for the traffic safety

Application	Social meaning
Practice	Traffic safety education
Screening	Checkup of physical fitness and recognition test
Rehabilitation	Training for the declining function
Human factor study	Analysis of traffic accident's factors
	Design of a safety car for pedestrians

motion of the subject, and a control computer [20]. Figure 27.3 shows the virtual traffic environment used in this system [21].

Human Factor of Older Pedestrians

Experiments were carried out with 15 subjects (nine younger subjects, six elderly subjects) in a total of 282 trials (excluding dropouts in the course of measurements

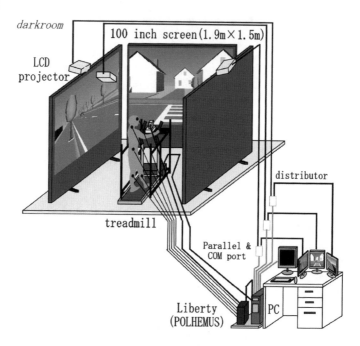

Fig. 27.2 Pedestrian simulator system: (**a**) block diagram of inspection system, (**b**) experiment scene

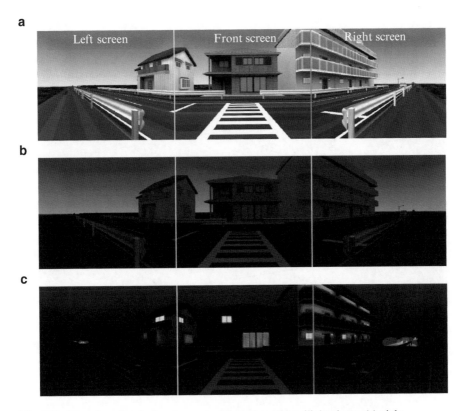

Fig. 27.3 Virtual road scene in cyberspace: (**a**) daytime, (**b**) twilight gloom, (**c**) night

and cases of violation of instructions) with the pedestrian simulator. There were 11 accidents, eight of which involved elderly subjects. A dangerous crossing was defined as a case in which a car passed within 1 m to the front or rear of the subject. Under the conditions of this experiment, most traffic accidents occurred in the daytime. There was only one accident at night.

Figure 27.4 shows the rate of traffic accident occurrence in each lane. The rate of accidents was five times higher for the elderly (1.7% for the younger subjects and 7.8% for the older subjects). All of the traffic accidents were due to a car approaching from the left side of the subject; accidents occurred in the far lane. Figure 27.5 shows the rates of accident occurrence for the elderly and young subjects as functions of the speed of cars approaching from the left (far) side and right (near) side. The rate of accident occurrence was higher when the speed of the car approaching from the left was higher that of the car approaching from the right. That is, traffic accidents were 1.3 times more likely to occur for the younger subjects under this condition and 1.1 times more likely for the elderly subjects.

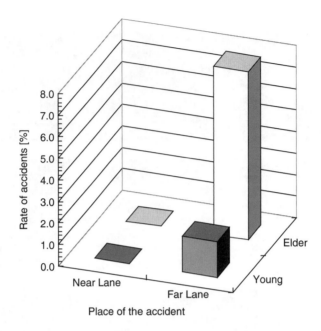

Fig. 27.4 Rate of accidents in each lane

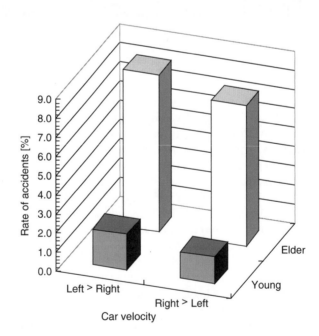

Fig. 27.5 Rate of accidents and car velocity for each group

Consideration of Strategy of Pedestrian Safety

Many of the traffic accidents reported for pedestrians occurred near their homes. From the human factor study using VR technology, the detailed situations of pedestrian traffic accidents become clear. Based on the risk factor of traffic accidents, we can develop effective assistive technology.

Business Opportunities in the Future Technology

There are three business opportunities in the process of reducing the traffic accidents of pedestrians in an aged society. The first business opportunity is the establishment of inspection technology. Health checkup technology using VR technique will be able to find the older adults who have risk factors of traffic accidents based on human factor study. This technique is not only useful for the prevention of traffic accidents but is also effective as a checkup technology for cognitive function. The second business opportunity is the establishment of training technology. Based on the results of tests, a proper training or rehabilitation program can be proposed in order to recover the declined ability of older adults. Recuperation of the cognitive function prevents older pedestrians from dangerous situations of traffic accidents. The third business opportunity is the establishment of the market of assistive devices that can compensate for an older adult's declining sense and cognitive functions. The bottom line is that the assistive devices should be developed based on each older adult's declining function. In the case where it is impossible to recover the ability, we will be able to develop assistive devices in order to compensate for the declined function. The important point is that the assistive technology has to be developed based on each declined function, and it doesn't have to be based on the latest technology.

Summary and Conclusion

Japanese society faces a lot of problems with the aging of the population. The percentage of elder people in traffic fatalities might be increased in all aged societies. However, we have been continuing the challenge in order to make an aging society affluent and vibrant. In this chapter, business opportunities in personal transportation for older adults have been discussed.

According to the statistics, the risk of traffic accidents involving older adults was extremely high during walking. In order to achieve traffic safety for older pedestrians, it is important to support the declining sense and cognitive functions. Unfortunately, there are no active safety technologies that can compensate for the declining sense and cognitive functions of the older pedestrian. One of the strategies for the prevention of pedestrian traffic accidents is an enhancement of sensibility (visual and aural) of older adults to harmful cars. For example, a lot of business automobiles in Japan have mounted additional LED devices on the front grille in order to increase their visibility for older adults. However, it is not enough for prevention of all pedestrian traffic accidents. I believe that we can develop more intelligent "Car-to-Pedestrian Friendly Interaction Systems" based on the human factors of older pedestrians.

Three business opportunities existing in the process of reducing pedestrian traffic accidents have been discussed. The first business opportunity is the establishment of inspection technology. The second business opportunity is the establishment of training technology. The third business opportunity is the establishment of the market of assistive devices that can compensate for the decline in the older adult's sense and cognitive functions. From the human factor study using VR technology, the detailed situations of pedestrian traffic accidents became clear. Effective assistive technology might be developed based on the risk factors of traffic accidents [21, 22].

References

1. Cabinet Office, *White Paper on Traffic Safety in Japan 2009* (Government of Japan, Tokyo, 2009). http://www8.cao.go.jp/koutu/taisaku/index-t.html
2. National Police Agency Japan, *Police white paper* (National Police Agency Japan, Tokyo, 2006). http://www.npa.go.jp/hakusyo/h18/honbun/hakusho/h18/pdfindex.html
3. Cabinet Office, *Annual Report on the Aging Society 2006* (Government of Japan, Tokyo, 2006). http://www8.cao.go.jp/kourei/english/annualreport/2006/06wp-e.html. Accessed 13 Jun 2008
4. K. Mitobe, T. Akiyama, N. Yoshimura, M. Takahashi, T. Ifukube, J. ITE **51**(6), 850 (1997)
5. K. Mitobe, T. Akiyama, N. Yoshimura, M. Takahashi, *T. IEE Jpn.* **118**-A(3), 245 (1998)
6. K. Mitobe, M. Kojima, Y. Terata, M. Takahashi, N. Yoshimura, Soc. Mater. Eng. Resour. Jpn. **12**(1), 16 (2004)
7. K. Mitobe, N. Yoshimura, B. Reimer, J.F. Coughlin, J. Jpn. Council Traffic Sci. **5**(1), 23 (2005)
8. N. Ooarata, K. Mitobe, N. Yoshimura, J. Jpn. Council Traffic Sci. **5**(1), 16 (2005)
9. Y. Terata, K. Mitobe, N. Yoshimura, *IEICE* **J87**-A(2), 296 (2004)
10. S. Ishida et al., in *Proceedings of 10th ITS World Congress*, Madrid, 16–20 Nov 2003 (IBEC, Birmingham, 2003)
11. T. Aoki, H. Kitamura, K. Miyagawa, M. Kaneda, *Development of active headlight system*, SAE paper 970650, 1141 (1997)
12. T. Tsuji, IEICE **89**(3), 272 (2006)
13. T. Tsuji, H. Hattori, M. Watanabe, N. Nagaoka, IEEE Trans. ITS **8**(3), 203 (2002)
14. H. Hatakenaka, T. Hirasawa, K. Yamada, JSAE Trans. **38**(03–07), 15 (2007)
15. S. Hirai, H. Hatakenaka, I. Yamazaki, JSAE Trans. **38**, 6 (2007)
16. M. Mizohata, H. Kitagawa, Papers City Plann. **38**, 41 (2003)
17. K. Yonemitsu, S. Tsunenari, J. Jpn. Council Traffic Sci. **4**(2), 21 (2004)
18. A. Taniguchi, S. Fujii, J. Jpn. Soc. Civil Eng. D **62**(1), 87 (2006)

19. Nissan, *Nissan to test intelligent transport system using cell phones*, Nissan press release 17 Apr 2007. http://www.nissan-global.com/EN/NEWS/2007/_STORY/070417-01-e. html. Accessed 13 Jun 2008
20. K. Mitobe, J.F. Coughlin, N. Yoshimura, *IEICE* **J89-D**(10), 2174 (2006)
21. K. Mitobe, M. Saito, M. Suzuki, N. Yoshimura, TVRSJ **14**(1), 21 (2009)
22. Y. Terata, K. Mitobe, N. Yoshimura, TVRSJ **10**(1), 111 (2005)

Chapter 28
In-Vehicle Telematic Systems and the Older Driver

Joachim Meyer

Abstract The car is rapidly changing. In addition to its traditional driving-related functions it becomes a platform for various services and devices. Some of these are related to the driving task and can improve its ease, comfort and safety, while others are unrelated to driving, and allow the driver to engage in various activities while driving. The aging of the driving population, and the tendency of older people in many parts of the world to continue driving for as long as possible, pose major challenges regarding the design of such devices and their deployment in cars. Some advantages, as well as some limitations which these devices may have for older drivers are pointed out. Design of future in-vehicle telematic systems will have to consider these issues in order to provide maximum benefits for the older driver.

Introduction

The Aging Driver Population

Readily available transportation is one of the major determinants of older people's quality of life. It determines mobility and the ability to maintain adequate personal relations, to obtain services, and to engage in various activities outside the home. Public transportation can be used in urban, high-density housing environments, but the suburbanization of many countries causes large parts of the population to live in areas in which transportation becomes almost exclusively a matter of using one's privately driven car. The consequence is that older people increasingly tend to continue driving for as long as possible.

In the USA, one of the countries with the highest use of personal vehicles for transportation, the trend is clearly evident. An analysis of data from the National Household Travel Survey (NHTS) showed 89% of older Americans (age 65+) conduct their travel in personal vehicles. Older adults take fewer trips, travel shorter distances, and have shorter travel times than younger adults. However, the

F. Kohlbacher and C. Herstatt (eds.), *The Silver Market Phenomenon*,
DOI 10.1007/978-3-642-14338-0_28, © Springer-Verlag Berlin Heidelberg 2011

individually driven car remains the main means of transportation. Only 2% of travel is done by other means of transportation than using a privately owned car and walking [1]. Based on NHTS data, the total number of miles that people aged 65 and older are expected to drive in the USA will increase by 50% in the next 10 years and may double by 2040 [2].

The trend to continue driving for as long as possible is reinforced by a number of factors. Today's older generation is the first generation that grew up with almost universal drivers licenses and private cars. Also, there is a tendency towards active aging, which is supported by a steady decrease in disability with age. Even though more people may be diagnosed as suffering from diseases, such as hypertension or diabetes, the adequate management of these diseases allows them to function appropriately and without real disabilities (e.g., [3]). In addition, today's older people are better educated than previous generations, which makes it likely that they will strive for continuing independence and mobility.

These trends pose significant challenges to the automobile industry, as well as to society, which needs to decide how to cope with the changing characteristics of the driving population. It may have implications on transportation planning, the design of urban areas, the licensing and monitoring of drivers, and many other aspects.

The Changing Car

Not only is the driver population changing, the car is also undergoing major changes. In fact, driving a car today differs for the first time greatly from driving the first mass-produced cars. In the past, the driver obtained all information necessary for driving by looking through the windshield or the windows. There was little in the car a driver needed to direct attention to, except perhaps passengers. Today, drivers obtain more and more information for driving through alerting systems. Also, judging from trends in research, future cars will have enhanced and augmented vision systems that will support drivers when visibility is impaired, and which will increase the likelihood that the driver will see obstacles or other relevant information. The driving task itself is becoming automated to some extent, with features such as cruise control (which maintains constant speed) and intelligent cruise control (which also maintains constant headway from preceding cars). In addition, the car becomes a platform for various devices that combine computation and communication. These devices are often referred to as telematic systems.

The novel devices introduced into cars belong to three categories according to their relevance for the driving task:

1. *Vehicle control devices* are devices that are immediately involved in driving. They may provide information through enhanced vision systems, backward or blind-spot cameras, or they may alert the driver about potential dangers through various types of warnings. Other systems are involved in the control of the vehicle. These include adaptive cruise control systems or intelligent braking systems.

2. *Driving assistance devices* provide information that is relevant for driving, but does not immediately affect vehicle control. Examples are navigation and traffic advisory systems that provide information on congestion or accidents on the route.
3. *Driver Infotainment devices* allow the driver or passengers to receive entertainment, allow communication, or support driver comfort. These devices are unrelated to the driving task itself. Examples of these systems are car entertainment systems, cellular phones, and email and web access from the car.

The three types of devices are not independent, and are, in fact, often implemented in the same system, using the same displays and controls. These devices can potentially interfere with safe driving, but they may also support driving safety in that they allow the driver to obtain information in ways that are optimally designed for the driving environment.

The changes in driving and the introduction of telematic systems in cars are likely to pose major challenges for older drivers. They will have to adapt to these new technologies. This may be particularly problematic for older drivers, whose main advantage may be their long experience with driving, which makes them, overall, very safe drivers. New devices may require the learning of new skills and may make previous experience obsolete. Also, these devices are often initially introduced into high-end cars, which are usually bought by more affluent (and usually older) costumers. Thus the older driving population (50+) will be the first to gain experience with these systems and will have to deal with technologies that are still not mature.

The automotive industry and system designers will have to face these challenges when designing in-vehicle devices, as well as the services that will be provided through them. In order to make them appeal to costumers, they must be of value for the older drivers. However, perhaps the characteristics of the older driver may make the use of these devices particularly dangerous. This is a major dilemma with which manufacturers and societies have to cope. Below are some of the issues relevant for this dilemma and pointers to possible solutions.

Why Are Older Drivers Special?

Older people may differ from younger ones in numerous aspects (see [4], for an analysis of aging and driving). They belong to a different generation, which grew up with a different education system, different cultural values, and different technologies. This effect is often referred to as the cohort effect. Other differences may be related to the higher frequency of diseases and the consequent use of medication among older people. Some diseases and medication, such as medicine against hypertension or psychopharmacological drugs can negatively affect driving. A third, and probably the most important reason for age-related differences is changes in sensory and cognitive functioning.

Particularly prominent are changes in vision. The decrease in visual abilities begins after the age of 20 and continues throughout a person's life. Shinar and Schieber [5] already stated that all visual functions deteriorate with age; the amount, rate, and onset of deterioration vary widely between individuals and functions; while static acuity begins to deteriorate in the 60s, other visual abilities deteriorate earlier; and performance differences between individuals increase with age (see [4], for a more detailed description of age-related changes in vision). Major visual abilities that decline with age include visual acuity (i.e., the ability to resolve small details when viewed from a distance), dynamic visual acuity (i.e., the ability to observe the direction and speed of a moving object), and the ability to focus on near objects. Particularly severe are age-related changes in night vision, contrast sensitivity, and recovery from glare. Night vision, for instance, starts to decline when a person is in his or her 20s, and continues to decline at an increasing pace throughout a person's life. Another visual property that is relevant for driving and decreases with age is the useful field of view (UFOV), i.e., the width of the visual field over which information can be acquired in a quick glance.

Other age-related changes that may affect driving and the use of in-vehicle devices include progressive decrease in hearing that may start as early as 40. There are also complex effects of aging on attention. There is evidence that older adults have greater difficulties dividing attention effectively, compared to middle-aged and younger adults [6]. This is particularly relevant for in-vehicle devices, which almost necessarily require the driver to divide attention between driving and using the device. Some evidence of these difficulties was expressed in a UK survey of older drivers [7], many of whom indicated having problems with their car radio, while others stated that they don't have a problem with their radio, because they simply never used it when driving. Older drivers will be more strongly affected by the use of in-vehicle devices. Their driving is likely to be somewhat impaired by these systems, and they may compensate for this by driving slower and with longer headway [8].

The existence of aging-related changes in memory is well-established (e.g., [9]). The memory difficulties may affect the use of new in-vehicle technologies, for instance by making it more difficult to remember procedures for using the system or by interfering with the recall of names and codes that are used in speech-activated systems. Another domain where aging-related changes may impact performance is skill acquisition [10]. Generally skill acquisition becomes slower with age, and a person will find it difficult to alter familiar ways of performing certain tasks. On the other hand, the procedural memory for familiar tasks and skills may remain intact up to a very advanced age. Thus a person is likely to be able to perform complex sets of actions, such as playing a musical instrument or driving a car. However, he or she may find it difficult to acquire some new skills that require changes in well-established routines.

Aging is also accompanied by a general slowing in processing speed. This causes a lengthening of response times and slower actions and in particular slower responses to unexpected events (e.g., [11]). However, with respect to driving, studies on braking responses actually showed that response time was unaffected by driver age if drivers expected the stimulus to occur. Responses took longer and response time increased with age when events were unexpected [12].

A major problem for many older people is lowered flexibility. A recent extensive postal survey in the UK with more than 1,000 respondents identified as major problems that cause difficulties for older drivers issues such as turning the head and looking out of the rear windows (56.1% of drivers reported this as a problem), as well as vehicle ingress and egress [7]. The lowered motility of the neck and head is a likely cause of accidents in which an older driver either collides with an object that is behind the car when backing up or fails, when changing lanes, to see a vehicle that comes up from behind in a parallel lane. This, in particular, is an issue for which adequately designed in-vehicle devices, such as alerts and visual aids, can provide clear benefits for the older driver.

It is important to develop a sound understanding of the causes of differences between age groups, because the different causes will make it more or less likely that certain differences will continue to exist in the future. If an age-related difference is caused by a physiological process, it will probably remain an issue that will require consideration in the future. If, however, a difference is due to cohort effects, the difference will exist only for a limited period of time, and will eventually disappear. One possible example may be the use of computerized devices. Today's older population is often reluctant to use these devices, but this may not be the result of an age effect. The widespread use of computerized devices began in the 1980s, which may have been relatively late in the careers of current older people. Hence these people did not acquire the skills necessary to use these devices as part of their education or work. People who now approach the age of retirement are much more likely to have experience with computers and may eventually find computer-based devices in the car and in other domains very useful.

Designing Telematics for Older Drivers

A number of points need to be considered when designing and evaluating telematic systems and other in-vehicle devices for older drivers.

The Importance of Long-Term Evaluation

A major challenge for designers and manufacturers of new in-vehicle devices is the need to predict how these systems will affect driving (and in particular safety) and driver satisfaction. This prediction is particularly difficult because the effects of new technologies may change dramatically over time and may differ from the predictions derived from preliminary testing. Some technologies (such as the ABS system) had initial negative impact on safety, and some time had to pass before people learned to use the new technology correctly. During this learning period, drivers may misuse the new technology, which may cause it to constitute a safety hazard in the short run. Thus, technologies need to be evaluated in the long run. Even then a device that was shown to be potentially useful may not improve safety and perhaps even lower it. This may be due in part to changes in the way people use the technology after the device is introduced. It is therefore crucial to evaluate the costs and benefits of technologies in the long run and assess what intervention or policy change is most likely to generate the desired positive effects.

User-Centered Design

The introduction of new technologies for older drivers should be based on the notion of "user-centered design" (e.g., [13]). It requires the entire design process to be driven by the attempt to address the needs of the user and to adapt the product to the user characteristics. Usability considerations are of major importance for consumer acceptance and satisfaction in the design of almost all consumer products. However, in the context of in-vehicle technologies, they are particularly important because of the inherent safety issues related to these devices [14].

The design of novel in-vehicle devices requires the application of knowledge and insights from a number of disciplines. These devices are by and large computerized, and theories, research, and recommendations from the field of human–computer interaction (HCI or CHI), cognitive engineering, ergonomics and human factors engineering should be considered (for sources, see, for example, [15–17]). The different areas of research overlap, but the approaches and theoretical systems that were developed in each of them are sufficiently distinct to warrant a closer look at all bodies of literature. Even though there is extensive research in each of these fields, there are still large gaps in our knowledge on how to design in-vehicle devices, especially if these devices are to be used by older drivers.

Considering Older Drivers' Sensory Capabilities

As mentioned above, older drivers are likely to have diminished sensory capabilities compared to younger people. Design for older users should therefore strive to maximize contrast and illumination. Also, most older people have presbyopia and require the use of corrective lenses to view close objects. Hence, in-vehicle displays and devices that require vision of small details may be problematic. Drivers will not put on reading glasses to use a system and may find driving with bi- or multifocal glasses unpleasant.

One possible way to avoid the problems that arise with visual information displays for older drivers may be to choose auditory displays instead. However, hearing difficulties are fairly common among older adults, and this needs to be considered when auditory displays are designed. Overall there is some evidence that older drivers may particularly benefit from multimodality displays that combine visual and auditory information [18].

The Promise of Telematics for Older Drivers

The question of how to provide older drivers with an opportunity to drive for as long as possible, while minimizing the risks due to incapacitated and unsafe drivers, is a crucial topic that will require increasing attention in the future. One possible way to deal with this problem is through appropriately designed technologies. As Pauzie [19] pointed out:

1. Reducing the complexity of the driving task reduces the performance differential between young people and the elderly.
2. Optimizing in-vehicle systems (improving the legibility and intelligibility of information, simplifying dialog) with regard to the functional capacities of older drivers generally also benefits the rest of the user population.

There is ample evidence that older people will not automatically reject new technology that provides information and assistance, in particular if interacting with the system is intuitive. This acceptance extends even to technologically highly complex systems if these are easy to use.

It will be necessary to develop cars and technologies that can help older drivers deal with some of the changes that occur with age. Such systems, if designed and introduced properly, may allow an older driver to maintain her or his mobility for a longer time, improving their quality of life. These considerations are also crucial for the automobile industry, which needs to consider the characteristics of the changing driver population. Manufacturers who will adapt their cars to the needs of this population are likely to have a foothold in a growing and affluent market.

Clearly the issues will not be simply the development of new technological solutions. Rather, the successful implementation of these technologies will require the collaborative effort of specialists from a variety of disciplines. It will be necessary to implement the idea of user-centered design into the design process of these devices, considering the user from the very beginning. This will require the close involvement of specialists in the research of lifestyles, demographics, and consumer behavior, who will need to pay special attention to older consumers.

The new technologies will also require entirely new ways of thinking about methods for testing them. It is by no means assured that a technologically sound device that provides some benefits for the user will eventually be adopted. It is necessary to develop new models and methodologies to predict the complex reactions of a user to a new technological system and to adapt the system accordingly. One can, for instance, not simply assume that a system analysis that applies for the current usage patterns of a device will also apply when the device is altered. The benefits that are to be expected from a new technology have to be considered very carefully. A lane-change warning system can serve as an example. It alerts the driver when she or he intends to move into a lane in which there is another car. Such a system provides great benefits for older drivers who often find it difficult to turn their head. The installation of such a system should help drivers avoid collisions and should make driving safer. However, drivers can potentially develop strong reliance on such systems. In extreme cases drivers may initiate a lane-change maneuver without bothering to look, waiting for the warning system to cue her or him if the lane is occupied. Given that the warning system will not be perfect (no system ever is), collisions are still likely to occur, and in these cases manufacturers may be held liable. Thus, the introduction of such systems requires a careful analysis of all aspects of their possible use, a task that requires the development of adequate predictive tools.

The same applies to the design of telematic systems. Here, too, we are facing many unknowns regarding the effects of these technologies on drivers in various situations. The design of the device, the allocation of functions to it, and the design of the interface all require a thorough understanding of the interaction between users and technologies. This goes clearly beyond our current knowledge in this field. We need to expand the empirical basis for our work by collecting both field and laboratory data. In addition, we need to develop appropriate design methodologies that take into account the unique characteristics of the driving situations and the needs and properties of the driver. This will be particularly important for older drivers, who may have less ability to adapt to nonoptimal design of the system. Finally, we need models of the use of the automation and devices for predicting how users will respond to a certain system design. Such models will allow us to move from the unsystematic engineering of human-vehicle systems that is practiced today to a more systematic and model-driven technique that approaches the methods used in other fields of engineering.

The models have to consider not only older drivers' characteristics and the function of the system, but also the conditions in which the system is used. For instance, Lavie and Meyer [20] showed that an adaptive in-vehicle telematic system that adjusts its functioning to the driver's usual usage patterns eliminates the differences between older and younger drivers, as long as the driver encounters routine situations to which the system has adapted. In nonroutine situations, when drivers need to act differently from the way they usually act, the difference between older and younger drivers increased greatly, much beyond the difference that exists with nonadaptive systems. Thus, an adaptive system may provide benefits for the older driver as long as adaptivity is almost perfect, but if it is only partly correct, the negative consequences from using it may exceed its benefits.

However, not only the design process needs to be reconsidered. The introduction of new technologies into cars for older drivers also makes it necessary for car manufacturers to reconsider their responsibilities. More attention will have to be paid to the familiarization of the new driver with the technologies in the car. The best ways to do this are still fairly unclear. Possibly car sales will have to include the use of simulator or test-track driving to teach the driver how to respond to different events with the complex technologies. In addition, older drivers in particular will need to have the technologies customized to their particular needs. This can be done by the driver herself, but in all likelihood optimal customization should be based on the objective evaluation of a specialist. This will require the development and validation of tools to determine the optimal configuration for a driver. Also, specialists for customizing cars to the needs of individual customers may have to be trained. It is unlikely that current sales personnel can be expected to do this job appropriately, unless they receive the tools and knowledge for this additional service.

Summary and Conclusion

This chapter has presented a number of issues that are relevant for the design of in-vehicle telematic systems for older drivers. The appropriate design of telematic systems for older drivers is a delicate balancing act. It needs to consider the requirements of older drivers and their characteristics, but it may also involve changing usage patterns and needs through appropriate training and support. A schematic depiction of some of the relevant points is shown in Fig. 28.1.

The introduction of new in-vehicle technologies for older drivers requires us to expand the boundaries of our knowledge and our understanding in a wide variety of fields. It is likely that the insights gained here will be important in various domains,

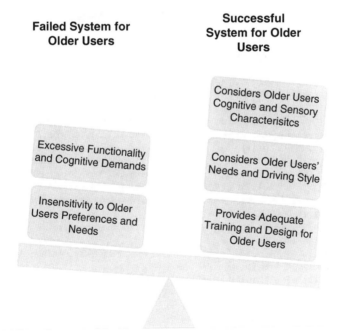

Fig. 28.1 Factors affecting the successful or failed introduction of an in-vehicle telematic system for older users

beyond the design of vehicles. Thus this may be an opportunity to develop some of the major technologies for the twenty-first century.

The new in-vehicle technologies, when designed for older users, are also likely to be one of the major business opportunities in the twenty-first century. Designing in-vehicle systems that are designed with the older user in mind and that are responsive to older drivers' needs can provide an important service for the older drivers and society, by increasing mobility and driving safety.

References

1. D.V. Collia, J. Sharp, L. Giesbrecht, The 2001 national household travel survey: A look into the travel patterns of older Americans. J. Saf. Res. **34**, 461–470 (2003)
2. NHTS Brief, *Older Drivers: Safety Implications* (U.S. Department of Transportation, Federal Highway Administration, Washington DC, May 2006)
3. K.G. Manton, E. Stallard, L. Corder, The dynamics of dimensions of age-related disability 1982 to 1995 in the U.S. elderly population. J. Gerontol. Biol. Sci. **53A**, B59–B70 (1998)
4. J. Meyer, Personal Vehicle Transportation, in *Technology for Adaptive Aging*, ed. by Richard Pew, Susan Van Hemel. National Research Council, Board on Behavioral, Cognitive and Sensory Sciences, Division of Behavioral and Social Sciences and Education. (The National Academies Press, Washington, DC, 2004), pp. 253–281
5. D. Shinar, F. Schieber, Visual requirements for safety and mobility of older drivers. Hum. Factors **33**, 507–519 (1991)
6. W. Brouwer, J.G. Ickenroth, R.W.H.M. Ponds, P.C. van Wolfelaar, Divided Attention in Old Age, in *European Perspectives in Psychology*, ed. by P. Drenth, J. Sergeant, R. Takens, vol. 2 (Wiley, Oxford, 1990), pp. 235–348
7. P. Herriotts, Identification of vehicle design requirements for older drivers. Appl. Ergon. **36**, 255–262 (2005)
8. N. Merat, V. Anttila, J. Luoma, Comparing the driving performance of average and older drivers: the effect of surrogate in-vehicle information systems. Transport. Res. F **8**, 147–166 (2005)
9. L.L. Jacoby, J.F. Hay, Age-Related Deficits in Memory: Theory and Application, in *Theories of Memory*, ed. by M.A. Conway, S.E. Gathercole, C. Cornoldi, vol. 2 (Psychology, East Sussex, UK, 1998), pp. 111–134
10. F.I.M. Craik, L.L. Jacoby, Aging and Memory: Implications for Skilled Performance, in *Aging and Skilled Performance: Advances in Theory and Applications*, ed. by W.A. Rogers, A.D. Fisk, N. Walker (Erlbaum, Mahwah, NJ, 1996), pp. 113–137
11. L.L. Falduto, A. Baron, Age-related effects of practice and task complexity on card sorting. J. Gerontol. **41**, 659–661 (1986)
12. P.L. Olson, M. Sivak, Perception–response time to unexpected roadway hazards. Hum. Factors **28**, 91–96 (1986)
13. A. Owens, G. Helmers, M. Sivak, Intelligent vehicle highway systems: A call for user-centered design. Ergonomics **36**, 363–369 (1993)
14. M. Flyte, The safe design of in-vehicle information and support systems: The human factors issues. Int. J. Vehicle Des. **16**, 158–169 (1995)
15. M.G. Helander, T.K. Landauer, P.V. Prabhu, *Handbook of Human–Computer Interaction*, 2nd edn. (Amsterdam, North Holland, 1997)
16. B. Shneiderman, C. Plaisant, *Designing the User Interface: Strategies for Effective Human–Computer Interaction*, 4th edn. (Addison Wesley, London, 2004)

17. C.D. Wickens, J.G. Hollands, *Engineering Psychology and Human Performance*, 3rd edn. (Prentice Hall, New Jersey, 1999)
18. Y. Liu, Effect of advanced traveler information system displays on younger and older drivers' performance. Displays **21**, 161–168 (2000)
19. A. Pauzie, Ageing population and ergonomics of innovative communicating technologies in driving. Recherche Transports Sécurité **81**, 203–212 (2003)
20. T. Lavie, J. Meyer, Benefits and costs of adaptive user interfaces. Int. J. Hum. Comput. Stud. **68**(8), 508–524 (2010)

Chapter 29
The Golden Opportunity of Silver Marketing: The Case of Housing and Financial Services

Kenneth Alan Grossberg

Abstract The unprecedented aging of Japan's population presents costs and opportunities for its future as a society and as a major economic power. Japan's seniors already control the largest portion of the nation's wealth,[1] but in the very near future they will also consume the lion's share of the social expense for care and living as they age and their proportion in the total population increases. In this chapter we examine two areas which promise commercial opportunities because of such a vast socio-demographic change linked to a huge pool of liquid assets. [2] Those areas are, firstly, catering to the financial needs of the country's senior citizens and, secondly, responding to their particular preferences and requirements for housing. In Japan's generally sluggish market for housing and financial services, the "silver market" provides one of the richest segments available, but successfully offering such services to this population requires skill, sensitivity, and an understanding of the evolving consumer mindset in Japan. In addition, the added impact of the recession of 2008 will make this target market even more difficult to persuade to part with their diminished personal assets, but it also opens opportunities for financial service providers whose offerings best suit the anxieties and fears of these aging investors.

---

[1]Dai-ichi Life Research Institute estimates that assets of Japanese baby boomers total ¥130 trillion, which is equivalent to 10% of all personal financial holdings in Japan. In addition to the amount of assets that they hold, between now and 2009 companies will have paid out about ¥50 trillion in retirement severance as workers reach age 60. According to a Dentsu survey, baby boomers are expected to spend about ¥11 trillion on travel after retirement, of which 90% would be for travel outside of Japan [18].

[2]Financial assets held by Japanese households rose to a record high of ¥1.56 quadrillion as of 30 June, 2007, with cash and deposits constituting 50% of that amount, a considerably higher percentage than in other advanced economies [7].

F. Kohlbacher and C. Herstatt (eds.), *The Silver Market Phenomenon*,
DOI 10.1007/978-3-642-14338-0_29, © Springer-Verlag Berlin Heidelberg 2011

Introduction

Japan is not unique among post-industrial societies in having an aging society, but it is surely *primus inter pares* in the extent to which the country's demographic bulge has shifted from youth to old age. As of 2005, the percentage of Japan's population at age 65 or older (20.1%) was higher than such "old" European nations as Italy (19.7%) and Germany (18.8%) and far higher than the relatively "young" USA (12.3%) [1]. By September 2007, the 65 and older population had grown to 21.5% of the population, with the number of Japanese of at least 80 years old topping seven million for the first time, 5.6% of all Japanese [2]. And, as time passes, Japan's character as the world's most geriatric society will likely become even more pronounced. From a public policy perspective, there are big problems ahead for Japan as the global community's eldest nation, but from a business and marketing point of view, such lemons can be the stuff of lemonade for the right industries. This research will examine two sectors that are related to each other – financial services and housing – which are already counting on the silver market to earn them substantial profits. "Housing" in this chapter refers to real estate offerings specially designed with the priorities of older Japanese in mind.

That the baby boomers are a veritable "pig in a python" demographically speaking is not news, and the looming opportunities presented because of their retirement from full-time employment and progressive aging have not eluded the attention of Japanese businesses. But, seeing opportunities and developing appropriate strategies to exploit those opportunities are not the same thing, and not every attempt to grow rich from the assumed needs or projected demand of Japanese baby boomers will succeed. Still, many enterprises are intent on turning that "silver" into gold. The banks, a major actor in this market, are trying to capture as much of the boomers' retirement pensions and savings as they can, and the residential housing developers have used a number of strategies to entice these older citizens to buy housing designed with them in mind (both in Japan and abroad) or to renovate (reform) their existing dwellings to make them more user-friendly for elderly residents.

The fortunes of many companies are riding on the extent to which their assumptions about senior citizens' consumption behavior turn out to be correct. Some firms have miscalculated as to the potential popularity of their innovations, and end up paying the price for not satisfying their targeted customers. One example of such a strategic error is the multigeneration house (*nisetai jutaku*) in its original incarnation, described later in this chapter. It was assumed by real estate developers that an appeal to the Japanese idea of togetherness – of having grandparents, children, and grandchildren all occupying the same house – would have great resonance with the Japanese. However, what they did not count on was the fact that the elder residents, whose financial contribution (of both land and down payment) was what usually made such expensive houses possible in the first place, would feel cheated and neglected after the three generations were actually living together in such housing for some length of time.

One example of the profits anticipated from the silver market can be seen in the financial arena. Companies have created financial instruments that cater to this market or, in the case of Goldman Sachs' Baby Boomer Basket E-Warrant, hope to profit in other ways from its growth. The ultimate success of some of these new products or services remains unclear. Goldman Sachs Japan designed the Baby Boomer Basket E-Warrant product to capitalize on the anticipated boom expected to result from the changing consumption preferences and needs of the elderly. Performance of the Baby Boomer Basket E-Warrant is linked to the share price of a basket of eleven companies that are predicted to gain disproportionately from the boomers' new lifestyle. Some of the 11 companies included are East Japan Railway (leisure travel), Konami (fitness clubs), Mitsbishi UFJ and Mizuho banks (financial management of boomers' pension and retirement nest eggs), and Toto (toilets and bathrooms) [3].

While the areas represented by these and other companies stand to gain from elder-spending during the next decade, it is still not clear how much this thrifty but status-conscious Japanese generation will actually spend, or where they will finally decide to put their hard-earned savings. And for those who were invested in securities and real estate, the heightened perception of risk resulting from the recession of 2008 will make them even more hesitant to commit their funds to vehicles which are not perceived as absolutely "safe." The banks and brokerages assume that they will have to put the money somewhere, and are intent on getting the lion's share of those funds. Likewise, the real estate companies are certain that the silver market is still willing to take the plunge to buy or renovate property that more fully satisfies their desires for comfort, privacy, and a richer life experience as they grow older.

Financial Services in Japan: Rethinking Customer Needs

It is almost a cliché to say that Japanese financial service firms (including banks, brokerages, and insurance companies) are behind the curve when it comes to offering state-of-the-industry, efficient service to their clients. This turned out to be something of an advantage when the "Lehman shock" of 2007–2008 revealed that Japanese banks were much less exposed to the subprime mortgage loan disaster that greatly weakened the balance sheets of banks from other countries. Although the lost decade that followed the bursting of the economic bubble in 1990 led to some soul-searching on the part of the large institutions, as well as ambivalent efforts to renovate their antiquated systems and priorities, culturally determined attitudes still prevent the rapid introduction of many internationally accepted practices. For example, banks still rely on the traditional seal (*inkan*) rather than customer signatures for official documents and have done little to transition to paperless systems. It must be acknowledged, however, that elder Japanese grew up with this archaic system based on the use of *inkan* seals instead of signatures and with passbook-based bank accounts with paper documentation used for every small transaction, so they are not necessarily seeking the same type of internet-based, automated service that has become popular with their younger compatriots. However, these seniors can recognize good service when it is offered to them, and the financial institutions are learning that to provide that service they must be more flexible than is their habit.

Change does not come quickly. After all, it took the better part of a decade before the excessively low interest rate returns on bank and pension accounts finally pushed Japanese seniors to explore new and riskier investments that offered the possibility of higher returns, and no doubt the worldwide financial troubles have chastened many of them for their boldness. From 2007, 8.4 million Japanese baby boomers are slated to start retiring, which has spurred the banks to expand their sales efforts into territory that is traditionally the province of stockbrokers. The domestic banks will not be alone. Foreign institutions also intend to compete for the Japanese boomers' yen. Prominently, Citigroup acquired Nikko Cordial's brokerage business and, with its 108 branches throughout Japan, thought that it could become a formidable rival [4]. But the financial disaster that befell Citigroup forced it to disgorge Nikko Cordial Securities soon after it was acquired, and the latter is now a unit of the Sumitomo Mitsui Financial Group Inc. The dream remains, however, and Sumitomo Mitsui Banking Corp. and Nikko Cordial Securities Inc. announced that they would join forces in marketing financial services to the wealthy, enlisting support from British bank Barclays PLC [5].

Another longtime player in the Japanese market, HSBC, has opened branches in Tokyo, and plans to expand to other large cities to grab a greater share of private assets [6]. The bank offers wealth management services throughout its network. It began offering private banking in Japan in 1996, catering to individuals with financial assets of more than ¥300 million, but the new service will target the 6.3 million people in Japan that the bank estimates have liquid financial assets of at least ¥10 million. This will bring it squarely into the middle-class boomer segment in direct competition with Japanese banks. Meanwhile UBS, the world's biggest money manager, opened its third branch in Japan in July 2007 and said it would target the ¥300 trillion in assets held by half a million Japanese households with assets of ¥200 million or more. According to the Bank of Japan, Japanese households still have 50% of their assets in cash or deposits, compared to 13% in the USA, so there is substantial room for growth in this business. Still, the BOJ admits that individuals are shifting their assets from deposits to higher-risk, higher-return government bonds and investment trusts. In 2007, investment trusts captured a record high of 5% of the total under management, expanding from 3.7% the year before [7].

Not only are the foreigners getting into the act, but the restructuring of Japan's financial services industry will bring complete deregulation of insurance product sales. That means that the banks can now offer one-stop shopping to customers interested in mutual funds, Japanese government bonds, and insurance policies, as well as the traditional bank products – loans and deposits. This includes a broadened mandate for the type of insurance products banks can to sell, beyond just the savings-type insurance that they traditionally have handled, and includes policies that offer payouts for illness or death. Bank of Tokyo-Mitsubishi UFJ, which owns the largest branch network in Japan (660 branches), now offers nearly every type of insurance to its customers. Mizuho Bank sells medical insurance policies, but all the banks know that they must recruit experts from insurance companies who are knowledgeable about these products in order to ensure the success of this initiative [8].

The impact of the global financial meltdown will be felt, but will not deter these institutions from their long-term strategic goal of capturing baby boomer assets.

The Japanese providers of financial services are aware that this silver market has unique needs and wants, and they are experimenting with different ways to attract senior citizens to their different company banners. In this, they are trying to leverage the boom in services, which now accounts for some 30% of Japan's GDP and almost 60% of total consumption spending. Health-related services, such as fitness, golf, and various self-indulgent therapies and treatments are of course very popular, but entertainment and lifestyle-related recreation is also in heavy demand [9]. That being the case, some of the marketing attempts used by the banks still seem to be counter-intuitive, but that is what makes the Japanese market so fascinating and difficult in general. For example, banks have created affiliation groups for different types of diversions that enable the clients to share experiences with others who are retired or semiretired, or empty nest couples with reduced obligations to their children and workplace. Sumitomo Mitsui Banking Corporation set up an organization called "Next Club 50s" to appeal to this particular segment. To join the club, a bank customer must have more than ¥5 million yen on deposit and be at least 54 years old. On the pretext of having a wine-tasting or learning how to make sushi, these customers are introduced by SMBC to the company's investment trusts. These are products that the bank is using to get this age and income cohort accustomed to putting at least some of their savings into instruments riskier (but potentially more rewarding) than time deposits. With some 8.4 million Japanese baby boomers expected to retire soon, banks like SMBC want to be able to retain as much of their retirement pensions in-house as possible [10]. Since the newly retired share many generational experiences, it makes sense to consider their needs as forming a cohesive core, and since they have more leisure time than any previous Japanese generation, they can be appealed to by combining financial concerns with recreational activities. In addition, as the least individuated of Japan's current generations, they are considerably less resistant to being treated as a group. It might even reduce apprehension to accepting the investment trust, because others of their generation are also being solicited at the same time and during the same recreational activity.

The past decade has seen many of Japan's leading banks and insurance companies merge into ever larger entities to protect themselves from the financial ruin that threatened when the financial bubble burst in the 1990s. As a consequence, the number of institutional choices available to Japanese seniors continues to narrow, and is considerably more limited than the options available to their American or European counterparts. Since those institutions traditionally moved "in convoy," it was hard for those consumers to find any point of differentiation in the products on offer. In addition, the fact that the return on savings during the past decade has been infinitesimal compared to what it will take for the increasingly long-lived baby boomers to be self-supporting means that a note of desperation has crept into Japanese seniors' search for a way to fund their retirement needs, which also encourages the financial institutions to create new products for them.

Even the conservative Japan Post, the world's biggest financial institution with €1,164 billion (¥187,000 billion) of customer monies has launched a suite of investment trusts from a variety of domestic and foreign asset managers (including Nomura, Daiwa, Goldman Sachs, Nikko, DIAM, Sumishin, and Fidelity). After struggling internally with such a major shift in strategy, it then took Japan Post a lot of time and effort to try to persuade its traditionally risk-averse customer base to buy the new products. The fact that a real market for them now exists, however, is seen in the results: Japan Post actually exceeded its annual sales target for 2006–2007 a month ahead of schedule, and doubled that target for 2008 to ¥1,100 billion. What is perhaps most important is that Japan Post has proved something no one would have believed possible only a few short years ago: that Japanese are willing to buy riskier investments than just savings accounts at their local neighborhood post office [11].

One reason why the financial service firms had been at all successful in selling the new investment trusts was because the long upward trend of global equity and property prices calmed investor fears. A rising tide raises all ships. Those halcyon days are now over, but their success is also attributable to the fact that the banks and Japan Post committed a lot of resources to the task. The insistent drumbeat of their sales pitch that Japan's retirees must begin to invest and not just save has begun to move older Japanese to reallocate their asset portfolios towards a higher risk/reward profile. Because interest rates in Japan have remained at historic lows for the past decade, it has been relatively easy to persuade older depositors to take advantage of the more attractive returns currently available from even the most conservatively managed investment trusts.

There is a double-edged sword inherent in marketing these riskier products, and the danger signs were already evident several years ago. As of 2007, 25% of Japanese customers who purchased investment trusts from major banks or brokerages were not satisfied with the service rendered, because of sales fees that are too high or a dearth of postpurchase information and insufficient explanation of the risks associated with the products. Significantly, the level of customer satisfaction was much higher when investment trusts were bought from online brokerages or directly from the mutual fund company [12]. So, the giants of Japan's financial community must not underestimate this target market as they did for so many decades when a highly regulated system gave them the advantages of an oligopoly without the possibility of credible foreign competition. The world is changing, and the silver market is a cohort that will vote with its assets and take its wealth elsewhere if not treated properly.

The banks had extra motivation since October 2007 to improve their service because a new law was passed whose intent is to protect elderly customers from sharp practices when buying investment trusts and other risk products. Now, selling risk instruments to seniors without first confirming that they understand how the products work could subject the seller to government penalties, so banks are working to ensure compliance. Sumitomo Mitsui Banking Corp. requires that customers aged 70 or older be accompanied by a family member when purchasing a variable annuity. Bank of Tokyo-Mitsubishi UFJ explains the risks involved at least twice to customers over 70 when selling investment trusts and variable annuities. Some banks are also strengthening their after-sales service, such as Mizuho Bank, which is starting to increase the frequency of visits to customers over 70 to explain the investment performance of their holdings to less than 6 months between calls [13].

The subprime mortgage bubble, which burst in late 2007 and continues to work its way through the international financial system, affecting Japan as well as the USA and other advanced economies, only serves to strengthen the call for caution and attention to legal and ethical constraints on financial product marketing to elder citizens on limited or fixed incomes. There are no doubt older Americans in danger of losing the roof over their heads in the fallout from the subprime mortgage implosion, and this issue must also be taken into consideration when marketing housing to retirees in Japan.

Marketing Real Estate to Older Consumers

One's house is truly one's castle, and this becomes even more so as we age and our mobility declines. Sometimes, when children grow and leave the family home, it becomes obvious that we might be happier, more comfortable, or better served by a different type of housing. This sentiment became the stimulus for a mass movement in the USA over the past quarter century, with a major shift of retirees to properties that had been developed with them in mind, in Sun Belt states like Florida, Texas, and California where they were offered adults-only communities that promised them a carefree lifestyle. Japan has not been immune to the impact of this cultural shift, but the importance placed on family members as caregivers of their own elderly at first created a somewhat different twist on the concept of senior housing.

The high cost of living in Japan proper has also created an opportunity for marketing housing solutions outside of Japan to Japanese baby boomers. This movement occurred in the UK on a large scale, where thousands of retired British subjects became permanent expatriates in Spain and Italy. Also, in the USA increasing numbers of American retirees on fixed incomes have been buying condominiums in Panama and Costa Rica because they provide cheaper alternatives for growing old comfortably than are currently available in the USA proper.

However, housing alternatives for the silver market must take into account both the economic and the social aspects of their lives. For most Japanese boomers, their peak earning years are over and, depending on their financial situation, they will either have to live on a limited fixed income or be able to call on rather substantial liquid assets for their retirement lifestyle. In either case, the issue of appropriate housing requires a consideration of the fact that the strength of the Japanese family unit is in fact weakening, though perhaps not to the degree that can be seen in the USA. Hard evidence about how much more these baby boomers want to distance themselves from their children's lives, and vice versa, than was thought possible only a few years ago can be found in the data on the decline of coresidential living arrangements among contemporary Japanese families.

Between 1975 and 1995 the proportion of Japan's over-65 population living together with their children fell from 72 to 49%, and there was a corresponding increase in the percentage of older Japanese living alone (from 7 to 12%) and in couple-only households (almost doubling, from 15 to 28%) [14]. These trends have continued and, if anything, may have even accelerated. Developers and marketers of residential properties saw an opportunity to sell a type of housing to these older Japanese that fused the ideal of keeping the entire family under one roof with the reality that parents and married children are frequently less willing to compromise their privacy than in previous generations. The existence of such contradictory emotions led to the creation of the multigeneration house.

The "two-generation house" (*nisetai jutaku*) was a concept that was supposed to provide parent and child with separate housing units under the same roof, and the Japanese government added its seal of approval for this model by legally stipulating that the two families in the dwelling had to be related to each other. Of the ten major housing companies, the three largest in 1994 (Sekisui House, Misawa Home, and Daiwa House) reported that approximately one third of their orders were for *nisetai jutaku* (see pp. 60–61 in [15]). Similar to the pace and direction of deregulation in financial services, with housing policy as well, the not-so-subtle influence of the Japanese government is apparent in the way the industry is allowed to develop and in the specific products it offers to fulfill the anticipated needs and desires of the baby boom generation. A not irrelevant issue encouraging the proliferation of *nisetai jutaku* housing was the fact that the housing company would be able to secure an advantageous "two-generation loan" to finance the construction of this type of residence (see p. 62 in [15]).

But, there was trouble in paradise that within a decade led to questioning the very rationale for the two-generation home. The parents felt cheated, because their assets had been a major reason why such housing could be created, but they perceived little benefit from the close proximity with the family of their offspring. The marketing of this housing involved promoting an unrealistically harmonious view of three generations living together in an almost idyllic environment. The reality was that "the anticipation of the elderly couple in the sharing of their grandchildren was not matched by the reality of being left alone with them" as perpetually available babysitters (see p. 64 in [15]). The adult children gained more from this arrangement than did their elderly parents, who felt their freedom of movement was constrained by the expectation that they would always be willing to take care of their grandchildren, even as their own grown-up children paid them little attention except when they were needed.

In a reaction to the negative feedback from the multigenerational home, the real estate industry began to realize that a change in marketing strategy was needed. Out of this necessity was born the promotion of technologically advanced and user-friendly housing for the elderly. Behind such an initiative lay the recognition that elderly parents had been the financial senior partner in the joint household situation from the start, often because they owned the very land upon which the house was built (see p. 65 in [15]). So, in the mid-1990s homes with safer, more convenient features for elder residents began to appear in Japan. Some of these amenities included wider corridors (to accommodate wheelchairs), the elimination of thresholds and steps within the house between rooms, installation of railings in bathrooms and along walls, and the use of extra large and easy-to-read switches for lights and fixtures (see p. 66 in [15]).

The development companies learned that the ideological emphasis on a multi-generational family living together as in the past is not the great selling point they had assumed it would be. Japanese seniors are waking up to the altered emotional landscape of the family in the twenty-first century and are more interested in finding a housing solution that suits their own needs, rather than one which keeps the family "together" under terms unfavorable to their autonomy and freedom. This altered emphasis matches the government's recognition that families can no longer be shamed into taking care of their elder members, a technique for social control that had been used successfully countless times in Japan's recent past. Public agencies or private services increasingly will have to pick up the slack as fewer young Japanese are willing or able to make the sacrifices required to take care of their aging parents.

A third type of solution for the housing needs of the baby boomer generation – besides the multigeneration home or the "reformed" dwelling – lies not within Japan itself but beyond its borders. Although Japan has the world's oldest population, it is not the pioneer in this activity. The British have long been relocating outside of the British Isles to the warmer climes and cheaper living available on the coasts of Spain and in Italy, as well as other Mediterranean locations. The USA has the advantage of being a large, continental country with its own Sun Belt perfectly suited for the golf courses, hot tubs, outdoor pools, tennis and shuffleboard courts, and the easy living touted by retirement communities consisting of homes and condominiums built specifically for the older buyer. Language and culture, of course, are not a problem for Americans and Canadian "snowbirds" who simply migrate south or west. Nevertheless, the high cost of living in the USA has encouraged Americans to look abroad too, mainly south of the border in Central America and the Caribbean, for environments boasting both a warm climate and a low cost of living. Panama, in particular, has become extremely popular as a long-stay destination for such retirees.[3]

---

[3]Sinpatanasakul [17] describes in detail why Panama is the number one destination for Americans seeking a low cost of living country to retire. The visa program offered by Panama, known as the "pensionado" program, provides retirees with discounts that have no serious competition anywhere else. As long as retirees are able to document a minimum monthly pension of US$500 (in addition to US$100 for each dependent), they are eligible for the pensionado visa offering the following benefits:

Import duty exemption for household goods

Tax exemption to import a new car every 2 years

For the Japanese who choose to move abroad to find pleasant and affordable surroundings, the different languages, cultures, and level of health and other services available are important considerations, and constitute substantial obstacles to the marketing of this real estate option. To date, not many older Japanese have actually migrated to the Philippines, Malaysia, Thailand or other countries that have tried to attract them in order to bring their foreign exchange into the various domestic economies. Nevertheless, the idea keeps growing, and these three Southeast Asian countries in particular seem to think that attracting the Japanese baby boomer expatriate is a viable marketing proposition. Each has devised a different program with varying financial and visa requirements (see Table 29.1).

The concept of overseas migration for the retired was introduced to the Japanese population in 1986, when the Japanese government proposed a project called "Silver Colonies" to build towns and villages for Japanese pensioners in Australia. That project never materialized because of Australian opposition. In 1992 the Japanese Long-Stay Foundation was established to facilitate long-stay tourism abroad. Southeast Asian countries began to see the economic virtue of this idea after the slump caused by the economic crisis of 1996. The crisis proved a stimulus for Malaysia, Thailand, and the Philippines to launch individual programs that created special visa categories for retirees. However, purchase behavior and incentives vary with different income groups. Japanese with higher incomes prefer to travel to various countries for a "look-see" before they decide on where to eventually settle, while less affluent retirees tend to move directly to a country because of the lower cost of living there ([16] as cited in [17]).

For these various initiatives to succeed, a health and welfare infrastructure that is Japanese-friendly must be erected. Having healthcare facilities staffed with Japanese speakers is one way Thailand has tried to make itself more attractive to the potential Japanese long-stay prospect. The relative lack of security in some of these countries when compared to Japan is another issue that must be tackled to set the risk-averse Japanese baby boomers' minds at ease. So, this is still a work in

---

50% off entertainment anywhere in the country (movies, theaters, concerts, sporting events)
30% off in-country bus, boat, and train fares
25% off in-country airline tickets
50% off hotel stays Monday through Thursday
30% off hotels stays Friday through Sunday
25% off restaurant bills
15% off at fast-food restaurants
15% off hospital bills (if no insurance applies)
10% off prescription medicines
20% off medical consultations
15% off dental and eye exams
20% off professional and technical services
50% reduction in closing costs for home loans
25% discounts on utility bills
15% off loans made in your name
1% less on home mortgages for homes used for personal residence
20-year property tax exemptions on all newly constructed homes

Table 29.1 Long-term Japanese expatriate resident requirements and conditions in three Southeast Asian countries [17]

	Thailand	Malaysia	Philippines
Visa name	Thai second home	Malaysia my second home	Special resident retiree's visa
Visa duration	Permanent	10 years	Permanent
Financial requirements	Monthly income of US$1,650 or deposit of US $25,000	Local deposit of US $87,000 (under 50); US$43,000 (over 50)	Monthly pension of US $800 + local deposit US$10,000 (over 50)
Property ownership	60/40 Thai/foreigner	Yes	60/40 Filipino/foreigner
Tax policy	Offshore income is tax-free	Offshore income is tax-free	Offshore income is tax-free
Cost of living	Rank 127th	Rank 114th	Rank 141st
Health care	Outstanding	Advanced	Advanced
Politics and crime:			
Political stability	0.55	0.51	−0.49
Terrorism index	1	1	4
Crime index	Ranked 14th	Ranked 34th	N/A
Language	Thai	English, Malay	English, Filipino

progress, but if economic conditions continue to favor an overseas cost-of-living, it is one option that Japan's silver citizens may well begin to take more seriously.

Summary and Conclusion

Enabling Japan's aging population to (1) sustain and support itself from its accumulated savings, and (2) enhance its quality of life are two goals that can best be served by innovative product development on the part of the financial services and real estate industries, but with serious attention also paid to the safety of those products, given the recent history of financial meltdowns. To summarize the key points that have been discussed in this chapter:

- The rapidity with which Japan is becoming a geriatric nation means that it must be a pioneer in creating solutions for enabling its elderly to grow old in physical comfort and financial security, or suffer the consequences of failing to do so. In this review we have examined some of the initiatives that promise to reward the creative marketer, while simultaneously fulfilling this promise of a better life for the country's seniors.
- One area of these innovations is designing financial instruments that answer the need for higher returns without unduly increasing the older investor's risk. This issue has taken on new urgency with the global impact which the recent recession and financial meltdown has had on the developed world's banking and securities industries. The crises of the past two years jeopardized not only the retirement nest-egg of millions of senior citizens in the USA, Japan, and the

European Union, but the very financial structures of those countries as well. The new cautious environment means that marketing financial services to the elderly will increasingly emphasize legal and ethical constraints on risk exposure. This will be in addition to the current Japanese focus on designing products that offer an attractive return, and on providing ancillary services that attract seniors to particular banks or financial institutions in order to capture a larger share of their investment business.

- Another initiative involves creating new and renovated housing options that are elder-friendly, including the packaging of practical offerings that would make it possible for seniors to move abroad in order to enjoy an affordable retirement lifestyle not possible on a fixed income in Japan proper. Quality of life issues relevant to older Japanese will receive increasing attention from Japanese firms that develop real estate and renovate (reform) older properties. This trend may also influence the way the residential real estate industry evolves elsewhere in the world, such as in the USA and Europe, where the population is aging more slowly but will have similar needs in the not-too-distant future as they bulk larger in those countries' total populations, and where inexpensive overseas housing alternatives might become more mainstream choices.

Time will tell which of the many options will capture the imagination – and the pocketbooks – of Japan's aging boomers. However, they are so important to the Japanese economy that their needs cannot be denied. The more attentive and creative marketers will win the competition for their patronage, as the financial services and residential real estate industries continue to transform themselves to accommodate this major consumer market.

References

1. Japan has highest ratio of elderly, government, *International Herald Tribune* (11 July 2007)
2. People age 80 and over top 7 million, *The Japan Times* (17 Sept 2007)
3. D. Turner, Money follows Japan's baby boomers, *Financial Times* (31 Jan 2007)
4. M. Nakamoto, Bid reflects a shifting climate, *Financial Times* (7 Mar 2007)
5. Nikkei, 15 Feb 2010
6. M. Yasu, F. Flynn, HSBC to expand in Japan, *International Herald Tribune* (6 Sept 2007)
7. Household assets hit record ¥1.56 quadrillion in June, *The Japan Times* (19 Sept 2007)
8. Banks gear up for insurance deregulation, *The Nikkei Weekly* (3 Sept 2007)
9. Consumers splurging on services, *The Nikkei Weekly* (19 Feb 2007)
10. M. Nakamoto, Pension attention: why the investment pots await Japan's big savings switch, *Financial Times* (12 Jan 2007)
11. D. Turner, Japanese experiment lures the risk-averse, *Financial Times* (23 Apr 2007)
12. Mutual fund buyers express discontent with banks, brokerages, *The Nikkei Weekly* (27 Aug 2007)
13. Law prompts banks to heighten protection for elderly customers, *The Nikkei Weekly* (1 Oct 2007)
14. J.M. Raymo, T. Kaneda, in *Changes in the Living Arrangements of Japanese Elderly: The Role of Demographic Factors*, ed. by J.W. Traphagan. J. Knight. Demographic Change and the Family in Japan's Aging Society (SUNY, New York, 2003), pp. 27–52

15. N. Brown, in *Under One Roof: The Evolving Story of Three Generation Housing in Japan*, ed. by J.W. Traphagan, J. Knight. Demographic Change and the Family in Japan's Aging Society (SUNY, New York, 2003), pp 53–71
16. M. Toyota, A. Bocker, E. Guild, Pensioners on the move: social security and trans-border retirement migration in Asia and Europe, ASEF-Alliance Workshop, spring 2006, *IIAS Newsletter* no. 40 (2006)
17. A. Sinpatanasakul, *Senior expatriate tide: marketing overseas housing to the retired*, MBA thesis, Waseda University, 2007
18. P. Rial, Around the markets: Leisure companies may benefit as Japanese baby boomers retire, *International Herald Tribune* (23 Feb 2007)

Chapter 30
The End of Mass Media: Aging and the US Newspaper Industry

Mark Miller

Abstract The Baby Boom generation – the largest in US history – grew up with mass media, and is by far the largest constituency for newspapers, television, and magazines. But, as audiences age and fragment, the economic foundation of these traditional media is challenged. The pain is especially sharp in the newspaper industry, giving rise to worries about the future of American journalism.

Introduction

The Baby Boom generation represents the last gasp for mass media in the USA. Boomers – the largest generation in American history – grew up with television, newspapers, and magazines, and they are the largest constituency for traditional media. However, the generations following Boomers are far less loyal, spreading their time across a wide array of new digital information choices. The pain of audience erosion has been felt most sharply in the newspaper industry, which has had the greatest difficulty attracting younger readers. Surprisingly, even older audiences (Boomers and seniors) have begun to shift their attention away from printed newspapers towards new media choices. That erosion, along with advertiser perception that older consumers are less desirable marketing targets, has rocked the economic foundation of the US newspaper publishing industry. Revenues from advertising and circulation have been falling at an accelerating rate during the recession. Investors have fled newspaper stocks, leading to a wave of industry consolidation via mergers and acquisitions.

It's ironic that the newspaper industry finds itself being punished for its audience, since Boomers are by far the most affluent American demographic segment. However, quality of audience hasn't helped newspapers convince youth-obsessed advertisers to stay on board. And investors worry – correctly – that newspapers simply won't be able to replace Boomer readers as they age and die. Indeed, a good deal of evidence points to continued fragmentation of audiences for news, entertainment, and other content as Boomers age out of the market in the coming

F. Kohlbacher and C. Herstatt (eds.), *The Silver Market Phenomenon*,
DOI 10.1007/978-3-642-14338-0_30, © Springer-Verlag Berlin Heidelberg 2011

decades. Large, mass audiences will be harder to find for all traditional media companies. Instead, media companies will find themselves responding to customer demands for customized access, and serving niche markets. The newspaper subscriber gives way to Internet users who access a story or two on a website via news integrators like Google News. Television viewers who once sat down for 2–3 hours of programs at a time now download just one show they want from the Internet. Music lovers don't buy the full CD of their favorite artists, just the individual songs they want.

Fragmentation poses a threat to all traditional media, but the threat to newspapers is especially alarming. The large editorial budgets and staffs of newspapers historically have been the most important source of the unbiased fact-gathering that is the foundation of news information flow in the US. As newspapers fall victim to fragmentation and ebbing revenue streams, it's not yet clear what new form of robust newsgathering organizations will take their place.

Newspapers face a long, difficult transition from print to success in digital media. In order to survive that transition, they will need to find a way to retain their core, older print audience as long as possible – and to convince advertisers of their value.

The US Boomer Market

Baby Boomers have dominated and shaped America's economic, political and social scenes, partly due to their sheer numbers. Born in the post-war years 1946 to 1964, Boomers account for 78 million adults, the largest generation in US history. However, the impact of Boomers also stems from a unique perspective shaped, in particular, by the coming-of-age experience of older Boomers. As young adults in the 1960s and 1970s, Boomers led the charge in massive social and political upheaval that included the civil rights and anti-war movements, feminism and women's rights, sexual freedom, drugs, and rock music. As they have moved through different stages of life, they've continued to remake their social environment. From an economic perspective, Boomers have driven sales of various industries: baby food in the 1950s and 1960s; blue jeans, fast food and rock music in the 1970s and 1980s; mutual fund companies and retirement funds in the 1990s.

In the same sense, the Boomer generation identity is linked with the explosion and dominance of mass media in the second half of the twentieth century, particularly television:

> Television separated the Boomers from every previous generation. Mass production and technological advances in the 1950s allowed most American families to own a set...in 1948 there were fewer than 400,000 TV sets in the country. Four years later there were nearly 19 million. By 1960 nine out of every ten American homes had a TV, and the average set was turned on for at least six hours every day...according to the political scientist Paul Light, the average Baby Boomer had viewed between 12,000 and 15,000 hours of television by age 16 [1].

Now, media companies face the stark reality that their most loyal audience is aging, and that the US population profile is turning more gray. The oldest Boomers turned 60 in 2006; by 2011, the number of the country's adults age 50–69 will be roughly equal to the number of adults age 30–49, according to the US Census Bureau (Fig. 30.1)

An aging customer base generally is a worry for any business, and mass media is no different. The industry relies on revenue from advertisers who, in turn, typically are hunting for young customers. The idea is to capture "customers for life" when they are in their prime as consumers. Marketers tend to see older consumers as set in their brand preferences, winding down their activities and pursuits – and not really buying much of anything [2].

The Boomer generation puts such traditional marketing thinking to the test. Just as they have put their unique stamp on every other phase of life, Boomers show signs of remaking life beyond 50. Most tell researchers and journalists that they envision an active and engaged post-50 lifestyle. Most Boomers plan to keep working in "retirement," to stay active or because the income is needed. At the same time, they intend to pursuing new passions such as travel, learning, and volunteer activities [3]. Boomer net worth has been diminished sharply by the recession, due to the plunging value of housing and retirement portfolios. However, they remain the most affluent US demographic segment; they account for 36% of the adult population, but account for a disproportionate share of wealth and consumer spending in a wide array of categories.

Newspapers have an especially commanding share of Boomer readers, who should be a premium marketing target for advertisers. Among adults age 50–59 years of age, 52% read a newspaper daily, and 60% are regular Sunday readers [4].

Still, newspapers have had trouble selling what should be a premium-marketing target to advertisers. Just the opposite, in fact: media buyers extract discounts from publishers due to the aging of their audiences [2].

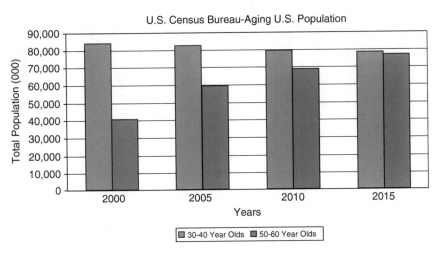

Fig. 30.1 US Census Bureau – aging US population

The Fragmenting Media Audience

At the heart of the newspaper industry's dilemma is the explosive growth in the number of consumer information options. The Internet, PDAs and MP3 players, video games, and social media websites all compete for the time and attention of consumers. And, they take time away from traditional media. Consider the following trends [5]:

- Prime-time network television declined 30% in the 10-year period ending in 2005, and the number of hours watching broadcast television overall dropped 15%.
- Total magazine circulation has been sliding since 2000.

Meanwhile, overall US Internet penetration is now at 60%. Some 45% of Americans now spend 4 h per day or more online *outside of their working hours,* a figure that rivals television usage: 65% of Americans watch 4 h or more of television per day (Fig. 30.2) [6].

Social media and websites where users create their own content are also seeing soaring use that steals time from traditional media. About 45% of Americans now use sites such as MySpace and Facebook.[1]

Although younger Americans are leading the charge in adopting new media, Boomers are definitely along for the ride. And why not? Boomers have embraced – and invented – all sorts of new technology and information platforms in their lifetimes: the personal computer, e-mail, cell phones, video cameras, MP3 players

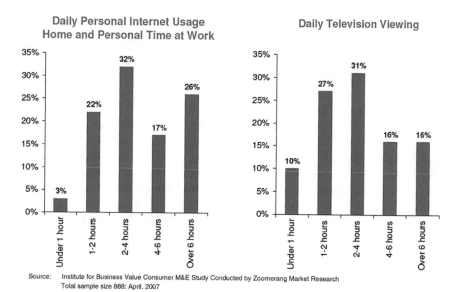

Source: Institute for Business Value Consumer M&E Study Conducted by Zoomerang Market Research
          Total sample size 888: April. 2007

Fig. 30.2 Nearly 45% of users spend over 4 h per day online for personal use; TV rivaled in attention, though 65% still watch over 4 h per day

---

[1]*Source:* IBM Corp.

and DVDs, just to name a few examples. Why would a generation so comfortable with new technology turn away from it just because they've started turning 50 or 60?

So, it should come as no surprise that 65% of Americans age 50–64 are online [7], or that time online is pulling them away from print media. As recently as 1999, 72% of US adults aged 55 and older read a daily newspaper; by 2008, that figure had slipped to 57% [8].

It's not just new media that are fueling this decline. There's striking evidence that older consumers are simply losing interest in following news. As Table 30.1 shows, the number of older Americans who feel the need to "get the news every day" fell sharply over the period 1995 to 2005. Although the reasons for this decline aren't entirely clear, some analysts point to a general societal turnoff to political and media institutions:

> Over the last 17 years, consumers of news and information have come to perceive the media as biased, inaccurate, and unprofessional. While at least one-half of all adult Americans in 2004 tended to believe their daily newspaper, believability ratings have been falling over the last several years and lag behind network television. According to the Pew Center for People and the Press, 'the public's evaluations of media credibility also are more divided along ideological and partisan lines. Republicans have become more distrustful of virtually all major media outlets over the past four years, while Democratic evaluations of the news media have been mostly unchanged.' [5]

The shift away from news is an especially negative development for newspapers, which have counted older Americans as their stronghold audience. The picture doesn't get any brighter when one projects forward to look at the media habits of younger age cohorts.

People form their news and information habits at a fairly young age, and those habits tend to stick as they age. Since 1972, the National Opinion Research Center at the University of Chicago has been asking Americans whether they read a newspaper daily as part of its well-regarded general social survey (GSS). The data reflect falling readership levels across age groups. The number of Americans age 20–29 who say they read a newspaper every day had fallen from 46% in 1972 to 21% in 2002. Clark Martire and Bartolomeo, an industry research firm that has analyzed the GSS data, predicted that 9% or fewer of 20–29 year olds would be daily newspaper readers by 2010 [9]. The age groups maintain a fairly consistent newspaper-reading habit as they age, but no age groups showed sizeable gains in readership as they grew older. In essence, newspapers are failing to replace readers as they age and die.

Impact on the Industry

The impact of falling readership has been unmistakable, using any number of yardsticks:

- *The number of newspapers.* There were 1,422 daily newspapers in the US in 2007, compared with 1,763 in 1960 [8].

Table 30.1 "I need to get the news every day": change in percentage from 1995 to 2005 by income group

"I need to get the news every day"	Total (%)	Young[a]			Family[b]			Mature[c]		
		UY	MY	LY	UF	MF	LF	UM	MM	LM
1995	50	52 (100)	39 (76)	39 (76)	50 (97)	44 (85)	37 (73)	66 (127)	61 (117)	59 (115)
2000	44	33 (100)	36 (107)	34 (101)	44 (131)	35 (109)	31 (94)	56 (167)	55 (165)	56 (167)
2005	42	38 (100)	32 (83)	32 (85)	45 (118)	35 (93)	32 (83)	59 (154)	48 (127)	47 (123)
Point change, 2005–1995	−8	−14	−8	−7	−5	−8	−6	−7	−12	−12

Source: Newspaper Association of America, Synovate Consumer Opinion Panel

[a]*UY* Upper-income young, *MY* middle-income young, *LY* lower income young

[b]*UF* Upper-income families, *MF* middle-income families, *LF* lower-income families

[c]*UM* Upper-income mature, *MM* middle-income mature, *LM* lower-income mature

- *Circulation.* Total morning and evening daily circulation stood at 52.3 million in 2006, down from 58.8 million in 1960.
- *Market penetration.* In 1950, 123% of US households bought a newspaper daily [10]. That's not a typographical error; rather, 1.23 newspapers were bought per household. By 1990, penetration had plunged to 67%, and in 2000 it was just 53%.
- *Advertising.* Total print newspaper advertising revenue was projected to end 2009 at $26.0 billion, down from $48.6 billion as recently as 2000 [11].
- *Market valuation.* Investors have fled newspaper stocks in recent years. For example, the average monthly adjusted price of shares in New York Times Co. fell 25% from January 2008 through the end of 2009.[2]

Newspapers have tried to get into the act online, but with middling results. Among the five highest-traffic US news sites in 2009, only one – the New York Times – was a newspaper website; the highest-traffic news sites were MSNBC, Yahoo!, CNN and AOL News [8] One reason for the unimpressive audience growth at newspaper sites is their mediocre website design and content. In fairness, newspaper websites operate in a vastly different competitive environment than their print counterparts. Most American cities today have just one major newspaper; a handful still have two or three local print competitors. On the Internet, newspapers find themselves competing with a vast array of news providers in a truly global market.

Even when newspapers do win the battle for online eyeballs, the revenue generated is far less than in print. Newspapers need two to three dozen web users to replace the revenue generated by a single print reader [12]. That reflects not only the loss of newspaper print circulation revenue, but online ad rates that are far lower than in print.

Future of Print Journalism

The threat to newspapers raises serious concerns about the future of serious, research-based journalism in the USA. Although magazines and some television news organizations remain committed to maintaining substantial reporting and research staffs, large editorial budgets at newspapers historically have provided the information underpinning most independent journalism in the USA. Overall newsroom employment has plunged [10], and battles between editors and corporate management have occurred repeatedly in recent years at major newspapers such as the Los Angeles Times as economic pressure grows. New York Times Co., which is well-known in the industry for lavish editorial budgets and high-quality journalism, has faced increasing pressure from investors seeking improved financial results

---

[2]*Source*: Finance. yahoo.com

[13]. Many industry observers believe the pressure will accelerate as the industry's economic underpinnings continue to weaken in the years ahead – and that news-gathering will suffer.

"The core issue is, who will pay for the reporting that is the fundamental basis for public discourse?" says Ken Doctor, author of Newsonomics: Twelve New Trends That Will Shape the News You Get (St. Martin's Press, 2010) and a former top editor and executive with newspaper publisher Knight Ridder:

> There is a fundamental difference between reporting and commentary. The emergence of blogging has made it possible for people outside newsrooms with real knowledge to comment and analyze, and get their thoughts to audiences. The problem is the original source reporting. What do people opine about? The news. The best reporting on that news feeds the commentary. Newspaper journalists have a different legacy than other journalists. They come to work every day to find out what is happening, and they don't tilt their reporting to suit advertisers, politicians or business executives. Their value system is one of no fear or favor, and that's what is threatened here.[3]

Summary and Conclusion

Newspaper publishers may be able to survive in a highly-competitive digital environment, but the transition to success will be painful and long. While fighting that battle, these companies would do well to re-focus on their core audience of Boomers, the last loyal mass audience and one with demographic characteristics advertisers *should* love. For a start, newspaper publishers need to find ways to halt the erosion of that older print audience. Then, they should lead a media industry charge to convince advertisers that Boomers have the money and want to spend it – and that newspapers are the place to reach them.

References

1. S. Gillon, *Boomer Nation: The Largest and Richest Generation Ever, and How it Changed America* (Free, New York, 2004)
2. P.L. Norton, The Last Laugh, *Barron's*, 26 Feb 2007
3. Harris Interactive, Merrill Lynch, Age Wave, *The New Retirement Survey* (Merrill Lynch, New York, 2005). http://www.ml.com/?id=7695_7696_8149_46028_46503_46635. Accessed 18 Jun 2008
4. Newspaper Association of America: *The Source: Newspapers by the Numbers* (NAA, Vienna, VA, 2006). http://www.scribd.com/doc/2293801/Newspapers-by-the-numbers-2006. Accessed 18 Jun 2008
5. Newspaper Association of America. *Growing Audience: Understanding the Media Landscape* (NAA, Vienna, VA, 2006). http://growingaudience.com/downloads/GALandscapeExec-Summary.pdf. Accessed 18 Jun 2008

---

[3]Author's personal communication with Ken Doctor on 26 September, 2007.

6. IBM, US Consumer Research Digital Entertainment and Media (IBM Institute for Business Value, April 2007). http://www.ibm.com/iibv
7. Pew Internet and American Life Project, *Older Americans and the Internet* (Pew, Washington, 2004). http://www.pewinternet.org/report_display.asp?r=117. Accessed 18 Jun 2008
8. The Project for Excellence in Journalism. *The State of the News Media 2008: An Annual Report on American Journalism* (PEJ, Washington, 2008). http://www.journalism.org. Accessed 9 Feb 2010
9. J. Bartolomeo, *Time bomb: the challenge of the next generation* (INMA, Dallas, 2002). http://www.inma.org/members/ppt/bartolomeo.ppt. Accessed 18 Jun 2008
10. The Project for Excellence in Journalism. *The State of the News Media 2004: An Annual Report on American Journalism* (PEJ, Washington, 2004). http://www.journalism.org. Accessed 18 Jun 2008
11. Silicon Valley Insider, U.S. Advertising Revenue by Medium, 27 Oct 2009. http://www.businessinsider.com/us-advertising-spending-by-medium-2009-10. Accessed 9 Feb 2010
12. E.T. Patterson, *Creative Destruction: An Exploratory Look at News on the Internet* (Joan Shorenstein Center on the Press, Politics and Public Policy, Harvard University, 2007). http://www.ksg.harvard.edu/presspol/carnegie_knight/creative_destruction_web.pdf. Accessed 18 Jun 2008
13. S. Ellison, How a money manager battled New York Times, *The Wall Street Journal* (21 Mar, 2007). http://online.wsj.com/public/article/SB117441975619343135-n166azU72Y6GkdTvl-v4nWSeWWWo_20080319.html. Accessed 18 Jun 2008

Chapter 31
Material Innovation in the Japanese Silver Market

Junichi Tomita

Abstract By means of a case study, this chapter argues what the material innovation process in the Japanese silver market should be like. Material suppliers are continuously attempting to contribute to an aging society through material innovation. Although they are not always successful in their intentions to meet the needs of users, they at times discover the actual needs of the users, which are slightly different from the perceived needs. Subsequently, these suppliers work on improving the new materials so as to meet the actual needs of users by developing a close contact with them. The case of superabsorbent polymer (SAP), studied in this chapter, is a typical example of this. We term this material innovation process an emergent process. The SAP "AQUALIC CA" launched on the market by Nippon Shokubai Co., Ltd., in 1983 is a raw material that facilitated the popularity of disposable diapers in the Japanese market. It also currently holds a large share in the American and European markets. However, it was not originally designed for use in disposable diapers, and the process it underwent from development to marketing was not linear. This case study describes how after failure in its technological development and supply agreements, success was finally achieved. Further, it indicates the effectiveness of developing evaluation technologies in the process through an end-user oriented approach. As a result, this study should prove to be a valuable aid in helping material suppliers in understanding effective innovation management.

Introduction

What should the material innovation process be like? What is effective innovation management for material suppliers? In recent times, the silver market is growing in Japan, and material suppliers are required to contribute to an aging society through material innovation. For example, nursing care goods such as furniture, food, and sanitary products are composed of several materials. Material suppliers often attempt to develop new materials. Although they are not always successful in

F. Kohlbacher and C. Herstatt (eds.), *The Silver Market Phenomenon*,
DOI 10.1007/978-3-642-14338-0_31, © Springer-Verlag Berlin Heidelberg 2011

their intentions to meet the needs of users, they at times discover the actual needs of the users, which are slightly different from the perceived needs. Subsequently, these suppliers work on improving the new materials so as to meet the actual needs of the users by developing a close contact with them. The case of superabsorbent polymer (SAP), studied in this chapter, is a typical example of this. We term this material innovation process an emergent process.

Disposable diapers first appeared in Sweden during World War II as an alternative to cloth diapers. After the war, panty-type disposable diapers were sold in the USA, and became highly popular. In the USA and Europe, with the abundant availability of wood as a resource, flocculent pulp was used as an absorbent material in these diapers. As many women had already advanced into playing active roles in society, the use of disposable diapers instead of those made of cloth allowed such working women to save time. Consequently, disposable diapers became highly popular in the USA and Europe before they attained similar popularity in the rest of the world. In Japan, however, the widespread use of disposable diapers came about much later, and until around 1980, most diapers were made of cloth.

Under such circumstances, the SAP "AQUALIC CA," launched on the market in 1983 by Nippon Shokubai Co., Ltd. (hereinafter Nippon Shokubai), began to be used as a diaper material due to its low cost and excellent absorption characteristics. As a result of the adoption of this material, disposable diapers have become highly popular in Japan, and, at the same time, the use of SAP has increased in the American and European markets.

Moreover, at present, the demand for adult disposable diapers is growing in order to support the independence of elderly people, improve the comfort level of incontinent patients, and minimize the workload on nursing care.

Currently, more than one million tons of SAP products, including AQUALIC CA, are consumed worldwide. Based on the estimation of 10 g SAP/diaper, one million tons of SAP can amount to 100 billion disposable diapers. Assuming that each child uses an average of four diapers per day, or an average of 1,500 diapers per year, these 100 billion diapers cater to the needs of as many as 65 million children.

Thus, SAP has now become the primary raw material used in disposable diapers. However, AQUALIC CA by Nippon Shokubai, one of the major SAP products, was not originally developed for use in disposable diapers. The process it underwent from development to marketing was not linear. Nippon Shokubai experienced many failures during technological development and subsequent supply agreements before finally meeting success.

Here, we examine the factors underlying the successful development of this product, as well as the process it underwent that led to its success. Further, this study indicates the effectiveness of the accumulated evaluation technologies in the process by an end-user oriented approach. Consequently, it is supposed that this study will be a valuable aid to material suppliers in understanding effective innovation management.

Market and Product

Market

Figure 31.1 shows the production volume of disposable diapers in Japan during the 12 years 1997–2008. In comparison with the production volume for adults, the production volume for children is much larger. However, the former increased rapidly since 2002. Moreover, the population structure in Japan has currently witnessed drastic changes in that the number of births has declined, but the number of elderly people over the age of 65 has increased. According to a report of the Ministry of Internal Affairs and Communications in Japan, by 2030, there will be 35 million elderly people, comprising 30% of the entire population of Japan. Further, the number of elderly nuclear families has also increased. Under these conditions, disposable diapers for adults will be more important in supporting the independence of elderly people, improving the comfort level of incontinent patients, and reducing the workload on nursing care.

Currently, approximately 10 g of SAP is used to produce one diaper. Therefore, 20 billion disposable diapers for children can be manufactured with 200,000 tons of AQUALIC CA. A child uses an average of four diapers per day or an average of 1,500 diapers per year. Hence, these 20 billion diapers can fulfill the needs of as many as 13 million children.

In 1983, Nippon Shokubai launched AQUALIC CA on the market as a SAP product. It is a type of powdered polymer called a lightly cross-linked acrylic acid polymer; moreover, for the first time in the world, it is manufactured by employing the bulk aqueous solution polymerization method. Ninety percent of the AQUALIC CA manufactured is currently used in the production of disposable diapers. In terms of the production volume of disposable diapers, about 80% of the total manufactured quantity is used for children's diapers, about 10% for adult diapers. Other uses include sanitary napkins, pet products (as an alternative to sand for cats, pet sheets,

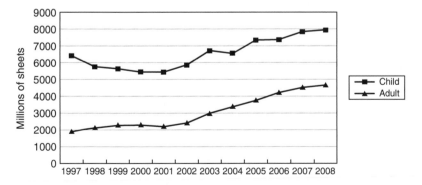

Fig. 31.1 Production volume of disposable diapers in Japan. Source: Japan Hygiene Products Industry Association

etc.), food-related products (drip-absorbent sheets), household products (disposable portable body warmers), cables (waterproof tapes for optical cables), water-retention materials for soil management, etc.

Due to its unique characteristics, described in a later section, the market share of AQUALIC CA was about 25% of the global SAP market as of 2007; it was competing with BASF of Germany for the leading position in the market. The size of the global market has reportedly reached around one million tons, or approximately 150 billion yen in value based on a rate of 150 yen/kg.

Over the past decade, the global demand for SAP has been growing at a pace exceeding 10% annually, and Nippon Shokubai has increased its production capacity accordingly (see Fig. 31.2). In 2005, the company started production at a new plant in China with a production capacity of 30,000 tons/year.

Product

Disposable diapers basically consist of a top sheet through which water can pass freely, a water-absorbing core, and a back panel that is impermeable. AQUALIC CA is used in the absorption core. Until the beginning of the 1980s, approximately 70 g of pulp was used in the absorption core. Later, the core weight was reduced to 40 g with the introduction of a SAP such as AQUALIC CA.

The use of AQUALIC CA provides advantages such as free absorbency, high maintenance capacity, high complementarities, and low cost.

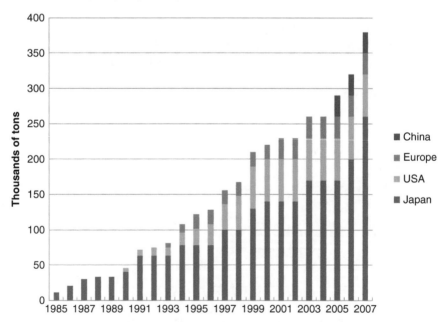

Fig. 31.2 SAP production capacity of Nippon Shokubai (volume in tons) [1]

First, it can swell considerably in volume by absorbing water (strong absorbency), and yet, it does not leak the absorbed water even under constant pressure. For this reason, when used in diapers it not only prevents the leakage of urine but also prevents the buttocks of children from becoming soiled.

Second, its capacity to disperse liquid is excellent. To increase liquid dispersion, the absorption concentration of the polymer should not be too high and the absorption speed should not be too fast. If the absorption concentration is further increased, the efficiency of the diaper decreases due to gel blocking. If the absorption speed is too fast, absorption occurs only at that portion of the diaper that has come into direct contact with urine and thus decreases the sustainability of the diaper. AQUALIC CA serves as a balance between such factors.

Third, it complements the urine absorbency of pulp. SAP can further absorb the urine after it has been absorbed by the pulp, thereby drying up the pulp and enabling its reuse.

Fourth, its cost of production is low because it can be easily mass-produced. The conventional manufacturing method (i.e., the reverse phase suspension polymerization method) was inferior in terms of its process ability after polymerization, drying ability, and mass production. The novel polymerization system and manufacturing method developed by Nippon Shokubai have greatly improved productivity.

AQUALIC CA is now widely used in the manufacture of adult disposable diapers. According to Kajiwara and Osada [2], these diapers can be divided into four types: panty-type, flat-type, supplementary pad-type, and pad-type. The panty-type diaper is an adult diaper that is most widely used. The adult panty-type diaper is similar in structure to the disposable diaper manufactured for children. The flat-type is used along with a diaper cover or a net panty. The supplementary pad-type is placed onto a diaper in order to improve the absorption capability of the diaper. These three types exhibit strong absorption and are thus used for those who require considerable protection. In contrast, the pad-type diaper has weak absorption capacity and is used by those who do not face a serious problem. The production volume of pad-type diapers has tripled over the last decade because of its high usability and low cost.

History of SAP and the Development of Disposable Diapers

SAP has evolved alongside the development of disposable diapers for children. Disposable diapers first appeared in Sweden during World War II as an alternative to cloth diapers. As in those days cloth and detergents were scarce in Sweden, the feasibility of using the country's abundant wood resources for diapers was studied. Disposable diapers are said to have originated from tissue-disposable diapers.

After the war, panty-type disposable diapers were sold in the USA, and became highly popular. In the USA and Europe, where there existed abundant wood resources, flocculent pulp was used as an absorbent material in diapers. As many women had already advanced into playing active roles in society, the use of disposable diapers enabled such working women to save the time that would have otherwise been spent washing cloth diapers. Consequently, disposable diapers became highly popular in the USA and Europe before they attained similar popularity in the rest of the world. In Japan, however, the widespread use of disposable diapers came about much later, and until around 1980, most diapers were made of cloth.

The development of SAP itself dates back to the 1960s in the USA. In those days, research on SAP in the USA focused on the water-retention materials used in soil management. The first patent for the use of SAP in disposable diapers was filed in the USA in 1972. Subsequently, in 1974, a research laboratory affiliated with the Department of Agriculture published a report stating that starch–acrylonitrile graft polymer, which used starch, was useful as a SAP.

Based on this report, Sanyo Chemical Industries, Ltd., began research on SAP. In 1978, it commercialized a SAP, and Daiichi Eizai Co., Ltd., began using this material for sanitary napkins. At around the same time, Procter & Gamble (P&G) entered into the Japanese market and began selling its disposable diapers named "Pampers." In those days, SAP had not yet been used in disposable diapers; applied research on SAP was also underway in Japan.

In such an environment, Unicharm Corp. began selling disposable diapers using SAP in 1981. Although, the product contained only a small amount of SAP, it stimulated the disposable diapers market in Japan. In 1983, Nippon Shokubai commenced the commercialization of its SAP product and in 1984, successfully launched a production plant with a capacity of 10,000 tons/year, a considerably large mass-production plant. Sanyo Chemical Industries, Ltd., the largest SAP supplier in Japan at the time, had a plant with an annual SAP production capacity of only several hundred tons.

In 1985, following the example of Kao Corp, P&G began selling disposable diapers using a large amount of SAP. As mass production commenced, the price of SAP began to decline, and the volume of SAP usage increased. Since then, the popularity of disposable diapers has sharply risen in Japan and, at the same time, the use of disposable diapers with SAP has also increased in the USA and Europe (see Fig. 31.2).

More than 90% of SAP is currently used for sanitary materials such as disposable diapers; moreover, most of this SAP is composed of lightly cross-linked acrylic acid polymers. Since this material has characteristics suited to disposable diapers and is low in cost, it has become the mainstream material used in the production of SAP. Other types of SAP have limited usage in industrial applications.

Background of the Development of AQUALIC CA

Development of Sodium Polyacrylate

As its name suggests, Nippon Shokubai (literally, "Japan Catalyst") is a company that specializes in catalyst-related technology. Since its inception, it has manufactured phthalic anhydride from naphthalene (1941), maleic anhydride from benzene

(1952), and ethylene oxide from ethylene (1959), using catalyst-based vapor-phase oxidation technology in each case.

In 1970, for the first time ever, the company succeeded in the development of acrylic acid from propylene. The research began with the aim of developing propylene acid, but failed. Instead, it developed acrylic acid. Tsubakimoto and Shimomura, both polymer (high-molecule) researchers, repeatedly developed and modified prototypes based on such accidental findings, finally succeeding in developing sodium polyacrylate (also known as polysodium acrylate or PSA).

Today, acrylic acid is an accessible material. However, until Nippon Shokubai developed a new manufacturing process, it used to be expensive because of the considerably complex methods used in its production. Specifically, acrylic ester was formerly compounded using acetylene and alcohol (in a process known as the improved Reppe method). The compound was then hydrolyzed to extract acrylic acid. This method was used by Rohm and Haas Company, Toagosei Co., Ltd., and other suppliers.

On the other hand, the manufacturing method developed by Nippon Shokubai extracts acrylic acid directly through vapor-phase oxidation of propylene, and is suited to mass production, enabling the manufacturing of acrylic acid at a low cost. Interest in polymer-based materials as alternatives to water-soluble phosphoric acid-based compounds increased due to a movement in Japan that was aimed at reducing the use of phosphorous, for example the amount of phosphoric acid contained in detergents. Under these circumstances, Nippon Shokubai succeeded in developing a low-molecule weight PSA (a product named AQUALIC L) in 1972, and sold it as a detergent builder or colorant dispersant.

In 1973, the company succeeded in developing a high-molecule weight PSA (HPSA), and marketed it for use as a flocculation and viscosity enhancer as well as a food additive. The technological experience gained in developing HPSA led to the subsequent development of a SAP. HPSA was initially difficult to mass produce. However, as mentioned later, the manufacturing method of HPSA was similar to that of SAP. Nippon Shokubai developed a super-low molecular weight PSA in 1976 and a medium-molecule PSA in 1982, increasing the sales of the AQUALIC family of products.

Development of Polymer for Sanitary Napkins

After the commercialization of HPSA, Yoshida, who was in charge of development, supplied samples to help identify new applications other than those mentioned above. Subsequently, he received the following request from a sanitary product manufacturer: we want sanitary napkins (leakproof sheets) that can be flushed away with water, and would like to try HPSA as its leakproof sheet. Sanitary napkins were made with plastic film in those days, and this made it impossible for users to dispose of them by flushing them down the toilet.

Three researchers including Shimomura commenced work on the development of a prototype using a compound of HPSA and the cross-linked acrylic acid polymers. As the alkalinity of HPSA was too strong, the product was bad for skin; therefore, researchers mixed the cross-linked polyacrylic acid with HPSA in an attempt to neutralize it. After a leakproof test was performed by Shimomura – his wife consented to be a test sample – a prototype sheet satisfying the target specifications was developed. However, some problems were encountered in the method used to manufacture the sheet for use in sanitary napkins, ending in its commercial failure.

Although the prototype could not be commercialized it was named AQUALIC CA, with the second element of the name being derived from an abbreviation of "catamenial absorbent." The research on SAPs continued; this was because it coincided with the research policy (domain) of Nippon Shokubai: "Efficient use of our own raw material (acrylic acid) and our own technology (HPSA)."

The researchers' focus on absorbency was based on the fact that the development of HPSA had repeatedly failed due to swelling, as it was not water-soluble. Shimomura believed that this characteristic could be exploited by using it as an absorbent and a leakproof material. This is a typical example of an accidental byproduct being created while developing a possible new application, just as in the development of the "Post-it."

Later, Shimomura discussed with Yoshida the possibility of using it as an absorbent; Yoshida suggested that it might be able to replace the flocculent pulp used in disposable diapers. Thus, the development of AQUALIC CA for disposable diapers began.

At the time, approximately ten suppliers in Japan were planning to launch SAP businesses using their own raw materials and their own manufacturing methods. Nippon Shokubai had already begun selling acrylic acid to customers, and some of these customers were developing SAPs. Some people within Nippon Shokubai voiced their opposition to the launching of its SAP business, arguing, "We will have to compete with our customers." For these reasons, the researchers decided to look for new customers who had no conflicting interest or to sell AQUALIC CA to customers by stressing the advantages it offered over rival products.

Development Process of AQUALIC CA

Invention of a New Manufacturing Method

The development of AQUALIC CA for use in disposable diapers began in 1978 and involved three researchers including Shimomura. These three researchers had developed cross-linked acrylic acid polymers in the previous year. At the time, they belonged to the No. 3 Laboratory of the Central Laboratory, which consisted of approximately 30 researchers. All of the researchers had a bachelor's or master's degree in chemistry. As the mainstream research themes at the laboratory were focused on the study of other high-polymers, SAP research was considered relatively offbeat and was not recognized as an official research theme. However, since

Shimomura could boast of having commercialized two research outcomes by 1973, the three researchers were able to work on SAP research without facing major constraints.

During the initial stage of development, SAP was also used in a method in which it was mixed with flocculent pulp in the manufacture of disposable diapers. First, Tsubakimoto, the manager of the No. 3 Laboratory, proposed a method that involved immersing an acrylic acid monomer into flocculent pulp by employing a special mixer. However, due to certain problems with the process, the method was not successful. Subsequently, Shimomura polymerized a monomer–water solution alone, employing a special mixer designed for different purposes. The process was successful and, it resulted in creating a polymer that had a texture similar to that of cooked rice. This was in 1980. A bench-scale plant was established in that year and the number of research members was increased to four.

This aqueous solution polymerization method was an epoch-making manufacturing method that greatly improved the productivity of SAP. Under the conventional method, referred to as stationary gel polymerization, drying the polymerized gel was to some extent difficult and the gel had to be cut into small pieces. Further, the gel had to be polymerized slowly and sliced thinly in order to dissipate heat, which would otherwise result in the degradation of the performance of the gel; the heat that was released during the process of polymerization increased the temperature and significantly lowered productivity.

The manufacturing method developed by Shimomura, on the other hand, could create a polymer that was of the size of a grain of rice during the initial process itself, eliminating the necessity to cut the gel into smaller pieces. Moreover, heat was readily dissipated, as the size of the particles was small. For these reasons, Shimomura's method was suited to mass production. This manufacturing method resolved most of the problems faced in the conventional manufacturing method. However, a problem was discovered in the absorption mechanism. Specifically, the diaper became wet and sticky at points subjected to the weight of the child after it had absorbed urine, making proper absorption impossible. To ensure that urine was absorbed properly, it was found necessary to disperse the urine evenly throughout the diaper.

Shimomura suggested making the surface of the gel particles "as hard as an eggshell." Moreover, he proposed a method of cross-linking the gel by adding a food additive to the polymerized particles. If the surface of the gel when swollen with water is solid, gaps are readily created, making uniform dispersion easier. His idea of adding a food additive was derived from his past experience in the development of SAP for sanitary napkins. In the development of the napkins, he compounded HPSA which was used as a food additive, successfully polymerizing and cross-linking HPSA in the presence of other food additives.

Since sanitary napkins are classified as quasi-drugs, approval from the then Ministry of Health and Welfare (now the Ministry of Health, Labour and Welfare) was necessary before they could be marketed. Shimomura believed that the use of food additives would make it easier to obtain government approval, and instructed his subordinate researchers, including Irie, to try this surface cross-linking method.

As a result, the surface was successfully cross-linked using this method, considerably increasing its absorption capacity. In subsequent research involving a different theme, Irie and Masuda succeeded in achieving granulation using only water, improving the appearance of its surface.

Thus, the competitiveness of the SAP product was enhanced by improving its productivity through the new aqueous solution polymerization method and by improving its properties through the surface processing method. These inventions were eventually extremely beneficial to the future of the SAP industry. However, as mentioned earlier, government approval for quasi-drugs was necessary in order to market SAP for use in sanitary napkins. The researchers visited universities and hospitals to collect data on safety, stability, analysis methods, etc., and repeatedly visited the ministry for negotiations. They finally received approval in 1983.

Development Cancellation Crisis and an Opportunity for a Large Contract

Subsequently, Nippon Shokubai received an inquiry concerning AQUALIC CA from a major sanitary product manufacturer. The researchers including Shimomura continued their development work; they were all highly motivated. Approximately 6 months later, however, the manufacturer in question announced that it would produce SAP on its own. Following this announcement, the response of the top management was to discontinue the development of SAP. Nevertheless, the researchers including Shimomura opposed this idea, and persuaded their manager to not discontinue the development. As a result, a decision was made to continue with the research, but only with a few research members.

Subsequently, Nippon Shokubai received an inquiry from a major Japanese cosmetics company regarding the use of AQUALIC CA in sanitary napkins. This prompted a decision by the top management of Nippon Shokubai to commercialize AQUALIC CA by aggressively creating sample products; moreover, a pilot plant with a production capacity of 1,000 tons was constructed in 1983. However, the company initially received very few inquiries and the operating ratio of the plant was at a very low level.

In late 1983, an inquiry was received from another major global sanitary product manufacturer, "P," for 10,000 tons of SAP. The production of 10,000 tons of SAP was considered to be a massive operation in the functional polymers industry, where an annual production of 1,000 tons was considered large.

Shimomura and the other researchers looked for a new manufacturing method to further improve productivity. During this process, his manager Tsubakimoto suggested continuously polymerizing the material instead of using the conventional batch method. Shimomura began developing a continuous polymerization method using various approaches, including modifying machines and visiting food industry exhibitions, food processing plants, etc. Subsequently, he suggested applying automatic sushi-making robot technology and developed a prototype polymerization system. The prototype system turned out to be highly practical, and the number of researchers working on the continuous polymerization method was then increased to six – three researchers each on the day and night shifts – in order to develop the production system. Finally, the continuous polymerization system was completed.

Although they were all researchers, these six people worked on the entire process, from finding new applications to approaching the users. Undoubtedly, it is the workers who are on the site who actually manufacture the product; however, it is the researchers who determine the facility conditions and product quality. Researchers with such experience have reportedly been able to develop a broad range of expertise in areas such as surveys, users, manufacturing methods, and patents in addition to expertise in their own special fields. Such a development method can be very effective with regard to functional chemical products, which require close contact with users.

Risks Involved in the Massive Supply Agreement

In February 1984, Nippon Shokubai shipped samples to company P for evaluation of the performance of AQUALIC CA produced by the continuous polymerization method, and received approval with regard to the specifications from P. In March, Nippon Shokubai signed an agreement to deliver 10,000 tons of the product, and began construction of a new production facility at the Himeji Plant. The researchers, including Shimomura, received an internal company award for their achievements.

In June of that year, however, P requested Nippon Shokubai to increase the order by an additional 10,000 tons to a total of 20,000 tons. A majority of the Nippon Shokubai directors opposed the request, saying that the risks were too high. Shimizu, the then director of the laboratory, and Shimomura were asked to attend the board meeting, and were requested by President Ishikawa to offer their opinions. Shimomura emphatically replied, "No problem. We should do it." President Ishikawa received the acquiescence of the board, and signed the agreement for an additional 10,000 tons in September.

By October, the new facility at the Himeji Plant, which had a production capacity of 10,000 tons, had almost been completed. Subsequently, on 31 October, while attending the regular end-of-month technical meeting, Tsubakimoto and Shimomura were suddenly called in by their superior, and informed that a telex had been received from P reporting that a serious problem had been discovered. The message stated that the performance of Nippon Shokubai's SAP was inferior to that of rival products.

The researchers – Tsubakimoto, Shimomura, and Irie – immediately flew to the USA. Andy Scott, the contact person for P, informed them that although the required specifications were met, the performance of the product when used in diapers was poor. What they had meant by "specifications" referred to the properties of SAP and not the performance of the diapers; moreover, P was unaware of the actual performance of the diapers until the SAP was actually applied to the diapers that it had produced.

For Nippon Shokubai, this raised the risk of losing the investment in the new 10,000-ton facility and putting the entire company in a difficult situation. The researchers' manager instructed them to improve the continuous polymerization method without making any changes to the production facility. However, the researchers including Shimomura felt that the texture of the gel created by the continuous polymerization method differed from that created by the batch method. They therefore decided to work on improving productivity by using the batch method in parallel with the continuous polymerization method. Further, they decided to keep this a secret from their manager. The researchers frequently traveled back and forth between the laboratory in Suita and the plant in Himeji, maintaining close correspondence with the manufacturing group. During the months of November and December, they carried out improvement work on weekends as well, as if each week consisted of "two Mondays, Tuesday, Wednesday, Thursday, and two Fridays."

As a result, they discovered that the productivity could be improved by using the conventional batch polymerization method. This result was reported at the end of the year to Vice President Nakajima, the head of the project. The researchers again flew to the USA with the new samples on 8 January. P reportedly performed a sample test using babies as test subjects. Test users had not meant "lead users," but common end-users. The test sample of babies couldn't suggest an idea of new diapers. The test proved that the performance of AQUALIC CA was much superior to the one of the rival products, and the researchers including Shimomura recognized that AQUALIC CA was truly successful.

Nippon Shokubai commenced the delivery of SAP to P in mid-1985, approximately 6 months after the agreed date. The agreement had stipulated that failure to deliver or purchase SAP by a predefined date would involve the payment of a penalty, as large amounts of capital investment had been made by both parties. However, as both parties had encountered problems of their own such as quality and defects in production lines in the initial stages, Nippon Shokubai was fortunate to be spared the burden of paying a huge penalty. From around August onwards, the company began to produce and deliver SAP smoothly.

First-Mover Advantage by Developing Evaluation Technologies

As mentioned later, the production of AQUALIC CA increased alongside the growth in demand. One of the reasons for the increase in production was the evaluation technology that the company had developed ahead of its competitors. The simplest evaluation method used for testing disposable diapers is the teabag method. In this method, a teabag is first emptied; subsequently, it is filled with the prototype polymer and immersed in water. Following this its weight is measured to determine its absorption strength. This measuring method was first developed by Nippon Shokubai and is now used throughout the world.

The "test of absorption strength under constant pressure" is said to be considerably more important for diapers. A diaper is subjected to pressure when used by a child who is lying down; therefore, it should be able to properly absorb urine under such pressure. Moreover, the absorbed liquid has to be uniformly dispersed throughout the diaper. Nippon Shokubai focused on such functions in the initial stages of development itself, and developed the surface cross-linking technology well before users (diaper manufacturers) requested such specifications.

Using this pressure test, the analyses by Nippon Shokubai proved that the request by diaper manufacturers for a fast absorption speed was, in fact, erroneous. The absorption speed was generally considered as "the faster the better." However, a polymer that hardens within a short period, if used in a diaper, will intensively absorb urine only where the diaper has actually come into contact with the urine. This makes the life span of the diaper shorter, even though the absorption speed will be faster. Nippon Shokubai learned through its tests that the polymer used in a diaper should gradually absorb and disperse the liquid throughout the diaper and dry the absorbed liquid.

The company later clarified another misunderstanding concerning absorption capacity – represented by claims such as "absorbs 1,000 times its volume." A polymer is generally conceived to be better if a larger amount of liquid can be absorbed by a smaller quantity of polymer. However, after absorbing the liquid, a polymer with high absorption capacity will swell and transform into a gel-like object that is as soft as tofu. This gel block prevents further liquid from being absorbed into the diaper. For this reason, Nippon Shokubai reduced the absorption capacity to only 300–400 times its volume.

Even if the specifications provided for the polymer are met, it does not necessarily guarantee that the performance of the diapers will be satisfactory. Since diapers are used over extended periods, they have to absorb urine repeatedly instead of only once. Specifications generally define values that apply to momentary use; however, it is also necessary to collect evaluation data pertaining to long-term use.

As mentioned above, premises that were initially considered to apply to the disposable diaper industry successively turned out to be inaccurate. As illustrated by the example of company P, diaper manufacturers also did not have a sufficient understanding of the functions that were actually required of diapers, nor of the technology to effectively use polymers. Shimomura stated: "That is why Nippon Shokubai's new ideas and technologies were accepted by customers."

Subsequently, Nippon Shokubai developed and improved its SAP by understanding the potential needs of children with respect to disposable diapers; moreover, it offered these new features and improvements to disposable diaper manufacturers while developing evaluation technologies by collecting feedback data. This suggests the importance of such perspectives as an end-user oriented approach, which takes into consideration the hierarchical nature of customer relationships. Specifically, in developing its products, Nippon Shokubai, a SAP supplier, not only had to listen to the requests from diaper manufacturers, its immediate customers, but also had to consider the performance of the diapers that were actually used by children, the end-users of the diapers.

Becoming the De Facto Standard

Since P, the world's largest sanitary product manufacturer, had decided to use Nippon Shokubai's SAP, major chemical suppliers throughout the world followed Nippon Shokubai's methods such as the use of acrylic acid as a raw material, and the adoption of the aqueous solution polymerization method and the surface cross-linking method. Thus, AQUALIC CA became the de facto standard in terms of both product and manufacturing method.

In reminiscing, Shimomura stated the following:

> Company P purchased AQUALIC CA for 10 years without any complaints. During that period, P did not mention anything about the product's performance – good or bad. They simply said that it was about the same as any new rival product. However, as the rival products did not utilize the surface cross-linking method, the researchers at Nippon Shokubai were confident that such rival products were inferior to AQUALIC CA in performance. But, as other companies started to catch up with AQUALIC CA after about 10 years, P, for the first time, started to request SAP suppliers to change their SAP specifications by incorporating the advantages of AQUALIC CA. In retrospect, it is apparent that AQUALIC CA boasted the highest performance among all SAP products at that time.

The production of AQUALIC CA has steadily increased in Japan since 1985. Production capacity grew at a rate of 10,000 tons annually until 1988 (see Fig. 31.2). Subsequently, in 1990, Nippon Shokubai began production abroad. In 1990, it established a joint venture (NAII) with Alco of the USA, and constructed a plant in Tennessee. In 1993, it established a joint venture with BASF of Germany and began SAP production there. Subsequently, in 2000, it constructed its own SAP plant and began production in Belgium. During these years, the global demand for SAP increased at an annual rate of more than 10%; Nippon Shokubai expanded its production capacity to meet this rising demand. In 2007, the company boasts the world's largest production capacity, amounting to 410,000 tons , from facilities that include a plant under construction in China and other plants in Japan, Europe, and the USA that are currently being expanded.

Moreover, currently, the demand for adult disposable diapers is growing in order to support the independence of elderly people, improve the comfort level of incontinent patients, and reduce the workload on nursing care. The adult panty-type diaper is similar in structure to the disposable diaper meant for children. The amount of SAP used is in the range of 13–20 g and that of pulp is in the range of 50–70 g. The concentration of SAP used in adult diapers is lower than that used in the ultrathin disposable diapers meant for children [2].

Many diaper manufactures are presently developing adult disposable diapers that have better leakage prevention and reduced thickness, through the improvement of the absorption core. Moreover, improvements in product design to make the use of diapers more comfortable are also being carried out by using a test sample of adults. A high gel strength and fast absorption speed are two indispensable properties of SAP when developing high-performance cores meant for adult diapers. Moreover, many SAP suppliers, including Nippon Shokubai, are developing such polymer gels. Improvement in the comfort level reduces the amount of workload on care providers, and further protects the privacy of the individual.

Summary and Conclusion

This case study demonstrated the innovation process of the SAP AQUALIC CA developed by Nippon Shokubai. AQUALIC CA is a raw material that has helped to increase the popularity of disposable diapers in Japan and currently holds a share of about 25% of the global market, thus making it one of the most internationally competitive functional chemical products in recent years (see [3, 4] for the definition of functional chemical products).

Recent research on product development has demonstrated that "team 'kimeko-makai' management (detailed management)" [5], "'customer of customers' strategy" [6], "management of customer system" [7], and "evaluating capability" [8] are potentially effective with regard to functional chemical products.

This case study describes the innovation process that led Nippon Shokubai from repeated failures in the technological development and supply agreements of PSA, HPSA, etc. to eventual success. It was not a linear process, but an emergent one. Further, it suggests the gaining of a first-mover advantage by developing evaluation technologies through the end-user oriented approach. Moreover, since users do not have sufficient technological capabilities to appropriately evaluate and use raw materials embodying a novel technology such as AQUALIC CA, raw material suppliers have to develop evaluation technologies by maintaining close correspondence with users right from the early stages of development in order to gain a competitive advantage. This study should prove to be a valuable aid in helping material suppliers understand effective innovation management. In other words, they need knowledge and know-how beyond their product coverage [9].

It could be also applied to other industrial goods such as components or equipments. Innovation for new final products or new system products needs both component knowledge and architectural knowledge that integrates multicomponents or equipments [10]. Generally, component suppliers have the former, system manufacturers have the latter. However, the innovative technology needed for system product innovation, such as in the auto industry, is not the same as the broader and deeper knowledge needed for component innovation [11]. So, component suppliers also have to accumulate evaluation technologies by close contact with users from the early stages of development. It should be a valuable aid for various industrial goods suppliers to understand effective innovation management.

It could be also important for system manufacturers to try to differentiate their new products from the early stages of development by close contact with suppliers having high evaluation technologies.

References

1. T. Shimomura, in *Koukyuusuisei polymer no gijutsu to kaihatsu monogatari*. (Technology and development story of superabsorbent polymer) Catalyst symposium of The Japan Petroleum Institute, 3 Mar 2004 (in Japanese)
2. K. Kajiwara, Y. Osada (eds.), *Gels Handbook* (Academic, New York, 2000)
3. K. Fujimoto, K. Kuwashima, in *Kinousei kagaku* (Functional chemicals), ed. by Kinousei kagaku sangyou kenkyuukai (Kagaku kougyo nippou, 2002), pp. 87–143 (in Japanese)
4. Kinousei kagaku sangyou kenkyuukai (Functional chemical industry research group), (eds.) *Kinousei kagaku* (Functional chemicals), (Kagaku kougyo nippou, 2000) (in Japanese)
5. K. Kuwashima, Akamon Manage. Rev. **4**(9), 459 (2005) (in Japanese)
6. K. Kuwashima, Kenkyuu gijutsu keikaku. J. Sci. Policy Res. Manage. **18**(3/4), 165 (2003) (in Japanese)
7. J. Tomita, T. Fujimoto, The Customer System and New Product Development, in *Management of Technology and Innovation in Japan*, ed. by C. Herstatt, C. Stockstrom, H. Tschirky, A. Nagahira (Springer, Berlin, 2005), pp. 73–84
8. J. Tomita, Seisanzai ni okeru teiangata seihinkaihatsu (A triad interaction model for industrial product development), Ph.D Dissertation, The University of Tokyo, 2008 (in Japanese)
9. S. Brusoni, A. Prencipe, Managing knowledge in loosely coupled networks: Exploring the links between product and knowledge dynamics. J. Manage. Stud. **38**(7), 1019–1035 (2001)
10. R.M. Henderson, K.B. Clark, Architectural innovation: The reconfiguration of existing product technologies and the failure of established firms. Admin. Sci. Q. **35**(1), 9–30 (1990)
11. A. Takeishi, *Bungyo to kyoso.* (Division of labor and competition) (Yuhikaku, Tokyo, 2003) (in Japanese)

Chapter 32
Effective Gerontechnology Use in Elderly Care Work: From Potholes to Innovation Opportunities

H. Melkas

Abstract The use of information and communication technologies (ICT), including safety alarm technologies, is increasing. Its influence on service personnel in elderly care has implications on the possibilities of rooting technological innovations into care work. Human impact assessment methodologies have been employed to assess competence related to technology use, needs for orientation into technology use, and well-being of care personnel. Safety alarms are considered useful both for actual care work and for the administrative part of the care organization. Care personnel appear not to be fully informed as to technical characteristics and the resulting organizational changes. At individual and work community levels, regular human impact assessment of new technologies may stimulate their adoption by the professional carers. This chapter is based on empirical research in a large research and development project in Finland. The research focused on safety telephones and high-tech well-being wristbands. Potholes (problems and shortcomings) lying in safety alarm systems were identified – taking into account the technology as well as services and organizational networks. The potholes may also be looked into as sources and opportunities for potential future innovation. Social, organizational, process and marketing innovations – combined with technology – are significant parts of the innovation activity related to the aging of the population.

Introduction

Implementing information technology requires changes in work practices and in collaboration among organizations, as well as in knowledge and skill levels of personnel [1–6]. Since technology and care service are commonly not felt as being connected [7], the introduction of such technologies may lead to fatigue, loss of work motivation, additional costs, unwillingness to use the technology, or a decrease of well-being at work [3, 8–10], resulting sometimes even in premature loss of experience and professional skills of elderly workers in the workforce [11, 12].

F. Kohlbacher and C. Herstatt (eds.), *The Silver Market Phenomenon*,
DOI 10.1007/978-3-642-14338-0_32, © Springer-Verlag Berlin Heidelberg 2011

This chapter includes results of empirical research on the impact on workers and workplaces within elderly care in Finland of safety telephones and a high-tech well-being wristband that monitors vital signs, in order to find factors to speed up adoption of technological innovations in care organizations.

The Finnish population is aging rapidly. According to population forecasts, one out of four Finns will be aged over 65 in the year 2030. High pressure is placed on services for the elderly. Safety telephones and wristbands that enable a call for help by pushing just one button increase the possibilities for an aging person to continue to live in her or his own home, even when there is a need for assistance. Aging people usually wish to live at home as long as possible, and safety alarm systems are part of today's structure of elderly care in Finland. Feelings of insecurity and fear are among the most common reasons for moving into a block of service flats or an old-age home. Safety alarm systems increase the user's feeling of safety and security, and their use has increased in private homes. They are also utilized in institutional settings to facilitate the work of care personnel, who can provide help more quickly in cases of need, such as when an aging person has fallen on the floor and is unable to get up without assistance [9].

Of the some 70,000 safety alarm systems in use in Finland today, more than half have been acquired by private citizens at their own expense. The rest are owned or maintained by municipalities as part of the public service provision. Safety alarm services are offered by private companies (in specific geographical areas or nationally), municipalities, foundations, nongovernmental organizations and co-operatives [9].

The system of safety alarm services includes a call center that receives alarm calls and gives guidance to customers or, if necessary, calls out a service provider who goes to the aging person's home to provide help. The call center also receives notifications concerning technical faults or service needs related to alarm appliances. Call centers may be tiny internal units in old-age homes or blocks of service flats that serve only the residents, large centers that serve thousands of customers from all over the country, or something between, such as municipal centers [9]. The services focused on in this chapter are provided within blocks of service flats or in home care.

A safety alarm customer may call for help by pushing the button on her/his wristband or pendant. The customer is then connected to the call center and may communicate by speech with the person in charge at the center. The service provider must arrange a quick and effective response to an alarm signal at all times. The type of response depends on the type of reason for alarm call. Typical responses are verbal advice, visit by a safety helper, or calling out emergency services (such as ambulance) [9].

Safety alarm systems are concrete examples of gerontechnology. Gerontechnology means research, development, and implementation of specific technologies (devices or environments) for the benefit of the whole aging population or its parts [13, 14]. Gerontechnology has five roles in supporting aging people [15]:

- Preventive: gerontechnology solutions aim at preventing weakening of health
- Supports strengths: gerontechnology develops methods and devices that help in reaching a wider benefit from aging people's strengths at work, in leisure time, in learning and social interaction
- Compensates for weakening abilities: gerontechnology produces methods, devices and products that compensate for weakening senses or ability to move
- Supports care work: gerontechnology provides technology for care workers to support their work
- Furthers research: gerontechnology helps aging people indirectly by supporting scientific and clinical research

This chapter focuses on the fourth role – the role that supports care work. The research methodology is described in the Appendix. Altogether, 78 workers were targeted in their relation to current and future use of safety alarms. Their customers were using a traditional safety telephone or a high-tech well-being wristband that automatically monitors the user's activity level 24 h a day by measuring micro- and macro-movement, skin temperature, and skin conductivity. It contains a manual alarm button, but will also trigger an alarm if and when the user is unable to do so. If desired, the system also provides an automatic notification when the wrist unit is removed or reattached (Fig. 32.1). The wrist unit continuously monitors its own performance, automatically transmitting alarms of any connection problems.

Effects of safety alarm use were investigated with the help of human impact assessment methodologies [16, 17]. Questions asked related to, for instance, linkage of technology to health (including perceived health), social effects such as trust and commitment, and to time use, information flows and network collaboration [9, 18], feelings of participation, as well as economic situation at the workplace. Results are presented qualitatively.

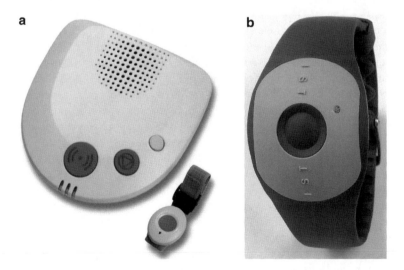

Fig. 32.1 The safety telephone (**a**) and the well-being wristband "Vivago WristCare" (**b**) that were tested (photographs by Miratel Oy and IST Oy)

Results of Empirical Research on the Use of Safety Alarms

Organizational Issues

In certain blocks of service flats, the safety technology is felt to be useful and vital for work, whereas in some others it is felt to cause harm and a notable amount of extra work – instead of help. Extra work is caused by so-called needless alarms made by customers, and false alarms made by accident or due to technical failures, such as false routing of alarm calls due to the structure of the building (walls, etc.). The caregiver also has to prepare a written statement on received alarms on a personal computer.

In addition to general organizational issues, substitutes and managers were specifically addressed. Lack of abilities among substitutes influences time use, as the permanent staff has to spend time on guiding them and supervising their work. Disagreements in the work community may be caused by a situation where some of the personnel are more committed to use of an appliance or a system and know it better.

Some typical positive answers concluded that unnecessary visits to customers have ended, work motivation has increased, tasks and time use at work can be planned better if the system is well learnt, welcome changes are brought to work, and customers feel that they are heard and get help. The work of the care worker on the night shift is felt to become easier if she/he can deal with the matter on the phone with the customer. Customers have the possibility to live a peaceful life of their own and receive services only when they wish.

The safety technology provides increased tools for managers. They can monitor the needs for help of customers and the reactions of care workers, and assess whether these meet. They can also monitor overall workload better. It is motivating for both care workers and managers that when a care worker writes an alarm record, including the work done to respond to it, it makes her/his work visible in a new way.

Some typical negative answers concluded that due to safety alarms, the work schedule and thoughts get mixed up. Recording of alarm calls causes extra work. All personnel at the workplace are not committed and do not take responsibility for this matter. Substitutes usually do not know the customers, so there are easily misunderstandings, and the information received on the phone cannot always be trusted. Substitutes in very short employment relationships have difficulties in being able to participate in the system and utilize it properly, due to lack of time to get acquainted with it. Those among the personnel who have good knowledge must be ready to answer the questions of substitutes.

Negative answers also revealed that customers are visited at 2 h intervals (in blocks of service flats), but still they call; the meaning of the wristband is forgotten or misunderstood. The financial cost of the system in comparison with the real benefit was felt to be in contradiction, and this could cause pressure in managers' expectations with regard to employees and their work.

Ethics of technology were also addressed. Customers may feel lonely when there is only the safety phone and no-one comes to visit them. The care worker cannot always come right away to help the customer, and some customers may not call even if they have a real need for help.

Trust, Skills and Motivation

There may be problems in answering an alarm call made by a customer. Transferring calls for help from one caregiver to another through the phone that first receives them has been problematic. This transfer requires pushing a series of numbers in a situation where the caregiver may be in the process of helping another customer.

False guidance from producers of alarm systems concerning waterproofness and use during washing, bathing, and a sauna visit threatened secure functioning. Care workers do not have accurate and sufficient knowledge of these technical characteristics that have a significant impact on secure functioning. They may give the elderly user guidance such as that using the alarm device is all right in all circumstances. Care workers feel that it is a great benefit that the device can be carried at all times; when they trust that the customer can get help anywhere, they are slightly less concerned about the customer's well-being. This is, however, based on inaccurate information. Such matters highlight the importance of continuous orientation and training of personnel, as well as responsibility from the producers of appliances.

Still, the impact of introduction of new technology on professional self-esteem is considerable. Lack of adequate skill and knowledge levels leads to feelings of insufficient capabilities. This, in turn, may lead to decreased motivation, fear, and distress.

Some typical answers concerning trust, skills, and motivation included decreased work motivation, because you cannot trust the system completely. Senior personnel felt more uncertain in using technological aids and even had fears. Senior personnel may feel that new things are "useless" and difficult to learn. Technology causes a feeling of ignorance and "insignificance." Constantly keeping up with the development of technology is difficult to handle, also for managers. Senior personnel may hand technology-related tasks over to younger and more capable workers. Managers are concerned with how care workers cope at work.

Workers thus ask for more or better training. Different professional groups' needs must be mapped to find out who really benefits from training. It is important to try to organize different study plans for people with different backgrounds and abilities. There must be cooperation in learning: the young learn from the older, and the older learn from the younger. Everyone at the workplace should be able to take part in training, as safety alarm systems have an impact on different professional groups. The system is burdensome if orientation into use is not given – to substitutes, for instance.

Inability to analyze different kinds of sleep diagrams of the well-being wristband exists quite often. An experienced nurse may be able to analyze a customer's health condition on the basis of the curves and assess the impact of medication, but this is not self-evident. The curves are felt to be partly easy but partly difficult to understand, and training is required to make use of them efficiently.

Services Rendered

Additional effects of safety telephones and well-being wristbands are, inter alia, effects on feelings of health, atmosphere in the workplace, time use, and attitudes, as well as effects on opportunities to participate in, contribute to, and influence the work community. A well-being wristband may be seen as a uniting factor in the work community – "our thing" that influences the atmosphere in the workplace positively.

Some typical answers were those highlighting everyone's commitment to respond to alarm calls. Safety alarm systems enhance coping at work, and in line with training, they function as a creator of community feeling at work. Systems keep the brain vigorous and give an opportunity to develop one's competence. On the other hand, junior personnel felt that "one can feel to be 'above others' when this area at work is well-learnt."

However, the service system outside the workplace should also be taken into account. Its practical significance depends on the type of the safety telephone system – whether it is an internal system in one municipality or based on services purchased by a municipality from a commercial company [9]. Also, caring family members and relatives are addressed. Some typical answers concluded that near relatives are satisfied because they know that safety is secured. Some relatives suppose that the "machines" play a bigger role in monitoring of customers' health condition than they actually do.

Discussion: How to Avoid Potholes?

New Individual Competence Requirements

In spite of problems and drawbacks, the employees focused on often feel that receiving and recording safety alarm calls is easier than normal use of computers. This may be due to regarding safety systems as a direct help and tool for elderly care, and seeing the ability to utilize them more as a professional skill than the use of computers as such. Safety alarms are assistive devices in daily use, accepted as part of work. They are felt to save time and financial resources, bring smoothness to planning of work, and maintain customers' independence and self-management.

Experiences of using safety alarm systems may, however, be quite different depending on the individual employee. Some feel that a certain procedure such as recording an alarm call is cumbersome, while others do not think so.

Fears and doubts of personnel are mainly related to situations where the safety technology does not function, or where customers are unable to use it with personnel on duty far away. In many workplaces, a safety telephone is "the caregiver" of an elderly person at night, their only link to the surrounding world. Some employees feel distressed because of this situation, as they suspect that all elderly people cannot manage with a mere safety telephone, but need another human being to be close by. In short, the technology is not fully trusted.

Still, the ability to use safety alarm technologies has become a central competence area. It has been found in earlier research that conditions are present to involve home nurses more explicitly in the introduction of assistive devices to their patients [19]. This finding is supported by our results. It is not only a question of care in this competence area, but also of the ability to guide customers in their use of technology. Professional carers such as nurses are indeed important contributors to the use and integration of technological innovations in social and health care [20].

Strength of Orientation

Most of the negative effects of safety alarm technology use could have been eliminated or relieved by means of good orientation, based on foresight information and assessment, as reported earlier [10, 21]. Introduction of technology into the workplace may have a significant impact on professional self-esteem. Without an appropriate level of skills and knowledge, feelings of insufficiency and incapability arise, leading to lowered motivation, fear, and distress. Poor abilities and possibilities to use technology have caused severe conflicts in some workplaces. The conflicts may, on the surface, seem to be due to something other than technology use, so solving them may be very difficult and depart from false assumptions.

The most significant factor related to introduction of technology that motivates an individual employee is the benefit that she/he gets from using it. Different types of impact of technology use are often indirect and difficult to identify. The skill level of each employee is different, and employees have different attitudes towards changes at work. Introduction of technological innovations to the workplace is development work in the same way as creating a quality management system or introducing team work. A technical device is not born and used in a vacuum: behind the technology, there is an organization and service activities, and a user with her/his own values and working (or living) environment. This is especially important when orientation is taken care of by an outside consultant or trainer. Producers of appliances and systems often organize initial training, but that kind of training rarely takes into consideration the specific needs of an individual workplace – let alone an individual employee. It is even more problematic to find a common language and a suitable starting level for a trainer who does not work in the care sector.

Orientation into technology use is one central area in introduction of technological innovations into work. Orientation should depart from individual employees' needs, and cover all aspects of assessment of work processes, technical orientation, and security issues, as well as support after the introduction of a device or a system. Continuous orientation is especially important for those in temporary employment relationships.

Orientation should not stop where technology has been brought to use and the necessary skills have been learnt. A well-managed orientation system includes assessment and updating of skills when systems or devices are updated and renewed. The different stages of the continuous orientation process need to have a clear beginning and end but, as a process, it should go on in the workplace in one way or another all the time [10].

When considering the necessary skills, relevant questions are views of the role and usefulness of technology in the workplace. What are the aims of introducing it? It is not uncommon that the aims are unclear to various stakeholders [22]. A foresight assessment should also cover the necessary level of competence of individual employees. Is it sufficient if basic skills are learnt, or should every employee also be able to take care of more demanding tasks, such as taking out various types of reports from the system of well-being wristbands?

Importance of Impact Assessment

Areas that are directly or indirectly related to technology use may be well-identified with the help of human impact assessment methodologies. If a decision is made to introduce well-being wristbands, including their accessories, in a block of service flats, this implies changes in work processes. Impact assessment produces information to support decision-making and development (Fig. 32.2). In the case of technology use, an assessment to be made before its introduction is the most

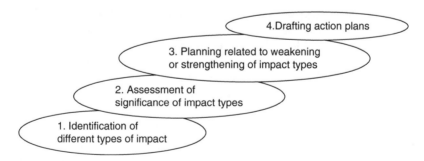

Fig. 32.2 A typical impact assessment process

beneficial. A central principle in impact assessment is collaboration; it gives personnel an opportunity for participation and dialogue. Impact assessment takes into consideration views of different groups of workers and of individual workers.

According to experiences from empirical research, results of impact assessments make attitudes, expectations, fears, and values visible – ready to be discussed and targeted in development efforts [17, 21]. In the use of technological innovations, experiences and views are highly varied. Impact assessment processes also give a lot of information for the benefit of planning orientation and training that were found to be essential. The social and health care sector is hierarchical, and a positive assessment culture has hardly been developed for individual workplaces of this sector in Finland.

The impact of technology use on care workers may be dependent on the ways in which customers use technology. Safety alarms are a typical example. If a customer uses the safety alarm too often or too seldom, it has an impact on the care worker. If the customer forgets to use the alarm altogether, perhaps due to beginning dementia, it has an impact on the care worker. According to the empirical research results, rather than drawing conclusions on impacts of technology use at a general level it is essential to pay detailed attention to impacts on care workers at an individual workplace, and thereafter to weakening of negative impacts and strengthening of positive impacts.

In introduction and impact assessment related to technology, managers have a central role in many ways. They must be able to assess and supply useful technologies at a suitable pace of introduction into the work processes of each individual employee. This would be a big step on the road to effective adoption of new, innovative technologies. In addition, regular human impact assessments of technology are expected to lead to savings in acquisition, training, orientation, and other costs; however, they are still commonly seen as an unnecessary extra cost. There is still a lot to be done to further sober application of technological innovations, including a holistic view of their suitability for customers and employees alike.

Other Factors

In order to avoid potholes in effective use of technological innovations, ethical questions and acceptability of technology use in care work should be targeted in discussions at workplaces. Care workers have many questions and concerns related to these themes, and they need attention in joint discussions between and among workers and managers. This was found to enhance sober and efficient application of technology as well as well-being at work.

Awareness among municipal authorities of preconditions of technology use in elderly care is one further factor to be developed if potholes are to be avoided. In Finland, municipal decision-makers draft strategies for elderly care, but managers at workplaces may have difficulties in implementing them. Care workers usually have no knowledge of the strategies, although they should provide the guidelines for practical work. Issues related to use of technology in elderly care are described at a superficial level, if at all. Impacts of technology use are not taken into account. There are most often formulations that technology use will be increased, but considerations of what this means in practice in the daily lives of care workers and customers are missing.

Increased use of technological innovations in elderly care requires comprehensive and coherent transmitting of actual attitudes and practices from decision-makers and managers to care workers. Wrong or inappropriate decisions lead to expensive solutions that may even weaken the quality of the service experienced by customers and lead to burn-out among care workers, as their work processes change.

Technology Use: Like Assembling a Mosaic

This chapter is based on research concerning employees in elderly care. In related research, many impacts on other groups have been identified (e.g., [23, 24]). For instance, managers and decision-makers need (1) novel competences and new knowledge (e.g., competence to give guidance in technology use and competence to assess impacts), (2) network management skills (to manage service networks consisting of the public, private and nongovernmental third sectors), (3) process management skills (e.g., acquisition, introduction, orientation and follow-up processes related to technology use), (4) change management skills (e.g., common rules of the workplace with regard to technology use), and (5) information and knowledge management skills (increase in information on the elderly person and other types of information – Who handles it? How? Where? and When?).

Potholes in effective use of technology in elderly care have been summarized as follows [22]:

- *Impact assessments* on technology use are missing, although they should form part of development of service quality
- Lack of awareness concerning the need for *competent and tailored orientation into technology use* (including elderly people, their near relatives, care work community – and the service network, where appropriate)
- Insufficient consideration of *aims, operational processes, ethical issues and acceptability of technology* (attitudes of different people)
- *Awareness-raising needed among decision-makers* concerning elderly care, technology use in it and impacts of technology use; opportunity costs are not considered
- *Public discussion on technology use is black-and-white* (negative–positive), although it should cover 'all colours' (different types of users, needs, and aims of use)
- Suitability of technology for all age groups – *Design for All thinking* should be encouraged and *users' views* incorporated into technology development (not just those of "experts" and young users)

The more technological is the device, the more challenging becomes the management of the whole of the use. It is time to vigorously start striving for a holistic approach to technology use in elderly care; otherwise the danger is that when technology becomes increasingly fragmented, technology-related competence and knowledge are also broken up into smaller and smaller pieces that drift further apart from each other. Technology use is a mosaic that needs to be planned and assembled in broad-based cooperation [22].

From Potholes to Innovation Opportunities

Innovations have traditionally been seen to be linked to high-technology fields of industry, but lately, the definition of innovation has been expanded more and more. One expansion has been to introduce and emphasize social innovations alongside the traditional technological or product innovations. Innovations related to aging are a broad phenomenon, and there is an increasing social demand for them. When developing and implementing the technology for aging, related innovation processes cannot be merely technology-driven by nature.

It is thus necessary to broaden the insight of technological innovations to be linked to other perspectives of innovation. Contexts have an impact on seeing the innovation potential in assistive technology. Broader perspectives and a holistic approach offer new platforms for innovation potential linked to a single product [25]. Social, organizational, process and marketing innovations – combined with technology – are significant parts of the innovation activity related to aging of the population.

The potholes – problems and shortcomings – in safety alarm systems can also be seen as opportunities and drivers for innovation, because triggers for innovation often arise from practice-based situations – for example, bad experiences with regard to reliability of technology or unsatisfactory service situations. Innovations in the social and health care sector are often responses to problems perceived (see, e.g., [26]) rather than careful foresight. A more conscious change in the way of thinking concerning potholes as opportunities for innovations could, however, be made. After all, Drucker [27] noted that systematic innovation begins with the analysis of sources of new opportunities. Understanding and opening up the diversity of aspects of safety alarm systems is also needed in developing the innovation *processes* – ways of *creating* new innovations and implementing and embedding of innovations, for example new models for integrating the service system into the aging people's everyday lives and the work practices of the care workers [25].

Pekkarinen and Melkas [25] categorized potholes in safety alarm systems into the following types:

- Technological pothole
- Service pothole
- Process pothole

- Organizational pothole
- Marketing or supply pothole
- Social pothole
- Ethical pothole

These were then used to sketch 'bas' (shared concrete or virtual spaces for interaction and knowledge creation; cf. knowledge management; [28]) for techno-logical, service, process, organizational, marketing or supply, social and ethical innovations. This is one way to achieve a more conscious change in the way of thinking concerning potholes as opportunities for innovations. Various innovation types usually coexist, and pure types hardly exist – for example, supporting independent living of elderly people is a very broad innovation topic – but dividing innovation roughly into types ensures that innovation is looked at from different perspectives, and may also contribute to distinguishing cause–effect relationships and coimpacts of various innovations [25].

Summary and Conclusion

Healthcare and social care form a large, societally highly important sector. It is especially large in Northern European countries in comparison with many others but, anywhere in the world, questions concerning social and healthcare interest both scientists and the general public. The sector is also an important employer, whether organizations represent the public, private, or the third sector. In many countries, this sector is undergoing major changes, and suffers from lack of financial resources as well as of personnel. Many other types of changes take place in individual organizations of the sector: technological innovations are introduced in an increas-ing amount to cope with the workload, collaboration between the three sectors is increasing, and the existing personnel often face problems in coping at work.

This chapter has focused on issues that typically cause potholes in the introduc-tion and use of technology in care work. In care organizations, abilities related to technology use have not yet become a central competence area at work, but the most important abilities are knowledge and skills related to care work itself and to illnesses. The view of competence in technology use as part of care work should, however, be widened. On the basis of results of empirical research conducted in Finland on safety telephones and high-tech well-being wristbands, this chapter illustrates the multifaceted influence of technology use on service personnel in elderly care. This influence has implications on the possibility of rooting techno-logical innovations into care work.

Regular human impact assessment of new technologies may stimulate their adoption by professional carers. Most of the negative effects of safety alarm technology use could be eliminated or relieved by means of good orientation based on foresight information and assessment. The effectiveness and economic significance of technology use consist, for instance, of the impact of employees' well-being on productivity, and of sober utilization of technology in work processes. Detailed attention has to be paid to impacts on individual care workers, and thereafter to weakening of negative impacts and strengthening of positive impacts.

This chapter shows what technology use may mean in practice in the daily lives of care workers and their customers. When employees become familiar with technological innovations by having enough time and space to learn, they can also adjust technology to their own needs. Impact assessments and related needs for orientation are not as such tied to any particular sector, workplace, profession, or theme or change being assessed, so their potential usability and applicability in developing and investigating services and work communities are much larger than could be described in this chapter. It is a question of rooting a general positive assessment culture into services, workplaces, and the development of one's own work.

A positive assessment culture and identification of potholes also serves as a valuable basis for recognizing opportunities for novel, holistic innovations with regard to technology use. They may be, for instance, service, process, organizational, marketing or supply, social and/or ethical innovations, or combinations of those.

Acknowledgments The empirical research was financially supported by the National Workplace Development Programme (TYKES) of the Finnish Ministry of Labour.

Appendix: Methodology

The empirical research focused on eight workplaces of care personnel, of which seven were blocks of service flats (sheltered accommodation) and one was a unit providing home care. Financing was public (four cases) or other (four cases: foundations and nongovernmental organizations). Some of the organizations included were eager to try out new technologies, others were not for or against, while some resisted new technology use or had very little experience so far. The workplaces were located in different parts of Finland and employed 7–60 persons from different professional groups (mainly assistant nurses and nurses). The care workers focused on had both permanent and temporary employment relationships. Altogether, 78 workers were targeted in their relation to current and future use of safety alarms. The customers were given a traditional safety telephone or a high-tech well-being wristband (Vivago WristCare) that automatically monitors the user's activity level 24 h a day by measuring micro- and macro-movement, skin temperature, and skin conductivity. It contains a manual alarm button, but will also trigger an alarm if and when the user is unable to do so. If desired, the system also provides an automatic notification when the wrist unit is removed or reattached (Fig. 32.1). The wrist unit continuously monitors its own performance, automatically transmitting alarms of any connection problems.

Effects of use of safety alarms were investigated with the help of human impact assessment methodologies that were originally developed for the planning of physical environments. They consist typically of four phases (1) identification of different types of impact by filling in forms, discussing, and/or interviewing, (2) assessment of significance of the different types of impact, (3) planning concerning weakening or strengthening the different types of impact, and (4) drafting action plans [16, 17, 21]. From May 2005 to September 2006, eight impact assessment processes were undertaken in the care organizations by three researchers. A typical assessment process lasted for approximately half a year with several assessment events.

There was only one man among the professional carers involved, as the workplaces were female-dominated. The share of older employees over 45 years of age was fairly large. The employees participated in the assessment processes by filling in pre-prepared forms in groups of 2–3 employees, or individually in certain cases. They also participated in subsequent discussions on the results of the assessment. Questions asked related to the linkage (impact) of technology to health (including perceived health) and to social effects, such as trust and commitment, time use, information flows and network collaboration [9], attitudes and disagreements, feeling of participation, meaningfulness of work, need for training, services, economic situation at the workplace, and other possible types of impact (image of the workplace, and private life of the professional). Results were analyzed qualitatively.

References

1. R.B. Cooper, R.W. Zmud, Information technology implementation research: a technological diffusion approach. Manage. Sci. **36**, 123–139 (1990)
2. F.D. Davis, R.P. Bagozzi, P.R. Warshaw, User acceptance of computer technology: A comparison of two theoretical models. Manage. Sci. **35**, 982–1002 (1989)
3. H. Jurvansuu, J. Stenvall, A. Syväjärvi, *Information Technology and Workplace Practices in Health Care: An Assessment of TEL LAPPI Project (in Finnish)* (Ministry of Labour, Helsinki, 2004)
4. R. Miettinen, S. Hyysalo, J. Lehenkari, M. Hasu, *From Product into Tool at Work? New Technologies in Health Care (in Finnish)* (Stakes, Helsinki, 2003)
5. G.L. Rafnsdottir, M.L. Gudmundsdottir, New technology and its impact on well-being. Work **22**, 31–39 (2004)
6. G.L. Rafnsdóttir, L.R. Sigurvinsdóttir, Cyberfeminism in the Nordic Lights, in *Digital Media and Gender in a Nordic Context*, ed. by J. Sundén, M. Sveningsson (Cambridge Scholars, Newcastle, 2007), pp. 223–242
7. A. Barnard, Philosophy of technology and nursing. Nurs. Philos. **3**(1), 15–26 (2002)
8. T. Cox, A. Griffiths, S. Cox, *Work-Related Stress in Nursing: Controlling the Risk to Health.* Working paper CONDI/T/WP.4/1996 (International Labour Office, Geneva, 1996)
9. H. Melkas, *Towards Holistic Management of Information Within Service Networks: Safety Telephone Services for Ageing People.* Doctoral dissertation (Helsinki University of Technology, Helsinki, 2004). http://lib.tkk.fi/Diss/2004/isbn9512268868/. Accessed 6 Jan 2007
10. A. Raappana, M. Rauma, H. Melkas, Impact of safety alarm systems on care personnel. Gerontechnology **6**(2), 112–117 (2007)

11. N.S. Ghosheh Jr., S. Lee, D. McCann, Conditions of work and employment for older workers in industrialized countries: understanding the issues. *Conditions of Work and Employment Series No.* 15 (International Labour Office, Geneva, 2006)
12. J. Siltala, *The Short History of Worsening Work Life (in Finnish)* (Kustannusyhtiö Otava, Helsinki, 2004)
13. H. Bouma, Gerontechnology: Emerging Technologies and Their Impact on Aging in Society, in *Gerontechnology: A Sustainable Investment in the Future*, ed. by J. Graafmans, V. Taipale, N. Charness (IOS, Amsterdam, 1998), pp. 93–104
14. T. Harrington, M. Harrington, *Gerontechnology: Why and How* (Shaker, Maastricht, 2000)
15. J. Kaakinen, S. Törmä, *A Pilot Study on Gerontechnology: The Ageing Population and Opportunities Related to Technology (in Finnish)* (Office of the Parliament, Helsinki, 1999)
16. T. Kauppinen, K. Nelimarkka, A review of Finnish social and health impact assessments. J. Environ. Assess. Policy Manage. **6**(1), 1–17 (2004)
17. T. Kauppinen, K. Nelimarkka, *Human Impact Assessment (HuIA) as a Tool of Welfare Management* (National Research and Development Centre for Welfare and Health, Helsinki, 2004). http://info.stakes.fi/NR/rdonlyres/8028AF2D-4E9D-4965-B9B9-E3E2FF6626DB/0/huiatrainingmaterial.pdf. Accessed 20 Jan 2008
18. H. Melkas, Analyzing Information Quality in Virtual Networks of the Services Sector with Qualitative Interview Data, in *Challenges of Managing Information Quality in Service Organizations*, ed. by L. Al-Hakim (Idea Group, Hershey, 2007), pp. 187–212
19. M. Roelands, P. Van Oost, A.M. Depoorter, A. Buysse, V. Stevens, Introduction of assistive devices: home nurses' practices and beliefs. J. Adv. Nurs. **54**(2), 180–188 (2006)
20. J. Webster, J. Davis, V. Holt, G. Stallan, K. New, T. Yegdich, Australian nurses' and midwives' knowledge of computers and their attitudes to using them in their practice. J. Adv. Nurs. **41**(2), 140–146 (2003)
21. H. Melkas, A. Raappana, M. Rauma, T. Toikkanen, *Human Impact Assessment of Technology Use in Workplaces of Elderly Care Services (in Finnish)* (National Workplace Development Programme Tykes, Helsinki, 2007)
22. A. Raappana, H. Melkas, *Teknologian hallittu käyttö vanhuspalveluissa: opas teknologiapäätösten ja teknologian käytön tueksi/ Helhetssyn vid användning av teknologi inom äldreomsorgen: handbok till stöd för teknologibeslut och användning av teknologi* (Holistic View of Technology Use in Elderly Care Services: Handbook to Support Decisions Concerning Technology and Use of Technology; in Finnish and Swedish) (LUT Lahti School of Innovation, Lahti, 2009)
23. H. Melkas, Informational ecology and care workers: Safety alarm systems in Finnish elderly-care organizations. Work: A Journal of Prevention, Assessment and Rehabilitation **37**(1), 87–97 (2010)
24. H. Melkas, S. Pekkola, S. Enojärvi, S. Makkula, *Vanhusten hyvä kotona asuminen: tutkimusta kuntatuottavuudesta, älykodeista ja apuvälinepalveluprosesseista* (Good Living at Home of the Elderly: Research on Municipal Productivity, Smart Homes and Service Processes Related to Assistive Devices; in Finnish). Liitu tutkimusraportti 17. (Lappeenranta University of Technology, Lahti Unit, 2008)
25. S. Pekkarinen, H. Melkas, Safety alarm systems and related services: From potholes to innovation opportunities. International Journal of Service Science, Management, Engineering, and Technology (accepted to be published, forthcoming)
26. P. Cunningham, *Innovation in the Health Sector: A Case Study Analysis.* Innovation in the Public Sector. Report; D19. (European Commission, PUBLIN, 2005). Available online at: http://www.step.no/publin/reports/d19-casestudies-health.pdf. Accessed 25 June 2009
27. P.F. Drucker (N. Stone, ed.), *Peter Drucker on the Profession of Management.* Harvard Business Review Book Series (Harvard Business School Press, Cambridge, 1998)
28. I. Nonaka, H. Takeuchi, *The Knowledge-Creating Company: How Japanese Companies Create the Dynamics of Innovation* (Oxford University Press, New York, NY, 1995)

Chapter 33
Senior Educational Programs to Compensate for Future Student Decline in German Universities

D. Schwarz, J. Steidelmüller, and C. Hipp

Abstract Most industrialized countries are currently facing a shrinking and aging population. Germany's population is expected to fall from about 82 million people in 2008 to, at worst, 65 million people in 2060. Simultaneously, the average age of the population is increasing. In particular, the coming years in East Germany will be characterized by an expected strong decline in the number of young people and a significant increase in the number of elderly. However, demographic change does not automatically imply negative consequences but also creates room for opportunities. In this chapter, we explore opportunities to enlarge the purpose of the educational silver market by an economic component because of two developments (1) current and upcoming generations of seniors increasingly spend their spare time studying intellectual and cultural subjects, and (2) traditional universities will experience a shortage of students. We propose incentives to include more people aged 65 and over in educational issues, and thus to create a win-win situation for third agers and institutions of higher education.

Introduction

Europe has just entered a critical phase in its demographic evolution, and each additional decade in which fertility remains at its present low level will imply a further decline in the European Union of 25–40 million people, in the absence of offsetting effects from immigration or increased life expectancy [1].

As the German Federal Statistical Office for the German case reported, the share of people aged 19 years or less will fall from nearly 19% in 2008 to about 16% in 2060, while the share of people aged 20–64 years will fall from 61% to about 50%, and the share of people aged 65 and older will rise from 20 to 34% (see p. 16 in [2]). The results are based on the assumptions of the "middle variant" of the population projection, i.e., a constant birth rate of 1.4 children per woman on average, increased life expectancy of an infant male to 85 years and of an infant female to 89.2 years by 2060, and annual net migration of a minimum of 100,000 people

F. Kohlbacher and C. Herstatt (eds.), *The Silver Market Phenomenon*,
DOI 10.1007/978-3-642-14338-0_33, © Springer-Verlag Berlin Heidelberg 2011

beginning in 2014 and a maximum of 200,000 people beginning in 2020 (see p. 7, 11 in [2]). This indicates that the average age of the population will rise from 43 years in 2008 to about 52 years in 2060, and that the population will fall from about 82 million in 2008 to between 65 and 70 million in 2060 (see p. 5, 16 in [2]). The situation in East Germany seems to be even more dramatic. While the shrinking of the population in West and South Germany is more moderate, the shrinking of the East German population is considerable primarily due to internal labor migration and secondly due to the collapse of the birth rate after 1990. As Fig. 33.1 shows, migration from East Germany to the old Federal States (North, Central, and South of Germany) is not predicted to stop during the next few decades.

People aged between 18 and 30 years seem to be the most mobile: in contrast, people aged 50 years and over show the least mobility. Therefore, the East German population will shrink, firstly as a result of the missing potential parents and thus a new generation of children, and secondly because of age. The share of people aged 65–74 living in the new Federal States will increase by 8% from 2002 to 2020, while the share of people aged 65 and over will increase by 31.3%. Simultaneously, the East German population will shrink by almost 8%, which means a loss of slightly more than 1.3 million people between 2002 and 2020 [3]. In contrast, the share of people aged 65 and over living in the old Federal States will increase proportionally, by only 22.6% from 2002 to 2020, while the total number of people will rise from 65.5 to 66.4 million people during the same period [3].

"The triumph of public health, medical advancements, and economic development over diseases and injuries that had limited human life expectancy for millennia" has brought many challenges with regard to aging societies (see p. 5 in [4]). This development means thinking about the inclusion of older people at all levels of society, as well as economic issues. Thus, the authors of this chapter look at the educational market for retired people and the benefits for institutions of higher education in East Germany, which suffers from a lower number of young students.

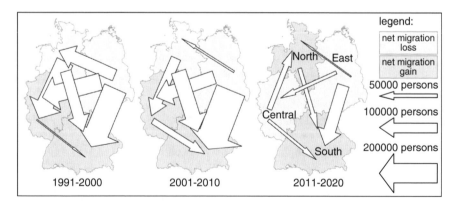

Fig. 33.1 Germany's internal net migration from 1991 to 2020. Source: Federal Office for Building and Regional Planning [3]

The Third Age

There are many categorizations of "age" and the decades of life in the literature. With regard to elderly adults, the terms "young-old" and "oldest-old," or "third age" and "fourth age," have become increasingly popular [5–9]. It is also a fact that there is no agreement about the lower and higher age limits of the respective classifications. Figure 33.2 gives an overview of a few existing definitions (Fig. 33.2).

While statisticians hardly criticize these categories, gerontologists have argued about this subject for several years. Apart from research problems in defining groups of interviewees, they fear that the extreme category is associated with negative stereotypes and the period of final dependence, decrepitude, and death (see pp. 369–370 in [5], p. 6 in [4]).

With regard to the topic of this chapter, we prefer to apply a more open definition of age. Following the arguments from Swindell, third agers "are no longer tied to the responsibilities of regular employment and/or raising a family" (see p. 419 in [9]), as they are in relatively good health, retired, socially and politically engaged (see p. 217 in [11], p. 409 in [12], p. 192 in [13], p. 643 in [10]), and aspire to achieve personal self-fulfillment (see p. 28 in [14]). They enjoy a more vigorous life than previous generations (see p. 409 in [12]), are willing to engage in honorary work and to spend time in consumptive activities such as education. A survey initiated by the Federal Statistical Office of Germany listed the daily activities of people aged 60–69. Apart from time spent on physical recreation and sleep, older people spend their time mainly in voluntary work and personal hobbies. About 31% of senior citizens aged 60–69 are experienced in performing or currently perform voluntary services, which indicates that elderly people are willing to participate in educational courses to prepare for these services (see p. 13 in [15]) (Fig. 33.3).

Even if some researchers ascribe the characteristics mentioned to the term "third age" (e.g., [8, 9]) and others to the term "young-old" (e.g., [13]), the age of retirement seems to be the lower limit of both terms. While eligibility for social security benefits in Germany has dropped to between 58.5 and 60 years (see p. 177

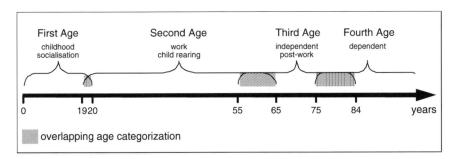

Fig. 33.2 Visualization of age categorizations. Author's illustration according to the definitions from [5, 8, 10]

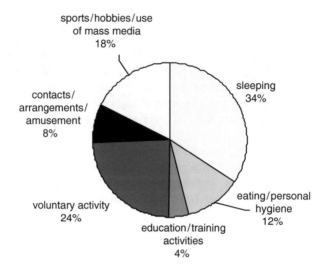

Fig. 33.3 Daily activities of senior citizens aged 60–69. Author's illustration according to data from [16]

in [17], p. 9 in [18]), the collapse of the German social security system will lead to a successive rise in the regular retirement age to 67 years from 2012 on. Thus, the lower limit of the third age category will shift naturally.

As we have already pointed out, the number of people aged 60 and over will increase in the future. The relevance of the "silver market" is rising and results, among other things, in the University of the Third Age (UTA) movement (see p. 409 in [12]).

Universities of the Third Age

Historical Survey

Models of learning for elderly people have a history of at least 40 years. The first generation of senior educational services appeared in 1960, to serve as a cultural leisure activity to occupy seniors and promote their social interaction (see p. 338 in [19]). The Institutes for Learning in Retirement (ILR) seem to have resulted from this generation, established in 1962 in New York City (see p. 54 in [20]). The second generation of senior educational services originated in the 1970s, and focused on the development of life experiences of seniors to prepare them to intervene in social issues (see p. 338 in [20]). The activities of the University of Toulouse probably belong to this generation, as the term "University of the Third Age" was proposed first in 1973 by Pierre Vellas, when the university offered low-cost summer programs for retired persons (see p. 57 in [20], p. 410 in [12], p. 178 in

[21]). This French model of UTA was characterized by engaging retired adults in forms of self-programmed learning, organized and presented by university staff and funded by the government (see p. 178 in [21], p. 57 in [20]). This first UTA had four major objectives [22]:

1. To contribute to raising the level of physical, mental, and social health and the quality of life of older people
2. To provide a permanent educational program for older people in close relation with other age groups
3. To initiate research into age issues
4. To set up education programs in gerontology for present and future decision makers, including Community Information Programs to promote the awareness of age issues in each person in our society

Lemieux identified a third generation of senior educational services, or better, a next generation of UTAs, which emerged in the 1980s (see p. 338 in [19]). The aim was to develop a curriculum for seniors who are retiring earlier and earlier, are better educated, and are demanding credited university courses for their tuition.

The UTA models spread rapidly around the world, including Australia, New Zealand, Canada, the USA, Argentina, Germany, the Czech Republic, Poland, the UK, Scandinavia, China, and Japan (see p. 57 in [20], [23]). However, they are different with regard to their organizational objectives, form of organization, approach to learning, field of study, admission requirements, and offers of certificates such as a baccalaureate or diploma (see p. 411 in [12], pp. 5–8 in [11]).

Case Box 1

One example of the different UTA concepts is the "University of the Third Age Online" (U3A Online). The idea to use the Internet to deliver UTA services came from a group of UTA leaders from Australia, New Zealand, and the UK (see p. 418 in [9]) in 1997. It was originally funded by the Australian Government in 1999, has continued to receive funding from the Australian Government, and has enjoyed considerable support to provide educational services for older people anywhere in the world who are isolated either geographically or through physical or social circumstances [24]. The courses are generally organized as follows: they require no previous knowledge of the subject areas, no exams are taken and no degrees are awarded, they have been developed by knowledgeable volunteers, and they require Internet access and basic computing skills [24]. The original concept of the virtual UTA has been reinforced by cooperative activities with UTA colleagues in other parts of the world who run their courses online with participants, e.g., from the UK, Australia, New Zealand, the USA and Germany (see p. 427 in [9]).

The UTAs in China are another example. "Since the end of the Cultural Revolution, Chinese governments have regarded education as important for helping the more than 100 million older Chinese to adapt to social change" (see p. 434 in [23]). China was thought to be the country with the largest number of UTAs, namely 19,300 UTAs and 1.81 million members by the end of 2002 [25]. A wide variety of UTAs have been set up since the 1980s, supported by government with funding, premises, and guidelines for the management of UTAs [25]. The first UTA was established in Shangdong Province in 1983 [26]. Swindell and Thompson figured out that there are both very prestigious and more traditional universities, and the majority of China's UTAs are associated with recreational centers (see p. 434 in [23]).

To promote the development of UTAs in China, the China Association of Universities for the Aged (CAUA) was established in 1988. It now has 207 member UTAs, publishes a magazine on lifelong learning, and has established a research group for the development of UTA textbooks [26].

The demographics of an aging society and the increasing demand for social activities have posed new educational challenges (see p. 173 in [21]). There is great potential, first because of the baby boomer generation that is already retired or will retire in the next few years. Second, there are many interested learners resulting from increased longevity (see p. 537 in [27]). Moreover, there are positive psychological and medical findings related to education in later life phases with regard to the maintenance of well-being and productivity [23, 28], enhancements of coping strategies, and prevention of unnecessary decline (see p. 448 in [29], p. 403 in [12]). According to UNESCO, which has initiated the concept of lifelong education, it is assumed that "learning is something that all people do and want to do, for reasons which are intrinsically valuable to their human existence and quality of life" (see p. 174 in [21]). Additionally, elderly people have a need for appropriate services and material goods, and education is itself one of those services (see p. 313 in [30]) or, in a new term, one of those "silver market" services. All of these facts could be a sign of a fourth generation of educational services – a generation that focuses on the following aspects:

- From a social perspective, to ensure the quality of life of older people, to meet their potential of interests and their demand for participation in social life through learning and honorary teaching [22].
- From an economic perspective, to support public institutions of higher education that suffer from a lower number of young students caused by demographic effects through study fees and allocation of governmental funds.
- From a socio-political perspective (see p. 78 in [14]), to gain a future-oriented voting public (see Chap. 4, p. 2 in [31]), and to improve the level of physical, mental, and social health to reduce costs of the health-care system.

Senior Educational Services in Germany

The supply of education for retired adults in Germany is manifold and somewhat confusing (see p. 153 in [14], p. 23 in [32]). Wenzke listed the big five providers of educational services in Germany (see p. 158 in [14]):

- Institutions for senior citizens, such as day-care centers, senior clubs, and service centers (20%)
- Admitted senior groups (13%)
- Educational institutions, e.g., senior universities (13%)
- Adult education centers (12%)
- Cultural and municipal institutions (9%)

While the number of providers, and thus the complexity of offers, has increased during the past few years, the participation of third agers, and obviously their learning motivation, are still relatively low (see p. 24 in [32]). This raises the question of whether the low participation is caused by the inactivity of elderly people and/or caused by unavailable or unattractive offers [32].

Focusing on UTAs, Saup [33] provided an overview of study offers for seniors at German institutions of higher education. A few universities in the former Federal Republic of Germany (e.g., Dortmund, Oldenburg, Mannheim, Frankfurt, Bielefeld, Münster, and Marburg) started in the 1980s with educational services for third agers. The number steadily increased from 35 universities in 1994 to 42 in 1997 and 50 in 2001 (see p. 13 in [33]). Meanwhile, this number of senior universities has increased further.

Considering the past years, younger third agers are increasingly interested in educational programs (see p. 15 in [33]). The average age of seniors participating in the programs offered in 2001 dropped to 63 years, possibly due to the lower age of retirement in the past (Fig. 33.4).

Older adults have three study options at UTAs (see p. 18 in [33]). Firstly, interested persons can register as *ordinary* students, presupposing the university entrance diploma, participate in required courses, and take examinations. Saup

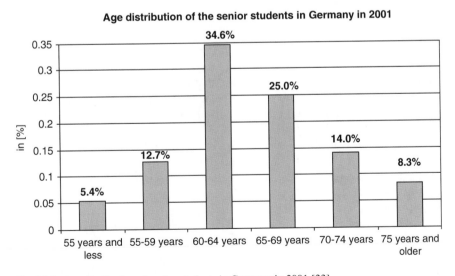

Fig. 33.4 Age distribution of senior students in Germany in 2001 [33]

estimated that 3,500–6,000 senior citizens (age not specified) were registered in 2001. Secondly, third agers can participate in education as *regular* guest auditors. Normally, no entrance certificate is required, and the training finishes without any examinations or educational achievements. The participants are free to choose generally offered fields of science without entrance limitations. Thirdly, UTA candidates can register as *specific* guest auditors. This program provides special advisory courses, regular courses, postprofessional training, and lecture series. The content and duration of study is not determined. These and other factors related to this kind of senior study differ from university to university. Being a specific guest auditor seems to be the most attractive program, since about 25,000 students were registered in that group in 2001.

The current generation of third agers has an agenda for studying. For example, they intend studying to compensate for the gap in previous education, to renew study abilities, to qualify for honorary work or even to extend employability, to satisfy the need for participating in a desired study, to improve image, to be able to continue communicating with younger generations or grandchildren, to discuss philosophical questions, to maintain physical and mental mobility, and simply to avoid loneliness (see p. 59 in [34], p. 15 in [33], Chap. 4, p. 4 in [31]).

Teaching these competencies (with regard to competence profiles in senior education, see [35]), German UTAs are linked primarily to universities and are quite academic in nature, because university professors often conduct these programs [23]. They finance their senior programs from their own resources as well as participation fees (see p. 186 in [36]), because they get no financial support from the government (see p. 12 in [37]).

Case Box 2: UTA at the University in Cottbus

The UTA at the Brandenburg Technical University in Cottbus, located in the southeastern part of the Federal State Brandenburg, was founded in 2001 to establish a place for education, meeting, and activity (see p. A11 in [14], [38]). Since 2001, the program has focused on building competencies helpful in everyday life, and competencies to qualify for honorary or regular employment (see p. 117 in [14]). The offer for third agers from 2002 to 2005 mainly included (see p. A179 in [14], [38]): sports courses (23.8%), lectures and series of lectures (19.3%), lectures held by professors or practitioners including discussions (17.3%), computer courses (15.7%), self-organized working and project groups (10.5%), sightseeing (8.1%), and participation as guest auditors in generally offered lectures. There are no admission requirements, but a semester fee of €30 is required (see p. 339 in [14], [38]).

In recent years, participants in this UTA program increased from 87 persons in 2001 to 1,186 registered senior students in 2006 [39]. This, in addition to the increasing demand for courses and lectures, means lecturers can hardly meet this demand in addition to their main responsibilities. Therefore, the UTA Cottbus relies partly on the help of the alumni of BTU and of senior students to pass on their knowledge and experience to others (see p. A190 in [14]).

According to the assumed fourth generation of UTAs, there are two main aims. The first, from a social point of view, is to meet the demand for senior education caused by the increasing potential (e.g., see p. 9 in [40], p. 24 in [15]) of third agers in the next 5–15 years. Since German UTAs are mainly university-linked (see p. 436 in [23]), the second aim is to help universities that suffer from a lower number of students. This means compensating for the expected decreasing number of young students and, thus, the decreasing funds of the federal government through senior students' tuition charges and other currently undefined funds. In short, there is a need to create a win-win situation.

Strategies to Enlarge the Benefit for German Universities

As mentioned in the "Introduction," both the number of third agers and probably the number of senior students – ceteris paribus, other things being equal – in East Germany will increase. Simultaneously, net income will decrease, as a result of demographically required reforms in the German social pension program (see p. 197 in [41]). Thus, expensive educational offers will probably not be affordable for the majority of UTA clientele. This dilemma leads to the consideration of strategies to finance this social responsibility of educating and developing retired persons through attractive leisure activities, and thus to recruit senior students and raise the total number of students at universities.

Application for governmental support. Education must be seen as a form of social policy (see p. 410 in [12]) and should, at least partly, be financed by the government. It is a social responsibility to care for elderly people and to protect them as long as possible from age-related impairment. That, in turn, could positively affect the social security system through reduced health-care costs, which should be a major incentive for the government to bankroll the initiative.

Realization of a unique program. The UTA needs to have a competitive advantage compared to other providers of senior educational services. A competitive advantage is not manageable if many competitors have the respective resources (see p. 155 in [42], p. 6 in [43]). As Barney defined: "Even if a resource is valuable, rare, and costly to imitate, if it has strategically equivalent substitutes that are themselves not rare or not costly to imitate, then it cannot be a source of sustained competitive advantage" (see p. 47 in [44]). This unique selling proposition (USP) campaign (for example by establishing a unique and attractive program) comes along with an adequate price policy. When the university succeeds in creating a competitive advantage, it improves its reputation. Thus, sponsors will potentially support this concept. For example, learning activities for seniors at Canadian UTAs are sponsored by federal initiatives, provincial initiatives, or community-based programs (see p. 454 in [29]).

Analysis of demand. UTA clientele should be interviewed to establish their intention and learning preferences regarding content (see Chap. 2 in [31]), time (see p. 409 in [12], [45]) and so on. For example, it does not seem conducive to run adult education programs in the evening, when some older people may be reluctant to leave home. Senior students have an "autonomous educational will" (see Chap. 4, p. 2 in [31]) that could be realized in the above-mentioned unique program.

Enlargement of the offer. In addition to the regular program, a virtual UTA that provides intellectually challenging courses for isolated or handicapped older people as well as for conventional UTA members could be interesting (see p. 414 in [9]). In Australia, the first "UTA online" started in 1999, and by the end of the first year, nearly 300 members belonged to that organization [9]. With regard to the limited mobility and circuitousness of the trading area, this enlarges the target group as well as the inclusion of unemployed and interested people. They should have the opportunity to participate in educational courses in order to use the whole capacity of the UTAs. UTAs in France have done this already (see p. 5 in [23]).

Establishment of an incentive policy. Elderly people aspire toward self-fulfillment, individualism, immediacy, and community (see p. 177 in [21]). Some adults have not had the chance to study or to study a desired scientific field. As Picton (see p. 409 in [12], [45]) identified, many retired persons left school at a very early age, perhaps due to socioeconomic imperatives or lack of opportunity to pursue education beyond the basic level. Thus, it is relevant to develop a specific curriculum like a Bachelor of Arts (see pp. 339–341 in [19]) or a PhD program for senior students. These educational achievements allow senior students to teach, such as in adult education centers, or even to work as senior consultants. Maybe there is a demand for more than low-cost learning opportunities. Additionally, this prompts universities to think about different tuition fee strategies.

Establishment of networks. Cooperating with municipal senior institutions could reduce costs through the use of synergies or declining administrative tasks. In addition to the sharing of effort in organizing programs and marketing campaigns, a clear and convincing concept of senior educational services would result (see p. 117 in [14]).

Improvement of information. While conducting research for this article, it was difficult to get up-to-date information about the respective UTA programs, or even to find the respective UTA Web sites. The fact that today's third agers are mostly unpracticed in working with computers, and that these sites are not very user-friendly or self-explanatory, is problematic. Improving the availability of information could be an important step toward improving the image of UTAs.

Boost of honorary work. Last, but not least, voluntary work should be mentioned. Specific offers could be operated by experienced senior students themselves (see p. 414 in [9], p. 644 in [10], p. 454 in [29]). Often they are motivated to transmit their life experiences (see p. 182 in [21]) and experience self-fulfillment (see p. 357 in [46]). It is necessary to boost honorary work (see p. 19 in [15]) to enlarge the variety of educational courses and simultaneously reduce costs.

Summary and Conclusion

This chapter began by discussing the demographic change regarding a shrinking of the population, particularly in Germany and East Germany. The projections of statistical offices have shown that the number of people living in Germany is expected to shrink. Simultaneously, the average age will increase in East Germany, caused by the migration of young people, and thus of potential parents, to other parts of Germany. Therefore, there seems to be a high potential for educational offers for older people. In the second section, we focused on the definition and classification of the term "third age." Many statisticians and gerontologists deal with that topic, but there is no agreement about the limits of each age category. Therefore, we defined retired people who are interested in intellectual free-time activities and social engagement as third agers. These individuals are interested in gaining new competencies, particularly in the field of social science, and in exchanging life experiences. For these people, UTA were established. In the section "Universities of the Third Age" we briefly outlined the history of these UTAs and hypothetically enlarged Lemieux's three-generation concept of UTAs by a fourth generation. We argued that the aims of the UTA, particularly in East Germany, were twofold. Firstly, to ensure that older people have the opportunity to continue living in dignity, to provide conditions and contexts at least equal to those available for younger age groups (see p. 461 in [8]), and to address their potential interests and demand for participation in social life through learning and honorary teaching. A second aim is to support public institutions of higher education that suffer from a lower number of young students, through senior students, the study fees of UTA clientele, and the additional allocation of governmental funds. This compensation seems to be possible, since German UTAs are often university-linked.

Next, we described the German system of educational services for senior citizens. As a short case and example, we mentioned the UTA at the Brandenburg Technical University Cottbus.

In "Strategies to Enlarge the Benefit for German Universities" we focused on the creation of a win-win situation for third agers, who may choose attractive educational services from a wide palette, as well as for universities, which get steady low funds for registered students from the federal government. Therefore, we proposed some strategies to enlarge the benefit for universities and thus to be able to ensure the availability of the UTA program and steadily improve it. As Swindell reasoned, keeping the brain active in later life may lead to measurable improvements in health and well-being (see p. 427 in [9]). Elderly people have a need for appropriate services such as education (see p. 313 in [30]) and, therefore, education must be seen as a form of social policy and social responsibility that is at least partly financed by the government.

What we learned from this chapter about UTAs, particularly the East German difficulties to recruit students, or rather UTA clientele, is not easily transferable to other countries. That is because UTAs all over the world differ in their organizational objectives, form of organization, approach to learning, field of study, admission requirements, offers of certificates (see p. 414 in [12], pp. 5–8 in [11]), and government support. But, we pointed out that motivational factors play a key role in increasing the number of senior students. Our remarks regarding the analysis of demand, virtualization of educational courses, and improvement of the availability of information about the UTA could also provide valuable stimulus for other countries, on the one hand, to satisfy senior students' needs and, on the other hand, to use institutions of higher education to their full capacity.

References

1. W. Lutz, Science **299**, 1991–1992 (2003)
2. Federal Statistical Office Germany (ed.), *Bevölkerung Deutschlands bis 2060: 12. koordinierte Bevölkerungsvorausberechnung* (FSO, Wiesbaden, 2009)
3. BBR, Federal Office for Building and Regional Planning, in *Raumordnungsprognose 2020/2050: Ausgabe 2006.* (BBR, Bonn, 2006)
4. K. Kinsella, D.R. Phillips, Popul. Bull. **60**, 1–42 (2005). www.prb.org
5. B. Bytheway, J. Soc. Issues **61**(2), 361–374 (2005)
6. P. Laslett, *A Fresh Map of Life: The Emergence of the Third Age* (Harvard University Press, Cambridge, MA, 1991)
7. R.A. Settersten, K.U. Mayer, Ann. Rev. Sociol. **23**, 233–261 (1997)
8. J. Smith, Eur. Rev. **9**(4), 461 (2001)
9. R. Swindell, Int. J. Lifelong Educ. **21**(5), 414–429 (2002)
10. E. Timmer, M. Aartsen, Soc. Behav. Pers. **31**(7), 643–656 (2003)
11. European Federation of Older Students at the Universities (eds.), *EFOS News*, **1**, 5 (2007)
12. V. Minichiello, Int. Rev. Educ. **38**(4), 403–416 (1992)
13. B.L. Neugarten, Ann. Am. Acad. Polit. Soc. Sci. **415**, 187–198 (1974)
14. B. Wenzke, *Produktivität im Alter: Bildung zwischen Institution und Selbstorganisation*, PhD thesis (Brandenburg Technical University Cottbus, 2007)
15. BMFSFJ, German Federal Ministry of Family, Seniors, Women and Youth (eds.), *Bildung im Alter: Ergebnisse des Forschungsprojektes* (BMFSFJ, Berlin, 2004)
16. H. Engstler et al., Alltag *in* Deutschland: Analysen zur Zeitverwendung, in *Conference Proceeding Zeitbudgeterhebung 2001/02, 16–17 Feb 2001*, ed. by Federal Statistical Office Germany (FSO, Wiesbaden, 2004), pp. 216–246
17. A. Börsch-Supan, R. Schnabel, Am. Econ. Rev. **88**(2), 173–178 (1998)
18. J. Gruber, D. Wise, *Social Security Programs and Retirement Around the World, in NBER Working Paper Series, Working Paper 6134* (National Bureau of Economic Research, Cambridge MA, 1997)
19. A. Lemieux, Educ. Gerontol. **21**(4), 337–334 (1995)
20. L.K. Hebestreit, *An Evaluation of the Role of the University of the Third Age in the Provision of Lifelong Learning.* Dissertation, University of South Africa (2006). http://etd.unisa.ac.za/ETD-db/theses/available/etd-06042007-115106/unrestricted/thesis.pdf. Accessed 18 Jun 2008
21. A. Williamson, Int. J. Lifelong Educ. **16**(3), 173–184 (1997)
22. P. Vellas, *The First University of the Third Age.* http://worldU3A.org/aiuta/vellas-uk.htm, 2007-10-31
23. R. Swindell, J. Thompson, Educ. Gerontol. **21**(5), 429–447 (1995)
24. U3A Online, *A Virtual University of the Third Age* (Griffith University, Queensland, 2008). http://www3.griffith.edu.au/03/u3a/. Accessed 18 Jun 2008
25. J. Thompson, *The Amazing University of the Third Age in China Today* (U3A, UK, 2002). http://worldu3a.org/worldpapers/u3a-china.htm. Accessed 18 Jun 2008

26. ICT, *ICT-in-Education Toolkit, Sustaining Lifelong Learning, 2007*. http://www.ictinedtoolkit. org/usere/p_page.php?section_id=175#footnote47. Accessed 18 Jun 2008
27. F. Kolland, Educ. Gerontol. **19**(6), 535–550 (1993)
28. M.W. Drotter, Educ. Gerontol. Int. Q. **7**(2), 105 (1981)
29. B.S. Clough, Educ. Gerontol. **18**(5), 447 (1992)
30. D. Radcliffe, Educ. Gerontol. **8**(4), 311–323 (1982)
31. D. Meynen *Lässt sich das Seniorenstudium modularisieren? Ansätze zu einer wissenschafts-didaktischen Theorie des Studiums im Alter* (Learning in Later Life, 2003). http://www.uni-ulm. de/LiLL/5.0/aufsaetze/daniel_meynen/seniorenstudium_modul.htm. Accessed 19 Jun 2008
32. C. Sommer, H. Künemund, *Bildung im Alter: Eine Literaturanalyse*. Forschungsbericht 66 der Forschungsgruppe Altern und Lebenslauf (FALL). (Freie Universität Berlin, 1999). http:// www.fall-berlin.de/index.html?/fdl3.htm. Accessed 18 Jun 2008
33. W. Saup, *Studienführer für Senioren*, ed by Bundesministerium für Bildung und Forschung (BMBF, Bonn, 2001). http://www.bmbf.de/pub/studienfuehrer_fuer_senioren.pdf. Accessed 18 Jun 2008
34. H. Hirsch, Altern. Higher Educ. **5**(1), 57 (1980)
35. S. Kade, Altersbildung und Kompetenz, in *Altersbildung an der Schwelle des neuen Jahr-hunderts*, ed. by R. Berghold, D. Knopf, A. Mörchen (Echter, Würzburg, 1999), pp. 129–135
36. K.P. Wallraven, in *Handbuch Altenbildung: Theorien und Konzepte für Gegenwart und Zukunft*, ed. by S. Becker, L. Veelken, K.P. Wallraven (Leske + Budrich, Opladen, 2000), pp. 186–188
37. I. Dummer, Senior Studies at the Christian-Albrechts-University in Kiel. EFOS News **1**, 12 (2007)
38. ZfW (ed.), *Seniorenuniversität* (BTU, Cottbus, 2008). http://www.tu-cottbus.de/btu/de/ weiterbildung/kindersenioren/seniorenuniversitaet/. Accessed 18 Jun 2008
39. ZfW (ed.), *Vortrag zum 5jährigen Bestehen der Seniorenuniversität* (BTU, Cottbus, 2006)
40. J.U. Prager, A. Schleiter, *Älter werden – aktiv bleiben: Ergebnisse einer repräsentativen Umfrage unter Erwerbstätigen in Deutschland* (Bertelsmann, Gütersloh, 2006). http://www. bertelsmann-stiftung.de/bst/de/media/CBP_Umfrage_03.pdf. Accessed 18 Jun 2008
41. BMFSFJ, German Federal Ministry of Family, Seniors, Women and Youth (eds.), *Fünfter Bericht zur Lage der älteren Generation in der Bundesrepublik Deutschland: Potenziale des Alters in Wirtschaft und Gesellschaft: Der Beitrag älterer Menschen zum Zusammenhalt der Generationen* (BMFSFJ, Berlin, 2005)
42. L. Argote, P. Ingram, Organ. Behav. Hum. Decis. Process. **82**(1), 150–169 (2000)
43. J.B. Barney, E.J. Zajac, Strateg. Manage. J. **15**(special issue), 5–9 (1994)
44. J.B. Barney, Acad. Manage. Rev. **26**(1), 41–56 (2001)
45. C.J. Picton, Trans. Menzies Found. **8**, 113–118 (1985)
46. M.J. Graney, W.C. Hays, Educ. Gerontol. Int. Q. **1**(4), 343–359 (1976)

Boppel, Michael; Boehm, Stephan; Kunisch, Sven (Eds.):

From Grey to Silver
Managing the Demographic Change Successfully

1st Edition., 2011, XX, 228 p., Hardcover
ISBN: 978-3-642-15593-2

Demographic change is one of the most crucial issues of our time. This book sheds light on the demographic implications companies face. Based on an integrated framework, the book investigates three important perspectives: An economic and social perspective helps organisations and managers better understand the basic parameters of demographic change and its influences on the labour market. A human resources and leadership perspective reveals how age management can help retain employees of different age groups as motivated and productive workforce members. An innovation and marketing perspective examines how companies can exploit the potentials that senior customers offer. A combination of research-driven and practice-oriented chapters makes this book a profound and an interesting read. It primarily addresses executives from various organizational fields, including HR, marketing, and management. Professional trainers, scholars and students of economy and business will also gain valuable insights.